Canadian Entrepreneurship and Small Business Management

SECOND
EDITION

Canadian Entrepreneurship and Small Business Management

D. Wesley Balderson
University of Lethbridge

IRWIN
Toronto • Chicago • Bogotá • Boston • Buenos Aires
Caracas • London • Madrid • Mexico City • Sydney

Senior sponsoring editor: Roderick T. Bannister
Sponsoring editor: Evelyn Veitch
Developmental editor: Elke Price
Product manager: Murray Moman
Project editor: Rita McMullen
Assistant production manager: Jon Christopher
Art manager: Kim Meriwether
Compositor: Carlisle Communications, Ltd.
Typeface: 10.5/12 Times Roman
Printer: R. R. Donnelley & Sons Company

ISBN 0-256-12357-8
Library of Congress Catalog Card No. 93-78563

Printed in the United States of America

3 4 5 6 7 8 9 0 DOC 0 9 8 7 6 5

Preface

Canadian Entrepreneurship and Small Business Management, 2nd Edition, is a result of many years of teaching entrepreneurship business classes at the college and university level; working closely with numerous owners of small businesses in a consulting role; direct, personal small business management experience; and, of course, the experience with the successful first edition. I have attempted to improve on the first edition by making this edition more interesting and instructional, practical and theoretically sound, and rigorous yet easy for the student to follow and absorb.

To accomplish these sometimes diverse aims, the text incorporates standard small business start-up and management fundamentals and introduces the reader to many Canadian entrepreneurs and their businesses through the more than 45 real-life small business incidents and 14 profiles of Canadian entrepreneurs. Each individual profiled started his or her business small. All have succeeded, and some have expanded into large businesses.

Numerous cases illustrate the small business management concepts discussed in the text. These concepts are stated at the beginning of each case in the *Instructor's Manual* to aid in teaching. Each case proceeds in a logical order from start-up of the business, to management of the existing business, and finally to planning for the future.

The second edition introduces several improvements to the first edition based on professor and student feedback. Specifically, the second edition includes

- More application-type questions in the end-of-chapter material.
- Greater depth in the following chapters: The Small Business Decision (Chapter 2), Organizing a Business (Chapter 4), Franchising (Chapter 6), Financing the Small Business (Chapter 7), Personnel Management (Chapter 11), and Managing Growth (Chapter 13).

- The addition of several new short cases and five longer comprehensive cases. For convenience, the shorter cases are included within the text at the conclusion of each section rather than at the end of the text.
- Over 40 new incidents or examples from Canadian business that illustrate the concepts discussed.
- The updating and/or replacement of the previous small business profiles at the beginning of each chapter.
- The updating of all statistics, examples, and information about programs, regulations, and taxes.
- New material on such issues as the future of small business, female entrepreneurs, entrepreneur leadership styles, and business plan preparation.

This text will be appropriate for any entrepreneurship or small business management class at the college or university undergraduate or graduate level. It can also be adapted easily to continuing education classes for those who are thinking about or are currently involved in running their own businesses. In many cases, the text will also be a useful resource or reading book for practitioners outside the classroom setting.

Canadian Entrepreneurship and Small Business Management, 2nd Edition, is divided into four parts. Each part covers an essential aspect of starting and/or managing a small business.

Part I provides background information essential to the decision to undertake small business ownership. Chapter 1 reviews the characteristics of small business and its contribution to Canadian society. Chapter 2 covers areas required for a personal evaluation of one's suitability for small business ownership. Chapter 3 presents a systematic procedure for determining whether a small business opportunity is feasible. It includes numerous sources of information essential in carrying out a feasibility analysis.

The four chapters in Part II discuss important aspects of starting or obtaining a business. Chapters 4, 5, and 6 review the three methods of establishing a small business. Chapter 4 discusses organizing the small business from scratch, including a special emphasis on the preparation of the business plan. Chapter 5 covers buying a business. Chapter 6 deals with franchising as a type of small business ownership. Chapter 7 discusses financing concerns in starting the business and includes a complete listing of sources of financing for entrepreneurs.

Part III includes five chapters that discuss the fundamental management practices in operating the already established business. Chapter 8, 9, 10, and 11 cover in detail the small business applications in marketing, finance, internal operations, and personnel management, respectively. Chapter 12 focuses on tax considerations for the small business owner-manager.

Part IV appropriately discusses future and long-term aspects of the small business. Chapter 13 deals with the principles underlying effective growth management. Chapter 14 discusses methods of terminating or transferring the ownership of the enterprise, with a special emphasis on family businesses.

The *Instructor's Manual* has been carefully prepared to provide the instructor with helpful information while allowing considerable flexibility. Notes relating to each chapter include the following components:

- *Conversion Notes*—compare the treatment of each chapter topic in this text with those of the two other leading Canadian texts.
- *Chapter Objectives*—reproduced from the text chapters.
- *Concept Checks*—key concepts summarized from text chapters.
- *Key Terms and Concepts*—from boldfaced words in chapter material.
- *Transparency List*—a list of transparencies appropriate for each chapter.
- *Answers to End-of-Chapter Questions.*
- *Case Solutions*—for end-of-part and comprehensive cases.

The solutions to the supplementary case questions are included toward the end of the *Instructor's Manual.*

Transparency masters, enlarged reproductions of the text materials, are included at the end of the *Instructor's Manual.*

Acknowledgments

Many people contributed to *Canadian Entrepreneurship and Small Business Management,* 2nd Edition. I am grateful to the many students and colleagues who have offered input and critical analyses of our small business course over the years. I also appreciate those owner-managers with whom I have had an opportunity to work in a consulting role. They have provided considerable insight regarding the pertinent problems small business owners face. Reviewers of the second edition and reviewers and users of the first edition also provided valuable suggestions. Reviewers include:

Perley Brewer, *New Brunswick Community College*

Maureen Gerber, *British Columbia Institute of Technology*

Brian Hobson, *Georgian College of Applied Arts and Technology*

Walter Isenor, *Acadia University*

Peter Kaglik, *Red River Community College*

Reid MacWilliam, *Mohawk College*

Lissa McRae, *Bishop's University*

John Morrison, *Seneca College*

Garfield Pynn, *Memorial University of Newfoundland*

Dennis Sullivan, *Fanshawe College*

Randy Vandermark, *British Columbia Institute of Technology*

Rick Wagman, *Saskatchewan Institute of Applied Science and Technology*

Several people made direct contributions to this text. Research assistants Cam Roberts, Patricia Elemans, Jim Seip, Susan Bruder, Rick Heyland, Donette Adamus, Michael Quinton, and Shilpa Morzaria collected data, checked references and permissions, and entered text material into the word processor for the first edition. Robert McLaren and Leisa Shea performed the same work for the second edition. Ronald Johnson, Chartered Accountant, reviewed the accounting aspects of the text, and Bernard H. Norton, B.A., L.L.B., a partner in the law firm of Fletcher and Norton, reviewed the legal topics for accuracy. Professor Gordon

Dixon, Associate Professor in the Faculty of Management, University of Lethbridge, reviewed the taxation chapter and provided valuable input. Norman Robinson allowed me to use his business as the basis for writing the comprehensive case. To all of these people I express my gratitude for their valuable contributions.

I thank those who authored some of the cases: Pat Elemans, Cam Roberts, and Rick Heyland, research assistants at the University of Lethbridge; R. E. Vosburgh, University of Guelph; Jim Mason, University of Regina; M. D. Beckman, Walter S. Good, and Caroline Dabrus, University of Manitoba; Stephen Tax, University of Manitoba; Ray Klapstein, Dalhousie University; Donald G. Ross, St. Francis Xavier University; Scott B. Fallows, Acadia University; and Malika Das, Mount Saint Vincent University. I also thank S. Shapiro, J. McCarthy, and Richard D. Irwin, Inc., for allowing some of their cases to be adapted for this text.

I thank the many authors and entrepreneurs who granted us permission to use diagrams, tables, profiles, and article excerpts to illustrate the text concepts.

I am extremely grateful for the support and assistance the School of Management at the University of Lethbridge provided in allowing computer research and secretarial time for this project. I thank Karen Erickson and Barb Driscoll, who typed and proofread parts of the manuscript and the *Instructor's Manual.*

I thank the staff of Richard D. Irwin, Inc., for their encouragement and support.

Finally, I thank my wife and seven children for the patience they have shown over the past four or so years. Much of my spare time (*their* time) was spent on this endeavour. Their support and encouragement assured me that it has been worth the effort.

Wes Balderson

Contents

Part II

Preparing for Small Business Ownership   102

4   Organizing a Business   105

5   Buying a Business   154

6   Franchising   178

7   Financing the Small Business   206

PART III

Managing the Small Business   251

8   Marketing Management   252

9   Financial Management   290

10   Operations Management   325

11   Personnel Management   351

PART IV

Looking to the Future   417

13   Managing Growth   419

Canadian Entrepreneurship and Small Business Management

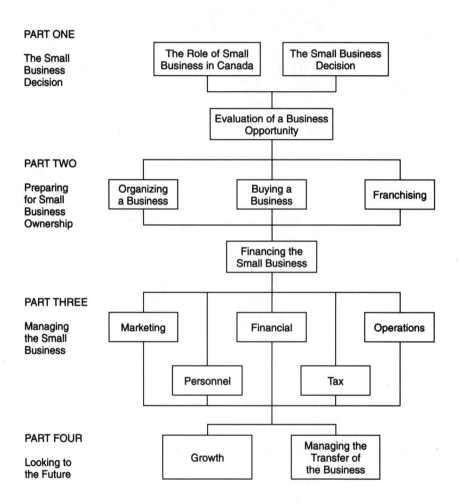

PART ONE

The Small
Business
Decision

| The Role of Small Business in Canada | The Small Business Decision |

Evaluation of a Business Opportunity

PART TWO

Preparing
for Small
Business
Ownership

| Organizing a Business | Buying a Business | Franchising |

Financing the Small Business

PART THREE

Managing
the Small
Business

| Marketing | Financial | Operations |

| Personnel | Tax |

PART FOUR

Looking to
the Future

| Growth | Managing the Transfer of the Business |

PART I

The Small Business Decision

The decision to start one's own business is a difficult one. It often involves leaving secure employment to face an uncertain financial future. Such a decision can have far-reaching effects on the physical, emotional, and financial aspects of one's life. To provide a better understanding of the implications of this decision, Part I discusses three topics.

Chapter 1 reviews the role of small business in Canadian society. It examines current trends and the probable future environment for small business.

Chapter 2 describes characteristics of successful and unsuccessful small businesses, including the personal capabilities the majority of successful entrepreneurs possess. The chapter also reviews the potential advantages and dangers of operating one's own business. Understanding this information can help one make an informed small business career decision.

Once an individual understands the relative merits of starting a small business and feels suited for such a career, he or she can do several things to find the best business opportunity to pursue. Generally, a considerable amount of information is needed to evaluate business opportunities. Chapter 3 presents ideas that can improve information collection and analysis skills to help the entrepreneur decide which opportunity to pursue.

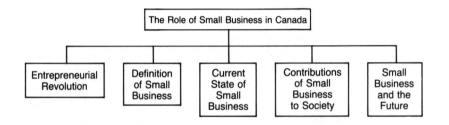

The Role of Small Business in Canada

Chapter Objectives

- To discuss the evidence of increased interest and activity in the small business sector.
- To review common methods of defining small business and explain why a definition is important.
- To understand the current extent of small business in Canada.
- To discuss the benefits a healthy small business sector can offer society.
- To explain the probable future environment for the small business community.

Small Business Profile

Catherine Enright

Acquaculture

Catherine Enright is an entrepreneur who has applied her education to help establish a new and growing industry in Nova Scotia. Enright was raised in Windsor, Ontario, and received her bachelor's degree in biology from the University of Windsor in 1974. While pursuing her master's degree at Dalhousie University in Halifax, she had an opportunity to work with a new type of commercial oyster that the federal government was attempting to introduce to the Canadian market.

In 1979, while still at the university, Enright started her own commercial oyster farm using the new oysters. Her business, Seafarm Venture, was a success and inspired other entrepreneurs to start similar businesses. Together they formed the Ostrea Edulis Cooperative Association, with Enright as president.

Since starting her business, Enright continued to pursue her university education, receiving her Ph.D. with distinction in marine biology in 1984 and an M.B.A. in international business in 1986, both from Dalhousie. She applied her training in biology to make improvements in the oyster production cycle. Her M.B.A. greatly helped her in running the management aspects of the business, including administering the company and developing an ambitious international business plan.

Enright's success in pioneering the commercialization of this product led to her selection by the government of Nova Scotia as the Acquaculture Co-ordinator for the province in 1990. In this position, she assists other small enterprises and co-ops in getting established and ensuring that the industry remains viable. Enright has been a member of the World Acquaculture Society for over a decade and a member of its board of directors since June 1990.

Catherine Enright has shown that a successful small business can make a significant contribution to society. Even in her current position with a large organization, she is able to continue her entrepreneurial activities in developing the industry.

Enright's success is a result of hard work and the often difficult application of university training to the operation of a business. Making money is not her main goal; rather, she says, "I like the idea of being involved in something that is new and exciting, something that is on the frontier."

Printed with permission of Catherine Enright.

Incident 1-1

After the Axe: Executives Turn Entrepreneur

Douglas Ludwig is one happy man. Each morning, from Monday to Friday, his large frame emerges from the back door of his elegant Toronto home and sinks into the comfort of his blue Oldsmobile for the morning drive to Hamilton, Ont. Once through the gates of a low-slung rope factory, he checks in at his office. That done, he invariably reaches for his grease-stained overalls before he heads for the shop floor to wrestle with one of his finicky rope-making machines.

Two short years ago, however, a different man appeared on the threshold. Back then, Ludwig donned standard executive gear—The Blue Suit. And when he stepped into his car, he drove not to Hamilton but to the gleaming towers of Bay Street in downtown Toronto.

Today, Ludwig is President of Cancord Inc., a rope manufacturer in Hamilton with 1987 sales of $1.5 million. Once upon a time, he was a high-flying executive with a brokerage house, earning $160,000 a year, juggling millions of dollars and dining in ritzy French restaurants. That world came crashing down in the spring of 1987, when Ludwig's American bosses decided to dump their Canadian managers.

Instead of trying to find a new job in the financial industry, Ludwig decided to buy a small business that made something tangible. As a result, he joined a growing legion of fired, laid-off or simply bored executives who have opted to run small companies rather than continue working among the corporate world's bigwigs. Says Ludwig, "Like many people, I liked the idea of doing my own thing—being a captain of one's own destiny and master of one's fate."

Source: Bruce Livesey, "After the Axe: Executives Turn Entrepreneur," *Profit Magazine,* March 1989, p. 34.

The Entrepreneurial Revolution

The 1970s and 1980s saw a reawakening of interest in small business, both in North America and abroad. The dream of starting small and developing a successful business, such as Catherine Enright did (see Small Business Profile), is shared by many. On the other hand, many individuals have become successful entrepreneurs out of economic necessity. An example of such an individual, Douglas Ludwig, appears in Incident 1-1.

During the past recessions, many individuals who lost their jobs and many college and university graduates unable to secure employment started their own businesses. Others chose to leave secure employment and strike out on their own because of a natural interest or a desire for a challenge. Incident 1-2 illustrates such an example. The importance of the small business sector of Canadian society is now more widely acknowledged than at any time since the

---

Incident 1–2

Life after the Ivory Tower

As a tenured academic, Andrew Benedek once enjoyed a lot of security and plenty of time off. As an entrepreneur, he doesn't have very much of either. Yet he has no regrets about the switch he made eight years ago. "I wanted to be useful to society in a more direct way," he says. "As an academic, I could only make an impact through my students. I wanted to make an impact myself."

Benedek was 37 when he left the faculty of McMaster University in Hamilton to found Zenon Environmental Inc. in neighbouring Burlington. Zenon makes water purification systems used by the medical, electronics, pharmaceutical and cosmetics industries.

He used his own savings, got backing from family members and mortgaged his house to the hilt. That raised almost $500,000. Later he got additional backing from the Ontario Development Corp., an agency of the provincial government. He was able to attract highly qualified scientists from universities and government departments. Now Zenon trains its own people and has a staff of 100, including 60 engineers and scientists.

In addition to its Canadian head office and manufacturing plant, Zenon has a U.S. sales office and has negotiated joint ventures and sales agreements with companies in Europe and Japan. Sales are approaching $10 million. Benedek says the water market is going to keep growing, and "we have some technologies that are very important to that market."

Source: Daniel Stoffman, "Life after the Ivory Tower," *Report on Business Magazine,* October 1988, p. 73.

turn of the century. Other countries have also shared in this growth and increased awareness in recent years.[1]

Since the Second World War, the philosophy in many circles has been that bigger is better in both business and government. As a result, government has increased in size and the climate for big business has improved. In the mid-1970s, however, the critics of "bigness" gathered more support as big government and big business failed to provide the expected panacea for society's economic problems. The result is that more people and more governments are looking to small business to provide a catalyst for their stagnant economies and enable faster economic growth.[2]

Although the rapid growth that characterized small business in the 1980s is unlikely to be sustained in the 1990s, small business will continue to offer a major benefit to the Canadian economy. The following sections provide specific evidence that the entrepreneurial revolution is alive and well.

FIGURE 1-1   Business Start-Ups and Exits, 1979–1989*

	Start-Ups	Exits	Net Increase
1979–1980	127,015	92,816	34,289
1980–1981	134,769	95,996	38,773
1881–1982	119,126	106,653	12,473
1982–1983	145,154	102,251	42,903
1983–1984	138,547	117,371	21,176
1984–1985	152,213	110,520	41,693
1985–1986	152,472	122,828	29,644
1986–1987	161,285	127,085	34,200
1987–1988	161,931	135,394	26,537
1988–1989	165,980	140,054	25,926

*Excludes public administration.

SOURCES: Entrepreneurship and Small Business Office, Statistics Canada.
Small Business in Canada, Industry, Science and Technology, Canada, 1991.

Increases in the Number of Business Establishments

Considerable research has been done to determine the number of new businesses established each year. This has proved a difficult, if not impossible, task because of the many different types of businesses as well as the varied methods of estimating business start-ups. Some indicators of business start-ups researchers have used are tax returns, new employer registrations, phone hookups, new incorporations, and business registrations.[3]

Figure 1–1 illustrates the increasing number of business start-ups in Canada during 1979–1989. As can be seen, the number of new start-ups increased by 34 percent during that period, despite the onset of the recession in 1989. Similar statistics for the United States show even more marked increases in business formations than in Canada.[4] Regardless of which indicators are used, it is evident that in recent years new businesses have increased between 5 and 12 percent per year.[5] Furthermore, the majority of these new business formations have been small businesses. For example, from 1978 to 1989 the number of Canadian companies with fewer than 50 employees grew from 582,000 to 906,592.[6]

Increases in the Number of Employees of Small Businesses

In recent years, the number of Canadians employed in small businesses has grown substantially (see Figure 1–2).[7] At the same time, employment levels in large businesses have remained the same or decreased. Clearly the trend of employment in Canada has shifted from larger to smaller organizations.

Increase in Government Interest and Programs

Today's best practices will be tomorrow's competitive imperatives. Business techniques that are successful today will establish benchmarks that define the competitive environment

---

FIGURE 1-2   Small Business Share of Employment, 1979 and 1989*

Under 50 Employees		Under 100 Employees	
1979	*1989*	*1979*	*1989*
34%	39.8%	40.8%	47.1%

*Including self-employed, excluding public administration.

SOURCE: Entrepreneurship and Small Business Office, Industry, Science and Technology, Canada, 1991.

of the future. Other companies wishing to position themselves in anticipation of that future can learn from what our more dynamic small businesses are doing today. And they can count on this Government to support them in their efforts to translate that knowledge into action.*

As the above quote illustrates, many politicians now recognize the importance of small business to a healthy economy and are beginning to offer various financial and nonfinancial programs to assist the small business owner.[8] Presently the Entrepreneurship and Small Business Office in the Department of Industry, Science and Technology coordinates and administers programs designed to aid small business at the federal government level. Likewise, all of the provinces have departments that perform the same function for small businesses within their jurisdictions. Appendix B of Chapter 3 gives a complete listing of these agencies.

Increase in the Number of Small Business–Related Courses at Colleges and Universities

The level of interest in small business–related courses at Canadian colleges and universities has risen dramatically in the past few years. The number of entrepreneurship courses in business schools has risen 56 percent since 1980.[9] By 1987, 67 institutions offered 143 courses, and the boom appears to be continuing.[10] Historically such courses typically were housed in management and commerce faculties and attracted only students of those faculties. However, as a result of the growing general interests in small business in recent years, many nonbusiness majors now take such courses.

Increase in Entrepreneurial Activities in Large Businesses

Recently many large, successful companies have developed or altered their organizations to promote creativity, entrepreneurship, and individual initiative.[11] These businesses have realized considerable productivity gains by encouraging this type of intrapreneurship. In their extensive study of successful large compa-

---

*The Honourable Tom Hockin, Minister of State, Small Business and Tourism, Government of Canada.

nies, which resulted in the best-selling book *In Search of Excellence,* Thomas Peters and Robert Waterman found that one characteristic of these organizations was their formal encouragement of entrepreneurship within and among departments. These companies were quick to recognize increases in productivity and innovativeness by rewarding employees who engaged in such entrepreneurial behaviour.[12] The very successful Post-It™ notepads manufactured by 3M Corporation and the Macintosh computer developed by Apple Computer are examples of this type of activity. The Small Business Profile at the beginning of this chapter illustrates that innovation and entrepreneurial activity can also occur through an individual leading a government agency.

Increase in Political Power of Small Business

Collectively, the small business community is a significant economic force in Canadian society. Several organizations are currently attempting to advance the small business cause through lobbying efforts and educational programs. The largest and most visible organization is the Canadian Federation of Independent Business, which boasts a membership of over 88,000. Such lobbying has resulted in many government programs and some legislation beneficial to small business. Many industry associations made up primarily of small businesses also are very active in lobbying activities and have influenced the directions of government initiatives.

What Is Small Business?

What size of business qualifies as a small business? This question is not easy to answer, because most organizations and agencies concerned with small businesses use different definitions. It is essential, however, to understand some of the common characteristics of these definitions to better appreciate what constitutes a small business. This can be important for at least the following reasons.

Comparison and Evaluation

To compare the performance of a small business to other small businesses, it is necessary to understand the sizes and characteristics used by data collection and dissemination agencies such as Statistics Canada and Dun & Bradstreet. Ensuring that firms are relatively the same size allows a more meaningful monitoring of sales levels, performance, and productivity in relation to other, similar firms in the industry. Currently Statistics Canada publishes operating data for incorporated and unincorporated businesses that have average net sales of $1 million or less.

Government Programs

Knowing how various government departments define a small business enables an entrepreneur to take advantage of the tax incentives and other government assistance programs designed for small business. Examples of differences in definitions among government agencies are given later.

Lending Programs

A small business owner needs to know the size of business lenders require to take advantage of favourable small business provisions in their lending programs. These programs are available to small businesses from the Federal Business Development Bank (FBDB), Provincial Government lending agencies, and the chartered banks.

In view of the foregoing, it is important to understand the criteria commonly used to distinguish a small business from a large one. At least four criteria are used to make this distinction.

1. Number of Employees.   Some government departments, such as the Federal Department of Regional Industrial Expansion, use the number of employees as their criteria. The Department of Industry, Trade & Commerce specifies a small business as one that employs under 100 people in a manufacturing industry and under 50 employees in a nonmanufacturing industry. The Ministry of State for Small Business also uses the guideline of 50 employees, while the Federal Business Development Bank considers a business that employs fewer than 75 to be eligible in its Counselling Assistance for Small Businesses Program. Other agencies, such as the Small Business Administration in the United States and Statistics Canada, specify much larger numbers of employees, ranging from 250 to 1,500 depending on the industry.[13]

2. Gross Sales.   Although the limits vary by industry, gross sales is a common basis for defining small business. The Ministry of State for Small Business uses $2 million in sales as a benchmark. The Small Business Loans Act in Canada applies to firms with sales of less than $2 million. The Small Business Administration in the United States uses the following gross sales guidelines:

Retailing: $3.5 million to $13.5 million

Services: $3.5 million to $14.5 million

Construction: $7 million to $17 million

3. Profits.   Revenue Canada uses operating profits as a guideline to define which businesses qualify for the "Small Business Deduction." This special deduction allows a reduced tax rate (the small business deduction is discussed in detail in Chapter 12). This limit is presently set at a net operating profit of $200,000.

4. Type of Management-Ownership Structure.   Another criterion used to define small business is the degree to which the owner is also the day-to-day manager of the business. With some exceptions, the majority of small business owners are also the managers.[14] Because the guidelines differ among industries and agencies, the Committee for Economic Development in the United States uses a slightly different and less specific approach in defining a small business. Its definition states that if any two of the following characteristics exist, the business may be classified as a small business:

1. Independent management (i.e., the owner is the manager).
2. Owner-supplied capital.
3. Local area of operations.
4. Relatively small size within its industry.

As can be seen, it is no easy task to define the size limits of a small business. The definition used will depend on the purpose and on the agency or program concerned.

Current State of Small Business in Canada

Although the size and extent of small business in Canada depends on the definition used, a review of the data compiled by Statistics Canada and the Small Business Secretariat illustrates that small business comprises a significant part of the Canadian economy. This data shows that

- Approximately 97 percent of all businesses operating in Canada are small businesses.[15] This percentage is derived by listing those businesses with under $2 million in gross sales.
- Approximately 29 percent of gross sales in Canada are made by small businesses.[16]
- Approximately 30 percent of gross domestic product is provided by small business.[17]
- Approximately 47 percent of the labour force is employed in small business.[18] This includes businesses with fewer than 100 employees.
- Approximately 28 percent of all business profits are made in small businesses.[19]
- Approximately 20 percent of all business assets are owned by small businesses.[20]

Young Entrepreneurs

In addition to the large general increases in the number of small businesses since 1974, two additional trends are worth noting. The number of small businesses owned by people under age 30 increased by 48 percent from 1974 to 1980 (whereas the increase in the number of small business proprietors increased by 25 percent during the same period).[21] According to Statistics Canada, over 38,000 business owners across Canada were under age 25 in 1986. In addition, almost

200,000 business owners were in the 25-to-34 age bracket, making up 24 percent of the total number of business owners. As a result, almost one-third of the entire business population are under age 35, indicating that business ownership is an attractive career option for many younger Canadians. In recent years, organizations such as ACE (Association of Collegiate Entrepreneurs) have been formed in Canada to provide networking and information for these young entrepreneurs.

Female Entrepreneurs

Women are also playing an increasingly important role in entrepreneurial activity in Canada. In 1988, 23.7 percent of small businesses were owned by women, up from 21.3 percent in 1981. This trend parallels the general growth in employment for women in Canadian society. The number of women entrepreneurs is increasing more rapidly than any other ownership factor.[22] This trend appears to be more evident in Canada than in other industrial societies.[23] In addition, almost one-third of the young-entrepreneur group discussed above is made up of women. Many of the incidents and profiles in this text illustrate the significant contributions of Canadian female entrepreneurs. Incident 1–3 on page 16 illustrates some challenges female entrepreneurs face.

Immigrant Entrepreneurs

A large number of Canadian entrepreneurs are immigrants to Canada or have parents who were immigrants. Over one-quarter of Canadian entrepreneurs fit into this category, the highest proportion of any country in a recent 11-nation study of entrepreneurs.[24]

Entrepreneurial Activity by Industry

As in other countries, the service industry in Canada is dominated by small businesses. Small firms also play a significant role in the retail and construction industries. The manufacturing industry is still dominated by large firms, although this trend is beginning to change as the momentum toward smaller organizations grows.

Figure 1–3 shows the level of small business involvement, including start-ups and survival rates for specific industries in Canada from 1979 through 1989.

Entrepreneurial Activity by Region

Although small businesses exist in all areas of Canada, some regions seem to be more fertile areas for growth. Figure 1–4 shows the regional share of small businesses in both numbers and number per 1,000 of population for 1979 and 1989.

FIGURE 1-3   Small Business Start-Ups by Sector, 1979–1989, and Business Birth and Survival Rates to 1989, Taken as a Percentage of the 1979 Base*

	Sector Share of Businesses with Fewer Than 100 Employees (%)	Number of Starts, 1979–89	Percentage of Total	Births	Survival
Primary	7.9	51,304	7.74	103.7	43.3
Mining	0.6	3,543	0.53	89.4	48.1
Manufacturing	6.1	35,645	5.38	82.3	52.5
Construction	11.9	77,293	11.66	95.6	40.3
Transportation/communications	4.2	27,236	4.11	97.9	43.2
Wholesale trade	5.8	33,468	5.05	79.6	49.5
Retail trade	15.9	101,871	15.37	88.1	39.5
Finance/insurance/real estate	6.3	39,325	5.93	95.4	46.9
Community services	8.4	44,192	6.67	87.7	70.2
Business and personal services	27.0	194,179	29.30	129.6	38.0
Unclassified	6.0	54,674	8.26	—	—
Total private sector	100.0	662,730	100.00	106.0	43.1

*Excludes public administration.

SOURCE: Entrepreneurship and Small Business Office, Statistics Canada.

FIGURE 1-4   Entrepreneurial Activity by Region

Regional Distribution of Canadian Small Businesses, 1979 and 1989 (%)*			Number of Businesses per 1,000 of Population		
	1979	1989		1979	1989
Newfoundland	1.8	2.3	Newfoundland	20.0	37.0
Prince Edward Island	0.7	0.7	Prince Edward Island	35.4	53.6
New Brunswick	3.0	2.9	Nova Scotia	25.1	35.5
Nova Scotia	3.4	3.4	New Brunswick	26.4	37.9
Quebec	25.2	25.2	Quebec	25.0	35.1
Ontario	35.4	34.6	Ontario	26.2	33.7
Manitoba	4.4	3.9	Manitoba	36.4	33.5
Saskatchewan	4.6	4.7	Saskatchewan	30.3	43.7
Alberta	11.2	11.2	Alberta	35.0	43.0
British Columbia	14.4	14.3	British Columbia	35.2	43.6
Yukon/Northwest Territories	0.4	0.3	Northwest Territories	28.8	33.6
			Yukon	47.1	56.3
			Canada	26.4	35.6

*Total may not add to 100 percent due to rounding and because some businesses are counted in more than one province.

SOURCE: Entrepreneurship and Small Business Office, Statistics Canada.

Incident 1-3

A Woman's Place Is on the Site

"Why," the banker asked Heather McLeod in 1984, "don't you open a boutique?" A 37-year-old woman selling skirts and blouses was something the banker could understand. A woman who wanted to start a manufacturing business to produce plywood forms for the construction industry wasn't.

Plywood forms are a specialized product used by builders to hold poured concrete while it hardens, but McLeod knew first-hand that nobody was meeting the demand for good-quality forms in Nova Scotia. She had worked seven years, first as an accountant and then in sales, for a company that made plywood forms, and her customers were telling her they weren't happy with the workmanship of the product they were getting.

"I thought—there's a good market here. Why don't I do something about it? If I don't, people from the States are going to move a plant up here." With her background and knowledge, she was dumbfounded that bankers should tell her she was in the wrong business. They were also unhappy that she wasn't married at the time, which meant no second income to support the new business. But she was able to get a mortgage on her house. She also "sold everything that wasn't tied down," including her car and her children's savings bonds, and got grants from the federal and Nova Scotia governments. Finally, she had a bankroll of $150,000.

In 1985, Superior Forming Systems and Supplies went into production in the village of Debert, near Truro. McLeod backed the quality of her product with a lifetime guarantee, and contractors, many of whom had encouraged her to go into business, were quick to place orders. Now she's expanding into New England and Ontario. Sales this year will pass the $1-million mark and she's investing more money in manufacturing. The company has 10 employees, including her husband of three years, who is vice-president.

McLeod says she loves working at her own business. At the height of the summer construction season she puts in a staggering 16 hours a day. "If you want to work from 9 to 5, you won't be successful," she says.

Source: Daniel Stoffman, "A Woman's Place Is on the Site," *Report on Business Magazine,* October 1988, p. 71.

Contributions of Small Business

The size of the small business sector is not the only reason this sector is important to Canada. The following sections discuss other significant benefits of small business to Canadian society.

Labour Intensity

Small businesses are generally more labour intensive than large companies. This means they typically employ more people to produce a certain level of output than a larger business does. In addition, small firms accounted for most of the new jobs created in Canada between 1979 and 1989.[25] It is estimated that this sector has produced another 1 million new jobs and virtually 100 percent of net job creation[26] between 1980 and 1990.[27] In this era of concern about employment levels, it is not surprising that current government policy includes incentives to promote the establishment of small businesses. Not only does small business provide significant contributions to employment; recent research indicates employees feel that small companies are better places to work than large ones.[28]

Innovations and Inventions

Individuals in small businesses have been responsible for a majority of the inventions and innovations society benefits from today. Many of these inventions have been made by Canadian entrepreneurs. As mentioned previously, even innovations of larger companies are often made by individuals within those organizations who are rewarded for their entrepreneurial creativity. Incident 1–4 illustrates the innovation of one Canadian entrepreneur.

Productivity and Profitability

Since the turn of the century, the conventional wisdom of economics concerning productivity in organizations has been that the larger the organization, the greater the opportunity to be more *productive* and *profitable*. As a result both business and government have tended to increase in size. However, the validity of this thinking has been seriously questioned in recent years and shown to be empirically weak. Figure 1–5 shows that in return on sales (profit to sales), a standard measure of profitability, small business scores substantially higher than all businesses in most industries.

Large businesses are also recognizing the gains in productivity associated with smallness. Of the eight attributes of success listed by Peters and Waterman in their study of successful corporations,[29] no fewer than six are commonly found in small businesses.[30] These six attributes are listed below.

1. Bias for Action. These organizations have found that a preference for doing something—anything rather than sending an idea through endless cycles of analyses and committee reports—encourages new ideas and creativity. This principle seems typical of most successful businesses.

2. Staying Close to the Customer. Small businesses learn customer preferences and cater to them. They are generally closer to and have more contact with the consumer. Larger organizations spend considerable amounts of money to maintain this closeness.

Incident 1-4

Cleaning Up with a Robot Vacuum

Selling science fiction isn't easy. As robotics designer Vivek Burhanpurkar learned, convincing backers and buyers to support innovation is a struggle when your product is more futuristic than familiar. Burhanpurkar designed a housekeeping robot with its own vision system that can vacuum any floor space. But developing a robot that can see requires investors who also have vision.

Burhanpurkar, a 27-year-old electrical engineer who founded Cyberworks Inc. in 1987, got his big break after taking an early prototype of "CyberVac" to a 1987 trade show in Cologne, Germany.

Burhanpurkar believes CyberVac is the world's first cleaning robot that uses sonar and artificial intelligence to vacuum a room. Competing systems need to be pre-programmed or follow an electronic pathway around a room. Burhanpurkar originally saw his robot as a household appliance, but is now targeting commercial clients. Negotiations are underway with three European contract cleaners and a U.S. hotel chain.

Burhanpurkar's idea was born in 1985. While studying at the University of Toronto, he devoted his thesis to robotics. The "A" he received encouraged him to leave school sans degree to try out his ideas. "I wasn't interested in designing bigger and better microwaves," he says. "I thought—Why not robots in the house? Science fiction stuff." After considering building a robotic lawnmower or a snowblower, Burhanpurkar settled on a battery-powered vacuuming robot.

Source: Jennifer Low, "Cleaning Up with a Robot Vacuum," *Profit Magazine,* March 1991, p. 32.

FIGURE 1-5 Return on Sales for Selected Industry Groups in Canada, 1990

| | Small Businesses | | |
Industry Group	Sales Level $100,000–$499,999	Sales Level $500,000–$2,000,000	All Businesses
Manufacturing	3.8%	4.9%	4.0%
Construction	6.9	6.7	2.3
Wholesale	4.6	3.9	1.8
Retail	2.5	2.9	3.4
Services	13.7	7.8	6.3

SOURCES: *Statistical Profile of Small Business in Canada (Statistics Canada),* 1987; *Corporate Financial Statistics (Statistics Canada),* 1987; *Key Business Ratios, 1987,* Dun & Bradstreet, Canada Ltd.

3. Autonomy and Entrepreneurship.   Breaking the corporation into small companies and encouraging each unit to think independently and competitively has become a strategy of many large businesses. The previously cited examples of 3M and Apple Computer illustrate the benefits of following this approach.

4. Productivity through People.   Creating in all employees the awareness that their best efforts are essential and that they will share in the rewards of the company's success is a major goal of successful companies. In small businesses, owner and employees typically share in the rewards of success and the disappointments of failure of their efforts.

5. Hands On—Value Driven.   Many organizations insist that executives keep in touch with the firm's essential business and promote a strong corporate culture. A recently popular method of management known as management by walking around (MBWA) testifies to the realization that management needs to be familiar with the firm's employees and the operation of the business. The successful owner-manager follows this principle faithfully.

6. Simple Form—Lean Staff.   Few administrative layers, with few people at the upper levels, are characteristic of many successful businesses. In many small businesses, employees have a direct line of access to the owner-manager. This arrangement increases the flexibility of the organization as well as employee morale.

Flexibility

Small businesses are generally able to respond more quickly than large businesses to changes in the economy, government policies, and competition. In addition, many markets can be served only by small businesses because they are too small or too localized for large companies to serve profitably. This situation alone presents countless opportunities for entrepreneurs.

Canadian Ownership

The content of Canadian ownership, a major concern of economic nationalists in Canada, tends to be much higher in small business than in large business.[31] Of businesses operating in Canada with less than $2 million in sales, fewer than 1 percent are foreign owned while over 99 percent are Canadian owned.

Small Business Health as a Link to Economic Growth

Considerable evidence exists that those economies that provide the most encouragement for entrepreneurship and small business have experienced the highest growth rates since the 1950s.[32] Recognition of this fact by many centrally planned economies has resulted in more encouragement of entrepreneurship with the associated potential of rewards for those engaged in this type of productive activity.[33] It may also have contributed to the dramatic changes that have recently occurred in these countries.

Social Contributions

Small business owners often have a long-term interest in the communities in which their businesses operate. As a result, they appear to contribute to those communities in nonbusiness ways to a greater extent than an employee of a large corporation might do.[34]

Small Business and the Future

An important question for present and future entrepreneurs, as well as for policymakers, is "What effects will future changes in our society have on the small business community?" As mentioned at the beginning of this chapter, the 1970s and 1980s were a period of entrepreneurial revolution. However, the 1990s are expected to determine whether this "revolution" was a passing phenomenon or a permanent adjustment to the Canadian business environment.[35] Several developing trends have potentially positive implications for entrepreneurs. At the same time, many of these trends will be advantageous only if entrepreneurs' actions are the result of insight, research, and careful planning.

Some of the more significant factors that will affect the future of small business are discussed briefly in the following sections.

Change

The world is now undergoing a period of rapid change, and this trend is expected to continue. Businesses today will carry out their various activities very differently than they will 10 years from now. This means that small business flexibility likely will continue to be a competitive strength for the entrepreneur.

As the following sections discuss, changes are occurring in technology, consumer demographics and buying patterns, and the competitive aspects of markets.

Technology

Technology has revolutionized the activities of both small and large businesses. Computers allow the entrepreneur to manage large amounts of information as effectively as a larger business. Such advances have signalled significant small business opportunities. Financial management and accounting, marketing research and planning, promotion, and consulting are areas where small businesses, many of them home based, have succeeded. As computer technology becomes more affordable, more small businesses will take advantage of computer applications in these areas.

New technology has also allowed small businesses to obtain subcontracts of many services from larger businesses and government organizations that are unable or choose not to carry out these activities themselves. Despite these potential opportunities, however, small businesses must be prepared to embrace new technology or face the possibility of obsolescence and lack of competitiveness. In a few industries, ignorance of technological change will not adversely affect performance.

Consumer Demographics and Buying Patterns

Canadian consumers are ageing, and their disposable incomes are growing. Of particular interest to most businesses is the "baby boom" consumer, born between 1946 and 1964. These people are the largest and most significant demographic group, comprising close to one-third of the Canadian population. This group is currently entering its highest income-earning period, resulting in large expenditures for certain types of goods and services. Although small in number, Canadian seniors hold close to 80 percent of personal wealth and are big spenders on travel, health and fitness products, and various services. The larger number of working women has created greater economic clout for females as well as heavier demand for time-saving products and convenience. All demographic groups in Canada are concerned about the environment and demand quality products at reasonable prices.

Each of these demographic and demand trends represents opportunities for entrepreneurs. Many examples of how entrepreneurs are responding to these trends are presented in the profiles and incidents in this text. Markets will become further fragmented as businesses attempt to satisfy consumer wants and needs. This increase in segmentation should favour small businesses that cater to these smaller, more specialized markets.

Competitive Aspects of Markets

Three major occurrences in the past few years have affected the already intensely competitive environment most small businesses face. The first is the Free Trade Agreement, which has liberalized trade between Canada and the United States. The second is the worldwide movement to global markets, augmented by recent developments in Eastern Europe. The third is the response to the growth of the small business sector by large business.

The Canada–U.S. Free Trade Agreement. The Free Trade Agreement will gradually remove trade barriers between Canada and the United States, but it will also eliminate protection for certain industries. In general, Canadian small business has been in favour of the agreement because of the large consumer market to the south that it opened up. Some Canadian entrepreneurs have already successfully penetrated this market. Many have found, however, that they must overcome other difficulties before they can effectively compete. These problems include higher Canadian taxes and distribution costs.

Free trade with the United States has also increased the competition from U.S. firms expanding into Canada. This trend has been most noticeable in the retailing industry. Although there will likely be adjustments in particular industries in the short term, the overall competitiveness of the affected industries is expected to improve. Consequences similar to those of the FTA are expected to result from the North American Free Trade Agreement (NAFTA) with the United States and Mexico.

Global Markets.   The world is currently experiencing a major shift to the globalization of markets. This means that the many small businesses will eventually include an international aspect in their operations. Current GATT (General Agreement on Tariffs and Trade) talks suggest that Canadian small businesses will find increased access to export markets as trade barriers come down. Although the trend toward trade liberalization has been evolving gradually over a number of years, the recent defeat of communism in the Eastern bloc has signalled a number of opportunities for entrepreneurs. Consumers in these countries have an insatiable demand for Western products and services. As remaining barriers and purchasing power problems are overcome, these areas will offer huge untapped markets.

Large Business Response.   Small businesses have always had difficulty competing with large businesses, particularly for such things as capital, raw materials, and labour. This situation is not expected to change appreciably in some industries. Financing problems continue to plague small businesses. Despite new programs, influence over suppliers by large businesses is strong, and wage rates paid by larger organizations and government are often too high for the smaller business to meet.

In addition to the difficulty of matching wage rates, the 1990s and beyond are expected to experience labour shortages. This will increase the competition for competent employees even more. Small businesses will need to find ways to retain top employees through nonfinancial methods. (Chapter 11 will discuss this further.) A recent survey of small business owners indicated that close to one-half see the labour shortage as a major concern for small business.[36]

One positive aspect is that many large businesses and government agencies are increasingly subcontracting the purchase of products and services to small business. There is also evidence that many small businesses are joining together through such means as industry associations in an attempt to be more competitive. Such a collaborative relationship, however, often runs against the grain of the entrepreneur's independent nature.

Recently large businesses in some industries have adopted strategies employed by smaller businesses to recoup lost market share. The adoption of entrepreneurial programs in product development, the increased attention to customer service, and the addition of some small business operating policies have enhanced the growth and success of smaller enterprises.

The Economy

The performances of many small businesses are directly related to the Canadian economy. During the recession of 1981–1982, net increases in the number of small businesses decreased (see Figure 1–1). This reflects the facts that it is harder for businesses to get established during such times and the number of failures increases because of lower revenues. The recession of the early 1990s has had a

---

Incident 1–5

The New Challenge of the '90s

Entrepreneurs will be talking about the 1990–91 recession long after the red ink flows black again. Panellists at the Profit Future Watch Roundtable agree this recession has reshaped the economy. "In southwestern Ontario, it's been the worst recession since the '30s and it's taken a real toll on the manufacturing industry," says John Cowperthwaite, national director of entrepreneurial services for Ernst & Young. "That's going to be a real problem for us in the future because I don't see that coming back. We lost jobs and it's going to be tough to regenerate those manufacturing positions." Also hard hit were retailers, and entrepreneurs will have to work harder than ever to provide value to watchful value-minded consumers.

The economy is changing. But *Profit*'s panellists, a stellar lineup of innovative and award-winning entrepreneurs, believe those who adapt and become tougher competitors will survive and prosper in the upswing. "You can bitch and yell about it, but the world is becoming more competitive," says Conald Ziraldo, president of Inniskillin Wines Inc. of Niagara-on-the-Lake, Ont. "If you want to stick around, you've got to join in." Our panellists suggest a three-step process to competing in the new '90s.

1. Get to know your market better, and deliver what your customers want.
2. Motivate your work force and reassess operations to produce the best products you can.
3. Look to export markets for future growth and diversification.

Source: Cathy Hilborn, "The New Challenge of the '90s," *Profit Magazine*, December 1991, p. 26.

---

similar effect on the performance of the small business sector. There is evidence, however, that those businesses that start during a recession have a greater chance of survival than those started during expansionary periods.[37] Incident 1–5 illustrates how entrepreneurs can cope with difficult times in the economy.

The Political Climate

During the 1980s, the political climate for small business ownership seemed to be improving. This was evidenced by attempts to reduce the burdens of paperwork and provide tax incentives to small businesses. These efforts will be discussed in detail in Chapter 12.

Federal government attempts to encourage entrepreneurship are also evidenced by incentives for immigrant entrepreneurs to enter the country. Special visas are provided for immigrants who invest in small business. In 1988 over $2.5 million was injected into the Canadian economy through this program.

Although there is considerable interest in government circles in reducing government involvement in business and encouraging entrepreneurial activity, as shown by recent government consultations,[38] most small business proponents are still waiting for significant action to take place.[39] In fact, the enactment of the goods and services tax (GST) has had a much more severe effect on small businesses than on larger firms. (Chapter 12 will discuss the GST further.) Continued collective lobbying efforts through such organizations as the Federation of Independent Business are required to achieve a political environment more conducive to the establishment and successful operation of the small business.

The Social Climate

Society tends to look more favourably on small business and entrepreneurial activities as a legitimate way to make a living. More and more college graduates are beginning their careers by starting their own businesses, joining the ranks of the many people who leave the once secure confines of large business to strike out on their own. Although this trend is expected to continue, adequate preparation and planning will be increasingly required to achieve success following this route.

The onus is now on entrepreneurs as prospective owner-managers to sharpen their skills in this competitive and rapidly changing society. An owner-manager in today's world cannot survive on guesswork. Numerous programs, courses, and types of assistance are available to allow the owner-manager to acquire this training. The remaining chapters in this book will cover the critical areas a prospective owner-manager should be familiar with in starting and operating a successful small business.

Summary

1. Many countries are turning to small business and private initiative to assist in their economic growth.
2. The entrepreneurial revolution is evidenced by the growing number of business establishments, employees in small businesses, government small business programs, college and university small business classes, and entrepreneurial activities of large companies.
3. Although defining a small business is difficult, a definition is important in comparing and evaluating small business as well as in taking advantage of various lending and assistance programs.
4. Some common criteria in defining small business are gross sales, number of employees, profitability, and type of management structure.
5. Small business accounts for 97 percent of all businesses, 29 percent of gross sales, 30 percent of gross domestic product, and 47 percent of the labour force in Canada.
6. Recent years have witnessed an increase in the number of small businesses established by young people and in the percentage of small businesses started by women.

7. Small business can provide jobs, innovations, high productivity, flexibility, a higher proportion of Canadian ownership, and more contributions to a society.

8. The climate for starting a small business should improve, however, competitive disadvantages may continue to negate this potential advantage.

Chapter Problems and Applications

1. Why do you think entrepreneurial activity has increased? Do you think these trends will continue? Why or why not?

2. Under what conditions would the various definitions of small business be more appropriate? (i.e., the level of profit may be used by Revenue Canada to determine the small business tax rate).

3. What is meant by the statement "Small business is the backbone of the Canadian economic system"? Give evidence to support this statement.

4. The computer consulting business is becoming more and more fragmented. In data processing, for example, there are hardware versus software consultants, batch versus time-sharing service bureaus, and mainframe versus microcomputer specialists. What effect does this type of industry fragmentation have on the small business community?

5. Ask three small business owners about their projections for the future of small business. What problems and opportunities do they foresee?

Suggested Readings

Bulloch, John F. "Competing in the Global Economy." *Journal of Small Business and Entrepreneurship,* July-September 1991.

Combined Impact of Old and New Establishments from 1971 to 1980. Regional Industrial Expansion. Ottawa, Ont.: Government of Canada, March 1984.

Drucker, Peter F. *Innovation and Entrepreneurship*: *Practice and Principles.* New York: Harper & Row, 1985.

Guidelines for the Development of Small Business in Canada. Toronto, Ont.: Canadian Federation of Independent Business, February 25, 1985.

Kao, Raymond. "The Market System and an Entrepreneurial Driven Economy," *Journal of Small Business and Entrepreneurship,* October-December 1991.

Small Business in Canada. Industry, Science and Technology Canada 1991. Government of Canada.

"Venturing into the 1990's." *Small Business Magazine*—special issue, June 1989.

Thompson, Pat. "Characteristics of the Small Business Entrepreneur in Canada." *Journal of Small Business and Entrepreneurship* 4, no. 3 (Winter 1986–1987), pp. 5–11.

The White Paper—Recent Cross Canada Consultation Inviting Submissions from Small Businesses. Ottawa, Ont.: Ministry of State for Small Business, Government of Canada.

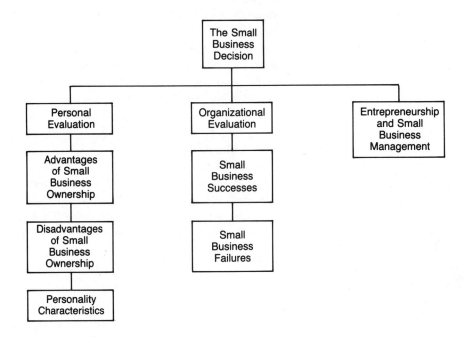

2 The Small Business Decision

Chapter Objectives

- To discuss the advantages and disadvantages of small business ownership as a starting point in making the small business decision.
- To review the personal attributes of a successful small business owner.
- To evaluate the small business decision from an organizational point of view.
- To explain the common reasons some businesses succeed and others fail.
- To discuss the types of environment that are conducive to successful small business opportunities.
- To identify the differences and similarities between an entrepreneur and a manager.

Small Business Profile

Lou MacEachern

Dalco-Servpro

Lou MacEachern was raised on a farm on Prince Edward Island. He dropped out of school after grade 7, but eventually completed his high school diploma and studied commerce at Dalhousie University. In 1952 he travelled to Calgary and worked before resuming his studies in high school and university. Although MacEachern had little money, his studies gave him confidence in his abilities. He gained experience in the cleaning industry for a few years and in 1964 started Servpro Disaster Restoration Ltd., which specialized in cleaning up after fires and floods. He later added Dalco Construction Ltd., which repaired flood and fire damage, and Commercial Salvage, which bought damaged goods for resale. MacEachern's companies grew dramatically and by 1991 they grossed $12 million. In 1991 he was selected as Alberta's entrepreneur of the year.

Lou MacEachern possesses many attributes of the successful entrepreneur. His guiding philosophy is hard work, regularly working "half days," as he puts it—from 6 A.M. to 6 P.M. He expects the same hard work from his employees and pays the better performers well, mostly through commission. Networking has been critical to his success, as he frequently visits with key clients, suppliers, and other businesspeople. MacEachern also displays another talent important to his success: salesmanship. He is very skilled at concluding a sale and acquiring unquestioned loyalty from his employees. Although he is very self-confident, he admits that even though he has worked hard, he has experienced a certain amount of good luck—"of being in the right place at the right time."

Finally, MacEachern, like many entrepreneurs, has little patience for government regulations and red tape. Perhaps this is part of the reason that his interest in Dalco-Servpro is for sale and he is looking to pursue other interests.

Source: Used with permission of Lou MacEachern.

The Small Business Decision: Personal Evaluation

In contemplating whether to start their own businesses, individuals are well advised to consider the potential consequences of such a move, both on themselves and on those closely associated with them. Failure to do this can lead to disillusionment, frustration, and an unsuccessful attempt to capitalize on a viable business opportunity. A good way to begin this evaluation is to learn the potential advantages and disadvantages of starting and operating one's own business. In addition, an understanding of the personality characteristics and abilities required of an entrepreneur, as well as an honest self-appraisal of one's own suitability, is essential in making an intelligent small business decision.

Advantages of Small Business Ownership

Running one's own business offers some unique advantages over being an employee. Numerous small business owners cite the following potential advantages.

More Personal Contacts with People.   Running a small business usually means making contact with a larger number of people, including customers, suppliers, and employees. Those who enjoy and are skilled at working with people find such interactions the most rewarding aspect of their business.

Independence.   Often independence is the primary reason for going into business for oneself. This includes the freedom to make one's own decisions without having to account to a superior. A recent study of successful entrepreneurs indicated that the majority started their businesses to "control their own lives" or to "be their own boss."[1] Entrepreneurs should realize, however, that even though they own their businesses, they still must answer to customers, suppliers, key employees, and creditors.

Skill Development.   Abilities in many functional areas of management are necessary in running a small business and can be developed during the process. Often the possession of such skills makes an individual more sought after in larger organizations. Today many progressive and innovative organizations look for employees who have had small business experience.

Potential Financial Rewards.   The higher risk associated with operating a small business offers the possibility of obtaining a higher financial return. Many small businesses are profitable enough to make their owners financially independent. Note, however, that the promise of financial reward is seldom the sole motivating force behind a small business start-up.[2]

Challenge.   Many people start small businesses for the challenge and feeling of personal accomplishment. A recent study of Canadian entrepreneurs' perceptions of the "ideal" work showed that work that offers a challenge is the most important factor.[3] Often these people left larger companies because their positions lacked the opportunities and challenges a small business can offer.

Enjoyment.   Most successful entrepreneurs enjoy what they do. In fact, entrepreneurs tend to get their best ideas from their hobbies.[4] This fact explains in part why financial rewards are not necessarily the prime motivation for establishing a business. It also partly explains the large amount of time entrepreneurs devote to their businesses. The small business profile of Lou MacEachern at the beginning of this chapter illustrates this principle. The level of enjoyment entrepreneurs get from running their own businesses is indicated by the fact that over 90 percent of Canadian entrepreneurs said they would start their own business again.[5]

Disadvantages of Small Business Ownership

While there are many advantages in owning and operating a small business, there are several often overlooked disadvantages, including the following.

Risk.   The failure rate of small businesses is very high. Bankruptcy statistics for Canada show that smaller firms face a greater danger of bankruptcy than larger ones.[6] It has been estimated that four out of every five small businesses fail within the first few years. There are many potential reasons for these failures, but the major causes appear to be inexperience and unbalanced management.[7]

Stress.   Studies show that small business owners have high stress levels, a high incidence of heart disease, and a high rate of divorce owing to the increased pressures of managing their businesses.[8] In owning a business, it is difficult, if not impossible, to confine concerns about the business to the workplace. Typically these pressures will affect one's personal life and family situation as well.

Need for Many Abilities.   The acquisition of the required skills, such as accounting, finance, marketing, and personnel management, is a difficult task that many owner-managers never master. This is particularly true for the countless businesses that start out very small. In these situations, entrepreneurs generally cannot afford to hire people with specialized expertise in these areas. Failure to acquire these skills, either personally or through recruitment, can seriously hinder the growth of the business.[9]

Limited Financial Rewards.   Although the possibility of high earnings exists, relatively few small business owners become millionaires. The financial rewards are often very meagre, especially during the first few years of a business. Even businesses that are growing rapidly are not necessarily as profitable as one might think.

Incident 2–1

Innovation, Design, and Hard Work

Interalia Associates Ltd. in Calgary is a textbook example of the industry of the 1980s. A high-tech telecommunications and microsystems engineering firm, Interalia started in 1975 with nothing but the expertise of some computer buffs and a lot of enthusiasm. It now does business all over the world.

"The average workday here is 10 to 12 hours, and we're always open Saturdays," says Cal Manz. "Competition is fierce. Our edge is our willingness to spend a lot on R&D, and the fact that everyone with the company can do anything—even our receptionist can solder circuit boards in the back room if necessary. This helps us offset some of our difficulties. For example, it's difficult for a small company to properly market an ideal product without spending millions, so we rely on the personal approach and repeat business. Also, we have to maintain a very large inventory because all of our chips have to be imported from the States or Japan."

Source: Adapted from Richard Sherbaniuk, "Innovation, Design and Hard Work," *Small Business Quarterly* 4 (1985), pp. 14–15.

People Conflicts.   Because owning a small business tends to require more contact with people, the potential for more *conflicts* with employees, suppliers, and customers arises. This factor could turn what is often thought of as an advantage into both a disadvantage and a frustration of small business ownership.

Time Demands.   At least initially, almost all small businesses require long hours of work. The work schedule in Incident 2–1 illustrates that an owner-manager of a small business often has a much longer workday than he or she would if working for someone else. A recent study of small business owners indicates that almost 50 percent work over 50 hours per week and 86 percent say they work on weekends.[10]

Personality Characteristics Required of a Successful Owner-Manager

What are the personality traits of the successful owner-manager? In his book *Peak Performers,* Charles A. Garfield estimates that 70 percent of the 1,500 peak performers he studied were entrepreneurs.[11] These individuals exhibited some common characteristics that confirmed the results of previous studies.

In discussing the following characteristics, note that no common personality trait applies to all successful entrepreneurs. Canadian entrepreneurs have many different traits and come from diverse backgrounds. Very few, if any, entrepreneurs possess all of the traits discussed next. These characteristics have been noted in observing entrepreneurs. On the other hand, possession of such characteristics does not guarantee success in small business.

Individuals contemplating small business ownership would do well to evaluate their own suitability to operate a small business by noting the following personality characteristics possessed by successful entrepreneurs.

Achievement Orientation.   Those who place a high value on achievement, competition, aggressiveness, and hard work may be ideal owner-managers. Such people tend to be disciplined goal setters and to have a bias for action. Entrepreneurs also tend to possess above-average focus and drive, as well as the initiative to make things happen. Because they are hard workers, they generally strive to maintain good health to sustain this high level of energy.

Risk Taking.   As previously mentioned, the very nature of small business suggests that entrepreneurs are risk takers, although they often do not think of themselves as such. Evidence shows, however, that successful entrepreneurs usually do take calculated risks. They do not fear failure but use it as a source of motivation.

Independence, Self-Confidence, and Self-Assurance.   Entrepreneurs tend to resent authority and to want to take credit or discredit for their own actions. Karl Vesper, the well-known spokesperson for entrepreneurship, states in his book *New Venture Strategies* that "The entrepreneur . . . has a basic human appetite to crave for freedom and power over his/her circumstances."[12] Incident 2–2 illustrates the independence exhibited by one Canadian entrepreneur.

Strongly correlated with independence as other characteristics of successful small business ownership are self-confidence and self-assurance. Often these traits are acquired through parents who were also small business owners. A recent study found that 35 percent of Canadian entrepreneurs had parents who owned businesses.[13]

Innovativeness.   Successful entrepreneurs tend to be creative and willing to try new ideas. They are not afraid to evaluate an idea in a nontraditional way and to ask questions such as "why not?" Such entrepreneurs are sensitive to new trends in society and potential opportunities that result from such trends. Interestingly, the major reason given by Canadian entrepreneurs for starting their own businesses was that they had found an attractive market niche and wanted to pursue it.[14] Entrepreneurs tend to be oriented toward opportunity. Incident 2–3 on page 36 shows how a Canadian entrepreneur asked "why not" and proceeded to create a successful business from this idea.

Strong Verbal and Numerical Skills.   Successful small business owners are able to communicate their thoughts well. Their numerical skills aid them in solving many of the problems that arise in operating a small business.

Incident 2–2

Go Vacations

"Go Your Own Way, Worldwide" is the slogan of Go Vacations Limited, a Toronto-based company that now serves vacationers from around the world by renting motorhomes and houseboats across North America. Under the crafty management of thirty-six-year-old Paul Doyle, this company has become one of the largest renters of recreational vacation vehicles (popularly known as RVs) in the world. In 1985, Go Vacations and a growing list of vehicle owners (for whom it manages and rents motorhomes, houseboats, and yachts) will gross about $10 million.

Few would have predicted such success for Doyle as a teenager. He was asked to leave two high schools in Toronto and quit after grade eleven. Always a bit of a rebel, he objected to such rituals as the Lord's Prayer and singing "God Save the Queen." Nevertheless, he did not lack scholastic ability. He completed and passed grades twelve and thirteen on his own, then took a degree in only two years at York University, majoring in fine arts and psychology.

After graduation he worked as a high school teacher and took a job renting and selling camping trailers in the summertime. It went so well that in 1973 he decided to leave teaching and make a full-time job of RV retail sales. "My parents believed in me, so I was able to start with $15,000 borrowed from a bank, with their home as collateral. In the first year I sold tent trailers and was able to gross $50,000 and put all of the money back into the business."

Source: Kenneth Barnes and Everett Banning, *Money Makers: The Secrets of Canada's Most Successful Entrepreneurs* (Toronto: McClelland and Stewart, 1985).

Whether or not they achieved a high formal education, successful entrepreneurs have usually acquired the necessary skills and knowledge from various sources. Increasingly however, the educational background of Canadian entrepreneurs is rising. One study found that over 56 percent of those operating small businesses had at least some postsecondary education.[15] Most successful entrepreneurs have above-average marketing and selling skills. This skill not only is helpful in promoting the business to customers but essential for obtaining debt or equity capital, securing suppliers, and maintaining employee loyalty. It is also very valuable in establishing networking contacts or sources of assistance for their operations.

Problem-Solving Abilities.   Entrepreneurs identify problems quickly and respond with effective solutions. Typically they rank above average at sorting through irrelevant details and getting to the heart of a problem. Incident 2–4 on page 37 illustrates how two Canadian entrepreneurs have solved the problems their business encountered.

Incident 2–3

Getting Rich by Keeping It Cheap

Steve Duffy and a friend went running one night, and discussed how dissatisfied each was with the job he had. They decided to go away for a weekend, and ended up in Baltimore, Maryland, where they were stunned by the advertisements in the paper. "The prices were so much cheaper than in Canada that we bought ten Commodore 64's originally for our family and friends, and brought them back home." They happily paid the exchange rate—which was then only about 18 cents on the dollar—as well as the duty and taxes demanded at the Canadian border. But they were still considerably ahead of the game: The Commodore keyboards which they paid $250 U.S. for were going for $800 in Toronto.

So the two young men—Martin Pahnke was the other—ended up selling the computers for $550 each, and they still made a clear $200 profit on each.

"We were very surprised that it went so well, and we went down to the States lots of times," says Duffy. The two men soon quit their jobs, and in August and September of 1983 they made an average of three trips a week to Baltimore. In the first three months they sold $50,000 in machines. By October 1 of that same year they opened their store, Computers for Less, which pretty much tells what they were offering. It cost less than $4,000 to open the place, which they paid for from the capital of their never-ending garage sales.

The modus operandi of Duffy and partner was really quite extraordinary, and the border guards must have been on a first-name basis with them rather quickly. From the moment their miniature, 250-square-foot store in the west end of Toronto opened, it was a huge success.

The next move for the 22-year-old was, of course, to start franchising. Requests for stores have poured in from Montreal, Halifax, and Vancouver, but Duffy is a bit reluctant to travel too far from Toronto. Unlike many entrepreneurs, Steven Duffy knows his own limits: "One of my traits is, I'm a perfectionist. I like to see things done well, clearly, and tightly. If they are lacking in any of those, it would be time to reorganize. Right now, it's moving quickly, but well. But I wouldn't be able to run thirty stores."

There you have it: a Canadian who was willing to deal directly with American distributors, eliminate the middleman, and pass on part of the huge savings to the customer. It should make everyone happy, except perhaps the Canadian wholesalers.

Source: Allan Gould, *The New Entrepreneurs—80 Canadian Success Stories* (Toronto: McClelland and Stewart—Bantam, Ltd., 1986), pp. 343–47.

Strategic Planning.   Successful small business owners tend to excel at setting business objectives and developing different ways of achieving them. They adapt to change easily and know their industries and products thoroughly.

Incident 2-4

Agents of Change

When all four of his suppliers cut him off on the same day, Glen Behl realized just how radically he had challenged the status quo among Winnipeg's fruit and vegetable distributors. Not that his tactics weren't commonsense. As co-owners of a $300,000-a-year produce store, Garden Grove Produce Emporium, Behl and brother-in-law Michael Gorun began wholesaling to restaurants in 1987 by doing the legwork no one else was doing.

"We found it strange," says Behl. "It's a very lazy industry." By force of habit, most restaurants had been buying produce from one of four big produce importers—all linked to large national supermarket conglomerates. No less complacent were the importers, who rarely paid sales calls or sent out price lists.

Seeing that market apathy as an opportunity, Behl, 29, and Gorun, 28, started doing their own importing. By buying lettuce, tomatoes, and grapefruit in bulk from their lowest-cost suppliers, they were able to offer local restaurants prices lower than their own suppliers were charging. By the end of 1988 Garden Grove Produce Imports Ltd. had 16 restaurants in its fold, and sales had sprouted to $1.3 million from $300,000 the year before.

But Garden Grove's tactics didn't go unnoticed for long. "We were selling to too many of these big suppliers' customers," says Behl. "In September, 1988, the whole thing blew up in our faces." The word came from the big importers' sales reps on a Friday morning. As of Monday, they could no longer sell to Garden Grove.

To this day, those original suppliers won't sell a carrot to Behl and Gorun. Garden Grove was forced to break with the industry once again, this time by sourcing its produce directly in the U.S. But fortune again favoured the innovators, and Garden Grove just kept growing. With sales of $3.5 million in 1991, it enjoyed five-year revenue growth of almost 2,000%, good for the 12th spot on the 1992 Fastest 50 (*Profit Magazine*). And its profits grew a respectable 604%, to $183,000.

Source: John Southerst, "Agents of Change," *Profit Magazine,* June 1992, pp. 38-39.

Perseverance. Because of the difficulties in starting and operating a small business, successful entrepreneurs tend to have perseverance. They do not quit amid adversity. One study found that successful entrepreneurs "average 3.8 failures before the final success."[16] Incident 2-5 shows how Mellanie Stephens, who established Kettle Creek Canvas Company, is attempting to bounce back.

To assess the suitability of their personalities for starting a small business, entrepreneurs should evaluate their own capabilities in the areas just described.

Incident 2–5

Up the Creek Again

It was a bitter parting when founder Mellanie Stephens was forced out of Kettle Creek Canvas Co. three years ago in a dispute over control with her silent partners. But the bitterness was nothing compared to what she felt when the 59 store clothing retailer was forced into voluntary bankruptcy last year. "It was pretty heartbreaking," says the 40-year-old Stephens, who launched the St. Thomas, Ont.–based clothing chain in 1979. "When I left, it was making money."

Stephens, who says she was forced out after selling control of the company to raise equity, blames Kettle Creek's failure on mismanagement and overspending on expansion. She's kept a low profile since her '88 ouster as she struggled to pay off a stack of personal and business bills, and went through what she calls "a kind of mourning period. It was tough; watching something that I put so much into for so many years go under was gross."

But that's all over now, as she re-enters the business with a new solo venture. Rural Route Dry Goods Inc. opened in a London, Ont., mall late last year selling the same kind of rugged and reasonably priced casual clothing on which Kettle Creek was based. The store also sells furnishings, quilts, bags, and even wooden furniture produced by a woodworker who shares her warehouse in Aylmer, Ont. As in the past, she's depending on quality to attract repeat business and favourable word of mouth. So far, the word seems good: the guestbook in the new store is replete with comments such as "Welcome back, Mel."

Also in mind are the lessons she took away from Kettle Creek. Topping the list: "Keep your costs down and put your money in your product." She's doing that with low overhead, employing home sewers and setting up the mail-order business in the warehouse she's renting for $500 a month. Next is to remember that "the most important thing in your business is your customer, not your product or your big, fancy office. That's something too many managers forget."

Source: "Up the Creek Again," *Profit Magazine*, March 1992, pp. 48–49.

Making a checklist allows a quantitative evaluation of these characteristics. An example of one such checklist appears in Figure 2–1.

The Small Business Decision: Organizational Evaluation

It is important not only to evaluate one's personal capabilities to operate a small business successfully but to investigate what makes some businesses succeed and others fail. The following discussion reviews what some businesses do right and

---

Figure 2–1   Personality Characteristics Checklist

1. If the statement is only rarely or slightly descriptive of your behaviour, *score 1*.
2. If the statement is applicable under some circumstances, but only partially true, *score 2*.
3. If the statement describes you perfectly, *score 3*.

Score

1. I relish competing with others. _____
2. I compete intensely to win regardless of the rewards. _____
3. I compete with some caution, but will often bluff. _____
4. I do not hesitate to take a calculated risk for future gain. _____
5. I do a job so effectively that I get a feeling of accomplishment. _____
6. I want to be tops in whatever I elect to do. _____
7. I am not bound by tradition. _____
8. I am inclined to forge ahead and discuss later. _____
9. Reward or praise means less to me than a job well done. _____
10. I usually go my own way regardless of others' opinions. _____
11. I find it difficult to admit error or defeat. _____
12. I am a self-starter—I need little urging from others. _____
13. I am not easily discouraged. _____
14. I work out my own answers to problems. _____
15. I am inquisitive. _____
16. I am not patient with interference from others. _____
17. I have an aversion to taking orders from others. _____
18. I can take criticism without hurt feelings. _____
19. I insist on seeing a job through to the finish. _____
20. I expect associates to work as hard as I do. _____
21. I read to improve my knowledge in all business activities.

A score of 63 is perfect; 52 to 62 is good; 42 to 51 is fair; and under 42 is poor. Obviously, scoring high here is not a guarantee of becoming a successful small business owner, since many other personal qualities must also be rated. But it should encourage you to pursue the matter further.

---

what others do wrong. The potential small business owner should incorporate those things successful businesses do right and avoid the mistakes other businesses have made.

Small Business Successes

Despite the high risk associated with starting a small business, many small businesses operate successfully today. Numerous examples of these successes appear throughout this book in the incidents and profiles. These examples illustrate many of the characteristics of successful businesses and their owners. The characteristics discussed next are compiled from reviews of successful small businesses.

Alertness to Change.   Small businesses that are flexible and plan ahead are able to adapt to changing environmental conditions more quickly and, in many cases, more effectively than larger businesses. The success of many small computer software companies is a good example. The computer industry is changing very rapidly, and the new needs that are emerging offer many opportunities for small business. The ability of the Duffys (see the small business profile in Chapter 4) to recognize a need and respond to it contributed to their success.

Ability to Attract and Hold Competent Employees.   Small businesses tend to be labour intensive, and thus the value of employees cannot be overstated. Small businesses face increasing competition from large firms and even the government in attracting and holding good employees. Those that have mastered this skill are generally more successful. Many of the owner-managers profiled in the text have retained their good employees by using creative personnel management techniques. Frank Stronach of Magna International (see the Small Business Profile in Chapter 11) has implemented personnel policies that allow the firm to retain its best employees—and have also helped Magna grow into a billion-dollar business.

Staying Close to the Consumer.   Business owners who have a good knowledge of consumers' wants and needs and are able to incorporate them within the operations of their companies tend to be more successful. This skill involves constant monitoring of and responding to the market. Molly Maid's success (see the small business profile in Chapter 6) can be attributed to the owners' knowledge of consumers' wants and needs. Molly Maid spends $80,000 a year on consumer research and is looking to expand into other areas.

Thoroughness with Operating Details.   Successful businesses have a very detailed and highly controlled operating plan, whether it be in the plant or out in the market. Goals, reports, and evaluations and adjustments are made constantly. College Pro Painters' success (see the small business profile in Chapter 3) can be attributed to the very thorough operating plan the owner set up while testing the business concept.

Ability to Obtain Needed Capital.   A potential constraint on the operation and growth of any business is a lack of funds. Businesses destined to succeed, however, often have little difficulty obtaining start-up and operating capital. Their owners are aware of the sources of available financing and are able to make an acceptable presentation of their requirements to both equity and debt sources as the situation requires. John Buhler (see the small business profile in Chapter 5) has successfully bought failing businesses and made them profitable. In so doing, Buhler has shown an uncanny knack for obtaining the needed financing.

Effective Handling of Government Laws, Rules, and Regulations.   Owners of successful small businesses keep abreast of legislation and programs that may affect their operations. They realize that ignorance of certain regulations can cost their organizations not only in a direct financial sense but—perhaps more important—in terms of a tarnished reputation or a missed opportunity.

Environments Conducive to Small Business Success

In addition to the preceding internal characteristics of successful small businesses are some important external situations that may give small businesses a competitive edge. Some of these environments are:

1. Businesses or industries in which the owners' personal attention to daily operations is essential to success. In a service business, for example, the expertise of the owner-manager is a major factor in generating revenue.

2. Businesses in which owner contact with employees is important to the motivation of staff and the quality of work done. Specialized or custom-made manufacturing processes or service businesses and other businesses in which employees have direct contact with customers fit into this category.

3. Businesses that are more labour and less capital intensive. Because of the above points, a business that relies heavily on people rather than machines to provide its product or service may be easier to manage if it is small in size. The retail industry is a case in point.

4. Industries that require flexibility. These include industries with high growth rates, erratic demand, or perishable products.

5. Markets in which demand is small or local, making large businesses generally reluctant to pursue them. Incident 2–6 illustrates how such a market may offer opportunities for small businesses.

6. Industries that receive considerable encouragement from the government in the form of financial, tax, and counselling assistance. Much of this assistance is directed at smaller businesses in the manufacturing, processing, and exporting industries. Such industries represent potential opportunities for small businesses.

In deciding whether to start a small business, the potential owner should investigate whether any of the above environments exist or might exist. Such conditions could be a critical factor in the success of the business.

Small Business Failures

Despite its considerable appeal, operating one's own business can be disappointing if not adequately prepared for. This section discusses some of the causes of small business failure. Hopefully prospective entrepreneurs will avoid making the same mistakes as they start their own businesses.

The situation described in Incident 2–7 on page 45 has been all too common in recent years. The number of business bankruptcies in Canada has been steadily climbing. (see Figure 2–2 on page 43).[17] Bankruptcy figures alone, however, do not give a complete picture of business failures. Many businesses are placed in

---

Incident 2–6

Austin Air

In December 1984 Austin Air, a small airline operating out of Timmins, Ontario, made its first commercial flight from Timmins to Toronto. Austin uses second-hand, turbo-propped Hawker airplanes. The largest of these planes hold 50 passengers, which makes them ideal for servicing the Timmins–Toronto run. The company now plans to extend its services by adding Kapuskasing to its run. This will allow Austin Air to fully utilize the seating capacity of its planes and help keep the competition out of Kapuskasing.

The demand for airline services in these areas is small enough that the major airlines are not interested in servicing them. However, several smaller companies are competing with Austin Air for passengers. Thus far, Austin Air's flights are faster and cheaper than the competition's despite price cutting by rival firms. With the recent deregulation of the airline industry, Austin Air, as a small airline, is in a very good position because it provides a quality service to a small, localized market.

Source: "Venture," CBC Television, July 1985.

---

receivership, and other business owners simply close their doors and walk away from their businesses when they fail.[18] Estimates indicate that in 1989 there were about 10,000 bankruptcies, but close to 140,000 businesses in Canada actually ceased operations.[19]

Businesses follow much the same life cycle that products do in that both go through start-up, growth, maturity, and decline phases. The majority of businesses that fail pass completely through this life cycle within five years of start-up. Therefore, a small business owner has little time to remedy serious mistakes. Information from Statistics Canada reveals that only about 55 to 60 percent of businesses are still operating three years after their establishment.[20]

Entrepreneurs need to understand the reasons businesses fail so that they can avoid similar mistakes. As Figure 2–3 on page 44 illustrates, 97.1 percent of business failures are generally related to incompetence or inexperience in managerial skills. More specifically, some of the areas of managerial incompetence found in failing small businesses include: budgeting, receivables and payables management, inventory management, fixed-asset administration, high debt load, and marketing. Chapters 8–11 are devoted to these principles of management, because failure to follow them contributes to the difficulties unsuccessful firms encounter.

FIGURE 2-2   **Trends in New Business Registrations and Business Bankruptcies, Fiscal 1980–1991***

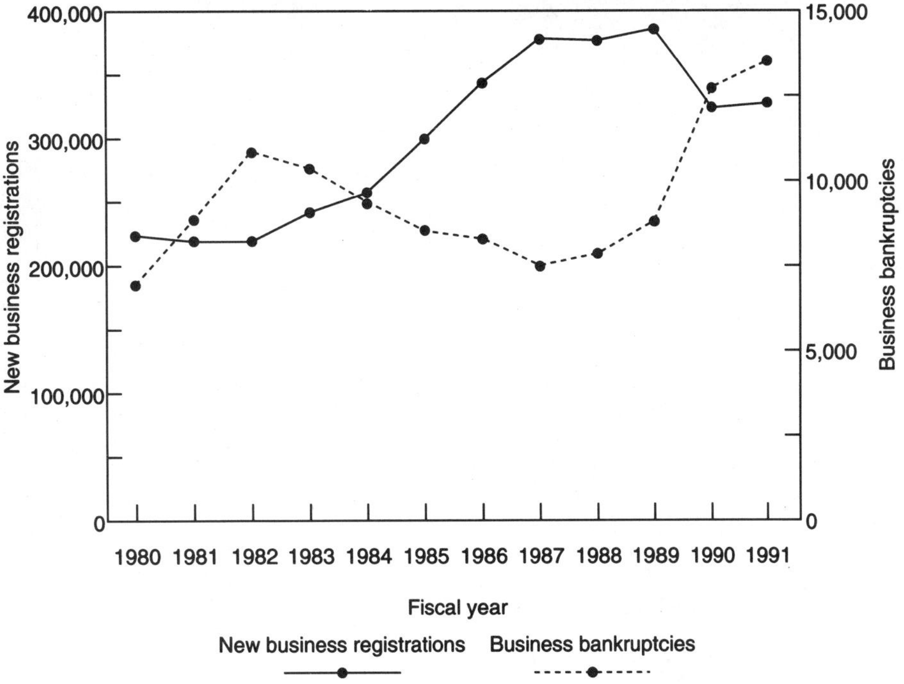

*Ending March 31 of the following year.

SOURCES: Consumer and Corporate Affairs, Canada, and Canadian Federation of Independent Business Research Department.

Entrepreneurship and Small Business Management

Up to this point in the text, the terms *entrepreneurship* and *small business management* have been used interchangeably. However, considerable confusion exists between these two terms, the types of skills they describe, and the type of training required to develop such skills. This section will distinguish between these terms. Understanding this distinction can be valuable in establishing and maintaining a business. Although they differ, both entrepreneurial and managerial skills may be necessary at different stages of the business's life cycle. This is the primary reason both types of skills and traits were discussed together earlier in this chapter.

Entrepreneurial Skills

Entrepreneurial skills are required to start or expand a business. The specific traits that describe entrepreneurship are creativity, flexibility, innovativeness, risk taking, and

FIGURE 2–3   **Classification of Causes of Business Failure in Canada, Total Year, 1983**

	Number	Percent			
	31	1.5	**Neglect**	Due to:	Bad habits
					Poor health
					Marital difficulties
					Death
					Other
	10	0.5	**Fraud**	On the part of the principals, reflected by:	Misleading name
					False financial statement
					Premeditated overbuy
					Irregular disposal of assets
					Other
	220	10.7	**Lack of experience in the line**	Evidenced by an inability to avoid conditions that result in:	
	339	16.4	**Lack of managerial experience**		Inadequate sales
Management Skills 97.1%					Heavy operating expenses
					Receivables difficulties
					Inventory difficulties
					Excessive fixed assets
					Poor location
					Competitive weakness
					Other
	517	25.1	**Unbalanced experience**	Some of these occurrences could have been provided against through insurance:	
	925	44.9	**Incompetence**		
	18	0.9	**Disaster**		Fire, flood
					Burglary
					Strike
					Employee fraud
					Other
	2,060	100.0	**Total**		

SOURCE: *The Canadian Business Failure Record* (Toronto: Dun & Bradstreet of Canada Ltd., 1984), pp. 1–19.

independence. Entrepreneurs who have a high tolerance for ambiguity and change tend to think and plan with a long-term perspective. Entrepreneurs are generally idea oriented.

Managerial Skills

The skills of a manager are useful in maintaining and solidifying the existing product/ service or business. The effective manager knows how to develop strategy, set organizational goals, and develop methods for achieving those goals. Managers require skill and knowledge in several functional areas of a business, including

Richard Thomas

Richard Thomas was optimistic about the new car dealership and gas station he had established in his home town of Kenora, Ontario. He had the only Chrysler dealership in the area and had just received approval from the bank to go ahead with the construction of a new building in an excellent location. He was confident that by offering gasoline at cut-rate prices he could increase customer traffic, which would eventually lead to sales of other accessories and, of course, automobiles.

Within a few months, however, problems started to surface. The cost of the new building exceeded projections, and Thomas had to use operating funds to complete construction so that he could begin operations. This led to a serious cash shortage. He could not meet operating expenses and service the current debt, which carried a high interest rate. In addition, Chrysler Corporation was experiencing its own difficulties, which were affecting its sales throughout Canada. Finally, although many people stopped to purchase gasoline, few bought anything else at Thomas's business. As a result, a year later Thomas was bankrupt and forced to give up the business that had once looked so promising.

Source: D. W. Balderson, University of Lethbridge, Alberta, 1992. Although this incident is based on a factual situation, the name and location have been changed.

finance, marketing, personnel, and operations. Such skills are most valuable after the business has been established.

As can be seen, although the skills the entrepreneur and the manager possess differ, they are nevertheless essential for the long-run success of the business. Entrepreneurial skills help get the business started, while managerial skills help ensure that the business continues to operate successfully. Entrepreneurial skills may be essential once again to promote growth of the business.

A major problem associated with small business is that individuals who have strengths in both areas are rare. Because most small businesses are started and operated by the same person, some skills or characteristics must be hired or otherwise acquired. Failure to do so may spell doom for the venture. A study by the Harvard Business School found that only one-tenth of 1 percent of the ideas patented and listed in the *Patent Gazette* had actually made money or could be considered successful.[21] This suggests that many of these businesses may have lacked the necessary managerial skills. Figure 2–4 summarizes the distinction between entrepreneurial and managerial skills and the situations to which they apply. Incident 2–8 illustrates how entrepreneurial characteristics are often not enough to maintain a business in a competitive environment. Part II of this text discusses essential considerations in starting a business (the entrepreneurial side),

Incident 2-8

Michael Cowpland

Michael Cowpland and his partner, Terry Mathews, established Mitel Corporation in the early 1970s. Mitel produced several products in the office automation and telecommunications industry, but its most successful product was a digital telephone exchange. Because of the high demand for its products, Mitel grew rapidly each year and by 1980 employed 6,000 people. Caught up in this growth, Cowpland, a skilled engineer, pushed onward, adding new products and moving into new markets.

By 1981, however, Mitel was experiencing difficulties with internal control and lack of attention to the organization's daily operations. In 1981 Mitel lost $110 million and was purchased by British Telecom. In retrospect, Cowpland indicates that he is the type of person who likes to initiate new ventures and get things started but lacked certain skills at managing the established organization.

Cowpland recently established a new company, Corel Systems Corporation, which is involved in electronic office publishing. Cowpland insists he has learned from his mistakes and will keep Corel small and manageable. Early indications are that this strategy is succeeding.

Source: "Venture," CBC Television, July 1985.

FIGURE 2-4   Small Business Skills

Type	Characteristics	Appropriate Situations
Entrepreneurial		
	Creativity and innovativeness	Generating ideas or solutions to problems
	Risk taking	Independence
		Starting new business
	Idea oriented	Expanding or adding new products
Managerial		
	Develops strategy and goal setting	Reaching performance objectives
	Prefers to know outcomes of actions or activities	Maintaining control of operations
	Team player	
	Works through others	
	Skills in finance, marketing, personnel, operations	

and these chapters refer to the individual as the *entrepreneur.* Part III covers the managerial skills required for the established enterprise (the management side) and refers to the individual as the *owner-manager* or the *small business manager.*

Summary

1. There are many advantages and disadvantages to owning a small business. Some of the most common advantages are frequent contacts with people, independence, skill development in many areas, potential financial rewards, challenge, and enjoyment. The possible disadvantages include high risk, higher stress levels, the need for many abilities, conflicts with people, limited financial rewards, and time demands.

2. Certain personality characteristics are associated with a successful owner-manager. These include an achievement orientation; risk taking; independence, self-confidence, and self-assurance; innovativeness; strong verbal and numerical skills; problem-solving abilities; strategic planning ability; and perseverance.

3. Environments conducive to small business success have the following characteristics: a good owner-manager rapport with employees, high labour intensity, personal attention to daily operations by the owner, markets requiring flexibility, markets in which demand is small or local, and industries that receive governmental assistance.

4. The major causes of business failure are generally related to incompetent or inexperienced management. Some specific areas where difficulties are found are budgeting, receivables and payables management, inventory management, fixed-asset administration, high debt load, handling personnel, and marketing problems.

Chapter Problems and Applications

1. What do you think are the most common reasons for small business failure? Investigate the causes of failure for a small business you are familiar with or for one of the examples in the text.

2. Which of the characteristics of successful small business owners do you think is the most important? Why?

3. How do managerial skills differ from entrepreneurial skills? When would an entrepreneur's skills be more useful than a manager's? Why?

4. Complete the checklist in Figure 2–1 on page 39. Do you possess the personality characteristics necessary for successful small business ownership?

5. What characteristics does Lou MacEachern in the Small Business Profile have? Are these characteristics managerial or entrepreneurial? Explain.

6. Interview a local small business owner about what he or she feels are the advantages and disadvantages of small business ownership.

7. Interview a local entrepreneur, and attempt to identify his or her entrepreneurial characteristics and leadership style.

Suggested Readings

Barnes, Kenneth, and Everett Banning. *Money Makers: The Secrets of Canada's Most Successful Entrepreneurs.* Toronto: McClelland and Stewart, 1985.

Bedard, George. "Telltale Signs of Trouble." *Small Business Magazine,* March 1987, p. 38.

Burch, John G. "Profiling the Entrepreneur." *Business Horizons,* September–October 1986, pp. 13–16.

Cook, James R. *The Start-Up Entrepreneur.* Toronto: Fitzhenry & Whiteside, 1986.

Drucker, Peter F. *Innovation and Entrepreneurship: Practice and Principles.* New York: Harper & Row, 1985.

Garfield, Charles A. *Peak Performers.* New York: Morrow and Company, 1985.

Gould, Allan. *The New Entrepreneurs—80 Canadian Success Stories.* Toronto: McClelland and Stewart–Bantam, Ltd., 1986.

Henderson, Carter. *Winners: The Successful Strategies Entrepreneurs Use to Build Their Businesses.* New York: Holt, Rinehart and Winston, 1985.

Kanter, Rozabeth Moss. *The Change Masters.* New York: Simon and Schuster, 1983.

Kao, Raymond W. Y. *Entrepreneurship and Enterprise Development.* Toronto: Holt, Rinehart and Winston, 1989.

Mancuso, J. *Have You Got What It Takes?* New York: The Centre for Entrepreneurial Management, 1986.

McMullan, W. Ed and Wayne A. Long. *Developing New Adventures.* Toronto: HBJ Publishers, 1990.

Rumball, Donald. *The Entrepreneurial Edge.* Toronto: Key Porter Books, 1989.

Toffler, Alvin. *The Third Wave.* New York: Bantam Books, 1981.

Vesper, Karl H. New Venture Strategies (rev. ed.). Toronto: Prentice-Hall, 1990.

COMPREHENSIVE CASE
THE FRAMEMAKERS: PART 1

Robert Norman faced a big decision. He was contemplating leaving his job running the family painting business to set up his own retail picture-framing store. As he thought about his dilemma, his mind wandered back to the events that had

---

This case, based on an actual small business situation (names and location changed), was written by D. Wesley Balderson, University of Lethbridge.

led up to the impending decision. He had been raised in a small town about 20 miles south of Brandon, Manitoba. His father was a painter, and Robert had worked in the painting business part time for several years. Upon graduating from high school, he completed a two-year business administration in interior design course at a college across the border in the United States. It was there that he met and married his wife, Teresa.

Although Robert had always thought he might come back to take over his father's painting business, he wanted to obtain some outside business experience first. As a result, he found a job in a Woolco store in Winnipeg after his graduation. Robert enjoyed working with people in the retail setting, but felt frustrated working for a larger company. He wanted to be on his own and dreamed of someday running his own business.

Finally, after two years with Woolco, the Normans decided to leave Winnipeg and return to Brandon, where Robert could begin to take over his father's painting business. His father was pleased with their decision and, since he was approaching retirement age, allowed his son to assume a major role in the business. Norman managed the business for six years. But although it provided a steady income, he could see that the growth possibilities in terms of income and challenge were limited. In addition, he soon realized he didn't like painting as much as he thought he would. As a result, he and Teresa started looking around for sideline opportunities to earn a little extra money. One they particularly enjoyed was assembling and selling picture frames.

One day, while in Winnipeg to obtain some water seal paint, Robert ran across a small retail store called U-Frame It. He went in to look around and talk to the manager about the business. He was impressed by the manager's enthusiasm and also noticed that the store was extremely busy. Robert immediately began wondering about the possibility of starting his own picture-framing store.

Excited by what he had seen, Robert returned to Brandon without even buying his water seal paint. Teresa was also enthused with the idea, as she was especially fond of framing. Robert's father was sceptical and, as Robert had expected, disappointed that his son wanted to leave the family business.

Robert needed to make his decision quickly. The manager of the U-Frame It store had indicated that the franchise chain was looking at Brandon as a possible site for another outlet sometime in the future.

Questions

1. What aspects of Robert Norman's background will contribute to his success if he decides to go ahead with the picture-framing store?
2. What further areas should Robert and Teresa explore before making this decision?

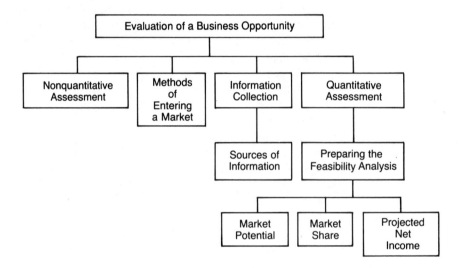

CHAPTER 3

Evaluation of a Business Opportunity

Chapter Objectives

- To review the nonquantitative aspects of evaluating business opportunities.
- To introduce the methods by which an entrepreneur can enter a market with a product or service.
- To discuss the types of information available to assist in the selection of a small business and illustrate how that information can be used.
- To provide a systematic way to quantitatively assess an industry and evaluate the financial feasibility of a specific small business opportunity.

Small Business Profile

Greig Clark

College Pro Painters

Greig Clark grew up in Thunder Bay, Ontario, and attended the University of Western Ontario in business administration. During each summer, he painted to earn the money he would need for the following semester. He found there was room in the industry for additional painters who provided quality work at a reasonable (lower) price. He also learned that he could make more money by hiring good people and giving them a considerable amount of responsibility than by doing all the work himself. Each summer brought his painting business more success and further expansion. While at school during the winter, Clark evaluated the possibility of developing his business into a franchise system. He even used the business as a project for one of his courses to assess its feasibility.

Clark accepted a full-time marketing position with General Foods upon graduating from the university but maintained his planning and summer painting operations in several locations. Many of these operations were successful, but many were disasters. In each of the unsuccessful cases, Clark learned from his mistakes and adjusted operations. Finally, in 1977, Clark decided to run one last test market in six centers. If they succeeded, he would quit his job at General Foods and go into the franchise painting business full time; if they did not, he would drop the idea once and for all. The results of the six test markets were positive. Greig quit his job, and his College Pro franchise was an astounding success.

By 1989 College Pro had become the largest residential painting company in North America, with 550 franchises and over $35 million in sales. In 1989 Greig Clark sold College Pro and has since established the Horatio Enterprise Fund, a venture capital company that invests in small start-up companies. Clark's philosophy remains the same as it was with College Pro: "I'm best at something when I'm working towards a greater mission." This greater mission involves "coaching" several businesses instead of being the "captain" on just one.

Printed with permission of Greig Clark.

Nonquantitative Assessment of Business Opportunities

Chapter 2 discussed methods of evaluating one's suitability for small business ownership. Much of this chapter deals with methods of quantitative evaluation. This section examines some nonquantitative factors to consider in the selection of a small business opportunity. These factors may influence one's selection and significantly alter the quantitative analysis.

Goals.   The individual should examine his or her personal goals regarding income earned from the business. The question to address is: How well will the type of business chosen allow me to achieve not only my financial goals but also my occupational status goals?

Content of Work.   The individual should assess his or her suitability for the business's working conditions. What type of work will the business involve? Will the business require hard physical work or considerable contact with people?

Lifestyle.   What type of lifestyle will the business allow? Will the hours be long or concentrated in the evenings or on weekends? Will the business allow family members to be involved? Remember that most small businesses take much more time to operate than the owner anticipates prior to start-up.

Capabilities.   In addition to the personal characteristics needed to run a small business that were discussed in Chapter 2, at least three other capabilities are required.

The first requirement is **good health.** As mentioned earlier, managing a small business usually involves long hours and is often physically and mentally stressful. One will need good physical health and stamina as well as the ability to withstand high levels of stress.

The second requirement is expertise in the **fundamentals of management,** including administration, marketing, and finance. While numerous courses can provide valuable training, many successful small business managers have acquired expertise in these areas through self-education.

The third requirement is a sound **financial base.** Except for some types of service businesses, one can seldom start a business with less than $10,000 to $50,000. This amount may, in fact, be only the equity portion, which qualifies the business to acquire the necessary capital.

Experience.   As the data in Figure 2–3 on page 17 illustrates, lack of experience and unbalanced experience are two major causes of business failure. One of the best preparations prospective small operators can make is to acquire work experience in the type of business or industry they plan to go into. An example of such an approach appears in Incident 3–1. In this example, an entrepreneur had some well-defined career goals and set out to obtain experience in the field prior

Incident 3–1

Roberta Cava—Training and Development Seminars

"Unlike most women, I set some goals for myself early in my career," she states. Re-entering the work force in 1973 following a divorce, after 13 years spent at home and with three children to raise, Ms. Cava was determined not just to "float" but to find a spot in the business world that promised both personal and financial rewards. Immersing herself in a personnel management job and a series of business diploma studies, she formulated an ambitious career plan that called for her to head a human resources department within 10 years and her own company within 20 years. In fact, it took just eight years to achieve both goals.

Source: Lois Bridges, "Roberta Cava: Training and Development Seminars," *Small Business Quarterly* 5, no. 3 (Summer 1986), p. 4.

---

to establishing her business. Another benefit of experience is the personal contacts one acquires while working in a particular industry. For many entrepreneurs, assistance from such sources can be invaluable in successfully establishing the business.

Many entrepreneurs establish their businesses and work in them part time while holding another job. This is an excellent way to gain experience and minimize risk. Although such an approach is not possible in some situations, many successful businesses originated from a part-time job. The profile at the beginning of the chapter illustrates how Greig Clark, the founder of College Pro Painters, accomplished this. Clark developed the College Pro concept and began operations while working at General Foods.

Breaking into the Market

Entrepreneurs have essentially three ways to enter a market by establishing a new business. The first is to *offer a totally new product to the market.* This involves "inventing" a product that meets a need not currently being fulfilled. Thousands of successful products have resulted from an individual's dissatisfaction with existing or a lack of existing products. An example of this type of product appears in Incident 3–2, which briefly describes one of Canada's Entrepreneurs of the Decade.

Many of the fad or novelty types of products also fit into this category. The need these types of products satisfy are often emotional or subjective rather than

---

Incident 3–2

Fox 40 Whistle

Over the years, Ron Foxcroft has refereed many boisterous basketball games. Frequently the noise was so loud that the whistle could not be heard. This caused considerable problems for the game and embarrassment for himself. Foxcroft thought, "There must be a better way."

Along with Joe Forte, another referee who had experienced similar problems, Foxcroft set out to develop a solution. He and Forte contracted a design consultant and a plastics manufacturer to come up with a whistle that could be heard over the noisiest crowds. The result was the Fox 40 whistle. The Fox 40 made its debut at the Pan American games in Indianapolis, Indiana. It was an immediate success and continues to sell not only to sports officials and leagues all over the world but to organizations such as police departments and military academies. Today Foxcroft's sales have reached $4 million in 81 countries. In 1992 Ron Foxcroft was selected as one of Canada's Entrepreneurs of the Decade by *Profit Magazine.*

Source: Adapted from Richard Wright, "Fox 40 Whistle," *Small Business Magazine,* June 1988, pp. 12–13.

---

rational. Products such as pet rocks and mood jewellery fit this description. Several periodicals provide product ideas (see Appendix A at the end of this chapter). Some companies sell ideas that have received preliminary market testing.

A second approach is to *offer an existing product to a different market or industry.* Phillip Kives, founder of K-tel International, was the master of this type of approach. His company achieved success initially by acquiring products currently sold abroad and marketing them in North America. Incident 3–3 illustrates another example of this method of starting a small business. Another form of this approach is to offer an existing product or service in the same geographical market, but to a different age or income group.

The third way to enter the market is to *offer a product or service similar to those already existing in the same market.* In this case, the prospective small business owner attempts to obtain some competitive advantage over the existing products or businesses in the industry to maintain viability. Perhaps the market is large enough to accommodate an additional business, or the level of satisfaction with existing businesses or products in the industry is low. Examples of this type of entry into the market include establishing a retail store that stocks brand-name, conventional merchandise and manufacturing a product so that it can be sold at a lower price. An example of this strategy appears in Incident 3–4.

Incident 3–3

Mother Finds Marketing Gold in Patented Garbage Bag Gizmo

Having started with a $20,000 remortgaged loan on her house, Donagh McNerney has run to over $7 million in sales, with energy to spare. Her company, Extrufix Inc., of Markham, Ontario, employs 70 people and had 1990 sales of $6 million in Canada, plus $1.25 million in export sales to the United States and Britain, Australia, and several other countries. Until just a few years ago, McNerney kept herself busy as a wife and a mother of three children.

Married at 20, McNerney led a fairly typical life until one day in the late 1960s, when her husband, Frank, who was in the plastic film extrusion business with Leco Industries, brought back from a business trip to Denmark 10 samples of a rack that could be installed inside a kitchen cupboard to serve as a garbage container—off the floor and out of sight. A roll of plastic garbage bags automatically replaced the previous bag as it was filled. Frank's employer wasn't interested, but when McNerney installed one in her kitchen, she could see the product's potential. "As a housewife, I was impressed," she says.

Frank suggested that she try to sell it. Since, her children were teenagers and she had been thinking of taking a job, she went to see the housewares buyers at Eaton's and Simpson's. She generated enough interest to begin taking royalties with the Danish patent-holder. Extrufix was on its way.

By 1970 the McNerneys had remortgaged their house for $20,000, added another $50,000 from a venture capitalist, and started working out of a small space in Frank's office. Within a year sales were $10,000. Frank quit his job and rented a 600-square-foot barn in Stouffeville, Ontario, as warehouse space, and the McNerneys plunged into business as partners.

Sources: Adapted from Ian Crysler, "Mother Finds Marketing Gold in Patented Garbage Bag Gizmo," *The Magazine That's All about Small Business,* November 1983, p. 6; *Canadian Key Business Directory* (Toronto: Dun & Bradstreet, 1992).

More will be discussed about carrying out an evaluation for this type of venture later in this chapter. Regardless of the approach used, it is important to look at the growth trends within the industry, the number of competitors and their relative market share, as well as their strengths and weaknesses prior to entering the market.

Collection of Information

The key to making a wise decision regarding which industry to enter and the type of business to start is the gathering and analysis of information. The more relevant

---
Incident 3–4

From Basement to Holt Renfrew

When Judy Osburn had her first child, she was appalled to discover that the only baby clothes for sale in Vancouver that she liked were European imports that cost $100 an item. Osburn, then 35, had been a retailer of women's clothes for 10 years but had no manufacturing experience. Still, she was certain she could produce children's clothes in Canada that were just as comfortable and stylish as the European imports, and at a reasonable price.

Unlike thousands of other Canadians who have had the same thought, Osburn actually went out and did it. With two partners, Jane Frazee and Anna Gustafson, she founded Bravo Children's Wear three years ago. The market they aimed at was women like Osburn and Gustafson who had decided in their 30's and 40's to have children before it was too late. These women would have both the inclination and the means to buy something better than the standard children's clothes made of synthetic pink or blue fabrics.

Bravo's founders were right. Sales are already at the $1.25 million mark and Bravo's comfortable, colorful all-cotton clothes are in such stores as Holt Renfrew in Canada and Bloomingdale's in the United States. Bravo also exports to Japan.

Source: Daniel Stoffman, "From Basement to Holt Renfrew," *Report on Business Magazine,* October 1988, p. 67.

---

the information, the greater the reduction of uncertainty about the results of this decision. Recent studies show that the overwhelming majority of small business owners do no formal marketing research, although many do informal, unsystematic information gathering.[1] Incident 3–5 illustrates a potential negative result of insufficient research prior to starting a business.

Some reasons entrepreneurs commonly cite for lack of research and investigation are that it is too time consuming, too expensive, too complicated, and irrelevant. While each of these claims has some substance, there are some simple, inexpensive, but effective methods of collecting and analyzing data available to the entrepreneur.

Sources of Information

The first thing entrepreneurs should be aware of is the many sources of information available to assist them in their investigations. Two general types of information can aid prospective small business owners in selecting the right small business. The first, **secondary data,** consists of data previously published by

Incident 3–5

If You Don't Make Mistakes, You Don't Make Anything

When software designers at Shana Corp. in Edmonton unveiled their dental-office software in 1985, the company's marketing executives waited for Canadian dentists to snap it up. But they were soon disappointed. The Shana Dental System sold neither as widely nor quickly as its inventors had anticipated. Despite its impressive ability to handle all the documentation of a dentist's office, it was complex, expensive and unproven. Shana's first foray into the software market was disappointing, but it wasn't fatal. The company has since hit its stride reaping annual sales of $700,000 with less expensive business forms software applicable to virtually any industry.

Every successful inventor has an inventory of failures—products that either didn't make it to market or failed to bring the expected flood of eager buyers. Often, the fault doesn't lie in the product. "The most common failures in new product development can be traced to inaccurate appraisals," says management consultant James Orr, founder of two successful manufacturing businesses he has since sold. "First, of the extent and nature of the potential market; second, of the need for the product; and third, of the competition." Common as miscalculations may be, however, they can provide invaluable lessons.

Shana fell victim to the first and second fatal flaws. Marketing vice-president John Murphy believed specialized software for all the documentation in a dentist's office would gain quick acceptance in a narrow niche. But at $3,000 a crack, the software appealed only to dentists who immediately understood its uses. Murphy and his partners didn't anticipate that most dentists would want to evaluate it for six months or more before staking their practice on it. After all, he admits, "if this (software) went down, the office could shut down for the day." As a result, Murphy and his partners misjudged the selling cycle, leaving the company strapped for cash while they waited for sales to pour in.

Source: Camilla Cornel, "If You Don't Make Mistakes, You Don't Make Anything," *Profit Magazine,* March 1991, p. 28.

another organization. The second, **primary data,** is data collected by the entrepreneur. The following sections discuss both types of information in detail.

Secondary Data

Secondary data takes the form of reports, studies, and statistics that another organization has already compiled. There is no shortage of secondary data to aid

---

FIGURE 3–1   Assessing Market Feasibility of Opening a Florist Shop in Toronto Using Secondary Data

---

Problem: To estimate the size of the market for a florist shop in Toronto.

Step 1: Determine the population in Toronto using Statistics Canada reports.

Area	Population
Census Metropolitan Area of	
Toronto	3,900,000
Ontario	9,066,000

Step 2: Determine the total retail sales for florist shops in Canada.

Retail Shop	Sales
Florist	$444,600,000 (1987)

Update sales to 1991 by increasing sales by the inflation rate (4%) for each year statistics are out of date (= $520,118,500).

Step 3: Calculate per capita sales for florist shops in Canada:

$$\frac{\text{Florist sales} - (1991 \text{ projection})}{\text{Canadian population} - (1991 \text{ census})} = \text{Per capita sales}$$

$$\frac{520,118,500}{27,296,859} = 19.05$$

Step 4: Apply the per capita projection to the Toronto market: 19.05 (per capita sales) × 3,900,000 (pop. of Toronto)

This shows that a total of $74,295,000 could be expected to be spent in the Toronto area in florist shops.

Sources: 1987 Statistics Canada, 1991 Census—Statistics Canada, 1992 *Market Research Handbook*—Statistics Canada.

the entrepreneur. A major problem, however, is finding information relevant to one's own situation. The secondary data available may be too general or may not apply to the type of business being established. Also, some reports are slightly out of date and thus will need to be adjusted to make them useful. Such data can be updated by projecting past trends.

Secondary information is inexpensive, which makes it very attractive to the prospective small business owner. Much of the secondary information available in Canada is provided by the federal and provincial governments. However, much valuable secondary information is available from private and semiprivate sources. Appendix A at the end of this chapter presents a complete listing of those sources most relevant for small businesses. Figure 3–1 gives an example of using secondary data to begin the feasibility analysis for a business. This example uses Statistics Canada reports to estimate market potential for a florist shop in Toronto.

In addition to obtaining published secondary information, entrepreneurs can consult several agencies for counselling in both starting up a business and ongoing operations. The most inexpensive and often most valuable source is the counselling provided to entrepreneurs by federal and provincial governments. The Federal Business Development Bank can provide start-up counselling as well as analysis of the already operating business. The latter service is offered through the Counselling Assistance for Small Enterprises (CASE) program. The CASE program is available to businesses employing fewer than 75 employees and uses retired businesspeople as consultants.

Most provincial governments also employ small business consultants to assist the small business (see Appendix B at the end of this chapter for the addresses of these agencies in each province). Many provincial agencies provide start-up and business plan preparation assistance similar to that offered by the federal government.

Another potentially valuable source of assistance comes from universities and colleges. Many universities have student consulting programs designed to aid the small business owner. Using the expertise of graduating or graduate students, these programs can assist in preparing feasibility analyses or evaluating a business problem for a minimal fee, usually the cost of materials used. (Appendix C at the end of this chapter lists universities in Canada that have such programs; several colleges offer similar services).

Other helpful counselling sources are lawyers, accountants, or bankers. Some of these sources may be more expensive than government services, however. Numerous consulting firms also specialize in small business operations.

In addition to the types of assistance just described, a new concept appears to promise considerable help in establishing new enterprises: the **incubation centre.** The incubation centre consists of an organization—usually a municipal or provincial agency—that provides essential services for new small businesses, either free or at minimal cost. Office space, secretarial services, computer capabilities, and financial and business counselling are examples of these services. Incident 3–6 illustrates how business incubators are assisting new businesses and providing employment for Canadian youth.

In 1992 approximately 500 incubators were operating in North America, including more than 1,000 incubator tenants, and estimates indicate that new incubators are opening at a rate of one per week.[2] Business incubators allow the small business community to work, individually or collectively, through the chamber of commerce and with municipal (city or town) governments, provincial governments, universities, and colleges. Statistics show that businesses receiving assistance from incubator centres have a 30 percent greater chance of success.[3]

Primary Data

Primary data is information collected through one's own research. Although usually more costly to obtain than secondary data, it can be more relevant to one's business and more current. Primary research is essential if secondary sources do not provide information required for the feasibility analysis. It may also be beneficial to supplement information obtained from secondary sources. Despite these advantages, small business owners have traditionally hesitated to do much primary research because of their lack of knowledge about how to do it and its relatively high cost.

Some research methods, however, are not complicated and can be of great value to the entrepreneur in evaluating the feasibility of a potential business

Incident 3–6

Incubating Entrepreneurs

In *Alberta Report*, April 13, Joanne Hatton described an innovative approach to promoting entrepreneurship. A group of free-enterprisers in Edmonton have joined the YMCA, IBM Canada, and all three levels of government in an effort to solve youth unemployment. Said Founders Realty partner Reginald Berry, who chairs the $1.4 million Youth Enterprise Centre, opened in March, "This will be a bastion of free enterprise."

The centre, the first of 10 in Canada, is housed in a newly renovated 40,000-square-foot warehouse that will accommodate up to 40 businesses. The program initially puts unemployed persons ages 16 to 30 through a 12-week business training course at the Northern Alberta Institute of Technology (NAIT). Their business plans must first be approved by a volunteer committee of local businesspeople. The centre, also referred to as a *business incubator,* provides entrants with rudimentary office equipment, pooled administrative services, warehouse or light manufacturing space, and the volunteer consulting expertise of local entrepreneurs and professionals. Nominal (50 cents per square foot) rents in the centre will rise to market rates as the participants approach profitability. The province and the private sector are contributing $75,000 apiece to a seed capital fund. The province is providing another $50,000 for centre renovations. "Without this program these kids would be drawing unemployment insurance," said Gerry Craig, the YMCA's vice president of program development. The centre, he emphasizes, offers help, not handouts. "If some businessman would rather be paying out money for UIC, then he's got a real problem." Indeed, the provincial government is so impressed with the concept of business incubators that it has unveiled a $3 million program to nurture their development in communities throughout the province.

Source: National Citizens Coalition, "Incubating Entrepreneurs," *Overview* 11 (May 1987).

opportunity. Three general methods that can be used to collect information through primary research: observation, surveys, and experiments.

1. Observation.   *Observation* involves monitoring the who, what, where, when, and how relating to market conditions. For the small business, this method might involve observing auto and pedestrian traffic levels or customer reactions to a product, service, or promotion. It may also entail simply observing sales or expenditure levels. The observation method may be fairly expensive, as it requires that time be spent in monitoring events as they occur. Another limitation of

---

FIGURE 3–2   Calculating a Representative Survey Sample for a Small Business

---

Step 1: The following chart can be used to determine the number of surveys that should be completed to achieve a 95 percent confidence level at .05 degree of precision.

Population Size	Sample Size
50	44
100	80
500	222
1,000	286
5,000	375
10,000	385
100,000 and over	400

Step 2: Choosing the respondents. If a phone survey is being conducted, there are two ways to choose the respondents. The first is to use the phone book and choose every *n*th individual. The second is to use a random number generator to come up with the phone numbers. Both of these methods have advantages and disadvantages, but both allow the surveyor to obtain a representative sample.

---

observation research is that it allows one to only make inferences about the reasons people respond in certain ways. There is no two-way interaction with the subject of the research that might shed light on such motivations.

2. Surveys.   To obtain more detailed information from potential consumers and to better understand their motivations in purchasing a product or service, a small business owner can carry out a *survey*. The entrepreneur should clearly define the objectives of the research prior to questionnaire construction and ensure that each question addresses one of the objectives. Usually it is not possible to survey each potential customer or the total market; therefore, only a part of the market is surveyed. It is essential, however, that the responses obtained be representative of the total market. Figure 3–2 illustrates a simple but accurate method for determining a representative sample for a research project for a small business. Many businesses have failed because the owners acted on their own feelings or the opinions of a few acquaintances. In some cases, these responses do not represent the opinions of the total market. Incident 3–7 illustrates how a lack of representative information from the market created a difficult problem for a small agricultural machinery manufacturer.

Occasionally, through design or necessity (e.g., limited funds), a nonrepresentative group of people are surveyed as part of the primary research project. This could involve surveying only experts or knowledgeable people in an industry rather than an equal cross-section of consumers. This method is also often used in surveying shopping mall customers. The most obvious drawback is that the findings may not be representative of the total market.

Three types of surveys are used to collect market information: mail surveys, telephone surveys, and personal interviews.

Incident 3–7

Kirchner Machine Ltd.

Kirchner Machine Ltd. is a well-known farm machinery manufacturer in Lethbridge, Alberta. It manufactures many successful tillage and haying implements and has built a solid reputation as a well-run small manufacturer in the farm machinery industry. In 1981 several farmers expressed concern to Kirchner about their inability to handle and transport large, round hay bales. These bales, commonly weighing about 1,000 pounds, had become very popular with farmers and ranchers throughout North America. However, they had to be moved to the stack or a larger truck one at a time, which was quite time consuming.

In response to this concern, Kirchner designed and manufactured a bale hauler that could be pulled with a tractor that could carry six bales. Named the Big Bale Fork, it was expected to add another successful product to Kirchner's line. Unfortunately, sales were disappointing. Although those who purchased the Big Bale Fork were satisfied, sales were too few and far between. One reason was that the firm had not carried out market research to assess total market potential for the product. Those who had purchased the hauler were too small a part of the market to make it economically feasible. Those who had suggested that Kirchner manufacture the Big Bale Fork were unrepresentative of the total market.

Source: D. W. Balderson, University of Lethbridge.

Mail Surveys.   Mail surveys are most appropriate when

- Only a small amount of information is required.
- Questions can be answered with "yes-no," "check the box" answers, or brief responses.
- A picture of the product may be required.
- An immediate response is not required.

One problem with mail surveys is their poor response rate—typically under 50 percent—and the lack of control over who fills out the questionnaire. Also, the preparer needs to make sure that the mail survey is not be too long or too complicated. Figure 3–3 shows a simple mail survey carried out for a small business to assess initial demand for a Japanese restaurant.

Telephone Surveys.   Telephone surveying has become the most popular survey method in recent years, most likely because of its low cost and quick response time. However, it is even more restricted than a mail survey in the amount and

---

FIGURE 3-3   **Mail Questionnaire: Japanese Family Restaurant**

---

1. Approximately how often does your family eat at a restaurant or dining lounge in the town of Oakville?*
    - a. _____ Less than once per month
    - b. _____ Once per month
    - c. _____ Once every two weeks
    - d. _____ Once per week
    - e. _____ Two–three times per week
    - f. _____ More than three times per week
2. Approximately how much do you normally spend when you eat out at a restaurant or dining lounge?
    - a. _____ $10 and under
    - b. _____ $11–$15
    - c. _____ $16–$20
    - d. _____ $21–$25
    - e. _____ Over $25
3. Are you familiar with the difference between Japanese and Chinese cooking?
    - _____ Yes
    - _____ No
4. If a family restaurant specializing in Japanese food were opened in Oakville, would you . . .
    - a. _____ Probably never go
    - b. _____ Definitely try it
    - c. _____ Patronize it regularly if food, service, etc. were adequate
5. Where would you prefer such a facility to be located?
    - a. _____ Downtown
    - b. _____ West Oakville
    - c. _____ South Oakville
    - d. _____ North Oakville
    - e. _____ Does not matter

Thank you very much for your time and cooperation.

---

*Name of the city has been changed.

SOURCE: Academy Management Services, Lethbridge, Alberta.

detail of information one can obtain. The telephone interviewer should follow a survey guide to ensure consistency. Figure 3–4 offers an example of a typical phone survey guide.

Personal Interviews.   The most expensive type of survey is the personal interview. While this method generally costs more and requires greater expertise, it is the best approach for obtaining more detailed information and opinion-oriented responses. As the number of people surveyed typically is smaller than in mail or phone surveys, this method is more suitable for interviewing knowledgeable people in an industry as opposed to surveying a cross-section of potential consumers. It may involve surveying one individual at a time or, as many large companies do, surveying several people together in what is called a *focus group*. The personal interview may be used for such purposes as testing a new product concept or advertisement or evaluating a company's image.

FIGURE 3–4   **Telephone Questionnaire Guide: Sporting Goods Rental Store**

A sporting goods store located in a city of approximately 58,000 people wanted to start renting summer sports equipment. The following survey was designed to determine consumer demand for such a rental business.

Survey number: Phone number:

Hi, my name is _____ ; I am presently conducting a survey to determine people's summertime leisure activities in the city. A few moments of your time to answer the questions would be greatly appreciated.

1. Can you tell me if you participate in any of the following activities during the summer? (*List equipment and responses*)
2. A lot of people ski in the winter because ski equipment can be rented at a fraction of its retail price. Are there any summer activities you would participate in if the equipment were available on a similar basis?
   a.
   b.
3. Are you older than 18 years of age?
   Yes ( )   No ( ) If no, record and terminate
4. Would you consider renting the following equipment if available at reasonable prices? Please indicate if you have the item. (*List equipment*)
5. Male ( )   Female ( ) Fill in for all respondents
6. Age: 18–25 ( )
           26–35 ( )
           36–50 ( )
           Over 50 ( )
7. Income: 0–$12,500   ( )
           $12,501–$20,000 ( )
           $20,001–$30,000 ( )
           Over $30,000   ( )

Thank you very much for participating in this survey.

SOURCE: Student Consulting Project, University of Lethbridge.

Entrepreneurs are often unsure about what types of questions to use in a survey. Some areas in which information should be attained are the following:

- Respondents' reactions to the product or service
- The price respondents are willing to pay for the product or service
- Respondents' willingness to purchase the product or service (usually answers to such questions are exaggeratedly positive and should be adjusted downward by as much as 20 percent)
- Frequency of purchase
- Level of satisfaction with current product or service
- Demographic characteristics of repondents

3. Experiments.   An *experiment* involves an attempt to simulate an actual market situation. For an inventor, it may mean letting a number of people try out a new product and then finding out their reactions. For a business, it may mean marketing a product on a limited basis and observing sales levels, or surveying to find out the level of satisfaction with the product or service. This method is fairly costly in that the product must be developed and marketed, albeit on a limited basis. The main advantage of experimental research, or test marketing, is that it measures what people actually do, not just what they say they will do, concerning the product. Small businesses have successfully used this method in taking prototype products to trade shows, exhibitions, or potential customers to assess potential acceptance.

The proper collection of secondary and primary data can be invaluable to entrepreneurs as they assess business opportunities. It can provide a base of data that, if analyzed correctly, may allow the capitalization of a successful opportunity or the avoidance of a disaster. The types of market research just described require an investment in time and money, but many successful entrepreneurs are convinced they are a worthwhile investment.

Although owner-managers often use these information collection methods prior to starting their businesses, they can and should use them on an ongoing basis after the businesses have been established to stay abreast of changes in market conditions. Many successfully established businesses have become complacent and as a result eventually failed because they lost touch with consumers and/or the market conditions. To avoid this, the small business should set aside the effort and money required to regularly collect and use relevant market information. Chapter 8 discusses this subject further.

Quantitative Assessment of Business Opportunities

Preparing the Feasibility Analysis

Once the entrepreneur has collected the relevant information about the market, the next step is to use this information as quantitatively as possible to assess the financial feasibility of the proposed venture. The purpose of this assessment is to determine whether the business will earn the amount of income the entrepreneur desires. The financial feasibility analysis as described in this section is most appropriate for starting a new business from scratch, but much of it could be applied to the purchase of an existing business or the operation of a franchise.

There are essentially three steps in estimating the financial feasibility of a proposed business venture. The first step is to determine potential revenue (demand) for the total market. The second is to estimate the share of total market revenue that the new business might obtain. The third is to subtract the associated expenses from the revenue estimate to arrive at a projected estimated net income for the prospective business. A more detailed explanation of the steps in calculating a feasibility analysis is presented next. A detailed example of such an analysis is given in Figure 3–5 at the end of the chapter.

Step 1: Calculate Market Potential

The purpose of this step is to arrive at a dollar or unit sales figure for the total market. It may involve three substeps:

1. *Determine the market area and its population.* Delineate the geographic area or target market the business will serve. This can be done by obtaining a map and marking off the size of the market. Then estimate the population (numbers) within that market that might conceivably purchase the type of product or service to be offered. This process yields an estimate of the size of the target market.

2. *Obtain revenue (sales) statistics for this market area for the product type or service.* Usually federal, provincial, or municipal governments have this information for many standard types of products or businesses. For example, Statistics Canada publishes retail expenditure and manufacturing data for many products and services. If total revenue or sales figures are not available for the proposed type of business or product, but per capita or per-family expenditures are obtainable, simply multiply this figure by the population estimate obtained in substep 1 (population of market × per capita expenditures).

If the product or service is new and no secondary data is available, use secondary data on a similar product. If there is no similar product, primary research—in the form of a survey, for example—may be used to assess consumer acceptance of the concept. If the results of such a survey indicate that a certain percentage of the market shows a purchase interest, multiply that percentage by the size of the market to obtain the market potential estimate.

3. *Adjust the market potential total as necessary.* If one is able to obtain actual revenue statistics for the market, usually the only adjustment needed is to update the data. As mentioned previously, secondary data is typically a year or two out of date. A simple way to update sales and expenditure data is to increase the amount of sales by the annual rate of inflation for the years involved. This might also include a forecast of trends that will affect demand in the future. Such trends could be included in the estimate.

If national averages of per capita expenditures are used, adjustments for local shopping patterns must be made. A common adjustment in this regard is to adjust for those living in the market area who purchase outside the market, and vice versa. For example, if it is estimated that 20 percent of the market buys the product or service outside of the market area, reduce the market potential by 20 percent.

Projections should include one-year and five-year estimates to reflect trends that may exist in the industry. Projections should also include trends with respect to growth of the competition that might affect future market share.

Step 2: Calculate Market Share

The purpose of this step is to estimate the percentage of the total market potential the proposed business will obtain. Because the method of calculating market share differs significantly depending on the type of business, market share calculations for retail, manufacturing, and service firms are illustrated separately.

Retail Firm

1. *Estimate the total amount of selling space in the market devoted to the merchandise the new business will sell (usually in square feet or metres).* This involves taking an inventory of space of competing stores (specialty and department stores) devoted to this product. This estimate may be obtained informally by observation or by asking the owners. In some areas, secondary information about retail selling space may be available through the municipal or city government or department.

2. *Estimate the size of the proposed store (in square feet or metres).* Most probably the entrepreneur will have a good idea of the size of the proposed store. The actual size, of course, may depend on the availability of outlets.

3. *Calculate the market share based on selling space as follows.* The information collected in steps 1 and 2 are now integrated in the following formula:

$$\frac{\text{Proposed store selling space}}{\text{Total market selling space (including proposed store)}} = \text{Percentage market share}$$

4. *Make adjustments to reflect any competitor strengths and weaknesses regarding the proposed store.* Typical adjustments might include the following:

   a. Decrease percentage share if the competition has a better location, is larger in size, or has considerable customer loyalty. A decrease in the percentage should also be made, because the proposed store is new and will take time to build customer loyalty.

   b. Increase percentage share if the proposed store will offer unique products, services, location, advertising, or other advantages over the competition.

The amount of the adjustments may be arbitrary and somewhat subjective, but typically they are fractions of a percentage of the market share.

5. *Multiply the revised market share percentage by the market potential estimate obtained in step 1.* The result is a dollar revenue estimate for the proposed business for the first year of operations. By applying market trends to this figure, a one- to five-year estimate can be obtained if required.

Manufacturing Firm

1. *Estimate the total productive capacity in the market for the product to be manufactured.* Typically this will be calculated in units, but it may be in dollars. This will involve estimating the production size of competitors (both domestic and foreign).

If the product is a new innovation and no competition exists, market share obviously is the same as the market potential calculated previously.

2. *Estimate the productive capacity of the proposed manufacturing plant.*

3. *Calculate the market share based on productive capacity.* The information obtained in steps 1 and 2 are integrated into the following formula:

$$\frac{\text{Production capacity of proposed business}}{\substack{\text{Total production capacity} \\ \text{(including proposed business)}}} = \text{Percentage of market share}$$

4. *Make adjustments to reflect any competitor strengths and weaknesses with respect to the proposed plant.* The market share percentage estimated in step 3 will likely need to be adjusted. The strengths and weaknesses of competitors should be determined and compared with the proposed business. Often primary research may be required to obtain this type of information.

Generally a higher market share can be obtained in industries in which competitors are smaller in size, the product can be differentiated from competitors' products, and primary research shows a particular level of dissatisfaction with existing products.

Market share will tend to be smaller if the industry is made up of a few large and powerful competitors who hold key contracts or where consumer satisfaction with the existing product is determined to be high.

Even though the existing market may look formidable, some sectors of the economy look favourably on purchases from small businesses. The federal government, for example, is a very large potential purchaser that should not be overlooked. These types of markets are discussed in Chapter 8.

For a manufacturing firm, success at obtaining key contracts may provide the certainty required to calculate the market share and bypass some of these calculations.

5. *Multiply the estimated market share percentage by the market potential estimate obtained in step 1.* This figure projects estimated dollar sales for the first year of operations. As in the retail example, industry trends can assist in estimating this figure for more than one year.

Service Firm

1. *Estimate the total capacity of the service available in the market area.* The base used to calculate capacity will vary depending on the type of service being offered. For example, restaurant capacity may be measured by number of seats, tables, or square footage; motel capacity by number of rooms; and beauty salon capacity by number of employees or number of workstations. It is important to determine which base most accurately reflects the service capacity. This estimate can be obtained by observing existing businesses or talking to owners.

2. *Estimate the service capacity of the proposed business.* This involves projecting the size of the proposed business in terms of service capacity.

3. *Calculate market share based on the capacity base.* The information obtained in steps 1 and 2 is integrated into the following formula:

$$\frac{\text{Proposed business service capacity}}{\substack{\text{Total market service capacity} \\ \text{(including proposed business service capacity)}}} = \text{Percentage market share}$$

4. *Make adjustments similar to those made for a retail store.* The adjustments in the service industry tend to be more significant than in retailing. The opportunity to differentiate from competitors in the service industry is much greater than in retailing, which tends to deal with more standardized products. Therefore, the percentage adjustments may be larger for service industry market share calculations.

Step 3: Calculate Net Income and Cash Flow

1. *Using the market share revenue figure obtained in step 2 as the starting point, calculate the expenses expected to be incurred for the business.* Most of these figures should be obtained by checking with suppliers and other, similar businesses. However, some secondary sources, such as those provided by Statistics Canada, provide typical operating statements for many types of small businesses.[4] Often these statements express expenses as a percentage of revenue and thus can be easily adapted to the proposed business.

Some of the more important required expenses are:

- *Cost of goods sold and gross profit percentages*—these can be obtained from secondary data but should be confirmed with suppliers.
- *Cash operating expenses,* such as rent, wages, utilities, repairs, advertising, and insurance. These expenses can also be obtained from secondary sources but should be verified by checking with vendors of these services, as they may differ for the market area of the proposed business.
- *Interest and depreciation*—a list of the costs of capital items (i.e., building and equipment) and total start-up costs will need to be made so that yearly depreciation and interest expenses can be calculated. Chapter 7 presents information on determining start-up costs and subsequent interest calculation.

One should remember that only the portion of these assets estimated to be used during that period should be included as the depreciation expenses. Using these start-up costs as a basis, an estimate of the amount of debt and annual interest costs using current rates should be determined.

2. *Subtract expenses from revenue to determine the projected net income from the proposed business in the first year and subsequent years, if required.* Once a projected income figure is calculated, the prospective entrepreneur is in a position to evaluate and compare this result with other types of available investments.

Return (income) as a percentage of investment (funds put into venture) can be compared to other types of businesses or safe uses of money, such as the return obtained by putting the funds in a bank. The rate of return of the business should be higher than bank interest, however, to compensate for the risk factor that accompanies a new business.

It is conceivable—and not uncommon—that the projected income for the new business will be negative, at least in the first few years of operation. Usually the entrepreneur is taking a long-term view of the business, and thus long-term projections may be required to evaluate financial feasibility. In addition to a net income projection, many feasibility analyses include a projected cash flow statement. This document is of particular interest to potential lenders and investors. The cash flow simply describes the cash in minus the cash out on a chronological basis. Usually cash flow statements are shown monthly (see Chapter 7). The sample cash flow in Figure 3–5 is shown on a yearly basis for simplicity.

A quantitative financial feasibility analysis for a retail pharmacy is presented in Figure 3–5. This example illustrates the steps described in the preceding sections.

FIGURE 3–5   **Feasibility Analysis for a Pharmacy in Lethbridge (approximately 3,000 square feet)**

Step 1: Calculate Market Potential

1. *Market area.* The market area is the population of Lethbridge plus outlying regions. This region includes towns within a 50-mile radius of Lethbridge. The population of this total market area is about 160,000. (Source: *Lethbridge Fingertip Facts,* 1991–92 edition, published by the city of Lethbridge.)

2. *Sales for market area.* The per capita sales for pharmacies in the market area can be determined through two sources. First, the actual sales figures may be published and available from the municipality concerned. Second, if that information is not available, find the per capita sales by taking Canadian or provincial sales of pharmacies divided by the respective population. This information is available from Statistics Canada.

$$\frac{\text{Pharmacy sales—Canada (1991)}}{\text{Population Canada (1991)}} = \text{Per capita pharmacy sales}$$

$$\frac{\$8,935,800,000}{27,296,859} = \$327.35$$

Once per capita sales have been determined, this number can be applied to the market area population.

$$
\begin{aligned}
\text{Lethbridge} &= \text{population} \times \text{Per capita sales} \\
&= 61,500 \times \$327.35 \\
&= \$20,132,415.00
\end{aligned}
$$

$$
\begin{aligned}
\text{Outlying area} &= \text{Population} \times \text{Per capita sales} \\
&= (160,000 \quad - \quad 61,500) \times \$327.35 \\
&\quad \text{(total market)} \quad \text{(Lethbridge)} \\
&= 98,500 \times \$327.35 \\
&= \$32,243,975.00
\end{aligned}
$$

(continued)

Since only 30 percent of people in the outlying area made their purchases in Lethbridge (primary research), multiply this figure by .3:

$$\$32,243,975 \times .3 = \$9,673,192$$
$$\text{Total market potential} = \$20,132,415 + \$9,673,192$$
$$= \$29,805,607$$

3. *Adjustments.* Typical adjustments might include updating secondary information regarding population and purchases by applying past trends.

Step 2: Calculate Market Share

1. *Estimate selling space in market.* There are a total of 25 pharmacies and pharmacy departments in Lethbridge, with a total estimated size of 75,000 square feet. (Primary research collected by observation.)
2. *Size of proposed store.* The size of the proposed pharmacy is 3,000 square feet.
3. *Calculation of market share.* Percentage share of the market:

$$\frac{\text{Proposed store selling space}}{\text{Total market selling space (including proposed store)}} = \frac{3,000 \text{ sq. ft.}}{75,000 \text{ sq. ft.} + 3,000 \text{ sq. ft.}} = 3.85\%$$

4. *Adjustments.* The percentage of market share would probably have to be decreased slightly, because the proposed pharmacy is new and would not have built up clientele and the reputation of an existing store.

Based on the above factors, market share has been adjusted to 3.0 percent.
5. *Multiply market share percentage by the market potential.*

Market share $\times$ Market potential = Estimated market share
3.0% $\times$ \$29,805,607   = \$894,168.21

Therefore, market share is approximately \$890,000.

Step 3: Calculation of Net Income and Cash Flow

NEW PHARMACY
Projected Income Statement

For the Period Ended December 1992		Percent of Sales	Source of Information
Sales	\$890,000	100.	From calculation in step 2
Less: Cost of goods sold	640,800	72.0	Dun & Bradstreet *Key Business Ratios* (1990)
Gross margin	249,200	28.0	
Expenses:			
Manager's salary	24,000	2.7	Primary information (talked to owners)
Employee wages (Schedule 1)	130,000	14.6	Schedule 1, Primary information
Fringe benefits	4,450	.5	Stats Canada operating results for pharmacies (1990)
Rent	26,700	3.0	Primary and secondary operating results (talked to owners and Stats Canada 1990)

(continued)

Utilities and telephone	8,000	.9	Primary (talked to owners)
Accounting, legal, taxes, and licence	4,450	.5	Primary (check agencies)
Insurance	4,450	.5	Primary and secondary (operating results, etc.)
Repairs and maintenance	4,450	.5	Stats Canada (operating results, etc.)
Advertising	4,450	.5	Stats Canada (operating results, etc.)
Bad debts	1,780	.2	Primary and secondary (talk to owners and Stats Canada)
Depreciation (Schedule 2)	16,000	1.8	Stats Canada (operating results, etc.), Schedule 2 and Schedule 3
Interest, exchange, and bank charges	7,120	.8	Stats Canada (operating results, etc.)
Office and store supplies	4,450	.5	Stats Canada (operating results, etc.)
Contingency	3,560	.4	Stats Canada (operating results, etc.)
Total expenses	$239,860	27.4	
Net income (loss) before tax	$ 5,340		

Schedule 1 (obtained through primary research)
Employee wages

1 Full-time pharmacist	35,000
1 Part-time pharmacist	17,000
2 Full-time cashiers @ $12,000	24,000
2 Part-time cashiers @ $7,500	15,000
1 Bookkeeper	18,000
1 Marker/receiver	13,000
1 Part-time stock/delivery boy (delivery expense included)	8,000
Total	$130,000

Schedule 2
Depreciation schedule
  Equipment cost = $80,000
  Capital cost allowance (CCA) = 20% (obtained from Master Tax Guide)

Year	Undepreciated Amount	×	CCA	=	Depreciation
1992	$80,000	×	.20	=	$16,000.00
1993	64,000	×	.20	=	12,800.00
1994	51,200	×	.20	=	10,240.00
1995	40,960	×	.20	=	8,192.00
1996	32,768	×	.20	=	6,553

The above process is continued until the entire item is depreciated.

(continued)

Schedule 3

Interest schedule

   Amount borrowed = $50,000
   Interest rate = 12%
   Interest 1992 = 50,000 × 12%   = $6,000
   Estimated bank and service charges = $1,120

Total $7,120

Schedule 4

Calculation of Cash Flow

NEW PHARMACY
Projected Cash Flow Statement
For Period Ended December 31, 1992

Cash inflow	
Beginning cash	$ 20,000
Bank loan	60,000
Cash sales	500,000
Payments on credit sales	200,000
Total cash inflow	780,000
Cash outflow	
Start-up costs	50,000
Merchandise purchases	550,000
Manager's salary	24,000
Employee wages	130,000
Fringe benefits	4,450
Rent (including deposit)	27,000
Utilities and phone (including deposit)	8,200
Accounting, legal, etc.	4,450
Insurance	4,450
Repairs and maintenance	4,450
Advertising	4,450
Interest and bank charges	7,120
Office supplies	4,450
Other expenses	4,450
Total cash outflow	$827,470
Net cash flow	$ (47,470)

Another potentially important part of the feasibility analysis, particularly for the manufacturing firm, is to estimate the level of production and sales required to break even financially. A detailed discussion of break-even analysis is included in Chapter 9.

FIGURE 3-6   Self-Assessment for a Small Business Opportunity

Personality:	Do I possess most of the personality characteristics of successful entrepreneurs introduced in Chapter 2?
Nature:	Does this business opportunity meet my occupational and lifestyle goals and interests?
Abilities:	Do I have the expertise in the fundamentals (financial, marketing, personnel, production) needed to manage this business opportunity? If I do not, am I able and willing to acquire or hire such expertise?
Experience:	Do I have experience with the business or industry? If not, am I able and willing to obtain it or find someone who can help me get started?
Financial base:	Do I currently have, or can I obtain, the necessary funds to finance the venture?
Feasibility:	Does the financial feasibility of the business opportunity meet my expectations and financial goals?

Once the feasibility analysis is completed, the prospective entrepreneur should have enough information to decide whether to pursue a particular business opportunity. The areas covered up to this point can be used to make this decision. Figure 3–6 presents a checklist for personal and opportunity evaluation.

Summary

1. Before deciding which small business opportunity to pursue, the entrepreneur must consider some nonquantitative factors such as his or her goals, the content of the work, the lifestyle the business offers, and the individual's capabilities and experience.

2. There are three ways to enter a market with a new product or service. The first method is to offer a totally new product. The second is to offer an existing product to a different market or industry. The third is to offer a product or service similar to those that already exist in the same market.

3. Two general types of information are available to aid a potential small business owner in selecting a business opportunity. The first and most inexpensive method is to collect secondary research about a potential market. Many government documents and other sources can provide valuable secondary data. When little current secondary data is available, prospective small business owners can collect primary data to help determine the feasibility of their businesses.

4. The purpose of an incubation centre is to provide otherwise costly services to small businesses at minimal cost. Office space, secretarial services, computer capabilities, and financial and business counselling

are examples of such services. Incubators allow the business community to work jointly with governments and universities.

5. Primary data is information collected through one's own research. Although usually more costly than secondary data, it can be more relevant and current to the analysis. Three general methods of doing primary research include observation, surveys, and experiments. Surveying usually is the most effective method for a small business.

6. There are three steps in estimating the financial feasibility of a proposed business venture. The first step is to determine potential revenues for the total market. The second step is to estimate the proposed business share of that total market. The third step is to subtract the associated expenses from the revenue estimate to determine an estimated net income for the prospective business.

Chapter Problems and Applications

1. Briefly explain the ways of entering a market. List examples that fit these methods other than those mentioned in the text.

2. J & J Inc. is thinking of developing a new coin laundry. The firm first needs to do some market research to determine the demand for the product. What kind of information should it collect?

3. What could Kirchner Machine Ltd. (Incident 3–7) have done to properly develop a financial feasibility analysis for the Big Bale Fork?

4. Why is it important to make adjustments in market potential and market share figures?

5. For a small business opportunity of your choice, show how you would evaluate the nonquantitative factors such as goals, experience, lifestyle, and content of work. How well does this business fit with these factors?

6. Design a simple mail questionnaire to assess demand for a carpet-cleaning business in your city.

7. From Dun & Bradstreet, *Key Business Ratios* (see Appendix A), find the "Return on Sales, Gross Profit and Current Ratios" for a jewellery store, a clothing manufacturer, and a grocery store.

8. Using secondary research, develop a market potential analysis for a bakery in your area.

9. The new bakery in Problem 8 has a proposed selling space of 500 square feet. The total amount of selling space devoted to bakery products in the city is 8,400 square feet. From the market potential estimated in Problem 8, find the market share in dollars for the new bakery.

APPENDIX A
SMALL BUSINESS REFERENCE BOOKS

Canadian Small Business Guide, CCH Canadian Ltd., 6 Garamond Court, Don Mills, Ontario, M3C 1Z5.

Market Research Handbook, Statistics Canada, Ottawa, Ontario.

Index to Federal Programs and Services, Supply and Services Canada, Ottawa, Canada.

Handbook of Grants and Subsidies of Federal and Provincial Governments, CCH Canadian Ltd., 6 Garamond Court, Don Mills, Ontario, M3C 1Z5.

ABC Assistance to Business in Canada, Federal Business Development Bank, 204 Richmond Street West, Toronto, Ontario, M5V 1V6, (416) 973–0062.

The Financial Post Canadian Markets, Maclean Hunter Ltd., 777 Bat Street, Toronto, Ontario, M5W 1A7, (416) 596–5585.

This book provides complete demographics for Canadian urban markets. It looks at 500 municipalities across Canada with populations greater than 5,000. It includes data on demographics; income; manufacturing activity; television, radio, and newspaper statistics; other economic statistics; average and annual growth rates of the population; and future population projections.

Handbook of Canadian Consumer Markets, The Conference Board of Canada, Suite 100, 25 McArthur Road, Ottawa, Ontario, K1L 6R3, (613) 746–1281.

This book includes data on provincial, rural, marital populations, and so on; employment; income; expenditures; production and distribution; and pricing.

Wayne D. Kryszak, *The Small Business Index,* Grolier, Inc., Sherman Turnpike, Danbury, Connecticut, U.S.A. 06816.

This book is an index to American and Canadian books, pamphlets, and periodicals that contain information on starting and running a small business.

Key Business Ratios, Dun & Bradstreet Canada Ltd., P.O. Box 423, Station A, Toronto, Ontario.

Contains key business ratios for over 800 different types of businesses. Also, the U.S. affiliate of Dun & Bradstreet publishes "typical" balance sheets, income statements, and "common-size" financial figures.

Small Business Source Book, John Ganly, Diane Seialtana, and Andrea Pedolsky, editors. Gale Research Company, Book Tower, Detroit, Michigan, U.S.A. 48226.

This book was designed as a first step toward finding information for anyone who is considering starting a small business. The book lists 100 companies as well as associations, sources of supply, statistical sources, trade periodicals, franchises, educational programs, trade shows, and conventions.

Statistics Canada, Head Office, R. H. Coats Building, Tunney's Pasture, Ottawa, Ontario, K1A OT6.

1. *Operating Results.* This report presents typical expenses, cost of goods sold, inventory, and net profit as a percentage of sales for many types of businesses. It presents results for both incorporated and unincorporated businesses and gives both mean and median results. Data is provided by both level of sales and province.

2. *Market Research Handbook.* This book presents data on selected economic indicators, government revenue, expenditures and employment, merchandising and services, population characteristics, personal income, and expenditures.

3. *Family Expenditure in Canada.* This report provides information on family expenditures in Canada for a very detailed list of items.

4. *Census Data.* This can be obtained from local city halls. Census data provides information on population growth rates, income level of schooling, and other facts. Census tracts for large centres can also be obtained from Statistics Canada.

5. *Small Business Profiles.* These provide complete financial operating reports for many small businesses.

Periodicals and Trade Magazines Particular to the Type of Business Involved.

For example, one would consult *Restaurateur* if opening a new restaurant. These magazines often provide typical start-up and operating costs for a business. In addition, there are several general small business periodicals, such as *Entrepreneur, Venture,* and *INC.,* that provide valuable ideas on starting a business.

Management Tips—A Guide for Independent Business, Royal Bank of Canada.

This series books offer guidence in starting and running a business. Topics covered include "How to Finance Your Business," "Pointers to Profits," and "Good Management—Your Key to Survival."

Managing for Success Series, The Institute for Small Business Inc., 1051 Clinton Street, Buffalo, New York, U.S.A.

This series contains 16 self-tutorials in business procedure written expressly for the independent business owner. It discusses important business topics such as financing, a do-it-yourself marketing plan, planning and budgeting, and advertising and sales promotion. It provides illustrative case studies and detailed examples and workbook and checklist pages that let you work out your business details along the lines given in the text.

Industry, Science and Technology Canada.

Provides several services for small businesses across the country. ISTC business service centres contain publications, videos, and computer databases, as well as counselling personnel.

Provincial Small Business Departments.

These offices can be very useful to someone who operates or plans to open a small business. They can provide information on sources of financing for small business, and so on. In Alberta, for example, the government publishes pamphlets on many aspects of running a small business, as well as "Kind of Business Files" (KOB), which contain data on 100 types of small businesses such as financial ratios, market trends, and so on.

Minding Your Own Business, Federal Business Development Bank, Management Services, P.O. Box 6021, Montreal, Quebec, H3C 3C3.

This is a series of guides to starting and running a small business. They provide information on areas such as forecasting for an existing business, managing your current assets, retail pricing, attracting and keeping your retail customers, and buying a franchise. The Federal Business Development Bank also publishes workbook case study pamphlets, which are used in training seminars for entrepreneurs. Some of these topics are "Total Quality Control," "Developing a Financial Forecast," and "How to Prepare a Market Study."

Suggested Periodicals for Small Business

Entrepreneur Magazine
Chase Revel
2311 Pontius Avenue
Los Angeles, CA 90064
(213) 477–1011

In Business Magazine
Jerome Goldstein, Publisher
Box 351
Emmaus, PA 18049
(215) 967–4135

INC. Magazine
Bernard Goldhirsh, Publisher
38 Commercial Wharf
Boston, MA 02110
(617) 227–4700

Journal of Small Business and Entrepreneurship
Faculty of Management
University of Toronto
246 Bloor Street West
Toronto, Ontario, M5B 2K3

Journal of Small Business Management
Bureau of Business Research
West Virginia University
Morgantown, WV 26506
(304) 293–0111

Venture Magazine
Arthur Lipper III, Chairman
521 Fifth Avenue
New York, NY 10175
(212) 682–7373

Success
Lang Communications
230 Park Avenue
New York, NY

Profit
CB Media Ltd.
70 The Esplanade, 2nd Floor
Toronto, Ontario

N.E.D.I. Notes
National Entrepreneurship Development
Institute
3601 St. Jacques West
Montreal, Quebec

Your Money
Maclean Hunter Ltd
777 Bay Street
Toronto, Ontario

Organizations and Trade Associations That Assist Entrepreneurs

Association of Collegiate Entrepreneurs
   (ACE)
University of Western Ontario
UCC Building, Room 268
London, Ontario, N6A 3K7
(519) 679–2111

Business Counselling Group
Communications Branch
Department of Industry, Science, and
   Technology
Entrepreneurship and Small Business
   Office
235 Queen Street
Ottawa, Ontario, K1A 0A5
(613) 941–4782

Business Information Centre
Federal Business Development Bank
204 Richmond Street West
Toronto, Ontario, M5V 1V6
(416) 973–0062

The Canadian Chamber of Commerce
120 Adelaide Street West, Suite 2109
Toronto, Ontario, M5H 1T1
(416) 868–6415

Canadian Council of Better Business Bureaus
2180 Steeles Avenue West, Suite 219
Concord, Ontario, M6P 4C7
(416) 922–2584

Canadian Federation of Independent Business
4141 Yonge Street, Suite 401
Willowdale, Ontario, M2P 2A6
(416) 222–8022

Canadian Organization of Small Business
Toronto Office
150 Consumers Road, Suite 501
Willowdale, Ontario, M2J 4V8
(416) 492–3223

Centre for Entrepreneurial Management
29 Greene Street
New York, NY 10013
(212) 925–7304

Federal Business Development Bank
Counselling Assistance for Small Business
901 Victoria Square
Montreal, Quebec, H2Z 1R1
(514) 283–5904

International Council for Small
   Business—Canada
204 Richmond Street West, 5th Floor
Toronto, Ontario, M5V 1V6

Small Business Network
52 Sheppard Avenue West
Willowdale, Ontario, M2N 1M2
(416) 221–8040

National Entrepreneurship Development
   Institute
3601 St. Jacques West
Montreal, Quebec
H4C 3N4
(514) 937–2228

National Small Business Institute
1070 West Broadway, Suite 310
Vancouver, BC, V6H 1E7
(604) 436–3337

Appendix B
Provincial Departments for Small Business

Alberta
Economic Development: Small Business
    Assistance
17th Floor, 10025 Jasper Avenue
Edmonton, T5J 3Z3
(403) 427–3685

British Columbia
Ministry of Economic Development
BC Enterprise Centre
750 Pacific Boulevard South
Vancouver, V6B 5E7
(604) 660–3900

Manitoba
Department of Business Development and
    Tourism and Small Business and Regional
    Development
155 Carlton Street
Winnipeg, R3C 3H8
(204) 945–2422

New Brunswick
Department of Commerce and Technology
Small Industry and Regional Development
Centennial Building
P.O. Box 6000
Fredericton, E3B 5H1
(506) 453–3606

Newfoundland
Department of Development and Tourism
Local Industry Support Services
Atlantic Place, Water Street
St. John's, A1C 5T7
(709) 576–2702

Northwest Territories
Department of Economic Development and
    Tourism
Business Development
P.O. Box 1320
Yellowknife, X1A 2L9
(819) 873–7229

Nova Scotia
Department of Development
200 Barrington St.
P.O. Box 1656
Halifax, B3J 2Z7
(902) 426–7850

Ontario
Ministry of Industry, Trade, and Technology
Hearst Building
900 Bay Street
Toronto, M7A 2E1
(416) 965–1586

Prince Edward Island
Department of Industry
Business Development
Shaw Building, P.O. Box 2000
Charlottetown, C1A 7N8
(902) 892–5445

Quebec
Ministere du Commerce
Exterieur et du Development, Technologique
Place Mercantile, 6e- 7e et 10e étages
770, Rue Sherbrooke Ouest
Montreal, H3A 1G1
(514) 643–5275

Saskatchewan
Department of Tourism and Small Business
Bank of Montreal Building
2103 11th Avenue
Regina, S4P 3V7
(306) 787–2207

Yukon
Department of Economic Development:
Mines and Small Business
Business Development Office
2131 Second Avenue
Whitehorse, Y1A 2C6
(403) 667–3011

APPENDIX C
UNIVERSITIES AND GROUPS THAT OFFER STUDENT CONSULTING PROGRAMS

These programs offer consulting projects for all aspects of business conducted by senior commerce/business students under the supervision of the university faculty. These programs have two purposes: (1) to provide a low-cost consulting service to small businesses and (2) to provide a useful and practical learning experience for senior commerce/business students.

Nova Scotia
Coburg Consultants
6152 Coburg Road
Halifax, B3H 1Z5
(902) 429–6555

British Columbia
Geoffery Dalton/Coordinator
Faculty of Business Administration
University of British Columbia
Burnaby, V5A 1S6
(604) 822–8500

David Boag
University of Victoria
P.O. Box 1700
Victoria, V8W 2Y2
(604) 721–6060

The Province of British Columbia has several Business Development Centres. For more information, contact Gary L. Bunney, Director of Academic/Technical Programs of the Ministry of Post-Secondary Education, (604) 387–6181.

Ontario
Professor Clem Hobbs/Faculty Coordinator
Carleton University/School of Business
Ottawa K1S 5B6

Professor P. Shonoski/Faculty Coordinator
Lakehead University
School of Business Administration
Thunder Bay, P7B 5E1

Professor Dave Gillingham/Faculty
Coordinator
Laurentian University
School of Commerce and Administration
Sudbury, P3E 2C6

Dr. R. S. Adamson/Faculty Coordinator
Wilfrid Laurier University
School of Business and Economics
Waterloo, N2L 3C5

Dr. A. W. Richardson/Faculty Coordinator
McMaster University
Faculty of Business
Hamilton, L8S 4M4

Reid McWilliam, Program Manager
Small Business Management Program
Mohawk College
P.O. Box 2034
Hamilton, L8N 3T2

Professor John McKirdy/Faculty Coordinator
Queen's University
School of Business
Kingston, K7L 3N6

Professor Jim Forrestor/Faculty Coordinator
Ryerson Polytechnical Institute
School of Business
50 Gould Street
Toronto, M5B 1E8

David Litvak/Faculty Coordinator
University of Ottawa
Faculty of Administration
Ottawa, K1B 6N5

Professor Wally Smieliauskas
SBC Faculty Coordinator
University of Toronto
Faculty of Management Studies
246 Bloor Street West
Toronto, M5S 1V4

Professor Murray Bryant
SBC Faculty Coordinator
University of Toronto
Faculty of Management Studies
246 Bloor Street West
Toronto, M55 1V4

J. F. Graham/Faculty Coordinator
University of Western Ontario
School of Business Administration
London, N6A 3K7

Dr. M. Ragab/SBC Faculty Coordinator
University of Windsor
Faculty of Business Administration
401 Sunset Avenue
Windsor, N9B 3P4

Dr. W. B. Crowston/SBC Faculty
  Coordinator
York University
Faculty of Administrative Studies
4700 Keele Street
Downsview, M3J 2R7

Ontario has several colleges and universities that run innovation centres. The innovation centre developed specifically for small business is listed below. For further information on other innovation centres, contact the Ontario Ministry of Industry, Trade, and Technology.

Ryerson Innovation Centre
Ryerson Polytechnical Institute
350 Victoria Street
Toronto, M5B 2K3

Saskatchewan

The University of Regina operates a student consulting service on an informal basis. Students involved in this service have completed a number of different projects for a small number of organizations. They are now considering formally establishing the student consulting service.

University of Regina
Faculty of Administration
Regina, S4S 0A2

Business Consulting Services
College of Commerce
University of Saskatchewan
Saskatoon, S7N 0W0

Manitoba
M.B.A. Student Consulting Program
(May–August)
Department of Business Development and
  Tourism
Winnipeg Enterprise Development Centre
1329 Niakwa Road, 2nd Floor
Winnipeg, R2J 3T4

Alberta
University of Lethbridge
Faculty of Management
4401 University Drive
Lethbridge, T1K 3M4

University of Calgary
Faculty of Management
2500 University Drive N.W.
Calgary, T2N 1N4

University of Alberta
Faculty of Business
202 Faculty of Business Building
Edmonton, T6G 2R6

Suggested Readings

Barnes, Kenneth, and Everett Banning. *Money Makers.* Toronto: McLelland and Stewart, 1985.

Davidson, Jeffery P. *The Marketing Source Book for Small Business.* New York: John Wiley & Sons, 1989.

Developing a Financial Forecast. Montreal: Federal Business Development Bank, 1991.

Do It Yourself Marketing Plan. Buffalo, N.Y.: The Small Business Institute, 1982.

Gorton, Keith, and Isobel Carr. *Low Cost Market Research: A Guide for Small Business.* New York: John Wiley & Sons, 1983.

Gray, Douglas A., and Diane L. Gray. *The Complete Canadian Small Business Guide.* Toronto: McGraw-Hill, Ryerson 1988.

How to Prepare a Market Study. Montreal: Federal Business Development Bank, 1989.

James, Jack. *Starting a Successful Business in Canada.* Vancouver: International Self-Counsel Press, 1982.

Kahn, Sharon. *101 Best Businesses to Start.* Garden City, N.Y.: Doubleday, 1988.

Kao, W. Y. "Market Research and Small New Venture Start-Up Strategy." *Journal of Small Business and Entrepreneurship,* Spring 1986, p. 36.

McDaniel, W., and A. Parasuraman. "Practical Guidelines for Small Business Marketing Research." *Journal of Small Business Management,* January 1986, p. 1.

Shook, Robert L. *Why Didn't I Think of That!* New York: Signet Books–Times Mirror, 1982.

COMPREHENSIVE CASE
THE FRAMEMAKERS: PART 2

After a few days of evaluating their small business decision, Robert and Teresa Norman decided to open the picture-framing retail outlet in Brandon. Robert had learned a great deal about the business from his visit with the U-Frame It franchise in Winnipeg. He convinced his father that the opportunity had promise. Both were aware that many people were now becoming do-it-yourselfers in home decorating.

His college training had taught Robert the importance of thorough investigation before starting a business. He realized he should do this even before deciding whether to start the business on his own or to become a franchise. He contacted the Professional Picture Framers Association (PPFA) and learned that the average customer spends $32 per visit at a framing store. In checking framing costs with the U-Frame It manager in Winnipeg, he confirmed this information. A typical per-customer profit statement for a framing shop was as follows:

Revenue	$32	(100%)
Materials	15	(47%)
Overhead (rent, utilities, wages, etc.)	9	(28%)
Profit per customer	8	(25%)

Robert knew there was one other framing store in Brandon, a city of 35,000. Using Winnipeg as an example, Robert calculated that a framing store could service a population of approximately 25,000 people and earn an acceptable profit.

Robert also attended an industry supplier seminar in Minneapolis. He was encouraged to learn that the do-it-yourself framing business was experiencing rapid growth throughout North America. While there, Robert learned about several picture-framing trade magazines and bought subscriptions for them. He also made valuable contacts with suppliers and other dealers.

Things looked more positive each day, so Robert closed down the painting business, and he and Teresa began making preparations to open their new store, which they would call The Framemakers.

Questions

1. What positive things has Robert done in investigating the feasibility of the new store?
2. What additional information might he have collected?

CASES FOR PART I

Abacus Computers	Petite Shop (A)
Alberta Dusters	Petite Shop (B)
Bramalea Realty Ltd.	Tom's Cleaning Company
Jane Smith	

Abacus Computers

L. Markle and R. E. Vosburgh
University of Guelph

Situation

Steven Faermann, sales manager with Abacus Computers at the Guelph store, is facing a difficult decision about Abacus Computers' current marketing strategy.

There have been an increasing number of customers coming into the Guelph store who are home computer users, that is, people who are interested in using a microcomputer for more than games but not for business reasons. These consumers express interest in using the home computer for personal budget and financial planning, keeping records of important transactions, itemizing and recording personal possessions for security reasons, education for the kids, recipe records, menu planning, and other related at-home uses. Steve does not know if Abacus Computers should branch out and try to capture this new market or if Abacus should maintain the current strategy and continue to focus on the business market.

Previously, Abacus Computers has taken the approach that the microcomputer home games retailer has met the needs of this new market. Now Steve is wondering if this new market is a viable marketing alternative. Steve is preparing his marketing strategy for the coming year and will have to access his budget requirements for advertising and promotion for the store. Therefore, he will need to make up his mind within the next two weeks.

The Microcomputer Industry

The industry has grown and expanded at a rapid pace in the last 10 years and is expected to continue to grow at the same pace for some time to come. There have actually been four major stages of development in the last 10 years. The first stage produced revolutionary hardware, but there was not much software available. The second stage developed powerful software and was followed by a third stage of integration of software and hardware. The final stage was characterized by computer designers creating unusual architecture within the equipment and by tricky programming.

Within the microcomputer industry there have been primarily two markets, the business user and the home game user. The business user uses the microcomputer along with software to meet the individual needs of the business. Common microcomputers for the business user are the Apple II and the IBM. The software available includes word-processing packages, accounting packages, stock-keeping records, and other related business functions. The home game user uses the microcomputer along with software primarily for games. Common microcomputers for the home user are the Atari, Intellivision, and the Commodore Vic 20. The software available includes numerous home games such as Space Invaders, Pac Man, Donkey Kong, and Tron and some education packages.

There appears to be a new market emerging in the microcomputer field, that of the home user who is not interested only in the game aspect of home computers, but in the practical applications of the microcomputer. This user is interested in using a microcomputer combined with the appropriate software to develop budget plans, educational packages for the kids, record-keeping, itemizing of household items, and numerous other home-related uses.

The Company

Abacus Computers initially began as suppliers of software equipment such as diskettes and printers to businesses in the Guelph area. There are two Abacus Computer stores, one in Guelph and one in Kitchener. Given the rapidly changing nature of the field, Abacus saw the opportunity to branch out into the sales of microcomputers. Since introduced into the two outlets two years ago, sales of microcomputers have been very successful and continue to grow. Abacus directs sales of both the microcomputers and the software to the business market as opposed to the personal home user.

Background

Given that Abacus Computers serves the needs of business, their marketing strategy has been to work with each company to design the appropriate computer package. The products which Abacus Computers offers are varied, and depending on the individual company or business user, the appropriate computer and/or package can be made available. With various microcomputers such as IBM or Apple, software such as VisiCalc®, an electronic accounting spreadsheet, and "languages" such as Basic and Pascal, Abacus offers the business user a wide variety in microcomputers, microcomputer packages, and software.

The prices of the microcomputers available through Abacus Computers are dependent on whether or not the business user wants just a microcomputer or a package consisting of a microcomputer, extra hardware, and software. For example, an Apple II microcomputer including a videoscreen, a disk drive, and the languages Basic and Applesoft would cost $2,895. To buy an Apple II microcomputer as described above with two basic software packages such as VisiCalc and Applewriter would cost an additional $610, for a total of $3,505.

A number of promotion and advertising methods are used by the Guelph Abacus Computers store to draw the business user market. Various methods used to date are: Direct mail to businesses in the Guelph area, advertisements in the *Kitchener-Waterloo Record* and the *Daily Mercury* newspapers, advertisements in the Centre in the Square programs, and some radio and point-of-purchase promotions, such as a free Apple booklet for consumers who come to the retail outlet.

Since their primary target market has been business users, Abacus Computers located their retail outlet in Guelph in the industrial basic at the northwest end of the city. The majority of commercial and industrial businesses in Guelph are located in this area. The Abacus Computer store location allows easy access for businesses and Abacus Computers salesmen in terms of service and sales.

The increasing demand for microcomputers, for both business and for personal home use, has resulted in an increasing number of computer consultants, software suppliers, and retailers of microcomputers in the Guelph area. This increasing competition is another factor which Steve is considering in the examination of the home user market. Consolidated Computer Inc. and Desktop Computer Inc. in the immediate Guelph area, and Computerland and Radio Shack in Kitchener and Burlington, are all suppliers in the Guelph area. These suppliers are directing their sales and service efforts to potential business and home users in the Guelph area. The first two, Consolidated Computer and Desktop Computer, as well as Radio Shack are primarily interested in the business users. However, they do provide sales, service, and support to the home users.

Since Abacus Computers is primarily concerned with the business market, Steve feels that there are other retailers which are meeting the needs of the serious home user. Steve is wondering, however, whether or not he should do some exploratory research to determine how viable this serious home user market is, particularly since there is an increasing number of competitors in the Guelph area directing their sales, service, and support to this home user market. Another alternative would be to go ahead and change some of the advertising and promotion Abacus currently uses to meet this new market and see what kind of response results. Steve realizes that he will have to make a decision one way or another, since he must have his marketing strategy and budget for the coming year ready in two weeks.

Questions

1. What information should Steve collect to make this decision?
2. If Steve were to pursue this new market, what changes would be necessary in his current marketing strategy?

Alberta Dusters

D. Wesley Balderson
University of Lethbridge

Background

In the summer of 1990 Jack Molnar, a real estate salesperson and sports enthusiast in the city of Lethbridge, Alberta, was contemplating the purchase of a franchise for that city in the Continental Basketball League. The Continental League teams, all located in the United States, were made up of players who were late cuts of National Basketball Association (NBA) teams or players with previous NBA experience. It was designed as a type of minor league for the NBA players and officials.

When Molnar contacted the president of the league, Jim Drummond, he met an enthusiastic response, as the league was eager to expand and locate a team somewhere in Alberta. Molnar checked with some business associates, who were also basketball enthusiasts, about the feasibility of the venture. With their support and encouragement he attended a league meeting where he learned, among other things, that the franchise fee was $40,000 (Canadian) and league statistics indicated that to break even the team would need an attendance of 1,200 to 1,500 spectators per game. The Canadian Basketball Association (CBA) was also excited by the fact that the NBA was starting to pay the CBA development money.

Because the deadline for entry into the league was drawing near and the preliminary information was positive, Molnar agreed to purchase a franchise for Lethbridge to start the 1990–1991 season.

Organization

Molnar went back to Lethbridge and, with his small group, incorporated a limited company called Blue-Green Sports Limited, which would purchase the franchise. Four preferred shares at $10,000 and 50 common shares at $1,000 were issued, which raised equity financing to $90,000. Additional funds were borrowed from the bank. The board of directors hired a general manager, a coach, and a secretary. The general manager, in charge of the day-to-day operations of the team, had a promotions background; promotions would be a major priority for the new team. The coach was hired from a Canadian university basketball team and had experience as a player in New Zealand.

The team was called the Alberta Dusters.

Area

Lethbridge is a city of 60,000 situated in an agricultural area in the southwest corner of Alberta, approximately 50 miles from the U.S. and B.C. borders. An additional population of about 50,000 people live within a one-hour drive of the city. This area of the province has had a long history of interest and support for basketball, one reason Molnar's group chose to locate the team in Lethbridge.

Competition

The Dusters' management believed the competition from the university, college, and high school basketball teams would be substantial and thus tried to avoid game conflicts where scheduling permitted. An agreement was reached with the high school league whereby some high school games could be played as preliminaries to the Dusters' home games. The Dusters felt this would enhance their attendance, as it increased their drawing power and avoided game conflicts. The high school league was less enthusiastic because of the distance it had to travel, but agreed to try the arrangement for a year.

Product

The team was made up of late cuts from the NBA and a couple of players with previous NBA experience. All players were recruited from the United States, with the exception of one U.S. citizen who had played university ball in Manitoba. The team was aligned in the West Division of the CBA along with teams from Anchorage, Alaska, Great Falls, and Billings, Montana. The Dusters were also scheduled to make one road trip during the season to play the East Division teams along the East Coast of the United States. Spectators generally voiced praise for the calibre of the play and the entertainment and excitement the teams provided.

Place

The Dusters decided to play their home games in the Lethbridge Sportsplex, which had a seating capacity of about 5,000. Although generally conceded to be the best facility in the West Division of the CBA, it was also the most expensive, costing the Dusters $1,500 per game (the other teams paid considerably less). Lethbridge had no other suitable facility available at the time as the university, college, and high school gymnasiums were already scheduled for the year. The other major tenant of the Sportsplex was the Lethbridge Hurricanes, a junior hockey team that played in the Western Canada Hockey League. The Dusters were able to schedule around the home games of the Broncos in booking the Sportsplex, but they forced the old-timers' hockey program in the city to readjust its scheduling to much later times, and this caused some discontent among members of this league. The rental paid to the Sportsplex included ushering, ticket sales, concessions, and novelties so the Dusters were not responsible for these functions.

Promotion

Promotion of the Dusters in year one was under the direction of the general manager and consisted of television spots (50 percent), radio (40 percent), and newspapers (10 percent). A program book was prepared and sold, but higher than expected printing costs caused the program to actually lose money. In-game promotions included the usual giveaways and contests at half-time, and they were generally considered successful.

Price

The ticket prices were set at $5.50 and $3.50 for adults and $2.00 for children, which were comparable to the Lethbridge Broncos hockey team's prices. Although this price was considerably higher than those for university, college, or high school games, it was felt that the much higher calibre of play would offset this price. The team advertised 237 season ticket holders, but only 118 were actually sold; the rest were given to shareholders and were part of promotions.

Results of Year One

Although there was much excitement at the beginning of the year, the team ended the year dismally both on and off the court. Both the general manager and the

---
FIGURE 1   Estimated Income Statement for 1990–1991

Revenue:
  Ticket sales (average 1,035 per game) $100,000
Expenses:
  Players' salaries $45,000
  Gym rental (Sportsplex)   33,000
  Administrators' salaries (general manager, coach,   30,000
    and secretary)
  Advertising   45,000
  Travel   30,000
  Training camp   15,000
  Telephone   17,000
  Miscellaneous   7,000
                                                                       _____
      Total expenses   222,000
Net loss   ($122,000)

---

coach quit toward the end of the season after considerable criticism from the board of directors. The team lost an estimated $122,000 in this first year of operation and finished last in the West Division of the CBA with an 11–31 won-lost record (see Figure 1).

Questions

1. What specific errors in marketing strategy were made in this case?
2. What additional problems caused the Dusters' poor financial performance?

Bramalea Realty Ltd.

D. Wesley Balderson
University of Lethbridge

Bramalea Realty Ltd. is a small, independent real estate firm located in Lethbridge, Alberta. Because of its success, the company recently decided to expand operations from residential real estate to office development. Management believed the decision to move into this area was sound because Alberta was experiencing a buoyant economy in the 1990s and all projections for business, population, and construction were very positive for the next decade. Although most of this activity was centered in Calgary, Edmonton, and points north, considerable spillover was affecting Lethbridge, which is located in the southwest corner of the province and has a population of 62,000.

Bramalea's accountant had noticed some figures in the *Financial Post Survey of Markets* indicating that Lethbridge's growth rate per decade was 35 percent—significantly higher than the Canadian average of 10 percent and even 1 percent higher than the Alberta average. In the same publication, he found that Lethbridge had a market rating of 86 percent above the national average, also higher than Edmonton and Calgary. This, he surmised, was a result of high retail expenditures per capita and a large retail drawing from the smaller communities surrounding Lethbridge.

Although Bramalea's management was a bit hesitant to move so quickly, they were aware that the demand for office space rose in proportion to population, income, and retail expenditures, and all these variables were rapidly increasing. The accountant pointed out that construction in Lethbridge was proceeding briskly and this would be an ideal time for Bramalea to enter this area of office development.

As a result, Bramalea purchased a site one block from the central business district, with plans to construct an office building. Although the site contained an old building, it would be replaced with a four-story office building of about 40,000 square feet.

Before going ahead with construction, Bramalea decided to do some research on the types of facilities prospective tenants would prefer (underground parking, recreation facilities, restaurant). They believed that acting on the results of this research would increase their chances to obtain the high early occupancy rate of at least 90 percent they would require to make the project financially feasible. Their investigation revealed the following, in addition to tenant preferences regarding amenities:

1. The population of Lethbridge was growing at a rate of 35 percent per decade (*FP Survey of Markets*) compared to the Canadian average of 10 percent.

2. The market rating index of Lethbridge was 86 percent above the national average in 1996 (*FP Canadian Markets*).

3. Per capita retail sales in Lethbridge in 1990 was $5,924, considerably above the Canadian average of $3,190.

4. Population projections for Lethbridge were as follows:

1990	60,000
1992	62,000
1994	64,000
1996	66,000

5. The present supply of office space in Lethbridge (1992) was estimated at 500,000 square feet, with a vacancy rate of 20 percent.

6. Averages for other cities in Canada showed an average of about 6.5 to 7 square feet per capita in office space at 90 percent occupancy.

7. There did not appear to be a great demand for restaurant or recreation facilities; the major preference was to be close to downtown.

In view of this information, Bramalea is still planning to proceed with construction of the building, but management is now a bit worried.

Questions

1. Should Bramalea be concerned about the results of its most recent research?
2. How should Bramalea have gone about assessing the market potential for the new office building?
3. What additional information, if any, is required at this point?
4. What would you advise Bramalea to do at this point?

Jane Smith

Jim Mason
University of Regina

Jane Smith was on the horns of a dilemma. Several of the better Canadian law and graduate business schools had accepted her and sorting them out was challenge enough. But something else was bothering her. Jane enjoyed operating her secretarial services company, but it had little potential, and she wondered if a small business career might not be best for her.

Jane realized that considerable research had been conducted on the personal traits and behaviour of entrepreneurs. This material would significantly improve a "seat-of-the-pants" guesstimate of her entrepreneurial potential. The key to her search was a realistic and thorough self-evaluation.

What Is an Entrepreneur?

Jane found many of the early studies interesting but not too useful. Richard Cantillon had characterized an entrepreneur as a person who bears risk; has the capacity to combine goods and services; organizes and supervises production; introduces new methods and new products; and searches for new markets, but Jane found this too broad. It applied to many people who wouldn't be considered entrepreneurs today. Adam Smith saw the entrepreneur as simply the supplier of capital. She felt better about Joseph Schumpeter's view of the entrepreneur as a creator of new combinations bringing about change. Her mother had always said that Jane did things differently and continually tried to change the world to suit herself.

Entrepreneurship was described as the ability to create an ongoing business where none had existed before. She wondered if this would include

- Someone who starts her own business rather than working for other people
- A person who buys an existing small business with the intention of making it grow or changing it significantly
- A limited partner in a small business, one not involved in day-to-day decisions but in the key decisions
- A professional in practice such as a doctor, consulting engineer, or accountant, or
- A franchisee

When Jane was a child many of the fathers of her friends worked in small organizations, mostly for themselves. Among the lawyers, doctors and dentists was an independent oil man and a small manufacturer. However, Jane was concerned that she had few established role models of self-employed women. One of her older friends, recently divorced, had started her own business, and Jane's mother had set up Calgary Home Economists last year for her consulting practice, but these were the exceptions. Jane was fascinated by the entrepreneurs profiled in *Canadian Business*. Perhaps they had some common characteristics.

What Are the Characteristics of Entrepreneurs?

Jane noticed that service-oriented entrepreneurs were significantly different from product-oriented ones. In addition, she found that technical entrepreneurs had different educational backgrounds than service or nontechnical entrepreneurs. Jane decided that across-the-board generalizations were, at best, risky—at worst, quite misleading. For instance, the demanding requirements for building a million-dollar venture would not be essential for establishing a mom-and-pop proprietorship.

Jane wondered which, if any, of these characteristics were evident before an enterprise was launched, and which resulted from the experience. It seemed to her that tremendous learning and personal growth would come from actually starting and managing your own company. Perhaps this was the best way to discover where she could excel and where she was weak. Certainly she could develop some skills such as goal setting, and learn some role requirements. Jane compared her own attributes to the characteristics she found in the literature. She was overwhelmed by the over fifty traits she had identified.

Timmons, Smollen and Dingee extensively examined the available research and theory about the characteristics of successful entrepreneurs. They found sufficient agreement to suggest fourteen dominant characteristics.[1] Jane thought about herself in light of each one.

---

[1]J. Timmons, L. Smollen, and A. Dingee, *New Venture Creation: A Guide to Small Business Development* (Homewood, Ill.: Richard D. Irwin, 1977).

Drive and Energy.   "Entrepreneurs have a high amount of personal energy and drive. They possess a capacity to work for long hours and in spurts for several days with less than a normal amount of sleep." Jane laughed. She had many experiences like this while she was studying for her B.Sc. in kinesiology. Her courses required a lot of papers, and she often found herself writing through the night. Delicate laboratory experiments were often done at night to avoid power surges. Besides, Jane never took the average course load. She always carried one or two extra classes each semester. In addition, she had worked several semesters to support herself while taking classes.

Self-Confidence.   "Successful entrepreneurs have a high level of self-confidence. They tend to believe strongly in themselves and their abilities to achieve the goals they set." People saw Jane as self-confident and competent. But deep inside she felt she was not the person they saw. She had trained long and hard as a competitive athlete and had won provincial championships, but often she'd had to remind herself, "I'm a graduate of the Outward Bound program and I can do anything" and then, "Gut it out." Although she was an excellent diver she had consistently placed lower than her coach expected. Jane had failed her diving test five times, and when she took Royal Conservatory exams her music teacher was disappointed with Jane's mark in the mid-80s.

Long-Term Involvement.   "Entrepreneurs who create high-potential ventures are driven to build a business, rather than simply get in and out in a hurry." Jane had set her sights on becoming a doctor. She had directed her studies and energy to that goal for years. In the process, however, she had shifted from honours math to physiotherapy to occupational therapy to kinesiology. Even then, she had thought about transferring into biology. Her mother always broke projects up into small tasks so Jane could complete them before her interests changed. Knitting a complex sweater was significant because Jane had completed it.

Money as a Measure.   "Money has a very special meaning to the professional entrepreneur: it is a way of keeping score. Salary, profits, capital gains, and net worth are seen as measures of how well the entrepreneur is doing in pursuit of self-established goals." Jane wasn't sure about this one. She always had made the money she needed for her trips, camps, and activities. She had the usual lemonade stands, paper routes and lawn-mowing businesses, and a few unusual enterprises— like rowing people about the lake one summer. But it wasn't money for money's sake. Her secretarial business had made just enough to do what she wanted. Terms like profit, capital gains, net worth didn't have much significance because she didn't know what they meant. However, money had recently become more important. Many of the women she worked with had been secretaries or clerks for twenty-five years. They were earning only a couple of hundred dollars a month more than when they started. If she was going to work, she wasn't going to get trapped in any female ghetto!

Persistent Problem Solving.   "Entrepreneurs who successfully build new enterprises possess an intense level of determination and desire to overcome hurdles, solve a problem, and complete the job." Jane was not intimidated by difficult situations. She had always felt the impossible just took a little bit longer. Yet Jane was realistic in recognizing what she could and couldn't do. She knew when and where to get help solving key but difficult tasks.

Goal Setting.   "Entrepreneurs have an ability and commitment to set clear goals for themselves. These goals tend to be high and challenging, but they are realistic and attainable." No doubt about it, Jane was a doer. She was goal and action oriented. Perhaps she did not always know how she was going to achieve her goals, but she believed in herself. Jane hated to waste time, so goals and priorities were useful ways to keep on track. She would sit down every semester in university and plot courses three semesters ahead. She wanted the best game plan to get out in a minimum amount of time—and she completed the four-year degree in three years.

Moderate Risk Taking.   "The successful entrepreneur prefers to take moderate, calculated risks where the chances of winning are neither so small as to be a gamble nor so large as to be a sure thing." Jane preferred situations that provided a reasonable challenge and a chance of success. Others may have seen her 150-mile solo backpacking trip as a ridiculous gamble. However, she'd arranged for friends to meet her every five days with more food. Jane believed her abilities and effort could overcome those things she set her mind to accomplish, yet she was not foolish. She liked to mountain ski in the back country, but she would check things out thoroughly before venturing out and in extreme situations she would accompany a more experienced skier.

Dealing with Failure.   "The ability to use failure experiences as a way of learning, and to better understand not only your role but also that of others in causing the failures in order to avoid similar problems in the future, is another important entrepreneurial characteristic." Jane smiled. Her mother had often said, "The person who has never failed at anything probably hasn't done much. You can be anything you want to be, but you have to try!" Her father, on the other hand, couldn't tolerate failure. Sometimes she had felt disappointed, even discouraged by a setback, but she'd pressed on. While intent on succeeding, she was always aware of the possibility of failing and letting down the family name.

Use of Feedback.   "Entrepreneurs, as high achievers, are very concerned about their performance, especially doing well.... Successful entrepreneurs demonstrate the capacity to seek and use feedback on their performance in order to take corrective action and to improve." Jane thought she fit this characteristic quite well. As a youth, she had particularly enjoyed individual sports like track and diving. She had little talent in art but liked to do crafts, and she found that needlework provided real personal satisfaction. Jane's father never worked around the home with her but Jane seemed to have a natural "mechanical" ability. Given a book, she could fix almost anything. Jane actively sought feedback from her teachers, coaches, and employers. Their expectations and praise motivated her almost as much as her own sense of accomplishment.

Taking Initiative and Seeking Personal Responsibility.   "The entrepreneur has historically been viewed as an independent and highly self-reliant innovator, the champion (and occasional villain) of the free enterprise economy." Jane was bright and particularly quick intuitively. She lost patience with slower thinkers. She would leap to creative solutions to problems. Even though she accepted responsibility for the success or failure of activities, she sometimes did it reluctantly. Although Jane didn't actively seek and take initiative in a power sense, she often found she would fill a vacuum where no leadership existed.

Use of Resources.   "Several studies have emerged in recent years which show that successful entrepreneurs know when and how to seek outside, as well as inside, help in building their companies." Jane thought about this. In starting her secretarial company, she had simply gone ahead and done it. She had not really looked for advice. In tackling new areas, Jane would first get a stack of how-to books from the library before seeking the extra insight from others. Looking for help was at odds with her idea of entrepreneurs as highly individualistic and self-reliant loners.

Competing against Self-Imposed Standards.   Jane saw competitiveness by itself as a misleading characteristic, and recognized the difference between competing with self and with others. She remembered several times when she had raced her boyfriend down ski hills, pushing so hard to win that they were dangerously close to being out of control. Competing simply to beat someone else could be destructive, even dumb. She had seen her older brother and sister competing with each other, and didn't like what it did to them. Jane felt that her standards were largely self-imposed. In the 880 or mile she ran against the clock rather than the other runners—there was a driving force in her to beat her last best time.

Internal Locus of Control.   "The entrepreneur does not believe the success or failure of a new business venture depends on luck or fate, or other external, personally uncontrollable factors." Neither did Jane. She felt personal success was within her control and influence. Her accomplishments were a matter of perseverance and hard work; luck had little to do with them.

Tolerance of Ambiguity and Uncertainty.   "Entrepreneurs have long been viewed as having a special tolerance for ambiguous situations and for making decisions under conditions of uncertainty." Jane always worked hard to reduce the uncertainty—planning her university course work three semesters ahead was typical. She had developed her communication skills to a high degree. When a boss gave her ambiguous assignments, she would draw him out skilfully until she knew what was wanted. Job security was not nearly as important as doing the best she could.

Where To from Here?

Jane reflected on her analysis. She had raised more questions in her mind than she had apparently answered. Her study of entrepreneurial characteristics was not exhaustive, but Jane wondered about the relative importance of the various attributes. She was concerned about how well she matched the entrepreneurial profile, and the presence or absence of particular traits. How did the various characteristics relate to the behaviours of successful entrepreneurs? How and to what extent could people change their motivation and behaviour? Was all the fuss about traits and behaviours purely academic? She wondered if so-called successful entrepreneurs had these characteristics before starting out, or if they were acquired in the process of becoming successful. What was her entrepreneurial potential? Could she answer these questions now? If not, how should she proceed?

Petite Shop (A)

D. Wesley Balderson
University of Lethbridge

Alice Wood was concerned. She had worked in a women's clothing store for several years and was now considering opening a store of her own. Her investigations had yielded considerable secondary information, but she was not sure how to go about estimating the potential for another women's clothing store in Prince George, British Columbia. Prince George was a city of 67,628, surrounded by a large trading area. Presently it had 22 clothing stores and 5 department stores that retailed women's clothing. During the past few years, she had been saving her money and learning all she could so that her Petite Shop ladies' wear store would be a success.

In anticipation of starting her own store, Alice had enrolled in a small business management course at a local college. The instructor had stressed the importance of market research and mentioned several sources of secondary information that could assist in determining market potential for a new business. Alice had obtained the reports she felt were relevant to her prospective business from the Provincial Department of Small Business and the city hall in Prince George. This information is presented in Figures 1 through 3.

FIGURE 1   **Selected Data for the City of Prince George**

Population	67,628
Number of households	22,625
Per capita income	$14,300
Retail sales	$352,570,300

SOURCE: *Financial Post Survey of Markets.*

FIGURE 2   **Estimated Retail Space for Selected Retail Establishments (in square feet)**

City of Prince George	
Food stores	1,200,000
Apparel stores:	
Men's clothing stores	145,000
Women's clothing stores	180,000
Hardware stores	600,000
Department stores	1,650,000

FIGURE 3   **Percentage Distribution of Family Expenditures, by Family Income, in Canada, 1991 (all families and unattached individuals)**

	Family Income			
	$20,000–$29,999	*$30,000–$39,999*	*$40,000–$49,999*	*$50,000–and Over*
Food	15.94%	14.82%	13.59%	12.87%
Shelter	17.45	16.36	14.49	14.25
Household operation	4.71	4.19	4.35	4.11
Household furnishings and equipment	3.54	3.40	3.69	3.71
Clothing	6.08	6.00	6.47	6.29
Transportation	13.81	13.62	14.09	13.46
Health care	2.20	1.94	1.80	1.67
Personal care	2.11	1.96	1.93	1.85
Recreation	5.11	5.06	5.09	4.85
Reading	0.60	0.61	0.56	0.53
Education	0.56	0.63	0.74	0.90
Tobacco products and alcoholic beverages	3.90	3.76	3.06	2.81
Miscellaneous	2.73	2.68	2.75	2.68
Personal taxes	13.64	17.60	19.49	21.62
Security	4.54	4.64	5.41	5.15
Gifts and contributions	3.07	2.72	2.48	3.24
Total expenditures	100.00	100.00	100.00	100.00

SOURCE: Adapted from *Statistics Canada: Family Expenditures in Canada, 1986* (Ottawa: Minister of Supply and Services Canada, Cat. 62–555, 1991).

Now that Alice had this information, however, she was not sure how to proceed. She did not want to retail all kinds of ladies' clothing but planned to cater to the "petite" woman who wore dress sizes 3 to 9. Alice herself was petite (5 feet, 1 inch), and she felt she understood the difficulties women of her size had in shopping for clothing. From her retailing experience, she estimated that about 60 percent of all clothing sales were in women's clothing and 20 percent of all women fit in the size 3–9 category. She arrived at her decision to select a store directed at the petite woman after she visited all of the 22 clothing stores in Prince George and the clothing departments of the city's 5 department stores. She estimated that only about 10 percent of clothing stores' stock was sized 3 to 9, and the five department stores devoted only about 6,500 square feet of selling space devoted to this size range. She believed a small shop of about 1,000 square feet could provide a much better selection to this market than those outlets presently provided.

Questions

1. Using the information provided, prepare an estimate of the market potential for the target market Alice Wood is aiming at.
2. What portion of this market potential could Alice expect for Petite Shop's market share?
3. What nonquantitative considerations should be brought into this analysis?

Petite Shop (B)

D. Wesley Balderson
University of Lethbridge

Now that Alice Wood had a better idea of market potential and market share for her proposed retail store, she wanted to be satisfied that the Petite Shop would provide an adequate return on her savings of $25,000. She began investigating the typical costs she would incur in operating the store. Alice thought she could operate her new store with one other full-time person and some part-time help at the estimated monthly cost of $2,000. In looking at potential rental costs, she came across a retail outlet for lease on a busy street in the central business district of Prince George that seemed ideal for the Petite Shop. She learned that the site leased for $20 per square foot, with no royalty payments except $550 per year to cover municipal taxes. The estimated utility expenses the owner provided were $300 per month, and the insurance for the retail shoe store that had previously been located there was $1,500 per year.

FIGURE 1   **Key Business Ratios, Canada—Corporations, 1990**

Line of Business	*Clothing, Women's*
(Number of concerns reporting)	(2,323)
Cost of goods sold	58.40%
Gross margin	41.60
Current assets to current debt	1.4
Profits on sales	2.7
Profits on tangible net worth	15.6
Sales to tangible net worth	5.9
Sales to inventory	5.7
Fixed assets to tangible net worth	63.6
Current debt to tangible net worth	127.6
Total debt to tangible net worth	177.3

Although Alice was excited about the potential of this site, she estimated she would need to spend approximately $12,000 for leasehold improvements, of which $8,000 would be depreciable items (20 percent). When obtaining the secondary information from the Prince George city hall, she learned that the business licenses would be $100. Alice estimated that all miscellaneous expenses such as stationery, bad debt expense, credit expense, and telephone to be about $5,000 per year. These figures were based on her experience in the store she currently worked in.

Alice knew she would have to borrow some money to purchase inventories. She visited her local bank and found out that the interest rate for a business loan was 10 percent. She also learned that until she had a more concrete proposal, her banker was not interested in considering her for a loan. He mentioned that in addition to leasehold improvements, she would need one-fourth of the year's cash expenses as operating funds. Although a bit surprised at the bank's reaction, Alice was determined to prepare such a proposal. She knew the new store would need to be promoted, but didn't know how much she should spend on advertising. The banker had suggested the average for ladies' clothing stores was about 2 percent of sales and had given her a copy of a recent Dun & Bradstreet financial ratio sheet to assist her (see Figure 1).

Alice now found herself in the same dilemma she had been in when determining market potential and market share. She had a lot of information, but was not sure how to proceed.

Questions

1. Using the information presented in "Petite Shop (A)" and this case, prepare an estimated income statement and return on investment calculation for the Petite Shop's first year of operation.
2. What areas has Alice overlooked in her investigation?
3. Given your analysis, what would you recommend to Alice?

Tom's Cleaning Company

E. Jerome McCarthy and Stanley J. Shapiro
Michigan State University and Simon Fraser University

Tom Willis is a 26-year-old ex-Army man and a lifelong resident of Brockville, Ontario. Brockville is a beautiful summer resort area situated on the St. Lawrence in the Thousand Island region. The permanent population is about 20,000, and this more than triples in the summer months.

Tom spent seven years in the Canadian Armed Forces after high school graduation. Returning home in June 1990 Tom decided to go into business for himself because he couldn't find a good job in the Brockville area. He set up Tom's Cleaning Company. Tom felt that his savings would allow him to start the business without borrowing any money. His estimates of required expenditures were $3,900 for a used panel truck, $475 for a steam-cleaning machine adaptable to carpets and furniture, $330 for a heavy-duty commercial vacuum cleaner, $50 for special brushes and attachments, $75 for the initial supply of cleaning fluids and compounds, and $200 for insurance and other incidental expenses. This total of $5,030 still left Tom about $2,800 in savings to cover living expenses while getting started.

One of the reasons Tom chose this line of work is his previous work experience. From the time he was 16, Tom had worked part-time for Joel Bidwell. Mr. Bidwell operated the only other successful carpet-cleaning company in Brockville. (One other company was in Brockville, but it was near bankruptcy.)

Mr. Bidwell prided himself on quality work and had a loyal clientele. Specializing in residential carpet cleaning, Bidwell has been able to build a strong customer franchise. For 35 years, Bidwell's major source of new business has been retailer recommendations and satisfied customers who tell friends about the quality service received from Mr. Bidwell. He is so highly thought of that the leading carpet and furniture stores in Brockville always recommend Bidwell's for preventive maintenance in quality carpet and furniture care. Often Bidwell is trusted with the keys to Brockville's finest homes for months at a time when owners are out of town and want his services. Bidwell's customers are so loyal, in fact, that a national household carpet-cleaning franchise found it next to impossible to compete with him. Even price-cutting was not an effective weapon against Mr. Bidwell.

Tom Willis felt that he knew the business as well as Mr. Bidwell, having worked for him for many years. Tom was anxious to reach his $20,000 per year sales goal because he thought this would provide him with a comfortable living in Brockville. While aware of opportunities for carpet cleaning in businesses, office buildings, motels, and so on, Tom felt that the sales volume available there was only about $8,000 because most businesses had their own cleaning staffs. As he saw it, his only opportunity was direct competition with Bidwell.

To get started, he allocated $600 to advertise his business in the local newspaper. With this money he was able to purchase two half-page ads and have enough left over to buy daily three-line ads in the classified section, listed under Miscellaneous Residential Services, for 52 weeks. All that was left was to paint a sign on his truck and wait for business to catch on.

Tom had a few customers and was able to gross about $100 a week during the first few months. These customers were usually Bidwell regulars who, for one reason or another (usually stains, spills, or house guests), weren't able to wait the two weeks required until Bidwell could work them in. While these people did admit that Tom's work was of the same quality as Mr. Bidwell's, they preferred Bidwell's quality-care image. During April and May Tom did get more work than he could handle when resort owners were preparing for summer openings and owners of summer homes were ready to open the cottage. The same rush occurred in September and October as resorts and homes were being closed for the winter. During these months, Tom was able to gross about $100–$120 a day working 10 hours per day.

Toward the end of his first year in business, Tom began to think about quitting. While he hated to think of having to leave Brockville, he couldn't see any way of making a living in the carpet and furniture cleaning business in Brockville. Mr. Bidwell had the whole residential market sewed up except in the rush seasons and for people who needed fast cleaning.

Questions

1. Evaluate Tom's approach to starting his carpet-cleaning business.
2. Why was he not able to reach his goal of $20,000 in sales?
3. Is there anything Tom could do to stay in business?

PART II

Preparing for Small Business Ownership

Once the entrepreneur has assessed an opportunity, the next important consideration is selecting from among three methods of assuming ownership of the business: organizing the business from scratch, buying an existing business, or signing a franchise contract. Chapters 4, 5, and 6 provide information to help evaluate each of these methods. The last, but equally important, start-up consideration is obtaining financing. Chapter 7 discusses the critical factors the entrepreneur should consider in obtaining financing needed to establish and operate the venture.

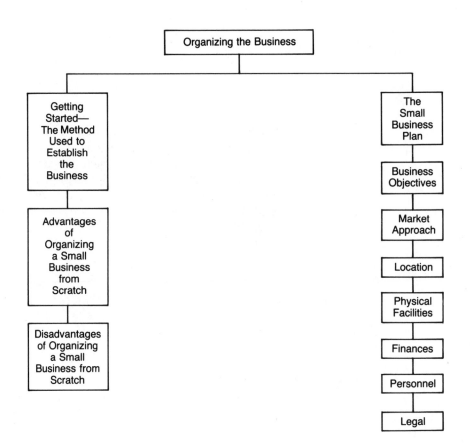

Organizing the Business

Getting Started—The Method Used to Establish the Business

Advantages of Organizing a Small Business from Scratch

Disadvantages of Organizing a Small Business from Scratch

The Small Business Plan

Business Objectives

Market Approach

Location

Physical Facilities

Finances

Personnel

Legal

Organizing a Business

Chapter Objectives

- To describe the advantages and disadvantages of organizing a business from scratch compared to purchasing a business or becoming a franchisee.
- To discuss the importance of formulating and following a business organizational plan.
- To review the essential components of a small business plan.

Small Business Profile

Peter Goudas

Goudas Food Products and Investments Ltd.

Peter Goudas's story is a classic example of the immigrant entrepreneur who, through hard work and intelligent planning, has created a successful business. Goudas arrived in Canada from Greece in 1967 without any money, family, or friends and very little command of the English language. However, with Goudas's background in engineering, he soon obtained employment with a company that needed a specialist who was experienced in metric.

While working with this company, he recognized that the plant could be operated more efficiently. Outside the job, he noticed a large demand for ethnic foods. The number of Canadians with an ethnic origin other than English or French was growing rapidly, and few companies seemed to be catering to them. Within three years he had saved enough money to act on his observations and buy a small factory, where he started packaging rice for this market. His product found a ready market, and because of this success, the Mr. Goudas line of food products has expanded rapidly (over 350 products), although rice (in 20 varieties) is still one of his mainstays.

Peter Goudas still works out of a small office in Toronto, but this setting hides the fact that he does business all over the world. Most of his products are imported. Many are also packaged elsewhere, but all enjoy popularity with ethnic Canadians.

In a business where the majority of new products fail, Goudas is successful because he made sure there was a market for his product before he introduced it, and he followed a meticulous approach to business planning. Such an approach provides a good pattern for budding entrepreneurs to follow.

Source: "Goudas Food Products and Investments, Ltd.," *Globe and Mail,* Tuesday, March 23, 1993.

Getting Started: Establishing the Business

Once the entrepreneur has assessed the feasibility of a business opportunity and found it to be favourable, the next step is to select the method of establishing the business. There are essentially three methods of establishing a small business. The first is to organize the business from scratch, the second is to purchase an existing business, and the third is to become a franchisee. This chapter discusses the essential steps in organizing the business from scratch and details the steps in creating a business plan. Chapter 5 deals with purchasing an existing business, and Chapter 6 covers franchising. Although the topics covered in Chapters 5 and 6 are treated separately, many of the aspects of business plan preparation covered in this chapter are applicable to the following two chapters.

In making the decision to organize a business versus buying a business or franchising, one generally opts for greater independence in the establishment and operation of the business. Figure 4–1 illustrates this concept.

The option of organizing from scratch is often chosen by the entrepreneur who wants the satisfaction of creating the business and adding his or her personal touch to all its aspects. It may also be the preferred route when few suitable businesses are for sale or there is little chance of obtaining a franchise for the market area. In making this decision, the entrepreneur should be aware of the advantages of organizing the business from scratch as well as the potential drawbacks.

Advantages of Organizing a Small Business from Scratch

Organizing the business from scratch offers several advantages. First, this option allows the small business owner to define the nature of the business, the competitive environment in which the business will operate, the appropriate market to reach, and the size and extent of operations to set up. In the small business profile that opens this chapter, Peter Goudas was free to handle each of these aspects for his new business.

Second, the owner can obtain the exact types of physical facilities—building, equipment, and location—preferred. Buildings and equipment can be tailored to meet requirements precisely. The owner can also choose the most appropriate location for the market, a very important competitve tool in retailing.

Third, the owner can obtain fresh inventory tailored to the target market. Thus, the risk of products becoming obsolete or difficult to turn over is minimized.

FIGURE 4–1   Methods of Establishing a Small Business

	Organizing	*Buying*	*Franchising*
Level of independence	Higher	Medium	Lower
Level of risk	Higher	Medium	Lower

Fourth, the owner can personally select and train employees for the business rather than having to rely on existing personnel of an established business.

Finally, the owner can develop his or her own information systems such as bookkeeping and the method of evaluating the operation. The owner also can take advantage of the latest technology in equipment and materials.

Disadvantages of Organizing a Small Business from Scratch

Starting one's own business also carries some substantial risks. First, the owner lacks historical information on which to base future plans. This can be a drawback if uncertainty regarding market demand, supplies, and operations exists. It is also generally more difficult to obtain financing if projections are based on estimates rather than on the extension of trends from existing operations.

Second, the advantage of personally assembling physical facilities can become a liability because of the time required. In some industrial situations in which prompt establishment is critical, one of the other methods of small business establishment—purchasing a business or signing a franchise contract—may be more advisable.

Third, a new business always has start-up problems or bugs that have to be worked out. Incident 4–1 illustrates some of the surprises one Canadian entrepreneur encountered in attempting to market his new product.

Fourth, establishing outside relationships with financial institutions, suppliers, and other key professionals is often time consuming. For example, new small businesses typically are not granted trade credit initially, whereas an existing business or franchise has far less difficulty. The savings in interest costs can be substantial.

Finally, the owner faces the risk that there will be insufficient demand for the product or service. Even if a feasibility analysis is to be carried out prior to business start-up, some uncertainty regarding the extent of the market may remain.

The Small Business Plan

> The data points to the crucial need for entrepreneurs to formulate business plans, not just for raising capital, but for organization and classification of long- and short-term goals. A business plan is a vital tool for entrepreneurs—a blueprint to be referred to again and again to keep business growth on course.*

The use of business plans by Canadian entrepreneurs is increasing. A recent study of 100 successful Canadian small business owners found that 53 percent utilized full-scale plans, 91 percent of which had a time frame and 98 percent of which were written down. On the other hand, only 4 percent of Canadian entrepreneurs did not prepare a business plan.[1] Incident 4–2 illustrates a systematic plan.

---

*Joe Mancuso, president of the Centre for Entrepreneurial Management.

Pressdent Takes On Toothpaste Multinationals—Again

When Ron Schiller confides jokingly that he's "a little crazy," it may explain his willingness to tangle a second time with the multinationals of the toothpaste world. Once again, Schiller is taking on Procter & Gamble Inc. (Crest), Colgate-Palmolive Canada (Colgate), Lever Bros. Ltd. (Aim, Pepsodent), and Beecham Canada Inc. (Aqua Fresh).

Round one went to the big four, who last year commanded 90 percent to 95 percent of the national toothpaste market of $90 million at retail, according to Lever's marketing manager of personal products, Murray Cresswell.

In October 1981, Schiller and his two partners had given the world its first liquid toothpaste, Pressdent. On January 14, only 15 months later, they were forced to appeal to their 75 trade creditors to settle claims of $579,069 at 25 cents on the dollar.

In order to come back and win a second battle it helps to know where you went wrong the first time. "Of course we know why we failed," Schiller snaps, ticking off, in his rapid-fire style of speech, "a series of failures we could not see."

They were failures that an experienced company would almost certainly have uncovered before venturing into the marketplace. Take the dispenser, for example. Pressdent is sold in a pump-action container, similar to liquid soaps. Unlike them however, toothpaste contains an abrasive, and in use this was found to clog the pump. A stronger spring is said to eliminate the trouble.

A second problem concerned waste. As much as 20 percent of the paste could not be pumped up from the bottom of the bottle. The interior of the container has been slanted, and Schiller says waste is now less than 10 percent.

Schiller also found difficulties in placing his product on the supermarket shelf in prominent display space—which is reserved for the high volume sellers of the larger companies.

As a result of these difficulties, Pressdent never really achieved success, and before long, the large toothpaste manufacturers introduced the pump technology that has become popular today.

Source: Adapted from Alan P. Gray, "Pressdent Takes On Toothpaste Multinationals—Again," *Financial Times of Canada*, January 31, 1983, p. 8.

To efficiently organize the business, the entrepreneur should follow a step-by-step plan. A systematic plan is essential not only in establishing the business but, as Dr. Mancuso indicates, also in obtaining required funding and in running the business's ongoing operations. Incident 4–3 illustrates the value of the small

---

Incident 4–2

A Plan for All Seasons

Richard MacArthur is a master of growth planning. Along with partners Michel Coutu and Yvon Malenfant, the vice-president of Montreal graphics equipment distributor Marathon Inc. guided his six-year-old firm from 1984 revenues of $1 million to $12 million in 1989—and into 15th place in the Small Business Fastest 50. Six-year-old Marathon now boasts a 10% share of the Canadian market for such products as printing plates, press-proofing systems and film. "Our goal from the start was to be a national distributor," says MacArthur. "But we knew we had to develop a regional presence first." And that, he says, required planning.

At Marathon, MacArthur drafted three comprehensive plans: a start-up plan to develop a regional presence; a growth plan to build on the customer base by broadening the company's products and services; and a long-term plan to become a national distributor. Each plan included assessments of competitors' strengths and weaknesses, customers and what motivates them, and finances—including forecasts for cash flow, receivables, profits and losses. With these blueprints in hand, MacArthur says the company knew where it was and where it was going. "If you lose your perspective," he says, "you kill yourself."

Entrepreneurs have to ensure that their plans are current and flexible enough to accommodate changes in the market, in the company's financial situation and in personnel requirements. In 1985, for example, MacArthur adjusted Marathon's budget five times, convincing his bankers of the need for more financing to increase inventory and hire new employees. Says MacArthur: "I didn't want to wake up in three months to find I didn't have any money in the bank."

Source: Joe Dangor, "A Plan for All Seasons," *Profit Magazine* June 1990, pp. 52–53.

---

business plan for one small firm. The basic steps in preparing a business plan are as follows:

- Establish business objectives.
- Plan the marketing approach.
- Select the location.
- Determine the physical facilities.
- Plan the financing.
- Plan the personnel.
- Investigate the legal requirements.

This chapter gives a brief overview of these steps. Chapters 8 through 11 discuss the operating aspects of these areas in more detail and should be consulted before beginning preparation of a business plan. Appendix A at the end of this chapter presents a checklist for a small business plan, and Appendix B shows an actual business plan following this format. Note that a business plan may also be critical when purchasing a business, obtaining a franchise, acquiring financing, and performing other essential activities of the business.

Establishing Business Objectives

The first step in preparing a business plan is to have clearly thought-out and formally written objectives for the business. To be effective, an objective must be specific. Specific and quantitative objectives allow meaningful evaluation of the business's performance. Objectives can be set in the following areas for the initial year and for a few years following start-up:

- *Business size.* This includes the size of the physical facilities, financial commitments, and number of employees.
- *Production levels.* The plan should include the number of products and product lines and unit production anticipated.
- *Performance levels.* Sales, market share, and profit level should all be estimated and may form part of the plan.

Planning the Marketing Approach

The second step in the business plan is to develop a marketing plan. Considerable information regarding the calculation of market potential and market share, both essential parts of the marketing plan, was provided in Chapter 3. The following additional key aspects of a marketing plan should be investigated prior to starting the business. Incident 4–3 illustrates how a marketing plan helped an Alberta company successfully enter the market.

Have a Clear Concept of the Target Market.   It is important that the prospective small business owner have a clear idea of who the target customer is and have a well-developed customer profile. This profile should include such demographic information as age, income, occupation, and social class, as well as certain personality and lifestyle characteristics.

After determining the target market, the owner can perform the steps discussed in Chapter 3—determining market area, market area population, market potential, and market share. Sometimes this information can be obtained using secondary data alone, but often some primary research will be required. Chapter 8 illustrates a more detailed target market profile.

Understand the Target Market's Needs, Wants, and Purchasing Habits.   Understanding the target market's needs, wants, and purchasing habits is essential in formulating a marketing strategy. Answers to the following questions may prove valuable:

Incident 4–3

Market Planning Helps Singles Sell Spindles

Ralph Single and his wife own and operate the Edmonton-based Spindle Warehouse, and the direct mail approach is part of the Singles' marketing plan. To date, it has brought good results. Ralph Single knows what marketing is. He describes it as "an organized plan to distribute your product to the consumer in a profitable manner." And, he says, "It's an attitude. If we didn't have a proper attitude, then we just couldn't make it."

"The best piece of advice we got when we were just starting our business was that we had to plan." As a result, they created a comprehensive and thoroughly researched marketing plan.

Now, halfway through their first year of operation, all this effort is paying off. Spindle Warehouse, which has exclusive distribution rights in Alberta and Saskatchewan for a high-quality line of wooden spindles, is prospering. According to Single, the company's overall approach to marketing has made the difference between success and failure in these days of high interest rates and construction slowdowns.

Source: "Market Planning Helps Singles Sell Spindles," *Small Business Quarterly,* June 1982, p. 6.

- Where does or where will the target customers purchase the product or service?
- When do or where will they purchase it?
- What product or service attributes influence the purchase decision?
- In what quantities will purchases be made?
- Most important, why do customers, or why will they, purchase the product or service?

Once again, the answers to some of these questions may be obtained using secondary data, but primary research may be required.

Be Aware of Any Uncontrollable Factors That Might Affect the Marketing of the Product or Service. Several factors external to the business can affect the marketing plan and should be investigated, including the following.

Exisiting or Pending Legislation Relevant to the Business. New laws relating to marketing practices such as advertising, pricing, and manufacturing can have a significant impact on the business and cannot be ignored. This information may be obtained from an office of Consumer and Corporate Affairs Canada or the equivalent provincial agency.

State of the Economy in the Market.   The prospective small business owner should investigate whether the state of the economy is in a recovery or recessionary period. This also can influence the effectiveness of the marketing plan. Statistics Canada and private reports can provide this information.

Extent and Strategies of the Competition.   The entrepreneur should attempt to evaluate the competition and look for competitor strengths over the prospective business. A recent study found that 33 percent of Canadian entrepreneurs omit this important aspect from their business plans.[2]

Cultural Norms of the Market.   The entrepreneur should ensure that the new business conforms to the social and cultural norms of the market. This is especially important for exporters and for companies moving into new markets.

New Technology That Might Affect the Business.   New technology should be reviewed and monitored regulary, as it can represent either opportunities for the business or detrimental competitor strategies. Trade magazines and competitor strategies are good sources of information concerning new technology.

Plan the Marketing Program.   After collecting the above information, the entrepreneur can formulate a marketing program. The essential aspects of the marketing program are as follows.

The Product or Service.   This includes such information as how the product or service is developed, sources of material, and level of quality, variety, and packaging.

The Distribution System.   This includes determining the path the product or service will take to reach the consumer and may involve selection of wholesalers and retailers.

Promotion.   This involves decisions regarding promotion budgets, advertising versus personal selling, and developing appropriate communications.

Pricing.   The development of pricing policies, including the calculation of specific price levels, should be planned.

These elements of the marketing program are discussed in more detail in Chapter 8.

Selecting the Location

The third component of a business plan is selecting the location for the business. In setting up a new business, the prospective owner needs to determine the trading area or city in which to locate. Then the owner selects the specific site within the trading area.

The Trading Area.   Several criteria are commonly used to select the trading area. Choosing the general trade area is often more critical for manufacturers than for retailers or service firms, whereas the selection of a specific site within the trade area is generally more important for retailers. The following information is valuable in selecting the trading area.

Economic Base.   Information on population, employment levels, income levels, retail sales, and house values within the trading area may be needed. These elements help small manufacturers determine the availability of employees and expected pay scales. For retail and service firms, they indicate the potential for future sales. One should also examine the trends relating to these key indicators. Most of this information may be obtained from secondary data such as the government sources listed in Chapter 3.

Attitude of Trading Area toward New Businesses.   Many communities are eager to attract new industry and offer various kinds of incentives for new businesses. While this benefit is usually more important for manufacturers, any small business owner should contact the local city administration or chamber of commerce regarding incentives. Often these agencies are aware of specific types of businesses their communities need.

Competition.   Competitive firms in a trading area should be noted. A retail or service firm with a fixed geographic market should evaluate various trading areas on the basis of *saturation levels* for the type of outlet it will establish. There are many methods of calculating the saturation index. A method commonly used in the retailing industry is to divide retail sales of all competitors by the selling space of the trading area:

$$\text{Saturation} = \frac{\text{Competing retail sales}}{\text{Competing retail space}}$$

The saturation index can be compared to other trading areas or industry norms. The higher the index, the more attractive the opportunity. The statistics needed to compute a saturation index can be obtained from city and provincial license and tax records, Dun & Bradstreet reference books, or personal visits.

Costs.   Obviously a key consideration in selecting a trading area is the cost of land and buildings. Another is the cost of required services and expenses once the business is operating. These include such items as utilities, business taxes, and insurance.

The trading area decision can be quantified to allow evaluation among several alternatives. Figure 4–2 shows an example of such a calculation.

The Site.   After selecting the trading area, the prospective owner should investigate the following items in selecting the specific site.

FIGURE 4-2 Evaluation of a Trading Area

---

1 = Poor; 5 = Excellent

Criteria	Trading Area A	Trading Area B
Economic base		
Attitude		
Competition		
Costs		
Other		
Total		

Accessibility. For the manufacturer, this means accessibility of transportation services for incoming supplies and materials, as well as ease of shipping the finished product. It might also include the site's accessibility to necessary services, employees of the business, and protection services such as the fire department.

For the retailer, proximity to major arteries and transit lines and availability of parking are important to ensure maximum customer traffic. Assessing traffic patterns, both pedestrian and vehicular, may be critical to success, especially for retailers of certain types of merchandise (Chapter 8 further discusses the location considerations for retail goods). Often the chamber of commerce can provide information on traffic flows.

Site Costs. The costs of sites within a community usually vary considerably. Generally the higher-traffic areas are more expensive to buy or lease. One should also investigate other possible costs such as utilities, taxes, and licenses.

Restrictions. When evaluating a site, any restrictive ordinances such as zoning by-laws should be investigated. Such restrictions may hinder current operations as well as future expansion.

Site History. The prospective owner should find out whether the site has had several tenants or owners over the years. If this is the case, he or she should investigate the reasons for the turnover before proceeding to purchase or lease the site.

Proximity to Other Businesses. Will the surrounding businesses have a positive or negative influence on the business? Levels of competitiveness complementarity are two significant factors. Figure 4–3 gives examples of the positive and negative effects of these factors for both noncompetitive and competitive businesses.

Physical Characteristics. Size, frontal footage, external facade, contour, and shape are all important considerations in site selection. The business should blend in with surrounding businesses, but it should also be distinctive.

FIGURE 4-3   **Influence of Neighbouring Businesses**

Positive Influence from Neighbouring Businesses	*Negative Influences from Neighbouring Businesses*
Complementary—for example, a pharmacy by a doctor's office	Uncomplementary—business such as a mortuary, tavern, or factory
Competitive—for shopping goods such as clothing, automobiles, and motels	Competitive—for nonshopping goods such as convenience stores

---

FIGURE 4-4   **Evaluation of the Site**

1 = Poor; 5 = Excellent

Criteria	*Site A*	*Site B*
Accessibility		
Costs		
Restrictions		
History		
Effect of other businesses		
Physical characteristics		
Other		
Total		

The evaluation form shown in Figure 4-4, similar to that for the trading area analysis, might be used in making the site selection decision.

The Buy-or-Lease Decision.   In selecting the specific site, a major consideration is whether to own or lease the premises. Because ownership is generally more expensive, most small businesses find that to reduce the already high risk at the initial stages, leasing is the more attractive option. The small business owner should investigate several factors before signing a lease contract.

Cost of the Lease.   The owner-manager should investigate the cost of the lease, how the rent is calculated, when the payments are due, and what taxes and utilities apply. Most leases are calculated on a per-square-footage basis. In retailing a percentage of gross sales is often added to the cost of the lease in the form of royalties.

Length of the Lease.   Questions concerning the length of the lease include: How long is the contract for? Is there a provision for renewal at that time? What notice is required for renewal, termination, or rent increases?

Restrictions.   Potential restrictions on the use of the property should be investigated. Can the site be subleased to someone else? Does anyone have the right to use a part of the property? Are there certain services or products that cannot be sold or manufactured at the site?

Repairs and Improvements.   Who is responsible for any repairs and improvements required? When the lease expires, who will own such improvements?

Insurance Coverage.   What insurance does the lessor have on the property? What about liability insurance coverage? What insurance coverage will be required by the lessee?

Running the Business from One's Home.   The final important consideration in site selection is the possibility of operating the business out of one's home. A recent study found that some business work is conducted at home in 23 percent of Canadian households and home is the primary base of business operations in 8 percent of Canadian households.[3] Incident 4–4 illustrates this increase.

Some situations are particularly suitable for a home-based business. First, if the business is started on a part-time basis, as many are, the costs associated with establishing a home office are minimal. Second, the lower costs associated with starting a business in one's home reduce the financial risks of a venture that may already carry a high degree of risk. Thus, a home office can serve as a temporary office until the business is more firmly established. Third, a home office is suitable for many businesses for which location is of minimal importance. Many service and some small manufacturing businesses fit in this category. Fourth, locating the business in the home offers several tax-related advantages. Chapter 12 gives more details on such advantages.

Determining the Physical Facilities

In preparing the feasibility analysis outlined in Chapter 3, the entrepreneur should already have prepared a detailed estimate of the total capital needed to acquire the building, equipment, furniture, fixtures, and possibly initial inventory. The size of investment in buildings and equipment is typically larger for a manufacturing firm, while the investment in inventory tends to be larger for the retail firm.

Prior to construction of buildings and purchasing equipment, the relevant building codes and construction standards should be investigated and required permits obtained.

In addition to these capital requirements and standards, a plan should be made of the operations flow within the business. This includes such factors as purchasing, inventory control, the production process, the interior layout, and distribution of the finished product. Chapter 10 discusses all of these items in detail.

Insurance.   One item that should be obtained prior to start-up is insurance coverage. Insurance is a method of transferring some of the risks associated with operating a business to another party—the insurance company.

Incident 4–4

Home Sweet Home

For 23 years, Henry Lorenzen worked in a downtown Regina office, first as an employee for an architectural firm, then eventually establishing his own practice. When the boom period of the 1970s occurred, Lorenzen had three employees and times were good. But when the recession hit in the early 1980's, business dried up and for Lorenzen, the writing was on the wall.

Instead of going into debt to keep his company afloat, Lorenzen laid off his employees and moved the business to an upstairs office in his home. He sold a lot of equipment and placed whatever was left in boxes. When business improved three years later, he decided against returning downtown and built a small studio in his backyard.

Lorenzen isn't alone in his decision to shy away from a downtown office and establish a business at home. More and more professionals are turning their backs on expensive commercial office space and are successfully operating a business from their own homes. Recent studies indicate that as many as 23% of Canadian homes or over 2 million people are involved in some way or another in operating a business at home. An increasing proportion are professional business people.

The reasons vary for this new trend. Ann Wells, president of the Ottawa-based Canadian Association for Home-Based-Business says reasonable starting costs, a desire for extra money and older people starting a retirement business are causing the upswing.

Since Lorenzen already had a client base established, moving home didn't affect his business. Since Lorenzen usually conducted meetings at his clients' offices, many clients didn't realize he worked at home.

Although his business didn't suffer from the move, Lorenzen admits it took extra organization to avoid conflicts between work and family. "You have to find out how much time they need, how much you need for your work, and keep the two separate," he says. "If you can't separate them, then it could be difficult."

Source: Pat Rediger, "Home Sweet Home," *Alberta Business Magazine,* April 1992, p. 2.

Types of Insurance.   Common insurable risks for a small business include the following:

Loss or Damage of Property.   This type of coverage protects the business in the case of fire, theft, and similar occurrences.

Business Interruption.   If one of the above problems occurs, this type of insurance protects the earning power lost due to the occurrence for a short period of time.

Liability and Disability.   This coverage includes bodily injury to employees or customers.

Life Insurance.   This insurance is usually bought in the form of a group insurance plan or occasionally key employee life insurance. Partners of a business may also desire to purchase life insurance for the other partner(s).

Failure to adequately plan for insurance can be costly for the small business. Incident 4–5 gives an illustration.

Insurance Decisions.   The entrepreneur faces three insurance-related decisions:

1. Determine what kind of insurance to purchase.
2. Determine how much coverage to take out.
3. Decide from whom to purchase the insurance.

In developing answers to these questions, the following rules of thumb commonly used in the insurance industry are helpful. The first and most important rule is: Don't risk more than you can afford to lose. In other words, if the prospective loss will put the business into bankruptcy or serious financial difficulty, insurance should be taken out. Usually the probability of occurrence of these losses is low, and the associated insurance premiums are also low. The maximum sustainable loss will, of course, vary from firm to firm and from time to time in a particular business.

A second rule of insurance management is: Don't risk a lot for a little. In implementing this second rule, the premium should be related to the potential loss and treated as savings or costs. For example, if comprehensive physical damage insurance on a $14,000 automobile costs $350 per year, the savings or return if the insurance is not purchased and the risk is assumed equals 350/14,000, or 2.5 percent. The owner is exposing a $14,000 investment to possible loss or damage for a 2.5 percent return, and that is risking a lot for a little. On the other hand, a driver who pays $150 a year for auto collision coverage with a $50 deductible, when the same coverage with a $100 deductible would cost only $125 per year, is paying a cost of $25/$50, or 50 percent for the second $50 of coverage. Here, from a cost point of view, the car owner is paying dearly for a small return. In the first case, the purchase of insurance is consistent with the rule; in the second, it is not. For this reason, it is usually advisable to purchase the largest deductible the business can afford. This can result in substantial premium savings.

The third rule is that insurance should be taken out only when absolutely necessary. Insurance always costs more than the expected value of a loss because the premium must also include the insurer's administration and selling costs, plus profit. This insurance is economically feasible only when the probability of loss is low and the severity of a potential loss is high. Therefore, in the opposite situation, the best approach may be to take preventative measures and build these losses into the cost or expense structure of the business.

Incident 4–5

The Policy That Never Was

On Oct. 12, 1989, a chemical spill caught fire at the 20,000-sq.-ft. plant of Medallion Pools Inc. in Orangeville, Ont., 50 km northwest of Toronto. The building, production equipment, and most of Medallion's inventory, burned to a crisp. Damage to the swimming pool manufacturer and installer: $2 million. Harrowing, thought owner Howard Hughes, but no problem; he was insured.

With $14,000 in monthly mortgage and equipment-loan payments to carry, Hughes and his wife and partner Mary laid off most of the staff and moved Medallion's few remaining operations into their home, awaiting a settlement of their claim. The fire had spared a few finished pools, and Hughes set about installing them at customers' homes.

But Hughes soon began to smell something worse than burnt rubber and epoxy. Two weeks after the fire, his insurance company's adjuster had only glanced at the file. Silence followed. In November, responding to Hughes' calls, the adjuster asked for sworn affidavits attesting to the cause of the fire and damage to assets. Hughes complied, and again met silence. When he sought an address or phone number for the insurer, the adjuster invited Hughes to sue him and send it care of his post office box. Soon after, Hughes discovered the Federal Bureau of Investigation had issued warrants for the arrest on fraud charges of two men linked with his insurer.

Through Toronto broker Mitchell & Ryerson, Hughes had purchased coverage from Antigua-based Firestone Insurance Co. through its Canadian agent, Amfirst Intermediaries of Canada Ltd. In Canada, only provincially licensed brokers can sell insurance, but they can use offshore underwriters. Hughes' policy cost $13,000—a savings of about $5,000 over coverage available from Canadian suppliers.

Last March, Hughes finally got a settlement—for about 55 cents on the dollar. Even that was obtained not through the original insurer, but by the Registered Insurance Brokers of Ontario obtaining a settlement from Mitchell & Ryerson through its errors and omissions insurance.

Source: "The Policy That Never Was," *Profit Magazine,* October 1991 pp. 20–21.

The fourth rule is to buy adequate coverage. The reason is that all property insurance contracts contain a co-insurance clause. The *co-insurance clause* states that if the amount of insurance purchased on the property is less than some stated percentage (usually 80 percent), the insured will share all partial losses up to the face value of the policy. The purpose of co-insurance is to encourage the small business owner to buy adequate insurance coverage for the business. For example, if a small business owner has a building with a current replacement value of $110,000 and a policy containing an 80 percent co-insurance clause, $80,000 of insurance is required for collecting on partial losses. If only $60,000 of insurance were purchased and a $10,000 loss occurred, the insurance company would pay only $60,000 (coverage)/$80,000 (co-insurance), or $7,500 of the loss.

The last insurance purchasing rule involves adequately investigating both the insurance company and the agent. Choosing an insurance company with financial stability, satisfactory claims service, and competitive premiums is important, and the selection of the agent may be even more critical. The agent should have a thorough knowledge of insurance, be located where he or she can provide prompt service on claims and enquiries, and possess a genuine interest in clients' needs. The agent should be questioned regarding the claim settlement procedures, cancellation procedures, and premium rates. Many insurance companies now have special policies tailored to small businesses.

Care should be taken to ensure that coverage is current. As replacement costs rise, the level of coverage should increase. Most insurance companies now adjust policies for inflation automatically.

Planning the Finances of the Business

Four major financial aspects of the new business should be planned in advance of opening.

Establish Capital Requirements and Make Feasibility Projections.   As indicated previously, these calculations are made when preparing a feasibility analysis. The results of these calculations form an integral part of the projected income statement for at least the first year of operations, and in some cases five years into the future. In conjunction with the income statement projection, enough information would have likely been obtained to prepare a projected balance sheet and cash flow statement. These statements are described fully in Chapter 9. It may be advisable for the entrepreneur to enlist the services of an accountant in completing these financial statements. Proper preparation of this financial data is key to obtaining funding from investors and lenders.

Determine Sources of Funding.   The projections discussed above provide an estimate of the funds required to get started and to operate the business. After calculating the required funds, the owner will need to determine a balance between his or her own funds (equity) and borrowed funds (debt). Because raising funds is such a critical area for the small business, Chapter 7 is devoted entirely to the types of funds required, sources of funding for the small business, and methods of evaluating those sources.

Plan the Accounting and Bookkeeping Systems.   An essential part of any business is recordkeeping. Bookkeeping is the recording and classifying of the internal and external transactions of the business. This may be an area that requires professional advice. Chapter 9 reviews the types of financial records kept and the different types of bookkeeping systems used by small businesses.

Determine Financial Evaluation Measures.   One area crucial to the success of the small business is the financial evaluation of operations. To perform this evaluation, the owner should determine the key indicators of the financial health of the business. These indicators include profit margins, return on investment, and inventory turnover. The owner should also set up a system of regular monitoring and reporting of these areas. This system may also require professional assistance to establish and is discussed in detail in Chapter 9.

Planning the Personnel

Chapter 11 discusses the operating details of personnel administration for a small business. Folllowing are the major considerations in organizing for the management of personnel.

Administrative Structure.   This involves setting up the responsibility and reporting procedure for all employees of the business. If there are only two owners, the administrative structure takes the form of a clear division of responsibilities. A business with several employees might require setting up an organizational chart.

Employee Recruitment and Training.   The plan for hiring, training, and managing those who will work in the business should be determined.

Personnel Policies.   Operating policies affecting employees should be stated explicitly and be formally prepared prior to the time the business begins operations.

Investigating the Legal Requirements

A small business can be significantly affected by the legal environment in which it operates. Considerable legislation in Canada applies to the ongoing management of the business. Typical areas covered are advertising and promotion, credit, sales contracts, pricing, distribution channels, personnel, and financial relationships. Legislation pertaining to each of these aspects of managing the ongoing business is covered in later chapters.

This section discusses the legal requirements relating to the establishment of the business that should be included in the business plan. Some of the most important aspects are selecting the legal structure, investigating which licenses are required, and filing for patent protection if necessary. The legal information provided here and in later chapters is intended not to replace the advice and

FIGURE 4–5   Advantages and Disadvantages of a Sole Proprietorship

Advantages	*Disadvantages*
1. Simple and inexpensive to start.	1. Unlimited liability.
2. Offers individual control over operations, profits, etc.	2. Often more difficult to obtain financing.
3. Fewer forms and reports to fill out.	3. The personal tax rate may be higher than the corporate rate.
4. Some tax advantages.	4. The life of the business terminates on owner's death.

direction of a lawyer but merely to provide a background with which the entrepreneur can work with such professionals more knowledgeably.

Legal Structure.   The owner must decide under which legal structure the business will operate. Five types of legal structures can be used.

1. Sole Proprietorship.   In the *sole proprietorship,* the business is owned by a single individual. Registration with the provincial government is normally required and can help protect the name of the business. Figure 4–5 lists the advantages and disadvantages of a sole proprietorship.

2. Partnership.   In most ways, *partnerships* are similar to sole proprietorships except that partnerships include two or more partners. Partnerships typically provide increased resources, but they also increase the possibility of conflict (see Incident 4–6). There are two kinds of partnerships a small business might use:

1. *Limited partnership.* In a limited partnership, one or more partners obtains limited liability in exchange for not taking an active part in the day-to-day management of the business or acting on behalf of the company. These partners, often called *silent partners,* usually provide only the financial investment as their part of the ownership interest. Small businesses are increasingly using this form of ownership because silent partners constitute an important source of equity funding. In addition, limited partnerships offer some tax advantages for the silent partner while retaining the positive aspects of sole proprietorship for the entrepreneur.
2. *General partnership.* In a general partnership, unlimited liability applies to all partners.

Figure 4–6 lists the advantages and disadvantages of partnerships.

3. Cooperative.   The *cooperative* is used infrequently by small businesses. In most respects, its strengths and weaknesses are similar to those of a corporation (see Figure 4–7). The distinguishing feature is that in a cooperative (which needs

Incident 4–6

When Partners Collide

When business partners feud, their company often suffers. But when the partners are also boyhood friends, it can become a gut-wrenching ordeal that affects everyone even remotely associated with the company.

Since starting Montreal-based Frisco Bay Industries of Canada Ltd. in 1970, Barry Katsof and Joel Matlin built a nation-wide clientele for their customized security systems used by banks and large corporations. By 1988, Frisco Bay registered sales of $13 million and employed 200.

Sensing the company's imminent transition to big-league player, Frisco Bay chairman and chief executive Katsof and Matlin, then president, began to discuss future strategy. But the partners, who had known each other since high school, soon butted heads. Discussions escalated into arguments, and eventually the two stopped talking to each other. The chill between the CEO and the president had fearful employees, wary suppliers and nervous customers speculating about the firm's fate.

"We had a difference in philosophy as to how to run the company," says Katsof. Meanwhile Matlin had invoked the "shotgun clause" in the partnership agreement, offering to sell his shares for $1.95 each, totalling $3.2 million. Katsof and Waxman had 30 days either to accept his offer or sell their share to Matlin for the same price.

Katsof scrambled for financial support by the Dec. 12 deadline. "It was a very, very stressful time," he says. "I wasn't sleeping well at night." He once booked a hotel room for a two-hour nap between meetings with potential backers.

In the end, Katsof and Waxman bought out Matlin. All lawsuits ceased and Matlin signed a two-year non-competition agreement. Everyone at Frisco Bay heaved a sigh of relief, says Katsof. "We were friends for more than 18 years. But I had to do what I had to do. When Joel left the company, we could concentrate 100% on growing the company again."

Source: Jennifer Low, "When Partners Collide," *Profit Magazine,* October 1991, pp. 25–26.

a minimum of six members), each member has only one vote, whereas in a corporation each voting share has a vote.

4. Corporation.   The *corporation,* or *limited company,* is becoming an increasingly popular form of structuring a small business. The corporation is a legal entity that is separate and distinct from the shareholders of the business.

The day-to-day operations of a corporation are handled by a manager who is appointed by and reports to a board of directors. The board of directors is elected

FIGURE 4-6   Advantages and Disadvantages of a Partnership

Advantages	*Disadvantages*
1. Simple and inexpensive to start	1. Unlimited liability
2. Pooling of financial and skill resources	2. Death of a partner terminates the partnership unless a provision to the contrary is specified in the partnership agreement
3. Tax advantages (i.e., income splitting)	3. Greater possibility for disagreements (buy-sell agreements should be drawn up in the event of that partner(s) wants to leave the business)

FIGURE 4-7   Advantages and Disadvantages of a Corporation

Advantages	*Disadvantages*
1. The continuity of the business exists even if owner dies.	1. The cost to incorporate generally ranges from $500 to $1,000.
2. The owners have limited liability.	2. There is a greater reporting requirement to government.
3. May have a manager with professional training or expertise.	3. Flexibility may be reduced because of the binding provisions of the corporate charter.
4. Easier to raise funds as lending and equity investors usually look more favourably to incorporate companies.	4. Losses cannot be deducted from other personal income of the owner.
5. The corporate tax rate on small businesses (see Appendix B in Chapter 12) can be lower than one's personal rate.	5. Lenders often require a personal guarantee, negating the advantage of limited liability.
6. Incorporation can assist in establishing commercial credibility.	
7. Liability insurance may be less expensive.	

by the shareholders. Often in very small businesses the manager, director, and major shareholder can be the same person. Many small businesses have found it valuable to enlist the services of lawyers, accountants, and other noncompeting businesspeople to serve on their boards of directors.

The vast majority of incorporated small businesses are private companies. For a business to qualify as a private company, the following conditions must exist:

- The right to transfer shares is restricted, usually requiring the approval of the board of directors.
- The number of shareholders is limited to 50. The company cannot sell new shares publicly.

Figure 4–7 lists the advantages and disadvantages of a corporation.

Steps in Incorporation.   Most entrepreneurs regard incorporation as a very complex process that requires a lawyer's assistance. While it is advisable for the small business to enlist the services of a lawyer to assist in incorporating the business, some entrepreneurs with relatively uncomplicated businesses have incorporated their businesses successfully on their own. Incorporating a business has four steps:

1. *Selection of a name for the business.* This name must be submitted to and approved by the provincial government department that handles incorporations (see Appendix C at the end of this chapter). The selection can be facilitated by having the government do a computer search to ensure that no similar names are currently being used.

2. *Development of the share structure, directors, restrictions on share transfers, and so on.* The owner must determine the number of shares to authorize, the number of shares to issue, the number of directors, the timing of meetings, and approvals required for shares to be bought or sold.

3. *A description of company operations.* This section describes what the business can and cannot do.

4. *Acquiring the necessary supplies.* This includes such items as the corporate stamp, the minute book, and the necessary journals and ledgers.

5. Joint Ventures.   A *joint venture* is an agreement between one or more sole proprietors, partnerships, or corporations to participate in a business venture. Although similar to a partnership in many ways, this increasingly popular form of business allows for individual ownership of assets in the venture. Such items as capital cost allowance can be used by either party, depending on the need. Other advantages and disadvantages are similar to those in a partnership (see Figure 4–6).

Licences and Taxes.   Prior to starting a business, the prospective owner should investigate the required licences and the taxes that may be payable to the government. Licences and taxes can be levied by federal, provincial, and municipal governments, and these requirements differ among various industries. Following are the most common licences and taxes that apply to the small business. For a more detailed listing, see Appendix D at the end of this chapter.

Federal Government

1. *Income tax.* The income tax is a tax on both companies and individuals earning income from a business operating in Canada. The rates vary by province and by industry (see Chapter 12). Although the income tax payments are made to the federal government, part of this amount is transferred to the province in which the business earns income. Some provinces now collect their own business income tax.

2. *Goods and services tax.* The goods and services tax (GST) is a value-added tax levied on many seller's of goods and services by the federal government. The tax, which currently is 7 percent of the sale price, is collected from the purchaser by the seller and remitted to the government on a quarterly basis. Although the GST has met considerable resistance from business and consumers, it has been an effective method for increasing government revenues. Certain exemptions from the GST, relating to size of the business and type of merchandise sold, are available. The small business owner should consult Revenue Canada for the information about how the GST applies to their businesses.

3. *Excise tax.* The excise tax is an extra tax imposed on certain goods sold in Canada. Payment is made by the manufacturer and is a hidden component in the cost of purchasing those goods.

Provincial Government

1. *Income tax.* A percentage of federal income tax payable is assessed by the provinces. Some provinces (Ontario, Quebec, and Alberta) collect this tax. In other provinces, the federal government collects the tax and remits the provincial portion to the province.

2. *Licences.* Many types of businesses require a provincial licence to operate. Some of these businesses may also need to get bonded.

3. *Sales tax.* Most provinces levy retail sales taxes on tangible property sold or imported. This tax is collected by the retailer from the purchaser at the time of the sale and remitted to the government in much the same manner as the goods and services tax. Many businesses have found the administration of the provincial sales tax more difficult since the introduction of the GST.

Municipal Government

1. *Licences.* Municipalities (cities) are authorized to licence all businesses operating within their boundaries.

2. *Property taxes.* Municipalities are also authorized to levy property taxes on the real estate on which a business operates.

3. *Business taxes.* Other taxes levied on businesses by a municipality might be for water use or other services.

Patents.   As many entrepreneurs create new products or processes, a critical measure to ensure their success is to secure a patent. A *patent* is a right granted by the government to an inventor to exclude others from making, using, or selling his or her invention in Canada for a period of 17 years.

It is important for the inventor to record the date of the invention and file for the patent as soon as possible. Registration of a patent may be made through a Consumer and Corporate Affairs office or the Commissioner of Patents, Ottawa-Hull, Canada, K1A OE1. In Canada, if the patent has been used publicly or sold within the previous two years, it may not be granted. A patent agent or lawyer can provide valuable assistance in the patenting process and may be essential if infringement on the patent occurs later. Careful screening to ensure that the invention is new, useful, and a result of inventive ingenuity are criteria used in the patent approval.

The specific steps required to register a patent are as follows:

1. Conduct a search at the patent office to ensure that the idea is not already registered.
2. File an application—the formal request for the patent, which includes a description of the idea.

A patent application may take from one to three years to receive an approval. Nearly 29,000 patent applications are received each year in Canada, and approximately 24,000 are approved. Once approved, a listing of patents is available for public perusal at most public libraries. Similar procedures for obtaining patents are followed in registering trademarks, industrial designs, and copyrights. Applications for these items are also obtained through Consumer and Corporate Affairs or the Commissioner of Patents.

Summary

1. Organizing one's own business has several advantages and disadvantages. The advantages of having a hand in determining the type of business, equipment, employees, inventory, and market are balanced against the disadvantages of uncertainty concerning demand, unforeseen problems, and the time required to establish the business.
2. The basic steps in preparing a business plan are establishing business objectives, planning the marketing approach, selecting the location, determining the physical facilities, planning the financing, planning the personnel, and researching the legal requirements.
3. Several criteria are commonly used when selecting a trading area, including the economic base of the trading area, the attitude of the trading area toward new businesses, the competition, and the costs involved in setting up.
4. Once the trading area is chosen, the owner chooses the actual site. Criteria in site selection are accessibility, site cost, restrictions, site history, proximity to other businesses, and physical characteristics of the site.
5. Because purchasing a site is generally more expensive, most small businesses find that to reduce the already high risk at the initial stages of the business, leasing is the more attractive option.

6. Prior to construction of buildings and purchase of equipment, the relevant building codes and construction standards should be investigated and the required permits obtained.

7. Insurance transfers some of the risks associated with operating a business to another party. The common insurable risks for a small business include loss or damage of property, business interruption, liability and disability, and life insurance.

8. Four major financial aspects of the new business should be planned in advance: the capital requirements and feasibility projections, sources of funding, the accounting and bookkeeping systems, and financial and evaluative measures.

9. The owner must decide under which legal structure the business will operate. The four types of structures that can be used are sole proprietorship, partnership, cooperative, and corporation.

10. The advantages of incorporation are continuity, limited liability, professional management, ease in raising funds, and some tax advantages. The disadvantages are the high cost of incorporating, increased reporting requirements, reduced flexibility, some tax disadvantages, and the requirement of a personal guarantee.

11. The most common taxes required by the federal government for small businesses are income taxes, the goods and service tax, and excise taxes. Provincial governments also impose income and sales taxes, and municipalities levy property and business taxes.

12. The provincial and municipal governments require business licences for most businesses operating in their jurisdiction.

13. The specific steps required to register a patent are to (1) conduct a search at the patent office to ensure that the idea is not already registered and (2) file an application, which includes the formal request for the patent and a description of the idea.

Chapter Problems and Applications

1. Investigate a small business that is for sale. What are the advantages and disadvantages to you of buying this business as opposed to starting a similar one from scratch?

2. You are thinking of opening up a small business consulting company. What uncontrollable factors might affect your decision? Explain.

3. The saturation index is useful to a prospective small business owner in selecting a trading area.

    a. Using the information in the following table, which trading area would you recommend to the prospective owner?

	Location		
	1	*2*	*3*
Number of customers for the store	100,000	50,000	25,000
Average purchase per customer	$5	$7	$9
Total square footage of the drugstore (including the proposed store)	20,000	15,000	10,000

    b. If you excluded the proposed store (3,000 square feet), which area would you select?

    c. Which index of saturation is more accurate—the calculation with the proposed store square footage or the calculation without it? Why?

4. Which variables are important in site location for a drugstore? Note: In answering this question, consider the variables in Figure 4–4 and rank them from 5 (most important) to 1 (least important). Justify your ranking on each variable.

5. Interview a small business owner about the details of his or her start-up plan. Find out what aspects were omitted from the plan that should have been included.

6. Choose a specific type of small business and obtain advice from an insurance agent on the types of insurance needed and the precise costs. Write a short report on your findings.

7. Contact your local patent office and find out the requirements for registering a patent.

APPENDIX A
CHECKLIST FOR A SMALL BUSINESS PLAN

1. Have specific business objectives been set? At the end of one or five years, what will the size of the business be in gross sales? In production level? In number of employees? In market share? In profit?

2. Has a marketing approach been developed?

    a. Who is the target market in terms of occupation? Income level? Education? Lifestyle?

  b. What is the target market purchasing behaviour for this product or
    similar products? Where are purchases made? When are purchases
    made? What quantities are purchased?

  c. Why does the target market purchase this product or similar
    products? Which characteristics are preferred? What other factors
    influence the purchase?

  d. What external constraints will affect the business? Existing or
    pending legislation? State of the economy? Competition? Social or
    cultural trends? New technology?

  e. Which product characteristics will be developed? Quality level?
    Amount of depth? Type of packaging? Patent protection? Extent of
    warranty protection? Level of service?

  f. How will the product get to the consumer? What channel of
    distribution will be used? Length of the channel? Intensity of
    channel distributors? Legal arrangement within the channel? Type of
    physical transportation?

  g. How will the product be promoted? What are the promotional
    objectives? Which media will be used? How much will be spent on
    production? Who is the target of the promotion? What is the
    promotional theme? What is the timetable for promotion?

  h. What price levels will be set for the product? Which pricing policies
    will be instituted? What factors will influence pricing? How
    important is price to the target market?

3. Has the location been selected?

  a. In what trading area or community will the business be established?
    What is its economic base? Its attitude toward new businesses? Its
    saturation level in terms of competing businesses? Its costs?

  b. What specific site will be selected? Is it accessible to supplies,
    employees, and the target market? What is the site cost? What
    restrictions on site use exist? What is the history of the site? What
    are the neighbouring businesses? What are the physical
    characteristics of the site?

4. Have the physical facilities been determined?

  a. What building, equipment, and start-up supplies will be needed?
    What are the costs? What are the depreciation rates of the fixed
    assets? Which building codes or standards are relevant? Which
    permits are required? What insurance is required?

  b. How will the physical facilities be organized? Is the production
    process efficient and safe? Has the interior layout been carefully
    planned? Is the exterior facade attractive?

  c. How will inventories be managed? What initial inventory is re-
    quired? How will inventory levels be monitored? How will
    inventory be valued? What method will be used to order
    inventory?

5. Has a financial plan for the business been made?
    a. What are the financial requirements of the business? What are start-up costs? Ongoing operating costs? What are projected sales, expenses, income, and cash flow?
    b. Which sources of funding will be used? How much equity? How much debt? Which sources will be used? Private? Commercial? Government?
    c. What bookkeeping system will be instituted?
    d. How will the financial information be used? Which accounts will be evaluated? How often? By whom?
6. Has a personnel plan been developed?
    a. What is the administrative structure? Is there an organizational chart? A responsibility and reporting procedure? Have job descriptions and specifications been developed?
    b. Have personnel policies been developed? What are the hours of work? Pay levels? Employee benefits? Conditions and standards of employment? Grievance procedures?
    c. How will the business recruit employees? Where will employees be found? How will they be screened? What guidelines will be used in selection? How will employees be trained?
7. Have legal requirements been investigated?
    a. Has the legal structure for the business been determined?
    b. Have the relevant licences and taxes been researched?
    c. Has patent protection been obtained, if necessary?

APPENDIX B
BUSINESS PLAN—RETAIL STOCKING STORE, THE SOCK HOP

Background

The Sock Hop is a store totally devoted to socks. The product is in the medium price range, and emphasis is on variety and quality. The Sock Hop will be located in the new Park Place Mall, Lethbridge, Alberta, which is close to the downtown core. The mall, which opened in August 1988, has a variety of products and services. It contains beauty salons, shoe repair shops, movie theatres, two anchor shops (Sears and Eatons), jewellery stores, men's apparel, ladies apparel, children's stores, toy stores, food fair, as well as many other specialty stores. Furthermore, a major food retailer (Food City) is located at one end of the mall.

The majority of the customers of The Sock Hop will be between the ages of 15 and 64, both male and female. The 1991 city census indicates that there are 48,436 people between the ages of 15 and 64.[1]

The owner-manager of The Sock Hop is Sharon Stockwell. She holds a management degree from the University of Lethbridge and has eight years of experience working in the retail clothing industry full and part time. She has prepared this business plan to assist in the start-up of this venture.

The feasibility analysis shows that The Sock Hop could be a viable business within five years as it becomes well known and builds a clientele.

Business Plan

The business plan provides a focal point for organizing the proposed venture. It serves as a guide in operating the business and in allocating available resources efficiently. The business plan consists of seven steps and each will be investigated separately in the following subsections.

1. Business Objectives

Objectives are the goals (long-range and short-range) that the business hopes to reach. The statement of clear objectives helps to model a strategy and to translate the company philosophies into action. The Sock Hop's business plan consists of a number of objectives.

The first objective relates to opportunity costs for the owner/manager. The owner would like to obtain returns that would exceed that of a salary obtained through alternate employment and the cost of capital on her equity investment in the business.

Therefore,

$$\begin{matrix} \text{Salary at} \\ \text{The Sock Hop} \\ (\$24{,}000) \end{matrix} + \begin{matrix} \text{Additional} \\ \text{profits} \end{matrix} > \begin{matrix} \text{Salary if} \\ \text{working for} \\ \text{someone else} \end{matrix} + \begin{matrix} \text{Cost of} \\ \text{capital on} \\ \text{equity} \end{matrix}$$

It should be noted that the cost of capital on equity investment is included because, had the person placed her life savings in a savings account, it would have been earning a stated interest amount. Thus, for the owner/manager to remain in the business the total tangible benefits derived from the business must be greater than they would have been without the business. This objective should be met in approximately five years.

The second objective is based on performance. Market share should increase from the present adjusted 22 percent to 33 percent within five years (medium term goal). It is hoped that as the business grows, it will have a loyal following of customers along with a good business reputation to overcome some of the weaknesses.

---

[1] City of Lethbridge Urban Study, 1991.

As a result, the sales and profits should also increase. The sales per square foot should increase from the present estimate of $278/sq. ft. As a way to increase overall profit, a minor objective is to increase the efficiency in selling the merchandise.

A third objective is a 10-year long-term goal for future expansion. By the year 2003, it is hoped that the owner will be able to work out a system to franchise The Sock Hop in Western Canada. By then, the "bugs" should be worked out in the system and a franchising plan can be established. This is dependent on the Lethbridge prototype store being successful.

A fourth (short term) objective involves the method of financing the business. The owner/manager of The Sock Hop will not be the sole contributor of equity capital to the business. However, she wishes to retain as much independence and control as possible while spreading the risk. Thus, even when equity capital is obtained, the owner/manager will retain in excess of 51 percent of the control, and there will be an option for the owner/manager to buy out other equity investors.

2. Market Approach

Description of the Target Market.   The geographic market area for The Sock Hop is Lethbridge. However, this must be further defined into a demographic target market, since a consumer-oriented marketing strategy is to be adopted by The Sock Hop.

For The Sock Hop, the target will be anybody between the ages of 15 and 64 who lives in Lethbridge. The income level, occupation, social class, and education are relatively irrelevant for this necessary product.

The fact that this target market will be interested in quality socks at a moderate price is important. Furthermore, The Sock Hop is targeted to those who are looking for variety and fashion in socks. In addition, a good part of inventory will be devoted to high-quality socks catering to the business community.

Uncontrollable Factors.   There are four uncontrollable factors that the small business owner must understand. The owner must gather information about these uncontrollables, predict or monitor trends, and adjust the internal operations to them.

Economy.   At this point, the economy in Lethbridge is positive. The type of merchandise that The Sock Hop is selling, however, tends to be recession proof. Because socks are not a high-cost item, the market should remain steady. The economic environment will be continually monitored, however, with respect to its effect on this business.

Competition.   There are several stores in Lethbridge that sell socks. A lot of these stores have built-up reputation and convenient location as strengths. Reputation is one of The Sock Hop's weaknesses. However, its main strength is greater variety, particularly in fashion socks.

The Sock Hop plans to monitor the competition closely through primary observation and by reviewing industry reports on a regular basis. Competitor reactions to its entrance into the market will also be noted.

Legal Restrictions.   The specific legal restrictions are discussed in the legal section of this paper. Keeping abreast of new and existing laws that affect retailers and the sock industry is important. Talking to middlemen in the industry and reading association magazines and newspapers are effective ways to monitor legal effects.

Social/Cultural Trends.   Since The Sock Hop has decided to adopt a consumer-oriented marketing strategy, it is imperative that new trends are monitored. Because the product is very fad oriented at times, trends are going to be vital, especially to the portion of the target market that is young and attracted by the fashion stock. In order to keep up with these trends, industry and fashion magazines, social statistics, and government reports will be of particular help. Furthermore, observing the competition and the general surroundings will help to keep The Sock Hop management up to date on lifestyle trends, demographic changes, and purchase patterns.

All of these uncontrollables have to be monitored, and the controllable elements of the business (product, price, place, promotions) have to be changed in anticipation of or in reaction to these.

Marketing Strategy

Product.   The product strategy for The Sock Hop involves offering a product that can be differentiated from the competition and that will ensure a reasonable profit, anticipating the market's changes in preferences, and continuing product innovations.

The product will be differentiated by being more fashion oriented. There will be more variety, greater selection, and better services offered at The Sock Hop than is found with competitors. The customer will be able to choose socks from both the fashion stock and the basic stock. There will be a full money-back guarantee to complete this total package offered to the customer—a package that will sway the consumer's choice toward The Sock Hop.

Socks are classified somewhere between convenience and shopping goods. This means that consumers will generally shop around and compare before making a purchase, with only occasional impulse purchases occurring. Thus product differentiation (real or perceived) is crucial.

Distribution.   It is an advantage that The Sock Hop is located close to other stores that carry socks, since it aids comparison. The Sock Hop is small and new and thus will have some disadvantages compared to department stores and chains. For this reason, it would be best for The Sock Hop to take part in a buying group. There are a lot of sock stores in Calgary and Edmonton, and many are operated as small businesses. The Sock Hop intends to investigate joining a buying group. In this way, it can obtain volume discounts, pass the savings on to customers, and thus remain competitive. Purchasing with a buying group will help keep a lower inventory, as slow-moving items can be purchased in minimum quantities.

In addition, The Sock Hop will use a more direct channel for purchasing, in accordance with the belief that the fewer the middlemen, the higher the profit margin available to the retailer. It will use a manufacturer/supplier in Canada if one with a good reputation for quality and dependability exists. The Sock Hop will avoid foreign suppliers if possible since it is their policy to buy Canadian.

In terms of getting the product to the consumer, The Sock Hop will sell to consumers directly. This will be possible because its location is convenient and it will be easy for customers to make sock purchases while shopping in the mall for other merchandise. In addition, The Sock Hop will offer excellent customer service as part of the total package, which will differentiate The Sock Hop from its competitors.

Pricing.   Price is *not* the means of differentiating The Sock Hop from the competition. The Sock Hop is competing on the basis of selection, quality, service, and specialization.

Sales will be held at various times of the year to improve overall profit, to promote certain items, to counter competition, to dispose of excess inventory of inactive stock, and to improve cash flow. However, in the long term, pricing based on the full cost will be used. The economic situation, competition, market demand, and the price sensitivity of the customers also have to be taken into account when establishing a markup percentage.

Promotion.   The objective here is to inform, persuade, and/or remind the target market. Five percent of sales has been devoted to advertising for the first year. This is in spite of the fact that the Dun & Bradstreet average for small businesses for advertising is 1.5 percent. Extra advertising support is needed in the first year of business because sales will not be large compared to those of other clothing stores, and the public needs to be informed about The Sock Hop and its total offering. In the next four years, advertising will be reduced to 3 percent of sales, but it will still be above the Dun & Bradstreet average.

A variety of advertising methods will be used. The normal outlets such as newspaper, radio, television, and the yellow pages will be used. Door-to-door flyer campaign will be considered, as Lethbridge is relatively small. For television and radio, The Sock Hop hopes to be involved in any promotional efforts in conjunction with the Park Place Mall.

At the start of the business, various contests can be held to get ideas on new designs for socks, which will help renew the product life cycle. In addition, sponsoring sock hops at the local high schools will improve public relations. This will be especially advantageous since the younger, fashion-conscious portion of the target market are high school youth. Moreover, a lot of these youngsters are innovators and thus have the power to influence a major portion of the target market.

As a promotion, The Sock Hop could start a Sock of the Month Club for loyal customers. The details of this will be worked out when and if the decision to go ahead with this promotion is made. The whole idea stressed here is the need for unique forms of advertising and promotion to add the special *sizzle* needed to set The Sock Hop apart from the rest.

Finally, price promotions can be used in busy months such as January, when clearances are usually held; during August and September, when it is back-to-school time; and during November.

3. Location

Trading Area

Economic Base.   The City of Lethbridge's economy is strongly based on agriculture. The agricultural economy is supported by the food processing, packaging, distilling, and brewing industries. The city has good road and rail connections to various markets as well as to producers, and these have been important in maintaining Lethbridge's economic position. In addition, Lethbridge is in a prominent position in its region, and growth is expected in the area.

Competition.   There is considerable competition in terms of the number of stores in the trading area offering socks, but it should be noted that these stores do not have a wide selection nor is much space devoted to the product. A factor working against The Sock Hop is that these other stores are already established, but in time The Sock Hop will have its own loyal customer following.

In terms of general retail and service competition in the trading area, there are 36 major retail/service clusters in Lethbridge, and they have been evaluated at a total of 3,479,000 square feet of retail and service space in addition to the square footage covered by Park Place.[2] The 3,479,000 square feet are allocated in the trading areas as follows:

> 2,650,000 sq. ft. in the city of Lethbridge
>
>   829,000 sq. ft. in the surrounding area, which comprises the trading area
>
> 3,479,000 sq. ft.

Attitudes of the Trading Area toward Having a New Business.   The new mall has increased the trading area and has shown a positive attitude toward development of the area. Lethbridge is moving ahead, and as a result most of the community is anxious for new businesses.

---

[2] Larry Smith and Associates Ltd., Market Study for the City of Lethbridge (September 1991).

Specific Site

Accessibility.   Park Place Mall is centrally located in the city of Lethbridge (north of the cental business district (CBD). There are major roads on all sides with good connections to the city. Careful consideration to traffic flows was given by the city before construction of the mall took place. Lethbridge is also well served by the major highway system serving Southern Alberta. Therefore, vehicular traffic is facilitated both in and around Lethbridge. The transit system facilitates customers who don't own vehicles. There is a major transit station downtown within walking distance of the mall. A proposal to move the station north of Galt Gardens has also been considered, which would bring this station on the street facing this mall. In addition, bus routes include the mall.

Thus, all customers will have good access to the site, which is fairly visible from the major thoroughfares (Stafford Drive, Crowsnest Trail, First Avenue).

Site Costs.   The specific site costs (information obtained from Park Place Mall administration and the city of Lethbridge) include the following:

Rent	$20–$30/sq. ft. per year ($30 × 400 sq. ft. = $12,000 per year)
Utilities	$5–$10/sq. ft. per year ($10 × 400 sq. ft. = $4,000 per year)
Business taxes	4.2% of fair rental value [4.2% × (400 × 30)] = $504
City business license	$53 per year
BRZ fees	$3.78 per month—$45.36 per year (0.75% of business tax)
Insurance	$87.39 per year

The total site and operational costs add up to $16,680.75.

Total rent of The Sock Hop will be $12,000 per year. In addition, the mall offices generally set a breakeven point for the store, and once this point is reached by the store, a royalty of 5 percent to 8 percent of sales in excess of breakeven point is charged in addition to the normal rent.

The typical term of this lease is between 5 years and 10 years. Since this aspect of the lease is negotiable, an attempt should be made to have the term reduced. In addition, advance rent of two months is required by the mall administration. In terms of recharges, the total cost of utilities, electricity, and upkeep of the common area is $4,000 ($10.00 × 400 sq. ft.).

Insurance for The Sock Hop covers the business contents such as merchandise, fixtures, furniture, and equipment. The insurance also applies to the actual business loss sustained by the owner and the expenses incurred to resume normal business operations. Thus, the insurance provides coverage when the damage caused by an insured peril results in the interruption of business. The money and securities are also covered against loss by robbery, safe burglary, and theft from a night depository in a bank or from the custodian. The insurance further covers liability for bodily injury and property damage claims arising out of the maintenance and use of premises.

Total insurance per year is equal to:

$$\$3.70 \times (\$23,618.77/\$1,000) = \$87.39$$

It should be noted that the mall administration insures the common area.

(The various taxes and licenses will be covered in the final section of this business plan.)

Restrictions on the Site.   The administrator at Park Place Mall did not allude to any restrictions on the site. Renovations may be done if prior approval is obtained from the mall head offices, and this approval time ranges anywhere from one week to one month. After approval, any renovations or improvements may be made as long as they are contained within the space indicated on the lease arrangement.

Site History.   There is no site history to the location because Park Place Mall is a new development.

Proximity to Other Businesses.   Park Place Mall has many products and services. This is advantageous in that it will generate customer traffic essential to the success of the business. Socks are defined as a shopping good, which means that consumers will usually shop around and compare before making the final purchase decision. Therefore, by locating close to competing businesses, consumers will be able to compare and choose the superior product. The Sock Hop offers good quality socks at a reasonable price, which, when compared to other stores, will draw a loyal following.

Furthermore, other stores will be selling complementary articles of clothing (shoes, pants), which will generate customer traffic for The Sock Hop by creating a need for socks. Other than the businesses in Park Place Mall, there are no other stores offering socks in the immediate vicinity of the site.

Physical Characteristics of the Site.   Most sites assigned by the mall administration would be advantageous since the traffic throughout the mall is heavy. An attempt will be made to obtain space that is not at the end of the mall to further facilitate customer traffic.

4. Physical Facilities

Start-Up Costs.   The start-up costs for a retail store are made up of two things—capital assets and inventory. The following is a detailed breakdown of the physical items required to furnish the store. (This list was obtained from Roll-It Catalogue, National Signs, and Consumers Distributing.)

Item	No.	Each	Total Value
Furniture and Fixtures			
Multi Merchandiser (48″ × 54″)	6	$507.00	$3,042.00
End Frame Pegboard (48″ × 66″)	4	146.65	587.00
Miscellaneous hardware (pegs)	1		1,000.00
Used Bargain Bunk	1	200.00	200.00
Counter	1	500.00	500.00
Sign	1	500.00	500.00
Filing cabinet (4 drawer, legal 24″ deep)	1	190.00	190.00
Desk (30″ × 60″, steel)	1	250.00	250.00
Swivel chair	1	50.00	50.00
Equipment (obtained from Cypress Business Equipment, AGT Business Office, Consumers Distributing, General Fasteners)			
Software (Bedford)	1	$ 300.00	$ 300.00
Computer and printer (IBM clone)	1	2,000.00	2,000.00
Cash register	1	1,200.00	1,200.00
Telephone installation	1	40.00	40.00
Adding machine	1	75.00	75.00
Pricing gun	1	80.00	80.00
Vacuum cleaner	1	280.00	280.00
Total			$10,294.00

Initially The Sock Hop will invest about 15 percent of projected sales in inventory. This is standard.

$$\text{Inventory} = \text{Sales} \times 15\%$$
$$\$13,324.77 = \$88,831.33 \times 15\%$$

Layout.   In the case of The Sock Hop, the layout is designed to display the merchandise effectively. While browsing is somewhat encouraged by the multi-merchandisers, there isn't enough selling space to encourage a lot of creativity in layout (see Appendix 1).

In this layout, two basic areas can be identified. These are the retail space and the back room space (washroom, staff room, storage, etc.). In the retail space there will also be dump bin displays near the areas of moderate customer traffic. The space itself will be divided between basic socks and fashion socks.

5. Financial

Feasibility Analysis

Target Market and Trade Area.   Geographically, the trade area for Lethbridge is delineated. The competitive influence of retail and service facilities in the city of Calgary limit the extension of the trade area to 70 kilometres to the north. To the east, competitive retail facilities in the city of Medicine Hat limit the trade area's extent to 95 kilometres. In the south, the trade area extends some 80 kilometres to the Canada–United States border. The trade area to the west extends 130 kilometres from Lethbridge. Here, it is primarily limited by the distance and driving times and is bounded by the Alberta–British Columbia border. The study by Larry Smith and Associates Ltd., referred to earlier, indicates that Park Place Mall expects to derive the majority of its sales volume (80 to 95 percent) from this area. The remaining 5 percent to 20 percent of market support normally reflects customer shopping derived from visitors, tourists, or people working in Lethbridge but not residing in the delineated trade area.

Socks for men and women are sold in a variety of department stores and chain stores. However, The Sock Hop can capture a reasonable share of the market because it will offer excellent quality socks in a wide variety at a moderate price. Furthermore, I believe that a good many shoppers will shop at The Sock Hop because it is a specialty shop (as, for example, The Tie Shop in Calgary).

Market Potential

- Total 1990 Lethbridge retail apparel and accessories sales were $32,260,000 (*Lethbridge Fingertips Facts,* 1990, p. 48). At an inflation rate of 4 percent per year (Alberta Retail and Service Trade Statistics), the retail sales for 1993 will be:

$$\$32,260,000 \times (1.04)3 = \$36,288,113$$

- The 1993 population of Lethbridge is 66,500 (city statistics).
- The 1993 population for the trade area excluding Lethbridge is 88,250 (city statistics).
- The amount of regional population which shop for socks in Lethbridge was estimated by clothing retailers to be 33 percent.
- It is estimated by clothing retailers and the personal experience of the owner-manager that between 3 percent and 5 percent of the expenditures on clothing are for socks. However, 3 percent may be on the high side for a low price item like socks, so a more conservative figure would be 2 percent. Based on these figures, the 1993 Lethbridge per capita socks sales figure can be calculated as follows:

$$\frac{\$36,288,113 \times 2\%}{[66,500 + (88,250 \times 33\%)]} = \$7.59$$

The market area for The Sock Hop can be safely defined as Lethbridge. Thus, in the remaining calculations, Lethbridge population figures will be used. Total market potential calculations:

- 1993 per capita socks sales in Lethbridge is $7.59 (as calculated above).
- 1993 population for Lethbridge is 66,500 (see above).

Therefore, the 1993 unadjusted total market potential figure for The Sock Hop can be calculated as follows:

$$\$7.59 \text{ per person} \times 66{,}500 = \$504{,}726.30$$

An adjustment must be made to this figure in order to take outshopping into account. *Outshopping* is the result of a consumer in a particular market area going to another area to make purchases. Based on interviews with store managers, the outshopping figure was said to be 20 percent. This is quite conservative, since the presence of Park Place Mall has two implications. Thus, the adjusted 1988 total market potential for Lethbridge will be:

$$\$504{,}726.30 \times 0.80 = \$403{,}781.04$$

This figure is the most accurate market potential figure. It takes into account inflation, outshopping buying habits (figure determined by primary research), and 1993 population figures.

Market Share.   No statistics were available on the amount of retail space devoted to socks. Therefore, estimates were obtained through primary research (see Appendix 2). The proposed store will have an area of 400 square feet with 320 square feet devoted to selling space. Based on these figures, the unadjusted market share of The Sock Hop should be the following:

$$\frac{320 \text{ sq. ft.}}{872 \text{ sq. ft.} + 320 \text{ sq. ft.}}$$

This figure represents the unadjusted market share available to The Sock Hop. In order to adjust the figure, the strengths and weaknesses on the various aspects of the business must be considered.

The major weakness of The Sock Hop is that it is a new store. It does not have a loyal customer following, has no reputation, and has plenty of established competition. In addition, this specialty store will more than likely have higher prices than some of the discount department stores selling socks.

The major strength of The Sock Hop is its location. It is going to be located in a new major shopping mall, Park Place Mall. The customer traffic in the mall is above average. The store will be in an attractive setting with good exposure. Furthermore, there is a vast amount of parking space available for the satisfaction of the consumers. The Sock Hop provides a variety of socks in one location that is convenient and pleasant for consumers. Another area of strength is the growing trading area. The outlook is very positive for the Lethbridge economy, and this can only aid The Sock Hop.

Based on this analysis, the adjusted market share can be said to be a very conservative 22 percent. This is based on present conditions. Hopefully in the future, this percentage will increase as the business becomes more established.

Projected Income.   The projected income statements for the next five business years are in Appendix 3 of this paper. The figures have been derived through primary and secondary research. The revenue figure was calculated by multiplying the adjusted market potential and the adjusted market share figures together:

$$\$403,781.04 \times 22\% = \$88,831.83$$

Financing.   This section pertains to the financing plan for The Sock Hop. Business start-up costs are needed in order to determine the financing needed. These costs are made up of the following:

CASE program	$ 400.00
Inventory	13,324.77
Incorporation fees	1,000.00
Physical facilities	10,294.00
Rent (last 2 months of lease + 1 month rent)	3,000.00
Total	$28,018.77

Most lenders require the borrower to prepare a financing proposal. This will provide answers to questions the lender will have about the owner and about the proposed business. Although business owners are anxious to obtain loans, it should be remembered that interest rates, amount of personal guarantee, repayment schedule, collateral, co-signor or guarantor requirement, capital expenditure restrictions, and payment penalties are all negotiable. In order for the lenders to know how a loan will be repaid, they need to look at income and cash flow projections for evidence of earnings that will support the loan. These are shown in Appendixes 3 and 4.

Sources of Financing.   The Federal Business Development Bank (FBDB) offers term loans to allow small business owners to acquire fixed assets such as land, building, machinery, and equipment. The loans are offered at floating rates or at fixed rates. FBDB may also provide assistance through its CASE program. CASE is a counselling service offered exclusively to small- and medium-sized businesses. This program employs experienced counsellors who advise the small business owner on any aspect of business.

The interest rate for the loan is approximately 13.25 percent with a minimum repayment period of four years.

The term of the amount borrowed must match the actual lifetime of what is being financed. Thus the inventory portion will be financed by an operating loan with a term of two years. This will be financing from a chartered bank. It should be noted that although $13,325 is being borrowed for this purpose, a lesser amount will be needed. This is because The Sock Hop will endeavour to finance a good portion of inventory from suppliers who, due to competition in the industry, are willing to market their products through new outlets. The remaining $7,500 will be borrowed from FBDB on a term of five years. The equity investment will thus be $7,500.

Accounting System. Rather than employ a bookkeeper, the manager of the business will record on a computer all transactions that occur every day. The Bedford accounting software will be used, which is priced at less than $300 (quote from computer dealer). The computer and a suitable printer priced at $2,000 will also be used.

The Bedford accounting software is a fully integrated package for the small business. It is easy to use and very user friendly. It consists of the Genera Ledger, Payroll, Receivables, Payables, and Inventory modules that are all posted, as applicable, through single entries. It is very versatile and easily adaptable to small business needs. It produces full audit trails and a number of other management information reports. The vendors have a good track record of maintenance and support. Computing magazines such as *PC Magazine* and *InfoWorld* have given good reviews to this software.

The services of a public accountant (C. A. or C. G. A.) will be utilized for annual reviews, for tax advice, and on special occasions when necessary. The business will follow Generally Accepted Accounting Principles in maintaining the financial records.

Credit Policy. The Sock Hop does not intend to allow any credit to customers, since it is not a practice in the industry. We do not intend to start a trend in this area, as the volume per customer would not justify it. However, we will accept all major credit cards (VISA, MasterCard, American Express, etc.). With this facility to customers, there would be no need to extend direct credit, which, in any case, would entail taking some risk on the part of The Sock Hop.

It must be mentioned here that credit card companies charge, on an average, 3 percent of sales charged. This is not excessive, and the cost can be easily justified as there is no risk on the part of the business. The possibility of reducing this charge to 2 percent and lower in the future exists with the increases in sales volume.

Financial Evaluation. Monthly financial statements will be prepared and reviewed by the owner-manager in an effort to monitor and evaluate progress. Several financial ratios will be calculated and compared to similar businesses as well as to previous performance.

6. Personnel

Administrative Structure. Since The Sock Hop is not a big store, initially the number of staff employed will be limited.

Store hours for The Sock Hop will be as follows:

Monday–Wednesday, 9:30 AM–5:30 PM.

Thursday and Friday, 9:30 AM–9:00 PM.

Saturday, 9:30 AM–5:30 PM.

Thus, the *basic* salary and wage expenses will be:

Store manager	$24,000.00
1 full-time clerk ($5.50 × 40 hr./week)	11,440.00
1 part-time clerk ($5.00 × 16 hr./week)	4,160.00
Total salary and wage	$39,600.00

With this staffing plan in mind, the organizational chart will be as follows:

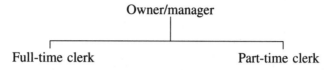

Owner/manager

Full-time clerk   Part-time clerk

Employee Recruitment and Training

Job Descriptions.   A typical job description is as follows:

Duties: Greets and helps customers, keeps shelves organized and stocked, rings up sales and bags items, responsible for opening and closing store when manager is away, cleans counters and vacuums.

Responsible to: Store owner/manager.

Requirements: Must have previous sales experience, be available to work nights and weekends, be able to use a cash register, be able to learn store procedures.

Personal: Must be friendly, dress and be groomed appropriately, be punctual and reliable.

Recruitment.   The channels of recruitment utilized by The Sock Hop will include write-ins (applicants), walk-ins, want-advertising, and educational institutions. Job application forms will be used to collect information about recruits. These application forms will attempt to gather information pertaining to personal data, employment status, education, skills, work history, memberships, awards, hobbies, and references.

The selection process consists of the following steps:

1. Preliminary reception of applicants in the form of a "courtesy interview."
2. A selection interview to evaluate the applicant's acceptability. This interview will evaluate such things as interpersonal relations skills and abilities.
3. Verification of the employment references.
4. A job preview. This will allow the potential employee to understand the job and the job setting before the hiring decision is made.
5. The hiring decision. Applications of candidates not hired will be kept on file for future openings. Retaining these applications will be useful if the

employer is charged with employment discrimination. The applications of those hired will also be retained.

Evaluation.   The first three months of employment are a period of observation for the employee as well as the owner-manager. The employee will receive professional sales training and will be taught the basics of The Sock Hop store procedures.

Beginning at the end of week 3 of employment, the owner-manager will initiate a coaching discussion. The employee's job performance will be evaluated, and discussions will be held to help the employee understand the job. In addition, any questions the employee has will be answered.

Coaching will continue at the end of week 8 and week 12 to aid the employee's progress and to evaluate his/her performance. The employee will receive regular coaching after this initial period with formal discussions at least every six months. This will ensure that the employee's efforts and abilities are being recognized and that he/she is receiving all the help required.

Training.   Training will be carried out by the owner-manager and will consist of three general areas. First, the employee will be provided with information about the business and its philosophy and goals. Second, the employee will receive training about the merchandise including such things as the material they are made of, washing instructions, etc. The third area of training involves the teaching of specific selling skills—such things as approaching the customer, presenting the merchandise, closing the sale, and suggestion selling.

In a small retail business, sales are directly related to how well customers get along with employees and how well employees anticipate and serve customers' needs.

Policies.   The following policies will be followed by The Sock Hop employees:

- An employee is assigned an identification number consisting of four digits to be used for all cash register operations.
- Work schedules will be posted at least one week in advance.
- Scheduling conflicts are to be reported to the manager as soon as possible.
- The wages for regular full-time clerks will consist of an hourly rate of $5.50 plus a 2 percent commission on sales.
- Similarly the wages for part-time clerks will be an hourly rate of $5.00 plus a 2 percent commission on sales.
- An employee who has completed six full months of continuous service by June 30th shall be entitled to one week's vacation during the summer vacation period.
- Any employee who has completed one full year of continuous service with the company by June 30 shall be entitled to two weeks *or* 4 percent of earnings as vacation pay (whichever is greater).

- Employees who have completed less than six months service with the company by June 30 must be paid 4 percent of their gross earnings from the date of hire until the last pay period in June.
- All full-time employees must receive vacation pay in the last pay period prior to leaving for their vacations.
- The employee will be expected to have a professional look. This includes proper grooming and appearance, clean and pressed clothing (no jeans), name tags, clean and proper footwear, and above all else, a *smiling pleasant attitude.*
- The Sock Hop emphasizes customer satisfaction. Therefore, the employee should ask all customers to retain their sales receipts. The Sock Hop will provide a full cash refund or merchandise exchanges on all returns with receipts.
- All staff will be entitled to a 20 percent discount on purchases from The Sock Hop.
- All purchases by staff members must be handled by the owner-manager. At no time is the staff member to "key in" their own purchases. These purchases are to be conducted during breaks or at the end of shifts.
- The phone is to be answered promptly, giving the store name and the employee's name. It is important that the employee be cheerful, helpful, and courteous.
- Personal calls are to be kept at an absolute minimum!
- The employee should practice the following prevention activities: (1) approach and greet all customers promptly and never leave the sales floor without coverage and (2) be aware of customers carrying merchandise from one location to another.

7. Legal Requirements

It has been decided that The Sock Hop will be an incorporated business. This decision was made after looking at the relative pros and cons of incorporation. The main reason for incorporating is the limited liability of shareholders. Thus, the owner is protected should the business fail. By incorporating, the owner is not risking her life savings. She is only liable for the amount invested in the business.

In addition, it will be easier to raise the needed capital in the future if the business is incorporated. There is also the advantage of business continuity should anything happen to the owner.

A final reason for incorporating relates to tax advantages. The corporate tax rate for small, Canadian-owned, private corporations is favourable. It is advantageous in that there is a 25 percent reduction from what larger businesses have to pay.

One of the disadvantages of incorporating is the cost (about $800–$1,000). This includes legal fees, registration, name search, minute book, and the seal for the company. Incorporating may also require increased reporting to the government and less flexibility.

Regulations. Since The Sock Hop is a retail store, the regulations that apply to it are those common to any regular small business in Lethbridge. The municipal government requires that the small business owner hold a business license ($53 per year). In addition, the city requires building and electrical inspections after renovations have been made. Municipal taxes include a business tax of about $504 per year and a Business Revitalization Zone (BRZ) fee of $45.36 per year, since the mall is within the BRZ. In addition, the small business is required to pay various taxes. The federal as well as the provincial government require the filing of yearly income tax returns. The federal GST will need to be collected on sales and remitted to the federal government.

APPENDIX 1

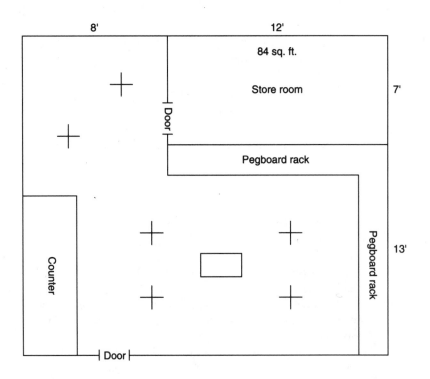

1 cm = 2 ft.

+ Multimerchandisers

☐ Bargain Bunk

APPENDIX 2
LIST OF STORES FOR MARKET POTENTIAL

Store	Number of Stores	Total Square Feet
Zellers	1	272 feet
Safeway	3	18 feet
Woolco	1	120 feet
Smartset	2	8 feet
Reitmans	2	8 feet
Eatons	1	42 feet
Sears	1	66 feet
Bi way	1	20 feet
Tip Top	3	24 feet
Jack Fraser	2	12 feet
Woodwards	1	24 feet
Mariposa	3	9 feet
Error factor	—	250 feet
Total		873 feet

APPENDIX 3
PROJECTED INCOME STATEMENT FOR FIVE YEARS

	1993 $	1994 $	1995 $	1996 $	1997 $
Sales	88,832	133,248	173,222	207,866	228,653
Cost of goods sold	44,416	66,624	86,611	103,933	114,327
Gross margin	44,416	66,624	86,611	103,933	114,327
Less expenses					
Rent	12,000	12,000	12,000	12,000	12,000
Staff wages	15,600	16,068	16,711	17,379	18,074
Owner's salary	24,000	24,000	24,000	24,000	24,000
Employee benefits	3,960	4,007	4,071	4,138	4,207
Advertising	4,442	3,997	5,197	6,236	6,860
Licenses and taxes					
Business licence	53	53	53	53	53
Business tax—4.2% of rent	504	504	504	504	504
BRZ fees	45	48	48	48	48
Credit card discounts	213	360	433	520	572

	1993 $	1994 $	1995 $	1996 $	1997 $
Repairs and maintenance	711	1,066	1,386	1,663	1,829
Utilities and occupancy costs	4,000	4,000	4,000	4,000	4,000
Professional fees	622	933	1,213	1,455	1,601
Office and store supplies	888	1,332	1,732	2,079	2,287
Telephone—Rent	115	120	124	129	135
—Estimated toll chgs	600	624	649	675	702
Insurance	87	91	95	98	102
Interest expense	2,593	1,594	1,396	398	199
Depreciation	2,059	2,059	2,059	2,059	2,059
Other expenses	1,777	2,665	3,464	4,157	4,573
Total expenses	74,269	75,521	79,134	81,591	83,804
Net income (before income taxes)	(29,853)	(8,897)	7,477	22,343	30,523
Income taxes	0	0	0	0	3,455
Income after income taxes	(29,853)	(8,897)	7,477	22,343	27,068

APPENDIX 4
PROJECTED CASH FLOW FOR FIVE YEARS

	1993 $	1994 $	1995 $	1996 $	1997 $	Totals
Cash in						
Net income	(29,853)	(8,897)	7,477	22,343	27,068	18,138
Add noncash items:						
Depreciation	2,059	2,059	2,059	2,059	2,059	10,294
Cash flows from operations	(27,794)	(6,838)	9,536	24,401	29,127	28,432
Equity contribution	35,000	15,000				50,000
Loan receipts—Operating	13,325					13,325
—FBDB	7,500					7,500
Total cash inflows	28,031	8,162	9,536	24,401	29,127	99,257
Cash out						
Loan repayments—Operating	0	6,662	6,663	0	0	13,325
—FBDB	0	1,500	1,500	1,500	1,500	6,000
Return of equity	0	0	0	20,000	30,000	50,000
Start up costs						
Legal	1,000					1,000
CASE counselling	400					400
Furniture and fixtures	10,294					10,294
Inventory	13,325					13,325
Two months' advance rent	2,000					2,000
Total cash outflows	27,019	8,162	8,163	21,500	31,500	96,344
Net cash flows	1,012	(0)	1,373	2,901	(2,373)	2,913

APPENDIX C
INCORPORATION OF COMPANIES AND ASSOCIATIONS

Federal
Registrar of Companies
Alberta Consumer and Corporate Affairs
Place du Portage, Phase 2
Ottawa-Hull, K1A OL5

Alberta
Registrar of Companies
Alberta Consumer and Corporate Affairs
Century Place
9803 102A Avenue
Edmonton, T5J 3A3

British Columbia
Registrar of Companies
Minister of Consumer and Corporate Affairs
940 Blanshard Street
Victoria, V8W 3E6

Manitoba
Corporation and Business Names
Registration Branch
Department of Consumer and Corporate
  Affairs
Woodsworth Building
405 Broadway
Winnipeg, R3C 3L6

New Brunswick
Registrar of Companies
Consumer and Corporate Services Branch
Department of Justice
P.O. Box 6000
Fredericton, E3B 5H1

Newfoundland
Registry of Deeds
Companies and Securities
Department of Justice
Confederation Building
St. John's, A1C 5T7

Nova Scotia
Consumer Services Bureau
5639 Spring Garden Road, 2nd Floor
P.O. Box 998
Halifax, B3J 2X3

Northwest Territories
P.O. Box 1320
Yellowknife, X1A 2L9

Ontario
Companies Branch
Minister of Consumer and Commercial
  Relations
555 Yonge Street, 2nd Floor
Toronto, M7A 2H6

Prince Edward Island
Department of Provincial Secretary
P.O. Box 2000
Charlottetown, C1A 7N8

Quebec
Department of Consumer Affairs
Cooperative and Financial Institutions
800 Place d'Youville, 6th Floor
Quebec, G1R 4Y5

Saskatchewan
Corporations Branch
Saskatchewan Justice
1871 Smith Street
Regina, S4P 3V7

Yukon
Department of Consumer and Corporate
  Affairs
P.O. Box 2703
Whitehorse, Y1A 2C6

APPENDIX D
JURISDICTION OF LICENCES AND TAXES

Topic	Comment	Jurisdiction		
		Municipal	*Provincial*	*Federal*
Licence and Permits				
City business permits		X		
Zoning by-laws	Applicable to certain provinces	X		
Land use regulations		X		
Business, school, water, taxes		X		
Provincial corporation income tax, estate taxes			X	
Capital tax (Ontario, Quebec, Manitoba, Saskatchewan, B.C.)	Applicable only to these provinces		X	
Quebec place of business tax	Applicable only to Quebec		X	
Sales and Excise Taxes				
Provincial excise tax	For consumer goods, must obtain a certificate from Department of Revenue, and vendor collects sales tax from consumer			X
Federal corporation income tax				X
Goods and services tax (GST)	Generally 7%, but certain goods exempted, e.g., foodstuffs			X
Revenue Canada Excise Branch Federal Sales and Excise Tax Office	Manufacturers or producers can obtain a manufacturing licence for sales tax exemption on raw material purchased			X
Export/import permit	All Canadian importers and exporters must obtain permit			X
Federal sales and excise taxes on imported goods	Levied on duty-paid value of some items			X
Custom duties on imported goods	Amount levied varies according to type of goods imported as classified by Canadian customs			X

SOURCE: Federal Business Development Bank, January 1980.

Suggested Readings

Dible, Donald. *What Everybody Should Know about Patents, Trademarks, and Copyrights.* New York: The Center for Entrepreneurial Management, 1986.

Drache, Arthur. "Life Insurance Can Save a Small Business." *The Financial Post,* April 2, 1990, p. 21.

Gray, Douglas A., and Diana L. Gray. *The Complete Canadian Small Business Guide.* Toronto: McGraw-Hill, 1988.

Hosmer, Larue T., and Roger Guiles. *Creating the Successful Business Plan for New Ventures.* New York: McGraw-Hill, 1985.

Kahn, Sharon. *101 Best Businesses to Start.* Garden City, N.Y.: Doubleday, 1988.

Mancuso, Joseph R. *How to Start, Finance, and Manage Your Own Small Business.* Englewood Cliffs, N.J.: Prentice Hall, 1984.

Orpen, Christopher. "The Effects of Long Range Planning on Small Business Performance: A Further Examination." *Journal of Small Business Management,* January 1985, p. 16.

Patents Questions and Answers. Canada: Consumer and Corporate Affairs, Ottawa 1986.

Starting a Small Business in Ontario. Toronto: Ontario Ministry of Industry, Trade and Technology, 1986.

Timmons, Jeffrey A. *New Venture Creation—A Guide to Entrepreneurship,* 2nd ed. Homewood, Ill.: Richard D. Irwin, 1985.

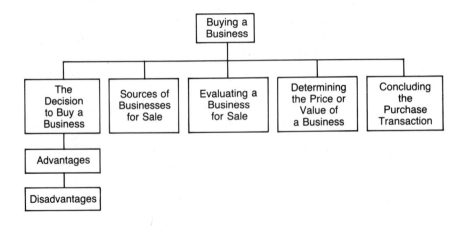

Buying a Business

Chapter Objectives

- To review the advantages and disadvantages of purchasing an ongoing business compared to the other methods of small business ownership.
- To describe the sources of businesses that are for sale.
- To explain how to evaluate a business that is for sale.
- To review the methods used in determining the price to pay for a business.

Small Business Profile

John Buhler

Farm King Allied Inc.

John Buhler was the second son of an immigrant Mennonite couple who settled in Morden, Manitoba, in 1927. While growing up, Buhler saw his father work many years for other people and never get ahead. As a result, he vowed as a grade schooler to become a businessperson and a millionaire by age 45.

By age 14, Buhler was earning money from several jobs, including driving a taxi, working in a garage, and managing three paper routes. After leaving school and working for the CPR (Canadian Pacific Railway) for seven years, Buhler purchased his first business, a small service station and auto wrecking company, in 1956.

Because these companies were in great difficulties, Buhler was able to obtain them at a good price. Strict cost cutting and hard work enabled him to turn them around. In 1970 he took over an ailing agricultural implement company, renamed it Farm King Allied Ltd., and managed it to a consistent profit just a few years later. Since that time, Buhler has purchased a car dealership, a cannery, and another farm machinery manufacturing business.

Several factors have contributed to John Buhler's success. First, he is an astute deal maker. For each of the ailing businesses, Buhler negotiated an attractive purchasing price, one that he knew would allow him to make a profitable business. In addition, he has taken advantage of government assistance in turning these businesses around, recognizing the importance policymakers place on employment in these communities. Buhler also sees through the layers of bureaucracy in an organization. In most of the companies he has purchased, he has instituted strict cost-cutting programs, often requiring the termination of several employees. Buhler typically adjusts the companies' products to be more responsive to consumer needs.

Finally, Buhler relishes hard work. He seldom sits still and visits his businesses constantly, ensuring productivity and efficiency. Buhler hasn't stopped there, however. He has continued to pursue various businesses, turning them around and providing badly needed jobs in the province.

_____

Incident 5–1

Die-Set Maker Tools Up for Global Markets

The opportunity he'd waited seven years for could not have come at a worse—or better—time. Clare Winterbottom, president of Anchor Lamina Inc. in Windsor, Ont., wanted to buy the company that had given him his start in the industry, rival Wheatley Manufacturing Ltd. of Windsor. He'd offered to purchase it in 1975, when he was its general manager, but it wasn't for sale then. Instead, he bought Anchor, a sleepy 15-year-old die-set maker and employer of nine, bleeding red ink on revenues of $400,000. As he steered Anchor into profitable waters—putting ownership into employees' hands, expanding its facilities, winning new customers and buying related companies—Winterbottom trained his eye on his former employer. In the throes of a recession in 1982, Anchor's sales had multiplied to $13 million, with profits of $270,000. And a financially-sinking Wheatley went on the selling block.

Says Winterbottom, "If we didn't buy it, someone else might have, and they would continue to compete with us. In slow recessionary times, we take the opportunity to position ourselves to move up with the next upturn in the economy."

Many entrepreneurs balk at spending money when the economy hits the doldrums: The survival instinct prompts them to tighten the purse strings. But expansion-minded owners like 56-year-old Winterbottom recognize the advantages recession shopping brings: business people are more open-minded about selling their firms—and more reasonable about their asking price.

Source: Cathy Hilborn, "Die-Set Marker Tools Up for Global Markets," *Profit Magazine,* October 1991, p. 10.

Purchasing an Existing Business

An alternative to organizing a business from the ground up is to purchase an existing business. Many entrepreneurs prefer this method of becoming a small business owner. Incident 5–1 describes an entrepreneur who bought a floundering business after a careful and thorough evaluation. Their experience and hard work turned the business around.

Advantages of Purchasing

Following are some reasons that buying a business may be an attractive alternative.

Reduction of Risk.   Chapter 2 mentioned that high risk is associated with starting a small business. Much of this risk can be reduced by purchasing an existing business. Uncertainty about the extent of consumer demand can be eliminated to a certain degree by examining past results of an existing business. Therefore, with proper investigation, the risk associated with purchasing a small business should be less than with a business organized from scratch.

Reduction of Time and Set-Up Expenses.   In an existing business, physical facilities such as building and equipment are already in place. The product or service is already being produced and distributed. Financial relationships and other important contacts have also been established. Each of these areas not only takes time to plan and organize but can be costly if unforeseen circumstances arise. Examples of such circumstances include lack of demand for the product or service, construction problems, production difficulties, and legal complications. Purchasing an existing business can minimize these potential problems.

Reduction of Competition.   Purchasing an existing business can eliminate a potential competitor. This may be an especially important consideration in a fairly stable market with only a few well-established competitors. Breaking into such a market with a totally new business may be difficult, and the potential small business owner should investigate the possibility of purchasing rather than organizing. Incident 5–1 illustrates this motivation for a Canadian company.

Capitalization of Business Strength.   Often a business for sale has a competitive strength that would be difficult to duplicate with a new firm. For example, the location of the business, a very important consideration in the retail and some service industries, may be excellent. Personnel, technology, or even the physical facilities of the business may be superior to those of competing firms. In such situations, buying a business that offers these advantages may be an attractive alternative.

Possible Assistance from the Previous Owner.   The previous owner may be willing to work for the purchaser of the business, or at least provide some assistance for a short time following the purchase. This type of help can be invaluable to the new owner.

Easier Planning.   Financial and market planning for a business is much easier when historical records are available. This information is not available for a start-up business. When approaching lenders or investors, projections from actual results of an existing business may generate more confidence than untested estimates.

Disadvantages of Purchasing

A prospective purchaser should also be aware of the potential disadvantages of purchasing a business. The situation in Incident 5–2 could easily have been

---

Incident 5–2

Partners Breathe New Life into Floundering Electronics Firm

In 1977, Bob Scott and Wes Stead, two high school friends from Owen Sound, Ontario, felt dissatisfied with their seemingly dead-end positions. So they sold their houses, boats, and other personal assets, moved into apartments, and bought a business they knew little about.

At the time, L. H. Frost Canada Ltd., an electronics component manufacturer in Oakville, Ontario, had annual sales of less than $1 million, and they were beginning to slide badly. The company had started in 1954 as a branch plant for a U.S. home appliance manufacturer. It had been sold in 1970, and between 1970 and 1976 ownership had changed hands several times. By 1977, its South American owner was running the plant at a loss. Customers were upset and, as Scott describes it, "goodwill was going to pot." Nevertheless, the firm had a 12,500-square-foot plant, fully equipped and staffed by 50 employees turning out electronic components such as transformers, chokes, relays, and coils. Though they knew little about the product lines, Scott and Stead had studied the company thoroughly, and they recognized its potential.

In the months before the purchase, Stead, then financial vice president of an electronics firm, had been looking for an acquisition for his employer. When he found L. H. Frost, he asked Scott, a graduate in electronics from Ryerson Polytechnical Institute in Toronto, to act as a technical consultant. Frost didn't fit the plans of Stead's employer, but it was just what interested Stead and Scott.

"We came down on a weekend and dug through all the sales files," says Scott, who was employed at the time in the marketing department of a fire alarms systems manufacturer in Owen Sound. "We looked at how many people they had, what kind of systems were in place, and found this wasn't a dying market." So, with about $100,000 in personal capital, a loan from the bank, and financing from the Ontario Development Corporation to cover 80 percent of the purchase price, Scott and Stead plunged in.

Source: Adapted from Curtis Rush, "Partners Breathe New Life into Floundering Electronics Firm," *Small Business*, November 1984, p. 8.

---

disastrous, as many small business purchasers have learned. Following are some of potential disadvantages of buying a business. Many of these problems concern the condition of the assets and other aspects of the business.

Physical Facilities.   The building and equipment may be old, obsolete, or below current standards. In addition, they may not be completely paid for or may have charges or liens against them. If the prospective buyer is unfamiliar with how to evaluate the condition of such facilities, he or she should enlist the services of a professional appraiser.

Personnel.   The business's employees may be incompetent or unmotivated. They may also resist the new ownership and reduce their productivity or even quit once the transfer of ownership is completed. The potential buyer is well advised to visit with current employees to ascertain their attitudes toward change.

Inventory.   The inventory may be obsolete or hard to sell. This factor may be especially critical in a retail store or a high-technology firm. Age of inventory can often be determined through internal records or by price tag coding.

Accounts Receivable.   The outstanding accounts may be uncollectible or at least costly and time consuming to collect. An evaluation of the length of time these accounts have been outstanding can be helpful in evaluating this potential problem.

Financial Condition.   The financial health of the business may be deteriorating or less robust than it appears in the financial statements. An in-depth evaluation of the firm's financial condition should always be conducted prior to purchase.

Market.   The market for the business's product or service may be deteriorating, or a strong, new competitor may be about to enter the market. In addition, such factors as the economic state, interest rates, or government policy could adversely affect the market.

Deciding on the Price.   The prospective owner may have difficulty negotiating a price to pay for the business or evaluating the fairness of the listed price.

Many of the above potential problems associated with buying a business can be uncovered through a detailed investigation of the operations of the business prior to purchase. Some of the key evaluation areas will be discussed later in this chapter.

Sources of Businesses for Sale

Where can the entrepreneur who has decided to purchase a business find out which businesses are for sale? The following are common sources.

Classified Ads.   Classified ads are found in local newspapers or financial or business publications. Figure 5–1 gives an example. Although numerous opportunities are publicly advertised, many of the best businesses to buy have been sold prior to the time they are advertised in the print media.

FIGURE 5-1   **Classified Ad for a Business Opportunity**

Lucrative Business for Sale

Manufacturer of picture frames and artists' supplies. Wholesalers to photo shops, artist stores, and craft
   shops. Growing business with established clientele, situated near Vancouver. Excellent investment
   potential. $150,000 negotiable. Please reply to:

The Financial Post
Box 444
777 Bay Street
Toronto, Ontario M5W 1A7

Government Departments.   The small business or industry department in most
provinces is usually aware of businesses for sale. They may also know of
communities that want to attract a particular type of business to locate there.

Real Estate Brokers.   Many entrepreneurs purchase their businesses with the
assistance of a broker whose job is to get buyers and sellers together and help
negotiate the sale. If the prospective purchaser knows a certain broker fairly
well, he or she might request that this individual be on the lookout for the type
of business desired. Brokers are aware of most businesses that are or soon will
be for sale, and some brokers even specialize in businesses.

Other Professionals.   Other professionals such as lawyers, accountants, and
bankers often know of businesses up for sale. Some prospective purchasers have
found excellent opportunities by sending these professional letters requesting
information about businesses for sale. In addition, organizations such as the
chamber of commerce may offer "match-up" services. One example is COIN
(Canadian Opportunities Investment Network).

Word of Mouth.   In their association with businesspeople, entrepreneurs often
learn about business opportunities through word of mouth. Executives of industry
associations often hear about owners who want out of their businesses, and
prospective buyers can contact these sources.

Evaluating a Business for Sale

As Incident 5–2 illustrated, a wise purchase decision may require considerable
investigation. The prospective buyer should look into several key areas of a
business before making a decision to purchase.

Industry Analysis

The entrepreneur should be well informed about the industry in which the business operates. Ideally this information should come from an extensive background or experience in that industry. Some specific areas to investigate are the following:

- Sales and profit trends of the industry
- The degree of competition, number of competitors entering or leaving the industry, and the nature of competitors' strategies
- The state of the economy in the market area and the extent to which changes in the economy affect the industry
- Legal restrictions currently affecting the operations of the business, as well as relevant pending legislation or political pressure
- Social concerns that may adversely affect the industry in the future

One or more of these areas could be significant in determining the future success of the proposed purchase. As a result, they should be thoroughly investigated unless the buyer has considerable experience in the industry.

The Previous Owner

The entrepreneur should ask the following questions about the previous owner of the business:

- Why is the previous owner selling the business? The often advertised reason, "because of poor health," may refer to financial rather than physical health.
- Is the previous owner a well-known and respected member of the community? Has this reputation contributed significantly to the success of the business? Will this success continue once that individual is no longer associated with the business?
- Will the previous owner be available—temporarily, at least—to provide assistance and advice to the new owner? This help can be invaluable, especially to a purchaser who lacks experience in the industry or market.
- Is the previous owner willing to finance the purchase by spreading it over a number of years? This may be helpful to the purchaser and advantageous tax-wise to the seller.
- What will the previous owner do after he or she sells the business? To guard against the previous owner starting a similar business in the same market area, the prospective purchaser might insist that a noncompetitive clause be included in the sales agreement.

Financial Condition of the Business

The financial condition of a prospective business is perhaps the most important area to evaluate. Care should be taken in evaluating the financial statements and assessing their validity. It is advisable to review not only the most recent year's financial statements but also those for past years. This process can reveal any trends and extraordinary circumstances. For instance, a general negative trend in profits during the past several years might suggest a lower value for the business, or at least the need for further investigation by the prospective buyer.

If the prospective buyer lacks a basic knowledge of accounting and an understanding of financial statements, it would be wise to enlist an accountant to assist in the financial evaluation. Some specific items to investigate, either by oneself or with the help of an accountant, are the following.

Validity of the Financial Statements.   Since some flexibility is allowed in preparing financial statements and a wide range of bookkeepers and accountants may be preparing them, the entrepreneur should assess the validity of the financial information obtained from the business. This can be done by insisting on audited statements and reviewing the methods used in recording such items as depreciation, inventory value, extraordinary items, repairs, owner's salary, and the treatment and terms of debt.

The prospective buyer should also investigate whether any potential hidden liabilities, such as liens or lawsuits, exist. Some industry experts recommend that if there is a possibility of such a liability but the amount is unknown, the purchaser should buy only the assets of the business. By doing this, the potential liability will accrue to the business itself rather than to the new owner.

Another task in assessing the validity of the statements is to review the income tax returns and bank deposits of the business. In addition, many prospective purchasers insist that the financial statements be audited to ensure their accuracy.

Evaluation of the Financial Statements.   Once the prospective buyer is satisfied that the financial statements are complete and accurately portray the operations of the business, he or she can evalutate the performance of the business as described in these statements. Sales, expenses, profit levels, assets, liabilities, and cash flow position are important items. Application of various financial ratios can help in comparing the performance of the business to those of other firms in the industry. Chapter 9 gives a detailed discussion of ratio analysis and other financial evaluation measurements. Appendix B in Chapter 9 illustrates the financial evaluation of a small business.

Naturally, one would hope the business is strong financially and profitable in its operations. In some situations, however, a business may be a good purchase even if it is unprofitable at the time of evaluation. This was illustrated in the Small Business Profile that opens this chapter and also in Incident 5–3. Such situations might be the following:

- The current owner is incompetent or lacks knowledge about the industry, and the purchaser has the competence and knowledge to turn the business around.

Incident 5–3

The Making of a Magnate

Six years ago, Gilles Labbe was a 26-year-old accountant with a decent salary but no assets to speak of. Today he's one of two major shareholders in Heroux Inc. of Longueuil, Que., which designs, builds and repairs aircraft landing gear. The switch from employee to entrepreneur has been a happy landing for Labbe because his share of Heroux is worth $36 million.

To get there, Labbe and his partner, Sarto Richer, needed the brains to see an opportunity and the courage to move swiftly at just the right moment. Heroux was a money-loser in 1982 when parent Bombardier Inc. appointed Richer, one of its veteran executives, to try to turn the division around. Labbe, who had done consulting work for Heroux, was soon hired as director of finance. By closing a plant, slashing employment and tightening financial controls, Richer and Labbe proceeded to turn a $549,000 loss into an $868,000 profit in the first year.

But by 1985 Bombardier decided to sell Heroux. Richer and Labbe wanted to buy it, but all they could scrape up between them was $100,000 and they needed $10 million. They approached the major Canadian banks and got nowhere. "They thought we were out of our minds," says Labbe. But several of the foreign banks have shown themselves to be more venturesome, so the Quebec pair approached one of those, Citibank Canada of Toronto. Outwardly, says Citibank vice-president Jim Hall, Labbe looked like a "hockey player from Quebec." But he quickly saw that Labbe had a deep knowledge of Heroux and was in total control of its operations.

The gamble paid off for everyone. In the past three years, Heroux's sales have shot up to $49 million from $14 million.

Source: Daniel Stoffman, "The Making of a Magnate," *Report on Business Magazine,* October 1988, p. 77.

- The industry is, or will shortly be, in a growth position that might improve the firm's profitability and/or resale value.
- The major contributor to the firm's unprofitability is lack of capital due to high interest rates, and the purchaser has the needed capital to inject into the business.

Condition of the Assets

Several assets of a business may require thorough inspection and, for nonliquid assets, possibly an appraisal by an independent appraiser. The fee for this service is generally reasonable and may be well worth it. Assets to value in this manner are the following.

Liquid Assets (Cash and Investments).   An important question to a prospective purchaser concerns how easily the liquid assets can be converted to cash. There may be special terms or conditions with respect to these assets, for example, the time period on a term deposit.

Accounts Receivable.   Have accounts receivable been aged? How many may be uncollectible? (Accounts receivable aging is discussed in more detail in Chapter 8.) Enlisting the services of a professional accountant to assist in this regard may be well worth the cost.

Inventory.   Is any inventory old, obsolete, or damaged? A detailed evaluation of inventory should be done by someone with knowledge and experience in this area.

Building and Equipment.   Are the buildings and equipment old or obsolete? Are they comparable to competitors' facilities? Are there any liens against them?

Real Estate.   What are the land taxes and service costs? If the premises are leased, is the lease transferable? What are the terms and conditions of the lease? Has the location experienced a high turnover of businesses in the past?

Goodwill.   What value does the owner place on goodwill? Is this value realistic and reasonable? Generally, goodwill costs should not exceed 20 percent of the cost of the assets, even for well-established businesses.

Quality of Personnel

The prospective purchaser should evaluate the efficiency of the business's personnel. How do they compare to employees in other, similar businesses? An important factor is personnel reaction to the new owner after the purchase. It may be wise for the buyer to meet key with personnel to better evaluate their reaction to the sale of the business.

External Relationships of the Business

The investigation should include a review of those organizations or agencies currently essential to the operations of the business. Will these relationships continue, and if so, under what terms or conditions? Some organizations to contact include suppliers, financial institutions, and key customers.

Condition of the Records

Other records to review are credit files, personnel files, sales reports, contracts, and customer lists. These items can be very valuable to the operations of the business and should be included with the business when it is purchased.

Appendix A at the conclusion of this chapter presents a comprehensive checklist of considerations in purchasing a business.

Determining the Price or Value of a Business

If the preceding evaluation of the business shows positive results and the prospective purchaser decides to buy the business, he or she must make a decision concerning the price to pay for it. Is the asking price reasonable? Should a lower counteroffer be made? Several methods can be used to arrive at a price for a business. In a free market, the right price is the one purchaser and seller agree on, or where demand and supply meet. When applied to a business purchase, this price is called the *market value*. To use the market value method effectively, the prospective purchaser must collect data on the market values of many similar businesses. In most markets, the number of sales transactions of similar businesses is fairly small; thus, little data may be available.

There are three other useful approaches to valuing a business. The first relies heavily on asset value. The second uses the earnings potential of the business as a basis for determining value. The third uses a combination of asset value and earnings potential. Each method can help the entrepreneur make a general estimate of the purchase price. It should be kept in mind, however, that the buyer, the seller, or the business may possess unique characteristics that cannot be incorporated into a formula. Such situations will require adjustments to a formula-determined price.

Asset Value

There are two approaches to valuing a business using value of assets as a base: book value and replacement value.

Book Value.   The book value method lists the business at the net balance sheet value of its assets minus the value of its liabilities (Chapter 9 provides the fundamentals of balance sheet assets and liabilities). This method generally understates the value of the business by a significant amount. For this reason, the book value price may form a lower limit to determining the price of the business.

Replacement Value.   The replacement value method lists the replacement cost of the assets as their value. Because the assets of an existing business typically are not new, the replacement value method tends to overstate the value of the business.

FIGURE 5-2   **Calculating Weighted-Average Earnings for a Business**

	Earnings	Weighted Average Earnings (Earnings × Weight Factor)				
Last year	$ 5,000	5,000	×	5	=	25,000
Two years ago	7,000	7,000	×	4	=	28,000
Three years ago	4,000	4,000	×	3	=	12,000
Four years ago	10,000	10,000	×	2	=	20,000
Five years ago	14,000	14,000	×	1	=	14,000
	$40,000			15		99,000

Average earnings   = $40,000/5 years = $8,000
Weighted average earnings = $99,000/15 = $6,600

When coupled with the liability side of the balance sheet, the replacement cost method may result in an upper limit to the price to pay for the business.

Earnings Value

The prospective purchaser is interested not only in asset value but also in how the business will perform in the future. Therefore, earnings potential is another factor to be taken into account in setting the price of a business. Pretax earnings or income should be used, as the tax rates vary by province and by industry.

It is also important to use average earnings in calculating earnings potential rather than just the most recent year's net income figure. Many analysts will use the previous five years' average of earnings. If earnings appear to be unstable from year to year, a weighted-average calculation might be used. The determination of average earnings using the weighted-average approach is shown in Figure 5-2. This method gives a greater weight to the most recent years' earnings in arriving at average earnings.

Two specific methods of estimating the purchase value of the business use earnings as a base.

Capitalization of Earnings Method.   This method is commonly used to arrive at a quick estimate of the price of a business. The capitalized value is found by dividing average earnings of the business by a specified rate of return expressed as a decimal. This specified rate of return figure can be obtained by using bank interest (a risk factor of a few percentage points should be added) or another required rate of return percentage for the investment. It can also be obtained by using average return on tangible net worth statistics from such sources as Dun & Bradstreet and Statistics Canada. Figure 5-3 illustrates the capitalization of earnings formula.

Figure 5-4 illustrates a calculation of capitalized earnings value using industry averages. This method measures the firm's ability to earn profits in

FIGURE 5–3   **Capitalization of Earnings Formula**

$$\frac{\text{Average earnings}}{\text{Predetermined interest rate or}} = \text{Capitalized value}$$
$$\text{rate of return required for investment}$$

FIGURE 5–4   **Capitalized Earnings Value**

Line of Business	*Net Profits to Tangible Net Worth as a Percentage**	*Capitalized Earnings Value†*
Retail		
Book and stationery stores	22.0	$ 45,450
Clothing, men's	12.9	77,520
Clothing, women's	12.8	78,125
Drugstores	20.7	48,310
Foodstores	10.8	92,595
Gasoline service stations	23.1	43,290
Hardware	14.5	68,965
Jewellery store	8.3	120,480
Manufacturers		
Appliances, small	18.4	54,350
Bakery products	17.8	56,180
Machine shops	19.7	50,760
Meat products	11.8	84,745
Sash, door, and millwork		
plants	29.0	34,480
Soft drinks	34.9	28,655
Sporting goods and toys	11.0	90,910
Construction		
Building contractors	23.3	42,920
Services		
Hotels	15.5	64,515
Agriculture, forestry, and		
fishing		
Agriculture	12.2	81,965

*Tangible net worth is net worth less intangibles, i.e., copyrights, goodwill, trademarks, and patents. This figure can be found in Dun & Bradstreet, *Key Business Ratios.*

†Represents the investment or tangible net worth required to earn $10,000 in profits after taxes, assuming the firm is operating at median level. Calculated in the following manner:

$$\frac{\$10,000}{\text{Net profit to tangible}} = \text{Capitalized earnings value}$$
$$\text{net worth as percentage}$$

SOURCES: Adapted from Paul Harmon, *Small Business Management—A Practical Approach* (New York: D. Van Nostrand, 1979), p. 76. Figures updated from Dun & Bradstreet, *Key Business Ratios,* 1990.

relation to the capital invested. For example, for a book and stationery store, it will take $45,450 paid for the business to earn $10,000 after taxes if the store was run at the median level. Figure 5–4 also illustrates Dun & Bradstreet averages for various industries.

FIGURE 5-5   Bank of America Formula for Determining the Price of a Business

---

Step 1: Determine the adjusted tangible net worth of the business (the total value of all current and long-term assets less liabilities).

Step 2: Estimate how much the buyer could earn annually with an amount equal to the value of the tangible net worth invested elsewhere. The rate should be similar to that which could be earned elsewhere with the same approximate risk.

Step 3: Add to this a salary normal for an owner-operator of the business. This combined figure provides a reasonable estimate of the income the buyer can earn elsewhere with the investment and effort involved in working in the business.

Step 4: Determine the average annual net earnings of the business (net profit before subtracting owner's salary) over the past few years. This is before income taxes to make it comparable with earnings from other sources or by individuals in different tax brackets. (The tax implications of alternate investments should be carefully considered.) The trend of earnings is a key factor. Have they been rising steadily, falling steadily, remaining constant, or fluctuating widely? The earnings figure should be adjusted to reflect these trends.

Step 5: Subtract the total of earning power (2) and reasonable salary (3) from this average net earnings figure (4). This gives the extra earnings power of the business.

Step 6: Use this extra, or excess, earning figure to estimate the value of the intangibles. This is done by multiplying the extra earnings by what is termed the "years of profit" figure. This "years of profit" multiplier depends on the following points. How unique are the intangibles offered by the firm? How long would it take to set up a similar business and bring it to this stage of development? What expenses and risks would be involved? What is the price of goodwill in similar firms? Will the seller be signing a noncompetitive agreement?

    If the business is well established, a factor of 5 or more might be used, especially if the firm has a valuable name, patent, or location. A multiplier of 3 might be reasonable for a moderately seasoned firm. A younger, but profitable firm might have merely a one-year profit figure.

Step 7: Final price = Adjusted tangible net worth + Value of intangibles.

Times Earnings Method.   This method arbitrarily multiplies average earnings by a number between 1 and 10, based on past sales and industry experience, to arrive at the price for the business. Small businesses are usually sold at between four and five times earnings according to the U.S. Small Business Administration. This number can vary significantly for very small businesses. Therefore, the advice of an experienced business broker or accountant valuator should be sought.

Combination Methods

Because both the asset value and the earnings value are important components of the price of a business, some methods combine both values. The best known of these methods is that used by Bank of America, shown in Figures 5–5 and 5–6. The Bank of America formula not only uses asset and earnings value but also addresses the difficulty of valuing goodwill. It also incorporates the opportunity cost of not buying a business into the price. This formula may be inappropriate in some situations, for example, when the earnings of the

FIGURE 5–6   Illustration of Bank of America Formula

	Business A	Business B
1. Adjusted value of tangible net worth—assets less liabilities (source: balance sheet of business)	$50,000	$50,000
2. Earning power (at 10%) of an amount equal to the adjusted tangible net worth if invested in a comparable-risk business, security, etc.	5,000	5,000
3. Reasonable salary for owner-operator in the business	20,000	20,000
4. Net earnings of the business over recent years—this means net profit before subtracting owner's salary	28,000	23,500
5. Extra earning power of the business (line 4 minus lines 2 and 3)	3,000	–1,500
6. Value of intangibles—using three-year profit figure for moderately well-established firm (3 times line 5) (1 for newer service business, 3 for average, 5 for well-established, successful business)	9,000	none
7. Final price (lines 1 and 6)	$59,000	$50,000 (or less)

In example A, the seller gets a substantial value for intangibles (goodwill) because the business is moderately well established and earning more than the buyer could earn elsewhere with similar risks and effort. Within three years, the buyer should have recovered the amount paid for goodwill in this example.

In example B, the seller gets no value for goodwill because the business, even if existed for a considerable time, is not earning as much as the buyer could through outside investment and effort. In fact, the buyer may feel that an investment of even $50,000—the current appraised value of net assets—is too high because it cannot earn sufficient return.

SOURCE: "How to Buy or Sell a Business," *Small Business Reporter* 8, no. 11 (San Francisco: Bank of America National Trust and Savings Association), p. 11.

business are temporarily negative or of secondary importance to the prospective purchaser.

Figure 5–7 shows another combination method sometimes used. This method is tailored to the unique characteristics of each industry and based on past experience.

As mentioned previously, determining the price of a business by using a formula may provide a good estimate of a business's worth, but the unique characteristics of each situation may alter the price actually offered and/or paid for the business.

The Purchase Transaction

Once a purchase price and other terms and conditions have been agreed on, the buyer should enlist the services of a lawyer to draw up the purchase agreement and

Figure 5–7   Combination Methods for Pricing a Business

Type of Business	Price Offering Range
Apparel shop	.75 to 1.5 times net + equipment + inventory
Beauty salon	.25 to .75 times gross + equipment + inventory
Fast-food store	1 to 1.25 times net
Grocery store	.25 to .33 times gross, including equipment
Insurance agency	1 to 1 times renewal commissions
Manufacturer	1.5 to 2.5 times net, including equipment + inventory
Restaurant	.25 to .50 times gross, including equipment
Retail store	.75 to 1.5 times net + equipment + inventory
Travel agency	.04 to .10 times gross, including equipment
Video store	1 to 2 times net + equipment

Source: Gustav Belle, *The Small Business Information Handbook* (New York: John Wiley & Sons, 1990), pp. 30–32.

close the transaction. This helps ensure that clear title to the business is transferred and postpurchase difficulties are minimized. The purchase agreement should cover the following areas:

- The purchase price, including principal and interest amounts.
- Payment date(s)—when and to whom payments are to be made.
- A detailed list of all assets to be included in the purchase.
- Conditions of the purchase—what nonfinancial requirements, if any, are part of the purchase? Many purchase contracts are signed subject to the purchaser obtaining suitable financing.
- Provisions for noncompliance with conditions, including penalties for breaches of the contract.
- Collateral or security pledged in the transaction (if the seller is financing the sale).

Negotiating the Deal

In purchasing a business, the first formal step is to make the offer to purchase. The offer may be made directly by the buyer or through a realtor or a lawyer. In either case, the offer to purchase should be made only after consulting a lawyer and an accountant. As part of the negotiating strategy, the potential buyer should have calculated (preferably financially) the maximum amount he or she can offer for the business. This value is generally somewhat higher than the original purchase offer. As negotiations continue, the purchase price or other aspects of the agreement may have to be altered.

The buyer is normally required to make a deposit of 5 to 10 percent of the purchase price as a show of good faith. This amount should be minimized at least until the seller has met the conditions of the agreement.[1]

Summary

1. The potential advantages of buying a small business include the reduction of risk, time, set-up expense, and competition; capitalization of business strength; possible assistance from the previous owner; and easier planning. Potential disadvantages include problems with physical facilities, personnel, inventory, and accounts receivable; deterioration of the business's financial condition or market; and difficulty in negotiating a purchase price.

2. The common sources for locating a business for sale include classified ads, government departments, real estate brokers, word of mouth, and professionals such as lawyers, accountants, and bankers.

3. The key areas an entrepreneur should investigate in carrying out an industry analysis are sales and profit trends, degree of competition, state of the economy in the market area, legal restrictions, and social concerns that may adversely affect the industry in the future.

4. Before making a purchase decision, it is important to understand the effect of the previous owner's reputation on the success of the business. It is also important to find out why the owner is selling the business.

5. To determine the financial viability of any business, one should analyze the validity of the financial statements, evaluate those statements, review the condition of the assets, review the personnel, study the external relationships of the business, and consider the existing records.

6. In some situations, a business may be a good purchase even if it is unprofitable at the time of evaluation. This may be the case if the current owner is incompetent or unknowledgable about the industry, if the industry is or will shortly be in a growth position, and if the main contribution to the company's lack of profitability is the lack of capital. In each case, if the potential owner can correct or improve the situation, the struggling business may be a viable purchase.

7. There are three general approaches to valuing a business. The first method uses the asset value to determine the price. The second method uses the earnings of the business. The third method uses a combination of assets and earnings.

8. When developing a purchase agreement, the buyer should make sure that the purchase price, payment date(s), conditions of purchase, and any provisions for noncompliance with terms are included.

Chapter Problems and Applications

1. John Van Goegh wants to own his own business. His area of expertise is the sporting goods market. He has checked into opening his own store

versus purchasing an existing store in the downtown area. The existing store is a seven-year-old proprietorship with sagging sales. There are four main sporting goods shops in the city (60,000 people). The existing business is in a prime location, and the market and product line are well established. The financial condition, however, includes a large amount of accounts receivable. With this information, John turns to you as a consultant. What advice would you give John regarding whether to purchase the existing business or start his own? What additional factors should he consider? Justify your answer.

2. You are investigating the purchase of a fertilizer manufacturing plant. The results of your analysis of the firm are extremely positive, except for an unidentifiable annual payment of $100,000. On further investigation, you learn that the $100,000 is being paid in fines for dumping toxic waste. The previous owner has determined that it costs less to pay the fines than it would to properly dispose of the waste by deep well injection. In light of recent government actions, how would this situation affect your decision to purchase? Explain.

3. Sally's Bar and Grill is available for purchase. Sally's earnings for the past five years were as follows:

Last year, $50,000
Two years ago, $60,000
Three years ago, $30,000
Four years ago, $40,000
Five years ago, $25,000

Determine the value of the business using the following methods (use current bank interest rates).
a. Capitalized earnings value
b. Times earnings value

4. Use the Bank of America price formula (Figures 5–5 and 5–6) to calculate a selling price for the following businesses:

ABC Company			*The Clothes Closet*		
Assets	=	$ 90,000	Assets	=	$ 65,000
Owners' equity	=	40,000	Owners' equity	=	30,000
Revenue	=	100,000	Revenue	=	103,000
Expenses	=	70,000	Expenses	=	55,000
Owners' salary	=	18,000	Owners' salary	=	40,000

5. Do an industry analysis for the existing grocery stores in your area. Complete your analysis using all the areas mentioned in the text.

6. From an advertisement in the paper, contact the seller of a business. Find out the price and other information pertinent to the sale. Does the asking

price seem reasonable? Check with industry averages to evaluate the performance of the business.

APPENDIX A
CHECKLIST OF CONSIDERATIONS IN PURCHASING A BUSINESS

The Industry

1. What are the sales and profit trends in the industry?
2. What is the degree of competition? What competitive changes have taken place?
3. What is the nature of competitor strategies?
4. What is the state of the economy in the market? How is the business's performance affected by changes in the economy?
5. What existing or pending legal restrictions affect the operations of the business?
6. What social or cultural concerns affect the industry?
7. Are there any potential competitive or trading area changes that might affect the business?

The Previous Owner

1. Why is the previous owner selling the business?
2. Has the reputation of the previous owner contributed to the success of the business?
3. Will the previous owner help you by providing assistance and advice after the sale?
4. Is the previous owner willing to finance all or part of the purchase?
5. Will the previous owner start a competitive business after the sale?

Financial Condition of the Business

1. Is the financial information provided accurate and indicative of the business's performance?
2. What is the past history of profits going back at least five years?
3. Has the business gained or lost market share in the past five years?

4. How do the various financial ratios for the business compare with industry averages?
5. Does the business have a strong identity with customers or clients? Can this identity be maintained?
6. What prospects does the business have for increasing market share and profitability in the future?
7. If the business is currently unsuccessful, what are the chances of improving it with an infusion of capital and/or managerial expertise?
8. What value does the business place on goodwill?

Condition of Assets

1. Are any special terms or conditions associated with the liquid assets?
2. Are the accounts receivable collectible?
3. Is the inventory old or obsolete?
4. Are the building and equipment up to date and paid for?
5. Are taxes and service costs paid on land?
6. Is the location good? Is it increasing or decreasing in value?
7. Is the lease good? What are the terms and conditions of the lease?

Quality of Personnel

1. Do the employees of the business compare favourably with the industry in productivity and expertise?
2. Will the employees stay on with the business after the sale?
3. Has the business been progressive in meeting competitive demands regarding wage rates and employee benefits?

Condition of External Relationships

1. Can favourable relations with suppliers be maintained?
2. Are financial sources appropriate and adequate? Can they be maintained?
3. Does the business have a strong support staff such as a lawyer, an accountant, and a consultant? Can these people be retained if needed?

Condition of Records

1. Can the purchaser obtain key records such as credit files, personnel files, customer lists, sales reports, and contracts?

Suggested Readings

Bunn, Verna A., and C. R. Steedman. *How to Buy and Sell a Small Business.* Toronto: Checkerbooks, 1987.

Coltman, Michael M. *Buying and Selling a Small Business.* Vancouver: International Self-Counsel Press, 1983.

Gray, Douglas A., and Diana L. Gray. *The Complete Canadian Small Business Guide.* Toronto: McGraw-Hill Ryerson, 1988, pp. 79–103.

Kao, Raymond W. Y. *Small Business Management.* New York: Holt, Rinehart and Winston, 1983, pp. 306–17.

Kingston, John P., and P. E. McQuillan. *Valuation of Businesses: A Practical Guide.* Toronto: CCH Canadian Ltd., 1986.

Lipay, Raymond J. *Accounting Service for Your Small Business: A Guide for Evaluating Company Performance, Obtaining Financing and Selling Your Business.* New York: John Wiley & Sons, 1983.

Szonyi, Andrew J., and Dan Steinhoff. *Small Business Management Fundamentals.* Toronto: McGraw-Hill Ryerson, 1983, pp. 302–309.

Thomas, Peter. "Negotiate to Win." *Profit Magazine,* October 1991, pp. 34–36. Publications, Toronto.

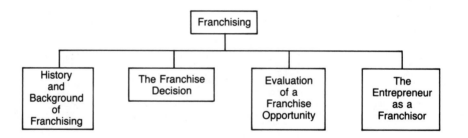

Franchising

Chapter Objectives

- To discuss the significance of franchising in the Canadian economy.
- To explain the various types of franchises available for small business.
- To list the relative strengths and weaknesses of franchising as a method of starting a small business.
- To explain how to evaluate a franchise opportunity.
- To discuss how to organize a franchising system.

Small Business Profile

Adrienne Stringer and Jim MacKenzie

Molly Maid International Inc.

In 1978 Adrienne Stringer, a former nurse, invested $2,000 to organize a maid service business. She believed changing lifestyles and the increasing number of two-income families had created a market for the business.

By 1980 Stringer's company, Molly Maid, was grossing about $100,000 and seeing further growth possibilities. Because she lacked finances to accomplish this growth, she decided she needed to obtain equity money, either from new partners or through a franchise system. As she investigated further, she thought the franchising system would more likely provide the necessary expansion funds. She entered into an arrangement with Jim MacKenzie to franchise the business. MacKenzie, a business graduate from Queen's University, purchased 80 percent of the business and immediately began developing a complete franchise system for Molly Maid. Stringer became the first franchisee.

Since that time Molly Maid has grown dramatically, employing over 2,000 maids and reaching sales of about $40 million in 1991. Molly Maid has sold more than 300 franchises in Canada, the United States, the United Kingdom, and Japan.

Molly Maid's success can be attributed to the recognition by Stringer and MacKenzie of an underdeveloped market and the business acumen needed to properly organize and administer the franchising system. A consistent dedication to marketing and consumer research has made the company the dominant maid service in Canada. In recent years, Molly Maid has also pursued international expansion aggressively.

Used with permission of Jim MacKenzie.

Incident 6–1

The New Franchises

One day before celebrating his 10th anniversary with Northern Telecom Ltd. in October 1989, 55-year-old advertising manager Conrad Heibey was fired. Falling victim to corporate cost-cutting was devastating, Heibey admits, but once the shock wore off, he started looking for work with another large company. After four months of fruitless searching, however, he decided "it was time at last to do something different with my life."

Heibey found his new niche in franchising. Last August he and his wife became proprietors of a Clock Gallery shop in Victoria, B.C., one of three franchisees of the 22-store Toronto-based retailer. Moving to the west coast was a longtime dream, and franchising helped him achieve it.

Through Canada's long slide into recession, Heibey isn't the only victim who has found an answer in franchising. With a weak economy forcing employers to slash payrolls, a new generation of experienced mid-level managers is eyeing the ranks of Canada's 25,000 franchisees. They see a $90-billion industry that's growing almost 20% a year—and they're scouting for the right opportunity.

Source: "The New Franchises," *Profit Magazine,* July-August 1991, p. 41.

History and Background of Franchising

Franchising is becoming an increasingly popular method of establishing and operating a small business. Many entrepreneurs find the opportunity to operate their own business with slightly less risk an attractive option (see Figure 4–1). Others enter franchising out of necessity, having lost jobs with larger organizations (see Incident 6–1). Franchising now occurs in most industries and is experiencing rapid growth in the service sector.

Not only has franchising been successful for the entrepreneur. Many large organizations also recognize that this method of doing business benefits their operations. Incident 6–2 illustrates the advantages of franchising for both franchisee and franchisor.

From the franchisor's point of view, franchising provides a source of capital and a stable and motivated work force, thus usually leading to higher performance. For the franchisee, it offers a turnkey operation with valuable assistance from the franchisor.

One dilemma the entrepreneur often faces is that as the business grows, funds are needed for expansion. As the profile at the beginning of the chapter illustrates, franchising is one answer to this financing question.

Incident 6–2

Branchising: A Chip off the Corporate Block

As the first franchisee in the Agnew Shoes store-franchise system, Ron Chapell knows that his performance will in many ways determine how the system grows. This wouldn't be an unusual state of affairs for a new franchise system, except that Ron has worked for the Agnew chain for 28 years.

After 111 years in business, Agnew Group Inc., based in Waterloo, Ont., has decided to franchise some of its 353 company-owned outlets. Five outlets have been franchised in 18 months, and Agnew hopes to have 50 franchised within another year as the program gets rolling.

Ross McCallum, a partner at Price Waterhouse in Toronto, is helping the Agnew group make the transition. He says Agnew's move is part of a trend to "branchise." "Branchising is simply defined as taking company stores and turning them into franchise outlets," says McCallum. "This is an especially attractive option for retail companies that are looking for hands-on owner-management to increase profitability."

There is a definite trend toward branchising, especially in the retail sector. McCallum says that the trend started after the October 1987 stock market crash as companies re-evaluated their financing options. McCallum says branchising allows corporations to lay out less capital and free up money for expansion or acquisitions. We will see, he says, more branchising in the future as retail companies that have saturated their primary markets look for new markets to tap.

Branchising also increases sales. A survey this spring of American branchises by Price Waterhouse consultants in Canada found that per-store sales increased an average of 20% to 25% after branchising. The best results came from stores where mediocre corporate managers were replaced with well-trained, motivated franchisees.

Source: Bev Cline, "Branchising: A Chip Off the Corporate Block," *Profit Magazine,* July-August 1989, p. 66.

In addition, expansion of a business usually requires the addition of new employees. The new employees often lack the same incentive as the owner to make the business succeed. Again, franchising has been the answer for many, as it was for the founders of Tea Masters (see Incident 6–3), who are credited with pioneering the first food franchising business.

Although the concept has been around for decades, franchising has experienced its most rapid growth in North America only since the 1950s. It began with the automobile manufacturers, oil companies, soft-drink bottlers, and breweries and has since spread to many different industries throughout the world. Through

---

Incident 6–3

The Family Franchise

Angelo Manousos stepped off the plane from Greece in 1966 with his wife and eight-year-old son, Paul. He had high hopes and no money. He soon found there was no demand for his trade, which was designing ships. After a typical immigrant's apprenticeship running a series of jug-milk stores, in 1979 he opened a takeout coffee-and-tea operation in an out-of-the-way nook beneath the Royal Bank Tower in the heart of Toronto's financial district. Today, his son Paul runs their chain of 11 Tea Masters stores, which have annual sales of $4.2 million. He and his father will add seven more stores this year and hope to have 50 stores by 1991.

To open the first store, Angelo mortgaged his house and sold his Canada Savings Bonds. That raised $70,000. He couldn't afford advertising, so he had to depend on satisfied customers spreading the word. But after six months, Manousos, his wife, Jenny, and Paul were wondering if their great idea was really all that great. They were working 13 hours a day for a dismal $100 in sales. Finally, people began to find the store and word got out: Manousos knew he had succeeded the day there was a lineup outside the shop by 7:30 A.M.

Paul, who has a business degree, began to franchise Tea Masters in 1981. He thinks the franchise system helps maintain quick, personal service. That's because "when the owner is there the staff tries a little harder." Hands-on management and good service are the major reasons for Tea Masters' success.

Source: Daniel Stoffman, "The Family Franchise," *Report on Business Magazine,* October 1988, p. 75.

---

franchising, many organizations with a proven concept or product were able to expand much more rapidly to meet demand. This growth was so rapid that toward the end of the 1960s, several problems developed in the industry that resulted in the formation of franchisee associations and the passage of legislation to protect the rights of both franchisees and franchisors.

Today about 40 percent of all retail sales ($432 billion) result from franchising in North America.[1] Estimates are that this figure may be as high as 60 percent of sales by the year 2000.[2] Franchise growth in Canada has paralleled the rapid growth in the United States, with approximately $69 billion in sales registered in 1988.[3] This trend is shown in Figure 6–1. A recent study by Price Waterhouse showed that franchising grew by 2 percent in 1991; the general economy, in contrast, declined. This trend is expected to continue, with 1992 franchise growth forecasted at 12.4 percent.[4]

An estimated 1,300 franchising companies operate 50,000 outlets in Canada today.[5] Figure 6–2 illustrates the industries in which franchising has had the most

FIGURE 6–1   **Franchise Sales in Canada (in billions)***

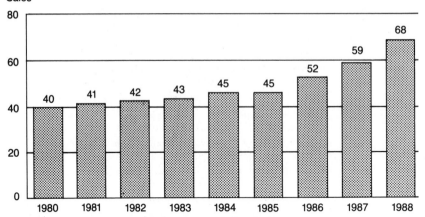

*Sales figures are estimates of the Canadian Franchise Association.

FIGURE 6–2   **Franchising by Industry**

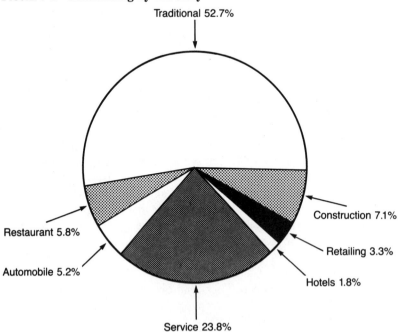

Source: *Market Research Handbook,* Statistics Canada, 1988, p. 191.

FIGURE 6-3   **Canada's Leading Franchising Companies**

Franchise	Gross Revenue	Parent	Type of Business
Canadian Tire	$2,986,900	Billes family	Retail hardware
Shoppers Drug Mart	2,843,600	Imasco	Retail pharmacies
McDonald's Restaurants of Canada	1,357,300	McDonald's Corp.	Fast food
Marlin Travel Group Ltd.	723,200	Several	Travel agency

significant impact. The percentages denote industry sales as a percentage of total franchise sales.

Franchises exist in almost all industries today. A major reason for the large recent increase in the number of franchises is expansion into the service sector, which is the fastest-growing sector in the Canadian economy. The profile at the beginning of this chapter exemplifies this trend. Figure 6–3 lists the largest franchises in Canada today.

What Is Franchising?

A common definition for a franchise arrangement is a patent or trademark licence entitling the holder to market particular products or services under a brand or trademark according to prearranged terms or conditions. Today many applications of this definition translate into a broad range of franchising relationships. The various types of franchises are grouped into three categories.

Manufacturer-Directed Franchise.   In this type of franchise, the manufacturer of a product grants a dealer the right to sell the product. This right, which tends to be geographically exclusive, often requires no initial fee. (See Figure 6–4 for further details of this type of franchising.) Manufacturer-directed franchising is common in such industries as automobile sales, gasoline distributorships, and farm implement dealerships. This type of franchising is successful only when the manufacturer has an established name, a solid reputation, and considerable consumer loyalty.

Wholesaler-Retailer–Directed Franchise.   In this arrangement, one member of the distribution channel, such as the wholesaler or retailer, initiates the organization of the franchise. The primary purpose of such an organization generally is to centralize many managerial and operational functions and take advantage of volume buying for a group of sellers. As with the manufacturer-owned franchise, there is usually no initial fee, but an equity investment in the franchise may be required. Figure 6–4 illustrates some of the other operating details for this type of franchise and the industries in which it is prevalent.

FIGURE 6-4   **Types of Franchises**

Title	Method of Franchising	Details of Agreement		Examples	
		Franchisor Provides	*Franchisee Provides*	*Industry*	*Company*
Manufacturer	Franchisee has right to sell product	Product sales support	Selling function	Automobile	Ford GMC
		Exclusive territory	Facilities	Farm machinery	Hesston John Deere
				Oil companies	ESSO GULF
Wholesaler-retailer	Franchisee owns equity in supplier company and purchases product from the franchise	Product and other technical assistance and service	Selling function Buys equity Board of directors	Retail grocery Hardware	Associated Grocers Home Hardware
Franchising company	Franchisee buys the right to sell service and/or product	Method of operations Training Location, building, etc. Financing Proven name Advertising	Fee Royalties Compliance with conditions of contract	Fast food Auto rental	McDonald's Kentucky Fried Chicken Avis Budget Hertz

Franchising Company.   This type of franchise usually involves a company that sells a product or service in exchange for an initial predetermined fee and an ongoing royalty. The franchisee gains the right to sell under the franchisor's name and receives the franchisor's assistance and managerial expertise. Franchising companies are commonly found in the retail and service industries. In recent years, many companies using this method of franchising to expand their operations have experienced rapid growth. Figure 6-4 provides further details of the franchising company arrangement.

Advantages of Franchising

Compared to the other two methods of starting a small business (buying and organizing), franchising offers many specific advantages.

Proven Market for the Product or Service.   Except for newly established franchises, a known market for the franchisor's product or service exists. Information about the performance of existing franchises is normally supplied or can be obtained by the franchisee. Such a track record makes it much easier to make projections for future operations.

FIGURE 6-5   Characteristics of Canadian Franchise Agreements

Contract Provision	*Percent Yes*	*Percent No*
Require franchisee to be owner/operator	79	21
Offer renewal option	88	12
Provide training	94	6
Offer financing	25	75
Franchisor owns franchise property	6	94

SOURCE: *Franchising in the Canadian Economy 1990–1992* (Toronto: Canadian Franchise Association and Price Waterhouse 1992), pp. 36–39.

The instant pulling power of the product also greatly helps the small business owner shorten the duration of the initial stage of the business, when the market is being developed and resulting revenues are low. A recent study by the University of Toronto showed that franchised businesses had higher sales per outlet than independents in almost all types of businesses.[6] Another study of franchisors found that during the last recession, franchised outlets were less affected than nonfranchised outlets.[7]

Services the Franchisor May Provide.   A franchising company typically provides many valuable services to a franchisee. Figure 6–5 shows the incidence of some of these services. A description of franchisor services follows.

Selection of Location.   Assistance in selecting the location can be very important, especially if location is critical to the success of the business, such as in retailing and often in the service industry. Often a franchisor has considerable site selection expertise that can be used in establishing the business.

Purchase or Construction of Site, Buildings, and Equipment.   The franchisor's experience and financial resources in this area may mean considerable savings of time and money. In addition to providing expertise, the franchisor may even purchase or construct the facilities for the franchisee.

Provision of Financing.   Some franchisors will provide financing for franchisees, and their association with the franchisees often helps obtain financing. For example, The Royal Bank, through its Franchise Assistance Program, allows favourable interest rates on franchisee loans because of a franchisee's association with a well-known franchisor.

Standardized Methods of Operating.   Standardized operating procedures and manuals are often part of the services the franchisor provides in the areas of cost accounting, control systems, and customer service standards. Such methods can

---

Incident 6–4

Franchise Performance

Why do franchises enjoy healthier sales figures? Buying into a system helps franchisees avoid many of the common mistakes made by new businesses. In the fast food industry, for example, poor inventory control can result in spoilage or not having enough food on hand. To help its franchisees, Toronto-based Mr. Submarine provides procedure manuals that cover everything from inventory control to a list of product shelf lives. "We cover all aspects of the business," says franchising director Thanos Dimitrakopoulos, up to and including "when to clean tables and take out the garbage."

Equally important are the economies of scale franchises enjoy in purchasing and advertising. With group advertising, for example, comes greater consumer awareness. "A typical single-unit store might spend 2% to 5% of gross revenues on advertising," says Stanley Brown, a franchise consultant with Laventhol & Horwath in Toronto. To get the same impact as a franchise organization with 18 stores, says Brown, an independent business would have to spend much more. Dimitrakopoulos agrees: "Every time we open a new location, it's an advertisement for the other 325."

Source: Excerpted from Gordon Brockhouse, *Profit Magazine,* July–August, 1990, p. 48.

---

result in considerable savings for the small business. Incident 6–4 illustrates how this service benefits franchisees in the fast-food industry.

Advertising.   Most franchisors will provide national advertising that may benefit the franchisee. Such a level of promotion may be difficult and costly for the franchisee to develop unassisted. As Incident 6–4 illustrates, group advertising brings greater consumer awareness.

Purchasing Advantages.   Because the franchising company purchases large volumes of inventories for its franchisees, it can pass the resulting cost savings on to franchisees on purchases made from the franchisor.

Training.   Most franchisors provide training to new franchisees. This may take the form of an instruction manual or thorough training at a franchisor's school. A McDonald's franchisee, for example, receives training at Hamburger University in Illinois and can even receive a bachelor's degree in Hamburgerology! Because of the extra training provided, franchising (as opposed to buying or organizing) is often more suited to someone who lacks experience in the industry. Incident 6–5 illustrates the advantages of such training for one franchisee.

Incident 6-5

The Franchise Advantage

When Dan and Sue Gillis left Toronto to head back to their native Nova Scotia to start a haircutting franchise in early 1989, they had precious little business experience. But by July, the pair had bought their salon and in October they opened for business.

To launch their Dartmouth franchise on time, Dan, formerly a geologist with a Toronto mining-consultant company, worked 15-hour days, seven days a week, installing chairs and mirrors, arranging phone service and hiring staff. While he had some previous experience, he didn't know what to look for in a hairstylist. But the task proved easy thanks to training courses put on by the franchisor, Mississauga, Ont.-based First Choice Franchise Services Inc. First Choice also provided marketing, advertising and technical advice. The help, says Gillis, was invaluable. So far, only two of the nine hairstylists he hired have left the franchise, not bad for a startup business in a high-turnover industry. And sales are growing by about 5% a week.

Thanks to his franchise connection, Gillis purchases products for retail sale, such as shampoo, conditioner and hair spray, at lower prices than his non-franchised competitors. That lets him shave 20% off prices his independent competitors charge for similar products.

Technical and management training, group advertising and ongoing support are important reasons why franchises often outperform independent businesses in the same industry.

Source: Excerpted from Gordon Brockhouse, *Profit Magazine,* July-August 1990, p. 47.

Because of the foregoing advantages, a franchisee's chance of success in the business is higher than with the other two methods of starting a small business. The franchising industry advertises a failure rate of only 4 to 8 percent, which is much lower than the rate for nonfranchised businesses.[8]

Potential Disadvantages of Franchising

Because of the apparent advantages just discussed, many individuals have signed franchise contracts. However, some suffered disillusionment and failure a short while later. Evidence shows the level of franchise litigation is growing. Often franchisees misinterpret the franchise agreement concerning such things as use of advertising funds, restrictions, and services provided by the franchisor. It is critical that the prospective franchisee be aware of the difficulties that can arise when one enters the world of franchising. Following are some of the more common dangers.

Lack of Independence.   In signing a franchise contract, the franchisee can expect to receive a certain amount of assistance from the franchisor. The franchisor will monitor the business, however, to ensure that the conditions of the contract are being met. This condition restricts the franchisee's freedom and independence.

Cost of the Franchise.   Most franchises have a price that often consists of an initial fee and ongoing royalties based on operations. To enter most franchise organizations, individuals will have to accumulate a certain amount of capital to either pay the fee or provide the facilities. Appendix A provides details on this subject, including the financial requirements of some of the better-known franchises in Canada.

Unfulfilled Promises.   Most franchising companies indicate they will provide such services as training and advertising. In some cases, however, this assistance does not materialize or is inadequate.

Restrictions of the Contract.   The franchise agreement may contain some restrictions that inhibit the franchisee's freedom. Such restrictions include the following.

Product or Service Offered.   The franchisee may not be allowed to offer for sale any products not procured by the franchisor.

Line Forcing.   The franchisee may be required to offer the franchisor's complete line of products for sale, even if some are not profitable in the franchisee's market area.

Termination.   The franchisee may not be able to terminate the franchise contract without incurring a penalty. The franchisee may also be prohibited from selling the business or passing it on to family members.

Saturation of the Market.   In some industries, franchising companies have allowed oversaturation to occur in a particular geographic market. This puts financial pressure on those franchisees operating within that market. If a franchisor has a large initial fee and no royalties, its major concern may be the selling of franchises rather than their ongoing success. Such franchises seem particularly vulnerable to oversaturation.

Lack of Security.   A franchisor may elect not to renew a franchise contract once it has expired or may terminate the contract prior to its expiry if the franchisee has violated the terms or conditions. Many franchising companies operate company-owned outlets as well as franchised outlets. The number of company-owned outlets is only about 18 percent of total franchise outlets, but recent figures show slight increases in this percentage.[9] Some argue that franchising companies take over the outlets after the franchisees have successfully established them.

Cost of Merchandise.   The cost of merchandise purchased from the franchisor may exceed the price the franchisee can obtain elsewhere. However, the contract may require the franchisee to purchase from the franchisor.

Effectiveness of Promotion.   Most franchisors provide promotion and advertising for their franchisees. In some situations, however, the promotion is not effective for the franchisee's market and may be time consuming and costly for the franchisee to participate in. Often a franchisee does not wish to participate in these programs but is required by the contract to do so.

Exaggeration of Financial Success.   Most franchising companies provide promotional literature for prospective franchisees. This information generally contains financial statements for the typical franchisee. In some cases, these estimates have been overly optimistic and the actual results for the franchisee are disappointing.

Evaluation of a Franchise Opportunity

In view of the potential disadvantages just mentioned, it is critical that a thorough investigation of the prospective franchise be made before signing the contract. Several key areas should be examined in evaluating a franchise. Information to assist in this decision can be obtained from several sources.

Industry Associations

Such organizations as the Canadian Franchise Association (Toronto), the local chamber of commerce, and various other industry associations may provide valuable information about a franchisor's history, reputation, operations, size, and number of operating franchises. Appendix B at the conclusion of the chapter lists several agencies that can provide assistance. Some publications also offer assistance, including the *Franchise Annual,* published by the Canadian Franchise Association in St. Catharines, Ontario; the *Franchise Yearbook,* published by *Entrepreneur Magazine;* and the *Info Franchise Newsletter,* published by Info Press in St. Catharines, Ontario.

Professionals

A prospective franchisee is well advised to enlist an accountant to review the financial side of the franchise to ensure that the information provided is accurate.

Often financial statements do not conform to Generally Accepted Accounting Principles (GAAP) or are unrealistic.

A lawyer's expertise should also be used in reviewing the terms and conditions of the contract. Because the franchising industry is becoming so specialized, it may be worthwhile to enlist a lawyer who is knowledgeable about franchising issues. The franchisee should ensure that his or her rights are protected and that there is a clear understanding of both franchisee and franchisor responsibilities regarding the following items:

- Initial fee—how much and when paid?
- Royalties—how much and when paid?
- Additional costs for training and management assistance
- The total investment required and how the balance will be financed
- Assistance offered by franchisor
- Product pricing fees
- Termination conditions—are they specific and realistic?
- Advertising provided
- Any merchandise requirements and/or restrictions
- Liability insurance—who carries it and what is covered?
- Geographic territory—what is the geographic territory of the franchise, and is it exclusive?

Other Franchisees

One of the most valuable sources of information for the prospective franchisee is communication with other franchisees from the same organization. Has the franchisee been happy in his or her association with the franchisor? Has the franchisor lived up to the promises made? How does the franchisor resolve difficulties that have arisen?

Government Agencies

The Consumer and Corporate Affairs departments or their equivalents at the federal and provincial levels of government may also provide information about the practices of franchisors. In addition, the provinces of Alberta and Quebec require franchisors to register and provide disclosure of information that could be helpful to the franchisee in this investigation. The industry division of Statistics Canada also offers a fraud checklist for potential investors.

Checking with the above sources can provide much valuable information to aid in the franchise decision. However, some final and critical questions remain. How much drawing power does the franchise name and product or service have?

Is the franchise fee worth the drawing power and services provided? The latter may not be a critical question for well-established franchises such as McDonald's or Dairy Queen, but it may be very important for a lesser-known franchise. Market research obtained through secondary sources or even collected by the prospective franchisee may provide enough information for evaluating the strength of the franchise's drawing power. Specific areas to investigate include industry trends, consumer acceptance of the concept, and franchisability of the concept.

Because the signing of a franchise contract is a major step for the entrepreneur, the investigation should be thorough. Appendix C at the end of this chapter provides a comprehensive checklist for the prospective franchisee to use in this evaluation.

The Entrepreneur as Franchisor

An increasingly popular method of entrepreneurship in franchising is not being a franchisee but selling franchises and becoming a franchisor. Incident 6–6 illustrates how one entrepreneur succeeded in this manner.

Before a prospective franchisor attempts to sell franchises, several requirements must be met. Is the type of business franchisable? What information is required? How much capital is needed? All of these questions should be addressed in the process of becoming a franchisor.

What Businesses Can Be Franchised?

Franchises abound in many industries today. This phenomenon is reflected in the following statement by the U.S. Commerce Department: "Any business that can be taught to someone is being franchised."[10] The franchise business must have a sound concept. The franchise should be distinct, be practical, and fill a need. It must also be easy to teach and clearly communicate to others. It must be capable of being replicated and transferred to other geographical areas. Suzy Okun, a co-founder of the franchise Treats, which specializes in desserts, elaborates on this idea: "We sell a concept. We take what the palate already knows, and we make it electric! We take what the customer has already seen and do it differently."[11] Consumer research may be required to solidify the concept. Estimates based on sound research will be much more attractive to the prospective franchisee.

How Does One Become a Franchisor?

Once the prospective franchisor is satisfied that the business is franchisable, he or she must take several steps to develop the franchise. Some of the most important steps are the following.

Incident 6-6

Lethbridge-Based Franchisor Turned the Rules Around

Dorsey Asplund suspects that the franchise organization he heads is unlike any other in North America. The driving force behind a Canadawide string of Minute Muffler shops, this 40-year-old Lethbridge entrepreneur has reversed just about every franchise "convention" in the book—apparently with total success.

Specialized muffler shops are relatively new in Canada. The Minute Muffler organization is only 15 years old; the oldest companies in this business have been in operation for no more than 20 years in this country.

Asplund started with a single shop in Lethbridge in 1969. Soon he had expanded into a small chain of half a dozen or so company-owned outlets. Franchising began in 1979, and now the company boasts 68 franchises across the country, including all but the original company-owned facility. "We will never give up our practical base," notes Asplund. "We chose franchising because we felt we have developed a better way of doing things that should be of interest to the industry and should be marketable as well."

The Lethbridge franchisor feels his company has survived, despite stiff competition from some formidable industry giants, because of its strength in research and development: "We basically lead the industry in R&D and any technical advances we make, we sell to our shops if they require them." Despite the inevitable "humps and bumps" encountered in establishing coast-to-coast franchises, Asplund notes, "We've only lost one outlet in our history."

That's an excellent record for this Alberta-based but nationally known franchisor.

Source: Adapted from Lois Bridges, "Lethbridge-Based Franchisor Turned the Rules Around," *Small Business Quarterly,* Spring 1984, p. 11.

1. Establish a Prototype.   The franchisor should set up and operate a prototype business long enough to iron out the bugs and get a clear picture of market demand. This business can also serve as a reference point for prospective franchisees to use in their evaluations. To be useful, the prototype should be earning a consistent profit.

2. Prepare the Necessary Information.   Information prospective franchisees will require includes promotional literature regarding the franchise and detailed financial data not only for the company but for a typical franchise. A prospective franchisee requires information on capital needed, potential income, cash flow projections, and future trends in the industry to make an informed decision. It is recommended that someone with accounting expertise be retained to assist in preparing this information.

3. Investigate the Legal Requirements.   The franchisor should investigate the legal requirements in setting up a franchising company. Some of these requirements might be:

- Registration and disclosure with government agencies. As mentioned earlier, some provinces require detailed information before franchising can begin.
- The required business licenses and incorporations.
- Other laws regulating the operations of franchises.

In addition, the franchise contract should be drawn up by someone with legal expertise to ensure that the rights of both parties are protected. The legal operations of the franchise and the responsibilities of both franchisor and franchisee are formalized in the franchise contract. The franchisor needs to decide which services and what assistance to provide, what restrictions to impose, and what to require from the franchisee in return. A more detailed listing of typical contract provisions appears in Appendix D.

4. Develop a Planned and Standardized Program of Operations.   Standardization of procedures is an essential part of a successful franchise and enables the franchisor to monitor operations more easily. The following quote about Molly Maid, the business profiled at the beginning of the chapter, illustrates the effective use of professionals in the development of the franchise system:

> MacKenzie made full use of experts in setting up his company. He used two well-known accounting firms, one to develop an internal accounting system, and the second to construct a package for franchisees. A legal expert on franchising developed the franchise agreement, and a firm specializing in trademarks and patents set up the rules for use of the logo.[12]

The operations manual is generally developed using the experience of the prototype business. As mentioned above, the methods or "system" used are typically the "service" that is franchised. The franchisor must ensure that the operations manual is understandable and easy to integrate into franchisee operations. The following quote about College Pro Painters (see the Small Business Profile in Chapter 3) shows the time and care taken in preparing the operations manual:

> After graduation in 1974, he took a year off to travel around the world, and started to put together a manual for the operation of College Pro Painters. Drawing on the knowledge he had acquired at school, he developed a chronology for starting a business and systematically attached every topic from "Business Plan" to "Close Down" in what would become his corporate bible.[13]

5. Obtain Adequate Financing. To franchise successfully, the franchisor will need capital to set up the prototype business, do the necessary market research, prepare the promotional literature and financial estimates, and develop the system of operations. A rapid expansion program may even require outside equity financing from a venture capital company or other financial institution.

Franchising in the Future

Franchising is expected to continue its rapid growth as new types of businesses incorporate franchising principles into their operations. Several trends are expected to surface in the future. The retail food industry, the largest sector of Canadian franchising, is expected to continue its growth, but in more specialized areas such as ethnic foods. As mentioned previously, more and more service businesses are expected to become franchises.

Some franchises are experimenting with "piggybacking," in which two or more franchises operate in one outlet. This concept has been tried with gas stations/convenience stores and restaurants/video stores. The practice of converting existing chain outlets to franchises, or "branchising" (see Incident 6–2) is expected to continue as chains search for new sources of interest-free capital.

Recent trends show a more sophisticated group of franchisees participating in the industry. These individuals tend to have higher educational qualifications and more business management experience. This trend is not only leading to higher success rates for franchises but also the creation of more organizations to protect franchisee rights.

Summary

1. Franchising has enjoyed phenomenal growth in recent years. One reason franchising is popular is the increased incentives for franchisees. Franchising continues to allow many organizations with a proven concept or product to expand much more rapidly to meet demand.

2. The three types of franchises are (*a*) the manufacturer-directed franchise, in which the manufacturer of a product grants a dealer the right to sell the product; (*b*) the wholesaler-retailer–directed franchise, in which one member of the distribution channel, such as the wholesaler or retailer, initiates the organization of the franchise; and (*c*) the franchise company,

in which a company sells a product, service, or system in exchange for an initial predetermined fee and an ongoing royalty.

3. Franchising offers the following advantages over the other two methods of starting a small business: a proven market, services such as selection of location, purchase or construction of the site, financing, standardized methods of operating, advertising, volume purchasing, and training. The potential disadvantages of franchising are lack of independence, cost of the franchise, unfulfilled promises, restrictions of the contract, saturation of the market, lack of security, cost of merchandise, and possible exaggeration of financial success.

4. Several key areas should be examined in evaluating a franchise. Information can be obtained from several sources, including the Association of Canadian Franchisors, professionals such as lawyers and accountants, other franchisees, and government agencies.

5. Becoming a successful franchisor entails five steps. The first step is to develop a franchise prototype to iron out any difficulties. The second is to prepare the necessary information for the prospective franchisee. The third is to investigate the legal requirements in setting up a franchise company. The fourth is to plan and standardize the program of operation to facilitate the monitoring of operations. The last step is to ensure that adequate financing is available to keep up with possible rapid expansion.

Chapter Problems and Applications

1. Contact a franchisor and obtain information about becoming a franchisee. Using the procedures discussed in this chapter, evaluate the attractiveness of this opportunity.

2. What possible benefits did Minute Muffler (Incident 6–6) realize in franchising its shops instead of expanding through chain stores?

3. Discuss in detail the steps you would follow in developing a maid cleaning franchise system.

4. Visit a local franchise in your city and ask the manager what he or she thinks are the advantages and disadvantages of franchising.

5. Using the same franchise as in question 4, gather information from government agencies and other sources about that franchise. From your collected information and the results of question 4, would you invest in a franchise of this company? Justify your answer.

APPENDIX A
A SAMPLING OF CANADIAN FRANCHISORS

Franchisor	Number of Units Owned	Total Units in Operation in Canada	Initial Fee	Royalty	Approximate Investment Required (cash and liquid assets)
Bonanza	—	51	$40,000	4.8%	$350–400,000
Budget Rent A Car	—	375	$15,000	10	Varies
Century 21 Real Estate	—	425	$20,000	6	$60–70,000
College Pro Painters	—	2%	—	10	$2,500
Dairy Queen of Canada	—	406	$30,000	4	$600–1,100,000
Magicuts	18	149	$18,000	7 (1.5 adv)	$60,000
McDonald's Restaurants	236	230	$250,000	9 (16 adv)	$650,000+
Midas Muffler	35	184	$25,000	5	$225,000
Ramada Inns	40	590	$35,000	3	Varies
Second Cup	3	147	$20,000	9	$175–225,000
Tim Horton	—	420	$15,000	3 (adv)	$230,000
Zippy Print	10	80	$40,000	5	$135,000

SOURCES: *Franchise Annual,* 1990; *Canadian Franchise Association,* St. Catharines, Ontario.

APPENDIX B
TRADE ASSOCIATIONS THAT ASSIST FRANCHISORS AND FRANCHISEES

Canadian Franchise Association
595 Bay Street, Suite 1050
Toronto, Ont., M5G 2C2
(416) 625–2896

International Franchise Association (IFA)
1350 New York Avenue
#900 Washington, D.C. 20005

International Franchise Opportunities
11 Bond Street
St. Catharines, Ont., L2R 4Z4
(416) 648–2923

Retail Council of Canada
Franchise Division
214 King Street West, Suite 212
Toronto, Ont., M5H 1K4
(416) 598–4684

Ontario Ministry of Consumer and
Commercial Relations
Investigation and Enforcement Branch
555 Yonge Street
Toronto, Ont., M7A 2H6
(416) 963–0302

APPENDIX C
A CHECKLIST FOR THE POTENTIAL FRANCHISEE: QUESTIONS TO ANSWER AFFIRMATIVELY BEFORE GOING INTO FRANCHISING

	Check if Answer Is Yes
The Franchisor	
1. Has the franchisor been in business long enough (five years or more) to have established a good reputation?	_____
2. Have you checked better business bureaus, chambers of commerce, government agencies, Association of Canadian Franchisors, industry associations, or bankers to find out about the franchisor's business reputation and credit rating?	_____
3. Did the above investigations reveal that the franchisor has a good reputation and credit rating?	_____
4. Does the franchising firm appear to be financed adequately so that it can carry out its stated plan of financial assistance and expansion?	_____
5. Have you found out how many franchisees are now operating?	_____
6. Have you found out the "mortality" or failure rate among franchisees?	_____
7. Is the failure rate low?	_____
8. Have you checked with some franchisees and found that the franchisor has a reputation for honesty and fair dealings among current franchisees?	_____
9. Has the franchsior shown you certified figures indicating exact net profits of one or more going operations that you have checked yourself?	_____
10. Has the franchisor given you a specimen contract to study with the advice of your legal counsel?	_____
11. Will the franchisor assist you with	
a. A management training program?	_____
b. An employee training program?	_____
c. A public relations program?	_____
d. Obtaining capital?	_____
e. Good credit terms?	_____
f. Merchandising ideas?	_____
g. Designing store layout and displays?	_____
h. Inventory control methods?	_____
i. Analyzing financial statements?	_____
12. Does the franchisor provide continuing assistance for franchisees through supervisors who visit regularly?	_____
13. Does the franchising firm have experienced and highly trained management?	_____
14. Will the franchisor assist you in finding a good location for your business?	_____
15 Has the franchising company investigated you carefully enough to assure itself that you can successfully operate one of its franchises at a profit both to it and to you?	_____
16. Have you determined exactly what the franchisor can do for you that you cannot do for yourself?	_____

SOURCE: Adapted from Wendell O. Metcalf, "Starting and Managing a Small Business of Your Own," *The Starting and Managing Series,* vol. 1, 3rd ed. (Washington D.C.: Small Business Administration, 1973), pp. 50–55.

Check if
Answer Is
Yes

The Product or Service

17. Has the product or service been on the market long enough to gain broad consumer acceptance? _____
18. Is it priced competitively? _____
19. Is it the type of item or service the same consumer customarily buys more than once? _____
20. Is it an all-year seller in contrast to a seasonal one? _____
21. Is it a staple item in contrast to a fad? _____
22. Does it sell well elsewhere? _____
23. Would you buy it on its merits? _____
24. Will it be in greater demand five years from now? _____
25. If it is a product rather than a service
    a. Is it packaged attractively? _____
    b. Does it stand up well in use? _____
    c. Is it easy and safe to use? _____
    d. Is it patented? _____
    e. Does it comply with all applicable laws? _____
    f. Is it manufactured under certain quality standards? _____
    g. Do these standards compare favorable with similar products on the market? _____
    h. If the product must be purchased exclusively from the franchisor or a designated supplier, are the prices for you, as the franchisee, competitive? _____

The Franchise Contract

26. Does the franchisee fee seem reasonable? _____
27. Do continuing royalties or percent of sales payment appear reasonable? _____
28. Is the total cash investment required and the items for financing the balance satisfactory? _____
29. Does the cash investment include payment for fixtures and equipment? _____
30. If you will be required to participate in company-sponsored promotion and publicity by contributing to an advertising fund, will you have the right to veto any increase in contributions to the fund? _____
31. If the parent company's product or service is protected by patent or liability insurance, is the same protection extended to you? _____
32. Are you free to buy the amount of merchandise you believe you need rather than required to purchase a certain amount? _____
33. Can you, as the franchisee, return merchandise for credit? _____
34. Can you engage in other business activities? _____
35. If there is an annual sales quota, can you retain your franchise if its not met? _____
36. Does the contract give you an exclusive territory for the length of the franchise? _____
37. Is your territory protected? _____
38. Is the franchise agreement renewable? _____
39. Can you terminate your agreement if you are not happy for some reason? _____
40. Is the franchisor prohibited from selling the franchise out from under you? _____
41. Can you sell the business to whomever you please? _____
42. If you sell your franchise, will you be compensated for the goodwill you have built into the business? _____
43. Does the contract obligate the franchisor to give you continuing assistance after you are operating the business? _____
44. Are you permitted a choice in determining whether you will sell any new product or service introduced by the franchisor after you have opened your business? _____

	Check if Answer Is Yes

The Franchise Contract *(continued)*

45. Is there anything with respect to the franchise or its operation that would make you ineligible for special financial assistance or other benefits accorded to small business concerns by federal, provincial, or local governments? _____

46. Did your lawyer approve the franchise contract after studying it paragraph by paragraph? _____

47. Is the contract free and clear of requirements that would call on you to take any steps that your lawyer thinks are unwise or illegal in your province, county, or city? _____

48. Does the contract cover all aspect of your agreement with the franchisor? _____

49. Does it really benefit both of you and the franchisor? _____

Your Market

50. Are the territorial boundaries of your market completely, accurately, and understandably defined? _____

51. Have you made any study to determine whether the product or service you propose to sell has a market in your territory at the prices you will have to charge? _____

52. Does the territory provide adequate sales potential? _____

53. Will the population in your territory increase over the next five years? _____

54. Will the average per capital income in your territory remain the same or increase over the next five years? _____

55. Is the existing competition in your territory for the product or service not too well entrenched? _____

56. Are you prepared to give up some independence of action to secure the advantages offered by the franchise? _____

57. Are you capable of accepting supervision, even though you will presumably be your own boss? _____

58. Are you prepared to accept rules and regulations with which you may not agree? _____

59. Can you afford the period of training involved? _____

60. Are you ready to spend much or all of the remainder of your business life with this franchisor, offering this product or service to the public? _____

APPENDIX D
FRANCHISE CONTRACT CLAUSES

The following are individual clauses commonly found in franchise agreements. The clauses are listed in the order in which they are most frequently found in a franchise agreement.

1. Term and Renewal
2. Site Selection
3. Franchisor Approval of Lease
4. Exclusive Territory
5. Trademark Restriction
6. Training by Franchisor
7. Franchisor Help with Operating
8. Operating Manual
9. Advertising by Franchisor
10. Advertising by Franchisee
11. Advertising, Control of
12. Royalty
13. Franchisor—Right to Inspect
14. Standard of Cleanliness
15. Standard of Operations
16. Franchisor—Right to Audit
17. Noncompetition
18. Confidential Information
19. Permitted Incorporation
20. Termination by Franchisor
21. Termination by Franchisee
22. Right of First Refusal
23. Sale Approval by Franchisor
24. Sale of Equipment to Franchisor

Suggested Readings

Brahim, A. Bakr. "Is Franchising the Answer to Small Business Failure Rate? An Empirical Study." *Journal of Small Business and Entrepreneurship* 3 (Fall 1985), pp. 48–54.

Franchise Annual. St. Catharines, Ontario: Canadian Franchise Association, 1988.

Franchise Directory. *Entrepreneur,* annual.

Franchise Financing. Toronto: Canadian Imperial Bank of Commerce. Useful information on financing a franchise.

Franchising in the Canadian Economy, 1990–1992. Toronto: Canadian Franchise Association and Price Waterhouse, 1992.

Gray, Douglas A. and Diana L. Gray. *The Complete Canadian Small Business Guide.* Toronto: McGraw-Hill Ryerson, 1988, chap. 7.

Jones, Constance, and the Philip Lief Group Inc. *The 220 Best Franchises to Buy.* New York: Bantam Books, 1987.

Knight, Russell M. "Franchising from the Franchisor and Franchisee's Point of View." *Journal of Small Business Management,* July 1986, p. 8.

"The Franchise 100—A Special Report on How Fast Growth Franchisors Add Units at Breath-Taking Pace." *Venture Magazine,* November, 1986, pp. 52–57.

Weinrauch, I. Donald. "Franchising an Established Business." *Journal of Small Business Management,* July 1986, p. 1.

Zaid, Frank, and Jerry White. *The Canadian Franchise Guide.* Toronto: Richard De Boo Publishers, 1986.

COMPREHENSIVE CASE
THE FRAMEMAKERS: PART 3

Robert and Teresa Norman immediately went to work organizing their new business. Robert had contemplated signing a franchise contract with U-Frame-It, but decided against it when he found out he would have to pay a $20,000 franchise fee just for the name and set-up assistance.

Robert's college training had taught him the importance of drawing up a business plan, so he prepared the following outline for their business:

- *Target market.* Robert thought the new store should cater to the price-conscious individual who wanted to save a few dollars by doing his or her own framing. What he had learned about the do-it-yourself market seemed particularly suitable for the new business.

- *Financial.* Based on data from the U-Frame-It franchise, Robert estimated start-up costs to be about $20,000. Since they were planning to lease space for the store, the capital requirements included only the purchase of shelves, fixtures, initial inventory, and tools. Because he and Teresa had $5,000 in equity to put into the venture, Robert expected to be able to borrow the remaining $15,000 from a local bank.

- *Personnel.* Robert and Teresa were hesitant to hire any employees until they were sure the business would be successful. In addition, they wanted to be totally involved in the business to better learn about all aspects of framing. The two would work full time, each doing whatever needed to be done.

- *Regulations.* Robert knew The Framemakers would need a business license, which they would obtain from the city hall. They would operate the business as a proprietorship until the need to incorporate became evident.

- *Layout.* After looking at the U-Frame-It shop in Winnipeg, Robert drew up an interior layout plan he believed allowed efficiency and convenience for the store.

- *Location.* Although there weren't many available locations in Brandon, Robert recognized the need to locate in a high-traffic area of the city. This would not only be convenient for regular customers but hopefully would attract some walk-in customers as well.

After developing this business plan, Robert began making contacts to get the business going. Within the next month, Robert was busy negotiating with suppliers, landlords, his banker, and the city hall to get the business started as soon as possible.

One particularly troublesome decision was the location. Brandon had three available locations, all in high-traffic areas of the city. The first was an older downtown outlet leasing for $500 per month; the second was space along a major artery into Brandon that rented for $600 per month; the third was in a small mall on the south side of the city and cost $550 per month. Although Robert and Teresa were partial to the mall location because it was closer to their home south of Brandon, they chose the space on the major artery on the advice of a friend who operated a business in the city. He had indicated that the most expensive space was usually the best because of the level of customer traffic.

Questions

1. From the information provided, evaluate the business plan Robert has prepared for his new business.
2. Weigh the relevant pros and cons for the Normans of operating a U-Frame-It franchise instead of starting their business from scratch.
3. What factors should the Normans have considered in selecting the location for The Framemakers? Did they make the right choice?

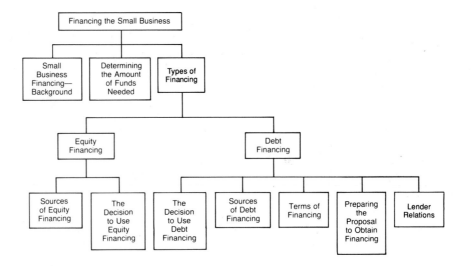

Financing the Small Business

Chapter Objectives

- To discuss the importance of outside funds to a small business.
- To illustrate a method for determining the amount of capital required.
- To identify the sources of equity and debt funds available to start and operate a small business.
- To explain the considerations in obtaining equity or debt financing.
- To discuss how to prepare a proposal to obtain financing for the small business.

Small Business Profile

Jim Brickman

Brick Brewing Company

J im Brickman is an entrepreneur who has successfully carved out a market niche in an industry dominated by large companies: the brewing industry. Although Brickman graduated from university with a degree in English, his early work experience was in advertising and marketing. During this time, he set up his own premium incentive business and learned about the marketing practices of many of his clients. One clearly emerging trend was consumers' need for quality and specialization, and Brickman wondered if such a concept would work in the brewing industry. He commissioned market research to test the concept of a small, regional, specialized brewery. When the response turned out to be positive, he began planning his business, to be located in Waterloo, Ontario.

Although the concept was sound and Brickman had the management capability, he had a very difficult time obtaining the financing to get the venture off the ground. The capital investment was large, and lenders were sceptical about the small brewery's ability to compete with the large brewers. Brickman was turned down by several banks before the venture capital division of one bank decided to invest in the business. He also received assistance from the Ontario Development Corporation. One reason for his ultimate success in obtaining financing was the quality of the proposal he prepared. He enlisted the services of an accountant to prepare a detailed and financially sound package for the financiers' evaluation.

Once Brickman overcame the hurdle of obtaining financing, Brick Brewing Company was established and enjoyed great success. Brick went public in December 1986, raising $1.8 million on the Toronto Stock Exchange. By 1991 sales topped $6 million. Brick Brewing sells everything it makes and is restricted only by the production capacity of the plant.

Used with the permission of Jim Brickman.

Incident 7–1

Consumers Hang Up on SUZY's Online Database

"My vision has always been to produce software that makes complex tasks easy," said Adrian Robson, founder of both companies (Bedford Software Ltd. and Stratford Software Corp.), in Stratford's 1989 annual report. Just as Bedford had given entrepreneurs financial control of their companies, Robson believed Stratford's online information services would help PC users run businesses, manage investments and communicate with each other.

Stratford's computerized information retrieval system, called SUZY, did deliver easy access to online information—but not to the masses Stratford envisioned. Initially, SUZY had everything going for it. Bedford programmers had worked on the product for a year prior to Stratford's debut, and Stratford started up with $2 million. But technical tie-ups kept SUZY off the market until April, 1990—six months late. By that time most of the money earmarked for marketing the new product had been spent.

Stratford's efforts to find equity financing were unsuccessful. By Nov. 30, 1990, Stratford recorded a six-month loss of $341,000. Management slashed staff from 15 to five, and replaced president Alex Morton with Thompson Mckie, a founding investor in both Bedford and Stratford. Mckie told a computer industry magazine last October that "undercapitalization was our downfall. . . . If we'd had the funds, we could have provided a greater number of features to make it more interesting and keep people on the system."

"The market was clearly there," adds Robson. "But every single database that gets put up probably has six months of R&D associated with programming it." With more funds, he says, Stratford could have hung on longer until it could reach break-even. "It's the difficulty of raising funds for startup high-tech companies that is a problem."

Source: Diane Lucklow, "Consumers Hang Up on SUZY's Online Database," *Profit Magazine,* March 1992, pp. 16–17.

Small Business Financing

The inability to obtain adequate funding has often been cited as a major small business frustration, if not a primary cause of some small business failures. Incident 7–1 illustrates the difficulties one entrepreneur encountered in obtaining financing to establish his software business.

Although many small businesses have experienced difficulties due to their inability to obtain needed funds, statistics show that financing woes are often a symptom of other management problems.[1] Lack of managerial competence and experience can often result in the following specific financial problems:

- Underestimating financial requirements
- Lack of knowledge of sources of equity and debt capital, leading to either an inability to obtain funds or the failure to obtain them at the lowest cost
- Lack of skills in preparing and presenting a proposal for financing to a lender or investor
- Failure to plan in advance for future needs, resulting in last-minute financial crises
- Poor financial control of operations, leading to failure in payment of loan obligations

This chapter will discuss each of these important areas to assist the entrepreneur in obtaining financing for establishing his or her business.

Determining the Amount of Funds Needed

The first step in securing capital (funds) for the business is to determine the amount of money needed. Any lender or investor will want to see evidence of a systematic and thoroughly prepared statement of fund requirements. In this regard, it is helpful to divide required funding into two categories: start-up costs and ongoing operating requirements. The entrepreneur's own funds available for the venture can then be subtracted from the projected required amounts to obtain the capital needed from outside sources, as shown in the following formula:

$$\text{Capital requirements} = \text{Start-up costs} + \text{Operating requirements} \\ - \text{Owner funds available for investment}$$

Start-Up Costs

Capital will be required to finance land, buildings, equipment, and other items needed to start up the business. The owner should obtain and verify quotes from sellers of these assets with owners of existing similar businesses. A contingency factor for potential price increases during the planning and start-up phase should be added.

Start-up capital will also be required to finance some of the operating costs during this period. Usually a delay in sales revenues occurs for a start-up business, but many operating expenses are incurred before the business begins operating. The entrepreneur will need to make estimates of these types of expenses and should include them in the capital requirements. Following are costs that often fit into this category:

- Initial inventory
- First few months' payroll, including owner's salary

FIGURE 7–1   Start-Up Cost Schedule

Item	Cost	Source
Land and buildings	No cost—leased	If purchased, a similar business or quotes from suppliers
Equipment	$ 34,000	Other similar businesses or quotes from suppliers
Initial inventory	70,000	Other similar businesses or quotes from suppliers
		Use the formula Inventory = Projected sales/Inventory turnover (300,000/4.3)
Wages (first 2 months)	6,000	Other similar businesses or current wage rates
Utilities and telephone		
First deposit	100	Quotes from provider
First 2 months	680	Quotes from provider
Rent (deposit)	500	Quotes from lessor
First 2 months	3,000	Quotes from lessor
Advertising agency or media	960	Quotes from advertising agency or media
Insurance (prepaid)	975	Quotes from insurer
Licences and permits	200	Quotes from municipal agency
Other prepaids	285	Other similar businesses
Total start-up requirements	**$116,700**	

- First few months' utilities
- First few months' rent
- Initial advertising
- Prepaid items such as utility deposits, rent deposits, and insurance
- Licenses and permits
- Any other operating costs that need to be paid before revenues are generated

Start-up costs may be difficult to project. Figure 7–1 illustrates a start-up cost projection. Note the sources of information used to prepare this statement.

Ongoing Operating Costs

The entrepreneur should prepare a cash flow statement to calculate financial operating requirements after the start-up period. A *cash flow statement,* explained in more detail in Chapter 9, is simply a record of all projected cash inflows and outflows. An example of such a statement appears in Figure 7–2. In this monthly cash flow for a hypothetical business, it has been calculated that up to $65,285 may be needed to finance operations. This occurs in the first month. If debt financing were used, the entrepreneur would most likely attempt to arrange a $66,000 line of credit (operating loan), with a lender to cover this amount when

FIGURE 7-2   **Sample Cash Flow Statement**

	Feb.	March	April	May	June
Opening balance	$ 0	$(65,285)	$(48,595)	$(31,905)	$(55,173)
Bank loan	35,000	0	0	0	0
Sales:					
Cash	12,000	12,000	12,000	13,750	13,750
Credit	0	12,000	12,000	12,000	13,750
Total receipts	$ 47,000	$(41,285)	$(24,595)	$ (6,155)	$(27,673)
Disbursements					
Furniture and					
fixtures	$ 34,000	0	0	0	0
Rent	1,500	$ 1,500	$ 1,500	$ 1,500	$ 1,500
Utilities	200	200	200	200	200
Promotion					
(2% of sales)	480	480	480	550	550
Telephone	140	140	140	140	140
Wages and salaries	3,000	3,000	3,000	3,000	3,000
Inventory	70,000	0	0	41,820	0
Maintenance and					
repairs	240	240	240	270	270
Professional fees	330	330	330	330	330
Insurance	975	0	0	0	0
Interest and					
bank charges	1,420	1,420	1,420	1,208	1,208
Loan repayment	0	0	0	0	0
Total disbursements	$112,285	$ 7,310	$ 7,310	$ 49,018	$ 7,198
Cash (+/−)	$ (65,285)	$(48,595)	$(31,905)	$(55,173)	$(34,871)

Note: 50% of monthly sales are cash and 50% are credit. The credit sales are collected in the next month.

required. Such a method of financing would allow the business to withdraw and deposit funds on an ongoing basis as long as the total amount withdrawn at any point in time did not exceed $66,000.

The Owner's Net Worth

After estimating start-up and operating capital requirements, the owner should prepare a personal net worth and capability statement. Preparing this statement not only will help determine the amount of the owner's funds to invest in the business but will probably be required by a lending institution if the owner needs to borrow the necessary capital. The essentials of the personal net worth statement are the same as those for a business's balance sheet. An example of a net worth statement appears in Figure 7-3.

FIGURE 7–2 (concluded)

July	Aug.	Sept.	Oct.	Nov.	Dec.	Jan.
$(34,871)	$(14,569)	$(36,839)	$(17,289)	$ 2,261	$(19,811)	$ 1,967
0	0	0	0	0	0	0
13,750	13,750	13,750	13,750	14,250	14,250	14,250
13,750	13,750	13,750	13,750	13,750	14,250	14,250
$ (7,371)	$ 12,931	$ (9,339)	$ 10,211	$ 30,261	$ 8,689	$ 30,467
0	0	0	0	0	0	0
$ 1,500	$ 1,500	$ 1,500	$ 1,500	$ 1,500	$ 1,500	$ 1,500
200	200	200	200	200	200	200
550	550	550	550	570	570	570
140	140	140	140	140	140	140
3,000	3,000	3,000	3,000	3,000	3,000	3,000
0	41,820	0	0	43,350	0	0
270	270	270	270	270	270	290
330	330	330	330	330	330	330
0	0	0	0	0	0	0
1,208	1,960	1,960	1,960	712	712	712
0	0	0	0	0	0	35,000
$ 7,198	$ 49,770	$ 7,950	$ 7,950	$ 50,072	$ 6,722	$ 41,742
$(14,569)	$(36,839)	$(17,289)	$ 2,261	$(19,811)	$ 1,967	$(11,275)

Determining Types of Financing

Two general sources of funds can be used to finance a small business. The first is *equity* or *ownership financing*. The second is funds obtained from borrowing, usually referred to as *debt financing* (including trade credit). Many small businesses use both forms of financing to get established. A recent study of entrepreneur start-ups found that 35 percent obtained debt financing from a lending institution, 18 percent from family members, 7 percent from external investors, 6 percent from retail companies, 5 percent from friends, and 5 percent from government agencies.[2] This section discusses each of these types of financing.

Equity Financing

Equity financing involves giving up ownership of the business in return for capital. The three sources of equity financing are private investors, corporate investors, and government.

FIGURE 7–3 **Suggested Format for a Personal Net Worth Statement**

Personal Net Worth Statement For: _____

As of _____, 19___.

Assets		Liabilities	
Cash on hand and in banks	$ _____	Accounts payable	$ _____
Savings account in banks	_____	Notes payable to banks	_____
Canada savings bonds	_____		
Accounts and notes receivable	_____	Notes payable to others	_____
Life insurance—cash surrender value only	_____		
Other stocks and bonds	_____	Installment account (auto)	_____
		Monthly payments $ _____	_____
Real estate	_____	Installment accounts (other)	_____
		Monthly payments $ _____	_____
Automobile—present value	_____	Loans on life insurance	_____
Other personal property	_____	Mortgages on real estate	_____
Other assets	_____	Unpaid taxes	_____
		Other liabilities	_____
		Total liabilities	_____
		Net worth	_____
Total	$ _____	Total	$ _____

Private Investors.   This source includes funds from friends, relatives, or private investors in exchange for shares in an incorporated company or for a percentage of ownership in a sole proprietorship. It is especially critical from an investor's point of view that there be a clear understanding of conditions, authority, and responsibilities of all the investors under such an arrangement. The investor's degree of involvement can vary greatly. Some investors expect only a reasonable return on their investment, while others expect to be full operating partners in the business in addition to receiving a return on their capital.

An increasingly popular form of private financing is the selling of ownership interest to the employees of the business. Many companies have found that in addition to providing a source of funds, this method of financing results in dramatic increases in productivity. Incident 7–2 illustrates such a situation.

Another form of private equity investment is the sale of shares in the business to anyone who is interested. This is known as *going public,* wherein shares in the company are sold on a public stock exchange. This form of financing was discussed in detail in Chapter 4. Generally, small businesses are not large enough to seek public equity for the business start-up.

Corporate Investors.   Many companies are interested in investing in a small business in the hope that the value of their investment will increase over time. Often they then sell their ownership interest back to the original owners when the owners are in a better position to finance the business independently.

Incident 7-2

Need Cash? Why Not Ask Your Employees?

There's been a flurry of renewed interest lately in profit-sharing plans for small businesses. For the employer, it's a means of encouraging increased productivity; for the employee, the lure is the scent of ownership. But surprisingly, little attention has been paid to a tax-effective profit-sharing strategy that has been available in some parts of the country for a number of years. The strategy involves having employees set up small business development corporations (SBDCs) in Ontario, or their counterparts in other provinces.

Take, for example, a small Ontario manufacturer so laden with debt that it can't get further credit and, therefore, is unable to fill incoming orders. In an attempt to save what is fundamentally a sound business from going under and, at the same time, get a piece of the action, 15 employees put up $10,000 apiece to form an SBDC. The SBDC invests the $150,000 in the company and receives, in return, 20 percent of the company's common shares. Under existing rules, the employees collect a tax-free grant of $45,000 (30 percent of $150,000) from the provincial government. They may then reinvest the $45,000 in the company via their SBDC, thereby triggering a further government grant of $13,500. Or they could distribute the $45,000 among themselves, reducing their net investment to $7,000 per person.

As part owners in the business, if the business prospers, the employees share in the rewards. The lure of entrepreneurship, the prospect of investment income, and the hope of safeguarding their jobs while contributing their expertise to a business they partly own add up to a powerful incentive. Meanwhile the business acquires not only capital and the capacity to grow, but also the assurance that its shareholder-employees will do their utmost to help it succeed. It's one of those rare situations where, barring an unexpected disaster, everyone ends up a winner.

Source: Ralph Selby, "Need Cash? Why Not Ask Your Employees?" *Canadian Business,* April 1984, pp. 128–29.

Companies whose major activity is investing in smaller and medium-size businesses are called *venture capital companies.* These companies use highly sophisticated evaluation techniques and accept only a small percentage of applications.[3] A venture capital company typically looks for a business within a growth industry, with sound management and the potential for a return on investment of between 20 and 40 percent.

In 1991, the 125 members of the Association of Canadian Venture Capital Companies invested some $268 million in 210 small businesses in Canada. The majority of the investments fell within the $200,000–$1,000,000 range.[4] For businesses that require smaller amounts of money, private investors (sometimes

Incident 7–3

Coaxing Financiers into the High-Tech Circuit

Early-stage funding is scarce for any business. Add technology to the equation and most investors run the other way. According to Venture Economics Canada Ltd. of Toronto, technology-based companies copped only 25% of the $343 million invested in venture capital in 1989, compared to 47% in 1985.

Ironically, the venture-capital industry owes its start to the sector on which it's now turning its back. A spate of U.S. high-tech successes in the early 1980s—such as software giant Microsoft Corp. and computer-maker Compaq Computer Corp.—prompted Canadian investors to seek similar returns at home. Bankers left their posts, says Venture Economics' product manager Pat McGrath, and began backing high-tech firms. But most of these investors didn't understand the technology they were backing and made mistakes—like funding companies without a real lead in their field.

These errors translated into losses. Within three years, comparisons revealed non-tech investments like mining and food services were outperforming high-tech deals. Five years ago, 35 venture-capital firms were funding high technology; today, there are 19.

Clearly, when high-tech entrepreneurs outnumber investors willing to back them, the investors can be choosy. You need to show that you can provide the returns they seek—at least 30% per annum over three to five years for high-risk investments. But the Canadian market alone will rarely provide these returns. The answer is to sell internationally—but it takes a good concept—and perseverance.

Source: Cathy Hilborn, "Coaxing Financiers into the High-Tech Circuit," *Profit Magazine*, March 1991, p. 42.

referred to as "angels") may be helpful. The small business profile in Chapter 3 illustrates Grieg Clark's attempt to meet this niche for small business financing. "Angels" are thought to invest some $1 billion per year in small businesses.[5] An entrepreneur seeking venture capital assistance should be aware of the areas of the business to which investors will pay specific attention. Normally such factors as the abilities and expertise of the management team, the level of development of the product or service, and industry trends are key elements in this evaluation.[6] Incident 7–3 illustrates some of the difficulties in obtaining venture capital.

Government. Traditionally the government has hesitated to provide equity funding to small businesses. However, programs have been developed in recent years that permit government funding and incentives for venture capital firms or allow for direct equity investment by the government in the business. Some of these programs and agencies are described next.

Federal Business Development Bank (FBDB).   As part of the New Mandate announced in 1983, the FBDB will participate with other investors as a principal in the provision of investment capital in businesses it views as promising. Generally the purpose of such financing is to provide an adequate equity base for the firm to receive funding from additional sources.

Canada Development Corporation (CDC).   CDC is a crown corporation set up by the federal government to act as a venture capital company. This agency, however, provides funds primarily for larger businesses and large-scale projects.

Provincial Programs.   Provincial governments have provided tax and rebate incentives for the formation of small business investment companies, which function similarly to venture capital companies. Examples of such companies were shown in Incidents 7–1 and 7–3. A brief listing of current provincial government equity capital programs appears in Appendix A at the end of this chapter.

Advantages and Disadvantages of Equity Financing.   Before proceeding to obtain equity capital, the entrepreneur should be familiar with the advantages and disadvantages of equity financing versus debt financing.

Equity financing offers the following advantages:

1. There is no obligation to pay dividends or interest. This flexibility allows the firm to invest earnings back into the business in its early years, when these funds are usually needed most.
2. Often the original owner benefits from the expertise the investor brings to the business in addition to the financial assistance.
3. Equity capital expands the borrowing power of the business. Most lenders require a certain percentage of equity investment by the owners before they will provide debt financing. Thus, the more equity a business has, the greater its ability to obtain debt financing.
4. Equity financing spreads the risk of failure of the business to others.

Disadvantages of equity financing include the following:

1. Equity financing dilutes the ownership interest of the original owner and leads to decreased independence. Because of this drawback, many owner-managers are hesitant to follow this route in obtaining capital.
2. With others sharing the ownership interest, the possibility of disagreement and lack of coordination in the operations of the business increases.
3. A legal cost may be associated with issuance of the ownership interest.

Debt Financing

Few small businesses are able to get established and continue operations without some sort of debt financing. About 30 percent of the $70 billion loaned to business

Incident 7–4

Rentown's Empire Crumbles under Demand-Debt Pressures

Gordon Reykdal built his business on easy credit. As president and co-founder of Edmonton-based Rentown Enterprises Inc., Reykdal's rent-to-own programs put big-ticket electronics items like TVs and stereos in the hands of those with big dreams, but limited means. Terms were easy, says Reykdal, and the company never did extensive credit checks.

But Reykdal no longer heads Rentown. Lured by the same easy credit that attracted its customers, the firm took on $29 million in debt to finance expansion. Its cross-country run ended in November, 1990, when Chicago-based Transamerica Commercial Finance Corp. called a $25-million demand loan. Two months later, it called the receiver.

Reykdal says Transamerica cited "a material adverse change in (Rentown's) financial position" when it called its loan in November. But he accuses Transamerica of financing the expansion with the intention of seizing control. Two of Rentown's minor shareholders, investment managers AGF Management Ltd. of Toronto and Montreal-based International Bankers Ltd., launched a lawsuit in February, alleging Transamerica backed Rentown until it consolidated the Canadian industry, and then stepped in itself.

Murray Sinclair, a former Rentown director and vice-president of Vancouver venture-capitalist Noramco Capital Corp., an early investor in Rentown, says the financing was poorly handled. "They used borrowed funds for capital expenditures, for leasehold improvements, for salaries, for advertising." There's no rate of return on that expenditure, says Sinclair. And the form of debt left Rentown vulnerable: "When you finance with just demand debt, you are asking for trouble."

Source: Mark Stevenson, "Rentown's Empire Crumbles under Demand-Debt Pressures," *Profit Magazine,* July-August 1991, p. 23.

---

in Canada is held by small businesses.[7] A national survey found that 85 percent of small and medium-size businesess used a bank for financial support, 75 percent have lines of credit, and 50 percent have loans.[8] Because of the high possibility that debt financing will be required, it is essential that the entrepreneur be aware of the advantages and dangers of using it. It is also important that he or she understand the sources of debt capital and the characteristics and requirements of various financial lenders. Incident 7–4 illustrates the consequences of poor debt management.

Advantages and Disadvantages of Debt Financing.   Some of the positive benefits of using debt are as follows:

1. It is possible to obtain a higher return on investment by using debt. If borrowed funds earn a higher return than the associated interest cost, it

------

FIGURE 7–4   Debt Financing and Return on Investment

Basic information:

  Amount to invest = $10,000

  Interest rate = 16%

  Investment cost = $10,000

  Estimated return per year = $2,500

Calculation of percentage return after one year

  1. If no debt was used:

$$\frac{\text{Return}}{\text{Investment}} = \frac{\$2,500}{\$10,000} = 25\% \text{ return}$$

  2. If debt was used (assuming only $2,000 was invested, $8,000 was borrowed to purchase the investment, and the interest on $8,000 is $1,280):

$$\frac{\text{Return}}{\text{Investment}} = \frac{(\$2,500 - 1,280)}{\$2,000} = \frac{\$1,220}{\$2,000} = 61\% \text{ return}$$

Note: The potential investment income that could be earned on the $8,000 not invested in the project could be added to this amount.

------

is possible to increase the overall return on investment for the business through debt financing. Figure 7–4 illustrates this concept. The $10,000 investment could be any productive asset or change in the business.

2. Interest costs in a business are tax-deductible expenses (assuming a profit is being made), whereas dividends paid as a result of equity ownership are not tax deductible.

3. Debt financing may allow greater flexibility in that there is no loss of ownership control.

4. Many small businesses have found it is often easier to obtain debt capital than equity capital.

Some of the potential negative aspects of debt financing are as follows:

1. Interest must be paid on borrowed money. Interest costs can be high, and high interest expenses are a common problem in many failing businesses. During the period from 1975 to 1985, interest rates in Canada were extremely high. This caused serious hardship to many small businesses, and the inability to pay interest costs resulted in the foreclosure and/or bankruptcy of many businesses.

2. Debt financing creates additional paperwork requirements for the entrepreneur, and the lender may monitor the business.

3. When using debt financing, the total risk of the venture lies squarely on the owner's shoulders. There are no other partners or shareholders to assume some of this risk.

Sources of Debt Financing.   Several sources of debt financing are available to small businesses, including private lenders, corporate lenders, private lending institutions, and government agencies.

Private Lenders.   One increasingly common source of debt capital for small business is the borrowing of funds from the owners of the business. These funds are called *shareholders' loans,* and they offer some unique advantages. A recent study by *Venture* found that 34 percent of small business owners made a start-up loan to their own businesses.[9] While the interest paid is a tax-deductible expense for the business, the repayment terms are often flexible. In addition, lenders often view shareholders' loans as equity as long as the funds are left in the company. Some believe this method combines the advantages of equity and debt financing.

Another source of private debt is borrowing from other individuals such as friends or relatives. As with shareholders' loans, it may be possible to structure flexible repayment terms.

Corporate Lenders.   In some circumstances, other companies may lend funds to a small business. Often these are larger firms that have established some connection or working relationship with the small business. One example of such funding would be the granting of trade credit by a company to a small business that purchases merchandise from that company. Most small businesses use this source of financing wherever possible. Trade credit for inventory is normally financed for 30, 60, or 90 days, with discounts for prompt payment. Equipment is usually financed for up to five years, with a 20 to 30 percent down payment required.

Another type of lender associated with accounts receivable is a factor. Factor companies purchase accounts receivable from a business at a discount. The business obtains needed cash, and the factor collects the accounts receivable. An increasing number of businesses in Canada are enlisting factoring companies to obtain short-term financing.

The sale and leaseback is another form of financing involving other businesses. In this arrangement, the business sells an asset to another company, which in turn leases it back to the seller. The advantage of the sale and leaseback is that the seller not only has the use of the funds of the sale but also benefits from the tax deductibility of the lease payments.

Regular Private Lending Institutions.   This category includes companies whose major purpose is the lending of funds. The most common of these firms are the following:

- *Trust Companies.* Trust companies are geared primarily for mortgages on long-term capital assets such as land, buildings, and equipment.
- *Credit Unions.* Credit unions are usually locally owned. They tend to be concerned primarily with personal loans, but in some communities they also provide significant financing to small businesses.
- *Finance Companies.* These are high-risk lenders that charge a higher rate of interest than other agencies. As with credit unions, the majority of their loans are personal loans.
- *Chartered Banks.* By far the largest source of small business financing is Canada's chartered banks. A recent survey of Canadian small businesses

indicated that 78 percent use bank financing.[10] At present six major Canadian chartered banks and a multitude of foreign-controlled banks operating in Canada account for nearly 80 percent of all small business lending. In many larger cities, some of these banks are even creating specialized business branches. The majority of small business loans range from $20,000 to $50,000.

Government Lenders.   Government agencies at both the federal and provincial levels lend money, provide grants, and give counselling assistance to small businesses. At the federal level, the major small business lender is the Federal Business Development Bank (FBDB). Initially government lending agencies were established to assist those small businesses unable to obtain financing from conventional sources because of high risk. In recent years, however, they have relaxed this attitude somewhat and become more similar to other lending institutions, although they still class themselves as high-risk lenders.

The potential advantages of approaching a government agency are the following:

1. The agency can finance higher-risk or lower-equity ventures, which characterize many small businesses.
2. Government lenders may be more willing to rewrite loan terms and conditions if the business gets into trouble. They also tend to be less quick to foreclose on a failing business.
3. Government agencies may provide a lower interest rate than the chartered banks. Many provincial government lenders fall into this category. FBDB rates, which are adjusted periodically, are usually similar to chartered bank rates.
4. Government lenders may provide some equity capital in the form of temporary ownership or grants, depending on the type of business and its location.
5. Government lenders may provide management counselling along with funding to assist the business.

Although the above advantages may make borrowing from government agencies attractive, there are some potential disadvantages of which the small business owner should be aware:

1. A government agency usually requires more information to review a loan application than other lending institutions do.
2. The time period required for approval of a loan tends to be a longer than with private lending institutions.
3. Most government agencies exert more monitoring and control over the businesses they lend to and often require regular reports on operations.

In addition to the government agencies established to provide both debt and equity financing, several specific federal government programs also provide

FIGURE 7–5   Matching Financing to Assets

Type of Loan	Sources	Use	Security	Loan Characteristics
Short-term (demand) loans	Banks, private sources, factoring houses, confirming houses	Receivables inventory (working capital items)	Assignment of receivables and inventory, personal guarantees, assignment of life insurance	Can be withdrawn on short notice; no fixed payment terms; interest, principal rates fluctuate
Medium-term (3–10 year) loans	Banks, term lenders, financial houses, leasing companies, foreign banks, private sources, government programs	Equipment, furnishings, vehicles, leaseholds, new business investments	Chattel mortgages, conditional sales contracts, or assignment of equipment insurance	Specific repayment terms; interest either fixed or floating with prime rate
Long-term (15–25 year) mortgages, bonds, debentures	Trust companies, foreign banks, private sources	Property, land, and buildings, new business investments	Collateral mortgages, assignment of property insurance	Fixed repayment terms; fixed interest rates

SOURCE: Geoffery Brooks, "Matching Your Financing to Your Assets," *Small Business Magazine,* September 1983, p. 38.

financial help for the small business. Appendix B at the end of this chapter briefly reviews those most helpful for the small business.

Most provinces also have various programs designed to provide financial assistance to the small business community. Appendix C at the end of the chapter reviews some of these programs.

Determining the Term of Financing

The small business owner should carefully evaluate the characteristics of the above sources of financing to ensure their suitability to the needs of the business. The length of term and type of financing required may assist in making the decision among lenders, as Figure 7–5 shows. The length of the term allowed by a lender is normally equivalent to the useful life of the asset, except in the case of land, which is often carried on a 20-year term.

An often costly mistake by some owner-managers make is to use funds obtained for long-term purposes to get them through short-term crises. Inevitably, this practice creates a more serious financial crisis a short while later. If capital requirements were underestimated, the owner should approach the lender again with this information and attempt to have the lender adjust the funds provided.

Incident 7–5

Reclino-Bath

Harold Taylor had a problem. He had withdrawn his total savings of $20,000 to purchase the mold required in the manufacture of a plastic bathtub accessory he had invented. To begin production, he needed additional funds but had been turned down by both chartered banks and government agencies. The lenders not only were unconvinced there was a market for the product but could see Taylor's lack of planning in estimating his financial requirements. They wanted him to prepare detailed information on what he needed and a projected statement of income based on objective research to estimate consumer demand for his product. Taylor didn't know where to turn. He lacked both the expertise to prepare the statements or do the research and the funds to hire an outside agency to do it.

Source: D. W. Balderson, University of Lethbridge.

Preparing a Proposal to Obtain Financing

Incident 7–5 describes an all too common situation for the small business. In attempting to obtain financing, a small business owner should be aware of those areas about which the lender requires information. In addition to completing the loan application, the owner should include the financial projections. A detailed and well-prepared loan proposal goes a long way toward ensuring the approval of a loan application.

Criteria Used in the Loan Decision

Most lenders make the loan decision by evaluating the following three criteria.

1. The Applicant's Management Ability. The lender will want to be sure the applicant has the skills, experience, and ability to make the business succeed. To evaluate the applicant's managerial ability, the lender will specifically want to know the following.

How Much the Applicant Knows about the Business. The lender will probably ask questions about the business or industry to ascertain the applicant's level of knowledge. The lender will also be interested in any previous experience the applicant has had that relates to the proposed business.

FIGURE 7–6   **Loan Proposal Format**

Program		*Financing*	
Land	$20,000	Bank loan	$60,000
Building	50,000	Own funds	20,000
Equipment	10,000	Total	$80,000
Total	$80,000		

How Much Care Was Taken in Preparing the Proposal.   The lender will want to see a detailed plan of what the loan is for, as well as a listing of the other sources of financing for the project. The steps of a business plan outlined in Chapter 4 should provide the basis for the financing proposal. Several statements will be required, and it is important that the applicant document the source of the information in those statements. The first statement is the lending proposal, which typically follows the format shown in Figure 7–6.

In addition to the lending proposal, the lender will probably want to see a proposed income and cash flow statement for at least the first year of operations, and probably longer. A balance sheet may also be required. These statements should be carefully prepared following the formats discussed in Chapters 3 and 9. As mentioned above, each item on the statement should be well researched and documented. The lender will want to know what provision has been made for the owner's salary and for potential contingencies. Often an entrepreneur is advised to enlist an accountant if he or she is weak in financial statement preparation. This and other requirements of preparing a lending proposal are discussed in Incident 7–6.

2.   The Proposal.   Obviously the lender will assess the idea or proposal itself. Using the income statement and cash flow projections, the lender will assess the chances of repayment of the loan. The lender will evaluate not only the specific business but industrial trends, including the extent of competition and the experiences of similar businesses. The lender may also check with experts in the industry. Many chartered banks now have industry specialists on staff to assist in this type of evaluation.

Some specific types of evaluation used in the lending industry are

- *Level of working capital*—the dollar difference between current assets and current liabilities. Working capital should be sufficient to meet current obligations as they become due and finance delays in revenue caused by such items as accounts receivable.
- *Current ratio*—current assets compared to current liabilities. A healthy current ratio is 2:1.
- *Quick ratio*—current assets less inventories compared to liabilities. A healthy quick ratio is 1:1.

Incident 7–6

Avoid Flash When Raising Cash

Phil Deck of Toronto investment banker Hurlow Partners Inc. goes to bat for entrepreneurs trying to raise funds. Often, he must first convince them that no investor is going to fall in love with their business the way they have. "Entrepreneurs have a difficult time putting themselves in the banker's position," Deck says. "Entrepreneurs are optimistic. They have to be. They're excited about their company; they're proud of what they've done." The trouble is, he says, "when you come right down to it, a banker's really not interested in the exciting parts of your business. To convince a potential investor, you have to persuade him he's making a sensible, rational, safe investment." And that means taking a serious approach, simply laying the straight facts on the table.

Bill McKenzie, investment officer with Edmonton-based Vencap Equities Alberta Ltd., suggests a credible introduction from an accountant or lawyer known to the investor can open the first crucial doors. Once you're in, keep it simple; a plain talking, no-frills presentation might give you an edge. "The best gimmick of all is to come with a plain, complete, precise business plan," advises Deck, "that lays out what you're going to do and how you're going to do it."

Be positive about your business plan, but not fantastic, says Bill Sharwood, Toronto financial consultant. It's a business document, not a fairy tale. You can't ignore the potential risks and problems. "Your memorandum can be facts with a flair, but the emphasis has to fall on the facts," he says. "Anything else is a snow job."

Source: Richard Wright, "Avoid Flash When Raising Cash," *Profit Magazine,* November 1991, p. 58.

- *Debt-to-equity ratio*—percentage of owner's equity compared to debt. A minimum debt-to-equity ratio is 4:1 (25 percent equity). For smaller businesses, most lenders prefer to see 50 percent equity.

Chapter 9 discusses each of these ratios in greater detail.

The lender will also want to see projections for the basic financial statements such as the balance sheet and income statement. The fundamentals of these statements are also covered in Chapter 9.

Because of the security position on the loan, the lender will want to know whether another lender is also providing funding for the project and, if so, what collateral it has taken as security for the loan. The lender will also want to ensure that the funds loaned will be secured by some form of saleable collateral. On capital assets, a lender generally allows only about 80 percent of the value of the assets as security. The reason is that if the lender needs to realize (repossess) on the security, obsolescence, selling, and administration costs will reduce its value.

Applicant's Background and Creditworthiness.   In addition to the project itself and the applicant's managerial ability, the lender will require some additional information in judging the applicant's creditworthiness.

Personal Information.   In filling out a loan application, an applicant is usually required to file information typically included in a personal résumé—items such as age, marital status, education, and work experience. (Be careful to check the legal implications of certain questions.)

Present Debt and Past Lending History.   The lender will want a list of the current state of any loans outstanding and may require information about the applicant's past loan history as well. Most lenders are members of credit bureaus that can provide a complete credit history of the applicant. Lenders will generally use this source to verify the information provided by the applicant.

Amount of Equity the Applicant Has Invested.   All lenders want to know the amount of the applicant's personal funds going into the project. Usually cash equity is required, but occasionally capital assets or even "sweat equity" may be acceptable. The amount of equity funds required will vary depending on the risk associated with the project, but as mentioned above, few lenders will provide financing if the applicant has less than 20 to 25 percent equity to invest in the business.

Will the Applicant Bank with the Lender?   Many lenders will request that the applicant's business accounts be transferred or opened with the lending bank. They may also require that a compensating balance be held in the account as collateral.

Lender Relations

Once financing has been obtained, it is important that the business provide up-to-date information to the lender regarding current operations and future plans. Regular financial statements and lease contracts can help establish trust between the banker and the owner-manager. Many businesses, such as the one discussed in Incident 7–7, have found that maintaining a close working relationship with lenders helps ensure adequate levels of financing in the long run.

What do entrepreneurs do if they have investigated both equity and debt sources and are unable to obtain the needed capital? Probably the first thing to do is find out the reasons for refusal and possibly rework the proposal to bring it more in line with the lender's requirements.

Changes may be necessary to make the proposed business more attractive to lenders and/or investors. One option that is increasingly being used to reduce the amount of funds required for capital purchases is to consider leasing or renting the asset. Leasing the asset generally does not require a down payment. The ability to obtain the lease is usually based more on the earning power of the asset

Incident 7–7

Dafoe & Dafoe

Heather Dafoe thinks their survival was due to two things. First, this was before the recession and the banks weren't as strict then. Second, they'd been meticulous about keeping the banks informed about everything they were doing. "We gave them complete year-by-year business plans and projections. We'd filed financial statements with them every month. We shared everything with them from the very beginning. I'm convinced to this day that the banks appreciated our forthright approach. It helped them to understand what we were trying to do. I really believe if you're open and honest with the banks, if you keep them informed all the time, if you give them more information than they need, that they'll stay on your side. That approach pulled us through then. To this day, we believe in full and honest disclosure in our financial dealings."

Source: Kenneth Barnes and Everett Banning, *Money Makers: The Secrets of Canada's Most Successful Entrepreneurs* (Toronto: McClelland and Stewart, 1985), p. 26.

and the business than on the background of the owner. Later, when the company is in a more stable condition, the owner may succeed in obtaining funds to make a purchase if he or she desires. Specific conditions of leases are discussed in Chapter 4.

Summary

1. Lack of managerial competence and experience can often result in such financing problems as underestimating financial requirements, lack of knowledge of sources of capital, lack of skills in preparing and presenting a proposal for financing to a lender, failure to plan in advance for future needs, and poor financial control in payment of loan obligations.

2. Start-up capital includes initial inventory, deposits, and first month's payments for payroll, utilities, rent, advertising, insurance, licenses, and permits. Accounts receivable and any other operating cost that needs to be paid before revenues are generated should also be planned for.

3. An essential step in determining the amount of capital needed is to calculate the owner's net worth. This helps determine the amount of

funds the owner(s) has to invest in the company and will probably be required by a lending institution.

4. Three general sources of equity financing are private investors, corporate investors, and government programs.

5. The advantages of equity capital over debt financing include interest obligation, expertise of the investor(s), expanded borrowing power, and spreading of risk. The disadvantages of using equity financing include dilution of ownership, increased potential of disagreements, and the cost incurred in the issuance of the ownership interest.

6. The potential advantages of debt financing over equity capital are a possible higher return on investment, deductibility of interest, flexibility, and ease of approval. The disadvantages include interest expense, additional paperwork, and lack of diversification of risk to other investors.

7. Sources of debt financing include owners of the business, corporate lenders, regular lending institutions, and government agencies.

8. Government agencies at both the federal and provincial levels lend money, provide grants, and offer counselling assistance to small businesses. These agencies are more willing to finance higher-risk businesses, may be more willing to rewrite loan terms and conditions, often provide lower interest rates, and may provide equity capital. On the other hand, government agencies usually require more information, tend to take more time to approve loans, may require more collateral, and usually exert more monitoring and control over the businesses to which they lend.

9. Criteria most lenders use in making the loan decision are the applicant's managerial ability, the proposal itself, and the applicant's background and creditworthiness.

10. If the entrepreneur cannot obtain financing, he or she should reevaluate the proposal and make any changes necessary to make the proposal more attractive to potential lenders or investors. The entrepreneur can also consider leasing instead of purchasing to reduce the amount of funds required.

Chapter Problems and Applications

1. Indicate whether each of the following is a start-up cost (S), an ongoing operating cost (O), or both (B).
   a. $1,000 for first month's rent
   b. $25,000 for store fixtures

     c. $1,000 for third month's rent

     d. Weekly cleaning fee of $250

     e. Purchase of $50,000 of inventory

     f. Payroll expense

     g. $50,000 for TV advertising

     h. Prepaid insurance

     i. Delivery expense

     j. Operating license

2. Assuming Adrian Robson's idea for Stratford Software is a good one (Incident 7–1), what could Robson have done to obtain the capital needed?

3. What are some potential drawbacks of the profit-sharing system as explained in Incident 7–2?

4. Imagine you are preparing a business plan for a small manufacturing firm in your province. Using Appendixes A and B, determine what programs are available for possible assistance. How could each program help your client's business?

5. *a.* Using Figure 7–5 as a reference, match the following list of assets to the type of financing, source, and loan characteristics needed.

    (1) Capital for building of manufacturing plant

    (2) Company car

    (3) Inventory purchase

    (4) Equipment (life expectancy two–three years)

   b. Why is it important to match financing to your assets?

6. Interview an employee at one of the government agencies that offer equity or debt financing to small businesses. Determine the purpose, the merits, and the weaknesses of that program.

7. Interview a banker to determine what he or she looks for in a loan application.

8. Using Figure 7–3, calculate your personal net worth.

APPENDIX A
PROVINCIAL EQUITY CAPITAL PROGRAMS

British Columbia

Small Business Venture Capital

Alberta

Small Business Equity Corporation

Saskatchewan

Equity financing available through SEDCO (Saskatchewan Economic Development Corporation)

Manitoba

Venture Capital Program

Ontario

Small Business Development Corporations Program
Venture Investments Corporations

Quebec

Societés de placement dans l'entreprise Quebecoise
Societés de developpement de l'entreprise Quebecoise

New Brunswick

Venture Capital Support Program

Nova Scotia

Nova Scotia Venture Corporations

Prince Edward Island

Small Business Development Corporations
Venture Capital Program

Newfoundland

Venture Capital Program

SOURCE: "Provincial Venture Capital Corporations: A Comparative Analysis," *Journal of Small Business and Entrepreneurship—Canada* 4, no. 5 (Fall 1986), p. 22.

APPENDIX B
FEDERAL GOVERNMENT ASSISTANCE PROGRAMS FOR SMALL BUSINESS

Program	Type of Assistance	Limits	Purposes	Contact Offices
Small Business Loans Act	Provides guarantees on loans for a variety of capital purposes.	No refinancing of existing debt. Annual revenues can't exceed $2 million. Interest: prime plus 1%. Maximum 10-year repayment period.	Improve and modernize equipment and buildings; purchase land.	All approved lenders

(continued)

Program	Type of Assistance	Limits	Purposes	Contact Offices
Program for Export Market Development	Shares costs of specific export marketing efforts. Encourages and assists export.	Provides up to 50% of the costs incurred by a company in penetration of new markets. Repayable if sales are made.	Specific project bidding; market identification; participation in trade fairs abroad; bringing in foreign buyers; export consortia development; sustained export market development.	I.S.T.C. regional offices
Self-Employment Incentive Program	Provides temporary grants while entrepreneurs establish business.	$200 per week.	To assist with living expenses while an entrepreneur establishes a business.	Employment and Immigration Canada
Atlantic Canada Opportunity Agency	Financial assistance for economic development and capital costs.	Varies by type of project and industry.	Improve the economic viability of businesses in Atlantic Canada and encourage entrepreneurship.	ACOA offices in Atlantic Canada
Western Economic Diversification Fund	Financial assistance through grants.	Maximum amount of assistance depends on which tier the applicant is in. Level of support depends on nature of the project, need for support, value, and government economic objectives.	Promote industrial and regional development in Western Canada.	I.S.T.C. regional offices
Industrial Research Assistance Program	Financial assistance through grants and technical assistance.	Varies according to which aspect of the program is applied for.	Increase the calibre and scope of industrial research and development through the use of available technology.	Industrial Research Assistance
Small Business Development Bank	Assistance through reduced interest rates on loans.	Eligible small business corporations that use all their assets in an active business. One-to-five-year loan. Specific time restrictions on past loans to qualify.	Relieve the financial burden of interest rates on the small businessperson.	All approved lenders

(*continued*)

Program	Type of Assistance	Limits	Purposes	Contact Offices
Technology Outreach Programs	Financial assistance.	Small businesses can access information, receive grants and loans for implementing new technology.	Promote innovation and use of new technology.	Industry Science and Technology Canada
Federal Business Development Bank	Loans and equity investment.	Extend debt financing to small businesses. Can also extend venture capital to small firms wanting to expand.	Increase viability of small business.	FBDB offices

APPENDIX C
PROVINCIAL GOVERNMENT FINANCIAL ASSISTANCE PROGRAMS AND AGENCIES FOR SMALL BUSINESS

Alberta

Small Business Assistance Program.   This program provides access-fixed-term loans (3 to 10 years) with fixed rates to qualifying small businesses throughout the province. Loans can be for refinancing or consolidating business debt or for improving, constructing, or acquiring capital assets. Limit $150,000.

Small Business Equity Corporation Program.   Essentially this program provides a cash grant of 30 percent of the capital invested by a resident Albertan or a refundable tax credit of 30 percent of capital invested by a corporation with a "permanent establishment in Alberta."

Alberta Opportunity Company.   This is a crown corporation that provides financial and managerial assistance. The AOC is a lender of last resort. Loans are made or guaranteed for capital assets, plant buildings, machinery and equipment, material and inventories, research and development, and general working capital.

British Columbia

B.C. Development Corporation.   The BCDC is a provincial crown corporation set up to further economic development in British Columbia through financial, advisory, and information services. Under its low-interest loan plan, the BCDC provides funds for establishing, modernizing, or expanding manufacturing and processing industries.

Small Manufacturers Assistance Program and Assistance to Small Enterprise Program. These programs create jobs by assisting with the establishment, expansion, or modernization of small manufacturers. They also give other assistance to small enterprises in the province. These programs provide interest-free, forgivable loans to British Columbia companies that may be used for start-up, expansion, or modernization.

Manitoba

Design Assistance for Small Projects. This cost-shared program will pay up to 50 percent of design costs to improve product, graphics, and packaging to a maximum contribution of $1,000.

Venture Capital Company Program. This program aims to stimulate the flow of equity capital into Manitoba businesses by providing an investment vehicle for the private sector. The province participates jointly on a 35/65 percent basis with private investors, who must contribute $25,000 at the time the venture capital company is registered and a minimum of $65,000 within one year.

New Brunswick

Department of Commerce and Development. The minister of Commerce and Development may provide financial assistance to aid and encourage the establishment or development of manufacturing or processing industries in the province. Assistance may take the form of a direct loan, bond guarantee, or acquisition of shares in a company.

Financial Assistance to Small Industry. This program makes interest-free, forgivable loans to new or existing industries for start-up, modernization, or expansion. Loans are calculated on the basis of approved capital costs.

Newfoundland and Labrador

The Newfoundland and Labrador Development Corporation. This crown corporation is funded jointly by the federal and Newfoundland governments. It is mandated specifically toward small business. The NLDC offers both term loans and equity finance, but it does not guarantee loans.

Northwest Territories

Small Business Loans and Guarantees Fund. This program gives loans and guarantees to small businesses in the territory that are not eligible for the Eskimo Fund or the Indian Business Loan Fund. Funds may be used for purchase and for improvement or expansion of land, buildings, equipment, and inventory.

Nova Scotia

Small Business Development Corporation. This program provides loans to businesses with annual sales of less than $2 million or employing fewer than 50 people. Interest rates are fixed for the life of the loan, and repayment terms are flexible.

Industrial Estates Limited Financing Program. This program provides appropriate loan financing to new or expanding manufacturing operations. The minimum loan financing available is $250,000. Repayment is normally by way of a 20-year amortization.

Product Development Management Program. This program assists manufacturers in developing new products and upgrading the design quality of existing products. Grants under the program provide up to 75 percent of the product development costs submitted by a consultant designer. The maximum grant is $15,000 per project.

Ontario

New Ventures. This program offers loans to new companies to a maximum of $15,000 if approved by a participating financial institution. These loans are guaranteed by the Ontario government (Ontario Ministry of Industry, Trade and Technology) and matched by the owner's equity.

Ontario Development Corporation. This agency and its complementary development corporations within Ontario stress the importance of small business and the desirability of a private sector share in small business financing. Although commencement of repayment may be deferred, loans may be interest free or at a rate lower than the ODC's prevailing rate.

Small Business Development Corporation Program. This program acts as a private sector investment firm in which individuals and corporations are encouraged to buy equity. These firms then invest in small businesses eligible under the act. Money invested may be issued only for expansion or improvement of fixed assets, development, or start-up debt. Corporations that invest in SBDCs are granted a credit of 25 percent against Ontario corporations' income tax.

Prince Edward Island

Department of Industry and Commerce. The PEI Department of Industry and Commerce administers five general assistance programs. Those occupied with direct assistance are run jointly with DREE. Eligible recipients of these programs are manufacturers and services in the small business sector.

Quebec

Quebec Industrial Development Corporation.   This crown corporation aims at spreading economic power within the population, improving and rationalizing the business structure. Assistance may come in the form of a rebate on the company's borrowing cost, a loan at the usual market rate, a loan guarantee, or acquisition of a minority interest in a company.

Small Business Assistance Program.   This program was established to assist firms that are usually profitable and well managed but face temporary working capital shortages. Financial assistance takes the form of an interest subsidy and loan guarantee.

Saskatchewan

Saskatchewan Economic Development Corporation (SEDCO).   This crown corporation is a major internal provincial government vehicle of economic development and as such deals with enterprises of all sizes and sectors. There is no upper limit on loans, and interest rates are set according to type of loan and current market conditions.

Labour Sponsored Venture Capital Program.   This aims to stimulate growth of the province's small business sector. It provides provincial tax incentives to both individuals and corporations that are willing to invest in Saskatchewan small businesses.

Community Bond Program.   This program provides financing for communities in the area of economic development.

Yukon

Yukon Small Business Assistance Program.   This program offers both financial and nonfinancial assistance to entrepreneurs wishing to start a new business as well as those seeking to expand an existing business. Financial assistance takes the form of loans and loan guarantees.

Suggested Readings

Assistance to Business in Canada (ABC) 1986. Montreal: Federal Business Development Bank, 1986.

Calof, Jon. "Analysis of Small Business Owners' Financial Preferences." *Journal of Small Business and Entrepreneurship,* Winter 1985–1986, p. 5.

Chase, A. G. *Small Business Financing.* New York: McGraw-Hill, 1983.

Gibson, Mary. "Financing for Your Small Business. Part I," *CA Magazine* 118, no. 2, February 1985, pp. 28–32, and "Financing for Your Small Business. Part II," *CA Magazine* 118, no. 3 (March 1985), pp. 44–53.

Gray, Douglas A., and Diana L. Gray. *The Complete Canadian Small Business Guide.* Toronto: McGraw-Hill Ryerson, 1988, pp. 145–63.

Knight, Russell M. "An Evaluation of Venture Capital Rejections and Their Subsequent Performances." *Journal of Small Business and Entrepreneurship,* Fall 1985, p. 18.

Knight, Russell M. "The Financing of Small High Technology Firms in Canada." *Journal of Small Business and Entrepreneurship,* Summer 1985, p. 5.

Mancuso, Joseph R. *How to Get a Business Loan without Signing Your Life Away.* New York: The Center for Entrepreneurial Management, 1986.

Mancuso, Joseph R. *How to Start, Finance, and Manage Your Own Business.* New York: The Center for Entrepreneurial Management, 1986.

Presenting Your Case for a Loan. Toronto: Thorne Ridell, Chartered Accountants, 1987.

Small Business in Canada. Industry, Science and Technology Canada, 1991, pp. 57–69.

Sources of Venture Capital in Canada. Ottawa: Department of Industry, Trade and Commerce, Government of Canada, 1987.

Comprehensive Case
The Framemakers: Part 4

After selecting their location, Robert and Teresa Norman began securing merchandise for their initial inventory in earnest. They soon learned, however, that suppliers wanted to be paid before making deliveries. Therefore, Robert approached his local bank's manager to obtain the money he needed to get started. Although he had known his banker for a long time, he was surprised to find a less than positive reaction toward his proposal. Robert requested a $15,000 business loan, with he and Teresa contributing $5,000 of their own money to the estimated $20,000 cost of the venture.

The bank manager asked Robert to go home and prepare a detailed description of his needs, as well as a projected operating statement for the first year's operations. Robert was upset by this negative reaction and decided to visit other banks to obtain the funds he needed. But he found out he would need to provide the requested information to obtain the money. He spent two days working feverishly and came up with the statements shown in Figure 1.

When he took the proposals to the bank, the manager seemed impressed but still would not give approval for the loan. Some uncertainties about the statements still bothered the banker. Finally, after two weeks of collecting information—and pleading—the Normans' loan for $15,000 was approved. A major reason for the approval was Robert's past dealings with the bank and his good credit standing. Now they could begin purchasing supplies to get started.

Before long, however, Robert realized he had underestimated many of his expenses. He learned, for example, that utilities, rent, and telephone all required initial deposits of $200. He also needed some additional supplies, even though he had overbought some unnecessary supplies from especially persistent salespeople. The landlord required the first and last months' rent before letting him move in. The equipment costs and inventory levels were higher than he had estimated. Finally, since the Normans had decided it would be better to incorporate their business, they faced additional legal costs for which they had not planned. The result of all these additions was that The Framemakers needed another $10,000—and the Normans hadn't even opened the doors!

Robert and Teresa didn't know what to do. They were hesitant to go back to the bank and ask for more money because of the difficulty they had had obtaining the first loan. On the other hand, they knew their chances of obtaining funding elsewhere were slim. On top of that, the time for the grand opening was rapidly approaching.

Questions

1. Evaluate the Normans' initial approach to obtaining financing for The Framemakers.
2. Assuming you are the banker, evaluate the financial requirements and projections Robert prepared.
3. What should the Normans do now?

FIGURE 1

THE FRAMEMAKERS
Financial Requirements, Year 1

Item	Amount	Source of Information
Inventory	$ 4,000	General estimate
Equipment and fixtures	7,000	Approximation
Opening promotion (trade show)	1,000	Price of booth
First month's rent	600	From landlord
Three months' salary		Estimated $1,500/month
(Robert and Teresa)	4,500	
First three months'		One ad in TV, radio, and newspaper
advertising	2,500	
Miscellaneous	400	Estimate
Total	$20,000	

THE FRAMEMAKERS
Projected Income Statement, Year 1

	Per Customer (Professional Picture Framing Association Figures)		10 Customers a Day for 240 Days
Sales	$32	100%	$76,800
Expenses	24	75	57,600
Profit	8	25	19,200

CASES FOR PART II

Garden City Petroleums
The Grounds Crew
Harris Sporting Goods
Ian's Futon Store

3-in-1 Kampkit
Nevada Bob's Discount Golf and Tennis
Sandra's Restaurant

GARDEN CITY PETROLEUMS

D. Wesley Balderson
University of Lethbridge

Bernie Gryant was a licensed mechanic working for a large garage in Coalbanks, a city of 55,000 in southern Alberta. Although he had worked with the same employer for seven years, he felt his chances for promotion were limited. Bernie lived on a small farm outside Coalbanks, and commuting each day was getting fairly expensive. All of these things had made him start thinking about opening his own business.

One day on the way home from work, he noticed a "for sale" sign on the old service station located on the highway just outside Garden City, a small town halfway between Coalbanks and Bernie's farm. The prospect of quitting his job and purchasing the business hit him immediately. The location was currently owned by a local fertilizer company. On talking to the owner, Rod Grainger, Bernie found out the asking price was $40,000, plus the value of the fuel in the tanks at the time of purchase. The owners also indicated a willingness to finance the purchase over three years at 10 percent per year if Bernie could provide a down payment of $10,000. Bernie didn't have $10,000 to invest, but he discussed the proposal with a good friend, Tom Duncan. Tom, a lawyer, agreed to enter a co-ownership arrangement with Bernie in return for the $5,000 needed for half of the down payment. They discussed the background of the proposal and obtained the following information:

1. The town of Garden City had a population of 1,500 but only one other gas station (affiliated with a major oil company). Although the owner of this station was very prominent in the community, he had no mechanic and was open only from 8 A.M. to 5 P.M. six days a week.

2. This station was the only outlet for bulk farm fuel within a 20-mile radius—and this was a farming community. If they decided to pursue the bulk fuel market, however, they would have to buy a bulk fuel truck.

3. Only one mechanic operated in Garden City; two others in the area did mechanical work from their farm garages.

4. Although the location of the proposed purchase was on the outskirts of Garden City, it was on the major highway between Coalbanks and the province's third major recreational area, Waterville National Park.

5. The present owner was willing to finance the purchase with favorable terms.

All of these points seemed positive, and Bernie and Tom agreed to make an offer subject to viewing the financial statements. The offer was accepted. Figures 1 and 2 show the income statement and balance sheet for the service station.

After viewing the financial statements, Bernie and Tom were a bit disappointed. However, although the business's income was low, they believed that with the addition of Bernie's mechanical capability, money spent on advertising, and the purchase of a bulk fuel truck, they could improve this figure substantially. They went ahead with the purchase.

Now, approximately six months later, Bernie is getting discouraged. He is working from 7 A.M. until 10 P.M. every day, and he feels profits are not as high as he had planned.

Questions

1. Evaluate the purchase of Garden City Petroleums. What further analysis should have been done prior to the purchase?

FIGURE 1

GARDEN CITY PETROLEUMS
Income Statement
For Year Ended March 31, 1992

Gasoline sales...		$215,480
Expenses:		
Cost of sales..	$185,162	
Bad debts..	1,008	
Depreciation..	2,000	
Equipment repairs..................................	1,206	
Insurance and taxes................................	3,000	
Office supplies and postage.........................	1,040	
Telephone and utilities.............................	2,025	
Wages and benefits.................................	15,000	
Total expenses................................		210,441
Net income...		$ 5,039

FIGURE 2

GARDEN CITY PETROLEUMS
Balance Sheet
March 31, 1992

Assets			*Liabilities*	
Cash	$ 1,191		Accounts payable	$ 1,658
Accounts receivable	8,425		Notes payable	5,000
Fuel in stock, 3/31/92	12,500		Total liabilities	$ 6,658
Other inventory	880			
Building and equipment			*Owner's Equity*	
Less: depreciation	18,000		Owner's equity	$36,338
Land	2,000			
			Total liabilities and	
Total assets	$42,996		**owner's equity**	$42,996

2. How could Tom and Bernie have gone about assessing the market potential and market share for this business?

3. Do you think the price paid for this business was too high, too low, or about right?

4. What recommendations would you make to Tom and Bernie at this point?

The Grounds Crew

Richard D. Heyland
University of Lethbridge

Brett Richards and Ron Williams were equal partners in The Grounds Crew, a light landscaping company operating in Hamilton, Ontario. Both were university students and operated the business during the summer months. After drawing up the business plans and using their savings to invest in some equipment, they started operations in April 1988. The business offered local residential and commercial property owners affordable, dependable, and top-quality lawn maintenance, light landscaping, and general yard work. There were other, similar firms in Hamilton, but Brett and Ron believed some of them lacked visibility and seemed to have problems dealing with their clientele. As a result, Brett and Ron decided they would develop their company by advertising and developing good customer relations. Although the partners reinvested little money in the business, it kept growing each year as old clientele returned and new customers were added (see Figure 1).

In the spring of 1991, encouraged by their past success, Brett and Ron decided to franchise their business in southern Ontario. They hoped that by providing prospective franchisees with an operations manual (see Figure 2) based on their own operations and some training, they could charge a $5,000 franchise fee with a 1 percent royalty on sales. With the operations manual and their expertise, they planned for each franchisee to achieve first-year gross sales of $9,000 and believed

Figure 1

	THE GROUNDS CREW Income Statement (Unaudited) Past Three Years		
	1989	*1990*	*1991*
Revenue	$36,000.00	$25,000.00	$12,000.00
Expenses			
Advertising and promotion	1,237.44	999.00	705.00
Workers' compensation	290.00	180.00	.00
Employee wages	7,630.61	4,350.00	.00
Gas	1,442.49	987.99	578.98
Taxes	1,283.89	564.88	.00
Miscellaneous	600.60	600.00	400.00
Equipment	1,540.00	1,590.00	2,000.00
Supplies	2,694.00	2,568.00	300.00
Total expenses	16,719.03	11,839.87	3,983.98
Net income	$19,280.97	$13,160.13	$ 8,016.02

FIGURE 2   Operations Manual

1. *Projected Sales.* The projected sales for the first-year franchisee are listed below. It is the franchisor's goal to have every franchisee achieve at least $9,000 in gross sales.

2. *Capital Requirements.* The capital requirements for the franchisee are also listed below. If working capital is scarce, renting is a possibility for the first year.

3. *Training.* One week of on-the-job training will be given to the franchisee. Here the basics of the business will be explained and illustrated.

4. *Communications and Reports.* The franchisee will be required to call the franchisor every two weeks at an appointed time to report the work done/estimated and the jobs to do. Some of the items reported will include gross income, amount spent on advertising, and the number of jobs completed.

Franchising The Grounds Crew
Franchisee Pro Forma Income Statement/Capital Requirements

		$7,000	$9,000	$11,000	$13,000	$15,000
Projected sales		$7,000	$9,000	$11,000	$13,000	$15,000
Less: Variable expenses						
Franchise royalty	1.0%	70	90	110	130	150
Fuel and auto	7.1	497	639	781	923	1,065
Advertising	4.7	329	423	517	611	705
Equipment rentals	2.3	161	207	253	299	345
Miscellaneous	4.1	287	369	451	533	615
Supplies	6.6	462	594	726	858	990
Total variable expenses		1,806	2,322	2,838	3,354	3,870
Less: Fixed expenses						
Equipment‡		1,200	1,200	1,200	1,200	1,200
Tools		275	275	275	275	275
Equipment depreciation*		144	144	144	144	144
Total fixed expenses		1,619	1,619	1,619	1,619	1,619
Total expenses		3,425	3,941	4,457	4,973	5,489
Net income[t]		$3,575	$5,059	$ 6,543	$ 8,027	$ 9,511

Franchise capital requirements	
Franchise fee	$ 5,000
Tools (crew kit)	275
Equipment	1,200
Registration and licensing	99
Advertising	423
Working capital	200
Capital requirements	$7,197

---

*Depreciation expense is applied to one three-year straight line on two lawn mowers, a trailer, and a power rake.

[t]Income tax not paid, but it will be nil if a student.

‡More would be needed if a trailer or truck were needed.

there would be a good supply of hard-working students who would be interested enough to make it profitable for them. They placed an advertisement in the local papers and waited to interview prospective franchisees.

Questions

1. Evaluate how well Brett and Ron developed their franchise system.
2. Would you be willing to become a franchisee of this business? Explain your answer.

HARRIS SPORTING GOODS

D. Wesley Balderson
University of Lethbridge

Bill Harris plans to open a sporting goods store in London, Ontario, as soon as he graduates from university there in the spring. He did a market demand analysis for such a store for one of his course projects at university and is confident the opportunity exists.

Bill's major problem is determining the amount of funds he will require. His father, who is quite wealthy, will give him $15,000 to invest as a graduation gift. He has located a store that rents for $1,000 per month (in advance) and has made an itemized list of the start-up costs as follows:

Merchandise (4 months, COD)	$50,000
Shelves, racks, displays	5,000
Remodelling	4,000
Cash register (used)	800
Check-out counter	500
Office supplies (4 months' supply)	200
Telephone: $25/month, $100 deposit, $25 installation fee	
Utilities: $100/month, $200 deposit	

Bill has made the following estimates:

- He can completely turn over his inventory every four months.
- In the first year, he plans a 60 percent markup on cost of merchandise.
- He can get by on a salary of $1,500 per month.
- He plans to hire one full-time employee at $1,000 per month.

- He plans to spend $2,000 in opening promotion in the first month and $200 a month after the grand opening for advertising.
- He estimates that 50 percent of his sales will be on credit and will be paid in 30 days.
- The interest rate is 15 percent, payable every four months.
- The depreciation rate is 10 percent.

Questions

1. Estimate how much money Bill will need from outside sources to start his business.
2. Assuming Bill receives start-up financing from a bank, as calculated in question 1, will he require an operating line of credit during the first four months of operation? If so, how much?
3. Should Bill pursue debt or equity sources of funds to get started?

IAN'S FUTON STORE

Patricia Elemans
University of Lethbridge

Ian Clarke is in his late 20s. Since graduating from the University of Toronto with a bachelor's degree in commerce, he has been working as assistant manager of a hardware store. Because the store is a family-owned business, Ian foresees no advancement opportunities there. Ian has always dreamed of owning his own store one day, but until recently has had no real idea of what type of store he wants.

A few months earlier, Ian came across an article on futons in the *Toronto Sun*. Futons are Japanese-style beds. The mattress is made solely out of cotton and noted for being nonallergenic, warm in the winter, cool in the summer, and very good for people with back problems. It is about eight inches thick and contains no springs, wires, and so on. The frame of the bed is relatively lightweight, and hence the bed is easy to move. The futon line includes a couch that folds down into a bed and is therefore suitable for bachelor suites, guest rooms, family rooms, and other temporary sleeping quarters. Another appealing feature of the futon is the price. Because the futon is relatively simple to manufacture and does not require a lot of materials, the production cost and resulting price are quite low. The futon runs about one-quarter to one-half the price of a regular box spring and mattress. Because the futon is low priced (comparatively) and very easy to move, it appeals to students, bachelors, and young families who move frequently or have limited space. There is also a line of accessories sold with futons, including pillows and quilts. These items are quite inexpensive and very attractive.

Although Ian had never heard of futons, he was intrigued by the article. This sounded like the perfect product for him to sell. He began researching futons, contacting manufacturers, doing a feasibility analysis, and setting up a business plan. All indications seemed positive. Since the futon was relatively new and had not yet been marketed in the Toronto area, he would have no direct competition.

Ian approached his father about the possibility of opening up a futon retail outlet in Toronto. His father was convinced of the potential of the idea and was willing to invest $20,000 in the venture. With these funds and his own good credit standing, Ian was sure he would have no problems obtaining a bank loan.

The only thing Ian really has to decide now is a specific site for the store. He has looked into three prospective locations.

The first location is in a shopping centre located in the suburbs of Scarborough. The centre has the highest traffic count of all the malls in the area, but this means the rent is quite high. The location would cost him a flat fee of $3,000 per month, plus various other costs. He must pay a proportion of maintenance costs for the mall, a proportion of mall taxes, and a proportion of mall advertising and promotions. These amounts are based on the size of the store relative to the size of the shopping centre. He must also pay 7 percent of gross sales to the mall; the total will be approximately $4,000 per month. The specific location has 2,000 square feet available. This is quite small, and although Ian could display his merchandise adequately, he would have limited space for storage of extra inventory. On the positive side, the site requires no repairs and Ian could move in immediately. Also, the only competition in the area would come from the anchor store at the end of the mall—Eatons, which carries furniture. Furthermore, the mall offers plenty of parking. The mall manager requires that Ian sign a five-year lease.

The second location is in a secondary business district. It is situated close to a residential area that consists mainly of apartment buildings and townhouses. The building has a total of 4,000 square feet and is 50 years old. This means there would be room for storage of extra inventory, so Ian would not have to order frequently. However, the building is not for rent; the owner is eager to sell it. The purchase would require a deposit of only $15,000 and affordable mortgage payments of $2,500 per month for 15 years. However, the building would require quite a lot of work. The previous occupant ran a furniture store, but it was set up more like a warehouse. Ian thinks the building would require partitioning into selling, storage, and office areas, as well as general renovations like new carpeting, paint, and some new fixtures. Another worrisome factor is that it is located close to two furniture dealers and one waterbed dealer. However, the area has a lot of drive-by traffic, and parking is plentiful.

The third location is on a string street located near the downtown area on a major traffic artery. The location Ian has in mind consists of 2,500 square feet, which he feels is adequate for displaying his merchandise and keeping enough inventory on hand to meet demand. The building can be rented for $2,300 per month. It would require some renovations, but Ian estimates these would not amount to more than $1,500. Also, he will be required to sign only a two-year lease. The previous occupant of the building was a jewellery store. The stores next to the site are a bakery and a confectionery. There are also a law office, an accountant's office, and a pizzeria on the same block. A factor that is very appealing to Ian is the absence of other furniture or bed stores in the immediate area. Because the building is close to the downtown area and has high traffic, limited parking is available.

Questions

1. What additional information should Ian obtain before deciding on a location?
2. What are the advantages and disadvantages of the various locations?
3. Where do you think Ian should open his futon store? Why?

3-IN-1 KAMPKIT

Rick Heyland
University of Lethbridge

George Allen, a resident of Winnipeg, Manitoba, spent 10 years trying to manufacture the 3-in-1 Kampkit in his spare time. He found many retailers and wholesalers that were willing to buy the product if he could manufacture it.

George had worked on drilling rigs and mine sites for many years; it was here that he saw the need for the Kampkit. The 3-in-1 Kampkit is a tool with a fibreglass handle and three attachable heads: shovel, pick mattock, and axe. A heavy-duty rivet holds a steel sheath onto the formed fibreglass handle. A forged steel wedge lock forms a positive lock for holding the axe, shovel, and pick mattock in place. George holds the patent rights for his invention.

The Kampkit is more cost effective, convenient, and durable than conventional tools. Rather than having three different bulky tools, the Kampkit comes all together in its own carrying case. It also assembles without tools. Replacing an axe head with the Kampkit takes minutes rather than hours.

George has found a strong interest in the product by some top hardware chains in Canada and the United States. The target market for this product is campers, recreational vehicle owners, mining companies, oil companies, and farmers. But George has been unable to get it manufactured.

George has made contacts throughout Canada, the United States, West Germany, Japan, and Sweden in an attempt to have the Kampkit manufactured, but has been unsuccessful. Initially George was looking for a manufacturer that could make the whole product, but manufacturing was so specialized that no one company could make it. As a result, George decided to try to find a group of manufacturers. Recently he found a manufacturer that could make the axe head, but it demanded $5,000 to make the die and a minimum of 10,000 units for an initial order.

Unfortunately, George has spent most of his funds on trying to determine the market and finding someone to make the product. He has calculated that to get an order of 10,000 units with all three heads, carrying case, and handle, he would need close to $250,000. George has tried everywhere to find an appropriate investor, but all prospects are either "a two-bit operation" or "want too much of the pie."

Questions

1. *a.* Where can George get the necessary financing?
   b. How can George get the necessary financing?
2. How would you recommend that George find a manufacturer for the 3-in-1 Kampkit?
3. If George can get the 3-in-1 Kampkit made, what distribution channel should he use to get the product to the consumer?

NEVADA BOB'S DISCOUNT GOLF AND TENNIS

D. Wesley Balderson and Rick Heyland
University of Lethbridge

James Durant had opened a small golf supply shop in downtown Saskatoon, Saskatchewan, in June 1991. Named Durant's Golf Accessories, it handled clubs, balls, bags, and carts, as well as a limited line of golf-related clothing. James, an experienced golfer himself, had done what he felt was a thorough job of assessing the market for the shop. However, after five months of operation and with winter approaching, the performance of the store was not what he had expected. The store was averaging only one-half of the projected $20,000 per month in sales. James was not sure why, but he suspected part of the problem was lack of awareness of his store among the golfing public. His product line included major brand name merchandise, and he was attempting to be price competitive. This was difficult, however, because of his lower volume of purchases, which resulted in higher merchandise costs. James believed he would have to advertise more but had put all of his savings (approximately $20,000) into getting the business started. He felt fortunate that thus far he hadn't needed to borrow any money.

In November 1991, James was contacted by the Nevada Bob's Discount Golf and Tennis franchise about the possibility of becoming the franchisee for Nevada Bob's in Saskatoon. Nevada Bob's is a well-recognized and respected golf and tennis supply wholesaler in the western United States and was in the process of expanding into Canada. James would be one of the first franchisees in Canada and would have exclusive rights for Nevada Bob's in Saskatoon.

Upon further investigation, James learned that Nevada Bob's would provide information on sources for merchandise at discount prices. He was not obligated, however, to purchase from these suppliers. James would also automatically receive any catalogue sales in the Saskatoon area that the franchise advertised nationally. The franchisor indicated this had amounted to $18,000 in 1986. James received from the franchisor a cash flow statement for a typical franchisee (see Figure 1), which looked very positive. He visualized that such performance would certainly be an improvement over his existing business.

The Nevada Bob's franchise would cost James $25,000, with an additional 2 percent royalty on sales. Although no formal training program or operations manual was available, the franchisor indicated they would help James if he needed some assistance. The franchisor has given James two weeks to make his decision.

Questions

1. If you were James Durant, what other sources would you contact? What information, if any, might you require, before making the decision?
2. What specific questions might be raised about the cash flow statement provided by Nevada Bob's?
3. What course of action would you recommend for James Durant?

FIGURE 1

NEVADA BOB'S DISCOUNT GOLF AND TENNIS
Statement of Projected Cash Flow as of 1989

Opening cash balance	$ 15,000	
Cash sales	876,000	
Cost of goods sold	(663,200)	
Total		$227,800
Cash disbursements		
Accounting and legal	$ 5,350	
Advertising	31,500	
Automotive	1,200	
Insurance	3,600	
License and dues	2,400	
Office and sundry	5,100	
Rent	24,000	
Credit card discount	8,760	
Repairs and maintenance	9,000	
Telephone and utilities	8,400	
Salaries	39,000	
Sales commission	3,600	
Travel and promotion	13,500	
2% royalty of gross sales paid quarterly	17,520	
Total		172,930
Cash balance		$ 54,870

SANDRA'S RESTAURANT

D. Wesley Balderson
University of Lethbridge

Sandra Williams worked as assistant department manager in the ladies' wear department of a large department store in Kingston, Ontario. She enjoyed her work but saw that chances of further advancement in her $21,000-a-year job were limited. For the past few years, Sandra had been thinking about starting her own business. As a teenager, she had worked summers in a fast-food franchise and had always desired to own her own restaurant. As she had two children, she resented having to work Thursday and Friday evenings and Saturdays and thought that by owning her own business she could more easily take time off to be with her family. Her husband, a schoolteacher, had supported her working in the past, but was a bit hesitant about Sandra risking her savings of $20,000 to go out on her own. They agreed, however, that Sandra should investigate a few possibilities and obtain as much information as she could about the restaurant industry in Kingston.

For the past six months, Sandra has visited with several of her friends, looked at some prospective businesses, and checked with public officials to find out what information was available. She has obtained the following information:

Population of Kingston	95,000
Per-family away-from-home food expenditures	$80/month
Number of families in Kingston	28,000
Number of restaurants in Kingston	110
Average square footage per outlet	1,500
Cost of goods sold as percentage of gross sales	50%
Bank interest rate	17%

Operating expenses, excluding rent, interest, and franchise advertising royalties, are estimated to be 35% of gross sales.

From several restaurant possibilities, Sandra has narrowed the decision down to three: a site in a new shopping mall, a downtown restaurant that is for sale, and a fast-food franchise. All three involve a greater investment than Sandra was planning on. To get sufficient funds, the Williamses may have to remortgage their house.

Possibility A

The first potential site is a new shopping centre just nearing completion in a new and growing part of Kingston. The centre is anchored at each end by two national department stores. The space Sandra is considering contains 3,000 square feet and carries a rental of $10 per square foot, plus a royalty of 2 percent of gross sales. Although the rental costs would be high, Sandra is confident that the mall would generate considerable customer traffic, which would outweigh the rental costs.

Also, the mall location is within a few minutes' drive from her home. However, the space is unfinished, and Sandra estimates she would need a minimum of $40,000 in equipment and $20,000 in leasehold improvements to get the restaurant started. Since not all the space was leased out, she was not able to find out how many other restaurants were planning to locate in the mall.

Possibility B

The second potential site is a 1,500-square-foot, busy downtown lunchtime café that is for sale. The present owner is asking $50,000 for the restaurant and is willing to finance the sale at $25,000 down and $10,000 per year for three years. The space had been leased at $12,000 annually and was due to be renegotiated in three years. The location of this restaurant makes it attractive to lunchtime and late-afternoon customers. The restaurant has operated successfully for six years and is located close to several large office buildings.

Possibility C

The third possibility is to sign a franchise contract with a national fast-food franchise chain that wants to expand into Kingston. The typical outlet size is 2,000 square feet. The initial franchise fee is $20,000, plus an additional $50,000 to be financed through Sandra's bank with the franchise guarantee, which would lower the interest rate by 2 percent. Sandra would also pay 6 percent of gross sales as a royalty. They would train Sandra in one of its company-owned outlets at no charge and help with the start-up of her own outlet. She would, of course, be constantly monitored by the franchise—a point that makes her a bit uneasy.

Sandra needs to make a decision soon. All three prospects might be lost if she waits too long.

Questions

1. How well has Sandra thought out and prepared for her decision to start her own restaurant?
2. Based on the information provided, which of the choices open to Sandra would you advise her to make?
3. What additional information should she obtain before making this decision?

PART III Managing the Small Business

Part II of this text dealt with issues relating to the organization and establishment of a small business. Once the business has been established, the owner-manager should follow several management fundamentals to ensure that the business stays viable and competitive. Part III discusses five of these management areas. Chapter 8 focuses on the marketing principles essential for understanding the market and getting the product or service to the consumer. Chapter 9 covers the recording and controlling of the financial aspects of the business. Both marketing and finance are areas in which many entrepreneurs lack training and competence. Chapter 10 discusses some fundamental components of the internal operations or production aspects of the business. Chapter 11 reviews the principles of personnel management applicable to the small organization. Chapter 12 outlines the most relevant tax considerations for the small business.

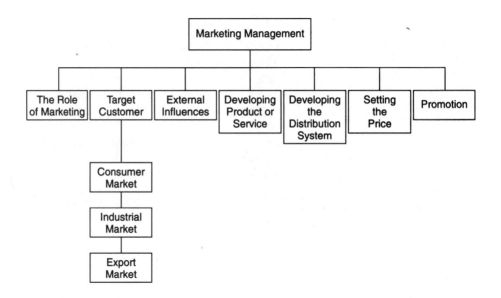

Marketing Management

Chapter Objectives

- To describe the role of the marketing function of a business enterprise.
- To discuss the importance of identifying and satisfying consumer needs.
- To explain the critical need for continual information gathering to ensure the long-run viability of the business.
- To discuss the components of a marketing program: product, price, distribution, and promotion.

Small Business Profile

John Cook

Sundance Bars and Restaurants Ltd.

John Cook has become a successful entrepreneur in Atlantic Canada by tailoring his product to the needs of his customers. Cook's success as an entrepreneur was not immediate, though, as he spent several years working for others and gaining business experience. Cook was born and raised in Newfoundland, dropped out of school in grade 9, and spent several years as a travelling salesman to supermarkets.

This work experience was not only valuable to John in terms of what he learned and the contacts he made, but he also became an expert on bars and restaurants which he frequented regularly as he travelled the province. His expertise was developed from "the patron's side of the counter."

John felt that many bars were not catering to their clientele as well as they could and eventually talked his father and brother into helping him get started with a pub near the campus of Memorial University. Big Ben's, as it was named, had a distinct English atmosphere and was an instant hit with customers. Encour-

aged by this success, the Cooks opened Uncle Albert's bar down on the waterfront a few years later. Once again the approach of tailoring the restaurant to the needs of the clientele proved successful.

By 1985 Cook had renamed his firm Sundance Bars and Restaurants Ltd. and had a small conglomerate of five establishments in St. John's and two in Halifax. Every one of the seven outlets had distinctive styles, menu and atmosphere which appealed to a specific market segment.

This type of strategy and the resulting success has earned John Cook the title of Atlantic Canada's bar tycoon as his restaurants grossed $5 million in 1985. A clear understanding of who the target market is and what their needs are has allowed Cook to become successful and is a good example to other entrepreneurs contemplating establishing a business.

Source: Kenneth Barnes and Everett Banning, *Money Makers! The Secrets of Canada's Most Successful Entrepreneurs* (Toronto: McClelland and Stewart, 1985).

The Role of Marketing Management in the Small Business

Marketing activities are often overlooked by owner-managers after the business has been established. Some possible reasons for this are: (1) Owner-managers do not fully understand what marketing is; (2) owner-managers may not think it is necessary—that is, they may believe that if they have a good enough product, it will sell itself; or (3) owner-managers tend to be so busy with the day-to-day activities and problems of the business that they do not take the time to assess the market and develop a marketing plan.

Regardless of the reasons for failing to apply marketing principles in the small business, it is critical that the owner-manager understand and apply those principles. The business will likely be unable to hire a specialist in marketing. Therefore, the owner-manager will have to do a considerable amount of marketing, not only to potential customers but to suppliers, employees, bankers, and perhaps even government agencies. Incident 8–1 illustrates how important marketing was to the successful establishment of one small enterprise.

The major purpose of this chapter, then, is to introduce the fundamentals of marketing that can help sustain the growth of the business. Some of the principles also apply to establishing a business and were mentioned briefly in Chapter 3. Other marketing principles form an important part of a business plan and were discussed in Chapter 4.

An owner-manager may become involved in the following marketing activities:

- Defining the target customer, target customer characteristics, and information concerning that customer's product/service wants and needs
- Understanding those influences outside the business that will affect its operations
- Developing the product or service
- Developing the channel(s) of distribution
- Setting price levels for the product or service
- Providing information or promoting the product or service to those who are influential in its purchase

This chapter will discuss the relevant aspects of each of these components of marketing separately. It is important to note, however, that these components need to be coordinated and managed together as a system to be most effective.

The Target Customer

In preparing the feasibility analysis in Chapter 3, we stressed the need to define the target customer. The ability of the entrepreneur to clearly identify the specific market is critical to success, as the Small Business Profile that opens this chapter

---

Incident 8–1

Doll Enterprise over the Hump

Ask Gerry Walker how he got involved in the business of designing sewing patterns for dolls, and he will reply it was simply through "naïveté." But when you ask for the longer version, he will tell you the story of an Albertan businessman who parleyed what was essentially a small segment of the home craft industry into a prospering, continentwide business venture in Calgary.

The idea for Dollcraft was first brought to light by Walker's wife, Linda, who is now president of the company. As an experienced seamstress, she believed she could create more interesting and better-quality doll patterns than most of the products on the market at the time. Linda's vision was to design dolls that combined practical construction for everyday use with aesthetic features, such as embroidered eyes, for doll collectors.

Packaging the product properly was vital to the success of the firm. Each 15 × 19 centimetre envelope (6 × 9 inches) contained a pattern with easily readable instructions, a picture of the finished product, and suggestions for clothing and accessories.

Even more important than packaging was effective marketing. Gerry originally sold his patterns through mail-order catalogues, but the Walkers got their first real break when a national distribution firm out of Montreal added Dollcraft. Walker next decided to try direct selling to retailers and convinced the Woodward's chain to carry his product. Today Woodward's remains Dollcraft's biggest client.

Source: Adapted from Brian Bergman, "Doll Enterprise over the Hump," *Small Business Quarterly,* Spring 1985, p. 6.

---

shows. This is important in calculating a quantitative estimate of the size of the market. The small business owner might attempt to reach and collect information about the following target markets:

1. The consumer market
2. The industrial market
3. The export market

Each of these markets has unique characteristics that must be taken into account in developing the marketing program.

The Consumer Market

The owner-manager should obtain information about several characteristics of the consumer market. Some characteristics that may be most helpful in developing the marketing program are the following:

1. *Demographic characteristics.* These include items such as age, income, education, occupation, and location of residence.
2. *Lifestyle characteristics.* This category includes such things as activities, interests, opinions, media habits, and personalities of target market individuals.
3. *Purchase characteristics.* These include what, when, where, and how much of the product or service the market purchases.
4. *Purchase motivations.* This area contains one of the most important items of information: It explains the reasons behind consumer purchases. In addition to understanding the "why" of the purchase, the entrepreneur should attempt to understand the factors that might influence the purchase. Common sources of influence are members of the consumer's reference group, social class, and/or family.

Once this type of information has been obtained, the development of the marketing program—including product characteristics, pricing strategy, distribution channels, and method of promotion—becomes much easier, and the program is usually more effective.

Much of the above information about the target customer can be obtained through secondary data or primary research, as discussed in Chapter 3. It is important for the small business owner to realize that collecting information about the target consumer is not a one-time event used only as the business is getting established. It should be used continuously to help the owner stay responsive to changes in consumer needs and wants.

Most successful companies, whether large or small, stay that way because they are close to the consumer and incorporate consumer wants and needs into their marketing programs.[1] This philosophy, called the *marketing concept,* has been taught in introductory marketing courses for a number of years. Many small businesses are successful initially because they fill a consumer need, but as they grow they often fall out of touch with their customers. This situation usually leads to difficulties, particularly in competitive markets.

Other companies define their consumer markets too broadly. As a result, their marketing programs may fail to satisfactorily meet the needs of any one group in the market. The practice of tailoring the marketing program to each specific market is known as *market segmentation.*

Figure 8–1 illustrates the target market information for a distinct market segment for a small restaurant. In this example, the owner-manager has selected a specific group of consumers toward whom to direct the marketing strategy. The demographic information needed to prepare quantitative estimates of feasibility (see Chapter 3) can be obtained from such secondary sources as government census reports. The information on lifestyles, purchase characteristics, and motivations might be obtained from industry marketing research reports, or the owner-manager may need to collect these data. This thorough consumer profile allows the restaurant owner to develop a market strategy that responds to the consumers' characteristics and needs. For instance, a high-quality, nutritious menu

---

FIGURE 8–1   Target Market for a Small Restaurant

The typical consumer has the following characteristics:

Demographics:
  Age: 30–49
  Income: higher than average ($40,000–$80,000)
  Occupation: professionals, managers
  Education: university graduates

Lifestyle:
  Activities: exercise and participation in sports, high social interaction; low on TV usage and high on
    reading; husband and wife both work, enjoy the outdoors, attend cultural events
  Interests: appearance, health, fashion
  Opinions: conservative economically, liberal on social issues
  Personality: achievement oriented, outgoing, independent

Purchase characteristics:
  What: higher-quality and higher-priced menu items
  Where: higher-class restaurant, international cuisine
  When: evenings and weekends
  How much: frequently eat away from home, 50 percent higher than national average

Motivations:
  Benefits sought: superior quality of food, service, atmosphere, variety of the menu
  Influencers: reference groups and social class the main influencers in choice of restaurant, through
    word of mouth

---

should be provided. Higher prices reflecting this level of quality would probably not affect demand negatively. Advertising showing young, socially active, and successful models might be effective. Testimonial endorsements may also have some influence. Incident 8–2 illustrates how one entrepreneur identified the needs of a specific target market in developing his business plan and thus was able to develop an appropriate strategy in launching the business.

The Industrial Market

The second type of market the small business might attempt to reach is the industrial market. This market includes companies, institutions, or even individuals who purchase the product to assist in the manufacture of other products. Government purchases, an ever increasing market for small business, are also classed as an industrial market.

In consumer markets, buying influences include the emotional as well as the rational. Industrial goods, on the other hand, are purchased primarily for rational reasons. Such characteristics as price, quality, dependability of supply, ability to manufacture to specification, speed of manufacture and delivery, and services offered are commonly considered in making industrial purchases. The purchasers, often acting as a committee, are well informed about the product category and are also aware of competitive offerings. Generally the information the purchaser requires is of a technical nature, requiring a well-trained and knowledgeable sales staff on the part of the small business.

Incident 8–2

Connors Brewing Company

After a squash game in early 1984, neighbours Bruce Parker and Sid Dickinson had a beer and sketched ideas for a new microbrewery. A business plan was born. By the time the Connors Brewing Co. of Mississauga, Ontario, opened its doors in March 1986, its plan had evolved into a large three-ring binder and briefcase of supporting files and Lotus® 1-2-3® disks.

When Parker wasn't putting Lotus 1-2-3 through its paces to deliver financial forecasts, he was pouring through books, magazines, and Statistics Canada data on the brewing industry; knocking on doors in Mississauga; talking to people in pubs; and interviewing students at York University in Toronto.

His research showed a target market of upscale, university-educated people, as many as 50 percent of whom were women. The market consisted of two general groups, one a discriminating group of recently graduated university students aged 21–27, the other 35- to 45-year-olds who "know what beer is all about." Connors then set about attempting to supply a product that responded to the target group's needs.

Source: Tim Falconer, "One Good Business Plan Leads to Another," *Small Business,* June 1986, pp. 14–18.

In attempting to reach the industrial market, the following areas should be investigated: (1) which companies and government agencies purchase from small businesses, (2) the influences on industrial demand, and (3) how the bidding-tendering process works.

Companies and Government Agencies That Purchase from Small Businesses.   Appendix A shows that a large number of purchases by some organizations are made from small businesses in Canada. Many of these organizations purposely look to small business to fill their product and service needs.

Influences on Industrial Demand.   Demand for industrial goods is derived from demand for the final product. Because of this relatively delayed response, industrial demand changes can be easier to predict than consumer demand changes. Some of the key indicators of industrial demand changes are:

- The state of the economy and its effect on the purchase of the end product
- Government legislation or regulations

- Potential competition for the purchasing company
- Specific bodies or agencies that exert influence on the purchases

Incident 8–3 illustrates the importance of the last type of influence to the success of a small manufacturer.

The Bidding-Tendering Process.   The small business owner should be aware of how the purchase decision is made and which criteria or specifications are used to make the decision in the industrial market. Because many industrial goods, particularly those purchased by the government, are purchased on a tender-bid basis, it is essential that the small business owner know how to prepare and submit bids within such a system.

The Export Market

Canada has always been known as a trading nation. In recent years, the value of exports has contributed an estimated 20 percent of Canada's employment and 30 percent of GNP.[2] Export sales increased from $40 billion in 1977 to $157.5 billion in 1992.[3] In the past, a large portion of exports have come from the primary and resource industries, which consisted of large companies and government agencies. Recently, however, many small businesses have successfully exported manufactured goods to foreign countries. Because of both the vast potential in these foreign markets and the considerable encouragement and assistance provided by the government, the small business owner should not overlook this option. The recently signed Free Trade Agreement between Canada and the United States is rapidly opening up new markets for Canadian small businesses.[4]

The small business owner who plans to export needs to investigate (1) the forms of government assistance available for exporting, (2) the unique characteristics of the foreign market, and (3) the mechanisms of exporting.

Government Assistance Available for Exporting.   Many government programs are designed to encourage and assist the entrepreneur who desires to export a product or service to another country. Some of the more active agencies and programs follow.

Department of Industry, Science and Technology.   This federal government department provides assistance in designing marketing plans, offers information and liaison with other government departments, and administers specific programs such as the following:

1. *Promotional Projects Program.*   This program promotes Canadian goods and services abroad through trade fairs, missions, and other foreign contacts.

2. *Program for Export Market Development (PEMD).*   This program shares part of the financial risk associated with foreign trade by providing grants to the entrepreneur for travel to identify foreign markets, participate in trade fairs, and bring foreign buyers to Canada.

3. *World Information Network for Exports (WIN Exports).*   This computer-based information system is designed to assist in matching foreign needs to Canadian capabilities.

4. *Technology Inflow Program.*   This program is designed to help locate, acquire, and adopt foreign technologies by promoting international collaboration.

5. *New Exporters to Border States (NEBS)—to U.S. South (NEXUS)—to overseas (NEXUS).* This program provides counselling assistance as well as organizing trade missions to businesses planning to export to these areas.

Export Development Corporation (EDC).   The EDC is a crown corporation of the federal government that essentially provides three services to exporters:

1. *Export insurance.*   This is a protection service for the exporter to ensure payment for export sales in the event of buyer default or detrimental foreign government action.

2. *Export guarantees.*   Guarantees can be provided to financial institutions to assist exporters in obtaining financing for the export operations.

3. *Export financing services.*   The EDC also has authorization to provide medium- and long-term financing for exporters to help them compete in the international marketplace.

Canadian Commercial Corporation (CCC).   CCC is another crown corporation that responds to requests from foreign governments and international agencies seeking Canadian goods and services by attempting to match those requests with suitable sources of supply.

Canadian International Development Agency (CIDA).   CIDA is a federal government agency that administers Canada's development cooperation programs around the world, many of which employ private consultants, contractors, suppliers, and manufacturers to underdeveloped countries.

Department of External Affairs—Trade Commissioner Service.   This referral service maintains an extended network of trade offices in other countries. Its primary focus is to assist Canadian companies seeking export markets. A directory of the trade offices throughout the world may be obtained through the Department of External Affairs or the Department of Industry, Trade, and Commerce.

Incident 8–3

Kemek Manufacturing Company

Kemek Manufacturing Company is a small manufacturer of basic chemicals and polymer resins located in Ontario. John Gorman, a bright, young engineer, has been working for Kemek as a research engineer in the polymer resins laboratory. His job is to do research on established resins to find new, more profitable applications for resin products. During the last five years, John has been under heavy pressure from top management to come up with an idea that would open up new markets for the company's foamed polystyrene.

Two years ago, John developed the "spiral-dome concept," a method of using the foamed polystyrene to make dome-shaped roofs and other structures. Kemek built a few domes to demonstrate the concept. Its salespeople, however, were unable to close any orders for the domes. Because of the investment the company had already made in the project, Kemek was concerned about the lack of orders and contacted several leading architects across the country.

Typical reactions were as follows:

It was very interesting, but you know that the Fire Inspector of Toronto will never give his OK.

Your tests show that foamed domes can be protected against fires, but there are no good tests for unconventional building materials as far as I'm concerned.

Building codes around Vancouver are written for wood and cement structures. Maybe when the codes change . . .

After this unexpected reaction, management did not know what to do. John Gorman realized that he failed to investigate the requirements of the building codes regarding the suitability of the new product. He also now recognizes that he should have made a greater effort to educate architects and engineers about the new concept, since these professionals are normally consulted by prospective purchasers of the domes before they adopt such products.

Source: Adapted from E. Jerome McCarthy and Stanley J. Shapiro, *Basic Marketing,* 3rd ed. (Homewood, Ill.: Richard D. Irwin, 1983), pp. 772–73.

Canadian Export Association (CEA).   The CEA is a national nonprofit association concerned with improving the environment for Canadian exporters. It provides information, contacts, education, and lobbying support for exporters.

Export Clubs.   Many cities have established export clubs that meet regularly to exchange ideas and information about exporting.

FIGURE 8-2   Key Areas for Developing a Foreign Marketing Strategy

1. What needs does the product fill in this culture?
2. What products (if any) currently meet these needs?
3. What are the differences in the way the product is used (consumed)?
4. What are the characteristics of the consumers who will buy the product?
5. Can the consumers afford to purchase the product?
6. What are the political or legal restrictions to marketing the product?
7. What are the distribution and media capabilities in the culture?
8. What language differences exist?
9. What nonverbal communications should be noted?
10. What information-collecting restrictions might exist?

Provincial Government Programs.   Most provincial governments actively encourage exports and may offer specific incentive programs to assist in this regard. The Department of Industry, Trade and Commerce or its equivalent in each province can provide information about their programs.

As we have seen, considerable assistance is available for a prospective exporter. Specific addresses of the above agencies are given in Appendix B. Incident 8–4 illustrates how assistance from such programs helped one entrepreneur develop a successful exporting venture.

Unique Characteristics of the Foreign Market.   A second requirement for success in exporting is to understand the peculiarities of the foreign market. Many companies have experienced difficulties in marketing internationally because they failed to obtain enough information about the various markets. Several of the agencies mentioned above can provide information to answer the questions listed in Figure 8–2.

Mechanisms of Exporting.   The agencies discussed earlier can also provide information about the mechanisms of exporting. Some of the essential features of an exporting arrangement are as follows:

- *Documentation.* Contracts, invoices, permits, insurance, and bills of lading must be drafted or obtained.
- *Methods of credit offered.* Letters of credit, accounts receivable, and consignment sales are often a part of the process.
- *Physical distribution.* The type of shipment, transfer of title, and inspection points will have to be determined.
- *Channel of distribution.* Sales representatives, government agencies, export agents, and trading houses will need to be identified and contacted.
- *Security.* Export insurance and guarantees must be obtained.

W.P.M. Handcrafted Log Homes Ltd.

Old-fashioned skills, plenty of Canadian timber, and drive are the key ingredients in the success of a small company that's doing big things. Handsome, hand-built Canadian log homes are finding a place in the hearts of Japanese buyers, and W.P.M. Handcrafted Log Homes Ltd. is filling a demand by shipping prebuilt log homes across the Pacific Ocean. The demand for the homes is growing, and owner William Murray expects his company to ship about 100 houses per year to Japan. This would mean $2 million a year in revenue for W.P.M.

The natural appearance of a log home also appeals to Japanese tastes, and the buildings almost sell themselves. "The trend there, as in North America, is to go back to natural things," says Murray.

Building and shipping the first model house to an exposition in Japan, including sales literature and other expenses, cost the company about $18,000. Some of that expense was defrayed by a grant from a federal government program, the Program for Export Market Development (PEMD). The company also received assistance from the federal government in making contact with businesspeople in Japan and Korea and in finding information about the potential market for log houses in both countries.

Source: Adapted from Peter Von Stackelberg, "A Touch of the North in the Far East," *Alberta Exporter,* October 1985, p. 12.

Because many of these items are complex, it is recommended that the entrepreneur seek assistance from the agencies mentioned earlier to ensure that he or she follows safe and proper procedures in carrying out the mechanics of exporting. Incident 8–5 shows how one firm learned this the hard way. Many Canadian exporters have found that one of the most effective ways to do business in another country is to strike a partnership with firms in that country. Incident 8–6 illustrates this strategy.

Influences External to the Market

In any market, several conditions exist that may have a significant impact on the small business but are outside the control of the owner of that business. Nevertheless, the owner-manager can do some things to effectively respond to these external influences:

Incident 8–5

Nautical Electronics Laboratories

A few miles from Nova Scotia's picturesque Peggy's Cove is Hackett's Cove. Noted for high technology rather than tourism, Hackett's Cove is the home of Nautical Electronics Laboratories Ltd. (Nautel), world renowned for its expertise in solid-state marine and aeronautical beacons and solid-state radio transmitters. Nautel is the largest employer in the area, with a payroll of 100 people.

The fledgling company came across an opportunity to bid on a tender put out by Canada's Department of Transport. It called for bids on the construction of aeronautical radio transmitters in solid-state form (without tubes). No such product existed then, and many larger companies, such as Phillips, deemed it an impossibility. But the founders of Nautel were convinced they could develop the new beacon. "Rather than saying it couldn't be done," says Dennis Covill, company president, "we tendered a bid which, in effect, gave the Department of Transport what it asked for." After a long process during which the unknown company had to satisfy delivery questions posed by the Treasury Board, approval finally came through for Nautel.

Covill says the company's major problem in the early stages was simply a lack of money. It had to provide a bank guarantee to the federal government for the original contract and would soon discover the pitfalls of doing business internationally. "Whereas domestically bills are usually paid in 30 days, some foreign countries took four or five months. The banks helped, but it was never easy. Eventually we learned to take precautions such as arranging export insurance, requiring letters of credit, and shipping overseas in batches that were progress billed."

By 1990, overall sales for Nautel were over $14 million.

Sources: Adapted from Kenneth Barnes and Everett Banning, *Money Makers! The Secrets of Canada's Most Successful Entrepreneurs* (Toronto: McClelland and Stewart, 1985), pp. 167–68; *Canadian Key Business Directory, 1992* (Toronto: Dun & Bradstreet Canada, 1993).

- Identify which external conditions affect the business.
- Set up a system to continually monitor the relevant external influence(s). For the owner-manager, this might mean regularly obtaining reports, newsletters, and studies that contain up-to-date information on these conditions.
- Adjust internal operations to respond to changes in these external influences most effectively.

Some of the most common external influences that can affect the small business and thus affect the information to be collected are the economy, the competition, legal restrictions, and the social and cultural environment.

Incident 8–6

To Russia with Hammer and Nail

For 20 years Dave Green has built 10 to 20 homes every year in the Regina area. He'd anticipated 1992 would be no different in the Regina market until a chance meeting at one of his show homes changed all that in the fall of 1991.

Representatives of a large Hong Kong based investment firm known as Vastqueen happened to ask him if he'd be interested in bidding on a massive Moscow housing contract. With the Regina housing market a practical standstill at the time, Green jumped at the opportunity.

The Hong Kong investors have struck a joint venture deal with the City of Moscow to build 1,500 single family homes over the next 3 or 4 years. Green's low overhead Terra Vista Construction company submitted a bid against two other large Canadian home builders, one based in Vancouver and the other from Toronto.

The people from Vastqueen liked Green's bid and before he knew it, in the fall of 1991 he experienced his first real culture shock of his life as he was invited to visit with Russian officials in Moscow.

Like the majority of successful projects in Russia, Vastqueen has entered in a joint venture with the Russian Construction Association to construct homes for the hordes of westerners moving into what's becoming one of the world's fastest growing capitalist societies. This joint venture has given Green the inside track on obtaining hard to get supplies. "I was told you could never buy kiln-dried lumber here, but I've seen it. You can buy insulation here practically the same as in Canada ... but the plants are hard to find because there are no signs and telephone books, so I'm very lucky to be working with the Russian Construction Association," the Regina homebuilder says.

Source: "To Russia with Hammer and Nail," *Alberta Business Magazine,* May-June 1992, p. 17.

The Economy.   The state of the economy in the market area is a critical external condition. For most products and services, market demand is directly related to upturns and downturns in the economy. The small business often is able to react more quickly than large businesses to changes in the economy.

Competition.   As mentioned in Chapter 1, a small business usually finds itself competing against larger firms over which it has no control. New technology used by competitors is another factor in assessing competition, especially in many growth industries. In some cases, the small business may gain competitive advantages because of its size. The Free Trade Agreement between Canada and the United States has not only opened up new markets for Canadian entrepreneurs but also increased competition for Canadian businesses as U.S. companies continue to enter Canadian markets. These situations were discussed in Chapter 2.

FIGURE 8–3   **Working with External Influences**

	Possible Characteristic External Influence	System to Monitor	Possible Internal Adjustment
Economy	Inflation rate Unemployment level	Collect relevant government and industry reports regularly	
Retail sales	Lower prices Increase advertising		
Competition	Define who competition is Define strengths and weaknesses of competitors Competitors' use of new technology	Own evaluation of monitoring (primary research) Competitors' new product offerings Competitors' reaction to your strategies	Product or service alterations Selection of specific target market
Legal restrictions	What laws affect your business What changes in laws are pending	Regular receipt of legislative changes from government documents and industry reports	Product or service alterations Promotional changes
Social and cultural	Lifestyle trends Demographic studies Purchase patterns	Industry and government reports recording social statistics and purchases	New products or services Distribution channel changes Promotional themes and levels

Legal Restrictions.   This potential influence includes the laws and regulations with which the business is required to comply. The owner-manager should keep up to date with any legislation that might affect business operations.

Social and Cultural Environment.   This factor encompasses trends in the culture in which the business operates that may affect demand. The culture may dictate norms the population is generally hesitant to violate or suggest new growth industries that can be attractive opportunities.

Figure 8–3 illustrates how a small business can work with these uncontrollable conditions.

Developing the Product or Service

As we mentioned at the beginning of this chapter, the product or service to be offered should be designed to meet target market demand. To ensure responsiveness to consumer demand, the owner-manager should think of the product or service in terms of the ways and extent to which it satisfies consumer need. A prototype of the product should be prepared and tested with a representative sample of the market. This type of information should be collected prior to finalizing the production decision.

Some major decision areas about which the small business owner should be knowledgeable when developing a product strategy are discussed next.

Develop Product or Service Policies.   Product policies should cover such items as quality level, product or service depth and width, packaging, branding, level of service, and warranties.

Decide How the Product Will Be Manufactured.   For many small businesses, contracting with another firm to manufacture the product is advantageous. This may be an especially viable alternative during the early stages of a business, when the risk is usually higher. Once the product has achieved market acceptance and the volume of production has increased, it may be more cost effective to acquire the manufacturing capability.

Understand the Product Life Cycle.   All products and services have a life cycle, as Figure 8–4 shows. As the product moves from the introduction to the decline stage in its life cycle, the marketing strategy for the product and even for the business may also change. This means changes may be required in pricing, in distribution, in promotion, and even in the product or service. Knowing that the product or service has a life cycle helps the owner-manager plan for any necessary adjustments to the marketing strategy when the maturity stage is reached. Such modifications can help prolong the life cycle of the product or service. Strategies include the following:

- Appeal to a new target market.
- Adjust the product or service to meet changes in customer needs.
- Increase promotion to enhance frequency of purchases.
- Emphasize different uses or characteristics of the product or service.
- Offer a new product or service.

Determine Factors That May Accelerate Product or Service Adoption.   Research shows that consumers generally adopt new products or services at different rates. Those who purchase first are the *innovators* or *early adopters*. These people often are the opinion leaders in a social group. The innovators and early adopters typically make up about 15 percent of the market, but they have a far greater influence because the rest of the market usually looks to this group before purchasing.[5]

After the small business owner has identified the innovators and early adopters within the target market, every attempt should be made to test market the product or service to that group first. If the early adopters accept the product or

FIGURE 8–4   Product Life Cycle

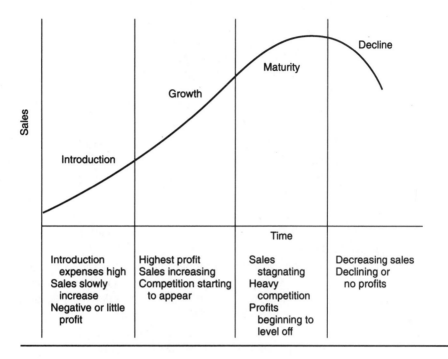

service, they may even do much of the initial promotion. Early adopters and opinion leaders also tend to be very vocal about the products and services they try and use. In addition, they tend to have higher income and educational levels, be more socially active, be more willing to take risks, and have greater exposure to printed media.

In addition to understanding the characteristics of innovators and early adopters, the small business owner should be aware of the factors that can speed up product adoption and attempt to capitalize on them. Following are some of the more important factors.

Relative Advantage.   If the product or service appears to have a significant advantage over existing ones, and if this advantage can be communicated effectively, it is more likely to have a faster adoption.

Complexity.   If the product or service is difficult to understand, the adoption rate is typically longer. In such a case, promotion should have an informational or educational content.

Divisibility.   A product or service that can be purchased in small amounts with a minimum of social or financial risk usually has a quicker adoption rate.

Communicability of Results.   If the results of using the product or service are quickly evident and easily communicated to others, its adoption will be more rapid.

In summary, the less risk associated with the purchase decision, the more rapid the adoption rate. The owner-manager therefore should do whatever possible to reduce such risk when introducing a new product or service. Providing information and offering a guarantee or warranty as part of the purchase are commonly used methods for reducing risk.

Understand How the Consumer Classifies the Product or Service.   Marketers use a standard classification system in categorizing consumer goods. This system can be valuable in developing the marketing strategy for the small business. The classifications are as follows:

- *Convenience goods.*   Convenience goods are purchased with minimal effort. They may be necessities, unplanned purchases, or emergency goods.
- *Shopping goods.*   Shopping goods are purchased only after comparison with similar products. Comparisons may be made on the basis of price if competing products are viewed as similar or in terms of quality or style if competing products differ.
- *Specialty goods.*   Consumers have substantial brand or product loyalty with specialty products or services. As a result, they are willing to spend considerable effort to locate and purchase the brands and products they desire.

Figure 8–5 illustrates strategy implications for each of these classifications. The focus of the marketing strategy is determined by how the target consumer classifies the product or service.

Developing the Distribution System

Many entrepreneurs develop an excellent product but lack the knowledge about the best way to get it to the consumer. Such a situation is illustrated in Incident 8–7. An effective distribution system should provide the product or service to the right consumer, at the right place, at the right time, and in the right quantity.

The *distribution channel* is the path the product or service follows from the producer to the consumer. It includes the different organizations or individuals who will assist in this movement toward consumption.

The small business owner needs to address three main distribution decision areas: the type of channel to use, the length of the channel, and the number of distributors authorized to sell the product.

FIGURE 8–5   **Strategy Implications for Consumer Good Classifications**

Type of Good	Price	Distribution	Promotion
Convenience	While usually lower-priced goods, the markups tend to be high Within a certain range, price is not important to consumer	Located close to consumers, either in relation to where they live or within the store Availability important to consumer	Promote availability Point-of-purchase displays for impulse goods
Shopping	For similar products the price must be competitive, as consumers are price sensitive For dissimilar products that are still competitive, price is not as important to consumer	Located close to competing products to aid comparison	Promote price advantage for similar products or quality/style advantage for dissimilar products
Specialty	Within a certain range, price is not important to consumer	Location not important to consumer	Promote outlets that carry the product or brand

Channel Options

A small business can follow essentially two channel paths, although various combinations of these types of channels are possible.

Manufacturer to Consumer (Short-Direct Channel).   This type of channel involves distributing the product or service directly to the consumer. The transportation and selling functions are carried out by the owner-manager or the sales staff. Often small businesses lack the financial capacity or expertise to hire and train their own sales forces.

Manufacturer to Wholesaler/Retailer to Consumer (Long-Indirect Channel).   In this type of distribution channel, the wholesaler or retailer purchases the product and resells it to another channel member or to the consumer. The manufacturer assumes less risk with this method but generally has less control over the distribution and a lower profit margin. The small business may use this type of distribution channel by going to a retailer or wholesaler directly or visiting a trade show attended by these intermediaries. Many products receive their initial start from successful trade show experience, as Incident 8–8 illustrates.

Channel Length

The decision regarding channel length will depend on the concerns of the manufacturer mentioned above. It also involves examining the product and market characteristics listed in Figure 8–6.

Incident 8-7

Hitchfinder Fencing Company*

George Mackenzie was a rancher from Pincher Creek, Alberta. For many years he had struggled with fencing problems on his ranch. As a result, he developed an electric fence with posts made not of conventional wood but of plastic PVC pipe. The big advantage of his fence, which he called the Hitchfinder, was its ease and speed of erection and dismantling. A rancher could pasture a part of his or her ranch and then move the complete fence to another part of the ranch in a few hours. Also, the cost was also considerably less than that for conventional fences.

George knew the product would be a sure-fire success. He obtained a patent, manufactured some quantities, and observed the enthusiastic reaction of those who tried it. However, George lacked business training, and had little idea how best to market the product. Should he sell to farm supply dealers? Should he hire a marketing firm to carry out the complete marketing of the product? Should he hire a salesperson? George didn't know which way to turn.

*This incident is based on an authentic situation, but the name of the individual has been changed.

Source: D. W. Balderson, University of Lethbridge, Alberta, 1986.

FIGURE 8-6   Deciding Channel Length

Direct/Short Channel (Manufacturer to Consumer)	*Indirect/Long Channel (Manufacturer to Wholesaler/Retailer to Consumer)*
Implications for Manufacturer	
More expensive to set up	Cheaper to set up
Greater potential return	Least return
More risk	Less risk
More expertise needed	Less expertise needed
Product Characteristics	
Perishable	Standardized
Technical	Inexpensive
Large, bulky	Proven demand
Expensive	
Market Characteristics	
Geographically concentrated	Geographically dispersed
Low product awareness	High product awareness
Sales effort required	Less sales effort required

Incident 8–8

Trade Shows and the Pet Rock

Experienced advertising men, Gary and Pat decided to help the item sell by making a point-of-purchase display at the annual trade show. Almost overnight they came up with a poster that perfectly captured the whimsy of the Pet Rock. The headline was simple: THEY'RE HERE—PET ROCKS! The 5-foot poster, painted in four colours, showed six copies of the same photograph of a rock, each with a different caption under it—Pet Rock Sitting Down; Pet Rock Standing Up; Pet Rock Playing Dead; and so on. The poster went in front of the display of the 12 prototype Pet Rocks.

Gary and Pat could not stay away from the show, the first test of the rock's appeal. "We lurked around," Gary says, "watching people's reactions. They'd walk in, see the poster, go over and pick up a box, and then they'd start reading the book, and they were just laughing their butts off! It was great! We knew. 'By God, we've done it!' And we'd find the nearest bar and celebrate."

Source: *Why Didn't I Think of That!* by Robert L. Shook. Copyright © 1982 by Robert L. Shook. Reprinted by arrangement with New American Library, New York, New York.

Channel Intensity

Another channel decision is how many distributors/dealers will be allowed to sell the product. Generally speaking, products that require greater selling effort, seller knowledge, and sales expertise are best distributed through a more exclusive type of arrangement. Standardized or convenience-type products usually call for a more intensive channel system. Because product availability is important in such a system, many dealers are allowed to carry the product.

Setting the Price for the Product or Service

Another marketing strategy variable within the control of the owner-manager is the setting of price for the product or service. Pricing is a critical part of the marketing strategy; the small business cannot afford to make a pricing mistake in a competitive industry.

To approach price setting effectively, one must understand the factors that affect prices. These factors can be classified as either external or internal. External influences, as discussed earlier, include the state of the economy in the market area, the extent of competition, possible legal restrictions, cultural or societal attitudes toward certain price levels, and target market demand. Typical internal influences on pricing policy are internal costs, the firm's long-run objectives, and pricing policies as set by the owner-manager.

FIGURE 8-7   **Cost-Based Pricing Methods**

Manufacturing Firm

Direct material cost per unit	$ 18.00
Direct labour cost per unit	21.00
Variable overhead (manufacturing)	10.00
Fixed overhead (factory)	30.00
Total manufacturing cost per unit	79.00
Selling costs per unit	3.00
General overhead (allocated per unit)	5.00
Total cost per unit	87.00
Desired profit	13.00
Selling price	$100.00

Retail Firm

Cost of merchandise	$ 50.00
Selling and storage (estimated)	20.00
Estimated markdowns	5.00
Desired profit	25.00
Selling price	$100.00

In retailing, the difference between the price and the cost of inventory is known as *markup.* In this example, it is $50 and is usually expressed as a percentage in the following manner:

$$\text{Percentage} = \frac{100 - 50}{100} = 50\%$$

Service Firm

Estimated cost of providing service per customer	$ 60.00
Estimated overhead costs per customer	20.00
Desired profit per customer	20.00
Selling price	$100.00

In setting price levels for the product or service, one may find that some of these factors are more influential than others. As a result, businesses use three general bases for price setting that take these influences into account: cost, demand, and competition.

Cost-Based Pricing

In *cost-based pricing,* the major influence is the cost of producing the product for the manufacturer, of purchasing and selling the product for the retailer, and of providing the service for the service firm (internal influence). Figure 8–7 illustrates the use of cost-based pricing in each of these types of business.

Once the costs have been determined, a percentage markup is added to reflect the profit objective of the firm. The owner-manager should realize, however, that the initial markup is seldom achieved. Markdowns and inventory shrinkage should be estimated (see Figure 8–7) and built into the markup calculation.

Demand-Based Pricing

Demand-based pricing uses consumer sensitivity to price as the major factor in arriving at the final price level (external influences). Usually primary research in the form of surveying will be required to assess acceptable prices for new products. Figure 8–8 illustrates the results of such a survey incorporated into a demand curve. Each point on the line shows the quantity demanded at the related price. For example, at a price of $30, demand would be 10 units; at $20, demand increases to slightly more than 15 units. In this example, the total revenue at the $30 price is $300 (30 × 10), whereas at $20 the total revenue is $320 (20 × 16). This situation can be described as price elastic. In *price-elastic* situations, price increases result in a negative effect on demand. For some types of products (convenience and specialty) and some industries (those with little direct competition), price may be less as important to the purchaser, and thus a change in price may not significantly affect demand. If this condition exists, it means the business has much more freedom and flexibility in setting prices than it would in a more competitive and price-sensitive situation.

For products and services already on the market, existing price levels and industry experts may provide valuable information to assist in setting demand-based prices.

Competition-Based Pricing

Firms in a growing number of industries are using *competitive pricing* in which the major consideration in setting prices is the price levels and policies of competitors (external influences). Many firms conduct ongoing price checks on the competition to guide their own pricing. The small firm may wish to set prices at a fixed percentage above, equal to, or below competitors' prices.

The small business owner should not rely too heavily on only one of the above methods of pricing. All these methods are important in most industries, and each should be taken into account when setting the final price for a product or service.

Promotion

Gone are the days of the philosophy "build a better mousetrap and the world will beat a path to your door." Today most businesses must actively provide information to the purchaser.

Types of Promotion

A small business can use essentially four methods to provide information about its product or service: advertising, sales promotions, public relations, and personal selling.

Advertising.   Advertising is a nonpersonal form of promotion. It is directed at a mass audience through various forms of media such as television, radio, newspapers, magazines, billboards, and direct mail. A small business owner should be aware of the strengths and weaknesses of each of these types of media and exactly when each is appropriate. This information is presented in Figure 8–9.

Sales Promotions.   Sales promotions are also nonpersonal forms of promotion but are directed at a much more restricted audience than advertising is. Examples of sales promotions are point-of-purchase displays, coupons and discounts, trade shows and exhibitions, and contests. All of these mechanisms are very effective forms of advertising for the small business, and some are relatively inexpensive.

Public Relations.   As Incident 8–9 illustrates, public relations, or publicity, can be a very effective form of promotion for the small business. This is particularly the case when the product or service is innovative or extraordinary in some way. This form of promotion may involve public-interest news stories, such as in Incident 8–9, sponsorship by the business of community projects such as sporting teams or events, or specialty advertising such as calendars, pens, hats, and the like. Public relations is generally inexpensive and can be very helpful in promoting not only the product or service but the business itself.

Personal Selling.   The conditions conducive to a short distribution channel or an emphasis on personal selling were discussed earlier in this chapter. Most businesses will require some personal selling as part of their marketing strategy. Owner-managers will undoubtedly be required to promote themselves, their

FIGURE 8–9   Advertising for Small Business

Media Type	Advantages	Disadvantages	Particular Suitability	Typical Costs

Newspapers	Flexible
	Timely
	Local market
	Credible source
		May be expensive
		Short life
		Little "pass along"
		Nonselective
		  audience
			All general retailers
			  or for definable
			  market areas
			  similar to
			  circulation
				One-page ad:
				  large market
				  ($1,200–$1,600)
				  small market
				  ($500–$600)
				  (prices dependant
				  on length of
				  contract)

Television	Sight, sound, and
	  motion
	Wide reach
		Cost
		Clutter
		Short exposure
		Less selective
			Definable market area
			  surrounding the
			  station's location
			  for certain products
				30 seconds of prime
				  time:
				  large local market
				  ($500–$700)
				  small local market
				  ($150–$200)

Direct mail	Selected audience
	Personalization
	Flexible
		Relatively expensive
		  per contact
		High "throwout" rate
			New and expanding
			  businesses; those
			  using coupon
			  returns or
			  catalogues
				Approximately $1 per
				  contact

Radio	Wide reach
	Segmented audience
	Inexpensive
		Audio only
		Weak attention
		Short exposure
			Business catering to
			  identifiable groups:
			  teens, commuters,
			  housewives
				30 seconds of prime
				  time:
				  large local market
				  ($150–$200)
				  small local market
				  ($35–$50)

Magazines	Very segmented
	  audience
	Credible source
	Good reproduction
	Long life
	Good "pass along"
		Inflexible
		Long lead times
		Costly
			Restaurants
			Entertainment
			Identifiable target
			  Markets
			Mail order
			Chains
				Approximately
				  $30,000 for
				  one-page,
				  four-colour ad in
				  Chatelaine (French
				  and English)

Outdoor	Flexible
	Repeat exposure
	Inexpensive
		Mass market
		Very short exposure
			Amusements
			Tourist businesses
			Brand name retailers
				1 month of prime
				  location billboard,
				  large market
				  ($2,000–$2,500)

Telephone
  directories
	Users in the market
	  for goods or
	  services
	Continuous ads
	Costs relatively low
		Limited to active
		  shoppers
		Limited visibility
		Not dynamic
			Services
			Retailers of brand
			  name items
			Highly specialized
			  retailers
				Inexpensive—
				  depends on size of
				  ad

businesses, and their products to customers, bankers, suppliers, and government agencies through personal selling. If salespeople are employed, they will need to be trained not only with respect to product or service knowledge but also in selling skills. Other aspects of training, supervision, and motivation of a sales force are discussed in detail in Chapter 11.

Incident 8–9

Publicity and the Pet Rock

Once the rocks were in production, Gary turned his attention to publicity. Since he had no money for advertising, he prepared news releases with a photo of himself surrounded by boxes of Pet Rocks. Marguerite, who was still not convinced Gary's idea would be profitable, approved of the photograph. "He had a great big smile on his face," she recalls, "like a Cheshire cat. It was as if he was saying, 'I'm going to put one over on the public.' "

Optimistically, Gary sent the release to major media. *Newsweek* picked the story up and sent a reporter and photographer to Los Gatos to do a half-page story on Gary and the Pet Rocks. The story included the fact that Neiman-Marcus had just then purchased four dozen Pet Rocks. "And the whole thing exploded!" Gary says. Retailers who read the story decided to follow the lead of Neiman-Marcus. And other major media followed *Newsweek*'s lead. By November 1, all 10,000 Pet Rocks were gone. With media interest increasing every day, Gary decided to go ahead with 50,000 more units. Before the printing was off the press, those units had been sold.

The snowballing publicity on the Pet Rock was helped by department stores, which decided to cash in on the public interest. John Gesicke, the Neiman-Marcus buyer, was one of the first to pose on a street corner with a Pet Rock on a leash. The photograph was picked up by the Dallas newspapers. Gary, well familiar with business wires, also sent out news releases through them to media across the nation. Soon he was being contacted by hundreds of magazines, newspapers, and radio and television stations from all over the country. Everybody wanted to write about the Pet Rock. It had become perhaps the biggest publicity blitz in the history of American business.

Gary was so much in demand that he once gave simultaneous telephone interviews to two radio stations. He appeared on such national television shows as the *Tonight Show* and *Tomorrow*. Since publicity like this cannot be purchased, it is impossible to put a price tag on its value—but an equivalent advertising blitz would have cost many millions. After the craze had ended, Gary was invited to address a marketing group in Los Angeles. "I told them I was very proud of the fact that I never spent a penny to advertise the Pet Rock," he says with a grin. "When they heard that they died laughing."

Source: *Why Didn't I Think of That!* by Robert L. Shook. Copyright © 1982 by Robert L. Shook. Reprinted by arrangement with New American Library, New York, New York.

Steps in a Promotional Campaign

How does the owner-manager prepare the promotional program for the product or service and/or the business? Following are the essential steps in carrying out a promotional program that can be used as a guide for the small business.

FIGURE 8-10   **Effectiveness of Promotion Types**

	Personal Selling	Sales Promotions	Public Relations	Advertising
Create awareness of product or business	Weak	Weak	Strong	Strong
Develop interest in product	Weak	Medium	Weak	Strong
Increase desire to purchase product	Medium	Medium	Weak	Medium
Achieve product purchase	Strong	Medium	Weak	Weak

1.   Set Promotional Objectives.   Specific objectives should be set prior to the promotion. Typical examples are the desired percentage increase in sales, the amount of traffic to be generated, and the percentage of awareness increase desired.

2.   Determine the Target of the Promotion.   While in many cases the target will be the ultimate consumer, often it may be a middleman in the distribution channel or another group that has considerable influence over the purchase.

3.   Understand the Target's Needs and Perceptions of the Product or Service.   Once the target of the promotion has been determined, it is essential that information be gathered about that group with regard to their needs, media habits, and perceptions of the product category or specific product or service. This information is very similar to the consumer profile discussed earlier.

4.   Develop the Relevant Theme.   The next step is to develop a theme for the promotion that will reflect responseness to target needs and perceptions and help achieve the promotional objective. It is important that only one theme be used, since too many themes or too much information can confuse the consumer and lead to unsatisfactory results.

5.   Determine the Method or Media to Use.   The decision about which promotional type to use often depends on the relative importance of creating awareness and/or closing the sale. Figure 8-10 lists the strengths of each previously mentioned type of promotion with respect to these purposes. As the figure illustrates, advertising and public relations and some sales promotions tend to be more effective in creating awareness, whereas personal selling tends to work better for achieving or closing the sale.

6.   Develop a Specific Promotional Message.   Once the theme and medium have been determined, it is possible to develop the specific type of message to be used. As Figure 8-9 points out, some types of information are not appropriate for certain types of media.

7. Setting the Promotional Budget.   Once the method of promotion is determined, it is possible to estimate the cost of the promotion. Several methods are used to determine amounts to spend on promotion. The most common approach is the percent of sales method. Standard percentages for various businesses can serve as a guide in using this method. (see Appendix C for examples). The percent of sales method is theoretically weak but simple to apply, which explains its high rate of use by small businesses. A business owner should remain flexible in using these percentages, however, as market and product conditions may necessitate a deviation from the averages.

8. Implement the Promotional Program.   An essential feature of implementing the program is proper timing. Certain times of the year, the week, and even the day may be inappropriate for promoting the product or service to the target market.

9. Evaluate the Effectiveness of the Promotion.   The owner-manager should attempt to evaluate the promotional effectiveness to aid in future promotions. Evaluating effectiveness is much easier if specific objectives such as those mentioned earlier are set. Observations of results and surveys may be used in this evaluation. The mechanics of using primary research methods were discussed in Chapter 3.

As this chapter illustrated, many aspects are involved in the marketing plan of a small business. The way all of these aspects are integrated so that they comprise a clear and coordinated strategy often spells the difference between a successful and unsuccessful business. Appendix D at the conclusion of this chapter provides a marketing plan checklist.

Summary

1. Marketing activities include defining the target customer's needs and wants, monitoring the relevant outside influences, developing the product or service, selecting the channel of distribution, setting the price, and developing the promotional program.
2. The three types of target markets a small business may attempt to reach are consumer markets, industrial markets, and export markets.
3. Information required in exporting includes the forms of government assistance available, the unique characteristics of the foreign market, and the mechanisms of exporting.
4. Some of the most common external influences affecting the small business are the economy, the competition, legal restrictions, and the social and cultural environment.
5. In dealing with external influences, the owner-manager must identify which external conditions affect the business and then set up a system to monitor and effectively respond to changes in those influences.

6. All products or services have a life cycle in which sales and profits increase and eventually decline. The marketing strategy will change as the product or service moves through its life cycle.

7. To reduce risk in the early stages of a product life cycle, some small businesses get other companies to produce their products.

8. Speed of adoption of a new product can be increased by developing significant advantages over existing products, reducing the product's complexity, providing for the purchase of the product in smaller amounts, and allowing the results of using the product to be quickly evident and easily communicated.

9. The classifications of consumer goods include convenience, shopping, and specialty goods. The marketing strategy will differ for each type.

10. The major decision areas in distribution include being aware of the channel options, deciding on the length of the channel, and determining the channel intensity.

11. In determining length of the distribution channel, the owner-manager should examine market and product characteristics as well as the firm's capabilities.

12. An intensive channel is used where product availability is important. Exclusive channels are found for products that need greater sales effort and support.

13. The three methods of setting price are cost-based, demand-based, and competition-based pricing.

14. Price elasticity is a measure of consumer sensitivity to various price levels. The owner-manager should determine how important price is to the consumer.

15. There are four methods of providing information about a product or service: advertising, sales promotion, public relations, and personal selling.

16. The essential steps in carrying out a promotional program are as follows: (1) set promotional objectives; (2) specify the target of the promotion; (3) understand the target's needs and perceptions of the product or service; (4) develop the relevant theme; (5) determine the method and/or media to use; (6) develop a specific promotional message; (7) set a promotional budget; (8) implement the promotional program; and (9) evaluate the effectiveness of the promotion.

Chapter Problems and Applications

1. Define the target market for Dollcraft (see Incident 8–1). What are the target market demographics, lifestyle characteristics, purchase characteristics, and purchase motivations (see Figure 8–1)?

2. Illustrate how W.P.M. Handcrafted Log Homes Ltd. (Incident 8–4) successfully completed the three steps in developing an export market outlined in the chapter.

3. Discuss the uncontrollable variables that might affect W.P.M. Handcrafted Log Homes Ltd. in its exporting of log homes.

4. Develop a marketing mix (i.e., product, promotion, price, distribution) for a bakery.

5. Where is Kellogg's Corn Flakes in the product life cycle? What has Kellogg done to prolong the life cycle of this product?

6. What could a new cereal company do to speed up the adoption rate for its cereals?

7. How would you classify the following products (see Figure 8–5)? How would you promote and distribute these products? Explain.
   a. Discount clothes
   b. Quality furniture
   c. Chocolate bar
   d. Bread

8. Develop a distribution system for Hitchfinder Fencing Company (Incident 8–7). Which channel should be used? What should be the level of channel intensity?

9. Which pricing system would you use for the following products? Why?
   a. Campbell's Soup
   b. Montreal Expo season tickets
   c. Patio furniture
   d. Automobiles

10. Using a scale of −1 to +1, how would you rate the following products for elasticity (−1 = inelastic, 0 = neutral, and +1 = elastic)? Justify your answers.
    a. Salt
    b. Porsche automobile
    c. Lawn mower

11. You have been approached to develop an advertising campaign for a new local discount golf franchise. The owners realize they need to develop awareness among consumers but have a very limited amount of funds available for advertising. Using Figure 8–9 as a guide, decide which media type to use for the advertising campaign. Justify your decision to use or not to use each media type.

12. Choose the promotional types (advertising, personal selling, sales promotion, and public relations) you would use for the following list of products. Explain why.
    a. Medical supplies
    b. Hula Hoop™
    c. Recreational vehicles

      d. Coca-Cola™

      e. Participation program (government fitness program)

      f. B.C. Lions (football team)

13. Interview a local small business owner and find out what his or her marketing strategy is. Determine the promotional strategy. Are these strategies similar to those discussed in the chapter?

APPENDIX A
ORGANIZATIONS THAT PURCHASE FROM SMALL BUSINESSES

Rank by Purchases	Organization	Annual Purchases ($ millions)		Estimated Percentage Purchased from Small Business
		1985	*1984*	
1	Federal government of Canada	$6,114	$5,178	31
2	General Motors of Canada	5,764	4,122	15
9	Canadian National Railways	1,300	1,000	30
14	Kmart Canada Ltd.	851	721	25
20	Ontario Hydro	721	751	82
28	Saskatchewan Wheat Pool	490	335	15
33	Union Carbide Canada Inc.	363	398	30
78	Harding Carpets Ltd.	75	75	15
82	Grand & Toy Ltd.	70	N/A	99

SOURCE: "Mission 86—Canada's Top 150 Purchasers," *The Magazine That's All about Small Business,* June 1986, pp. 49–53.

APPENDIX B
AGENCIES PROVIDING EXPORT ASSISTANCE

Department of Industry, Science and Technology
1st Floor, East Tower
235 Queen Street
Ottawa, Ontario, KIA 0H5

Export Development Corporation (EDC)
Box 655
Ottawa, Ontario, K1P 5T9

Canadian Commercial Corporation (CCC)
Bental Tower IV
P.O. Box 49158
Vancouver, B.C., V7X 1K8

Canadian International Development Agency (CIDA)
200 Promenade du Portage
Hull, Quebec, K1A 0G4

Canadian Export Association (CEA)
99 Bank Street Suite 250
Ottawa, Ontario, K1P 6B9

External Affairs and International Trade
Canada
125 Sussex Drive
Ottawa, Ontario, K1A 0G2

APPENDIX C
ADVERTISING AS PRACTICED BY SELECTED SMALL BUSINESSES

Type of Business	Average Ad Budget (percent of sales)	Favourite Media	Other Media Used
Gift stores	2.2	Weekly newspapers	Yellow Pages, radio, direct mail, magazines
Hair-dressing shops	2.0–5.0	Yellow Pages	Newspapers (for special events), word of mouth
Home furnishing stores	1.0–3.2	Newspapers	Direct mail, radio
Pet shops	2.0–5.0	Yellow Pages	Window displays, shopper newspapers, direct mail
Restaurants and food services	0.3–3.2	Newspapers, radio, Yellow Pages, transit, outdoor	Television for chain or franchise restaurants
Shoe stores	0.5–0.8	Newspapers, direct mail, radio	Yellow Pages (especially for specialty shoe vendors)
Bars and cocktail lounges	1.0–1.2	Newspapers (entertainment section), local magazines, tourist bulletins	Specialties
Bookstores	1.5–1.6	Newspapers, shoppers, Yellow Pages	Direct mail
Building maintenance services		Direct mail, door-to-door, Yellow Pages	Signs on company vehicles and equipment
Camera shops (independent)	2.0–3.5	Direct mail, handouts, Yellow Pages	Newspapers (except large urban)
Drugstores (independent)	1.0–3.0	Local newspapers, shoppers	Direct mail (list from prescription files)
Dry cleaning plants	0.9–2.0	Local newspapers, shoppers, Yellow Pages	Store front, ads, pamphlets on clothes care
Equipment rental services	1.7–4.7	Yellow Pages	

SOURCES: Adapted from Dennis H. Tootelian and Ralph M. Gaedeke, *Small Business Review* (Sacramento, Calif.: Goodyear Publishing Company, 1978), pp. 154–55; *Dun & Bradstreet Operating Statistics, 1990* (Toronto: Dun & Bradstreet).

APPENDIX D
CHECKLIST FOR A MARKETING PLAN

The Target Market

1. Has the target market been clearly defined geographically?
2. Has the target consumer been clearly identified?
3. What are the target consumer characteristics—age, income, education, occupation?
4. What are the target consumer lifestyle characteristics—activities, interests, opinions, media habits, personalities?
5. What are the target consumer purchase characteristics—what, when, where, how much of the product or service they purchase?
6. What are the reasons the target consumer purchases the product?
7. Are there any government programs that can assist in marketing to the target consumer?

The Environment

1. What economic forces will affect the business?
2. What is the competitive situation? How many competitors? What are relative market shares? What is the nature of competitors' strategies? What are competitors' strengths and weaknesses?
3. What legal restrictions will affect the marketing of the product or service?
4. Are there any social or cultural trends that will affect the business?
5. What adjustments have been made to accommodate any of the above environmental constraints?

The Product

1. What are the objectives and policies for the product?
2. How will the product be manufactured?
3. What is the estimated length of the life cycle for the product?
4. What can be done to increase rate of adoption of the product?
5. How does the target consumer classify the product?
6. What will be the product quality, depth, and variety?
7. What warranty and service standards will be set?
8. Does the product or service possess the features or characteristics the target consumer wants?

Distribution

1. What channel options are available to reach the target consumer?
2. Can the product be marketed better through a short-direct channel or a long-indirect channel?
3. Who are potential buyers for the product?
4. What trade shows exist for the industry?
5. What level of intensity should exist in the distribution channel?
6. Will the selected distribution channel provide the product to the target consumer at the right place, at the right time, and in the right quantities?

Price

1. What price policies have been set?
2. What price is the target consumer willing to pay?
3. How important is price to the target consumer?
4. What levels of markup are required to cover selling and overhead costs?
5. What are competitors' prices, and how do they compare with our product price?

Promotion

1. What are the objectives of the promotional program?
2. Does the theme reflect target consumer needs and attitudes?
3. What specific media will be selected to carry the message to the target consumer?
4. Does the product require personal selling?
5. How much will be spent on promotion?
6. What is the timing of the promotional program? Has a calendar timetable been prepared for this?
7. How will the results of the promotion be evaluated?
8. Will the business offer credit to the target consumer? If so, what procedures will be followed to screen, monitor, and collect accounts?

Suggested Readings

Banner, William. *Advertising and Sales Promotion: Cost Effective Techniques for Your Small Business.* Englewood Cliffs, N.J.: Prentice Hall, 1983.

Beamish, Paul W., and Hugh Munro. "Export Characteristics of Small Canadian Manufacturers." *Journal of Small Business and Entrepreneurship,* Summer 1985, p. 30.

Blake, Gary, and Robert Bly. *How to Promote Your Own Business.* Scarborough, Ont.: Canadian Small Business Institute, 1990.

Brannen, William. *Practical Marketing for Your Small Retail Business.* Englewood Cliffs, N.J.: Prentice Hall, 1981.

Bullock, John F. "Competing in a Global Economy." *Journal of Small Business and Entrepreneurship,* July–September 1991.

Davidson, Jeffrey P. *The Marketing Source Book for Small Business.* New York: John Wiley & Sons, 1989.

Dorff, Ralph. *Marketing for the Small Manufacturer.* Englewood Cliffs, N.J.: Prentice Hall, 1983.

Gray, Douglas A., and Diana L. Gray. *The Complete Canadian Small Business Guide.* Toronto: McGraw-Hill Ryerson, 1988, pp. 206–27.

"Marketing." In *Canadian Small Business Guide.* Don Mills, Ont.: CCH Canadian Limited, 1981, pp. 3001–3499.

Quagliaroli, John. *How to Write a Marketing Plan.* New York: Center for Entrepreneurial Management, 1986.

Small Business in Canada, 1991. Ottawa: Industry, Science and Technology Canada, 1991.

COMPREHENSIVE CASE
THE FRAMEMAKERS: PART 5

Saturday was the big day! Robert and Teresa had been able to obtain the needed financing after considerable difficulty and were now ready to open their store. The few weeks leading up to the grand opening were hectic. The interior remodelling and layout organization took longer than they had expected. Some of the inventory did not arrive on time. The Normans learned they needed many items they hadn't planned for. As a result of these difficulties, the opening had to be postponed for a few weeks.

Once ready, they placed advertising in newspapers, on radio, and even on television announcing the store's opening. Robert soon found out that the $2,500 budgeted for opening promotion didn't go very far. The quarter-page ad in the local newspaper totalled $500 for three days. Robert paid $700 for radio advertising the week before opening on the two Brandon radio stations. This included production costs. He also placed an advertisement on a local television station that cost $1,300, including production. Robert wished he had had more money for promotion but realized that if he hadn't purchased the lowest advertising rate, he wouldn't have received even the coverage he did. He wondered how other framing shops got much promotion done using the 1 percent of sales figure the Professional Picture Framers Association (PPFA) had suggested.

When Saturday rolled around, Robert and Teresa were a bit disappointed to note that the store wasn't as busy as they had hoped. In addition, several people who came in looked around and left without making purchases. Robert hoped this was characteristic of a typical store opening. Some purchasers of frames indicated that The Framemakers had good prices on the merchandise. Others, however, complained prices on some items were way out of line. This troubled Robert, as he had been sure to follow the suppliers' suggested retail prices on most of the merchandise. A few customers also complained of poor parking and of difficulty finding The Framemakers.

At the end of the day, Robert and Teresa were exhausted and disappointed. They had rung up sales of only $312. They were concerned about the negative comments they had received and wondered if this was just an occupational hazard or if the business had some real problems.

Questions

1. Evaluate The Framemakers' opening promotion program. Suggest any changes that might have improved its effectiveness.
2. Evaluate The Framemakers' pricing procedures. Make recommendations regarding what, if anything, should be done at this point.

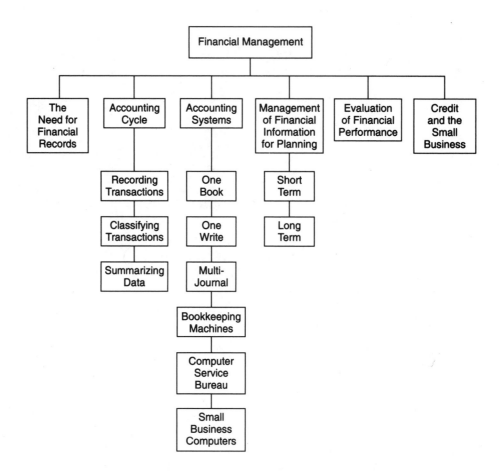

CHAPTER
9

Financial Management

Chapter Objectives

- To review the fundamentals of small business accounting.
- To discuss the various types of accounting systems a small business can use.
- To describe the considerations in purchasing a computer for the small business.
- To show how to develop and use budgets and financial planning tools.
- To illustrate how to evaluate and control the financial operations of the small business.
- To discuss the important aspects of credit management for the small business.

Small Business Profile

Doreen Braverman
The Flag Shop

In 1974 Doreen Braverman's career had been anything but entrepreneurial. She had worked as a telephone operator, receptionist, and teacher, as well as in advertising. Her decision to purchase a small premium and incentives business changed the direction of her working life.

The company she purchased—Vancouver Regalia, located in downtown Vancouver—did reasonably well, but Braverman became convinced that one of its products, flags, had more potential than the rest. She decided to focus on selling flags of all kinds to a ready market. Many businesses were adopting the use of flags; also, demand for flags from the government and private individuals was growing. Braverman renamed the company The Flag Shop and soon found that because of the high sales growth, she would have to make her own flags to ensure an adequate supply. She therefore added a silk screening business and moved into flag manufacturing with the establishment of Atlas Textile Print Ltd.

Growth of the companies has been steady. The Flag Shop has topped $2.5 million in sales, has over 40 employees, and has opened up five additional stores.

Braverman realized early in her entrepreneurial career that she would have to understand how to manage her business to make it remain successful. To this end, she earned an MBA degree by correspondence from the Canadian School of Management in Toronto. This training has helped her maintain tight financial control over The Flag Shop. She receives weekly sales and operations reports from her managers and prepares monthly reviews on the company's progress, which she compares to the planned budgets. Braverman recognizes the value of financial planning; she prepares annual plans three years in advance.

Doreen Braverman is also active in industry associations. While she has contributed considerably to these organizations, she has also gained valuable contacts and assistance from them. She is a strong advocate for free enterprise and believes the government should not subsidize businesses.

Braverman continues to work 50-plus-hour weeks and indicates that she "loves every minute of it."

Printed with the permission of Doreen Braverman.

Incident 9–1

Mall Expansion Folds Calgary Fan Retailer

There's more than a hint of irony in Rick Borden's voice as he recalls his company's early days. Fandango Ceiling Fans Ltd. got its start in a 10-ft. by 10-ft. kiosk in Calgary's Deerfoot Mall just before Christmas, 1983. Six years later, the specialty retailer had grown into a 15-outlet chain grossing more than $5 million on sales of Casablanca-style fans. But while sales had increased steadily, Fandango's profit picture was swirling into red. Borden had planned to boost his market share by franchising in major malls across the country. But he underestimated how demanding that growth strategy could be. High overheads and heavy losses finally took Fandango out of circulation last March.

For one thing, says Borden, overhead in the mall locations was "astronomically higher" than in storefront outlets. Wages were about 50% higher, he says, because of extended store hours—72 hours a week, vs. 48 hours outside malls—and rents averaged two to three times higher. To top it off, leasehold improvements at each new location ate up some $30,000 to $50,000.

Higher volumes also meant Borden had to source more of his product from the Far East, which boosted the inventory he was carrying between shipments. To offset the cost, he increased the markup on goods going to each store. Retail price hikes offset some of that, says Borden, but the markup "made it difficult for [individual stores] to become profitable." Sales increased to $4.6 million in 1988, but costs were rising faster. Profit plummeted to $50,000, partly because Borden had to buy back two franchised outlets after buyers ran out of cash.

The Royal Bank of Canada, which had backed Borden's venture from its early days, showed increasing concern. Fandango operated out of margin on its $750,000 line of credit during February, says Borden, and the bank started bouncing cheques: "When you're in a tight cash-flow position, and you're asking suppliers to bear with you, when [cheques start bouncing], they start to lose confidence real quick." When the bank called the loan, Borden put Fandango into bankruptcy early in March.

Source: Catherine Callaghan, "Mall Expansion Folds Calgary Fan Retailer," *Profit Magazine,* July-August 1990, pp. 16–17.

The Need for Financial Records

Incident 9–1 illustrates how financial management problems spelled disaster for a small business. This situation occurs often with small businesses. A recent survey found that from 24 to 45 percent of Canadian small business owners did not understand basic financial measurement ratios used in evaluating their businesses.[1] Failure to understand and manage the financial aspects of a business can be disastrous for the small business owner. The need for competence in this area is continually growing as new technology and greater competition in many markets necessitate closer monitoring of operations and quicker decision making. Keeping proper records can warn the owner-manager in advance of future financial difficulties and assist in planning the growth of the business.

Another reason for proper recordkeeping is to satisfy government requirements. While most owner-managers don't revere Revenue Canada, the fact that this agency requires accurate recordkeeping to calculate a business's tax liability may actually benefit the small business.

Recordkeeping is also necessary if a business must borrow money. Lenders will require that proper recordkeeping be followed to ensure that debt obligations are met.

The availability of accurate and current records of the operations of the business is also essential for the evaluation and control of business operations.

Small business owners may be tempted to neglect the financial aspects of the business in favour of the day-to-day operational aspects such as production, personnel management, and marketing. Often this is because they have an incomplete understanding of how to manage the recordkeeping system effectively. Understanding the managerial aspects of recordkeeping requires reviewing some basic accounting fundamentals.

The Accounting Cycle

Figure 9–1 illustrates the basic process by which transactions of the business are translated into financial statements.

Recording Transactions

Transactions are recorded chronologically (as they occur) in a record called a *journal.* Many types of journals are used. In a business where few transactions occur, these entries may be made manually. In many retail businesses, the daily cash register tape total may be used to record the revenue journal entries. The check register can be used to record payments or disbursements. In businesses with a large number of transactions, the journal may be kept mechanically by a bookkeeping machine or by a computer.

Accounting uses double-entry recording. This means the amounts of each transaction are recorded twice. This procedure accurately reflects the fact that each

---

FIGURE 9-1   The Accounting Cycle

Recording of Transactions (journal)	$\rightarrow$	Classification of Transaction Totals (ledger)	$\rightarrow$	Summarizing of Data (financial statements)

transaction affects two parts (accounts) of the business. Often a decrease in one means an increase in another. For example, if a desk costing $400 is purchased and paid for in cash, the amount of cash in the business decreases by $400 and the value of the office furniture in the business increases by $400. The use of double-entry accounting also allows double-checking of the accuracy of the entries.

Figure 9–2 illustrates how some typical recording entries might appear in a small business journal. In each of these transactions, for every increase in one account a corresponding decrease occurs in another account. At the end of the period, the totals of increases and decreases at the bottom of the page for a number of transactions should be equal.

Classifying Transaction Totals

Once the transactions have been accurately and properly recorded, the next step is to group or classify similar transactions together. These groupings or classifications are called *accounts* and are entered into a book called a *ledger.* The ledger keeps a running balance of the dollar amounts in each account so that the net totals may be known at the end of each period. Like journal entries, a ledger may be kept manually or by computer. Figure 9–3 shows some accounts of a typical ledger for service, retail, and manufacturing firms. The recording and classifying steps of the accounting cycle are usually referred to as *bookkeeping.* Many small businesses have found it valuable to hire an accountant to set up the bookkeeping system most appropriate for their businesses.

Summarizing Data

The third step in the accounting cycle (which is usually carried out by an accountant) involves taking the account totals from the ledger and putting them together to form the financial statements. These statements indicate the past

---

FIGURE 9–2   Typical Journal Entries

Jan. 1, 1992	Cash 2,000	
	Accounts Receivable	2,000
	Received from Bill Smith on account.	
Jan. 5, 1992	Equipment 4,500	
	Cash	4,500
	Purchased equipment for cash.	
Jan. 20, 1992	Inventory 2,000	
	Accounts Payable	2,000
	Inventory is purchased on account.	
Jan. 31, 1992	Accounts Payable 500	
	Cash	500
	Liabilities of $500 are paid with cash.	

FIGURE 9-3   Typical Ledger Accounts

Service Firm	For a Retail Firm Add These Accounts	For a Manufacturing Firm Add These Accounts
Sales	Sales Returns and Allowances	Machinery
Cash	Sales Discounts	Accumulated Depreciation: Machinery
Accounts Receivable Accounts Payable	Furniture and Fixtures	
Land	Accumulated Depreciation: Furniture and Fixtures	Cost of Goods Sold: Raw Materials Direct Labour Factory Overhead
Building		
Accumulated Depreciation: Building	Merchandise Inventory	
Office Equipment		
Accumulated Depreciation: Office Equipment Office Supplies Inventory Retained Earnings Salaries Expense Telephone Expense Advertising Expense Office Supplies Expense	Cost of Goods Sold: Purchases Purchase Returns Purchase Discounts Transportation In	
Depreciation Expense: Building		
Depreciation Expense: Equipment		
Miscellaneous Expense		
Salaries Payable		
Utilities Expense		
Licenses and Taxes Expense		
Insurance Expense		
Accounting and Legal Expense		

---

success and current position of the business. It is important that the small business owner understand what financial statements mean and how to use them.

Essentially three financial statements are important to the small business owner: the balance sheet, the income statement, and the cash flow statement.

Balance Sheet (Statement of Financial Position).   The balance sheet presents, in summary form, a snapshot of what the business owns and owes at any point in time. Those items the business owns are termed *assets,* and those owed are either *liabilities* (owed to sources outside the business) or *equity* (owed to owners). Figure 9-4 illustrates a balance sheet for a hypothetical small business. Assets and liabilities are generally listed in order of liquidity, with the most liquid being first.

FIGURE 9–4

SMALL BUSINESS CORPORATION
Balance Sheet
As of December 31, 1992

Assets

Current assets:

Cash	$ 3,449	
Accounts receivable	5,944	
Inventories	12,869	
Prepaid expenses	389	
Total current assets		$22,651

Fixed assets:

Land, buildings, and equipment cost	26,926	
Less accumulated depreciation	13,534	
Total fixed assets		$13,412

Other assets:

Investments	1,000	
		1,000

Total assets $37,063

Liabilities and Shareholders' Equity

Current liabilities:

Accounts payable	$ 6,602	
Other current liabilities	845	
Total current liabilities		$ 7,447

Other liabilities:

Mortgage payable	3,000	
Total liabilities		10,447

Shareholders' equity:

Common stock	15,000	
Retained earnings	11,616	
Total shareholders' equity		26,616

Total liabilities and shareholders' equity $37,063

Usually assets and liabilities are divided into current (to be consumed in one year) and noncurrent (in more than one year).

Income Statement (Statement of Profit and Loss).   The income statement shows the results of the operations of the business for a given time period. This statement, introduced in Chapter 3, is an integral part of the feasibility analysis and the business plan. The profit or income is determined by taking revenue from operations and subtracting expenses incurred in earning that revenue. Figure 9–5 illustrates an income statement for a hypothetical small business.

FIGURE 9–5

SMALL BUSINESS CORPORATION
Income Statement
For the Year Ended December 31, 1992

Net sales	$197,000
Cost of goods sold	123,000
Gross margin on sales	74,000
Operating expenses	
Selling expenses	
Advertising expense	1,200
Sales salaries expense	18,300
Depreciation expense—store equipment	2,000
Total selling expenses	21,500
General expenses	
Depreciation expense—building	3,000
Insurance expense	675
Miscellaneous general expenses	425
General salaries expense	7,200
Total general expenses	11,300
Total operating expenses	32,800
Net operating margin	41,200
Other expenses	
Interest expense	2,750
Net income before income taxes	38,450
Income taxes	14,450
Net income	$ 24,000

Cash Flow Statement and/or Statement of Changes in Financial Position. The importance and format of the *cash flow statement* was discussed in Chapter 7. This statement is similar to the income statement except that only cash inflows and outflows are shown.

In recent years, it has been common to examine not only the cash flow position of a firm but all of the asset/liability accounts over time. This practice has led to the popularity of a statement called the *statement of changes in financial position.* As the name implies, this statement presents balance sheet account changes from one period to the next. It can help explain why a business has a positive net income but a decrease in cash for the same period of operation, a situation that mystifies some small business owners. The examination of the statement of changes in financial position can be complex. An example of a cash flow statement for a hypothetical small business appears in Figure 9–6.

FIGURE 9–6

SMALL BUSINESS CORPORATION
Cash Flow Forecast 1992

	Jan.	Feb.	Mar.	Apr.	May	Jun.
Cash receipts:						
Sales in 1992	—	$ 5,000	$ 7,500	$10,000	$10,000	$10,000
Accounts receivable for 1991	$19,000	13,000	6,000			
Other:						
Equity funding		10,000				
Total cash receipts	$19,000	$28,000	$ 13,500	$10,000	$10,000	$10,000
Cash disbursements:						
Cost of sales						
Labour	$ 5,000	$ 5,000	$ 5,000	$ 7,000	$ 7,000	$ 7,000
Materials	400	800	800	1,000	1,100	1,100
Transport	300	400	400	500	400	400
Accounts payable from 1991	12,000	10,000	10,000	6,000		
Selling expense	400	800	800	800	800	800
Administration	250	550	550	550	550	550
Fixed-asset investment						
Long-term debt repayment			2,500			2,500
Income tax installment			3,000			3,000
Interest on debt						
Long-term debt			680			640
Bank loan (other cash source)	400	350	270	370	430	440
Total cash disbursements	$18,750	$17,900	$ 24,000	$16,220	$10,280	$16,430
Monthly cash surplus (deficit)	$ 250	$10,100	$–10,500	$–6,220	$ –280	$–6,430
Accumulated cash surplus (deficit) for 1992	250	10,350	–150	–6,370	–6,650	–13,080

Accounting Systems for the Small Business

Small businesses use several types of accounting systems today. Variations occur because of differences in size, type of business (retail, service, manufacturing), industry, number of transactions, and expertise of the owner. Following is a brief description of some of the more common general systems used.

One-Book System

The one-book system is most appropriate for the very small business with few transactions. It combines the recording and classifying steps of the accounting cycle into one step and presents this information on one page in a typical columnized ledger. Figure 9–7 illustrates a typical one-book system. In this example, the journal entry is recorded in columns 1 through 5 and the ledger

FIGURE 9–7   **Illustration of a One-Book Accounting System**

1	*2*	*3*	*4*	*5*	*6*	*7*	*8*	*9*	*10*
			Bank		**Revenue**		**Expenses**		
Date	*Description*	*Check Number*	*In*	*Out*	*Sales/Miscellaneous*		*Wages/Advertising/Other*		
Sept 1/92	Wages paid for August	25		5,000			5,000		
Sept 8/92	Sales for week 1		8,000		8,000				
Sept 12/92	Paid utility bill	26		800					800
Sept 15/92	Sales for week 2		6,500		6,500				
Sept 19/92	Paid advertising bill	27		400				400	

accounts are entered in columns 6 through 10. The double-entry procedure is followed, and column totals at the end of the period are taken to prepare the financial statements.

One-Write System

A simplification of the one-book system is the one-write or "pegboard" system used by many small businesses. The format is the same as that for the one-book system. However, special carbon checks are used so that when a disbursement check is made out, it automatically enters the name and amounts into columns 2, 3, and 4 of the journal. This eliminates one operation and reduces the potential for error in transposing the information from the check register to the journal columns. The ledger part of the entry is the same as that for the one-book system.

One-write systems are commercially available and are usually reasonably priced.

Multijournal System

For businesses that are larger or have a large number of similar transactions, the journal and ledger entries may be separated into two books. It is common for the business to use more than one journal, such as a sales journal, a disbursement journal, a payroll journal, and others. This practice can simplify the entry procedure and allow easy transfer of the journal totals to the ledger accounts.

The multijournal system, along with the one-book and one-write systems, is a manual system whose use is decreasing as more and more small businesses adopt automated systems.

Computer Service Bureau

An attractive option for many small businesses that cannot afford their own computerized accounting system is to use a computer service bureau. Most of these services are offered by accounting firms. For a monthly fee, a small business can take its journal and/or ledger totals to such a bureau and within a few days receive detailed financial statements for the period (usually monthly). Much of the bookkeeping will still need to be carried out by the business, but a good portion of steps 2 and 3 of the accounting cycle can be provided by the service bureau. The big advantage is that the details contained in the reports can be valuable in operating the business.

Small Business Computer Systems

Many small businesses are finding that computer systems are no longer reserved solely for large companies. Many have also realized great benefits from purchasing a computer, as Incident 9–2 shows. Not only has the cost of computers come down, making a computer affordable for the small business, but numerous software programs exist that are written especially for small businesses. Computer systems can manage several types of information requirements for a business. Some of the most commonly used operations are the following:

- *Word processing.* A simplified and efficient method for producing any written correspondence.
- *General ledger.* A complete bookkeeping/accounting system of all business transactions.
- *Database files.* Storing, monitoring, and retrieving of information on inventory, personnel, customers, and suppliers.
- *Payroll.* Simplified payroll systems, including cheque writing.
- *Financial planning.* Spreadsheet packages to prepare actual and projected financial statements.
- *Capital investment decisions.* Programs calculate interest costs, payback, and present values.

In all of these functions, the computer can allow for increased speed and accuracy of maintaining records, improved service to customers, improved and more timely information to managers, and reduced operating costs. Figure 9–8 reviews the specific applications and strengths of computers. Note that the selection of software is the most important aspect of the computer decision. Software that will carry out the operations the small business requires should be selected first, followed by the hardware on which the software will run. This ensures that the hardware is powerful enough to handle the demands the software places on the computer.

Despite the benefits, purchasing a computer does not automatically solve an owner-manager's financial problems. Many small businesses have purchased a computer only to find that it was the wrong decision. Such a decision is illustrated in Incident 9–3. It is important that the small business owner fully understand the potential pitfalls of computer ownership as well as the benefits. Some of the potential disadvantages include the following.

Cost.   Although microcomputer costs are coming down, an adequate total system for most small businesses could still cost over $3,000.

Incident 9–2

Computer Keeps Track of Nickels and Dimes

Bill Wright, owner-manager of Georgia Straight Collision Ltd. of Courtenay, British Columbia, barely broke even, despite revenues of $730,000. He says the problem was simply an inability to keep track of the company's spending. Says Wright: "We were moving too fast to keep track of the nickels and dimes, which quickly amounted to what we should have made in profit."

Wright decided to computerize the business so that sales and expense information, which had been slipping through the cracks, could be kept and analyzed. He selected a package called the Automotive Repair Management System (ARM), specifically designed for collision shops by 3M Canada Ltd., paying $12,000 for the software and $6,000 for the PC on which to run it. The system keeps track of inventory and the productivity of employees, and handles all paper work from purchase and work orders to the final customer bill.

If Wright had a reasonable handle on the business in 1984, he now has percentages down cold. The flat rates determined by the Insurance Corporation of British Columbia are stored right in the system, as are material and labour costs. Instead of relying on an annual analysis from his accountant, Wright can make most of his critical ratios appear with a couple of keystrokes.

Now approaching $1 million in revenue for 1985, with a 12 percent net profit margin, Georgia Straight boasts a second location and an additional line of business.

Source: Randall Litchfield, "Computer Keeps Track of Nickels and Dimes," *Small Business*, April 1986, p. 18.

FIGURE 9–8   **Some Benefits of Using a Small Business Computer**

Applications	Reduce Labour Expense	Shorten Billing Cycle	Carry Less Inventory	Increase Sales	Control Costs	Manage Cash	Plan and Control Growth
Accounts payable	X				X	X	X
Accounts receivable	X	X	X	X		X	X
Business modelling				X	X	X	X
General ledger	X			X	X		X
Inventory control	X	X	X	X	X	X	X
Order entry	X	X	X	X		X	X
Payroll	X				X		X
Word processing	X			X			

SOURCE: Data General Corporation, *The Insider's Guide to Small Business Computers* (Westboro, Mass.: Data General Corporation, 1980), p. 8.

Incident 9–3

Small Business Stumbles into the Computer Age

At a recent charity auction in rural Carroll County, Maryland, one local lawyer got away with what he considered a steal: a personal computer for $2,000. "Hot dog!" he thought. He could do all his client billings on the computer. Prize in hand, he strutted over to his corner computer retailer, Basically Computers Inc., in nearby Westminster. There he found out what he had really bought: a computer that lacked enough memory to run his legal billing system—and whose maker was extinct.

The lawyer's experience is all too common for small businessmen. While the rest of corporate America shifts into high gear in office automation, most small businesses are still casting about in the wilderness. For the handful that have already plunged ahead, the move to office systems is often filled with false starts.

Source: "Small Business Stumbles into the Computer Age," *Business Week,* October 8, 1984, p. 126.

Obsolescence.   The rapid changes in the computer industry are resulting in very short life cycles for most computers. Often, by the time a computer is purchased and operating, new, improved versions hit the market.

Employee Resistance.   Employees within an organization may resist the introduction of a computer. The owner may need to involve such employees in the decision and purchase process to help dispel any such resistance.

Capabilities.   Many types of computers are available, all with different capabilities and characteristics. Some computers cannot do what the small business owner requires them to do, as Incident 9–2 illustrated. Thorough investigation of the business's needs and computer capability is required to avoid this situation. Business owners should purchase computers with future growth and expansion in mind, recognizing the possible need to add to existing capacity.

Set-Up Time.   Installing a computer system, educating those who will use it, and eliminating the bugs will take time. It is recommended that the system previously used by the small business be continued for a short period of time in case such a problem arises.

Failure to Compensate for Poor Bookkeeping.   Some small businesses purchase a computer hoping it will clean up their bookkeeping systems. However, a computer will not help a bookkeeping system that is sloppy and inaccurate. After all, the same information entered on a manual basis must be entered into the computer. A common rule of thumb used in the computer purchase decision is that if the information generated by a manual system is accurate but takes a long time to prepare and retrieve, a computer may be of great assistance.

As the preceding discussion shows, the decision to purchase a computer is not one to be made haphazardly. It should be approached systematically and with thorough investigation. Appendix A presents a checklist for use in making the computer purchase decision.

Management of Financial Information for Planning

The first part of this chapter dealt with the fundamental aspects of collecting and maintaining the financial information within the business. This information is of minimal value, however, unless it is used to monitor, evaluate, and control current operations as well as plan for the future.

Short-Term Financial Planning

Short-term financial planning consists of preparing an estimated future financial result of operations of the business. This kind of plan is generally referred to as a *budget* and was described in Chapter 3 in the preparation of the feasibility analysis. Although budgets can provide many benefits to an organization, relatively few small businesses prepare or work with budgets. Using a budget, however, can be a very valuable financial tool for the following reasons.

Clarification of Objectives.   A budget forces an organization to anticipate future operations and set goals and procedures to accomplish them.

Coordination.   The budgeting process draws employees and/or departments together and brings them into the planning process to input into the budget information relevant to their responsibilities.

Evaluation and Control.   A budget allows the owner-manager to quickly determine discrepancies that may require investigation. Such an investigation is often called *variance analysis*. It also allows comparison of planned (budgeted) amounts with actual results, which can improve effectiveness in the long term. Figure 9–9 shows how a budget might be established and used. After the comparison of budgeted (planned) and actual results, attempts can be made to explain the reasons for any differences. Consequently, changes might be made to correct the differences or refine the budgeting process.

Long-Term Financial Planning

Three types of long-term financial planning decisions could affect the small business—decisions regarding capital investment, capacity, and expansion.

FIGURE 9–9

SMALL BUSINESS CORPORATION
Income Statement
For the Year Ended December 31, 1992

	Budgeted	Actual	Difference	Explanation
Net sales	$197,000	$180,000	$17,000	
Cost of goods sold	123,000	120,000	3,000	Material costs increase
Gross margin on sales	74,000	60,000	14,000	
Operating expenses				
Selling expenses				
Advertising expense	1,200	1,200	0	
Sales salaries expense	18,300	18,300	0	
Total selling expenses ..	19,500	19,500	0	
General expenses				
Depreciation expense—store				Additional equipment
equipment	2,000	4,000	2,000	purchased
Depreciation				
expense—building	3,000	3,000	0	
Insurance expense	675	1,200	525	Premium increase
General salaries expense	7,200	7,200	0	
Miscellaneous general				
expenses	425	600	175	
Total general expenses ...	13,000	16,000	2,700	
Total operating expenses	32,800	35,500	2,700	
Net operating margin	41,200	24,500	16,700	
Other expenses				
Interest expense	2,750	3,200	450	Rate increase
Net income before income	38,450	21,300	17,150	
taxes				
Income taxes	14,450	7,455	6,995	Marginal rate decrease
Net income	$ 24,000	$ 13,845	$10,155	

The Capital Investment Decision. Most long-term planning includes the question of future capital purchases. This may involve the acquisition of land, buildings, equipment, or even another business. The small business owner needs to have a simple but accurate way to determine whether the decision will be financially sound. Some of the more commonly used methods of estimating future return for capital investments are illustrated below.

Rate-of-Return Method. This method estimates the annual rate of return of the new investment. After this value has been determined, it can be compared to alternative investments. Figure 9–10 shows how a rate of return for a capital asset is determined.

FIGURE 9–10   Rate-of-Return Method

Steps	*Example*
1. Calculate total cost of investment.	$50,000
2. Estimated depreciable life of investment.	5 years
3. Calculate average value of investment over life. Beginning value ($50,000) plus end value (0) divided by 2 equals average value.	$\dfrac{\$50,000}{2} = \$25,000$
4. Estimate average annual profit over depreciable life (net of depreciation).	$10,000
5. Average profit divided by average investment.	$\dfrac{\$10,000}{\$25,000} = 40\%$

A reasonable rate of return on a capital investment is between two and three times the prime rate of interest. Using this criteria, the 40 percent rate of return in this example represents an attractive investment.

FIGURE 9–11   Payback Method

Steps	*Example*
1. Calculate total cost of investment.	$50,000
2. Estimate depreciable life of investment.	5 years
3. Calculate annual depreciation charge.	$10,000
4. Estimate average annual profit over depreciable life.	$10,000
5. Cost of investment divided by cash inflow (profit + depreciation).	$\dfrac{\$50,000}{\$10,000 + \$10,000} = 2.5$ years

The payback period for the capital investment would be 2.5 years. As this is considerably less than the depreciable life of the asset, it appears to be an attractive investment.

Present Value Method.   This method employs the time value of money in looking at future cash inflows and outflows. Future inflows and outflows of cash are discounted because cash held today is worth more than cash received or paid in the future. Present value rates are collected from present value tables, which most accounting and finance texts provide. The rate required to equalize discounted outflows (for the purchase of the assets) and discounted inflows (income from the assets) represents the discounted rate of return of the asset.

Payback Method.   This method, which is similar to the rate-of-return method, estimates the number of years required for the capital investment to pay for itself. Figure 9–11 illustrates how the payback method is used.

The Capacity Decision.   Another important financial planning decision for the small business, especially the small manufacturer, is the size and extent of operations. Financial management techniques related to capacity help answer such questions as how many units should be produced and how large the plant should be. A useful technique for answering these questions is break-even analysis.

The *break-even point* is the point at which the level of output (in units or dollars) is equal to fixed and variable costs. By applying break-even analysis, the small business owner can determine the minimum level of operations required to financially break even. The use of break-even analysis could form an important part of the feasibility analysis discussed in Chapter 3.

The formula for break-even analysis is as follows:

$$BEP = \frac{\text{Fixed costs}}{\text{Contribution per unit}} = BEP \text{ in units}$$

or

$$BEP = \frac{\text{Fixed costs}}{\text{Contribution as percent of sales}} = BEP \text{ in dollars}$$

where

Fixed costs = Costs that will not vary as production increases (e.g., costs of plant, equipment, and some overhead expenses)

Contribution per unit = Selling price − Variable costs

The resulting graph (Figure 9–12) illustrates at what price and output the break-even point occurs given fixed and variable costs.

FIGURE 9–12   Break-Even Analysis

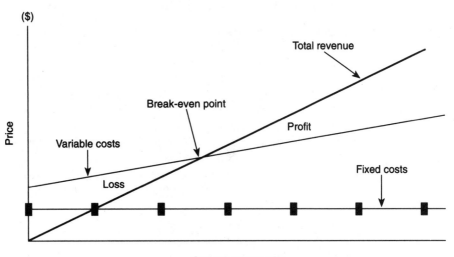

The Expansion Decision.   Break-even analysis can also be used to help the owner-manager decide whether to expand the scope of operations. The same formulas can be used, but only on an incremental basis as follows.

The Effect of Fixed-Cost Adjustments.

$$\text{BEP} = \frac{\text{Additional fixed costs}}{\text{Contribution per unit}} = \begin{array}{l}\text{Additional unit volume needed to} \\ \text{cover additional fixed costs}\end{array}$$

$$\text{BEP} = \frac{\text{Additional fixed costs}}{\text{Contribution as percent of sales}} = \begin{array}{l}\text{Additional sales volume needed to} \\ \text{cover additional fixed costs}\end{array}$$

The Effect of Variable-Cost Adjustments.   Another use of incremental break-even analysis is to measure the effects of changes in the components of the formula, such as variable costs. The following example illustrates this calculation:

$$\text{BEP} = \frac{\text{Fixed costs}}{\text{New contribution/unit}} - \frac{\text{Fixed costs}}{\text{Old contribution/unit}}$$

$$= \begin{array}{l}\text{Additional unit volume needed to} \\ \text{cover additional variable cost}\end{array}$$

$$\text{BEP} = \frac{\text{Fixed costs}}{\begin{array}{c}\text{New contribution as} \\ \text{percent of sales}\end{array}} - \frac{\text{Fixed costs}}{\begin{array}{c}\text{Old contribution as} \\ \text{percent of sales}\end{array}}$$

$$= \begin{array}{l}\text{Additional sales volume (in dollars) needed} \\ \text{to cover additional variable costs}\end{array}$$

Evaluation of Financial Performance

Quantitative evaluation of the performance of the business is an essential management task. Because they lack a financial background, many small business owners rely on their accountants to look after the complete financial end of the business. An accountant may be essential for preparing year-end financial statements, but few small businesses can afford ongoing financial management advice from this source. The small business owner is well advised to acquire a basic working knowledge of some key financial evaluation components of the business. This can enable the owner to monitor and control operations throughout the year, not just at year-end.

Several measures also can be used to evaluate the results found in the financial statements. Some of the more common techniques are described next.

Management of Current Financial Position

One critical problem many small businesses face is a shortage of cash to finance operations. Some small business owners find it hard to understand that as their businesses become successful and grow, this problem tends to create a strain on operating funds. Equally hard for many to understand is the situation in which the income statement shows a profit, but the cash position of the business has deteriorated.

The reason these situations occur is that most small businesses do not operate on a cash basis of accounting. (Some service businesses, farmers, and fishers do use cash basis accounting methods, however.) The system used is called an *accrual-based* accounting system. With an accrual system, a transaction need not involve a cash transfer to be recorded. For example, a sale of merchandise is recorded as revenue for income statement purposes whether it is paid for in cash or purchased on credit. Likewise, many noncash transactions may affect the income statement, whereas some cash transactions may not.

The above discussion illustrates the need to closely monitor the cash position of the business. As we saw, this is difficult to do by examining only the income statement. The balance sheet and cash flow statements are essential components of monitoring cash position.

If the cash position of the business needs to be improved, an effective way to do so is to reduce the length of time from payment for inventory to receipt of payment for the inventory once it is sold. This cycle has three essential components:

1. Time taken to pay accounts payable
2. Time taken to sell inventory
3. Time taken to receive payment for inventory

Figure 9–13 illustrates how to use these components in reducing this cycle for a hypothetical business.

Evaluation of Financial Statements

Once the financial statements have been prepared, several relationships between various account totals can assist in evaluating the operations of the business. This evaluation of relationships is called *ratio analysis*. It can be used to compare the financial performance of the business to those of other, similar businesses or to previous results for the same business.

Reports of financial ratios for other businesses are prepared by industry associations, Statistics Canada, and Dun & Bradstreet. These reports are collected from many businesses across the country; thus, when using them it is important to use comparable businesses from the same industry.

Financial ratios can also help in isolating and analyzing weaknesses within the business. Four categories of ratios are commonly used in evaluating a small business. Each will be discussed next; illustrations of these ratios for a small business appear in Appendix B.

Liquidity Ratios.   Liquidity ratios assess the business's ability to meet financial obligations in the current period. Two liquidity ratios are commonly used: the current ratio and the acid test or quick ratio. The calculations for these ratios are as follows.

$$\text{Current ratio} = \frac{\text{Current assets}}{\text{Current liabilities}}$$

FIGURE 9–13

SMALL BUSINESS CO. LTD.
Balance Sheet

Assets		Liabilities	
Accounts receivable	$100,000	Accounts payable	$ 40,000
Inventory	50,000	Bank loans	100,000
Fixed assets	140,000	Shareholders' equity	150,000
		Total liabilities and shareholders'	
Total assets	$290,000	equity	$290,000

SMALL BUSINESS CO. LTD.
Income Statement

Sales	$750,000
Cost of goods sold	500,000
Gross profit	250,000
Expenses	200,000
Net profit	$ 50,000

1. Time taken to pay accounts

$$= \frac{\text{Accounts payable}}{\text{Cost of goods sold}} \times 365 \text{ days}$$
$$= \frac{\$40,000}{500,000} \times 365 \text{ days}$$
$$= 29.2 \text{ days}$$

This means that, on average, it takes 29.2 days to pay for inventory purchased.

2. Time to sell inventory

$$= \frac{\text{Inventory}}{\text{Cost of goods sold}} \times 365 \text{ days}$$
$$= \frac{\$50,000}{500,000} \times 365 \text{ days}$$
$$= 36.5 \text{ days}$$

This means that, on average, it takes 36.5 days to sell the inventory.

3. Time to receive payment

$$= \frac{\text{Accounts receivable}}{\text{Sales}} \times 365 \text{ days}$$
$$= \frac{\$100,000}{750,000} \times 365 \text{ days}$$
$$= 48.67 \text{ days}$$

(continued)

FIGURE 9-13 *(concluded)*

This means that, on average, it takes 48.67 days to receive payment for inventory sold. The business cycle for this company is:

−29.2 days + 36.5 + 48.7 = 56 days

To increase the cash position, suppose the business was able to increase the accounts payable and decrease the turnover and receivable day totals for each component by five days. The result of these actions is shown in the paragraphs below.

1. *Time taken to pay accounts:* A five-day increase substituted in the formula would increase accounts payable from $40,000 to $46,849 with a resulting increase in cash of $6,849 by using the above formula. This five-day increase might have been accomplished by obtaining extensions from suppliers or simply not paying accounts payable until absolutely required.

2. *Time to sell inventory:* A five-day decrease substituted in the formula would decrease inventory from $50,000 to $43,150 with a resulting increase in cash of $6,850. Such a decrease might be as a result of increased advertising, more careful purchasing, or greater incentive to salespeople.

3. *Time taken to receive payment:* A five-day decrease substituted in the formula would decrease accounts receivable from $100,000 to $89,589 with a resulting increase in cash of $10,411. Such a decrease might be accomplished by increasing the intensity of collection procedures and/or submitting charge card receipts more often.

The total effect of these measures on the cash position of the company would be $6,849 + $6,850 + $10,411 = $24,110 increase. The owner-manager, of course, would have to balance this increase in cash against the costs of accomplishing the five-day increases or decreases.

SOURCE: Adapted from *Key Business Ratios, 1990,* Dun & Bradstreet Canada.

This figure, expressed as a ratio, should be higher than 1:1 and usually between 1:1 and 2:1.

$$\text{Acid test or quick ratio } = \frac{\text{Current assets } - \text{ Inventories}}{\text{Current liabilities}}$$

The quick ratio is more suitable for businesses that have a high level of inventories. A ratio of 1:1 is considered healthy.

If the liquidity ratios are lower than they should be, the business may have difficulty meeting obligations within the year and will have a hard time raising further debt capital.

Productivity Ratios.   Productivity ratios measure the efficiency of internal management operations. They include the inventory turnover ratio and the collection period ratio.

The calculation of the inventory turnover ratio is as follows:

$$\text{Inventory turnover } = \frac{\text{Cost of goods sold}}{\text{Average inventory at average cost}}$$

or

$$\text{Inventory turnover} = \frac{\text{Sales}}{\text{Average inventory at retail price}}$$

Inventory turnover reveals the number of times the inventory is turned over (sold) in a year. Average turnover rates vary considerably by industry but usually should not be lower than 2 to 3 times. An inventory turnover that is too low may reflect poor inventory buying in terms of either being overstocked or buying low-demand inventory.

The collection period is calculated as follows:

$$\text{Collection period} = \frac{\text{Accounts receivable}}{\text{Daily credit sales}}$$

This ratio reflects the average number of days taken for purchasers to pay their accounts to the business. Normal collection periods are in the 20-to-40-day range. If the collection period is too long, it may mean the credit-granting policy is too loose, the administration of billing is too slow, or the collection of accounts is too lax.

Profitability Ratios.   Profitability ratios measure the effectiveness of operations in generating a profit. There are four ratios in this category.

The first ratio is gross margin:

$$\text{Gross margin} = \text{Gross sales} - \text{Cost of goods sold}$$

This figure, usually expressed as a percentage of gross sales, can be used for comparisons. Gross margin for an individual product is calculated by subtracting cost from selling price and is commonly called *markup*. Average gross margins usually range from 20 to 50 percent. If gross margins are lower than they should be, the cause may be poor buying, failure to emphasize high-margin items, theft or spoilage, or price levels that are not current.

The profit on sales ratio measures profit as a percentage of gross sales:

$$\text{Profit on sales} = \frac{\text{Net profit (before tax)}}{\text{Gross sales}}$$

Typically the average percentages fall within 1 to 5 percent. A lower than average profit-to-sales percentage can reflect a problem with either pricing or expenses. Pre-tax profits are normally used, since the tax rates may vary by province and industry. In addition, reporting agencies that publish industry standards may use pre-tax profits as a comparison.

The third profitability ratio is the expense ratio:

$$\text{Expense ratio} = \frac{\text{Expense item}}{\text{Gross sales}}$$

Many specific expenses on the income statement may be expressed as a percentage of gross sales. These figures can then be compared to those for similar businesses.

Finally, the return-on-investment ratio reflects the profitability of the owner's investment:

$$\text{Return on investment} = \frac{\text{Net profit (before tax)}}{\text{Owner's equity}}$$

This ratio may be compared not only with those for other, similar businesses but also with alternative investments. If compared to the bank rate of interest, it is important to remember the risk associated with the business. Thus, the return on investment should be higher than the bank rate to compensate for this.

Debt Ratio.   Finally, the debt-to-equity ratio measures the solvency of the business, or the firm's ability to meet long-term debt payments:

$$\text{Debt to equity} = \frac{\text{Debt}}{\text{Owner's equity}}$$

Acceptable debt ratios vary, but generally speaking it should not be greater than 4 to 1. A lender normally will not provide further financing to a firm with a higher ratio.

Credit and the Small Business

A major concern for many small businesses in their attempt to reduce the length of the business cycle is control of credit. The owner/manager should understand the fundamentals of credit granting and management to effectively control receivables. Before deciding to extend credit, the owner/manager should be aware of the costs and potential difficulties involved in granting credit as well as the advantages of its use.

Advantages of Credit Use

The advantages of offering credit include the following:

- A credit program will undoubtedly result in increased sales and will probably be necessary to remain competitive.
- Credit customers are more likely to be loyal to the store or business than cash customers.
- Credit customers tend to be more concerned than cash customers with quality of service as opposed to price.
- The business can maintain a record of credit customer purchases and information about regular customers that can help in formulating future plans.

Disadvantages of Credit Use

A credit program can also create certain difficulties:

- There will generally be some bad debts when using a credit program. The number of bad debts depends largely on how strict the credit-granting policy is and how closely accounts are monitored.

- Slow payers cost the business in lost interest and capital that could be used for more productive investments. It is estimated that in many businesses, losses resulting from slow payers are greater than losses from bad debts.
- A credit program increases bookkeeping, mailing, and collection expenses. Purchase records need to be kept, statements mailed, and accounts monitored and collected. As a result, many small businesses decide against offering their own credit programs.

Management of a Credit Program

If the small business owner decides to use a credit program, some essential steps should be followed to ensure maximum effectiveness.

Determine Administrative Policies.   This includes such items as application forms, credit limits for customers, procedures to follow on overdue accounts, determining which records to keep, and deciding when to send statements.

Set Criteria for Granting Credit.   A small business owner-manager may want to assess many of the same areas a lender would evaluate in considering a small business loan, although perhaps not in the same detail. Some essentials would be past credit history, other accounts held, monthly income, references, and bank used. A small business is well advised to use the services of a credit bureau located in most cities or a commercial agency such as Dun & Bradstreet to evaluate customers' credit-worthiness.

Set Up a System to Monitor Accounts.   Proper management of accounts receivable involves classifying accounts by the length of time they have been outstanding. This process is called *ageing of accounts receivable*. Common categories used are under 30 days, 30 to 60 days, 60 to 90 days, and over 90 days. Experience shows that the longer an account is outstanding, the smaller is the chance of collecting it. Therefore, special attention should be paid to overdue accounts.

Establish a Procedure for Collection.   A uniform procedure should be set up regarding the use of overdue notices, phone calls, credit supervision, legal action, and/or a collection agency. Lax supervision of accounts has led to many small business failures, so this is an area of credit management that cannot be ignored. An example of such a collection policy appears in Figure 9–14.

One form of collection sometimes used by small businesses is a factoring company, which, as discussed in Chapter 7, can also be a source of small business financing. This type of company purchases accounts receivable for cash and attempts to collect them. In some cases, a factoring company handles the overall credit program for the business and even provides debt financing.

FIGURE 9-14   **An Example of a Collection Policy**

	30 Days	45 Days	60 Days	75 Days	90 Days
Communication	Letter, telephone; copy of statement	Letter, telephone; copy of statement	Letter, telephone	Letter, telephone	Registered letter or lawyer's letter
Message	Overdue account, please remit	Pay in 15 days or deliveries will be stopped	Deliveries stopped; pay immediately	Pay in 15 days or account will be turned over for collection	Action is being taken
Action	None	None	Stop deliveries	None	Use collection agency or small claims court

SOURCE: "Small Business Review," pamphlet (Toronto: Thorne Riddell Chartered Accountants, April 1981), p. 5.

Use of Bank Credit Cards

Because of the high costs and risks involved in operating their own credit programs, many small businesses find the most effective way to offer credit is to use bank credit cards such as Visa and Mastercard. The credit card companies assume the risk of bad debts and cover much of the administration costs of bookkeeping and issuing of statements in return for a fee—usually of from 2 to 6 percent of sales, depending on volume. Because of the high ownership of these cards by consumers today, most retail and service firms find their use essential to enhancing sales.

Some retailers are experimenting with debit cards. Much like the bank credit card, the debit card automatically transfers the sale amount from the customer's account at the bank to the business's account. The obvious advantages of debit cards are the quick repayment and reduction of accounts receivable.

Summary

1. The three-step process of the accounting cycle includes (1) recording the transactions (journal), (2) classifying the transaction totals (ledger), and (3) summarizing the data (financial statements).

2. The three financial statements important to the owner-manager of a small business are the balance sheet, the income statement, and the cash flow statement.

3. The common types of bookkeeping systems used by small businesses today are the one-book system, the one-write system, the manual multijournal system, bookkeeping machines, computer service bureaus, and small business computers.

4. Some of the more common operations computers can perform are word processing, general ledger, database files, payroll, financial planning, and capital investment decisions.

5. Some potential disadvantages of computer ownership are cost, obsolescence, employee resistance, restricted capabilities, and set-up time.

6. Short-term financial planning consists of preparing an estimated future financial result, or a budget, and comparing it to actual results.

7. The three types of long-term financial planning decisions are capital investment, capacity, and expansion decisions.

8. Ratio analysis enables the small business owner to compare the financial performance of the company to those of other firms in the industry and to the company's own past performance.

9. Common financial ratios include liquidity ratios, productivity ratios, profitability ratios, and debt ratios.

10. The advantages of offering credit are a likely increase in sales, increased store loyalty, and improved information about purchases. The disadvantages are bad debts, slow payers, and administration costs.

11. Essential aspects of administering a credit program are defining administrative policies, establishing credit-granting criteria, setting up a system to monitor accounts, and establishing a procedure for collection.

Chapter Problems and Applications

1. For the following transactions, indicate which accounts are changed and by how much.
   a. Feb. 14, 1992—Received $1,000 from Frank Johnson on account.
   b. Feb. 14, 1992—Purchased equipment for $1,500 (paid cash).
   c. Feb. 15, 1992—Paid owner Bill Cartwright $2,000 for January's salary.
   d. Feb. 18, 1992—Paid telephone bill of $90.87.
   e. Feb. 19, 1992—Bought ice cream on account, $395.00.

2. Evaluate what the lawyer in Incident 9–3 could have done to ensure the purchase of the right computer for his business.

3. Calculate the rate of return for the following investment. The total cost of the investment is $250,000, the depreciable life of the investment is 10 years, and the annual profit (net of depreciation) is $30,000. What considerations other than financial ones exist?

4. Assume the annual depreciation charge for the investment in Problem 3 is $25,000. Determine the payback period of the investment.

5. Determine the break-even point, in dollars, for an investment with fixed costs of $100,000 and an estimated contribution of 60 percent. How much revenue would it need to produce before you would invest?

6. *a.* From the balance sheet and income statement of Sam's Paint and Drywall, determine the following ratios.
   (1) Current
   (2) Inventory turnover
   (3) Profit to sales
   (4) Return on investment
   (5) Debt to equity

   b. From Dun & Bradstreet's *Key Business Ratios* on industry norms, evaluate each of the above ratios.

SAM'S PAINT AND DRYWALL
December 31, 1992
(in thousands of dollars)

Assets		*Liabilities and Net Worth*	
Cash	$ 12	Accounts payable	$ 15
Inventory	41	Notes payable—bank	4
Accounts receivable	18	Other	20
Total current assets	71	Total current liabilities	39
Fixed assets:		Long-term liabilities	39
Vehicles	10		
Equipment	15		
Building	22		
Land	23	Total net worth	63
Total fixed assets	70		
Total assets	$141	Total liabilities and net worth	$141

Income Statement
December 31, 1992
(in thousands of dollars)

Sales	$280
Less: cost of goods sold	186
Gross margin on sales	94
Less: operating expenses	81
Net profit	$ 13

7. Conduct an informal survey with three small businesses to find out which accounting system they use. Determine whether their systems are working effectively.

8. Why would a small gasoline retailer drop its credit program?

9. Dick's Draperies has gross sales of $15,000 per month, half of which are on credit (paid within 30 days). Monthly expenses are as follows: wages, $3,000; utilities and rent, $2,000; advertising, $300; and miscellaneous, $500. Inventory is purchased every three months and totals 30,000 for each order. Yearly expenses paid for in advance are insurance of $1,000 and a rent deposit of $700. Prepare a six-month cash flow statement for Dick's Draperies. What advice would you give this business based on the cash flow statement?

Appendix A
Checklist for Buying a Small Business Computer

1. Take an introductory computer course, or read a book on small business.
2. Invest in independent consulting advice.
3. Determine the potential benefits your organization can obtain from EDP.
4. Examine your existing systems and their deficiencies.
5. Define your information needs.
6. Estimate your current costs.
7. Prepare and send out a request for proposal.
8. Consider feasibility questions:
    a. Will it work?
    b. Will it pay?
    c. Will we use it?
    d. Will it cause adverse effects?
9. Avoid potential risks:
    a. Availability of proper personnel.
    b. Availability of suitable computer programs.
    c. Continued support of software.
    d. Expendability of the equipment.
    e. Security of the computer installation.
    f. Security of files and programs.
    g. Availability of a disaster recovery plan.
    h. Adequate formal management and personnel discipline.
    i. Careful selection of the computer system.

Source: Harvey S. Gellman, *A Buyer's Guide to Small Business Computers* (Toronto: The Canadian Information Processing Society, 1979), p. 12.

10. Deal carefully with suppliers:
    a. Get everything in writing.
    b. See a realistic demonstration.
    c. Check the suppliers' references.
    d. Negotiate a contract.
11. Develop and follow an implementation plan:
    a. Form a conversion and installation team.
    b. Involve top management.
    c. Plan your conversion carefully.
    d. Emphasize careful system testing.

Appendix B
Use of Financial Ratios for a Small Business (Automotive Dealer)

Ratio	Method of Computation	Motor Vehicle Dealer			Explanation
		Last Year	*Previous Year*	*Industry Average*	
1. Liquidity a. Current ratio	Current assets/Current liabilities	1.09 times	1.05 times	1.1 times	Satisfactory: This dealer has the same ability as is common in this industry.
b. Quick ratio	Current assets— Inventories/ Current liabilities	.33 times	.45 times	Not available	
2. Productivity a. Inventory turnover	Cost of goods sold/ Average inventory (at cost) or Sales/Average inventory (at retail)	7.41 times	7.41 times	6.0 times	Good: This dealer has a higher turnover rate than the average dealer. This may indicate a higher sales level or lower inventory levels.
b. Collection	Average inventory at retail/Daily credit sales	13.56 days	16.01 days	12 days	Fair: The collection period is longer than average which may indicate the need to tighten the credit policy; however, it seems that some action has already been taken.
3. Profitability a. Gross margins	Gross sales—Cost of goods sold or a percent of sales	10.71%	12.28%	16.70%	Poor: The inventory may be obsolete or company prices may be too low.
b. Profit on sales	Net profit (before tax)/Gross sales	.85%	−(.6%)	.6%	Good: Expenses are being kept in line.
c. Expense ratio	Expense item/Gross sales	11.69%	13.59%	Not available	Good: The company is making an effort to cut expenses.

(continued)

APPENDIX B *(continued)*
USE OF FINANCIAL RATIOS FOR A SMALL BUSINESS (AUTOMOTIVE DEALER)

Ratio	Motor Vehicle Dealer				Explanation
	Method of Computation	*Last Year*	*Previous Year*	*Industry Average*	
d. Return on investment	Net profit (before tax)/Owner's equity	10.49%	−1.74%	9.0%	Good: This company is more profitable than most in the industry. It is clear that action is being taken to improve profitability of this firm.
4. Debt a. Total debt to equity	Total debt/Owner's equity	325.89%	376.09%	398.20%	Good: This dealer depends less on debt financing than is common in this industry. An intentional move has been taken in this direction.

NOTE: / Denotes division sign.

Suggested Readings

Business Failure—You Can See It Coming. Toronto: Thorne Riddell Inc., May 1982.

Cohen, Jules A. *How to Computerize Your Small Business.* Englewood Cliffs, N.J.: Prentice Hall, 1980.

Coltman, Michael M. *Financial Control for the Small Business.* Vancouver, B.C.: International Self-Counsel Press, 1984.

Cornish, Clive G. *Basic Accounting for the Small Business.* Vancouver, B.C.: International Self-Counsel Press, 1985.

Cornish, Clive G. *Basic Accounting for Small Business: Simple Foolproof Techniques for Keeping Your Books and Staying Out of Trouble.* Vancouver, B.C.: International Self-Counsel Press, 1983.

Fundamentals of Record Keeping and Finance for Small Business. New York: Center for Entrepreneurial Management, 1986.

Korasik, Myron S. "Selecting a Small Business Computer." *Harvard Business Review* 62 (January-February 1984), pp. 26–30.

Petro, Louis W. "Mini Computer Systems for Small Business." *Journal of Small Business Management,* July 1983, p. 1.

COMPREHENSIVE CASE
THE FRAMEMAKERS: PART 6

Robert and Teresa were able to overcome their first-day blues as they continued to work hard, gain experience, and make adjustments to their operations. It seemed that business was picking up gradually as the first year progressed. However, six months after the opening sale, the bank called and indicated that The Framemakers' account was overdrawn beyond the authorized operating line of credit. This was especially alarming to the Normans because a bank payment was due soon. Robert visited the bank and, on the basis of the steady record of deposits and increasing sales, was able to obtain an increase in the amount of operating credit and postpone the bank payment until the end of the year. The bank manager indicated that he wanted to see The Framemakers' financial statements for the first year when they were completed.

During the last few months of the year, it seemed to the Normans that business had picked up considerably, especially during December. As a result, they were able to meet the bank payment at the end of December. Robert and Teresa were beginning to feel confident that their business was turning the corner. Robert gathered up the box of cash register receipts, invoices, and cheque register stubs and dropped it off at the accountant's office in January so the year-end statements could be prepared.

The Normans were shocked, however, when they received the statements about a month later (see Figure 1). Although business for the year had been slower than expected, they did not anticipate the $9,810 loss that had occurred. The Normans were concerned about the loss and were now very hesitant to take the statement to their banker. Robert contacted the industry association and obtained some operating results for framing shops to better understand what had happened. The data are as follows:

Current ratio	1.2 to 1	Collection period	5.8 days
Gross profit	70%	Debt to equity	.8 to 1
Profit on sales	20%		

Questions

1. Evaluate the Normans' financial management practices during the first year of operation.
2. In view of the industry statistics obtained, evaluate The Framemakers' statements and make suggestions for improvement.

FIGURE 1

THE FRAMEMAKERS
Statement of Income or Loss
For the Year Ended January 31

Sales revenue	$62,000
Less cost of goods sold	24,800
Gross profit	37,200
Expenses:	
Accounting and legal	748
Advertising and promotion	3,500
Auto costs	2,895
Bank charges and interest	2,500
Building maintenance and repairs	3,280
Depreciation	1,560
Equipment rentals	800
Office supplies	942
Rent	7,200
Travel	2,105
Utilities	3,480
Wages	18,000
Total	47,010
Net income	($9,810)

THE FRAMEMAKERS
Balance Sheet

Assets

Current:	
Cash	$ 872
Accounts receivable	3,601
Inventory	8,204
Prepaid expenses	350
Total current assets	13,027
Equipment and fixtures	7,773
Organization expenses	500
Total assets	$21,300

Liabilities

Current:	
Bank indebtedness	$15,000
Accounts payable	9,010
Current part of long-term debt	1,000
Total current liabilities	25,010
Long-term debt	6,000
Total liabilities	$31,010
Share capital	100
Owners' equity (deficit)	($9,810)

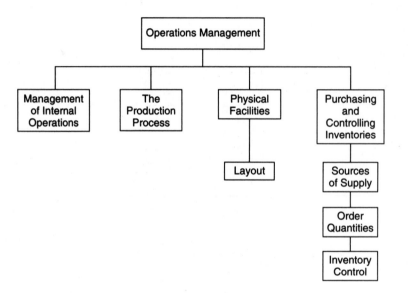

CHAPTER 10 Operations Management

Chapter Objectives

- To discuss the management of the components of the physical facilities of a small business.
- To explain the types of layouts used in small businesses.
- To illustrate methods of purchasing and controlling inventories in the small business.

Small Business Profile

Sylvia Rempel
Sun Ice Company

Sylvia Rempel has used her expertise as a seamstress and her creativity as an entrepreneur to become a very successful Canadian sportswear manufacturer. Raised in East Germany, Rempel came with her family to Alberta in the 1950s. Following her marriage, she took classes in and worked with garment manufacturing in Calgary while her husband, Victor, was going to university. She was later hired as a sewing instructor. When the family, which by this time included four children, took up skiing, she made them skiwear.

Rempel had noticed that much of the skiwear worn was not manufactured in Canada and believed there was a real opportunity for marketing her ideas. She made several items and tested them out in some ski shops in Calgary. The reception was enthusiastic, and Rempel's company, Sun Ice, was off and running.

Growth has been dramatic, with sales of $35,000 in 1978 growing to nearly $30 million by 1990 and close to 190 people on the payroll. Victor, who has since joined the company, has helped expand the business into the United States and other countries. Sun Ice has also branched out into many types of sports leisurewear, which totals 70,000 garments per year.

Sun Ice's dramatic growth was due in part to the combination of state-of-the-art manufacturing and Sylvia Rempel's meticulous eye for quality that oversees all operations. Sun Ice employs computer-assisted design and pattern making, robotic cutting, and overhead computerized material handling. Computerization allows the firm to compete with low-cost imports and produce quickly to meet retailer demands. Despite this mechanization, however, Sylvia oversees all aspects of design and production from start to finish.

During the past two years Sun Ice, along with most other Canadian garment manufacturers, has been hurt by the recession. Sales in 1992 dropped to $15.6 million, and for the second straight year the company lost money. Other factors that have hurt Sun Ice's performance were the mild climate during 1991–1992, the effect of the GST on consumer spending, and increased international competition. Despite the firm's difficulties Sylvia Rempel remains optimistic. Sun Ice has reduced expenses and, with no significant long-term debt, is poised to return to profitability when the recession subsides.

Management of Internal Operations

Operations management is one area in which many small business owners have their greatest strength. They know how to produce a quality product or provide a quality service, and their primary interest often lies with this aspect of the business. As mentioned in earlier chapters, the entrepreneur is typically weaker in the areas of marketing and financial management than in managing the production process.

The Production Process

The production process involves the conversion of inputs such as money, people, machines, and inventories into outputs—the products or services provided. Figure 10–1 illustrates this application for manufacturing, wholesaling, retailing, and service businesses. The owner-manager's task is to organize the production process of the business so that the outputs (products) can be produced efficiently. Incident 10–1 illustrates how one Canadian firm is accomplishing this.

The Priority Evaluation and Review Technique (PERT) and other flowchart systems have been developed to assist in organizing the production process. A simple example of such a system is shown in Figure 10–2 for a manufacturing firm.

FIGURE 10–1   Examples of Production Systems

Type of Business	Inputs	Process	Outputs
Apparel manufacturer	Cloth, thread, buttons	Store→Cut→Sew→Press→Ship	Dresses
Wholesaler	Large volume per order of each product	Store→Sort→Package→Ship	Smaller volume of a product in each order
Retailer	A volume of each of many products to the ultimate customer	Store→Customer display→Package	Low volume of a few products to each customer
Laundry (service firm)	Dirty clothes	Sort→Wash→Press→Store	Clean clothes

SOURCE: Adapted from Curtis E. Tate, Jr., Leon C. Megginson, Charles R. Scott, Jr., and Lyle R. Trueblood, *Successful Small Business Management,* 3rd ed. (Georgetown, Ont.: Irwin-Dorsey of Canada, 1982), p. 244.

Incident 10–1

Strite Makes Right

Joe Strite learned his trade making precision gauges for the manufacture of Mosquito and Lancaster aircraft during World War II. Now the owner of one of the most technologically advanced plants in Canada, he proudly turns in his hands an aluminum valve block plucked off one of his $550,000 Swiss-made metal machining stations. Inside the hatbox-sized cube, which will eventually house valves in a Pratt & Whitney jet engine, is a complex maze of grooves, holes and odd shapes. Each block is worth about $5,000. Manned by a lone operator, the computerized station performs all the necessary operations to mill, drill and machine the block out of a single piece of metal, right down to automatically changing its own tools from its selection of 64. "To do this kind of job takes the right kind of machines and lot of know-how," he says. "And I have to cover my costs."

Back in his office, the 67-year-old tradesman and founder of Strite Industries Ltd. in Cambridge, Ont., sits amid shelves crammed with byzantine metal shapes designed to fit the inner workings of aircraft and turbochargers, each made with microscopic tolerances for error. "We're not the cheapest," he says, reflecting on the tension between meeting the competition on both price and quality. "We can't be." Joe Strite chooses quality every time.

On the plant floor—now 72,000 sq. ft. following a seven-stage expansion that was also mostly self-financed—the days of meticulous manual measuring and cutting are fading. Workers plot designs on a computer-assisted design terminal. They program computers that control machines for cutting, boring, turning and grinding. Electric discharge machines (EDM) cut into tricky alloys of nickel, titanium, magnesium and aluminum with wire, like a cheese cutter. Another EDM, called a sinker, can plant tiny holes and shape complicated impressions in metal parts.

Parts coming off these lines are of dimensions accurate up to millionths of an inch, Strite says. To make sure, computerized vision systems, profile projectors and automated surface testers check the finished product. Because parts must be free of metallic burrs, they are checked individually under microscopes and painstakingly finished with emery cloth and tiny picks similar to dental instruments.

Source: John Southerst, "Strite Makes Right," *Profit Magazine*, July-August 1989, pp. 16–18.

Physical Facilities

Planning the physical facilities was discussed briefly in Chapter 3 as part of the preparation of the feasibility analysis. Selection of the location for the business was introduced in Chapter 4 as one of the steps in organizing a business.

FIGURE 10–2   Priority Evaluation and Review Technique (PERT)

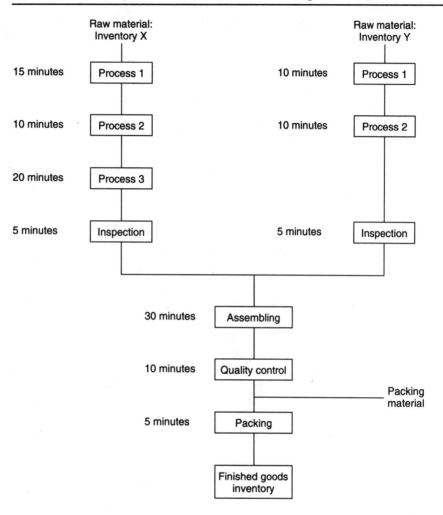

Total work time = 120 minutes

While it is not necessary to review that information again, it is critical for the owner-manager to recognize that the physical facilities must be closely monitored and maintained to ensure they are efficient and up to date. Locations are never static—populations, businesses, and traffic patterns shift continuously. This trend has caused many excellent locations to deteriorate over the years.

Some aspects of the physical facilities that should constantly be evaluated are illustrated in Figure 10–3. The figure ranks the importance of each physical facility characteristic based on the type of small business.

FIGURE 10–3   **Business Building and Site-Rating Table**

Factors	Retailing	Service	Manufacturing	Wholesaling
Building feature:				
Age	1	4	3	4
Space	1	3	1	4
Configuration	1	4	4	3
Appearance	1	3	3	4
Frontage	1	4	4	4
Access	1	2	1	1
Interior utilization:				
Floor space	2	3	1	1
Room dimensions	1	3	1	4
Ceiling heights	2	2	2	4
Stairways, elevators	3	3	1	1
Window space	1	3	4	4
Utility services	3	1	1	3
Improvement potential:				
Building exterior	1	3	4	4
Building interior	1	3	2	2
Site	1	2	3	4
Surrounding	2	2	3	4
Streets and walks	2	3	3	3
Access	1	3	2	1
Expansion	2	1	1	1
Site and environment:				
Street and service areas	1	2	2	3
Setback and frontage	1	3	4	4
Parking	1	2	2	3
Surrounding businesses	2	3	4	4
Area environment	2	3	4	4

Key to ratings: 1 = critical; 2 = very important; 3 = not ordinarily important;
4 = minimum importance.

SOURCE: John B. Kline, Donald P. Stegall, and Lawrence L. Steinmetz, *Managing the Small Business* (Homewood, Ill.: Richard D. Irwin, 1982).

Layout

Effective management of the interior layout of the business can greatly enhance productivity. Small businesses use several types of layouts. The layout selected varies by industry and by scope of operations. In determining layout, it is advisable to draw up a floor plan to better utilize available space.

Layouts for Manufacturing Firms

Here are some key areas to consider in planning the interior of a manufacturing plant:

- Location of utility outlets for machines
- Location of receiving and shipping areas for raw materials and finished goods
- Safety aspects
- Adequate lighting capability throughout
- Provision for ease of maintenance and cleaning of the plant

Essentially three types of layouts are used by small manufacturing firms: product layout, process layout, and fixed-position layout.

Product Layout.   The product layout is suitable for the business that manufactures just one or only a few products. It closely resembles the production line of a large factory. Figure 10–4 illustrates the floor plan of a typical product layout. The

---

FIGURE 10-4   **Product Layout**

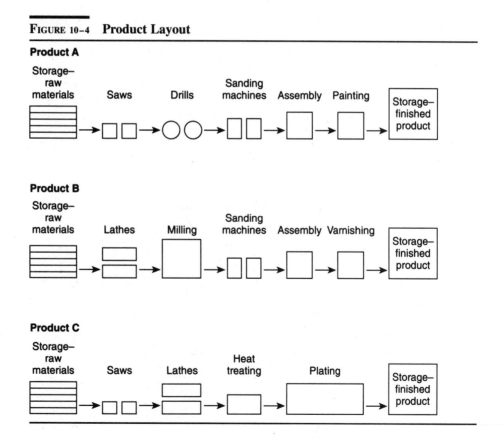

product layout generally allows for economy in both cost of and time required for production, as each part of the manufacturing process is carried out in sequence.

Process Layout.   The process layout is designed for factories that manufacture many different or custom-made products. In this layout, similar processes are grouped together and the product moves back and forth among those areas until completed. The process layout is often more expensive and requires more management time to ensure efficiency. Figure 10–5 illustrates a process layout for a small factory.

Fixed-Position Layout.   In the fixed-position layout, the product remains in a fixed position throughout its manufacture. The production processes move to the product. As one might expect, this type of layout is used for very large and cumbersome products and is used infrequently by the small business. Figure 10–6 illustrates the fixed-position layout.

Layouts for Retail Firms

As noted in Figure 10–3, interior layout is a very important factor in the success of a retail store. As Incident 10–2 on page 334 illustrates, sensitivity to consumer needs and shopping patterns is critical to the development of an effective layout. In planning the layout, the retailer will need to analyze several key areas.

Allocation of Selling versus Nonselling Space.   Experience in retailing shows that some areas of a retail store are more productive and draw more traffic than others. This phenomenon is illustrated in Figure 10–7 on page 335. Generally, the space

FIGURE 10–5   **Process Layout: Floor Diagram of a Small Factory**

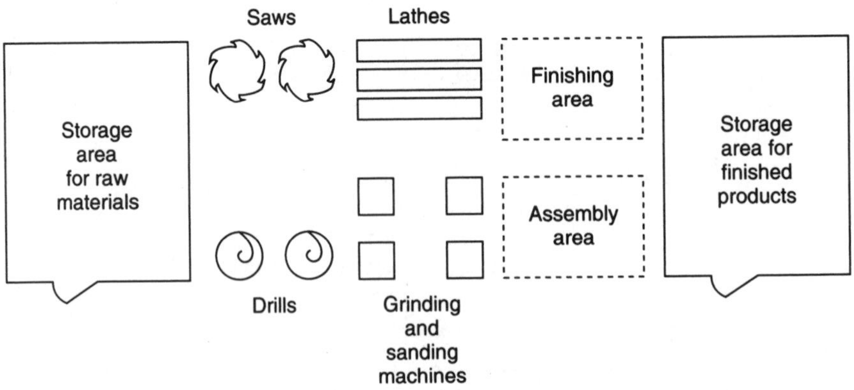

FIGURE 10-6   Fixed-Position Layout

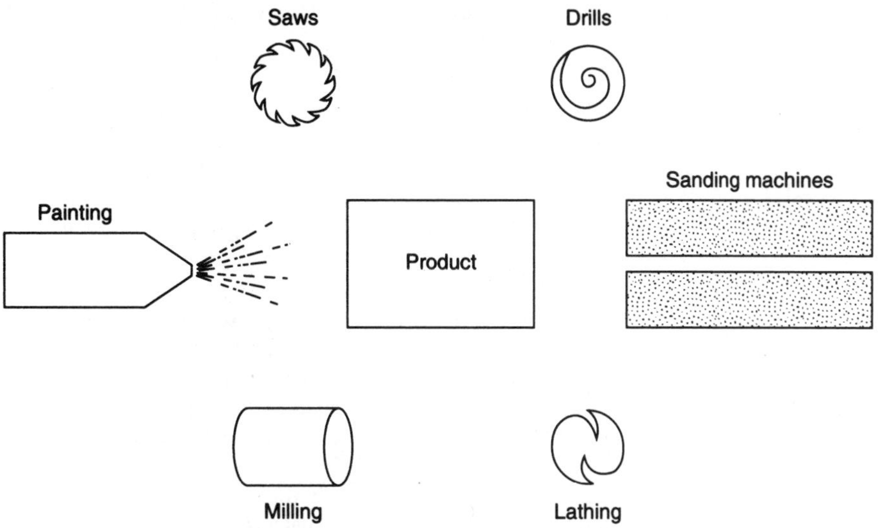

at the front and to the right is more productive space. Obviously, selling space should be planned for the most productive areas of the store.

Allocation of Space among Departments and/or Products.   The same principle discussed above should be applied in allocating space among departments and products, with the most profitable being placed in the high-traffic areas if possible.

Classification of Merchandise.   Chapter 8 discussed the classification of consumer goods—convenience, shopping, and specialty goods. Each merchandise classification may require a slightly different placement in the retail store based on the purchase motives associated with that class of goods. For example, convenience items are often found close to heavier customer traffic flow. Shopping goods might be placed by competing brands, and specialty or demand items at more inaccessible parts of the store.

Location of Displays and Products on the Shelf.   The small retailer should acquire expertise in a number of display techniques. Placement of merchandise on the shelf or counter can lead to increased sales, as certain areas are more productive than others. Merchandise placed at eye level and at the ends of aisles generally sells better.

Two types of layouts are used by retail stores: the grid layout and the free-flow layout.

Incident 10–2

Different Delis Serving Different Markets

A chain of six supermarkets, all within 50 miles of each other, all of them with delis, but six very different ethnic groups to serve. That's the challenge facing the management of Longo Brothers Fruit Markets Inc. Its stores, with their distinctive red and white decor, are spread out among the burgeoning communities north and west of Metro Toronto. Each deli strives to serve the special needs and traditions of the many ethnic groups in its market area.

Take the Oakville store, which opened in 1982. There are many residents of English heritage in this town bordering Lake Ontario. They are steady customers for English pork sausage, Scotch pies, tins of corned beef, Black Forest ham and other cold cuts from the deli case, plus their traditional cheeses—Stilton, Lancashire, extra strong Cheddar and double Cloucester. Cocktail size sausage rolls are a sell-out.

English products would have little success at Longo's new Woodbridge store, which opened in November. Ninety-five percent of its clientele are Italian. They have a passion for breads and rolls from the bakery and, of course, meats: mortadella, mild or hot Genoa salami, prosciutto and capicollo. Cheeses too, such as mozzarella, provolone and parmigiano. And every week more than 30 gallons of olives are sold in the store; so are at least 100 skinned rabbits plus 800 pounds of store-made Italian recipe sausage.

Responsibility for these six delis falls on deli purchasing/supervisor Nina Piruccio, who works out of Longo's centrally located head office in Mississauga. She started with Cara Foods, a catering firm at Toronto International Airport, in 1967 and then moved on to be an Air Canada commissary attendant. She joined Longo's 11 years ago and has been its chief buyer of deli products for four years.

Piruccio says that customers today lean towards purchasing smaller quantities of deli meats, yet they don't want to sacrifice freshness and quality. And customers want fast service too.

To meet these needs, the Woodbridge store now has its own vacuum packing equipment for pre-sliced deli meats and cheeses. The cuts and prices are the same as they are at the service counter, which is important, says Pirruccio. And it is essential that the product look fresh.

Source: Nick Hancock, "Different Delis Serving Different Markets," *Canadian Grocer,* April 1992, pp. 20–22.

Grid Layout.   The grid layout is organized with customer convenience and retailer efficiency in mind. Grid layouts have traditionally been used in stores like supermarkets and hardware stores. Figure 10–8 illustrates a grid layout.

Free-Flow Layout.   Some types of merchandise are purchased in a more relaxed atmosphere that allows customers more time to browse. For such merchandise it is

Figure 10-7   Rankings of Space Importance in a Typical Retail Store

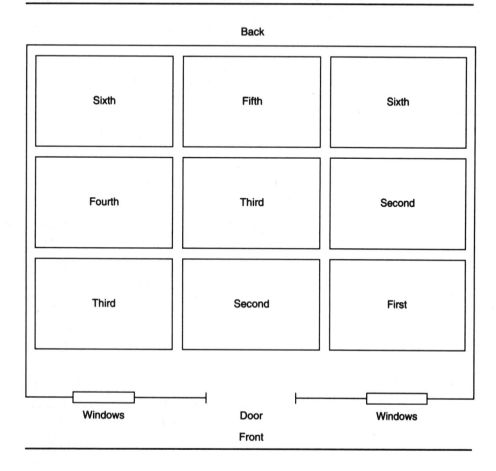

common to use the free-flow layout, illustrated in Figure 10–9. This type of layout is suitable for clothing and many specialty types of merchandise.

Many larger retail stores use combinations of the grid and free-flow layouts. Most small retailers, however, generally use one or the other type.

Layouts for Service Firms

Because the operations of service firms are so diverse, it is difficult to provide standard information on layouts. Some service firms, such as restaurants, more closely approximate the layouts of retail stores. Many of the principles discussed earlier for retailing apply here. For those service firms that are more similar to manufacturing firms, such as repair shops, the principles of manufacturing layouts may be more appropriate.

FIGURE 10–8   Grid Layout

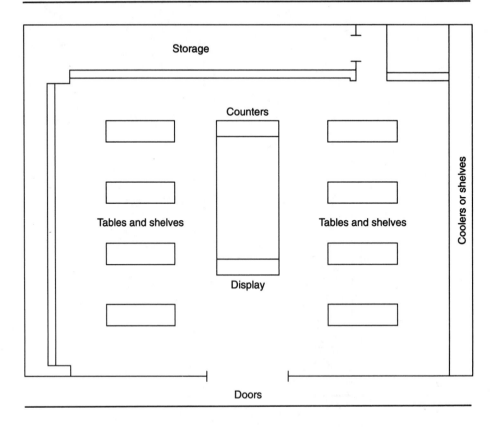

FIGURE 10–9   Free-Flow Layout

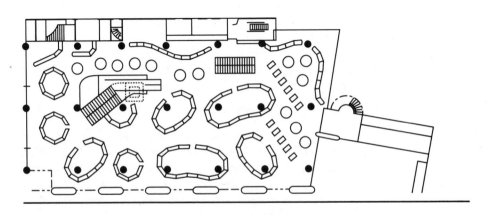

Purchasing and Controlling Inventories

The cost of purchasing and holding inventories can be substantial. Because a small business generally has limited economic resources, it is critical that such a firm give inventory management a high priority. The following sections discuss areas about which the small business owner should be knowledgeable in purchasing and controlling inventories.

Sources of Supply

Chapter 8 discussed various aspects of the distribution channel from the seller's point of view. The same principles apply in this section, but from the buyer's position. The owner-manager should know which suppliers are available. Purchases can usually be made directly from the manufacturer, from an agent of the manufacturer, from a wholesaler, or from a retailer. While sources vary considerably among industries, most small businesses purchase their inventories from wholesalers. Many owner-managers import merchandise that uses sources of supply from other countries. In this case, many of the concepts discussed in Chapter 8 with respect to the exporting section may be applicable.

One question most small businesses face is whether to purchase from one supplier or many. In purchasing from only one supplier, the buyer is assured of consistent quality and will probably receive favourable treatment such as discounts and guaranteed supply in case of shortages. On the other hand, other suppliers may offer lower prices from time to time. The business may also spread risk by purchasing from many suppliers. The small business owner must weigh these pros and cons in making this decision. Incident 10–3 illustrates the possible consequences of making the wrong supplier decision.

Evaluating Suppliers

Small business owners generally use certain criteria to evaluate suppliers. Following are some of the more common criteria.

Dependability.   The owner-manager should evaluate how dependable the prospective supplier will likely be. Dependability will undoubtedly be more important for some companies and even for some types of products than for others.

Cost.   Obviously the cost of inventories will play a major role in supplier selection for the small firm.

Services Offered.   Typical services offered by suppliers are delivery, discounts, credit, promotion, and technical assistance. Willingness and ability to provide these services may be an important factor in the selection of a supplier.

Incident 10–3

***

Bill's Service Station

Bill Andrews, owner of Bill's Service Station in Edmonton, Alberta, was in a dilemma. He ran out of antifreeze early in the winter of 1974, and most of his regular customers were growing impatient and going elsewhere to winterize their cars. In the past, Bill had prided himself on shopping competitively for antifreeze. To obtain the lowest prices, he frequently changed suppliers and had been able to pass some of this saving on to his customers. With the onset of the antifreeze shortage, however, this practice had come back to haunt him. Suppliers were providing the scarce product only to the retailers who had been loyal to them and had previously purchased larger volumes. Bill's Service Station was one of the first outlets to be cut off. Now Bill wished he had stayed with one supplier, even if it meant paying a few dollars more.

Source: D. W. Balderson, University of Lethbridge.

Determining Order Quantities

Estimating the quantities of inventories to order will require several essential items of information.

Order Lead Time. The time taken to process the order at both shipping and destination points, as well to transport the item(s), should be estimated. This is called *order lead time* and is illustrated by the distance between points B and C in Figure 10–10. Recently many businesses that require large stocks of inventory have instituted a just-in-time inventory policy. In this approach, the order is placed so that the inventory arrives "just in time" to be utilized in the production process. This system is appropriate for manufacturers that have computer capabilities, are confident in the dependability of suppliers, and require large amounts of inventory.

Sales or Production Estimate. The owner-manager will need to make a realistic projection of inventories to be sold or consumed in the manufacture of the finished product for the period. Methods of obtaining this type of information were discussed in Chapter 3. Such a rate of sale throughout the period is shown by the diagonal line A–C in Figure 10–10.

Minimum Inventory Levels Required. No business wants to run out of inventory, especially if the inventory consists of important items. It is therefore common to carry a minimum basic inventory for many items. Such inventory is often called *safety stock* and is shown as the distance between D and E in Figure 10–10. The size of safety stock usually depends on such factors as the importance of the inventory, volatility of demand, and dependability of sources of supply.

FIGURE 10–10   Order Lead Time

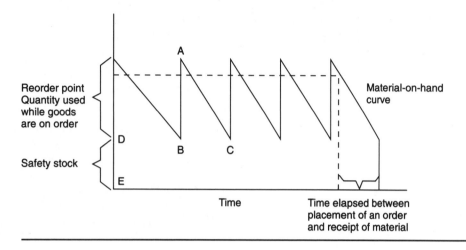

Inventory Currently on Hand.   The owner-manager should have an accurate estimate of inventories on hand. To monitor current inventory levels on a continuous basis, a perpetual inventory system can be used. Details of this type of system will be discussed later in this chapter. For many businesses, a perpetual system requires a computerized inventory system. As mentioned in Chapter 9, an increasing number of small businesses can now afford such systems. Once current inventory levels have been determined, the owner-manager can incorporate those amounts into various methods to determine order quantities.

Methods for Determining Order Quantities.   Some of the more common methods used to determine order quantities follow.

Minimum Turnover Method.   This method uses the inventory turnover formula (discussed in Chapter 9) for the business in determining amounts of inventory required. For example, if inventory turnover for the business is 4 (four times per year) and projected sales for the period are $200,000, the required inventory is calculated as follows:

$$\frac{\text{Sales}}{\text{Inventory}} = \text{Inventory turnover}$$

$$\frac{\$200,000}{\text{Inventory}} = 4$$

$$\text{Inventory} = \frac{\$200,000}{4} = \$50,000$$

Hence, the required inventory for the period is $50,000.

Maximum and Minimum Method.   Some small businesses set acceptable maximum and minimum limits on inventory levels. Whether inventory is measured in dollar amounts or number of units, reaching these limits indicates when it is time to order and specifies the amount to order. This method is used frequently by small businesses for merchandise of lower unit values.

Open-to-Buy Method.   This method of calculating order quantities, used extensively in retailing, uses the following formula (the components were discussed earlier):

$$\text{Open-to-buy} = \text{Planned purchases} - \text{Merchandise on order} - \text{Merchandise onhand}$$

where

$$\begin{aligned}\text{Open to buy} &= \text{Inventories that can be purchased} \\ \text{Planned purchases} &= \text{Planned sales} + \text{Estimated reductions} \\ &\quad + \text{Planned end-of-period stock} - \text{Beginning stock}\end{aligned}$$

Economic Order Quantity (EOQ).   This formula is used infrequently in small businesses but may be helpful for important items or in manufacturing businesses. It allows for the calculation of the minimization of the ordering and storage costs of inventory. Generally speaking, if ordering costs are higher (more frequent orders), storage costs are lower (less inventory required). Through this formula, the owner-manager can arrive at the least-cost combination of ordering and storage costs. The EOQ formula for dollar amounts is as follows:

$$\text{EOQ} = \sqrt{\frac{2AB}{i}}$$

where

$$\begin{aligned} A &= \text{Annual or period demand in dollars} \\ B &= \text{Costs of making an order in dollars} \\ i &= \text{Inventory carrying costs (storage costs) expressed as a} \\ &\quad \text{percentage of inventory value} \end{aligned}$$

For obtaining the economic order quantity in units, the formula is

$$\text{EOQ} = \sqrt{\frac{2\,AB}{PI}}$$

where

$$PI = \text{Unit price}$$

Although this formula has proved unwieldy for many small businesses in the past, the increasing accessibility of computers may allow more businesses to take advantage of the EOQ formula in the future.

FIGURE 10–11   A-B-C Analysis

	A Items	B Items	C Items
Percent of total inventory value	65%	25%	10%
Percent of total list of different stock items	20%	20%	60%
Inventory method used	Minimum turnover EOQ Maximum turnover	Minimum turnover	Eyeballing
Time allocation	Time-consuming and precision needed	Less time-consuming estimates	Rough estimates only

A-B-C Analysis.   This method of inventory management recognizes that some items of merchandise are more important to the business than others. The level of importance is influenced by such factors as higher sales, high unit value levels, higher profitability, or importance in the manufacture of the finished product.

With A-B-C analysis, the most important inventory (A items) is watched more closely to ensure they are managed efficiently. The B and C items, being less important, may require less detailed monitoring and control. Figure 10–11 gives an example of A-B-C analysis.

Administration of the Buying Process.   The owner-manager should be familiar with the mechanics of purchasing. Knowledge of the different kinds of discounts and purchase terms and conditions is essential, as are efficient receiving, checking, and marking of merchandise to minimize inventory costs and reduce shrinkage.

Inventory Control

As discussed earlier, efficient purchasing requires proper monitoring and control practices. Three essential aspects of inventory control are determining the unit of control, the method of valuing inventories, and the method of monitoring inventory levels.

Unit of Control.   Most firms keep track of their inventories by dollar amounts. This approach is called *dollar inventory control.* Dollar inventory control is suitable for firms with large amounts of inventory at a relatively low per-unit value.

Some businesses that have relatively small amounts of inventory keep track of inventories in numbers of units. This method is called *unit control.*

FIGURE 10–12   Valuation of Inventories

Sales − Cost of goods sold − Other expenses = Net income

where

Cost of goods sold = Beginning inventory + Purchases − Ending inventory

Using the relationships in these formulas, one can see that if ending inventory is overstated, cost of goods sold will be understated by the same amount and net income overstated by that same amount. Therefore, a valuation error of $100 will translate into either an overstatement or an understatement of net income by $100.

Valuation.   Generally accepted accounting principles allow inventories to be valued at the lower of cost or market value. It is very important that an accurate valuation of inventory levels be calculated, because, as Figure 10–12 shows, inventory levels directly affect the net income of the business at the end of the period.

Monitoring.   There are essentially two methods of monitoring inventories. The first, periodic inventory, involves physically counting and recording the merchandise to determine inventory levels. Periodic inventory calculation is required at least once each year for income tax purposes. It is costly and time consuming to carry out, however, so most businesses use this method no more frequently than required.

The second type of inventory monitoring, perpetual inventory, involves continuous recording of inventory increases and decreases as transactions occur. Historically this system was feasible only for a small business with low levels of high-unit-value inventory. Recently, however, microcomputer database management programs have made the perpetual inventory system a reality for many small businesses, as Incident 10–4 shows.

Security of Inventory.   Preventing loss of inventory (shrinkage) is a major challenge for most small businesses. The business should develop a detailed procedure for ordering, receiving, marking, handling, and monitoring all inventories. The system selected will vary depending on the type of business. Incident 10–5 illustrates the problem of inventory shrinkage.

Incident 10–4

Creative Stockkeeping Can Boost Your Bottom Line

Monarch Industries Ltd., a Winnipeg manufacturer of pumps, cement mixers and hydraulic cylinders, has known the pinch of high inventory levels. Just two years ago, each of the company's six locations in Canada and the United States carried $100,000 to $150,000 in stock, stored in 5,000-sq.-ft. warehouses. Despite this massive investment, says Monarch's distribution director Gordon Sepke, the company had difficulty keeping track of stock. When a branch location took an order, head office had no record of it until the bill of lading was sent. "We were always one to three weeks behind because of the paper lag," Sepke says. If a customer wanted a product that wasn't in stock in Winnipeg, Monarch had to fax to telex each of its branches to find out whether they had it.

About two years ago, Monarch began to computerize and centralize its inventory control system. Now, salespeople and customers fax, mail or phone (on a 1–800 line) orders to Winnipeg, where they are shipped from a master warehouse. Distributors have replaced the branch warehouses. At Winnipeg's request, they receive, package and send fast-moving products that customers need immediately. As a result, inventory has been sliced to $50,000 per branch.

Now, when Monarch's distributors send an item, they notify head office by fax and the computer updates the inventory level that evening. "We have a set level of stock at each of the locations," says Sepke. "I get a printout on Friday mornings that tells me what stock has to be replenished and I ship it to those locations." A monthly computer report helps Sepke identify fast-moving items to be kept on-hand by distributors and allows him to make accurate forecasts so the plant doesn't get choked up with excess materials. Customers are happier, and Monarch, which boasts about $35 million in annual revenues, saves about $1.2 million a year—money it can pour back into the business to make it even more competitive.

Source: Camilla Cornell, "Creative Stockkeeping Can Boost Your Bottom Line," *Profit Magazine,* October 1990, pp. 48–49.

Incident 10-5

Retailers Fight Losing Battle against Shrinkage

While Canadian store owners fight cross-border shopping, they are losing another battle on their doorsteps: the war on shrinkage. The Retail Council of Canada estimates retailers are losing $6 million a day—a whopping $2 billion annually—to customer and employee theft and careless accounting.

According to the council's 1991 Shrinkage Survey, the median level of shrinkage rose to 1.5% of sales in 1990, up a full 17% from 1.28% of sales in 1990. The council suggests the increase may be due in part to a steady rate of theft coupled with a recessionary decline in paid sales.

Thieves are more likely to target stores with centralized check-outs or outlets that sell a large assortment of items from a small space, says retail council vice-president Mel Fruitman. Family clothing stores are the hardest hit, with a shrinkage rate of 2.2% of sales, while supermarkets rank the lowest with a rate of 0.25%. Small firms with sales under $1 million estimate two-thirds of shrinkage is due to customer theft; stores with sales of over $100 million pin just one-third of shrinkage on shoplifters, pushing much of the blame on employees and on bookkeeping errors.

The key to reducing shrinkage lies in education. "We have to get away from the euphemism 'shoplifting,' and call it what it is—theft," says Fruitman. "Most people wouldn't think of approaching a cashier and demanding $50, but shoplifting amounts to the same thing."

Source: Jennifer Myers, "Retailers Fight Losing Battle against Shrinkage," *Profit Magazine,* October 1991, p. 8.

Summary

1. The production process involves the conversion of inputs such as money, people, machines, and inventories into outputs—the products or services provided.

2. The physical facilities must be continually monitored, as the conditions that contribute to their effectiveness will not remain static.

3. The three types of layouts used by small manufacturing firms are the product layout, process layout, and fixed-position layout. The product layout is used when the business manufactures large numbers of just one or a few products. The process layout is designed for factories that manufacture smaller numbers of many different or custom-made

products. The fixed-position layout is used for very large or cumbersome products.

4. In planning the interior layout of a retail store, the retailer needs to analyze the allocation of selling versus nonselling space, the allocation of space among departments and/or products, classification of the merchandise, and the location of displays and products on the shelf.

5. The two types of layouts used by a retail store are the grid layout and the free-flow layout. The grid layout, typically used in a supermarket, is organized with customer convenience and retail efficiency in mind. The free-flow layout has an atmosphere more relaxed and conducive to browsing. This type of layout is suitable for clothing and many specialty types of merchandise.

6. It is important for the small business manager to be aware of the sources of supply. One question most small businesses face is whether to purchase from one supplier or many. The owner-manager understand the relative merits of using one versus many suppliers.

7. In estimating the quantities to order, the essential items of information required are the order lead time, the sales or production estimate, minimum inventory levels required, and the inventory currently on hand.

8. Some methods used to determine order quantities include: the minimum turnover method, which uses inventory turnover calculations; the maximum and minimum method, which indicates the time and amounts to order; the open-to-buy method, used in retailing; the economic order quantity, which calculates the minimization of the ordering and storage costs of inventory; and A-B-C analysis, which prioritizes types of inventory.

9. Three essential aspects of inventory control are determining the unit of control, determining the method of valuing the inventories, and determining the method of monitoring inventory levels.

Chapter Problems and Applications

1. What kind of layout should be used for the following manufacturing firms?
   a. Golf club manufacturer
   b. Independent bottler
   c. Bob's Machine Shop
2. What kind of layout should be used for the following retail firms?
   a. Clothing store
   b. Motorcycle shop
   c. Small grocery store

3. Answer the following questions regarding the location of food items in a grocery store.
   a. Where are the bread and milk located? Why?
   b. Where are the chocolate bars and other candy located? Why?
   c. Where on the shelf are the top name-brand items located? Why?
   d. Where are the high-margin items positioned in the store and on the shelf? Why?

4. Visit a small retail store or manufacturing plant, and evaluate the layout.

5. Frank Newhart is opening a new video store, but he has not determined which VCR supplier to use. Frank has narrowed the choice to two sources. Supplier 1 is newly established and sells the units for $260 apiece. Supplier 2 is a well-established firm and sells the units for $275 each, with a 7 percent discount on orders over 50. Evaluate each supplier from the information given. With this information, develop different scenarios in which Frank would choose supplier 1 or supplier 2.

6. Rick Smith, owner of Smith's Men and Boys' Wear, must determine how much inventory to purchase and in what amounts. For the upcoming year, he has forecast $500,000 in sales. He has calculated that the average ordering cost is $50, and the average inventory holding cost is 5 percent. His average inventory turnover is 3.4.
   a. Calculate the per-order quantities in dollars.
   b. Calculate the required inventory for the year.
   c. How many times during the year should Smith order?

7. Interview three business owners to determine which inventory ordering system they use and why.

8. Interview a small business owner to learn why he or she selected a particular supplier. Find out what criteria were important to the owner in making the choice.

Suggested Readings

Berman, Barry, and Joel R. Evans. *Retail Management: A Strategic Approach.* New York: Macmillan, 1983, pp. 38–46.

Hodgetts, Richard M. *Effective Small Business Management.* New York: Academic Press, 1982, pp. 143–60.

Kao, Raymond W. Y. *Small Business Management—A Strategic Emphasis.* New York: Holt, Rinehart and Winston, 1983, pp. 208–23.

Siropolis, Nicholas C. *Small Business Management.* Boston: Houghton Mifflin, 1986, pp. 509–21.

Total Quality Control: A Winning Strategy for Small Business. Montreal: Federal Business Development Bank, 1990.

COMPREHENSIVE CASE
THE FRAMEMAKERS: PART 7

Although The Framemakers' financial statements for the first year of operations were disappointing, sales had picked up during the last few months by enough to allow the Normans to make their bank payment. The Normans also were learning that the majority of their customers appeared to be repeat business. Thus, instead of experiencing a post-Christmas slump, sales continued to climb steadily. Now Robert and Teresa were sure the business had turned the corner.

The increased sales made it necessary to hire two employees and substantially increase the money spent on inventory. The inventory ordering area troubled Robert. It seemed that at the same time they had too much of some inventory, they frequently ran out of some of their more popular items. Both Robert and Teresa had initially placed orders when they thought an item was getting low. They tried to order a week before they expected the item to run out to allow for the seven days' delivery required for their supplies, which came mostly from Ontario or the United States.

Another inventory problem was determining the amount to order. Frequently they ordered a larger amount of inventory on some items than they thought they needed. Some suppliers, however, required a minimum-volume purchase to grant a discount, and others would not deal with them unless the order was substantial. The Normans also differed on which inventories they thought were needed. Robert felt Teresa ordered too much of some items that she especially liked to work with herself. He hesitated to bring it up, however, as they were already experiencing enough strain.

To deal with these problems, the Normans hired another employee and implemented a card system to control inventories. However, it became clear toward the end of the second year that the card system had failed to solve the inventory problems. Inventory always seemed to be behind, and frequently cards were not updated as items were sold.

Robert realized he had to do something about the problem. The Framemakers' inventory turnover figure and gross profit had been far too low in the first year, and if a better system were not adopted, he suspected it would be worse the following year.

Robert investigated the possibility of purchasing a computer to help solve these inventory difficulties. Despite the company's still weak cash position, he found an inexpensive used Apple II computer that the salesperson said would be adequate for their needs. The Normans were pleased they would finally be able to get better control over the business.

The implementation of the computer system turned out to be another disappointment. First, the employee who had developed the card system for inventory control and would be doing much of the ordering was sceptical about the benefits of the computer, continued to make errors, and eventually quit. The Normans also found that the computer they had purchased lacked the capacity to handle their expanded inventories. Finally, some information concerning inventory and the accounting system had been completely lost when entered on the computer and then cancelled.

Robert and Teresa not only continued to worry about inventory control but were completely disillusioned with the computer. They were considering scrapping it altogether and going back to their manual system.

Questions

1. Why did The Framemakers experience inventory management problems? Aside from purchasing a computer, what could the Normans have done to alleviate these problems?
2. Evaluate the Normans' computer purchase decision and its implementation.

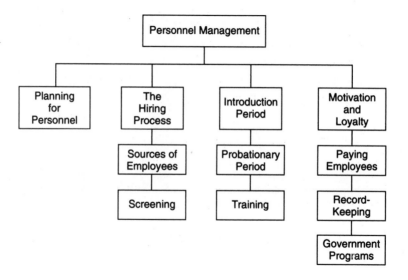

Personnel Management

Chapter Objectives

- To explain the importance of personnel management to the small business.
- To illustrate the methods of planning for hiring and training of employees.
- To discuss skill areas the owner-manager can strengthen to improve personnel management practices within the small organization.
- To illustrate principles of effective personnel management for the small business, such as motivation, remuneration, and evaluation.
- To review the procedures of administering a small business payroll.
- To review the legal requirements relating to personnel of the small business.

Small Business Profile

Frank Stronach

Magna International

Frank Stronach was born in Austria and grew up during the war years. At age 14, he began an apprenticeship in tool and die making at a large factory in his home town. Eager to see the world, Stronach arrived in Canada in 1954 with nothing more than a suitcase and $200 in his pocket. He first worked as a dishwasher and then held a number of tool-making jobs before opening his own small business in 1957.

Stronach's one-person tool shop grew rapidly over the next several years. As he hired people to help with its growth, Stronach realized that to perform at peak productivity, employees needed to feel they were part owners of the business and could share in its success. This realization prompted Stronach to implement employee ownership and profit-sharing programs. As a result of this unique operating philosophy, known as Fair Enterprise, Magna International Inc. today is a $3 billion business with more than 16,000 employees worldwide who share in the company's record-high profits. The organization is well known for its motivated employees and high productivity rates.

Frank Stronach believes that Magna's Fair Enterprise philosophy, enshrined in its corporate constitution, is the real blueprint for success. According to Stronach, "Magna is a corporation which is constantly searching for new ways to make a better product for a better price while recognizing the importance of human capital."

Used with permission of Frank Stronach.

Personnel Management and the Small Business

Management in an organization has often been defined as getting things done through other people. The small business owner is a personnel manager even if his or her main strength or interest lies in the production, financial, or marketing aspects of the business.

Often the small business owner is reluctant to learn personnel administration fundamentals because he or she believes these principles apply only to larger organizations. The result is often personnel problems such as frequent turnover of staff, lack of motivation and initiative, lack of harmony among employees, high absenteeism, frequent grievances, and high overall employee costs. The incidence of these problems appears to be high in small business. A recent study of 77 successful entrepreneurs indicated that owner-managers' number one headache was personnel.[1] The same study pointed out that the demands of running the business usually prevented owner-managers from paying as much attention to their employees as they should. Another study, conducted by the Canadian Federation of Independent Business in 1989, found that over half of small businesses had difficulty finding qualified labour.[2]

As the business grows, the owner-manager's work load generally expands. Because there is a limit to what one person can do, the business may suffer if the owner fails to hire new employees and delegate responsibilities to them.

The reputation of a business in the community can be affected by employees' satisfaction with their jobs. The level of employee satisfaction can be enhanced or lowered by the owner-manager's use of personnel management principles. This is especially true in the retail and service industries. Motivated and competent personnel are one characteristic of a business that the competition may find difficult to duplicate.

Given all these factors, it is essential that the owner-manager have some knowledge of personnel administration principles to sustain the success of the business. This chapter covers planning for personnel, hiring, and ongoing personnel management in the small business.

Planning for Personnel

There are essentially four personnel planning steps in an organization. This section discusses each of these steps briefly.

Determe Personnel Requirements.   The first step in planning for personnel is to determine the number of jobs or tasks to be done, the level of expertise required, and the number of people needed to perform those tasks. This process may already have been carried out as part of the feasibility analysis discussed in Chapter 3.

Set Organizational Structure.   The second step in personnel planning is to integrate tasks and employees so that the owner can visualize how the different parts of the plan will work together. This formalized plan is commonly called an *organizational chart.* In the very small (two- or three-person) business, the organizational chart may simply be a division of responsibilities, as in Figure 11–1. In a larger business, the organizational chart shows the lines of responsibility for each member of the organization. An organizational chart for a small retail store appears in Figure 11–2.

Each business possesses unique characteristics that dictate how to set up the organizational chart. Some of the more common approaches are to organize by (1) function performed, such as sales, purchasing, or promotion; (2) type of merchandise or department, as in Figure 11–2; and (3) geographic territory.

In setting up the organizational structure, some rules of thumb have been found to contribute to a successful operation:

- Each employee should report to only one supervisor. This arrangement is called *unity of control* or *command.*
- Similar functions should be grouped together if possible.
- There is a limit to an individual's span of control. *Span of control* is the number of people who can be directly supervised by one person. The

FIGURE 11–1   Division of Responsibilities for a Very Small Business

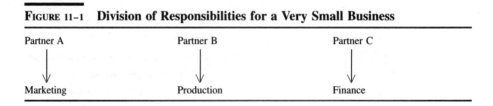

FIGURE 11–2   Organizational Chart for a Retail Furniture Store

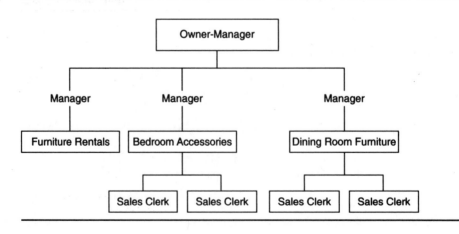

proper span of control varies according to the combined characteristics of the manager, the subordinates, and the job.

Prepare Job Descriptions.   The third step in personnel planning is the preparation of job descriptions and specifications. Before hiring employees, a detailed listing of the job or task duties (job descriptions) must be made. The job description briefly explains what is to be done, how it is to be done, and why it is done. This information goes into the job specification—a statement of the skills, abilities, physical characteristics, and education required to perform the job. As mentioned earlier, part of the job description may be included in the policy manual. Figure 11–3 illustrates a job description and specifications for an employee of a small business.

Develop Personnel Policies.   The fourth step in personnel planning is to formally develop personnel policies. Including these policies in an employee policy manual can help prevent many personnel problems. For the very small business, this may simply be a list of some do's and don'ts; a larger business may provide a booklet to each new employee.

Policy manuals are used infrequently in small businesses. The uncertainty that can result may create serious employee difficulties. The common areas to be covered in a policy manual are described below. Minimum standards for many of these areas are set by government labour departments in each province.

- *Job descriptions* clearly outline the duties, responsibilities, and reporting lines for employees, as mentioned previously.
- *Working conditions* include such things as hours of work, coffee breaks, and other expectations of management.

FIGURE 11–3   Job Description and Specifications Sales Manager, Hardware Store

Job duties (description):
  Reports to the general manager.
  Directly responsible for floor salespeople.
  Suggests markdowns on slow items.
  Controls inventory.
  Authorizes merchandise returns.
  Occasionally meets with suppliers to learn about new products.
  Maintains good customer relations at all time.
  Takes care of written correspondence concerning sales.
  Does any other task relevant to the job as requested by the general manager.
Personal requirements (specifications):
  High school diploma or equivalent.
  At least two years' experience in a similar job.
  Initiative; "instinct" for sales; convincing manner; aptitude for managing people.
  Self-disciplined; good appearance; willing to work overtime.

- *Holidays and leaves* outline statutory holidays, paid vacations, and procedures for taking a leave of absence.
- *Remuneration and pay* consist of a listing of details of the payroll such as date of payment, time periods included, and reviews of pay levels.
- *Employee benefits* provided by the firm, such as bonuses, profit sharing, medical-dental insurance plans, and employee discounts should be clearly stated.
- *The grievance procedure* consists of a description of the procedure employees are to follow if they have a concern or grievance within the organization.

The Hiring Process

Once the personnel plan has been developed, the next step is to review various sources for potential employees and make the selection.

Sources of Employees

Following are some potential sources of employees for the small business.

Recruitment from Within.   For most organizations, recruiting from within the firm is the most common course if current employees have the qualifications. Hiring an outsider to perform a supervisory job instead of someone within the organization usually has a negative and disruptive effect on the business.

Other Businesses.   To reduce training costs, employees from competing firms or similar industries can be hired. Such employees generally will have some background about the industry and/or business that can be easily transferred. The recruiter, however, will have to use this approach carefully to avoid a negative reaction from the competition, particularly in smaller markets.

Employee Referrals.   Present employees may be asked to recommend acquaintances to fill available jobs. This method has the advantage of some prior knowledge of the individual's background. It may have a negative effect, however, if the new employee proves unsatisfactory.

Advertising.   Some small businesses advertise for employees in local newspapers. The cost of this type of advertising is minimal.

Employment Agencies.   Employment agencies sponsored by provincial governments are one source. Canada Manpower offices also have lists of employees looking for work. This can be a potentially valuable source of employees, particularly for positions that do not require highly technical expertise. Private employment agencies typically are not used by small businesses to recruit employees, but they may be helpful in recruiting highly skilled employees.

Educational Institutions.   Some small businesses that require employees with technical expertise use universities or colleges as sources. These sources can be helpful in manufacturing and some service businesses and are increasingly being used in retailing.

The Screening Process

Once potential employees have been identified from one or more of the above sources, the owner-manager faces the task of selection. Several screening devices can be used to aid in the selection of employees.

Application Form.   Many small businesses do not use an application form. If new employees are hired infrequently, such a formal document may be unnecessary. However, the application form can be a valuable screening tool and a time saver for the owner. An application form need not be lengthy to be useful, as Figure 11–4 illustrates. The owner-manager must be careful not to violate provisions of the Human Rights Act in preparing the application form.

The Employment Interview.   Although the application form may screen out several potential employees, an interview is usually required in making the final decision. The employment interview is particularly important for jobs requiring interpersonal contact, as it allows the interviewer to judge appearance, poise, and communication ability. A helpful tool in interviewing is an interview guide, which focuses the discussion and provides a constant base of information with which to compare applicants. Figure 11–5 illustrates an interview guide. Again, human rights legislation precludes the use of certain questions during an employment interview, and the owner-manager should be aware of such legislation.

Checking References.   The third screening device is the checking of references. Most application forms require the applicant to list both personal and business references. As might be expected, business references are more valuable because they provide information regarding the individual's past work record. Incident 11–1 illustrates the value of checking references for one small business.

Checks made by telephone or in person with business references are preferred to written responses. The writer of a letter of reference may have little or no idea of the requirements of the job. Also, past employers are sometimes reluctant to write uncomplimentary letters of reference. Specific questions should be asked about the candidate's performance, as well as about whether employers would consider rehiring the person.

Tests.   Many large businesses use various types of intellectual, ethical, and physical tests as part of the screening process. Some specific tests being used

FIGURE 11–4   Application for Employment for a Small Business

Name_____   First Name_____

Address (Home)_____   Tel._____

Address (Work)_____   Tel._____

Social Insurance No._____

Languages: Spoken_____   Written_____

Secondary Education

Years	School	City	Diploma

Postsecondary Education

Years	School	City	Degree

Work Experience
(begin with most recent)

From_____To_____   Employer_____

Title_____   Nature of Duties_____

_____   Salary_____

Reason for Leaving_____

Work Experience

From_____To_____   Employer_____

Title_____   Nature of Duties_____

_____   Salary_____

Reason for Leaving_____

Other Information

References:	Name	Address	Title
1.			
2.			
3.			
Signature		Date	

FIGURE 11–5   Interview Guide for a Small Business

Job:
Applicant:
Interviewed by: Date:

Check off or comment on the items you observed or found out. Do not guess at the other items; leave them blank. Not all items are relevant for every job. Your answer should be "yes" or "no," "we cannot hire," "maybe," or "not certain." You can qualify your yes or no under "Comments."

	Yes/No	*Comments*

Evaluate the applicant on the following:

1. Work experience necessary to perform the job satisfactorily.
2. Skills with machines, tools, equipment.
3. Skills with job procedures.
4. Experience with special projects.
5. Formal education.
6. Trade or vocational education.
7. On-the-job training.
8. Will need training for this job.
9. Ability to get along with supervisor.
10. Ability to get along with fellow employees.
11. Ability to work as a member of a team or work group.
12. Applicant's comments about former supervisor.
13. Applicant's plans.
14. Attendance record.
15. Punctuality.
16. Safety record.
17. Health.
18. Physical strength to perform job.
19. Good work habits.
20. Supervisory experience.
21. Prefers to work alone.
22. Primarily interested in money.
23. Prefers nonfinancial rewards.
24. Likes the work.
25. Blames others.
26. Flexible; can adjust to changes.
27. Has a part-time job.
28. Off-the-job activities.

---

increasingly in small businesses are proficiency and skill tests (to perform a particular trade, craft, or skill), vocational interest tests (to assess long-term interest in the job or company), aptitude tests (to determine how a person might perform on a given job), and polygraph tests (to measure level of honesty). Because some of these tests are technical, the owner-manager should seek professional assistance in administering them.

Incident 11–1

Home Hardware

The owner of the Home Hardware store in Magrath, Alberta, was looking for an assistant manager for hardware. After interviewing several applicants, the owner decided to hire an individual who had several years' experience in a hardware store in a distant town. All indications were that this individual was the best choice. Before making the offer of employment, the owner decided to check with the previous employer. He was grateful he did, because he found out that the chosen applicant had an unsatisfactory work record as well as questionable honesty. As a result of this reference check, another applicant was chosen and proved to be an excellent employee.

Source: D. W. Balderson, University of Lethbridge.

Notification of the Hiring Decision

Once the hiring decision has been made, an offer of employment should be made to the successful applicant. This notification should be in writing, with a clear indication of the terms and conditions associated with the job. Most businesses require written confirmation of acceptance of the offer by the applicant.

All unsuccessful applicants should also be notified. Failure to provide this courtesy can have a detrimental effect on the reputation of the business.

Personnel Management

Once the employee has been hired, the owner-manager's responsibility is to see that he or she is properly trained, satisfied enough with the working conditions to continue working there, and—probably most important—motivated to work hard and show initiative. Most small businesses are not in a position to hire a professional personnel manager to ensure that these desirable conditions exist. However, the owner-manager can foster these conditions by using the concepts of personnel management discussed in this section.

The Introduction Period

The first few months on the job are crucial to the employee's overall satisfaction and length of stay with the business.

The First Week.   One of the most frequently mentioned characteristics of good working conditions is the way the owner-manager makes the employees feel like part of the organization.[3] Much can be done in the first week to communicate to the employee that he or she is a valued member of the business. The new employee should be introduced to co-workers, shown the locations of employee facilities, informed of any company regulations, and encouraged to ask for additional information if needed. The employee should be talked to frequently during the introductory period, not simply left alone to read the company policy manual as larger companies sometimes do.

Many employers find it helpful to set some short-term goals toward which the employee can work within the first week or two. These goals can be discussed at the conclusion of the agreed-upon time. This communicates not only that the employer is interested in the employee but also that the business is results and goal oriented.

The Probationary Period

Most employers find it advantageous to use a probationary period of three to six months for new employees. The probationary period allows the employer to further assess the new employee's suitability for the job. At the conclusion of a satisfactory probation period, the employee becomes permanent and may be entitled to a pay increase and other benefits of a permanent employee.

Training

The purpose of the training program is to increase productivity. In addition, successful training programs can reduce employee turnover, allow for less supervision, and increase employee morale. Properly trained employees acquire a sense of worth, dignity, and well-being, as well as increased skill levels. Businesses use many forms of employee training. Some of the more common are discussed next.

On-the-Job Training.   This is the least structured and most frequently used method by small businesses. It is perhaps the best method of training for routine and repetitive types of work. The business may assign another worker to work closely with the new employee in a buddy system or apprenticeship.

Formal Classroom Training.   Businesses use many varieties of formal classroom training, but only a few have been used by small businesses. One such system is a cooperative type of program with an educational institution. This allows the employee to attend classroom instruction and training on a part-time basis. In Canada, the government provides financial assistance for employee training programs. These programs will be discussed later in this chapter. Some businesses hold periodically seminars in which they bring experts from various fields to the business.

The Owner-Manager as Personnel Manager

Leadership Style.   The first step in this process is a self-evaluation to obtain an understanding of one's own leadership or management style. Sometimes the owners are so preoccupied with running the technical or market side of the business that they give little thought to the kind of leadership example they set for employees.

Among leadership styles of entrepreneurs, several styles appear to be successful. A recent study of Canadian entrepreneurs found five different types of leadership. Figure 11–6 describes each type.

The effectiveness of the owner-manager's leadership style may vary depending on the characteristics of the business and its employees. However, certain styles generally are more successful in the long run. Whatever the owner-manager's style, concern for both the people within the organization and the production process is important. The resulting team management approach found in many Japanese companies is particularly adaptable to the small business.

Time Management.   A second critical aspect of successful people management is efficiently managing one's own time. Time management is often difficult to apply in the small business. So many operating crises and interruptions take place in the normal course of a day that the owner-manager may feel much of the advice in time management literature is impossible to employ. However, some basic time management concepts can be used successfully in the small business. Some of the more important concepts are discussed below.

Recognize the Importance of Time.   Much time wasting results from a failure to recognize the importance of one's time. The first step in improved time management, therefore, is to have a sincere desire to use time more efficiently.

Reexamine and Clarify Priorities.   Priority planning may be long or short term. Long-term planning involves setting objectives that the owner and business are projected to meet over a period of months or years. Long-term objectives,

---

FIGURE 11–6   **Leadership Styles in Canadian Small Business**

Solo	Osmosis	Managerial	Systems	Figurehead
Does everything	High level of control over business, but does spend time developing managers	Sets objectives and lines of authority	Develops systems and direction	Owns business but has little to do with it
Little delegation		Controls results but delegates more on procedures	Allows employees to set some objectives and determine how they are met	Complete delegation
Very small firms	High level of contact with employees	Less employee contact		

discussed in Chapters 3 and 4 as part of the establishment plan of the business, provide direction for the firm.

Short-term priority planning deals with the utilization of time on a daily or weekly basis. It involves prioritizing tasks and working on those that are most important.

Analyze Present Time-Consuming Activities.   This step requires keeping a diary of the daily activities of the owner-manager. Most people find the results of this step surprising. Often they find they spend time on less important items at the expense of more important ones. One small business owner spent several hours arguing over a $25 increase in building rental instead of using that time to evaluate the suitability of the overall location.

Implement Time Management Principles.   The owner-manager may be able to eliminate common time-wasting traps and become more efficient in his or her use of time by implementing the following practices:

- Avoid procrastinating on difficult but important decisions in favour of easier but less important ones.
- Use the most productive time of the day for the more important decisions or analyses. For some people this may be early in the day, and for others it may be later. Many have found it beneficial to schedule routine or enjoyable tasks during their least productive time.
- Read only relevant information. Stop reading and start searching. Use travel, waiting, or otherwise unproductive times for reading.
- Use letters less and the telephone more. If possible, handle letters only once in a given period of time.
- Operate with a minimum of meetings. Make sure meetings are results oriented and have definite starting and ending times.
- Delegate as much work as possible, recognizing that the owner-manager is still ultimately responsible for the decision or action. A more detailed discussion of delegation in small businesses appears in Chapter 13.

Motivation and Loyalty

Successful managers are able to generate strong loyalty from their employees. They also succeed in motivating employees to work hard and be creative. They have open communication lines that provide a comfortable work environment (see Incident 11–2). It is no accident, however, that these conditions exist in some companies and not in others. Some owner-managers understand and are able to apply some critical principles in human relations management. Two important principles concern working conditions and employee needs.

Working Conditions.   Employee satisfaction with general working conditions has been shown to reduce employee turnover. Although these factors may have

Incident 11-2

All-Star Employers

When Helma Gansen and Roxanne Lindsay founded the interior-design firm, Gansen Lindsay Design Consultants Inc., they hoped to employ six designers by 1992. Picking up clients such as the Bank of Canada, Gloucester Hydro, the minister of national revenue and accounting giant Thorne Ernst & Whinney, they hit that target in three months. Their payroll now numbers 12.

Lindsay and Gansen say there's no secret to their success. They promise top quality work, on time and on budget. They hire the best talent they can find, and provide a workplace where those employees can excel.

The secret of creating that environment is communication. Gansen Lindsay's team, all trained designers, share a compact, open-concept office that encourages collegiality and group problem-solving. In return, they receive constant feedback, encouragement and training—as well as above-average pay. Now Gansen and Lindsay are talking of extending partnerships to designers who show special promise. This is so far ahead of schedule that they don't know how to do it, but a lawyer is looking into the paperwork.

Attitudes like this carried Gansen Lindsay to the top of the Small Business's roster of 50 Best Bosses. But Lindsay and Gansen speak for almost all the Best Bosses when they say they treat their employees well because they are the firm's most important asset. "This company is totally people-oriented," says Gansen. "Without our employees, we can't function."

Lindsay says their employees are paid 20% more than comparable designers, "to show that we care" and keep them on board. The firm can afford this, adds Lindsay, because she and Gansen have yet to take a salary. And they are now devising bonuses, such as paying designers a portion of the amount saved when they bring in a project under budget.

Gansen Lindsay also stresses continuing, constructive feedback. Every Thursday morning, the staff crowds into the tiny boardroom-lunchroom to discuss projects, problems and grumbles. It's no holds barred, says senior designer David Gibbons. "If there's a problem, it's out on the table and gets solved right away. There are no negative aspects, no negative vibes in the air."

More importantly, the two partners meet each employee four times a year to review his or her progress, suggest ways of getting ahead, and discuss any questions or grievances. "We talk about where things are going, for them, and for us, how they feel about the people, the company, the work," says Lindsay. It's not easy to find the time, she admits. "You have to make time for your employees. You have to force yourself to make the time."

That effort is paying off. "The word is out on the street that this is a very good place to work, and coming on strong," says David Gibbons. "People are starting to knock on our doors."

Source: Rick Spence, "All-Star Employers," *Profit Magazine,* November 1989, pp. 32–33.

Incident 11–3

Berwick-Ferguson Payroll

Diana Ferguson moved her operation out of her house into an office and hired her first staff. Like many other entrepreneurs she found the transition from loner to manager not as easy as she had anticipated. "It took me a while to realize that employees do not look at the company through your eyes. No matter how capable your employees may be, the fact is, it's not their company, so they usually do not put the same care and energy into everyday tasks as you do."

Ferguson soon solved the problem of motivating her employees. She installed a healthy profit-sharing plan. In 1984 her 10 employees earned an 18 percent bonus over normal annual salaries, and in 1985 it will amount to almost 30 percent. Although she has retained ownership of 85 percent of the company, the remainder is held by two employees. These moves to give employees a stake in the company's success help imbue the entire establishment with a spirit of teamwork. "In a company like ours, everyone does everything. We get the job done, and we don't let a hierarchy stand in the way."

Source: Kenneth Barnes and Everett Banning, *Money Makers! The Secrets of Canada's Most Successful Entrepreneurs* (Toronto: McClelland and Stewart, 1985), p. 180.

---

minimal motivational impact, they are important in developing loyalty to the organization.[5] Some working conditions that may have this effect are the physical characteristics of the workplace, the level of supervision, relationships with co-workers, and company policies.

Employee Needs. Understanding employee needs and providing the means whereby employees can fulfill unmet needs can be a powerful motivational tool for the owner-manager.[6] These needs include adequate pay, feeling a valued part of the organization, the possibility for advancement, extra responsibility or authority, recognition by management, esteem by peers, a sense of achievement, and the challenge of the job.

One real challenge to the owner-manager is to encourage employees to have the same interest and enthusiasm for the business that she or he has. Incidents 11–3 and 11–4 illustrate how two entrepreneurs have accomplished this.

Paying Employees

Small business owners face stiff competition from large companies and even the government in paying their employees. Many think they cannot afford to meet this

Incident 11–4

Regional Steel Works Inc.

Fred Simser closed his three-year-old Ottawa steel-fabrication business in 1981 and moved to Thunder Bay, Ont., to coach platform and springboard diving. Within two years his team ranked among the best in Canada. Having trained other coaches to continue his work, he returned to Ottawa in 1984 and calmly started up his business again.

Producing and installing everything from three-tonne steel beams to ornamental railings, the firm is now one of Ottawa's top three steel fabricators, with a staff of 35 and revenues of $5 million. His success in both diving and steel emerged from the same philosophy. "In coaching or running a business, the challenge is exactly the same: motivation. Athletes want to know that somebody cares, and it's the same with employees."

Simser has studied motivation since taking up coaching 15 years ago at the age of 26. And he says most managers have it wrong. "A lot of bosses are of the impression that motivation is financial reward," says Simser. "That's partly true, but mostly false. People are motivated by a feeling of belonging, and by recognition for a job well done. If you feel that you're an integral part of a company and that your participation is not only appreciated but acknowledged, then you get up in the morning saying "Boy, what can I do for the company today?", instead of "Do I have to go in?""

A trail of ground-in dirt leading from the shop floor up the stairs to Simser's office attests to the open-door policy that underlies his people strategy. Simser talks to almost all his employees every day, even chatting with the installation crews at 7 A.M. before they head to their job site. He makes sure everyone knows what they're expected to do, setting out clear goals every Monday morning at a meeting with senior staff.

Simser is also quick to reward performance: "I don't think a week goes by that someone doesn't get a bonus of some sort." He may pay $100 or more for money-saving suggestions, excelling in a project, or for changing a vacation schedule to complete a job. Sometimes he'll pay a bonus for no reason at all. His only rule: never do the same thing twice.

More formally, Regional's seven top employees own non-voting shares that pay dividends four times a year. And senior employees benefit from a profit-sharing plan that has paid individuals as much as $40,000 a year. "When you have a company where people are motivated," says Simser, "one person will do the work of three or four."

Source: Rick Spence, "Regional Steel Works Inc.," *Profit Magazine,* November 1989, p. 34.

competition. However, the value of a key employee cannot be overstated for many small businesses. As a result, many owner-managers have recognized that they must be competitive in paying key employees.

Employees are concerned not only about absolute but also relative wage levels. This means employees are usually aware of and concerned about their level of pay relative to those of their co-workers. Employee pay levels are very difficult to keep confidential in a small business. Often a wage increase for one employee will be seen by other employees not as a reward for that employee but as a decrease in pay for themselves. This, of course, can cause unrest within the organization.

Wage levels are generally set using external and internal factors as a guide. Externally the owner-manager may want to assess wage levels in similar or competing industries. Many provincial governments publish wage survey data that can assist in this regard. Most owner-managers can find out what the wage levels are in their communities through an informal survey. Other external considerations in arriving at wage levels might be cost-of-living increases, the demand/supply situation for employees, and government regulations. Internal considerations employers use in setting salary levels are ability to pay, employee performance levels and requirements, and, as just mentioned, relative pay relationships.

Remuneration for employees can offer employees security and also have a motivational effect. There are many methods of paying employees, each with advantages and disadvantages. The owner-manager needs to tailor the pay plan to meet the needs of employees and the goals of the organization. Figure 11–7 lists some of the more common methods of paying employees in small businesses and

FIGURE 11-7   Salary Plans for Small Businesses

Type of Plan	How Calculated	Advantage	Limitation	Types of Businesses Using the Plan
Salary	Per hour or per month	Security Simple	Lack of incentive	Many businesses— routine tasks
Commission	Percent of sales	Incentive	Lack of control	Automobile sales Housing industry Some retail products requiring extra selling effort
Cash bonus on individual performance	Bonus upon reaching objectives or quota	Security Incentive	Can be complicated	Retailing Manufacturing
Profit sharing on company performance	Percent of profits distributed	Incentive Cooperation in organization	Can be complicated Amounts too small to motivate	Manufacturing Retailing
Stock bonus	Predetermined percent to employees based on objectives	Long-term interest in organization Incentive	Some employees want only cash	Manufacturing

Incident 11–5

Magna International

Magna International has adopted a plan of distributing the ownership interest of the company to its employees through a profit-sharing plan. It is a plan whereby the employee can buy into the company after a certain length of time working for the organization. For those that have ownership interest they receive a percentage of the profits. Magna is a manufacturer of plastic bumper facia for GM, Ford, and Chrysler and has over 60 plants in Canada. They use the Japanese "just-in-time" delivery method of manufacturing. As the orders come in they make, check, and deliver the orders in a day. It requires exact timing and the cooperation of all departments. The faster the employees work, the more each plant sells and the more profitable the employees are. The system requires loyalty to the company, and in return the company pays special attention to human relations. The profit-sharing system has worked very well and has allowed Magna to become one of the most successful companies in Canada.

Source: CBC Corporation, "Venture" series, March 4, 1985.

describes their advantages and limitations. Many organizations use combinations of these plans.

Incident 11–5 illustrates how the use of some of these options dramatically increased the productivity of Magna International.

Fringe Benefits

Although a recent survey found that fewer than half of Canadian small businesses offer incentive plans,[7] increasingly a small business needs to provide fringe benefits to attract and retain employees. Some benefits becoming common in industry today are employee discounts, pension plans, disability and life insurance, and dental insurance. If the smaller business has enough employees, it may be able to qualify for group insurance plans that reduce the cost of providing this benefit. Frequently these plans are available through industry associations.

Other work-related fringe benefits the business might offer to increase employee satisfaction and motivation are job rotation, flexible hours, and employee suggestion systems.

Job Rotation.   With job rotation, employees are periodically allowed to exchange jobs with other employees. Used in factory situations, this program can not only increase employee interest and motivation but also assist in training workers.

Incident 11-6

Camco

What do you do when you're losing competitive ground to the Japanese, and you can't seem to improve your plant inefficiencies? Camco Industries, a manufacturer of microwave ovens, thought they would ask their employees. After all, who should know the production lines better? With the employees' help they developed a program called Orange Plus, which means Orangeville (name of the city in Ontario where the plant is located), and the Plus denotes "Productivity Lets Us Succeed." Camco has increased productivity 25 percent in one year. Employee suggestions, which are implemented and save the company money, earn the employees one half of the saving. The other half goes to the company. In the first year 337 ideas were given by employees and 170 of them were adapted. The savings were estimated at $1 million, which meant an extra $1,600 for each employee. Camco management claims that no productivity expert could have saved them $1 million in one year. Camco, through its employee suggestion program, has regained its competitive edge.

Source: CBC Corporation, "Venture" series, March 11, 1985.

Flexible Hours.   Some firms have experienced increases in productivity by allowing employees a work schedule other than the 9-to-5 schedule common in many industries.

Employee Suggestion Systems.   Many companies have some form of employee suggestion system. Recently some companies have taken this idea a step further by offering employees money to implement their suggestions. The National Association of Suggestion Systems reports that some 3,000 formal suggestion systems operate in the United States, generating over 300,000 ideas and saving companies more than $800 million annually. Incident 11-6 illustrates a Canadian company that found success using this approach.

Controlling and Evaluating Employee Performance

Many of the practices previously mentioned may contribute to a more motivated and loyal work force. It is essential, however, that this motivation be directed toward the achievement of the firm's objectives. In this regard, the owner-manager needs to effectively evaluate progress toward goals and objectives and inform employees of their progress. This can be done through a regular performance appraisal.

Another method that can accomplish this is the management by objectives approach (MBO), which is used in many organizations. A simplified version of MBO that is suitable for the small business is described in *Putting the One Minute Manager to Work.*[8] The five steps in this method (called the PRICE system) are as follows:

- *Pinpoint:* Define the performance area to be evaluated (i.e., sales for a retail clerk).
- *Record:* Set up a system to monitor and record performance in that area (i.e., the cash register tape).
- *Involve:* Manager and employee jointly set goals and a strategy for reaching those goals in that performance area (i.e., dollar sales per month).
- *Coach:* The manager observes performance periodically, perhaps making suggestions but allowing the employee considerable freedom to work toward the agreed-on goals.
- *Evaluate:* At the end of the agreed-on time period, an assessment of performance is made; positive results are rewarded, and future goals are set.

— Create standard not just someone's opinion.

As can be seen, the value of the PRICE system is the clear line of communication between employer and employee in directing the employee toward goals and evaluating his or her progress.

Handling Grievances

Employee grievances, or concerns, arise in most organizations. They can have a negative effect on the morale of the organization, but they can also be positive and helpful if handled properly. Following are some principles for effective grievance management:

1. Implement a precise method whereby employees can express grievances. It is important that the organizational lines of authority be followed in this case. If at all possible, the grievance should be expressed to the immediate supervisor. This procedure should be laid out in the policy manual.
2. Employees need assurance that expressing their concerns will not jeopardize or prejudice their relationship with the employer. A wise employer will recognize that many grievances are legitimate and, if acted on, can help the organization.
3. There should be minimal red tape in processing complaints. Employees need to feel that someone is really listening to their concerns.
4. Owner-managers need to understand that some employees may be hesitant to raise a concern directly. In these situations, the suggestion box is effective.

Unionization and the Small Business

Most small businesses do not have unions operating within the organization. As the firm grows, however, and as employees become further removed from the owner, the possibility of union-related activity increases. The owner-manager should recognize that unions are formed when a majority of employees believe that a union would better serve their employment needs than the existing system. Effective human relations policies can go a long way toward discouraging union establishment in the firm. Some small businesses in certain industries may be required to hire unionized employees.

In both of these situations, there are certain requirements for both the employer and the union as set out in the Labour Relations Act in each province. Some of the more common aspects of collective bargaining that may affect the small business owner are the following:

- The contents of an agreement must deal with wages, benefits, and working conditions.
- Both parties must meet and bargain in good faith. However, an employer need not reveal company data that he or she prefers to keep confidential.
- The owner cannot discriminate against an employee for union involvement.
- Both employers and unions are bound to the terms and conditions of the collective agreement.
- Disputes concerning interpretation of the agreement must be resolved by an arbitrator.

Government Requirements and Assistance

The owner-manager should be aware of relevant government labour laws and programs that affect the management of personnel. A brief discussion of such laws and programs for all levels of government follows.

Federal Government

The federal government provides training and employment programs to 400,000 Canadians each year. Through the Canadian Jobs Strategy program, approximately $1.7 billion is spent to increase training and expand opportunities.[9] Some specific programs of Jobs Strategy include the following:

- *The job entry program* provides training for unemployed or undertrained people for up to one year.
- *Skill shortage and skill investment programs* provide financial assistance and training for up to three years for skill upgrading as a result of technological change within the company.

- *The job development program* provides training and financial assistance for the unemployed, disadvantaged persons, women, disabled persons, mature people, and visible minorities.
- *Innovation programs* provide funds to test new solutions to labour market–related problems.
- *The Community Futures Program* helps finance local committees for development training and employment initiatives in areas experiencing economic hardship.

For more information on each of the above programs, contact the local Canada Employment Centres.

The federal government also has some legislation in the areas of employment standards and hiring practices. Because of some overlaps in jurisdiction with the provinces, details are discussed in the next section. Appendix A at the end of this chapter illustrates these jurisdictions for the various programs and standards.

Provincial Governments

Each province in Canada, through its manpower or labour department, has set labour standards with which every owner-manager should be familiar. Appendix B lists the agencies that administer these standards in each province. Some of the more important areas that the provinces administer are discussed briefly below.

Job Discrimination.   Each provincial government has passed legislation concerning human rights in the workplace. Entitled Bills or Codes of Human Rights and administered by provincial human rights commissions, provincial legislation has jurisdiction over businesses not federally owned or regulated. Like its federal counterparts, these provincial regulations are designed to prevent discrimination in the workplace.

Pay and Employment Equity.   Recently some provinces have enacted legislation to ensure equality of pay and employment opportunity regardless of gender, race, religious affiliation, or ethnic origin.

Working Conditions and Compensation.   Numerous legal requirements govern the conditions under which retail employees work. Of importance to the small business owner are wage and hour requirements, restrictions on the use of child labour, provisions regarding equal pay, workers' compensation, unemployment benefits, and the Canada Pension Plan.

Employment Standards.   Both the federal and provincial governments administer a considerable amount of legislation related to employment standards and labour relations. At both levels of government, ministries of labour have primary responsibility in this field of regulation. In addition, both levels have legislation that allows for the establishment of unions and collective bargaining agents in the form of provincial labour relations acts and the federal Canada Labour Code. The Canada Labour Code also deals with many aspects of fair labour standards, labour relations, dismissal procedures, severance allowances, and working conditions. Similarly, each province enforces statutes covering minimum wage rates, hours of work, overtime, holidays and leaves, termination notices, employment of young people, and information requirements on the statement of earnings and deductions.

Employment Safety and Health.   Employment safety and health programs are designed to reduce absenteeism and labour turnover. Most provinces have passed industrial safety acts to protect the health and safety of workers. These laws govern such areas as sanitation, ventilation, and dangerous machinery. In addition to legislation, provincial governments, as well as employers, provide programs and training designed to accomplish similar purposes.

Workers' Compensation.   Workers' compensation is an employee accident and disability insurance program required under provincial law. It covers the employees who are accidentally injured while working or are unable to work as a result of a disease associated with a particular occupation. While these programs vary among the provinces, they generally provide for medical expenses and basic subsistence during the period of disability. Employers help pay for the program through assessments from the Workers' Compensation Board. The assessment rates, which many provinces have recently increased, represent a substantial operating expense; thus, they must be planned for and managed with considerable care.

Wage Subsidy Programs.   These programs provide financial assistance for up to six months for small businesses that hire unemployed persons.

Provincial Training Programs.   These programs provide job training and skill development incentives to upgrade the labour force. Often such programs include a wage subsidy to small businesses that hire new employees. Contact your provincial labour department (see Appendix B) for details of these programs.

Municipal Governments

Local or municipal government regulations related to industry generally are confined to such areas as licensing, zoning, hours of operation, property taxes, and building codes. For example, one issue of current debate relates to Sunday openings of retail stores. Generally jurisdiction has been left to the municipal government by the provinces. This issue has significant implications in terms of operating costs and competitiveness.

Municipal authorities also exercise an especially strong influence over food establishments. For instance, a municipal licensing system for restaurants and other food services establishments may be in effect. Also, health inspectors may make periodic and sometimes unannounced inspections. (Any store that sells wine, beer, and/or liquor may require a license from provincial liquor-licensing authorities.)

Recordkeeping for Employers

Every employer should maintain an employee file that includes such information as the employee's original application form, work record, salary level, evaluation reports, and any other pertinent information. One of the most important employee recordkeeping tasks for the owner-manager is completing the payroll. There are several essential steps in managing a payroll system for employees.

Employee Remittance Number.   As an employer, the owner-manager collects employee income tax on behalf of the government as a deduction from the employee's wage. Before remitting this amount to the Receiver General, the employer must obtain a remittance number, available by contacting the nearest office of Revenue Canada. Along with the remittance number, the appropriate tax deduction tables and forms will be provided.

Payroll Book.   The employer should obtain a payroll book or record that contains space for recording time worked as well as all of the required deductions. These books can be obtained from most business supply or stationery stores.

Monthly Remittance.   As mentioned above, each payday the employer is required to make the appropriate deductions and remit them, as well as the employer's share of Canada pension (2 times the employee's share) and unemployment insurance (2.4 times the employee's share), to Revenue Canada. This remittance is made on a prescribed form similar to that in Figure 11–8. This form contains the remittance number, the current payment amount, and a cumulative record of payments to date.

Year-End Statements.   At the end of the calendar year, the employer is required to total and reconcile the year's remittances with Revenue Canada's totals. This is done on a T4-A summary form provided by Revenue Canada.

   It is also the employer's responsibility to fill out for each employee a record of earnings and deductions for the year on the T4 slip. The T4 slip (see Figure 11–9) is completed by reviewing totals from the payroll book and is required to be sent to the employee by the end of February of the following year.

FIGURE 11-8 Remittance Form

Revenue Canada Taxation — Revenu Canada Impôt S

REMITTANCE FORM - FORMULE DE VERSEMENT

PD7AR REV. 78

6

FOR MONTH OF: / POUR LE MOIS DE: ______19__

ENTER AMOUNT OF PAYMENT / INSCRIRE LE MONTANT DU PAIEMENT $

H COMPANY LTD
203 FRINGE ST
NOWHERE

010 101

TBX 00000 0 TBX 00000 0 S

NAME, ADDRESS AND OWNERSHIP CHANGES
CHANGEMENTS DE NOM, D'ADRESSE ET DE PROPRIÉTAIRE
Please enter details of any changes not reported previously.
Prière d'indiquer le détail des changements non signalés antérieurement
New Name / *Nouveau nom* ______
New Address / *Nouvelle adresse* ______
Postal Code / *Code postal* ______
If ownership of business has changed enter effective date.
Si la propriété de l'entreprise a changé, en indiquer la date de prise d'effet. ______

DISTRIBUTION OF REMITTANCE (INCL. EMPLOYER C.P.P. & U.I. SHARES)
RÉPARTITION DU VERSEMENT (Y COMPRIS PARTS PATRONALES DU RPC ET DE L'A.-C.)

TAX DEDUCTIONS	C.P.P. CONTRIBUTIONS	U.I. PREMIUMS
$	$	$
DÉDUCTIONS D'IMPÔT	*COTISATIONS AU RPC*	*PRIMES D'A.-C.*

SIGNAL	L.P. CODE / *CODE P.P.T.*	NO. OF PAYTS. / *NBRE VERS.*	MONTH / *MOIS*	YEAR / *ANNÉE*
	1			

Revenue Canada Taxation — Revenu Canada Impôt

PD7A REV. 78

TAX DEDUCTION — CANADA PENSION PLAN — UNEMPLOYMENT INSURANCE REMITTANCE RETURN
DÉCLARATION DE VERSEMENTS CONCERNANT LES DÉDUCTIONS AU TITRE DE L'IMPÔT, DU RÉGIME DE PENSIONS DU CANADA ET DE L'ASSURANCE-CHÔMAGE

H COMPANY LTD
203 FRINGE ST
NOWHERE

010 101

EMPLOYER NO. / *N° DE L'EMPLOYEUR*	TBX 00000 0
DATE	08 AUG 1992
YEAR / *ANNÉE*	1992
REMITTANCE / *VERSEMENT* $	175.12
TOTAL TO DATE / *TOTAL À CE JOUR* $	1,407.14 CR

TAX DEDUCTIONS	C.P.P. CONTRIBUTIONS	U.I. PREMIUMS	CURRENT REMITTANCE
			$
DÉDUCTIONS D'IMPÔT	*COTISATIONS AU R.P.C.*	*PRIMES D'A.-C.*	*VERSEMENT COURANT*

IMPORTANT—SEE REVERSE
RETAIN THIS PART FOR YOUR RECORDS

J.S. HODGSON
DEPUTY MINISTER OF NATIONAL REVENUE FOR TAXATION
SOUS-MINISTRE DU REVENU NATIONAL POUR L'IMPÔT

IMPORTANT — VOIR AU VERSO
CONSERVEZ CETTE PARTIE

FIGURE 11–9   T-4 Slip

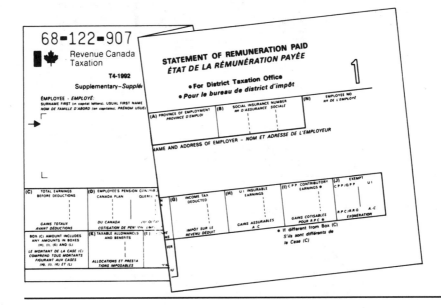

Summary

1. Sound personnel management is a key to the success of a small business, because motivated and competent personnel is one aspect of a business that may be unique and difficult to duplicate.

2. The organizational chart integrates tasks and employees so that the owner can visualize how the different aspects of the plan will work together.

3. An effective way to prevent many personnel problems is to have a policy manual covering such areas as job description, working conditions, holidays and leaves, remuneration, and employee benefits.

4. Some potential sources of employees for small business are recruitment from within, other businesses, employee referrals, advertising, employment agencies, and educational institutions.

5. The screening devices used in hiring employees include an application form, the employment interview, references, and various kinds of tests.

6. An interview guide helps focus the interview and provides a constant base of information with which to compare applicants.

7. Much can be done to ensure that a new employee has a smooth transition into the job. The new employee should be introduced to

co-workers, shown the locations of employee facilities, informed of any company regulations, and encouraged to ask for more information if needed.

8. The owner-manager should apply the following concepts of personnel management: assess his or her leadership style, work on time management by avoiding procrastination on important decisions or tasks, assess priorities, and use the most productive time of the day for the more important decisions.

9. Two important principles of human relations management are to provide satisfactory working conditions and to understand and provide for employee needs.

10. Compensation plans used by small businesses are straight salary, straight commission, cash bonus plans, stock bonus plans, profit-sharing plans, and combination plans.

11. Some common fringe benefits available to employees are job rotation, flexible hours, and employee suggestion systems.

12. A simplified version of the MBO process applicable to small business, the PRICE system, includes the following five steps: (1) pinpoint, (2) record, (3) involve, (4) coach, and (5) evaluate.

13. Some important principles in grievance management are to have a clear method of expressing grievances, assure employees that expressing their concerns will not jeopardize or prejudice their positions, ensure a minimum of red tape in the grievance process, and provide a method for nonvocal or hesitant employees to use the process.

14. The steps in administering a payroll system are to obtain an employee remittance number, obtain a payroll book, make the appropriate deductions and remit them with the employer's share to Revenue Canada, total and reconcile the year's remittance at the end of every calendar year, and send out T-4s.

Chapter Problems and Applications

1. Discuss the relative advantages and disadvantages of the various compensation plans used in small businesses.

2. Referring to the Magna International example in Incident 11–5, what industries can you think of in which profit sharing would be less successful? Why?

3. Discuss the relative advantages and disadvantages of the different types of fringe benefits for a small manufacturing company. If possible, interview employees of such a business to find out which of these benefits are the most attractive.

4. Recently a small business increased the wages of its employees, but its productivity is still inadequate. What could be some possible reasons for this low level of productivity?

5. ABC company employee deductions for July are UIC $98.72 and CPP $110.17. For what amount would the employer be liable?

6. Interview two small business owners to find out their personnel policies and how they communicate those policies to their employees.

7. Ask three employees of small businesses what they like and dislike about their jobs. What personnel policies could be used to remedy the dislikes?

8. Determine how three employees of various small businesses were recruited for their present positions. What seems to be the most popular source to recruit employees for small businesses? Why?

Appendix A
Labour Legislation Jurisdiction

Topic	Comments	Municipal	Provincial	Federal
Minimum age; contact provincial department of labour	Varies among provinces		X	
Minimum wage; contact minimum wage commission	Each province has its own industrial relations legislation		X	
Hours of work, annual vacations, holidays; contact provincial department of labour	Varies among provinces; general standard is two weeks; other holidays depend on the province		X	
Workers' compensation; contact provincial workers' compensation commission	Contributed by employer		X	
Industrial safety and health; contact provincial department of labour	Major jurisdiction from provinces; some federal jurisdiction		X	

(continued)

Topic	Comments	Jurisdiction		
		Municipal	*Provincial*	*Federal*
Unemployment insurance; contact Canada Employment and Immigration Commission	Contributed by employer			X
Canadian pension plan; contact Revenue Canada, District Taxation Office	Except in province of Quebec, where contributions are made to Quebec Pension Plan and both employer and employee contribute			X
Employment equity	Contact provincial department of labour; Ontario has legislation Some federal guidelines		X	
Hours of operation	Contact city hall	X		

APPENDIX B
PROVINCIAL LABOUR DEPARTMENTS

Alberta
Department of Labour
10808 99 Avenue
Edmonton, T5K 063
427–2723

British Columbia
Ministry of Labour
Parliament Building
Victoria, V8V 114
327–1986

Manitoba
Manitoba Labour
Norquay Building, 401 York Avenue
Winnipeg, R3C 0P8
945–4079

New Brunswick
Department of Labour and Human Resources
Chestnut Complex, 470 York Street
P.O. Box 6000
Fredericton, E3B 5H1
453–2342

Newfoundland
Department of Labour
Beothuk Building, Crosbie Place, St. John's
Mailing Address: Confederation Building
St. John's, A1C 517
576–2722

Northwest Territories
Labour Standards Board of the Northwest Territories
P.O. Box 2804
Yellowknife, X1A 2L9
873–7924

Nova Scotia
Department of Labour
5151 Terminal Rd., 6th Floor
P.O. Box 697
Halifax, B3J 2T8
424–6647

Ontario
Ministry of Labour
400 University Avenue
Toronto, M7A 1T7
965–4101

Prince Edward Island
Department of Fisheries and Labour
Sullivan Building, 16 Fitzroy Street
P.O. Box 2000
Charlottetown, C1A 7NB
892–3493

Quebec
Ministère du Travail
425, Rue St. Amable
Quebec, G1R 4Z1

255, Boulevard Cremazie
Montreal, H2M 1L5
543–2422

Saskatchewan
1870 Albert Street
Regina, S4P 3V7
787–2396

Yukon
Workers' Compensation Board
3rd Floor, 4110 4 Avenue
Whitehorse, Y1A 2C6
667–5877

Suggested Readings

Baumback, Clifford M. *How to Organize and Operate a Small Business.* Englewood Cliffs, N.J.: Prentice Hall, 1988, pp. 308–56.

Blanchard, Kenneth, and Spencer Johnson. *The One Minute Manager.* New York: Berkley Books, 1982.

Dolan, Shimon L., and Randall S. Schuler. *Personnel and Human Resource Management in Canada.* New York: West Publishers, 1987.

Philip, Mark A. *The 100 Best Companies to Work for in Canada.* Toronto: John Wiley & Sons, 1987.

Small Business in Canada. Industry, Science and Technology Canada, 1991, pp. 57–69.

Sullivan, Daniel J., and Joseph F. Lane. *Small Business Management: A Practical Approach.* Dubuque, Iowa: Wm. C. Brown, 1983, pp. 267–76.

Szonyi, Andrew J., and Dan Steinhoff. *Small Business Management Fundamentals.* Toronto: McGraw-Hill Ryerson, 1983, pp. 267–76.

Tate, Curtis E., Jr.; Leon C. Megginson; Charles R. Scott, Jr.; and Lyle R. Trueblood. *Successful Small Business Management.* Homewood, Ill.: Irwin-Dorsey of Canada, 1982, pp. 171–226.

COMPREHENSIVE CASE
THE FRAMEMAKERS: PART 8

Throughout the second year of The Framemakers' operation, sales and customer traffic continued to increase steadily. When the financial statements were returned from the accountant, gross sales in year 2 had exceeded first-year sales by a whopping $30,000—almost a 50 percent increase.

This was especially gratifying to the Normans. They had worked much harder than they had anticipated and had experienced many unforeseen problems. In addition to the inventory difficulties, one of their biggest concerns in year 2 was their employees. They had a difficult time attracting good employees. It seemed wage rates were too high, particularly with government agencies and larger businesses. The Framemakers could not afford to pay those kind of wages. Its total wage bill was already higher than the industry average for similar-size stores. Subsequently, those employees who were hired appeared unmotivated and unknowledgeable. They dealt poorly with customers, as the large number of customer complaints confirmed. As a result, either through employee resignations or firings, considerable employee turnover had occurred. New employees were sought through ads in the local newspaper and seemed to be in ample supply.

Firing employees had caused tense moments between Robert and Teresa on more than one occasion. Teresa tended to be the tougher of the two and would often reprimand employees and even let them go without Robert's knowledge. The most serious problem, however, was Robert's growing disillusionment with having any employees at all. He would complain to Teresa, "Why can't they take some interest in the job? They constantly watch the clock, ask for time off for this or that, and dress and behave so carelessly around the customers. Maybe we would be better off to stay small so we could do all the work ourselves!"

Questions

What are the causes of the Normans' personnel problems? What recommendations can you make for solving them?

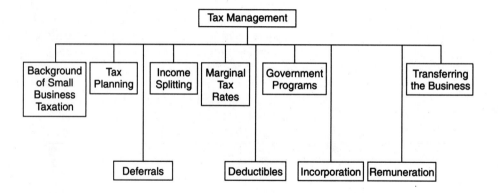

Tax Management

Chapter Objectives

- To explain the importance of understanding the Canadian tax system.
- To discuss key tax management principles the owner-manager can follow.
- To describe specific tax-related programs that apply to small business.

Small Business Profile

Gordon and Sonia Jones

Peninsula Farms

The story of Peninsula Farms, Ltd. shows how two unlikely entrepreneurs attempted to escape from the fast lane and big-city life by moving to the country. Although the move still left them very busy, Gordon and Sonia Jones are now doing something they enjoy.

In 1972, the Joneses left successful consulting and teaching careers in New York to move to Lunenburg, Nova Scotia, as Sonia had been offered a teaching position at Dalhousie University in Halifax. Although Gordon was planning a semiretirement, it wasn't long before he had purchased a few milk cows and found they produced more milk than the Joneses needed. Upon learning that government regulations would not allow them to commercially sell milk without an expensive quota, they turned to yogurt.

So skillful were the Joneses at yogurt making that within five years they developed a successful business selling to local stores. In 1979 they were offered an opportunity to distribute their yogurt to Sobey's, a major chain, and later to two other eastern Canadian chains. The Joneses realized they would have to change their operations to accommodate this increase in demand. They doubled the size of their plant with the help of a government grant from the Department of Regional Industrial Expansion. By 1992 they had sales of over $2 million (25 percent of the maritime market) and employed more than 40 people.

In 1991 the federal government classified single-serve yogurt as snack food and added the 7 percent GST. Sales for Peninsula Farms dropped nearly 50 percent. The Joneses and others in the industry lobbied vigorously to have the GST removed by pointing to studies showing that most yogurt is eaten in the home. Although they succeeded, the lobbying and internal adjustments were expensive, and sales have never recovered to pre-GST levels.

The Joneses remain undaunted, however, and have added frozen yogurt in addition to looking for new international markets. Their persistence and ability to adapt to government programs and taxes have helped them succeed and should contribute to Peninsula's future growth.

Sources: Anne Templeman Kluit, *Profit Magazine,* July-August 1986, pp. 18–20; Jennifer Myers, *Profit Magazine,* September 1992, p. 29.

Taxation and Small Business

Chapter 4 presented a brief outline regarding the tax requirements of a small business. It was noted that various types of business and property taxes are levied by federal, provincial, and municipal governments. The calculation of and liability for most of those taxes are relatively straightforward and will not be discussed again in this chapter. Income taxes, however, can be more complicated, be more subject to interpretation, and have a greater impact on the planning and cash flow of the business. This chapter therefore focuses primarily on this area.

The income tax was instituted in Canada as a "temporary" measure in 1917. But income taxes not only are here to stay but are becoming increasingly complicated and generally more burdensome for most Canadians:

> The average Canadian family pays more than 52 percent of its income in taxes. With changing governments, high unemployment and crippling interest rates every consumer must find ways to save on tax bills and manage money more effectively.[1]

Individuals who reside in and corporations that operate in Canada are liable for federal and provincial income taxes. These taxes are applied on income that is received or receivable during the taxation year from all sources, less certain deductions. Federal and provincial tax agreements govern the procedures by which the federal government is empowered to collect taxes and remit portions to the provinces. Some provinces, including Quebec and Alberta, now collect their own corporate income taxes.

Because of the complexity of tax principles and the frequency of legislative changes concerning taxes, a detailed treatment of tax management for small business is beyond the scope of this book. This chapter briefly discusses some general tax management principles and programs. While it is essential that owner-managers have some knowledge of these principles in managing and planning their businesses, they are strongly advised to seek professional advice in preparing tax returns and investigating methods of minimizing tax liability.

Some owner-managers may not be overly concerned with income taxes and thus may do little tax planning. This lack of concern may be due to one of two factors. First, the business may currently have no tax liability; in other words, it is losing money. This situation, of course, will be only temporary because the business will eventually become profitable or cease to exist. Second, the owner-manager may not understand the impact of taxes on the cash flow of the business. As Figure 12–1 illustrates, an increase in the tax rate of only 10 percent translates into a tax liability that would require an additional $100,000 in sales to offset. When the owner-manager understands the full effects of a lower or higher tax liability, he or she will want a working knowledge of tax principles and programs.

FIGURE 12-1   **Impact of Tax Rate on a Business**

Taxable income	$50,000
Increase in tax rate from 20% to 30%	20% of 50,000 = $10,000
	30% of 50,000 = $15,000
Increased tax liability	15,000 − 10,000 = $5,000
Profit as a percentage of sales	5%
Sales required to offset tax	5,000/5% = $100,000

NOTE: The extra $100,000 in sales would also incur an additional $1,500 tax liability.

General Tax Management Principles

The owner-manager should be aware of nine fundamental areas of tax management.

Continual Tax Planning

One of the most disturbing aspects of tax statement preparation for the owner-manager is learning that he or she has incurred an unnecessary tax liability. This situation usually arises because the accountant received and prepared the return too late to take advantage of favourable programs and deductions.

It is critical, therefore, that the owner-manager be aware of the tax consequences of business operations throughout the year, not just at or after the year end. Up-to-date income statements (as discussed in Chapter 9) can assist in forecasting income trends, allowing some advance tax planning. Incident 12-1 illustrates the difficulties a lack of tax planning can create.

Revenue Canada requires that income tax be paid in instalments throughout the year. Individuals operating proprietorships and partnerships are required to remit quarterly instalments for the amount of taxes they incur. Corporations must submit monthly instalments based on their estimated tax liability. Again, prior planning will be required to allow compliance with this regulation.

Tax Deferral

One unwritten rule of tax management concerns tax deferral. This means that one should attempt to put off paying taxes as long as legally possible. There are at least two good reasons to defer taxes. First, one has the use of the tax money for the period of the deferral. This money can be put to productive use in the business or other investments. Second, tax laws may change, resulting in a decreased liability in the future.

Several specific programs facilitate deferral of tax liability. Some of these programs will be discussed later. Choosing the fiscal or tax year end of the

Incident 12–1

The Taxman Always Rings Twice

Colette Arsenault has made a career out of knowing what research and statistical analysis to sell to the international forest industry. But when a new service she tried to introduce flopped, it triggered the most frustrating experience of her career: a Revenue Canada audit.

Two Revenue Canada auditors stationed themselves at Arsenault Consulting full-time, sifting through two years of company records. Arsenault had to enlist her external accountant to sit with them for a week, pouring over every receipt, contract and log-book entry.

The auditors were polite and businesslike, says Arsenault, but they came at a bad time. When her employees should have been working flat out to beat the recession, she says, they were being asked by the auditors to justify and explain line items, or were distracted and worried by the auditors' presence.

The auditors earned a meagre payback, uncovering $2,000 in taxes owing. But the accountant alone cost Arsenault $2,000 more and she figures the company's sales and wages were lost for the full week, "when everyone was running around working with Revenue Canada." None of that includes the stress Arsenault endured while her business and reputation went under the microscope.

Source: "The Taxman Always Rings Twice," *Profit Magazine,* October 1991, p. 27.

business is one practice that can benefit the small business, particularly a proprietorship or a partnership. It is not necessary to use the calendar year in calculating income from the business. Revenue Canada, on the other hand, assesses a tax liability on income earned (year-end income) for the calendar year. Therefore, if the year end of the business was December 10, 1992, the liability to Revenue Canada will arise for the 1992 calendar year and require payment by April 30, 1993. However, if the year end is moved back to January 10, 1993, one month later, the liability arises in the 1993 calendar year, with payment due by April 30, 1994. As can be seen, the selection of the year end for the business may allow the deferring of tax liability for almost one year. See Figure 12–2 for an illustration of this example.

Income Splitting

The tax system for individuals in Canada is a progressive system whereby a higher taxable income results in a higher percentage tax liability (see Appendix A for current federal tax rates in Canada and Appendix B for provincial tax rates).

FIGURE 12–2   Tax Deferral by Selecting Year End

No Tax Deferral	*Tax Deferral*
Year end of business: Dec. 10, 1992	Year end of business: Jan. 10, 1993
Business income to be taxed in this year: 1992	Business income to be taxed in this year: 1993
Tax to be paid by: April 1, 1993	Tax to paid by: April 1, 1994

FIGURE 12–3   Income Splitting

Business income = $25,000

A. If one person declared the income:	B. If two people split the income:
Income = $25,000	Income = $25,000
Tax rate = $4,438 + 25% of $1,504	Partner A = $12,500
Tax liability = $4,813	Partner B = $12,500
	Tax rate for each = $1,201 + 19% of $4,668
	Tax liability A = $2,088
	Tax liability B = $2,088
	Total liability for A & B = $4,176

Tax savings by splitting income = $4,813 − $4,176 = $637.

Because of the progressive nature of taxes, splitting incomes between spouses and other family members or among partners will result in a reduced overall tax liability, as Figure 12–3 shows. If done within a family, the spouse and/or children will likely be taxed at lower rates, which would further reduce this tax liability.

Care should be taken when splitting income within the family to ensure that wages paid to the spouse or children are a reasonable amount considering their contribution to the business and that payroll withholding taxes, if applicable, are deducted.

Marginal Tax Rates

The marginal tax rate is the tax rate applied by Revenue Canada to the next dollar of income earned. Knowledge of an individual's marginal rate can be helpful in planning income and expenses. For example, if an owner-manager has a marginal tax rate of 30 percent, he or she knows that each dollar of income earned will incur a tax liability of 30 cents, whereas each dollar of expense incurred will save 30 cents in tax liability. Thus, awareness of the current marginal rate allows the owner-manager to calculate the after-tax effects of extra income and expenses.

Another benefit of knowing the marginal rate is the possibility of moving that rate to a lower bracket by incurring some additional expenses prior to year end—provided, of course, that the expenses are necessary. Like income splitting, this principle has the most value for the proprietorship and partnership.

Deductibles

The small business owner should be familiar with those expenses that are deductible in the calculation of taxable income. The onus is on the taxpayer to keep proper records, since the burden of proof for these expenses lies with him or her. This means the owner-manager must keep receipts of business expenses. An often neglected aspect of this practice is the failure to obtain or keep receipts of expenses for which the owner-manager paid personally on behalf of the business. These expenses may seem too small to justify keeping track of them. However, if the tax rate is 25 percent, a mere $4 expense unrecorded can result in an increased tax liability of $1.

According to generally accepted accounting principles, an expense is defined as a payment or a liability created to earn income. To determine whether certain expenses are deductible the owner-manager should consult an accountant, Revenue Canada, or such publications as the *Master Tax Guide* published by Commerce Clearing House. Some of the more common small business expenses that may require explanation follow.

Accounting and Legal Expenses.   Only those expenses incurred to earn income are deductible. Expenses incurred to incorporate the business or prepare a personal tax return are not deductible.

Advertising.   Advertising expenses are deductible only if used in Canadian media and targeted to Canadian consumers.

Business Entertaining.   Business entertaining expenses incurred in one's home are not deductible. Neither is the purchase of club memberships or yachts. Other types of legitimate business entertaining, however, are deductible.

Automobile Expenses.   For a personal auto, the portion of expenses used for business purposes is deductible, but records must be kept to verify those amounts. Usually the business portion is the mileage expended on business travel.

Interest Expense.   Interest expense is deductible for business loans but not for personal loans. Some experts counsel that to maximize this deductible, personal savings should be used to finance personal expenses if possible, rather than business expenses.

For a corporation, another interest-related matter is a loan to the business by a shareholder. This is a fairly common form of financing a business, because it offers some significant advantages. The interest is a deductible expense to the business, but the repayment terms may remain flexible depending on the ability of the business to pay and the wishes of the owner-lender. In a sense, the shareholder's loan combines the advantages of both debt and equity financing.

Repairs and Improvements.   Repairs are deductible expenses, but improvements should be depreciated at the specified CCA rates. CCA (Capital Cost Allowance) rates are percentages that can be subtracted from a capital asset cost and allocated as a business expense. It is often unclear what portion of the expenditure is a repair and what portion is an improvement. An accountant should be consulted in making this allocation.

Office Expenses.   Office expenses are deductible and can be an important area for the owner-manager whose office is in the home. In such a case, a portion of household expenses such as utilities, mortgage interest, insurance, repairs, and taxes can be listed as business expenses. The portion to deduct depends on the size of the office relative to the size of the house. Care should be taken in including depreciation as an office expense, since it could be deemed to be recaptured and added to taxable income.

Government Tax-Related Programs

Numerous government programs and policies in Canada affect the tax management practices for the small business. Following is a summary of some of the more important items for the owner-manager.

Special Tax Rate Deductions

Small Business Deduction (SBD).   The small business deduction is 16 percent of active business income for an incorporated, Canadian-controlled, private business. This special rate applies to the first $200,000 of income each year. Figure 12–4 illustrates the significance of this program for a small business.

Manufacturing and Processing Deduction.   This program provides for an additional reduction of 6 percent in tax liability for any business involved in the manufacturing or processing industries. This deduction is available for income that is not eligible for the SBD mentioned above (only for income over the $200,000 limit cited above). Beginning January 1, 1994, this deduction increases to 7 percent.

Investment Tax Credits.   Only the Atlantic provinces and the Gaspe are eligible for investment tax credits on purchases of qualified property. All taxpayers are eligible for tax credits on qualified scientific research expenditures (SRTCs). Canadian-controlled private corporations may apply for a 35 percent SRTC, while all other taxpayers may apply for a 20 percent SRTC. In the Atlantic provinces and the Gaspe, the rates for SRTC are 35 and 30 percent, respectively.

FIGURE 12-4   **Effect of the Small Business Deduction**

Business income = $50,000

No small business deduction:	Small business deduction:
Tax rate = 38%	SBD = 38% − 16% = 22%
Tax liability = $19,000	Tax liability = $11,000

Difference in tax liability = $8,000

Deferral Programs.   Some programs that allow tax deferrals have been very popular with owner-managers of small businesses:

1. *Deferred profit sharing.*   DPS allows for a deferral of part of the business profits that have been registered for payment in the future to employees. The payment amount is taxable to employees only when received, but is a deductible expense in the year in which it is set aside or registered.

2. *Registered retirement savings plan.*   RRSPs allow the owner-manager to put money into a registered plan that will be taxed only when received at a future date, presumably when the taxpayer is in a lower tax bracket. Recent budget changes have increased the contribution limits of RRSPs.

3. *Bonus deferral.*   This program permits the business to deduct as an expense an accrued bonus or wage but allows a certain time period (recently reduced to 180 days) to pay the amount. This amount is not taxable until received. The bonus deferral thus may effectively allow the business an expense in one year, but defer tax liability in the hands of the recipient to the following year.

Accelerated Capital Cost Allowance.   This program allows an increased depreciation rate (capital cost allowance) to be applied as noncash expenses to certain classes of assets in calculating taxable income. Capital cost allowance rates can be obtained from an accountant or the tax department or by consulting the *Master Tax Guide.*

Small Business Financing Programs.   For the incorporated business, these programs allow the business to borrow money from a chartered bank at a reduced interest rate. This is made possible because of special tax treatment these banks receive from Revenue Canada. Only businesses unable to obtain ordinary debt financing are eligible for this program.

The Incorporation Question

One decision regarding the establishment or growth of the business that owner-managers face is incorporation. Chapter 4 discussed the relative merits and weaknesses of the proprietorship, the partnership, and the incorporated company. Some significant differences in tax treatment also exist among these different forms of business.

As mentioned above, with the small business deduction the tax rate for an incorporated business is about 25 percent. If the business is a partnership or a proprietorship, the business income is brought into the owner-manager's personal tax return. This return includes various other personal deductions and exemptions. The individual's personal rate may be higher or lower than the rate for an incorporated business. If the minimization of tax liability were the major concern, the owner-manager would pursue incorporating when the tax rate for the business was lower than the personal rate. The incorporation question is influenced not only by the tax liability for the different legal forms of business; many government programs are available only to incorporated businesses.

The Remuneration Question

Another difficult decision owner-managers must make is how to be paid by the business. In the proprietorship and the partnership, payment to the owner is treated as a drawing from the business and is not a deductible expense (or taxable income). In the corporation, an owner can be paid with a salary or with dividends. These methods of payment receive significantly different tax treatment as Figure 12–5 illustrates. The owner-manager should consult with an accountant prior to making a decision in this area. Future federal budgets have changed the difference in tax treatment of salary and dividends. Currently surtaxes imposed by the federal and some provincial governments result in a slightly higher income tax paid when remuneration is taken in dividends if the owner's taxable income exceeds $55,000.

Transferring the Business: Capital Gains

Many small business owners wanting to transfer their businesses to others have encountered considerable difficulty. Some tax considerations significantly affect how the business is transferred. Recent tax changes involving capital gains exemptions have made it much easier to transfer the business to family members or others. This topic is discussed in more detail in Chapter 14.

FIGURE 12–5   Dividend versus Salary Income

Corporate income	$ 1,000	$1,000
Salary	−1,000	—
Taxable income of corporation	—	1,000
Corporate tax @ 23%	—	230
Available for dividend payment	—	770
Income to shareholder	1,000	770
Dividend gross-up @ 25% of dividend received	—	193
Net income	1,000	963
Personal tax @ 29% on salary or dividend	290	279
Less: dividend tax credit @ 13⅓ of grossed-up dividend	—	−128
Net federal tax	290	151
Plus: provincial tax (50% of net federal tax)	145	75
Total personal tax	435	226
Corporate tax	—	230
Personal tax	435	226
Total tax	$ 435	$ 456

Summary

1. Basic tax knowledge allows the small business owner to save money that would otherwise be paid in taxes.

2. Continual tax planning ensures that the owner-manager is aware of the tax consequences of business decisions throughout the year rather than just at the year end.

3. The reasons for tax deferral are that (*a*) the owner-manager has the use of the tax money for the period of deferral and (*b*) tax laws may change, resulting in a decreased liability in the future.

4. Because of the progressive nature of taxes, splitting incomes between spouses and other family members or among partners will reduce the overall tax liability.

5. The nine fundamental areas of tax management of which the owner-manager should be aware are (*a*) continual tax planning, (*b*) tax deferral, (*c*) income splitting, (*d*) marginal tax rates, (*e*) deductibles, (*f*) knowledge of government tax-related programs, (*g*) the incorporation question, (*h*) the remuneration question, and (*i*) capital gains.

6. A deductible expense is defined as a payment or a liability created to earn income.

7. Some of the more important government tax-related programs are the small business deduction, manufacturing and processing deductions, investment tax credits, deferral programs, accelerated capital cost allowances, and small business financing programs.

8. One key consideration in the incorporation question is tax liability. If a partnership or a proprietorship is being taxed at a higher rate than an incorporated company, it would be beneficial to incorporate to reduce tax liability.

9. In an incorporated company, it may be preferable to draw dividends instead of salaries to reduce tax liability.

Chapter Problems and Applications

1. Explain why the year-end date is significant in tax planning.

2. The year end for Wave Waterbeds is soon approaching. The proprietor, Tom Newcombe, estimates that the company currently has taxable income of $5,500. He would like to purchase a new cash register worth $2,000. Determine the tax liability if Newcombe purchases the cash register before or after year end (use Appendix A); cash registers are depreciated at 20 percent. When would you advise Newcombe to purchase the cash register? Why?

3. The owner-manager of L.A. Construction has just incurred the following expenses. Which expenses are tax deductible?
   a. Incorporation expenses
   b. Advertising expense in the United States and in Canada
   c. Truck repairs of $2,000
   d. Costs of maintaining a residential phone used for business purposes

4. What is the tax liability for the following proprietorships' taxable incomes?
   a. $5,496
   b. $10,942
   c. $34,999
   d. $63,000

5. Which variables affect the decision to incorporate?

6. Determine the tax liability for the following companies.
   a. A Canadian-controlled incorporated company with $25,000 taxable income
   b. A Canadian-controlled incorporated company with $25,000 taxable income that qualifies for a small business deduction
   c. Same as part b, but the business qualifies for the 5 percent manufacturing credit
   d. A proprietorship with taxable income of $25,000

7. Ask a consultant or an accountant when a business should incorporate. What are the important considerations?

8. Discuss with an accountant the advantages and disadvantages of the different owner compensation methods in a corporation.

9. Calculate the marginal tax rate for yourself or for someone you know.

APPENDIX A
FEDERAL INCOME TAX RATES FOR INDIVIDUALS

Taxable Income	Tax Rate*
Up to $29,590	17%
$29,591–$59,180	26
$59,181 and over	29

*The taxable income brackets are indexed to the annual inflation rate in excess of 3 percent. A surtax of 5 percent must be added after taking any applicable credits into account. The 1992 federal budget decreased the basic surtax to 3 percent effective January 1, 1993.

APPENDIX B
PROVINCIAL TAX RATES FOR INDIVIDUALS

The personal provincial tax rate, with the exception of Quebec, is a percentage of basic federal tax.

	Effective January 1, 1992			
	Other Corporations		**Small Canadian-Controlled [a] Active Business Income**	
	Mfg.[k]	Non-Mfg.	Mfg.[k]	Non-Mfg.
Federal rates[b]	23.8%	28.8%	12.8%	12.8%
Provincial rates:				
British Columbia	15.0%	15.0%	9.0%	9.0%
Alberta	15.5	15.5	6.0	6.0
Saskatchewan	16.0	16.0	10.0[c]	10.0[c]
Manitoba	17.0	17.0	10.0[d]	10.0[d]
Ontario	14.5	15.5	10.0[e]	10.0[e]
Quebec[j]	6.9	6.9[i]	3.75[f]	3.75[f]
New Brunswick	17.0	17.0	9.0	9.0
Nova Scotia	16.0	16.0	10.0[g]	10.0[g]
Prince Edward Island	15.0	15.0	10.0	10.0
Newfoundland	17.0	17.0	10.0[h]	10.0[h]
Northwest Territories	12.0	12.0	5.0	5.0
Yukon Territory	7.5	10.0	2.5	5.0

Note: At the time of publication of this book, the provinces had not yet released their budgets for 1992. Provincial corporate tax rates for 1992 are therefore subject to change.

[a]Canadian-controlled private corporations (CCPCs) eligible for the federal small business deduction.

[b]The rates include the 3 percent federal corporate surtax applicable to all federal tax net of applicable logging tax credits and special credits for investment corporations and credit unions. The 3 percent federal surtax does not apply to a non-resident-owned investment corporation or to the capital gains refund received by a mutual fund or investment corporation.

[c]Canadian-controlled private corporations incorporated after March 26, 1986, and before April 1, 1992, may be granted a two-year tax holiday on up to $200,000 of active business income.

[d]Qualifying small businesses incorporated after August 8, 1988, and before January 1, 1993, are subject to a tax holiday in which the 10 percent rate will be phased in at 2 percent per year, beginning with the second taxation year.

[e]A new surtax is levied on corporations claiming the Ontario small business deduction. The surtax is equal to the lesser of (1) 3.7 percent of taxable income in excess of $200,000 and (2) the Ontario small business deduction claimed.

[f]Canadian-controlled private corporations incorporated after May 1, 1986, may receive an exemption from income on their first $200,000 of eligible business income earned during their first three years.

[g]A two-year tax holiday applies to new businesses incorporated after April 18, 1986, and eligible for the federal small business deduction.

[h]Qualifying new small businesses incorporated after April 2, 1987, but before April 2, 1991, are exempt from corporate income tax for three years.

[i]Active business income only; nonactive business income is taxed at 14.95 percent up to August 31, 1991, and 16.25 percent thereafter.

[j]These Quebec rates actually became effective on September 1, 1991.

[k]The February 25, 1992, federal budget reduced the manufacturing and processing rate (before the 0.84 percent surtax) from 23 to 22 percent on January 1, 1993, and to 21 percent on January 1, 1994.

SOURCE: *The Practitioner's Income Tax Act,* 2nd ed. (Toronto: Thomson Professional Publishing, 1992).

Suggested Readings

Beam, R. E., and S. N. Laiken. *Introduction to Federal Income Taxation in Canada,* 13th ed. Don Mills, Ont.: CCH Canadian Limited, 1992.

Canadian Master Tax Guide. Don Mills, Ont.: Commerce Clearing House, yearly.

Corporate Tax Return Handbook. Toronto: Canadian Institute of Chartered Accountants, 1992.

Fisher, S. Brian, and Paul B. Hickey, eds. *The Canadian Personal Tax Planning Guide.* Toronto: Thomson Professional Publishing, 1992.

Kao, Raymond W. Y. *Small Business Management.* New York: Holt, Rinehart and Winston, 1983, pp. 342–50.

Peat Marwick. *Tax Planning for the Owner-Managed Business, 1986–87.* Toronto: Peat Marwick, November 1986.

Siropolis, Nicholas C. *Small Business Management.* Boston: Houghton Mifflin, 1986, pp. 534–51.

Touche Ross. *Personal Tax Planning Ideas, 1986–87.* Toronto: Touche Ross & Company, 1986.

CASES FOR PART III

BOUCHARD'S MARKET

D. Wesley Balderson
University of Lethbridge

Bouchard's Market opened a new store in Quebec City in January 1991. Although the firm had been in business for three generations, the neighbourhood in which the original store stood had become shabby, and many of its loyal clientele had moved to the suburbs. The present owner, Pierre Bouchard, decided to follow the population move. The new store was located in a small shopping centre adjacent or close to more than 70 four-story apartment buildings that housed over 400 families. Many more apartment buildings were under construction, as well as three- and four-bedroom, single-family homes in several nearby housing developments. The nearest competition was located approximately two miles northeast of the present shopping centre.

In preparation for the grand opening, Pierre Bouchard purchased many varieties of canned juices, fruits, and vegetables. In addition, he carried a number of varieties and lines of cheeses, frozen foods, other dairy products, fruits, vegetables, and meats. To display and sell all the stock, it was necessary to use valuable aisle space as islands for various bulk cheeses, canned fruits, and dry groceries such as potato chips, pretzels, and the like. The store size was 55 by 90 feet. The store layout, shown in Figure 1, is as follows:

- A: display area for crackers, breads, and cookies
- B: refrigerated area for frozen foods, frozen desserts, and packaged cheeses
- C: display area for olives, pickles, other condiments, canned fruit, and fruit juices
- D: display area for canned vegetables, canned fish, breakfast cereals, and dried fruits.
- 1: island display for bulk cheeses
- 2, 3: island display for soft drinks
- 4: area for shopping carts

FIGURE 1   **Present Store Layout**

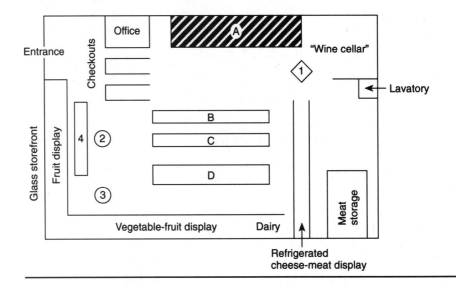

The store employed eight full-time people. These consisted of six clerks and two assistant managers—one manager for meat and dairy and the other for grocery, produce, and frozen foods.

During the first four weeks of operation, it was found that:

1. There were far too many employees for the type of work needed.
2. There was far too much congestion of shoppers at certain in-store locations.
3. There was a build-up of customers at the checkout stations.
4. Many customers inquired as to where to find various food items.
5. Several of Bouchard's employees indicated that some changes needed to be made to the interior layout of the store.

After receiving this input, Bouchard was not sure what to do. The present layout seemed unsatisfactory, but he did not want to spend a lot of money making changes.

Questions

1. Based on Figure 1 and the observations of the first four weeks, what are the weaknesses of the present store layout?
2. Develop a layout that might solve these problems.
3. How should Pierre Bouchard go about implementing such changes?

Source: Adapted from A. Edward Spitz, "Stacker's Market," *Retailing: Case Problems* (Columbus, Ohio: Grid, 1975), pp. 7–9.

Cape Breton Boat Rentals

Donald G. Ross
St. Francis Xavier University

On May 1, 1989, Bruce MacLean, owner of Cape Breton Boat Rentals, was preparing a weekly cash budget to determine his operating line of credit requirements for the upcoming summer rental season.

Company Background

Cape Breton Boat Rentals, established in June, 1988 at Munro Park, North Sydney, Nova Scotia, was set up to rent canoes, kayaks, sailboards, sailboats, paddleboats, and motorboats to tourists and local residents. MacLean thought Munro Park was an ideal site as it provided a good traffic location on Seaview Drive (for customers wishing to take the water craft away) and a good beach location (for those customers seeking to rent on-site).

In 1988, Cape Breton Boat Rentals operated seven days a week from June 17th to September 5th; MacLean's younger brother, Malcolm, ran the shop. By all accounts, the company's services were well received by the public. Many customers had praised the fair prices, adding that the service "should have been available long ago." July write-ups in the Cape Breton Post and August radio coverage seemed to echo expressions of satisfaction with the new business.

Despite this favourable reception, the company's first year of operations was disappointing. Sales reached only $14,699, less than half the projected sales revenue of $33,000. The poor sales performance combined with expenses of $22,024 produced a first year loss of $7,325 (Figure 1) and a tight liquidity position (Figure 2). To reverse this poor performance in 1989, MacLean planned a number of changes. He expected these changes to substantially improve revenues while holding expenses steady; if successful, these moves would lead to the realization of the projected income statement set out in Figure 3.

Revenue Projections

MacLean made several risky assumptions in projecting increased sales revenues for 1989. He was relying on: (1) better weather for rentals, (2) customer acceptance of a substantial increase in prices, (3) increased market development as a result of a tripled advertising budget, and (4) increased revenues from an extended operating season.

MacLean knew that low sales in 1988 were not caused by a lack of rental equipment. In fact, on only one sunny weekend in August had almost all of the

FIGURE 1

CAPE BRETON BOAT RENTALS LIMITED
Income Statement
Year Ended April 30, 1989

Revenue		
Rentals	$12,857	
Sale of Rental Property	1,655	
Miscellaneous	187	
Total Revenue		$14,699
Expenses		
Advertising	820	
Automobile	1,837	
Cost of Rental Property Sold	1,377	
Depreciation	7,672	
Insurance	556	
Interest & Bank Charges	2,047	
Land Rent	500	
Maintenance	1,329	
Miscellaneous	292	
Motorboat Gas & Supplies	661	
Office Supplies	291	
Telephone & Utilities	907	
Wages	3,735	
Total Expenses		22,024
Net Income (Loss)		$ (7,325)

SOURCE: Company records.

company's equipment been used; on average only about 10% of the company's equipment was out on rental. MacLean felt instead that low sales in 1988 were mostly due to the poor July weather—he believed this factor alone had reduced the season's sales by 25%.

He also felt that insufficient advertising during the company's first season had hurt sales. He therefore intended to triple his advertising budget to $2,500 for 1989. This would enable him to: (1) distribute brochures to the major tourist bureaus, campgrounds, motels, and restaurants at the start of the season as he had done in 1988, (2) double, from May to August, his first season's advertising in the local daily newspaper, the Cape Breton Post, and (3) introduce radio spots on CJCB to increase demand during the six week peak period from July 2nd to August 12th (weeks 8 through 13). (Peak season demand was double that of low season.) He expected an additional 25% in sales from the increased advertising.

To further boost revenues, MacLean planned a 25% across-the-board increase in rental fees for 1989. Although the increase was steep, the new fees would still be below prices MacLean had observed in the Halifax-Dartmouth area and in

---

Figure 2

CAPE BRETON BOAT RENTALS
Balance Sheet
April 30, 1989

Assets		
Current Assets		
Cash	$ 663	
Inventory	504	
Prepaid Expenses	121	
Total Current Assets		$ 1,288
Rental Property		
Gross Rental Property	42,045	
Accumulated Depreciation	(6,542)	
Total Rental Property		35,503
Fixed Assets		
Gross Fixed Assets	6,366	
Accumulated Depreciation	(1,032)	
Total Fixed Assets		5,334
ACOA Grants Receivable		1,344
Organizational Costs		
Gross Organizational Costs	850	
Accumulated Amortization	(98)	
Total Organizational Costs		752
Total Assets		
Liabilities & Net Worth		
Current Liabilities		
Accounts Payable	$ 143	
Accrued Interest Payable	712	
Loans Payable	7,000	
Due to Shareholders	2,927	
Total Current Liabilities		$10,782
Long Term Liabilities		
LT Portion of Loans Payable		9,200
Net Worth		
Common Shares		150
Contributed Surplus	31,414	
Accumulated Deficit	(7,325)	24,089
Total Net Worth		24,239
Total Liabilities and Net Worth		$44,221

Source: Company records.

FIGURE 3

CAPE BRETON BOAT RENTALS LIMITED
Pro Forma Income Statement
Year Started May 1, 1989

Revenue		
Rentals	$26,862	
Sale of Rental Property	2,500	
Miscellaneous	200	
Total Revenue		$29,562
Expenses		
Advertising	2,500	
Automobile	2,000	
Cost of Rental Property Sold	2,000	
Depreciation	6,500	
Insurance	584	
Interest & Bank Charges	2,400	
Land Rent	500	
Maintenance	1,500	
Miscellaneous	300	
Motorboat Gas & Supplies	100	
Office Supplies	300	
Telephone & Utilities	19,000	
Wages	4,250	
Total Expenses		$23,934
Net Income (Loss)		$ 5,628

SOURCE: Company records.

similar operations in Prince Edward Island. Consequently, he didn't feel that the company would lose any sales because of the price increase.

Finally, MacLean felt that revenues in 1988 were unnecessarily restricted by too short an operating season (82 days). To secure a longer operating season (91 days) and capture the spring fishing boat market, he decided to open on May 19th, the start of the Victoria Day weekend, and to stay open Friday through Monday until Canada Day (weeks 1 through 7). Thereafter, the company would operate seven days a week until it closed on Labour Day (week 17). MacLean also felt that each additional business day would not only generate increased sales, but would lessen the impact of bad weather on total 1989 revenues.

Expense Projections

Advertising expenditures for the season comprised: (1) $250 for brochures to be printed the first week of May (payable the last week of June); (2) $875 for the "business card" advertisement running Tuesday, Thursday, and Saturday in the

Cape Breton Post ($125 payable in the last week of June and $250 payable the last week of each month following); and (3) $1,375 for radio advertising. (Because the company had not previously used radio advertising, the terms of payment called for $350 the first week of July, $350 the last week of August and the remainder the last week of September.)

The $2,000 expected automobile expense was based on the costs incurred in using MacLean's own automobile and is comprised of car operating costs of $1,000 (spread evenly over the season) and a $1,000 fee for use of the automobile (MacLean would draw this out at the end of the season). The company's insurance is payable in one lump sum the second week of July.

Interest and bank charges of $75 were paid on the last week of every month to the Royal Bank of Canada (RBC), which handled the company's operating accounts and held a demand note for $4,000 from the company which was to be repaid at the end of the 1989 season. An additional combined payment of $1,500 interest and $3,000 principal was due on October 31st to the Northside Economic Development Assistance Corporation (NEDAC), which provided term financing to the company at a fixed interest rate of 11¾%.

Land rent was payable as follows: $100 on June 30th, $200 on July 31st, and $200 on August 31st. Maintenance costs were expected to total $1,500: $500 to cover a major engine overhaul payable on the first week of June and $1,000 incurred equally over the season. Motorboat gas and supplies expense was projected to drop to $100 over the season because this cost was going to be passed along to the customer in 1989. The cost of office supplies would be paid in the last week of June. Telephone and utility charges were expected to be incurred equally over the season and would be paid the last week of each month, starting in June.

To prepare the shop for opening, Malcolm would commence work on Sunday, May 14th (beginning of Week 1) and would work until Saturday, September 9th (end of Week 17) when the shop would be closed for the winter. Wages would be paid at the end of each two week period (commencing in Week 2).

Rental Stock Adjustments

To increase rental revenues by an additional $1,500, MacLean had arranged to purchase a used 35 hp motorboat for $2,500 cash on May 15th. He believed this would bring in at least another $1,500 in rental revenues. To finance the purchase MacLean planned to sell some surplus canoes and small outboard motors over the season.

Question

Prepare a weekly cash budget for Cape Breton Boat Rentals for the 1989 season, and advise MacLean of his operating line of credit requirements.

Additional Information.   MacLean planned to include all preseason payments in the first week and all cash receipts and payments after the end of the season in the last week. MacLean required a minimum cash balance of $1,000 at the end of each week to cover any contingencies.

All sales were for cash; no credit was allowed. Sales tax of 10% would be collected and remitted monthly to the Province of Nova Scotia in the third week of the month following collection.

When preparing the cash receipts from sales figures, MacLean calculated the low season cash receipts on the basis of being open for only four days a week and the peak season receipts at twice the low season daily sales rate.

SOURCE: This case was prepared by Professor Donald G. Ross of St. Francis Xavier University for the Atlantic Entrepreneurial Institute as a basis for classroom discussion and is not meant to illustrate either effective or ineffective management. Some elements of this case have been disguised.

DREAM DRAWER

Cameron Roberts
University of Lethbridge

Victor Goodman is in his mid-40s and has lived in Windsor, Ontario, all his life. A foreman for a large cabinet manufacturer, he has worked for the same company for 18 years. Recently he became intrigued by the possibility of making a simple drawer insert he had invented into a profit-generating venture. The idea was spawned from his ongoing struggle to find the proper utensils in his kitchen drawer. He had tried using different loose-fitting plastic inserts to keep the utensils sorted, but before long the drawer usually returned to being a complete mess. What started out as a simple request for a pickle fork inevitably turned into a pile of scrap metal on the floor.

Goodman knew that if the utensils could be properly sorted and secured in their own appropriate, attractive wooden stalls, the irritation that accompanies a junk drawer would be eliminated. Over the next few months, whenever he had spare time, he was in his basement shop creating different prototypes. These eventually went to his relatives, all of whom were very happy with the inserts and declared them a dream come true.

The drawer sorter, later to be named the Dream Drawer, could be made to match any wood cabinets customers had in their kitchens. The Dream Drawer consisted of a two-level system that held the utensils at a 17-degree angle so that handles could be easily gripped and the utensils removed. The furthest tier contained a series of slots that held the knives so that only the handles were exposed, making it impossible to cut one's hand (which often happened while rummaging through a junk drawer). The front and back tiers had special partitions that held spoons and forks securely in their proper spaces, eliminating any chance of mayhem (see Figure 1).

FIGURE 1

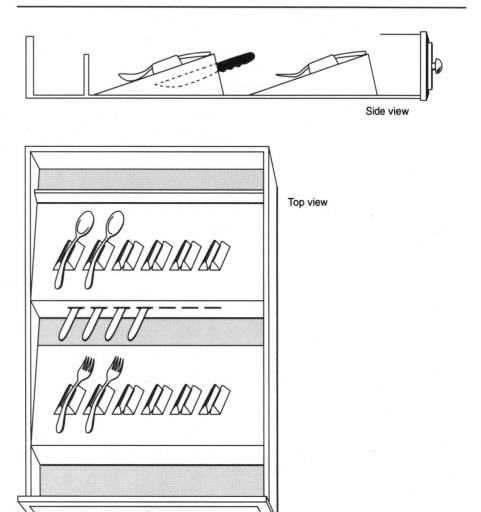

Side view

Top view

What made the Dream Drawer unique was the metal adjusters underneath the tiers. They allowed the insert to increase or decrease in length or width, enabling it to fit any standard drawer available on the market (most drawers vary in size by only a few inches). As the system expanded in width, additional slots and lips became available from within the present system. At the front and back of the insert was storage space to hold ill-fitting or special items such as can openers, potato peelers, and skewers. The Dream Drawer was unique, tastefully attractive, and very neat. It would probably appeal to the homemaker who was conscientious, disciplined, and highly organized.

Goodman went to a patent lawyer to find out about protection laws for his product. The lawyer told him the design of his product could be protected but another, different design approach to the same problem could be marketed by someone else, which the patent on Goodman's insert could not prevent.

Nevertheless, Goodman decided to go ahead with the project. His brother-in-law, Reggie, who was very personable and had a sales background, decided to join ranks with Goodman on this new business venture.

The company where Goodman worked was largely industrial and usually did work brought in from various contractors. Goodman discussed his idea with the people at the company, and they all encouraged him to go ahead with it. The company had the production facilities and capacity to produce the insert, but they were not set up for its marketing application.

Together Goodman and Reggie came up with $60,000, mostly from personal savings. After considerable work they decided they had enough money, an innovative product, and access to production facilities. The only problem was how to market the Dream Drawer.

Question

Develop a marketing strategy for the Dream Drawer.

JOHNSON CONSTRUCTION COMPANY

D. Wesley Balderson
University of Lethbridge

In September 1991, Hal Johnson realized a lifelong dream by starting his own construction company. He had worked for several construction firms in the province of Quebec over the years, and prior to the time he started his own firm, he had been a foreman on several large projects. He was a hard worker and had developed a reputation as a capable and sought-after foreman by many companies. Since starting Johnson Construction Company, Hal succeeded in obtaining several profitable contracts, which kept him very busy.

One day he was visiting with a friend, George Derocher, over lunch. The following conversation revealed that things were not so great at Johnson Construction.

George: How is your business doing, Hal? You've sure been busy lately.
Hal: Yes, we've got lots of work, but you can't imagine the problems I've had with employees. I never dreamt it would be such a hassle.
George: What kinds of problems are you talking about?

Hal: Take your pick! When we started up and got our first contract I needed six labourers, so I ran an ad in the paper. I got 19 applicants, and I was surprised that most hadn't finished high school. Even the ones I hired were lazy and undependable. I spent half my time replacing those who quit or whom I fired. Since then things haven't really improved much.

George: Maybe you should spend more time training them.

Hal: More time? As it stands now, I have to be with them almost constantly on a job and tell them what to do every step of the way. If I leave one of them in charge when I have to be away, the others resent it. It seems like they're always bickering with each other.

George: I wonder if you should train a foreman to supervise the workers.

Hal: I tried that. The work that he supervised was poorly done, and on top of that he padded his hours. I even noticed a few tools missing. When I confronted him with it, he up and quit.

George: Can't you spend a little more money and find some better-qualified and motivated employees?

Hal: My labour costs are too high already! Even though I don't hire union workers, I have to pay pretty close to those rates, and they are high. Once in awhile a hard worker will come along, but before long peer pressure from the others seems to drag him down to their level.

George: It sounds pretty hopeless.

Hal: The worst part is that just last month I gave all my employees a bonus. I distributed it based on how long they had worked for me and thought I had explained it to them. However, after I gave it out, several of them were upset, and I even had two quit on the spot. Can you believe that? I'm seriously considering shutting down the business and going back to work for my old firm.

Questions

1. Why do you think Hal has gotten into this situation?
2. What recommendations would you make to Hal?

JOSEPHINE'S FASHIONS

D. Wesley Balderson
University of Lethbridge

As part of his course requirements in completing his MBA at Simon Fraser University in British Columbia, Darren Richards had received a student consulting assignment with a small clothing manufacturer in Vancouver. The firm had been in operation a little over a year and had received funding from the government agency funding small businesses. However, it was experiencing cash flow problems. There was a concern that the business, Josephine's Fashions, would have to either close or obtain additional funds.

Josephine Chan had emigrated to Canada from Hong Kong about five years earlier. Being a hard worker and having worked in a clothing factory in Hong Kong, she got a job immediately at a dress-manufacturing factory. After three-and-a-half years, she accumulated some funds and decided to start her own small business making selected clothing primarily for the large Oriental population in the Vancouver area. Chan had an obvious talent for selecting fabrics and designing garments and, through her family and friends, developed a reputation as a skilled seamstress.

Chan located her business in the Chinatown district of Vancouver in a leased space of about 1,800 square feet. To make renovations, buy equipment, and pay other initial expenses, she had borrowed $5,000 and put $2,000 of her own funds into the venture. She had hired two full-time employees, paying them $4 per hour to assist in sewing the clothing items. The production process was simple: Each employee and Chan would make a garment from beginning to end.

Darren Richards visited Josephine's Fashions to assess the situation and determine what could be done to solve the cash flow problem. He was impressed with the product line, which exhibited quality craftsmanship. Josephine's produced primarily two garments. The first was a Chinese-style dress retailing at $55, and the second was a kimonolike robe retailing at $45. Sales were based almost entirely on word of mouth, as Chan spent no money advertising. In examining the production process, Darren noticed numerous interruptions occurred as family and friends of the workers frequently came by to visit. He estimated, however, that on average the dresses took four hours to make and the robes took three hours. The average dress took about three yards of material, and the robes averaged four yards. The fabric for both items cost Chan about $6 per yard.

Richards was concerned about the management of the firm. Although Chan had hired two full-time employees, she often hired family or friends to help for a few days at a time when they, as she put it, "needed some money." He was most concerned, however, with the financial procedures Josephine was following. Because there was no recordkeeping system, he had difficulty determining paid and unpaid bills from the assortment of receipts, scraps of paper, invoices, and notes Chan kept. Deposits and withdrawals from the bank account had been made but not recorded. Chan's salary was not recorded, but Richards learned that she withdrew $200 per week. Credit sales were frequent and informal, with Chan allowing customers to take garments without leaving a down payment. Richards spent considerable time wading through this data and finally came up with the approximate statements shown in Figure 1.

FIGURE 1

JOSEPHINE'S FASHIONS
Balance Sheet
As at January 31, 1991

Assets		*Liabilities and Owner's Equity*	
Current assets:		Current liabilities:	
Cash	$ 95	Accounts payable	$ 8,450
Accounts receivable	3,815	Current portion of debt	1,000
Inventory	4,765	Total current liabilities	9,450
Prepaid expenses	275	Long-term liabilities	
Total current assets	8,950	Debt	4,000
Fixed assets:		Total liabilities	13,450
Equipment	3,500	Owner's equity	(1,000)
Total assets	$12,450	Total liabilities and owner's equity	$12,450

Income Statement
For Year Ended January 31, 1991

Sales:		
352 dresses	$17,600	
298 robes	11,920	
Other miscellaneous	5,200	
Total sales		$ 34,720
Cost of goods sold:		
Dresses	6,336	
Robes	7,152	
Other miscellaneous	2,500	
Total cost of goods sold		15,988

JOSEPHINE'S FASHIONS
Income Statement
For Year Ended January 31, 1987

Expenses:		
Wages (including Josephine's)	20,400	
Rent	4,800	
Utilities and phone	3,200	
Interest	1,000	
Repairs and maintenance	3,000	
Total expenses		32,400
Total cost of goods sold and expenses		48,388
Net profit (loss)		$(13,668)

Questions

1. Briefly evaluate Josephine Chan's approach to starting her own business.
2. Examine the pricing system for Chan's clothes.
3. Assuming miscellaneous clothing and robe sales stay the same, how many dresses would have to be sold for Josephine's to break even?
4. Evaluate the financial statements prepared by Darren Richards in both form and content.
5. What kind of financial recordkeeping system would you advise for Josephine's?

TED MILLARD

Cameron Roberts
University of Lethbridge

Ted Millard is a hard-working, self-employed salesperson of restaurant and hotel supplies in Alberta. When the company he worked for went into receivership five years ago, Millard was the northwestern representative for the manufacturing firm, covering an area northwest of Edmonton and the Peace district of northern British Columbia. Even when he had worked for this company, Millard had always thought about being self-employed and decided to develop the ideas he had while on his travels. He saw a viable market for restaurant and hotel supplies, such as soap utensils and paper products, because of the many complaints he received about the difficulty of getting these products. There were no distributors in the area, and businesses frequently complained to Millard about how hard it was to get any personal service when ordering supplies. They either had to travel south or correspond by mail or phone, which was expensive and time consuming. Also, they were never assured that what they ordered would be what they would receive. Having made many contacts and friendships within these businesses, this seemed like a natural business for him to start.

Grand Prairie, Alberta, was a good location from which to set up a business. It was a central point close to most northern communities in both Alberta and British Columbia. The market area would consist of a 300-mile radius east, west, and north of Grand Prairie. Millard set up his proprietorship out of his home and usually spent four or five days a week on the road travelling among his customers, many of whom already knew him from his previous job.

Over the past five years the business has prospered, due largely to Millard's hard work and personality. Millard took an interest in people and was confident in what he was doing. The success of the business exceeded all projections. Recently, however, Millard has found himself paying higher income taxes based on his personal tax rate of 30 to 35 percent. As the following table shows, Millard's net income has increased considerably over the years.

	1988	*1989*	*1990*	*1991*	*1992*
Net income before tax	$20,000	$29,000	$37,000	$55,000	$68,000

Millard's projections for the next two years show gross income in excess of $80,000. Because his business is doing so well, the workload has increased so much that two years ago he asked his wife, Dorothy, to take care of the books and do general secretarial tasks. His only child, Peter, has just finished a two-year business administration course and hopes to get into his father's business. Millard would like his son to take over the business, but he wants to retain some control over the operations until Peter proves he can do the job.

Millard has been concerned with the large chunk of income he has to pay to the government in taxes: "A third of my income is going to those bureaucrats in Ottawa. Who am I really working for?" (See Table 1 for tax rates.) He has decided to get assistance from an accountant and possibly a lawyer to see if they can help him with this predicament.

Questions

1. What do you think the accountant's and lawyer's advice to Ted Millard will be? How can he avoid paying so much tax?
2. What would be the best way for Millard to bring his son into the business?

TABLE 1

Income	*Personal Tax Rate*
$10,000–$14,999	15%
$15,000–$19,999	20
$20,000–$24,999	25
$25,000–$29,999	30
$30,000+	35

West Hardware Store

D. Wesley Balderson
University of Lethbridge

West Hardware is a small hardware store located in Weyburn, Saskatchewan, an agricultural community with a population of about 9,000. Merchandise stocked includes automotive and farm supplies, furniture and appliances, sporting goods, plumbing and electrical supplies, and giftware.

The owner is David West, a prominent businessman in the community who also owns another business that occupies a large portion of his time. Because of this, West has delegated considerable authority to the manager of the store, John Burns. In July 1991, West and Burns decided to hire a new employee to be trained as an assistant manager. They first discussed the possibility of promoting one of the store's existing employees, but Burns thought none of them would be suitable as assistant managers because they were either too old or did not want the extra responsibility. Doug Burns, John's uncle, was already 63 years old and, though working full time, had indicated he wanted to work fewer hours and begin to ease into retirement. Sue Mikita, 52, had been with the company for 12 years but had concentrated on the giftware side of the department. Burns did not think she had an adequate knowledge of the farm supply side of the business, which produced the most revenue in the store. Ruth Huddy, 61, had worked for the company for only 6 years, mostly part time, and although she was very competent and knowledgeable, Burns felt she was also too old to fill the position. The only other employees were part-time students who worked Saturdays and summers.

West and Burns decided to advertise for an assistant manager in the local paper. This resulted in a few enquiries but no applicants who met the two criteria Burns and West considered most important: familiarity with the people in the community and a knowledge of agriculture. West and Burns met again in August to discuss the lack of prospects. West suggested that he might contact Noel Branlen, an acquaintance who lived in Weyburn, about coming to work for the company. Branlen currently worked in a town some 25 miles away, and perhaps he could be attracted back to his home town. Branlen was young—only 25—and knew the people in the community. West approached him and found out he was interested in working for him but required a salary higher than West and Burns had planned for this position. If they agreed to pay the salary he requested, Branlen would be paid a higher wage than the other hardware department employees except Burns himself. Although West and Burns were worried about this, they decided to hire Branlen and requested that his salary be kept confidential. Branlen would be in a training position for approximately six months and would then assume the position of assistant manager of the store.

Things went smoothly at first, but after a few months it was evident to West that some problems were surfacing. West noticed antagonism between Branlen and the other three regular employees, and so did the store's customers. In discussing Branlen's progress with Burns, West learned that Branlen was frequently late for work, his appearance was unsatisfactory, he was very slow in gaining essential product knowledge, and Burns had had several complaints from customers about him. In addition, Branlen himself had contacted West directly and expressed his disillusionment with the job and with his supervisor, John Burns. He indicated that Burns was not providing adequate training for the products or the authority to order inventory, set prices, and so on. Also, when Burns had his day off, several sales were lost because none of the employees knew the information customers required. Branlen also mentioned that as assistant manager he shouldn't have to sweep the floors as he had been required to do on several occasions. He further requested that he be granted time off two afternoons a week to take a management course at a local college to help him prepare for the managerial aspects of his job.

West discussed the problem again with Burns, who said that as soon as Branlen proved himself he would be given the requested authority—and he was very opposed letting Branlen take time off for a management course, so this request was turned down.

Toward the end of November, Branlen contacted West to see if he could take some of his holidays just before Christmas. When West mentioned this request to John Burns, Burns was very opposed because this was the busiest time of the year for the store; furthermore, in the past employees had worked for a year before they took their holidays. However, West allowed Branlen to take the holiday.

The store got through the Christmas rush and inventory taking without serious incident, but things got progressively worse thereafter. Nine months after his hiring, Branlen handed in his resignation, saying he was going back to the university. West was relieved that this problem employee was leaving and hoped that the same problems would not recur next time.

Question

Comment on the possible reasons why Noel Branlen's employment did not turn out successfully.

WINSTON'S JEWELLERS

Patricia Elemans
University of Lethbridge

Winston's is a jewellery store located in Kamloops, British Columbia. Kamloops is a city of approximately 70,000 people. Ten to 40 percent of its retail trade comes from the 25 surrounding agricultural communities. The total trading area of

Kamloops is approximately 200,000 people. During the past three years, the area has experienced severe droughts and thus poor farming conditions. This situation, coupled with generally poor economic conditions, has had an adverse effect on sales at Winston's.

Winston's opened its doors in 1985. A five-year lease was signed at this time and was renewed for five more years in 1990. The store was opened with an image that Fred Winston believed was consistent with his own lifestyle: upper-class.

Centre Mall, where the store is located, was the highest-traffic mall in Kamloops in 1985. Its retail mix catered to the middle- and upper-income consumer. Winston's was designed to appeal to this market as well. All aspects of the store's marketing targeted the "discriminating" consumer. Winston's carried a superior-quality, distinctive product, ran professionally produced television advertisements, employed a knowledgeable, experienced sales staff, used prestige pricing, and limited the number of sales promotions. Also, Fred Winston was the only certified gemologist in the city, meaning he was the only person in Kamloops qualified to complete jewellery appraisals. The other jewellery stores sent their merchandise to Creston, approximately 200 kilometers away, to be appraised, which took approximately two weeks. Winston's could have items appraised and returned to customers within 24 hours.

For the first four years of operations, Winston's enjoyed considerable success. Sales in the store climbed steadily. Over time, however, the market in Kamloops changed. Competition for the jewellery market increased. The number of stores selling jewellery rose from 13 to 17 in four years. Of these, two stores catered to the upper-income market. One store was a prestigious chain store that had been in Kamloops for five years. The other was a well-established, independent store owned and operated by a local businessperson who was well known and respected in the community. This store has been open for approximately 15 years.

The composition of Centre Mall's patrons also began to change. The upper- and middle-income consumers were now shopping at the newer mall in Kamloops. Centre Mall was now patronized predominantly by middle- and lower-middle-income consumers. Due to the changing clientele of the mall and the increased competition, Winston's began changing certain aspects of its marketing program to appeal to this new market. Initially the store brought in low-priced, lower-quality jewellery items. In 1984, in an effort to overcome slumping sales due to bad economic conditions, Mr. Winston decided to introduce giftware to the store's product line. The gift items were of average quality and could be purchased at most other jewellery stores and in some department stores. Also at this time, Mr. Winston introduced a "buy now and pay later" plan for customers. On approved credit, customers had one of two options. With no down payment they could take the merchandise they wanted and pay nothing for four months, at which time the balance was due. The second option was to take the merchandise and begin making 12 equal, interest-free monthly payments. The plan met with good response in 1989 and was continued into 1990. Most of the people who took advantage of the plan were in the lower- and middle-income ranges. The average value of items purchased on the plan was $700.

In early 1991, one of Winston's direct competitors closed its doors following the owner's retirement. The store had been open for more than 25 years and had captured approximately 25 percent of the upper-income jewellery market. The closing of this store, coupled with two large diamond sales of $12,000 and $10,000 in December 1990, led Mr. Winston to believe that there was a large market that was not being catered to. This was the upper-income market, who he felt were "floating around" and had not yet decided where to bring their business. Mr. Winston decided he wanted to attract these people to his store. Since he was not quite sure how to go about doing this, he hired a consultant to help him develop a marketing plan to attract this "floating" market.

Questions

1. What marketing-related problems does Winston's face?
2. What would you, as the consultant, suggest to Mr. Winston to get his business back on the right track?

PART IV Looking to the Future

Part IV focuses on management of the small business for the long term. If a business is being managed effectively and increasing sales and profitability have resulted, the owner-manager will face the question of expansion. If growth of the business is desired, some changes will be required within the organization. Chapter 13 discusses the preparations needed in such a situation.

Chapter 14 (appropriately) discusses the methods of transferring ownership of the business to someone else. Many key considerations in this regard have legal and tax effects that can have far-reaching consequences for the owner-manager. An option other than transferring of ownership to another person is to involve family members in the business. The majority of small businesses are in fact family owned and operated. Thus, Chapter 14 also examines the special characteristics of such businesses.

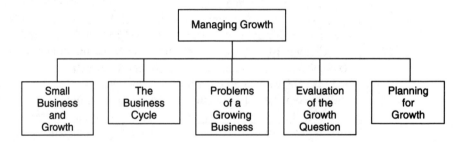

CHAPTER 13

Managing Growth

Chapter Objectives

- To describe the potential problems that success and growth can bring to the small business.
- To review the characteristics of the stages in the business life cycle.
- To discuss how to sustain the business despite the difficulties created by growth.
- To illustrate the importance of planning for growth.

Small Business Profile

Jim Pattison

Jim Pattison Group

Jim Pattison was born in Saskatoon, Saskatchewan. He moved with his mother and father to Vancouver, British Columbia, when he was 6 years old.

Pattison started learning about business by travelling with his father through the province of British Columbia demothing pianos. At the same time, his mother taught him at home during his grade 1 year. While attending public school Pattison held several jobs, including selling garden seeds, radios, magazines, and newspapers door to door. He later worked as a bellhop at the Georgia Hotel. Pattison attended the University of British Columbia. He financed his education by selling used cars to fellow students and washing cars at a used-car lot.

In May 1961, Jim Pattison mortgaged his home and put his life insurance policies up for collateral to borrow $40,000 from the bank to finance the purchase of a General Motors franchise located at the corner of Cambie and 18th Avenue in Vancouver. But he was not content to have just one dealership. After careful consideration, he realized he had the capabilities and the drive to expand his business activities. He set to work arranging the financing to get involved in many successful ventures over the next 31 years.

The Jim Pattison Group of companies now has more than over 13,000 employees and over $2.8 billion in sales annually. It is the fourth largest privately held company in Canada and the forty-fifth largest company in Canada. Currently the group has investments in Canada, the United States, and Europe and is involved in a wide variety of industries in five diverse areas: transportation, communications, food products, packaging, and financial services.

Recently Pattison was chairman and president of the Expo 86 Corporation, which he served in a volunteer capacity. He was appointed to the Order of Canada in 1987 and to the Order of British Columbia in 1990.

Pattison's friends and associates attribute his success to hard work, enthusiasm, and the courage to take a calculated risk. Pattison has been especially astute at examining, planning, and organizing for the growth possibilities of his organization.

Used with permission of Jim Pattison.

Small Business and Growth

As Incident 13–1 illustrates, short-term success and subsequent growth do not always lead to a trouble-free business operation. Often success and growth may compound the complexities and difficulties of managing the business.

To avoid the pitfalls of growth, the owner-manager should take to ensure long-term viability early in the life of the business. First, the owner-manager needs to understand the life cycle of the business to effectively plan for the future. Second, he or she should be aware of some of the more common growth problems a business is likely to face. Finally, the owner-manager should take certain specific steps in planning for growth of the business.

The Business Cycle

The business cycle of the small enterprise is similar to the product life cycle discussed in Chapter 8. For many small businesses that have only one or two products, the business cycle and the product life cycle may be one and the same. Figure 13–1 illustrates the shape and characteristics of a life cycle for a small business. The vertical axis represents the growth index, usually measured by gross sales, market share, or profitability. The horizontal axis measures the time taken to pass through the stages of the cycle. The length of time a business stays in one stage depends on several variables. Many small businesses take several years to move through the life cycle, while others pass through all four stages within a couple of years. This phenomenon is common in high-technology industries. The characteristics of the stages of the business cycle are discussed next.

Introduction.   Stage 1 is the start-up stage of the small business. It is characterized by expenditures made for both product development and introductory promotion and by low profits, particularly at the beginning. Stage 1 also usually includes a narrow market, a very limited product line, and involvement in most aspects of the business by the owner-manager.

Growth.   Stage 2 of the business cycle, growth, is usually characterized by the establishment of a market share, or acceptance, and expansion of the product line or markets. It may also take the form of internal or external expansion, such as a merger or franchising. During this period, sales grow at an increasing rate. At the end of the growth stage, however, competitive pressures begin to take their toll, necessitating changes in business strategy.

Maturity.   Stage 3 is characterized by a levelling of sales due to increased competition and/or a decrease in demand. During this stage, the owner-manager

Incident 13–1

Growing Pains

When Shapes Dance and Activewear's sales were exploding from 2,000 units a month to 5,000, the business was really beginning to take off.

But the growth had brought a negative side. The co-owners and the 10 employees were strained and frustrated trying to meet the increase in orders.

Marilyn Wohl and Ines Zagoudakis started Shapes in 1979 as a part-time operation—cutting, knitting, and sewing garments in Zagoudakis's living room. Three years later they were in business full-time manufacturing sweaters, bathing suits, leotards, jumpsuits, and leg warmers.

With the extra orders the 10 inside workers in the Shapes factory, who make and ship sample garments for pieceworkers, could not keep up with the faster pace. Wohl and Zagoudakis became frustrated when the staff could not complete the extra orders on time. What they didn't realize was that their workers were not at fault. It took an efficiency expert to show them that the workers were hampered by a chaotic routine.

Like many other owner-managers whose businesses enjoy rapid growth, Wohl and Zagoudakis had so much to think about that they paid less attention to their employees, and their employees' jobs, than they should have. The orders piled up and the employees found themselves working harder than ever but with less recognition for their efforts.

As the owner-managers expanded the staff they realized they would fail if they continued their bad habits, such as disorganization and lack of long-range planning. So they made two major changes to the operation. First they rearranged their factory's layout and routines. Then they implemented better methods of storing and recording inventory and collecting receivables. Most employees stayed with Wohl and Zagoudakis as their firm grew, but it took the owners time to learn how to keep them happy and to deal with the growing pains.

Source: Paul Weinberg, "Growing Pains," *Small Business*, May 1984, pp. 26–36.

---

must make some important strategic decisions to avoid moving into stage 4, decline. Of necessity the strategy of the business will become more competitive. Such a strategy may involve adding new products, expanding to new markets, or adjusting or improving existing products in some way. The goal of such actions is to lengthen the life cycle, as illustrated by the increase in sales during the decline stage of the adjusted life cycle in Figure 13–1.

Decline.   As Figure 13–1 shows, stage 4 involves a decrease in both sales and profits. Unless action is taken to reverse this trend, the business will fail.

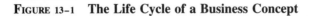

FIGURE 13-1   The Life Cycle of a Business Concept

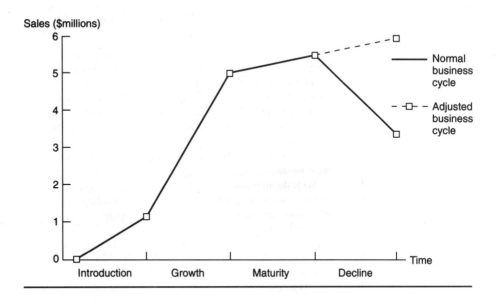

Figure 13–2 shows an example of the growth of a business and subsequent operational and strategy changes that should take place. The actual dollar level of sales relating to the stages of the life cycle will vary depending on the growth of the market, the type of industry, and the owner's objectives. However, Figure 13–2 points out the need to deal quickly with the changes that growth in sales can create.

Problems Created by Growth

To be able to anticipate growth difficulties and make plans to minimize them, the owner-manager should be aware of some of the problems that can be expected to accompany growth. These are discussed below.

Owner-Manager Fatigue and Stress.   Stress levels rise when the scope of the business and the magnitude of its problems increase.

Lack of Communication.   As the scope of operations grows, the former closeness between owner and business dissipates. Many owner-managers have resented this loss of closeness and even curbed their growth objectives as a result (see Incident 13–2).

Lack of Coordination.   Various aspects of the business may become specialized and less integrated with the overall operation as a business grows. This often results in increased conflicts among departments and/or individuals within the

Incident 13–2

Roots Shoes

Michael Budman and Don Green, founders of Roots Shoes, experienced astounding success in the late 1970s. However, they found that as the business grew to meet demand, they were losing touch with their employees and the operations within the manufacturing plant. As a result, they concluded that things were moving too fast, and they cut back on the size of their operations so they could stay small enough to keep running things themselves.

Roots Shoes is still very successful, and Budman and Green have maintained the closeness with their employees that enables them to provide motivation and a positive relationship. Although the firm has expanded into several successful clothing lines, the staff has remained small, totalling 150 employees in 1991.

Sources: CBC Corporation, "Venture" series, July 29, 1985; *Canadian Key Business Directory,* Dun & Bradstreet Canada, 1992.

FIGURE 13–2   Stages of Growth

Approximate Sales Level	Market	Product	Owner-Manager
0–$750,000	One market	One or limited line	Involved in day-to-day aspects of the business such as buying, selling, and financial management
$750,000– $2,000,000	Expanding into new markets	Adding new products in same category	Some organizational change allowing supervisor to oversee greater part of day-to-day operations Greater need for financial evaluation Greater need to obtain capital to finance growth Some delegation required Development of managers
$2,000,000 +	Established markets; continued expansion to new markets	Adding new products in different categories	Managers run day-to-day operations and report to owner Communication and information important Training for management development Establishment of proper controls

SOURCE: Ronald W. Torrence, *In the Owner's Chair: Proven Techniques for Taking Your Business from Zero to $10 Million,* © 1986, p. 259. Reprinted by permission of Prentice Hall, Inc., Englewood Cliffs, New Jersey.

Incident 13–3

Managing in a Maelstrom

If you didn't know better, you'd be overjoyed to have your company match the growth record of Clearly Canadian Beverage Corp. From 1986 to 1991, the Vancouver-based producer of sparkling flavoured mineral water saw sales explode 768% to $71.4 million in 1991, good for 32nd place on the Fastest 50. But Clearly Canadian's glass is still overflowing: In the first six months of fiscal 1992, revenues reached almost $90 million, and management says they could well top $200 million for the year ending June 30, 1992.

It looks great on a bar chart, but breakneck growth spells pandemonium for those trying to run the company. Problems abound as they learn to develop a management structure that can keep the firm running with some semblance of control while growth accelerates. Sure, it sounds like a nice problem to have in these dreary times, but how fast-growth companies manage their surge plays a key in whether they'll still be around to set records a few years from now.

At Clearly Canadian, president Doug Mason has maintained a consistent strategy that enables his company to cope with soaring sales with just 34 employees. From bottling and warehousing to manufacturing Clearly Canadian's distinctive silk-screened bottles, he contracts out virtually every stage of the operation. As a result, suppliers share in Clearly Canadian's management challenges, as well as its more obvious gains. "We use a lot of outside organizations," says Mason. "Growth has been more prevalent in the organizations we assign distribution, manufacturing and marketing rights to than in Clearly Canadian."

In-house, Clearly Canadian looks after administration, marketing strategy and quality control. "We operate more in think-tank mode than people-expansion mode," says Mason. This approach has its advantages. For one thing, it keeps things simple at head office, a tremendous benefit considering the constant changes and adjustments fast growth demands. Even more important, though, because suppliers have invested so much of their own money in Clearly Canadian's expansion, these subcontractors become partners, with more than enough incentive to ensure the brand success.

Source: Leslie Ellis, "Managing in a Maelstrom," *Profit Magazine,* June 1992, p. 46.

---

organization. Employees who in the early stages of the company life cycle performed many duties are often reluctant to give up some of those responsibilities to specialists. Such resentment often leads to conflicts within the organization. Incident 13–3 shows the importance of control in the rapidly growing firm.

Shortage of Cash.   Growth and expansion often require financing that the business has not yet generated. Merchandise may have been sold but cash not yet

Incident 13–4

Low Price Proves Right for Tynex's Innovative Drinkware

Tynex president Jack Burnett is using the latest in plastics technology and equipment to establish a new, year-round market for plastic drinkware. And with a $10,000 profit on 1990 sales of $244,000 he's proving Canadian manufacturers can compete—if they muster the right blend of technology, shrewd marketing and strategic investment.

Burnett started on the Enviroware trail three Christmases ago with a decision to buy glasses for friends who owned a swimming pool. Enviroware glass is crystal clear, impervious to detergents and tough enough to withstand the rigors of microwave ovens.

Production began in February, 1990. Sales of logo-bearing coffee jugs for the ad specialty market topped $200,000 that year, and paid for a fall launch of mass-market drinkware. A national roll-out followed, with listings in some 233 Safeway stores and another 100 western Canadian grocery stores. On the strength of its debut, Tynex recently won shelf space in 70 stores in Oregon and Washington state.

Now, the company faces a critical stage in its evolution. Cash flow is tight. And the partners need some $500,000 for working capital and a second injection-moulding machine to meet demand. Gordon Kirkland, a marketing consultant with Deloitte & Touche in Vancouver, is concerned that sales will grow more quickly than Tynex can manage. "If they stop delivering to major customers, they're going to lose shelf space," he says. "They have to understand that marketing is more than just selling product—it's everything from quality control through to inventory control and distribution systems."

Source: Diane Lucklow, "Low Price Proves Right for Tynex's Innovative Drinkware," *Profit Magazine,* September 1991, p. 16.

received, even though cash is still needed to acquire new inventories. Incident 13–4 illustrates how this lack of cash contributed to difficulties for one small business.

Low Profitability.   Low profitability is common in rapidly growing businesses. Several of the fastest-growing companies in Canada lost money in 1991, and others earned small profits.[1] Considerable expenses have been incurred in research and development of markets during the growth period.

Breakdowns in Production Efficiency.   Declining production efficiency, as evidenced by unmet schedules, increases in quality assurance problems, and consumer complaints, is common in rapidly growing companies.

Lack of Information.   Lack of information with which to evaluate the business's performance often accompanies rapid growth. As the owner-manager becomes increasingly removed from day-to-day operations and the scope of the business outgrows manual information retrieval, a more automated system is often required to generate the required data.

Decreasing Employee Morale.   Lower employee morale results in higher employee turnover and absenteeism. New people are added to the firm to accommodate growth, but they often receive insufficient training. Existing employees work harder in growth companies and may not receive adequate recognition for their efforts. This situation can lead to employee discontent.[2]

Any one of the above problems can spell disaster for an otherwise potentially successful small business. To prevent such problems, the wise owner-manager can prepare himself or herself and the business to handle growth in several ways.

Evaluating the Growth Question

The owner-manager should answer four important questions before proceeding to expand the business.

Is the Business One That Can Grow?   A preliminary step in dealing with the question of growth is to evaluate whether the product or business is one that can grow. Restricted markets or products that have volume production restrictions are difficult to expand. Many service businesses that rely on the special expertise of their owners also fit into this category.

Is the Business Owner Prepared to Make the Effort?   Expanding a business will require additional time and effort on the part of the owner-manager. The decision the owner-manager must make is whether he or she is ready to increase effort and prepare for the stress or be content with a smaller but less demanding business. Many successful small businesses have chosen not to grow for precisely this reason.

Does the Owner-Manager Have the Capabilities to Grow?   The owner-manager should assess whether the needed capital, labour, and expertise can be obtained to effectively deal with growth. Some of these specific areas will be discussed in the following section.

How Should the Owner-Manager Pursue Growth?   If growth is desired, several approaches may be taken in pursuing it. The most common strategies (some already mentioned) are as follows:

- Pursue new markets for the product or service. This may involve different geographic or demographic markets.
- Increase sales of existing products or services by increasing the frequency of use. This can be done through increased promotion.

- Add new products or services or modify existing ones.
- Find new uses for the product or service.
- Acquire other small companies.

Planning for Growth

Once the decision to expand has been made and the method of expansion has been determined, a plan for growth should be developed. A *growth plan* is a blueprint of future actions. Planning is an essential but often overlooked part of management. A recent survey found that only 5 percent of all companies do formal short-term and long-term planning, and almost 50 percent do little or no formal planning.[3]

Some small business owners fail to plan for the future because they do not understand what a plan is. A plan is more than short-term sales forecasts and budgets. It includes setting long-term objectives and outlining procedures for reaching those objectives.

In addition, most small business owners feel snowed under by the daily operations and often think planning is a nuisance. However, small business owner-managers who are able to periodically step back from the organization and objectively assess its overall direction are generally better able to cope with the environmental changes that will affect the business.

Finally, in many industries conditions change so rapidly that plans have to be altered frequently. The need for constant adjustment discourages many small business owners.

The Expansion Plan

Chapter 4 discussed the essential elements of the start-up business plan. Many similarities exist between the start-up plan and the expansion plan. The steps in the expansion plan are as follows.

1.   Set Objectives.   The first step in the planning process is to set the objectives the business is to accomplish. As mentioned previously, it is important to set objectives specifically so that the outcomes can be measured. Objectives may include dollar sales, market share percentage, or dollar profits.

2.   Determine Alternatives.   The second step includes identifying possible strategies to achieve the set objectives. It also involves forecasting the possible outcomes of different alternatives.

3.   Select the Best Alternatives.   Alternatives should be selected with a view toward long-term success. The components of this success are the company's capability and the potential growth of the area.[4]

Understanding the Requirements of Growth

Rapid growth will necessitate some fundamental changes within the organization. Some of the requirements of growth are discussed next.

Greater Management Depth. The owner-manager must realize that an expansion of management depth must accompany the expansion of the business. This will require more skills or harder work on behalf of the owner-manager. Because he or she may already be stretched to the limit, such expansion usually consists of training subordinates to handle some of the managerial responsibilities. This involves training and delegation, two personnel practices owner-managers are often hesitant to incorporate into their management styles. As Figure 13–3 illustrates, the owner must spend more time thinking and less time doing. This also means he or she must move from task delegation to functional delegation, allowing key people to manage various functional areas of the business. Greater management depth can also be achieved through the use of functional specialists outside the company such as accountants, lawyers, directors, or mentors.

Intelligent Expansion.   A common problem among small business owners is that in their effort to succeed, they start too many diverse projects. They often do so

---

FIGURE 13–3   Managerial Activities

Percent of time spent on daily work activities

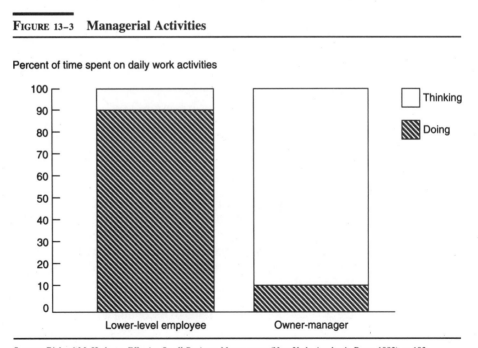

SOURCE: Richard M. Hodgets, *Effective Small Business Management* (New York: Academic Press, 1982), p. 193.

Incident 13–5

K-Tel International

With hindsight, it is easy to say that success spoiled K-Tel. Indeed, in the five years prior to 1981, the company sold more than 15 million LPs and tapes in 34 countries. Its sales jumped from a modest but respectable $23 million in 1971 to $178 million in 1981, precipitating a diversification frenzy that unhappily coincided with a blitz of economic bad news from which the company and Phillip Kives are still trying to recover.

It wasn't just that K-Tel got into oil and gas exploration when the bottom began to fall out of energy prices. Leaping headlong into a business with which it had no experience, K-Tel soon was involved in oil and gas exploration and development programs in Alberta and six U.S. states, including an extensive program in the Anadarko Basin of Oklahoma. Not content to be an oil baron, Phillip Kives plunged into real estate, just as interest rates began to take off.

In 1983 losses of $37 million led the banks to put K-Tel's Canadian subsidiary into receivership. To his credit, Kives accepts much of the blame for K-Tel's difficulties. He is able to pinpoint where the problems began. "I should have taken control at an early stage," he says, "but I let the situation get out of hand."

Source: Roger Neuman, "Death (and Rebirth) of a Salesman," *Report on Business Magazine,* May 1986, pp. 75–78.

without evaluating whether they have the productive or marketing expertise and resources to accomplish the expansion. They may also ignore the potential effects of unplanned expansion on their existing products. The decision to expand should incoporate continuity, experience, and intelligence. Incident 13–5 illustrates the tragic result of neglecting this fact for one of Canada's formerly most successful entrepreneurs.

Additional Capital.   Any expansion in the business will require additional money to finance added productive capacity, inventory, or personnel. Unless the business has a solid debt-equity ratio and a steady cash flow, it may have difficulty obtaining this needed financing. Chapter 7 discussed sources of financing. Incident 13–6 shows how one Canadian firm grew rapidly because of its ability to obtain the needed capital.

One way to achieve high growth even with limited capital may be to franchise the business or the idea. Although becoming a franchisor requires a certain amount of capital (see Chapter 6), franchising may allow a firm to expand rapidly without large amounts of funds.

Incident 13–6

Growth Gurus

When John Aldred stepped down as president of a flourishing manufacturing business in Calgary to start his own company, he luckily met the guardian angel that would help him succeed. Nick Ross, partner with Toronto accountants Ernst & Young, shared a mutual friend in an old room-mate of Aldred's. After meeting Aldred, Ross got so excited with the budding entrepreneur's plans that he did an unusual thing for an arm's-length CA; he staked him $30,000 in seed capital from his own pocket.

But Ross's participation didn't end when he signed the cheque. Along with investment banker Rob Williams, a senior vice-president at ScotiaMcleod Inc. in Toronto, Ross took a seat in 1980 on Aldred's new board and offered his five years of experience advising independent businesses on matters of finance and strategic planning. Together, the consultants helped Aldred develop a business plan and arrange financing. Later, as the company grew, they encouraged Aldred to hire strategic managers, develop computerized accounting, cost-control and production systems, and negotiate venture-capital deals when the firm decided to expand.

Much of Ross's contribution was in the vital area of raising money, and it is here that Ross says most entrepreneurs need help. "Many owners don't understand the financial side of their business because they more often come from the operational or marketing side. But you simply can't plan adequately without a good grasp of your company's financial performance, and requirements. If you don't have it, then you're best to contract it."

By 1985, the company craved even more capital. Rather than load up the debt side of the balance sheet, Ross advised Aldred to attract money by surrendering equity to a suitable partner. He used his connections to help Aldred find one in the form of Toromont Industries Ltd., a Toronto manufacturer of industrial refrigeration systems, which understood the compressor business. Today, Aldred sits comfortably atop an $85-million company of which he owns 40%.

Source: Randall Litchfield, "Growth Gurus," *Profit Magazine,* June 1990, pp. 62–64.

Financial Information.   Often increased sales obscure the fact that the profitability of the business is declining or even negative. As the business grows, it is increasingly difficult—but more important—for the owner-manager to obtain accurate information about the profitability and productivity of the business. The use of computers by many small businesses has greatly helped in this area. Owner-managers should regularly project future financial requirements so that cash shortages do not occur.

Organizational Change.   As the owner-manager realizes he or she can no longer be involved in every aspect of the business, the organizational structure will require alteration. This is necessary to establish a clear understanding of reporting and responsibility centers in the business. The aim is to reduce the owner's span of control and allow more of his or her time for the planning and long-term strategy development of the business. It can also allow the owner more time to foster coordination within the firm.

At the same time, the owner-manager must resist the temptation to "overdo" the bureaucracy of the organization. An entrepreneurial culture (which likely contributed to the business's success in the first place) must be retained if growth is to continue.

Implementing Managerial Controls.   As a business grows, it becomes more difficult to control. Through the use of informational and organizational methods, a system of goals, performance levels, and evaluations must be put into place. As discussed in Chapter 10, the integration of computers into the small business's operations has greatly enhanced the owner-manager's ability to control all aspects of the business. Such measures as ratio analysis, inventory turnover, margins, and cost controls are examples.

Monitoring the External Environment.   The final growth requirement is that the owner-manager focus greater attention on the external environment of the business. These external forces serve as a guide to the long-term strategic planning in which the owner-manager now must engage. Important external forces, discussed in Chapter 8, are technological change, competition, consumer demand, social and cultural norms, legislation, and the state of the economy.

Summary

1. To acquire the knowledge to deal with growth problems, the owner-manager should address three areas. First, the owner-manager must review the business life cycle. Second, the owner-manager should be aware of the common growth problems that arise. Third, the owner-manager must know the steps he or she can take to plan effectively for growth.

2. The four stages of the business cycle include the introduction, growth, maturity, and decline stages.

3. Problems to anticipate as a result of growth are the owner-manager's increased fatigue and stress, lack of communication, lack of coordination, shortage of cash, low profitability, a breakdown in production efficiency, lack of information, and possible decreasing employee morale.

4. In deciding on growth, the owner-manager should ask four important questions:
   a. Is the business one that can grow?
   b. Am I prepared to make the effort?
   c. Do I have the capabilities to handle growth?
   d. How should I pursue growth?

5. Growth planning is often overlooked because of the failure to understand the planning process, lack of time, and the constant changes occurring in the industry.

6. The three steps in developing an expansion plan for a small business are (1) setting objectives, (2) identifying all the possible strategies or alternatives for achieving the objectives, and (3) choosing the best and most viable alternative.

7. The requirements of growth are greater management depth, intelligent expansion, increased capital, financial information, organizational change, decreased management control, and increased attention by the owner-manager to the external environment of the business.

Chapter Problems and Applications

1. Describe the business cycle for and Shapes Dance and Activewear (Incident 13–1).

2. Which of the problems created by growth as described in the chapter could apply to Shapes? Explain.

3. The owner-managers of a small, successful hair-cutting company want to expand their business. Their growth objective is to have 35 percent of the local hair-cutting market in two years' time.
   a. What steps could they take to determine the feasibility of their expansion?
   b. Outline a brief expansion plan.

4. What recommendations for expansion would you make for the following companies? Justify your answers. How does your recommendation differ from what actually happened? Why does it differ?
   a. Roots Shoes (Incident 13–2)
   b. Clearly Canadian Beverage Corporation (Incident 13–3)
   c. Tynex (Incident 13–4)
   d. Shapes Dance and Activewear (Incident 13–1)

5. What requirements for growth would be necessary for further expansion of Shapes Dance and Activewear?

6. Interview the owner-manager of a successful small business, and evaluate the potential for further growth. Would you recommend expansion for this firm? Why or why not?

7. Visit three small businesses that you suspect have varying sales levels. Determine the market, product, and degree of owner-manager involvement in each business. Are your results significantly similar to those in Figure 13–2? Explain.

Suggested Readings

Anderson, Robert L. *Managing Growth Firms.* Englewood Cliffs, N.J.: Prentice Hall, 1987.

Brandt, Steven C. *Entrepreneuring—The 10 Commandments for Building a Growth Company.* Reading, Mass.: Addison-Wesley, 1982.

Sexton, Donald L., and Phillip M. Van Auken. "Prevalence of Strategic Planning in Small Business." *Journal of Small Business Management,* July 1982, p. 20.

Siropolis, Nicholas C. *Small Business Management.* Boston: Houghton Mifflin, 1982, pp. 317–32.

Torrence, Ronald W. *In the Owner's Chair—Proven Techniques for Taking Your Business from 0 to $10 Million.* Englewood Cliffs, N.J.: Prentice Hall, 1986.

Touche Ross. *Planning for Expansion—A Guide for Owner-Managers.* Toronto: Touche Ross, 1984.

COMPREHENSIVE CASE
THE FRAMEMAKERS: PART 9

After four years of operations, The Framemakers had developed into a thriving business. Despite their problems and difficulties, Robert and Teresa Norman were proud of its performance. Sales had reached $175,000, almost three times what they had been in the first year (see Figure 1). Sales were appearing to stabilize, however, and the Normans suspected The Framemakers had saturated the market in Brandon. Robert disliked the idea of this ceiling on sales and profits and was looking to expand operations. He was investigating three possibilities for expansion. Each would require additional financing. Even though interest rates were in the 15 percent range, Robert believed his banker would lend him the money on the basis of The Framemakers' past success and a possible rate of return of at least 20 percent.

The first expansion possibility involved the purchase of the other frame shop in Brandon, The Art Studio, which was rumoured to be for sale. Robert had

---

FIGURE 1

THE FRAMEMAKERS LTD.
Income Statement
For the Year Ended January 31, 199X

Revenue:		
Sales	$175,000	
Cost of goods sold	70,250	
Gross profit	104,750	
Expenses:		
Accounting and legal		$ 1,200
Advertising		3,500
Auto		3,900
Bank charges and interest		8,100
Repairs		2,200
Depreciation		3,800
Office supplies and miscellaneous		1,200
Rent		23,150
Travel		2,700
Utilities		3,750
Wages and benefits (includes $27,000 for the Normans)		47,500
Total expenses		101,000
Net profit		**$ 3,750**

contacted the owner and obtained some financial information (Figure 2). The owner would not give complete financial statements without a down payment, which the Normans were hesitant to provide. Although this business was smaller than The Framemakers, it had a prime downtown location that Robert thought would generate walk-in traffic. The asking price was $75,000. With the addition of the second store, The Framemakers would have a monopoly on the framing business in Brandon. The present owner indicated that he wanted to move to Toronto, where he saw greater opportunities for a successful business.

The second option particularly intrigued Robert: to get into the business of manufacturing oak picture frames. Through his contacts in the industry, he had learned of a frame-manufacturing business in the United States that was for sale. The company, Frame-Line Manufacturing Company, had been operating only three years, but partnership problems and the owner's personal financial difficulties had forced him to sell. The plant had several key contracts with large retailers in the United States and Canada that Robert hoped to be able to maintain. The oak frame, which averaged $25 (U.S.) retail per unit, had few other manufacturers and competed with the lower-priced, plastic imitation wood frames that were currently popular and that The Framemakers stocked. Robert thought it would be feasible to move the plant to his home town south of Brandon and still maintain the Canadian and U.S. markets for the frames. What Robert particularly liked about this opportunity was the growth potential in sales, which appeared to be far greater than in the retailing business. (Financial information on the manufacturing plant appears in Figure 3.) The asking price for the manufacturing business was $30,000 (U.S.). Robert thought that if he chose this option, he might have to sell The Framemakers so that he could devote full attention to establishing the manufacturing operation.

FIGURE 2

THE ART STUDIO
Financial Statements

Assets

Equipment	$ 14,000
Inventory	18,000
Total	$ 32,000

Liabilities   None

Gross sales were about $110,000 per year.

Robert estimated profits (excluding owner's wages) to be about 10% of sales. He felt that about $10,000 of the equipment and inventory was of minimal value.

FIGURE 3

FRAME-LINE MANUFACTURING CO.
Financial Information
(all figures in U.S. dollars)

Assets

Equipment (estimated life, five years)	$30,000
Inventory	2,000
Gross sales (200 frames per month)	60,000 per year but growing at 15% per year
Exchange rates	$1.00 U.S. to $1.30 Canadian
Freight and duty to ship equipment to Canada	$12,000

The third option was to organize a franchising operation using The Frame-makers as the prototype. With the industry growing, Robert believed that there was potential for another franchisor in the industry. He estimated he and Teresa would need $50,000 to develop the literature, contracts, and promotion and thought he could sell franchises for $10,000 each.

Questions

1. What areas should Robert and Teresa consider before they seriously investigate the three expansion opportunities?
2. Evaluate the suitability of the asking price or establishment costs for each opportunity. What nonfinancial aspects of each option should the Normans consider?

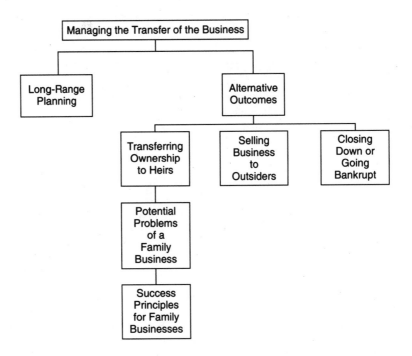

14 Managing the Transfer of the Business

Chapter Objectives

- To discuss the importance of planning for the long-term future and possible transfer of ownership of the small business.
- To review the unique characteristics and problems of owning a family business and passing it on to family members.
- To explain the critical considerations in selling the business to someone outside the family.
- To discuss information pertaining to the closing down of the business.

Small Business Profile

Harry Bondar

Hunter's Sport Shop Ltd.

How can a retail store in a town in rural Saskatchewan gross $50 million in sales? Harry Bondar has found the secret with Hunter's Sport Shop Ltd.

Bondar was born in Prince Albert, Saskatchewan, in 1922. After receiving his education and serving in the navy, he returned to the prairies, used his veteran's loan, and bought a small sporting goods store in North Battleford in 1946. For the next 20 years he learned the business, the market, and the merchandise. By 1970 he had branched out into boats and recreation vehicles, products that stimulated a substantial growth in his business. The firm moved to a larger, 100,000-square-foot location and dramatically increased inventories, staff, and market reach. Recently the company has also moved into manufacturing.

Harry Bondar possesses many characteristics that have helped make him one of Canada's most successful entrepreneurs. He rec-

ognizes the importance of being close to the consumer and responding to demand. In retailing, a major part of meeting this demand is good service. Bondar acknowledges that service is "the backbone of our business."

Harry Bondar likes to be in close control of the business, which is one reason he has rejected suggestions to franchise. Nevertheless, he recognizes that he needs good people to assist in the management of the business. As a result, Bondar has brought two sons and a daughter into the business. They have assumed responsible positions in the company and make take over the business once Bondar decides to retire. Bondar believes it is important for them to gain some experience with the organization and to allow him to train them and assess their abilities and interest.

In 1992 a disastrous fire destroyed Hunters in North Battleford—but Bondar remains undaunted in his desire to rebuild the business.

Used with permission of Harry Bondar.

Long-Range Planning

As mentioned in Chapter 13, relatively few owner-managers engage in formal long-range planning. One reason is the unpredictability of the future due to changes in the economy, technology, consumer demand, and legislation. However, one outcome that is predictable for small business is the fact that the owner-manager will not be able to manage the business forever. Someday the business will be transferred to others or closed down. Because of the time, effort, money, and commitment owner-managers have put into their ventures, they generally want the business to continue to grow and prosper and hope to realize a financial gain for their efforts in starting and building the organization.

To ensure this continuity for the business, the owner-manager needs to plan early for the time when he or she will no longer be in charge. Many small business owners are uncomfortable about this prospect. As a result they often procrastinate, avoiding the issue until shortly before the transfer of ownership is a necessity. Given today's legislation and tax laws, however, such a lack of planning can be extremely costly and damaging to both the owner-manager and the new owners of the business.

The entrepreneur should be familiar with the possible outcomes for the business, the relative merits of those outcomes, and some key implications of each.

Alternative Outcomes for the Business

The owner-manager can anticipate three possible outcomes for the business: transfer of ownership to heirs, selling the business to outsiders, and closing down the business on declaring bankruptcy.

Transferring Ownership to Heirs

Keeping the business in the family is a common method of transferring the business. Many small business owners desire to pass the business they have inherited or built up to their children. In most cases, this transfer occurs with considerable tension.[1] Because a family-owned business has many unique characteristics, it is important to review the problems and potential solutions in managing this type of organization.

Estimates of the extent of ownership within a single family indicate that approximately 70 to 90 percent of all businesses in Canada are family owned and operated[2] and employ close to 60 percent of the Canadian work force. Although a majority of these firms are small businesses, a significant number of family-owned large companies exists. Almost 35 percent of the Fortune 500 companies are owned or controlled by a single family.[3] Family ownership of a business in Canada is similar to that in the United States. A recent survey of the 500 fastest-growing private corporations in America undertaken by *Inc.* and *USA*

Incident 14–1

Problems of a Family Business

The most lethal of all deadly triangles in the family business is the father–son–son-in-law variety. Just ask the Jack Cates family. Jack Cates proudly carried on the tradition of a small wholesaling business called R. & J. Cates and Sons. Jack's son, Michael, was literally raised in the company, so when he graduated from an eastern university he exchanged his cap and gown for a sweatshirt and a place in Dad's business. Michael was the only son and had a promising future in the company. Less than three years later he was married to Susan Bellows, and he seemed to have everything going his way.

Jack's daughter Jennifer meanwhile was completing her college degree and had no immediate plans for the future. Jack wanted her to settle down and get married. That's where Frank Talbot comes into this story. After a one-year engagement, Frank, a middle-class travel agency accountant, married into this very affluent family.

This is where the problems began. By this time Michael had taken over much of the business and had been responsible for some large commercial hardware contracts. While Michael and Susan were living on top of the mountain and enjoying every luxury of life, Jenny and Frank were living in a small, modest apartment. Jenny wasn't used to living under such circumstances and approached her father to let Frank into the company. Jack, using his paternal instinct, hired Frank as an assistant office manager to train for the position of general manager. This was all right with Michael, and the three parties worked and played well together.

The problems began innocently enough. Frank, being a trained credit man, came down hard on some of the smaller, older customers that were accustomed to paying late. This upset Jack, and after keeping his feelings concealed for a while he laid into Frank about the problem. Michael also saw this as a way to vent his

---

Today found that the spouse and children are involved 33 percent and 28 percent, respectively, in the business operations of the other spouse.[4]

Despite the predominance of family businesses in Canadian society, relatively few survive into the second and third generations. It is estimated that only 30 percent continue into the second generation and only 15 percent into the third.[5] What are the reasons for this apparent lack of continuity? Observation shows that if some unique considerations in operating the family business are not recognized and planned for, they can cause considerable difficulties for the enterprise. Incident 14–1 describes such a situation. While it is an extreme example, it shows that family involvement in a business may have a detrimental effect not only on the business but also on family relationships.

Potential Problems in a Family Business.   Several problems may surface in the family-owned business. Recognition of these potential difficulties is essential for

Problems of a Family Business (*continued*)

frustrations and continued to put the heat on Frank. Frank began coming home every night heartsick. He took it out on Jennifer with a fury which frightened her and their two little children.

The tension between the two sibling families continued to mount, full of petty envy and jealousies. Urged by their wives, Michael and Frank continued their bloody battle. It continued with insulting memos, and their dislike for one another showed up in everyday operations and activities. Finally Jack called a meeting to settle the matter once and for all. After listening to Frank and Michael's future plans for the business, Jack announced that they would follow Frank's plan to move the whole operation to an industrial park where there would be much more room to expand. Then, with Michael in shock after his father followed Frank's plan, Jack announced that he was retiring and getting out of this mess and turning his chair over to Michael and pleaded with them to work together. Frank was shocked; he had just received a pat on the back and then boom—Michael was his boss. Hearing about her brother's promotion turned Jennifer cold, and she would not answer any of her parents' calls. She barred them from the house and would not allow them to see her children. Susan, in the meantime, nagged Michael to break Frank while he was down.

Both men were left disillusioned and lost interest in business. Contract bids went unanswered, and the company fell into dire straits. Conditions deteriorated so rapidly that Jack Cates was forced out of retirement to try and save the business. After several attempts, however, to get the boys to cooperate and save the business, Jack was forced to sell the company for a fraction of what it was once worth.

Source: Howard Klein, *Stop! You're Killing the Business* (London: Leviathan House Ltd., 1975), pp. 1–17.

the owner-manager and even for the other family members so that they can take steps to prevent them.

Higher Emotional Level.   Because of existing family relationships, some of the business decisions and evaluations may be more emotionally charged than they would be in a nonfamily setting (see Incident 14–1). For example, the evaluation of performance or supervision affecting a family member employee may be biased positively or negatively because of the relationship. Family members often bring their personal feelings and stress to the business, which often precludes them from making objective decisions.

Blurring of Roles.   In many family-owned businesses, the personal and business roles of individual family members may become blurred. For example, the chief executive officer of the business may in practice not really be in control because of his or her subordinate role in the family. This often occurs when children have "taken over" the business but their parents still exert informal control over both the children and the business.

Incompetence.   The problem of incompetence may arise in the family business in two areas. The first situation involves the relative who assumes the position of chief executive simply because of birthright. The experience, education, intelligence, and work ethic required to manage the business successfully may be lacking. The second situation involves hiring incompetent family members. Helping out an incompetent family member not only may lead to disappointment and damage to the business but can have a disruptive effect on the nonfamily employees.

Nonfamily Employee Attitudes.   One common characteristic of family-owned businesses is high turnover of nonfamily employees. Many young employees see no chance for promotion to management in the company because they are not part of the family. As a result, they may gain experience in the business and then leave for other organizations that offer the opportunity for promotion.

Objectives of Family Owners.   In most family businesses, more than one member of the family owns shares or has an ownership interest in the business. Because these owners may be from different generations, have different levels of involvement in the business, and have various backgrounds and needs, differences of opinion regarding the operations of the business are common.

For example, owners who are actively involved in building up the business often want to reinvest more of the earnings in the business. The nonactive owners or shareholders, on the other hand, may want their share of the profits to be distributed as dividends or payments to themselves.

Objectives regarding the growth of the business may also differ. Sometimes younger members of the family want to expand the business or make capital expenditures that older family owners are more conservative or cautious about making. Both situations can lead to conflicts that have a detrimental effect on the long-term progress of the business.

Planning for Succession.   The owner-manager has both a difficult task and an excellent opportunity in preparing children to become involved in the business. Some difficulties include providing the proper training, adequate motivation, and supportive atmosphere so that the child is able and wants to come into the business. Research shows that fewer than 50 percent of children who come from family businesses expect to return after receiving their college education, and only 20 percent plan to return to the business within five years of their graduation from college.[6] Other recent studies indicate that 70 percent of family businesses are either liquidated or sold after the founder retires.[7] It is apparently difficult for the parent to instill in the child the personal interest in the business the parent has. One school of thought is that parents may take too passive a role in attempting to interest their children in the business. They assume the children will find a

Incident 14–2

Charles Northstrup

Life in a family business has its ups and downs, but Brett Northstrup knew more about the downs. He had worked for his parents in the family furniture store all his life. "I grew up with the idea that I was going to work in the business; my parents told me the business was for me," said Brett. So there was never any leeway or choice as to what he was going to do as an adult. He was going to work there, so he did. But now, when it came time for his dad, Charles Northstrup, to retire, he wouldn't. He wanted Brett to take over the business, yet he didn't want him to do it because it was taking something away from him. Charles Northstrup now said, "I don't know if I ever will want to retire. I'd just take it a little easier someday, because I know I'd miss all the friends I've made, all the customers—they're just like friends. Besides, I'm not sure Brett can handle the business yet; he just doesn't run the business my way."

After 15 years with the business, Bret had finally had enough. He left and started over, leaving his parents to run the business their way.

Source: Rick Heyland, University of Lethbridge.

---

profession more interesting and rewarding for them.[8] A common scenario is that of the parent-owner who is unwilling to give up control or allow the child a say in the business. On the other hand, it is also common for the inexperienced child to want to make changes the parent believes will be detrimental to the business. Incident 14–2 illustrates such a situation.

Running a family business also offers a great opportunity to provide on-the-job training and background for the child that is not otherwise possible. The parent-owner can also assess the child's progress and level of preparation over a longer period of time than would be possible if hiring an outsider to manage the business. In addition, the owner-manager's business philosophy and style may be taught to the child who is apprenticing for management and ownership of the business. Incident 14–3 illustrates this situation.

Principles of Success for Family Businesses.   The preceding section has demonstrated the many difficulties that can arise in a family business. As was illustrated, these difficulties can be detrimental to the success of the business and damaging to family relationships. If one is involved in a family business or is contemplating bringing family members into the business, the following practices may help prevent some of the aforementioned difficulties from arising.

Recognize the Importance of Objectivity.   Evaluations and supervision involving family members should be done on an objective basis. Even if tempted to do

Incident 14–3

Rogers Cable Systems

Rogers Cable Systems is the largest cable network in the world. Through some inaccurate cost estimates and an aggressive expansion philosophy, the company had a $762 million debt in 1984. The bank had become nervous and asked the company to sell off some of its least profitable ventures. The banks will probably give 51 percent shareholder and president Ted Rogers the two years he is asking for to lighten the debt load.

There is another way to raise the necessary money. That would be to sell shares and raise some capital through equity rather than debt financing. But Ted Rogers is determined not to lose controlling interest in the company. The underpinning of his philosophy comes from his father, who had lost control of Canada's original radio company in the 1930s. Ted Rogers says, "My father's experience has been a towering influence in my life. There is no way I will lose control of the company. I think it is a credit to our country to have more ownership in dynamic companies instead of selling out."

Rogers seems to follow his dad's philosophy or at least learns from his dad's mistakes. The company, Rogers predicted, "will turn a profit by 1987." Although his prediction of profitability was optimistic, Rogers has continued to grow and by 1992 was the 109th largest company in Canada in sales.

Sources: CBC Corporation, "Venture" series, June 1985; *Canadian Business,* June 1992, p. 112.

---

otherwise, the owner-manager must attempt to separate family discussions and emotions from business activities. Care should be taken to ensure that consistent policies are followed for both family and nonfamily employees. Many owner-managers have found it essential to separate their children physically and functionally from themselves and one another to prevent such difficulties from arising.

Create Clear Role Structures.   The solution to the problem of the blurring of roles may be difficult to implement, as much of the control may be exerted informally. A clear definition of the roles, objectives, and responsibilities of all associated family members may help solve the difficulty. Separation of business and family goals and systems has also been recommended to alleviate this problem.[9]

Ensure Competence.   Because an incompetent owner-manager can spell disaster for the business, providing the heir with technical and practical training, along with increasing decision-making authority, is vital. This may involve encouraging the family member to acquire some necessary skills outside the business at a college, a university, or another business before returning to become fully involved. Many potential inheritors of businesses appear to follow this route to the ownership of the family business.[10] If a competent family member is not available, the remaining family owners may be able to persuade the owner-manager to let a more capable individual run the day-to-day affairs of the company.

If training does not improve the performance of incompetent relatives but for family reasons it is not possible to let the employee go, some owner-managers place such an employee in a position where he or she can do the least harm to the company.

Provide Incentives for Nonfamily Employees.   To maintain the loyalty of nonfamily employees and ensure that they stay with the company, the owner-manager will need to devise various rewards and incentives. These incentives can be financial or may involve including employees in decision-making and educational programs. It may still be impossible to retain an energetic young employee who desires to eventually rise to the top of the organization unless the owner-manager is prepared to give up some of the ownership or authority of the business.

Clarify Objectives of Family Owners.   To prevent disharmony resulting from differing objectives of family members, it is important to formally clarify the long- and short-term objectives of the company. These might include objectives for such areas as expansion and distribution of profits. Some firms distribute a set percentage of profits in dividends or reinvest a specified amount back into the business annually. Incident 14–4 shows how one Canadian entrepreneur planned for this problem.

Planning for Succession.   Care should be taken to nurture and prepare the child to take over the business with the same enthusiasm the owner has. This can best be done by including the heir in the business at an early age. It will also mean giving up a certain amount of control of the business, often before the owner-manager feels ready to do so. Incident 14–5 illustrates how this was done in one Canadian company. As mentioned earlier, it may be beneficial for the child to gain training and experience outside the business. Successful transfers between parents and children usually involve considerable compromise on the part of both parties.

Keeping Communication Lines Open.   Perhaps the most effective aspect of operating a family business successfully is open communication. Given many potential areas of conflict, differences of opinion must be communicated to the relevant parties before they develop into a serious problem. Formalized objectives, plans, roles, and procedures can accomplish this.

Tax and Legal Implications of Transferring the Business to Family Members. An increasingly complex consideration in transferring a business to heirs is the legal and tax implications. One specific tax consequence of transfers of business ownership within a family concerns capital gains. In Canada one-half of the capital gain (defined as the increase in value of the asset since acquisition of the

Incident 14–4

Keeping the Family in the Business

To keep the family name alive in the printing business, Lawrence Pollard, president of Winnipeg-based Pollard Banknote Ltd., mortgaged everything he owned. He borrowed $5 million in 1985 to acquire the technology needed to turn his 77-year-old printing house into a lottery ticket printer. Gambling on this new niche, he hoped, would not only bolster the firm's chances of survival, but pique the interest of his two eldest sons—John, 30, then in accounting, and Gord, 32, a corporate lawyer. "Young people," mused Pollard, then 56, "like to go where there's growth."

Pollard's gamble—and his insight into youthful ambition—paid off. John and Gord came back to bolster what is now a $35-million international "scratch and win" business. And Lawrence has a satisfaction shared by few principals of family businesses: knowing the company founded by his grandfather will carry on into the fourth generation.

To plan an orderly succession, Pollard drew up a detailed estate plan last year with his accountant. A heart attack he suffered in the first year of hectic changes helped him realize he couldn't take the future for granted: "My heart condition made me focus on my estate planning more."

The cardinal rule of Pollard's estate plan states only family members who work in the business may share in its spoils. That will leave out his two daughters, who chose not to work in the firm, and possibly a third son, Douglas, who is still in university. That condition improves the odds of company survival, says Pollard, because control passes to those who prove they're interested in running it. The children not involved in the family firm will inherit non-business assets.

Source: Jennifer Low, "Dad, When Are You Going to Let Go?" *Profit Magazine,* October 1991, pp. 28–30.

business or 1972, whichever is shorter) upon the sale is added to the income of the person disposing of the asset (business). This rule applies a "deemed disposition" rule (to family) in that the business is "deemed" to have been sold at market price whether or not the market price was actually paid.

In the past, the federal government allowed a tax-free rollover or capital gains deferral to spouse and children up to a maximum capital gain of $200,000. This applied to Canadian-controlled private corporations. If the heir sold the shares (or business) to someone outside the family, the capital gain would be realized and a resulting tax liability incurred. In the budget of May 23, 1985, the federal government introduced a $500,000 lifetime capital gains exemption, to be phased in gradually.

Incident 14–5

Dad, When Are You Going to Let Go?

Those who aren't ready to bow out when the next generation is anxious to take over could take a tip from carpenter Helmut Hinteregger, 48, and his wife Helen, 47, a bookkeeper. In 1969, they founded Concept Developments Ltd., an Edmonton-based builder of custom homes. Their two sons had helped with odd jobs on construction sites since they were kids, but Rick, 27, a business-administration graduate, finally joined in 1984, and son David, 23, a building engineering graduate, signed on in 1988. Over the past two years, "the boys," as Helmut calls them, proved their mettle when they re-costed for healthier margins and strengthened their roster of subcontractors by 40% to tackle more homes at once than their parents had ever dared. Rick, as general manager, and David, as construction manager, have helped boost sales from $1.6 million in 1985 to $8.8 million in 1990.

Their ambition is not in question. "Sometimes," says Hinteregger, they'd say, "Dad, when are you going to let go? We've got it under control." To recognize their sons' abilities, the Hintereggers gave them each 20% of the company last January. That, says Arch Pervin, a family business consultant, is a move that must be carefully planned. "Giving the kids a part of the company before they take control helps keep them interested," he notes. "But they have to have earned it. It's not a good idea to transfer all the ownership of management abruptly because the children need the model of mom or dad to guide them."

To make letting go a little easier, the elder Hintereggers plan a new enterprise of their own that will also ease Rick and David through the transition. While the sons are busy building homes, the senior Hintereggers will be buying and developing residential land.

Source: Jennifer Low, "Dad, When Are You Going to Let Go?" *Profit Magazine,* October 1991, pp. 30–32.

This provision allows for the transfer of ownership of the business with little capital gains consequence, whether or not the business is an incorporated company.

Obviously these changes have affected the tax consequences of transferring the business to heirs. While most of these changes have been positive from the point of view of the small business, they are complex and counsel should be sought from a legal and/or tax expert before making a decision in this area.

Methods of Transferring the Business to Family Members. In deciding which method to use in transferring all or part of the business to the heirs, the owner-manager first needs to clarify his or her own objectives in making the transfer. Some common transfer-related objectives are the following:

- The owner-manager wants to keep a reasonable amount of control over the business until the heirs are of an age and competence level to assume their responsibilities.
- Although the owner-manager wants to maintain control of the business, but also wants the heir(s) to maintain their interest and commitment to the business.
- The owner-manager desires to distribute the business assets (ownership) so that the heirs (if more than one) will recognize this distribution as fair.
- The owner-manager wants sufficient access to income or assets from the transfer of the business to maintain an adequate standard of living.
- The owner-manager wants to achieve an orderly transfer of the business to minimize the tax consequences for both parties.

Some of the most common methods of transferring ownership to the heir(s) are discussed next.

Through a Will.   When the transfer is made through a will, ownership of the business does not pass to the heir until the owner dies. This method may satisfy the owner's objective of maintaining control of the business, but it fails to address any of the other objectives mentioned. For example, serious tax consequences may arise if the business is unincorporated. In such a situation, the previous owner's income is calculated at the date of death. If the business has an irregular business cycle and a death occurs at the wrong time of the year, a large income (and higher tax liability) may result. The heirs would then have to deal with this tax liability.

Purchase and Sale of the Business.   This method may not satisfy the owner's objectives unless it takes place gradually over a number of years. Such an agreement can remain flexible within the family to accomplish the objectives of both the owner and the heirs. A "deemed disposition" is viewed to have taken place at market value whether or not that amount was actually paid. Purchasing the business gradually may provide an incentive for the heir and also allow the parent to maintain the desired control for the required period of time.

Gifting Program.   In the absence of gift taxes, part or all of the business may be gifted to the heir(s). The most common method of doing this is gradually, over several years. This option is likely feasible only if the owner is not dependent on proceeds of the sale for his or her income.

Life Estate.   A life estate is used primarily when the significant assets are real property. This method transfers the ownership or title of land or buildings to the heir, with the condition that the previous owner has a position of control until he or she dies. The extent of control can diminish as the heir becomes more involved in the business. Immediately upon the parent's death, the title automatically passes to the heir. This method accomplishes many of the aforementioned objectives.

Selling the Business to Outsiders

If the owner-manager is not able or does not wish to keep the business in the family, he or she may decide to sell all or part of the business to someone outside the family. This action, of course, could be taken at any time, not just when the owner-manager is ready to retire. Regardless of when the business is sold, however, the owner-manager should realize that the last few years' performance will affect the purchase price. Therefore, careful planning should be done to ensure that the business's performance is as positive as possible prior to the sale.

Many of the aspects of selling a business were discussed in Chapter 5 regarding the informational requirements of the prospective purchaser. The seller of the business must now prepare this information and make it available to a prospective buyer. Particularly important is information on the financial condition of the business as represented by the financial statements. A listing of any hidden assets or capabilities that do not show up on the balance sheet should be made. The asset valuation and earnings methods discussed in Chapter 5 can assist in setting an asking price for the business. Most buyers will thoroughly review these statements, particularly the earnings record, to determine how accurately they portray the business.

Another critical area in selling the business includes the terms of the sale. Timing of payments may have considerable tax consequences. Some of these consequences have been reduced, however, by the alternative minimum tax provisions. Often the purchaser wants the previous owner to remain in the business in an advisory capacity. This arrangement (with appropriate compensation) can be included in the purchase agreement.

One possible outcome of selling the business may apply to a partner or other owner. As mentioned in Chapter 4, a buy/sell clause should be a part of the partnership agreement. This clause should be carefully worded to account for future differences in the value of the firm.

Sometimes small businesses are purchased by larger companies in the form of a merger. The acquiring company is usually looking to expand or capitalize on some unique advantage or capability the small business has. For example, purchasing a small business may allow a company to capitalize on such strengths as a unique product, market access, or expertise it could not otherwise obtain. In many such situations, the owner-manager of the smaller business is retained in the organization. Often, however, this relationship is short-lived because the former owner is uncomfortable with his or her lack of independence in the new arrangement.

The owner-manager may want to sell only a part of the business. This is accomplished much more easily if the business is incorporated to allow a share transfer to take place. In such a case, the owner-manager may be able to retain control over the business while obtaining capital needed as payment for the shares.

Incident 14–6

International Verifact

The only product of International Verifact Inc. is a credit-card and cheque-clearing terminal that looks something like a medium-sized calculator. Called the Terminus I, it sits on the checkout counter of a store or restaurant or at a hotel front desk and permits the clerk to instantly clear any credit card transaction (it handles up to nineteen different cards). By punching the right code and running the credit card through the machine, which is connected to, say, VISA or Mastercard central terminals, a transaction can be cleared in seconds. Terminus I is even equipped with a device that notifies police if the card is stolen. It seems like an idea whose time has come.

"VISA was knocked out by our product and our enthusiasm," says partner Douglas Archibald, "and insisted we Canadians would teach the world a thing or two about product development. In a way, the people at VISA were right. At least we could tell the rest of the world that developing the product is the easy part."

The next step was to find the financing to keep the company afloat and to underwrite the expensive marketing push. They couldn't go to the banks for financing, because they were the ultimate customers, so the partners (Archibald's partner was Ian Cumming) met with several venture capitalists. But they were dissatisfied with the percentage of the company they would have give up to obtain the money they needed. "We would have been working for the venture capitalists, not ourselves," says Archibald.

Archibald and Cumming decided to raise money in the stock market. This meant going to the Vancouver Exchange, the only Canadian market that would list a fledgling enterprise with no track record. They went to an investment company in Vancouver with a fourteen-page draft proposal typed up by Archibald's wife the night before they left. "We had fourteen meetings in two days covering investment dealers and lawyers," says Cumming, "but we left Vancouver with a guaranteed agreement for the underwriting." It then took ten and a half months for the prospectus to be written. Finally, in January, 1984, shares were made available to investors and $600,000 was raised. International Verifact was off and running.

Source: Kenneth Barnes and Everett Banning, *Money Makers! The Secrets of Canada's Most Successful Entrepreneurs* (Toronto: McClelland and Stewart, 1985), pp. 79–80.

Going Public.   Sometimes a small business that has been successful but has a need or desire for a significant amount of capital sells shares to the public. In this case, the corporate status changes from a private to a public company. The advantages and disadvantages of this form of equity investment were discussed in Chapter 7. Incident 14–6 illustrates a Canadian business that successfully sold shares in the stock exchange. Going public may also allow control of the business to remain with the owner-manager if over 50 percent of the shares are not sold.

One or more of the following characteristics may indicate that the small business is in a favourable position to go public:[11]

- The company is in a popular specialized market.
- The company is in an above-average growth position.
- The business has a strong market niche and proven sales appeal in an emerging rather than a mature industry.
- The business can and does generate a return on equity of at least 20 to 25 percent.
- The company has at least $10 million in annual revenues.
- The company has strong management.
- The company has reached the point where it needs a substantial amount of capital for growth and expansion.

If the owner-manager finds it necessary or desires that the firm's shares be offered to the public, the services of an investment dealer may be helpful. An investment dealer (or underwriter) will assist the owner by acting as the marketer for the stock. The investment dealer can use an over-the-counter market, one that includes securities that are not sold on the stock exchange. If this method is followed, a reputable investment dealer with substantial connections throughout the investment community should be selected.

Alternatively, shares can be sold on the stock exchange. To obtain a listing, however, the business must meet several requirements, and many small firms lack the performance record needed to attract investors.

Closing Down or Going Bankrupt

The third possible outcome for the business—generally a result of unsatisfactory performance—involves closing down, being placed into receivership, or going bankrupt. These are, of course, the least desirable outcomes for the small business. As discussed in Chapter 2, however, each year many small businesses end up in this situation because of lack of profitability. Closing down is much easier for an unincorporated business than for a limited company. In theory, the incorporated company is required to file dissolution forms and notify government agencies. Although this is the case if the company does not have a large debt load, the incorporated company has more protection in a debt situation because of its limited liability.

Business Bankruptcy.   In 1990, 31,958 business bankruptcies were declared in Canada.[12] The majority of those failures were small businesses. If the business debts are significantly greater than assets and the earning power of the business is inadequate to service future obligations, the owner-manager may face two options.

First, a major creditor may appoint a receiver and the business placed in receivership. When a company is in receivership, the receiver enlists the services of another agency in an attempt to manage it out of financial difficulty. As this may be difficult to do, receivership is often a forerunner to bankruptcy.

The second option is to consult an accountant. If the accountant's recommendation is to see a licensed trustee for bankruptcy, an assignment usually takes place. When this happens, the debtor (the small business) assigns its assets to the trustee, who in turn meets with the creditors. The assets are converted to cash and distributed to the creditors to repay as much of the debt as possible. These assets are distributed using a priority system. Secured creditors—those who have signed security for some of the debt (including the trustee)—have first priority to proceeds of the deposition. Preferred creditors such as employees, landlords, or government departments have second priority, followed by ordinary unsecured creditors.

Frequently ordinary creditors may receive little or none of the money owed them. This is a significant point, since most small businesses themselves are ordinary creditors in their business dealings. Thus, they often lose out when a business with which they are dealing goes bankrupt.

If a proprietorship or a partnership of individuals goes bankrupt, the owner-manager is allowed to retain certain necessary assets. It is still possible for a bankrupt individual to start another business at a later date. In fact, some businesses enter into voluntary bankruptcy, which allows them to dissolve quickly and get reestablished. Once bankrupt, however, a person's credit rating is weaker than before, and obtaining debt financing may be difficult. A lawyer should be consulted if this type of bankruptcy is being contemplated.

Although bankruptcy is becoming more common, it can be a difficult and damaging experience that could have been avoided in 70 to 90 percent of the cases had financial difficulties been spotted and acted on early.[13] Owner-managers who have developed and are using financial management concepts such as those discussed in Chapter 9 should be in a better position to avoid bankruptcy.

Summary

1. Some of the more common methods of transferring ownership of a business to family members are through a will, a sale of the business to the heirs, a gifting program, and a life estate.

2. The unique problems of a family business are higher emotional levels, blurring of roles, incompetence, nonfamily employee turnover, differing objectives among family owners, and planning for succession.

3. The higher emotional level of a family business is natural because of the family relationship that already exists. This emotional level can result in a negative or positive bias toward other family members.

4. An incompetent family member employee can be sent to acquire some more skills at a college, a university, or another business before returning to become fully involved in the family business.

5. To maintain loyalty among nonfamily employees, the owner-manager will need to devise various rewards and incentives.

6. In a family business, it is important to set long-term objectives and to ensure that each family member understands his or her role in the business.

7. Succession in a family business can be facilitated by letting the family member gain experience outside the business and by allowing him or her increasing authority and control.

8. Given the many potential problems in a family business, it is essential to maintain open communication so that differences are discussed before they develop into serious problems.

9. If a business is transferred to another family member, one-half of the capital gain upon the sale is added to the income of the person disposing of the business outside the family, subject to rollover provisions. This rule applies regardless of what amount (if any) is paid for the business.

10. A recent federal government budget proposal allowing for a capital gains exemption will aid the owner-manager in transferring the business to outsiders or family members.

11. Sometimes a small business that has been successful but needs a significant amount of capital may sell shares to the public to meet financial needs while retaining control of the company.

12. A business that cannot be transferred can be closed down, be placed in receivership, or file for bankruptcy.

13. The priority order for distribution of assets in a bankruptcy case is secured creditors first, then preferred creditors, and finally ordinary creditors.

Chapter Problems and Applications

1. How could Charles Northstrup have satisfied both his son's career demands and his own desires and still effectively run their furniture store (Incident 14–2)?

2. Jim Duncan is the owner-manager of a local restaurant chain. In its earlier years, the three local family restaurants were very successful. Then the recession came, and the businesses haven't been doing as well. Jim is 60 years old and is thinking about retirement or

semiretirement. He has a son who has managed one of the restaurants, but he is not sure Jim, Jr., is ready for the problems existing in the whole operation. If you were Jim, Sr., how would you transfer ownership? Explain your decision.

3. *a.* What were the mistakes made and problems evident in the collapse of Jack Cates's business (Incident 14–1)?

   b. What would you have done in Cates's position to avoid those problems? Would it have helped to pay Frank and Michael the same salary? Why or why not?

4. Your father has just made you president of the family sand and gravel company. You want to computerize the payroll and the accounts payable and receivable, but your father doesn't see the need for the extra expense when expenses are already too high. What two problems exist here? How would you resolve this conflict as the newly appointed president?

5. Your parents have just made you the manager of your family's grocery store. Since the transition, problems have seldom been brought to your attention, and you have received little feedback on your instructions. What problems might be evident? How would you solve these problems?

6. Hamilton Rogers is the owner-manager of a successful machine shop. In the last year, he has promoted his sons to floor managers. Recently several employees have also left the company. What factors could be responsible for the employees leaving their jobs? How could Hamilton have prevented this problem?

7. Interview the manager of a family-owned and operated business. What unique problems are evident?

8. Interview someone who is a future heir of a family business and is now going to school or gaining business experience. What problems are evident from his or her perspective? Does this person want to go back to the business? Why or why not?

9. Pomaona Fastener Company has suffered several years of operating losses. Because of the unfavourable outlook for the firm, it filed for bankruptcy and was dissolved. On liquidation $570,000 was received, to be split among the following creditors:

Accounts payable	$100,000
Secured loans from bank	400,000
Accrued wages	10,000
Rent due on building	20,000
Government loan	300,000
Trustee's fee	10,000

What would be the priority of payment, and how much would each class of creditor receive?

10. Interview the owner-manager of a small business that recently went public, and find out what he or she learned through the experience.

Suggested Readings

Alcom, Pat. *Success and Survival in the Family-Owned Business.* New York: McGraw-Hill, 1982.

Barach, Jeffrey A.; Joseph Gantisky; James A. Carson; and Benjamin A. Doochin. "Family Business: The Next Generation." *Journal of Small Business Management,* April 1988, pp. 49–56.

Danco, Leon A. *Beyond Survival: A Guide for the Business Owner and His Family.* New York: Center for Entrepreneurial Management, 1986.

Deciding to Go Public—Understanding the Process and the Alternatives. Cleveland, Ohio: Ernst & Whinney, 1986.

Hartman, Chris. "Taking the 'Family' Out of Family Business." *Inc.,* September 1986, pp. 71–76.

Kantor, J. "How Can Entrepreneurs Maximize the Going Public-Offering Price? The Case of Ontario, Canada, 1978–1983." *Journal of Small Business and Entrepreneurship,* Spring 1986, p. 56.

Mancuso, J. *Inside Family Business.* New York: Center for Entrepreneurial Management, 1986.

Paisner, Marshall. "Myths about Succession." *Inc.,* October 1986, p. 146.

Rosenblatt, Paul C.; Leni DeMik; Roxanne Marie Anderson; and Patricia A. Johnson. *The Family in Business.* San Francisco: Jossey-Bass, 1985.

Stevens, Mark. "When to Take Your Company Public." *Entrepreneurial Manager's Newsletter* 7, no. 4 (1986), p. 4.

Ward, John L. "Keeping the Family Business Healthy." San Francisco: Jossey-Bass, 1987.

CASES FOR PART IV

Baker Hardware Ltd.   Millie's Hand Cooked Potato Chips
Bob's Restaurant   Weiss Manufacturing Company
James Macreary's Estate

BAKER HARDWARE LTD.

D. Wesley Balderson
University of Lethbridge

Baker Hardware Ltd. is a hardware store in the town of Souris, which is located in an agricultural area of southern Manitoba. Souris is 30 miles south of Brandon (population 55,000), which is the major trading centre for many smaller towns within a 60-mile radius.

Mr. Baker, the owner of Baker Hardware, is contemplating expanding his merchandise offering to include lumber and building supplies. Currently Baker's, in addition to a standard selection of hardware merchandise, carries paint and building tools; therefore, Mr. Baker thinks this new line would be fairly compatible.

Baker Hardware was a part of the Home Hardware network of dealers, a nationwide group of hardware stores and home centres located primarily in smaller towns and cities. For the past few years, Home Hardware had been encouraging its dealers to expand into building supplies. Concerned that there was another lumber yard in Souris (which happened to be next door to Baker Hardware), Mr. Baker had shown little interest in such a move in the past.

Recently, however, he became aware that this lumber yard, Banner Building Supplies, was for sale or would be closed down. Mr. Baker gathered information from both the owners of Banner as well as from Home Hardware and was in the process of making a decision. As Mr. Baker saw it, he had three choices: (1) purchase Banner Building Supplies, (2) expand into building supplies through Home Hardware on his own premises, or (3) maintain current operations (not expanding into building materials).

The Market

As previously mentioned, Souris was a small town of about 2,000 located in an agricultural area of southern Manitoba. The estimated population of surrounding area farms was 500. The town was located 30 miles southwest of Brandon, the major trading center for the area. Over the years, the retail communities in most of the small towns close to Brandon had deteriorated due to the strong competition of retailers there and the increased mobility of consumers. The building supply industry was no exception. Such chains as Canadian Tire and Beaver Lumber, which had outlets in Brandon, had attracted numerous customers from these rural communities.

The population of Souris consisted mainly of farmers, commuters who worked in Brandon, and professionals such as teachers who worked in the town. The town had experienced some growth in recent years because of its relaxed atmosphere and excellent recreational facilities. Projections indicated the population could reach 2,500 by the year 2000.

Baker Hardware

Baker Hardware had operated successfully in Souris for many years. Mr. Baker had purchased the store from his father, and with changes and modernizations, increased sales from $450,000 in 1975 to 800,000 in 1990. Although sales showed a significant increase, profits did not. The strong competition from hardware chains in Brandon in recent years had eroded Mr. Baker's profit margin. Baker Hardware's competitive strength had always been that it catered to the agricultural community. Unfortunately, farm incomes had experienced considerable volatility in recent years, and this trend directly affected Baker Hardware's profit performance.

Baker Hardware currently had 12,000 square feet of selling space and a large (8,000-square-foot) warehouse. Mr. Baker believed that if he went into building supplies he could, with some renovations, free up about half of the warehouse space to house the new merchandise.

Baker Hardware's current financial situation, while not serious, was such that if a capital investment were made, Mr. Baker would have to borrow to finance it. At the current interest rate of 14 percent, this was a concern for Mr. Baker.

Home Hardware

Home Hardware Ltd. is a well-established franchise system of dealer-owners located across Canada. Originating in southern Ontario, it has expanded to become a dominant small-town retailer of hardware merchandise. Recently Home Hardware moved into the building supply industry in an attempt to capitalize on the growth of the home center concept. Home has been encouraging its dealers to branch into this area, and many have done so.

Mr. Baker obtained from Home Hardware a list of the recommended product assortment for a home building supply dealer. A summary of this list, along with space requirements and markups, appears in Figure 1.

Home Hardware also suggested that Mr. Baker would need a forklift (estimated cost $15,000, used), a delivery truck (estimated cost $10,000, used), and a shed of at least 5,000 square feet (estimated cost $5,000).

FIGURE 1   **Recommended Home Building Supply Full Product Assortment**

Product	Cost	Suggested Markup on Cost	Estimated Turnover	Space Requirement
Insulation	$ 4,000	25%	4.0	600
Doors & mouldings (complete assortment)	6,000	30	2.5	900
Plywood (complete assortment, 2 pallets each)	10,000	15	5.5	2,100
Dry wall (complete assortment, 2 pallets each)	6,000	15	4.5	600
Cement	2,000	30	5.0	180
Roofing materials	5,000	25	3.5	600
Nails	1,000	30	5.0	120
Siding, soffit, facia	6,000	30	2.0	900
Dimensional lumber, 2×4, 2×6, etc. (complete assortment, 2 pallets each)	20,000	15	6.0	3,000
	$60,000			9,000

Banner Building Supplies

Banner Building Supplies was a family-owned business that had operated in Souris for over 40 years. It was owned by two brothers, both close to retirement age, who also owned a window and door manufacturing plant. As the manufacturing plant was much larger in size and scope of operations, the Banners had devoted most of their time and energy to this business. The retail building supplies outlet had, over the years, taken second priority in their business interests, although it provided a stable and needed outlet for the town.

Interest in selling the retail outlet resulted from two major factors. First, both brothers wanted to cut back on their work responsibilities, as both were approaching retirement age and had no family members interested in taking over the business. However, one brother had a son-in-law who was interested in the manufacturing part of the business. Second, the profitability of the retail outlet had suffered in recent years due to strong competition from larger hardware chains and home centres in Brandon. Some of these competitors could sell certain types of lumber and other supplies at lower prices than Banner's costs. The estimated profit and loss statement Mr. Baker obtained from Banners for 1990 is shown in Figure 2.

Currently Banner Building Supplies has approximately $75,000 in inventory (see Figure 3) and owns a large lot containing some sheds and a showroom next door to Baker Hardware. The estimated value of real estate and buildings is approximately $25,000. The company has no debt.

In looking at the merchandise requirements recommended by Home Hardware, Mr. Baker noted that Banner's inventory levels were different. Mr. Baker discussed this with the previous manager of Banner's and learned that some

FIGURE 2

BANNER BUILDING SUPPLIES
Estimated Income Statement for 1990

Sales	$230,000	
Cost of goods sold (85%)	195,500	
Gross profit		$34,500
Expenses:		
Wages	22,500	
Taxes and licenses	2,000	
Insurance	11,000	
Professional fees & admin.	500	
Utilities	2,000	
Fuel (trucks, etc.)	1,200	
Bad debts	1,000	
Depreciation	1,800	
Repairs & maintenance	1,000	
Misc. supplies	500	33,500
Net income before taxes		$ 1,000

FIGURE 3

BANNER BUILDING SUPPLIES
Inventory Estimate

Insulation	$ 6,000
Doors and mouldings	24,000
Plywood	12,000
Drywall	7,000
Cement	1,000
Roofing materials	2,000
Nails, etc.	1,200
Siding	2,000
Dimensional lumber	35,000
Paints	2,500
Tools and hardware	2,500
Carpet and linoleum	1,800
	$75,000

building supplies did not sell well in Souris. He informed Mr. Baker that the standard types of lumber (plywoods, 2×4's, etc.) were the steady sellers, although warpage caused considerable waste in dimensional lumber. He also mentioned that it was very difficult to compete with the city building centres for the large contractors' business. The major market for Banner's had been the small contractor (renovators) and the do-it-yourself customer.

Armed with the above information, Mr. Baker was determined to make a decision.

Questions

1. What other information should Mr. Baker obtain before he makes this decision?
2. Using the information provided, evaluate the alternatives Mr. Baker has identified. Be sure to evaluate the attractiveness of the proposed merchandise lines.
3. What other alternatives has Mr. Baker not explored?

Bob's Restaurant

E. Jerome McCarthy and Stanley J. Shapiro
Michigan State University and Simon Fraser University

Mr. Bob Wilson is the president and only stockholder of Bob's Restaurant Limited, a small, successful firm in the restaurant and recreation business in the small town of Wolfville, Nova Scotia, the site of Acadia University (population of 3,235 plus 4,050 students). Mr. Wilson attended the university in the 1950s and paid most of his college expenses by selling refreshments at all of the school's athletic events. As he expanded his business, he hired local high school students to help him. The business became so profitable that Mr. Wilson decided to stay in Wolfville after graduation. He rented a small building near the campus and opened a restaurant.

Over the years, his restaurant business was fairly successful. Mr. Wilson earned a $36,000 profit on sales of $1,462,500 in 1992. The restaurant now consists of an attractive 40-table dining room, a large drive-in facility, and free delivery of orders to any point on the campus. The only thing that hasn't changed much is Mr. Wilson's customers. He estimates that his restaurant business is still over 90 percent students and that nearly three-fourths of his sales are made between 6 P.M. and 1 A.M. There are several other restaurants with comparable facilities near the campus, but none of these is as popular with the university students as his "Papa Bob's."

As a result of the restaurant's success with the student market, Mr. Wilson has aimed his whole promotion effort in that direction, by advertising only through the campus newspaper and over the campus and local rock music radio stations. In an attempt to increase his daytime business, from time to time Mr. Wilson has used such devices as coupon meal books priced at 85 percent off face value. And he features daily "lunch special" plates. Nevertheless, he admits that he has been unable to compete with the university cafeterias for daytime business.

In 1989, when Mr. Wilson was seeking a new investment opportunity, he contacted a national manufacturer of bowling equipment and supplies about the feasibility of opening a bowling lanes operation. Wolfville didn't have a bowling alley at the time, and Mr. Wilson felt that both the local and university communities would provide a good market. He already owned a large tract of land which would be suitable for construction of the bowling lanes. The land was next to the restaurant, and he felt that this would result in each business stimulating the other.

The decision was made to go ahead with the venture, and to date the results have been nothing short of outstanding. Several local and university groups have formed bowling leagues. The university's men's and women's physical education departments schedule several bowling classes each term. And the casual bowling in the late afternoons and evenings is such that at least 12 of the 16 lanes are almost always in use. Some local radio advertising is done for the bowling lanes, but Mr. Wilson doesn't feel that much is necessary. The success of the bowling lanes has encouraged the developer of a small shopping centre in the residential part of town to make plans to include a similar facility in his new development. Mr. Wilson believes that competition won't hurt his business, because he has more to offer in his recreation centre.

Pleased with the profitability of his latest investment, Mr. Wilson decided to expand his recreational centre even further. He noted that both students and local citizens patronized his bowling lanes and concluded that the addition of an attractive, modern billiard parlour would also have a common appeal. There was one other poolroom in Wolfville. It was considered to be a "hangout" and was avoided by townspeople and students. He felt that by offering a billiard parlour operation, he would be able to supply yet another recreational demand of his market. He obtained a loan from a local bank and began to build a third building at the back of his land. The billiard parlour was outfitted with 12 tables, a snack bar, wall-to-wall carpeting, and a soft music background system.

Today, eight months later, Mr. Wilson is extremely disappointed with the billiard parlour operation. After the first two or three weeks, business steadily dropped off until now only one or two tables are in use even during the evening hours when business at the bowling lanes is at its peak. Promotion for the billiard parlour has been combined with promotions for other facilities, which are still doing very well.

In an effort to discover what went wrong, Mr. Wilson interviewed several of his restaurant and bowling customers. Some of the typical responses were:

A Coed: I had enough trouble learning how to bowl, but at least it's sociable. Pool looks hard and everyone is so serious.

A Fraternity Man: My idea of a good date is dinner at Bob's, then the movies or an evening of bowling. You just can't make a good impression by taking a girl to play pool.

A Wolfville Citizen: I've never allowed my children to enter the local pool hall. What's more, as a kid I wasn't allowed either, and so I've never learned the game. It's too late to teach an old dog new tricks!

Mr. Wilson is thinking about selling the billiard equipment and installing some pinball machines because he has heard they can be very profitable.

Questions

1. Why has Bob Wilson been successful in the past?
2. Why has Bob's latest venture been unsuccessful?
3. How could Bob ensure that the business succeeds in the future?

This case was adapted from E. Jerome McCarthy and Stanley J. Shapiro, *Basic Marketing,* 3rd Canadian Edition, 1983 (Homewood, Ill.: Irwin-Dorsey of Canada). Used with permission.

JAMES MACREARY'S ESTATE

D. Wesley Balderson
University of Lethbridge

James Macreary had built up a large farm retail store in Elmira, an agricultural community near Guelph, Ontario. He had followed the example of his parents and grandparents in working hard and persevering through good and bad times. His farm operations included 3,000 acres of prime agricultural land and a large livestock operation. He also owned a retail store in Elmira that employed 15 people full time and earned a steady but modest income. Over the years he had reinvested most of this income in the business, taking only a small salary for himself. He had an outgoing personality and was a well-respected businessman in the community.

Macreary stayed very involved in managing all aspects of the retail and farming business well into his 80s. His major concern was to ensure that the business keep operating successfully.

Macreary had three daughters but he didn't have a son. Two were married to farmers and lived close by, while the third lived in the United States. They seemed interested in helping Macreary, but because of lack of encouragement on his part, they never became very involved with his business interests. The husbands had all developed their own careers, and grandchildren were beginning to pursue careers that were taking them away from Elmira. In November 1989, at age 87, Macreary passed away.

A few days after their father's funeral, the three daughters met in the lawyer's office to settle the estate. None of them had any idea how the estate was to be divided. They learned that one-half of Macreary's estate was going to Mrs. Macreary, who was 85, and one-half was to be divided equally among the three daughters. This perplexed the daughters, as they did not know how to proceed in operating the business. Who would manage it? They were very hesitant to sell the assets, as they knew how much the business had meant to their father. He had mentioned many times that he did not want it sold.

In addition to this problem, the lawyer informed them that Macreary's proprietorship year end was on the day he died. Being a farmer, Macreary had used a cash basis for accounting income and usually incurred many expenses in December to reduce income for tax purposes. Having passed away in November, he had not yet had a chance to incur these expenses, and as a result he left an income of over $200,000. This meant that almost half would be a tax liability. There was not nearly enough cash in the estate to pay these taxes, and the daughters were concerned that they might have to borrow or sell some assets to pay them.

To make matters worse, the daughters were upset about the way the estate was divided. The two daughters living nearby felt they should have received more than they did. The third daughter thought she was entitled to one-third of the estate. All three were upset that their mother, age 85, had one-half of the estate. What might she do with it?

The family was in turmoil. They faced the prospects of trying to run a business they knew little about, a high tax bill, and resentment within the family.

Questions

1. What could James Macreary have done to avoid this situation?
2. What advice would you give to the family at this point?

MILLIE'S HAND COOKED POTATO CHIPS

Professor Scott B. Follows
Acadia University

In March 1990, John Miles and John Potter, equal partners in the Toronto-based food brokerage firm Betmar, purchased the assets and trademarks of Millie's Hand Cooked Potato Chips from a receiver. When the deal closed, Miles returned to his native Nova Scotia to re-establish the business. He expected to be able to have the unique chips back on the Nova Scotia market in six weeks. In order to turn the business around quickly, Miles needed to determine what had gone wrong. How could Millie's sales have increased from $500,000 to $3 million in three years and the company still have gone out of business?

John Miles had a wealth of experience in the confectionary business, having spent 23 years with Nabisco Brands as a sales manager and national account representative. After leaving Nabisco, Miles started Betmar, a brokerage company, with partner John Potter of the sales promotion company Nash Potter. Potter was the idea man and Miles made things happen.

Betmar was the successful bidder for the assets of Millie's: the machinery, a computer, the trademarks and a few supplies. The plant was not in working order, as the packaging machine had been repossessed in January 1989 due to a default on payments. In addition, the registration of the trademarks had never been completed, so the brand names were not legally protected. Betmar was to be a source of working capital for the first year.

Upon arriving at the plant, Miles discovered that there were no records or files and that he would have to try to understand what had gone wrong using only limited information. Based upon recent newspaper articles, previous conversations with Brian Shore (the former owner of Millie's), and interviews with former employees and retailers, Miles was able to piece together the following chronology of events.

Millie's was founded in 1984 by Brian Shore, a 38-year-old law school dropout who was a natural salesman. Shore had a history of entrepreneurial activity including building and selling prefabricated homes and producing New York–style soft pretzels which he sold from vending carts. The new company was set up under Mazel Mining Co., an existing shell company. This would enable Shore to use what little cash he had for the down payment on a delivery vehicle, a '79 Oldsmobile with the rear seat removed. Shore had been looking for a product which would generate revenue even in hard economic times. He turned to snack foods, stating: "When people don't have a lot of money, they buy a bag of chips and a six-pack of beer and go home and watch the hockey game rather than go out to a nightclub." Financing had been through a $30,000 loan from a silent partner (who left the business in March 1985), a $64,000 loan from the Toronto Dominion Bank (five other banks refused) and a $100,000 federal government small business loan.

Canadian retail potato chip sales in 1984 were $500 million and had been experiencing an annual growth rate of 5%. The highly competitive industry was dominated by three national producers: Hostess Food Products (General Foods), Humpty Dumpty (American Brands) and Frito-Lay (Pepsi-Cola Canada).

The Millie's chip was based on a 75-year-old Pennsylvanian Mennonite recipe which Shore altered to suit his taste. Conventional chip production used a continuous process where the potatoes were peeled using caustic soda, sliced, then dipped in a chemical bath or boiling water to bleach out the colour and finally fried in oil. Millie's used a batch process, slicing the chips directly into an open vat fryer and cooking them at a lower temperature for a longer time. The chips were hand stirred and the cooking time was determined by sight. "Our people get used to knowing when they're ready," said Philip Morris, Millie's production manager. No preservatives or monosodium glutamate were added and sunflower oil was used to make the chips cholesterol free. The result was a thicker, crispier, more nutritious and flavourful chip. Millie's was the only company with a hand cooked chip on the Canadian market.

The name "Millie's" came from Shore's partner's wife. Said Shore, "I liked the sound of the name and the look of the double *l*'s." Shore designed the white, red and blue package which pictured a woman with piled hair wearing a long dress and apron, stirring a cooking kettle with a ladle. The bag boasted "Natural Ingredients" and stated, "Millie's Hand Cooked Chips are made the old-fashioned way—hand cooked one batch at a time. This original method produces a potato chip that is golden crisp and crunchy with that tremendous natural potato flavour." Said Shore, " 'Naturals', like Millie's, have become a 'yuppie' product—they've developed a cult following." And, "I just figured that if I made a different potato chip, I'd get a niche in the market."

Millie's chips cost about 20% more to produce than conventional chips, but Shore felt, "If people like a product, they'll willingly pay a premium for it." The suggested price to the consumer was similar to national producers' prices but Millie's packages were smaller.

1984—The Beginning

Shipments from the 3,500 sq. ft. north-end Halifax plant, described by Shore as "a dump with a leaky roof," began in November 1984. Millie's offered three varieties: regular, Bar-B-Q and no salt. Two package sizes were available: a 32 gram snack pack (national producers used 48 grams) and the regular 180 gram bag (national producers used 200 grams). Shore spent no money on advertising but gave a lot of chips away hoping to generate word-of-mouth: "We don't need all the new and improved hoopla. If the people like it, they'll buy it, and they'll create the demand." The only promotion of Millie's chips was Shore's sales efforts. Said Shore, "We're purposely being unsophisticated, not hiring marketing guys and whatever."

1985—Modest Growth

Shore sold to health food stores, student pubs, and independent grocery and convenience stores in the Halifax–Dartmouth area because he had difficulty getting his product into the large grocery and convenience chain stores. He felt the chain stores should be obligated to stock a local product, and refused to negotiate shelf allowances in order to get listings. It was common trade practice for grocery retailers to expect incentive payments from manufacturers. Allowances lowered a retailer's costs and paid for in-store promotions and store advertising which featured the manufacturer's product. Shore fought tradition because he believed allowances discriminated against smaller companies with limited financial resources. Unable to achieve wide distribution, he began to look beyond the Maritime region for opportunities. In early 1985, Shore thought of producing a kosher chip for the annual Jewish religious holiday, Passover. He approached Steinberg's in Montreal, one of Quebec's largest grocery chains, and received a $30,000 order. By the end of 1985, Millie's was shipping chips throughout Nova Scotia and New Brunswick, and ended the year with sales of $500,000 and a profit of almost $20,000.

1986—Rapid Growth

The year 1986 brought tremendous consumer acceptance for the chips and growth for Millie's. Listings were obtained in the large grocery chains: Sobey's, The Food Group and IGA. This move expanded distribution to Prince Edward Island and Newfoundland. In order to increase volume, Shore positioned Millie's as the low-priced competitor. Moreover, prices were occasionally reduced further during selected promotional periods, and Millie's was often used by some retailers as a low price promotion.

Due to the large number of retail accounts in Nova Scotia and New Brunswick, Millie's contracted with independent general-line wholesalers to merchandise its product in major markets outside the Halifax–Dartmouth area (Fredericton, Moncton, and Saint John in New Brunswick; Truro, Bridgewater, Sydney and the Annapolis Valley in Nova Scotia). Merchandising entails order taking, delivering the chips, placing them on the rack in a presentable fashion and rotating the older chips to the front. The wholesalers received minimal direction and attention from Millie's. In contrast to Millie's, national producers used company vehicles operated by trained company employees.

Millie's made a number of changes in response to the growing demand for the product. It installed a new $200,000 form-filled packaging machine to speed up production. The product line was broadened to include "salt and vinegar" and "sour cream and onion," and the original snack bag was increased in size to 42 grams. In spite of $2 million in annual sales, Millie's barely broke even in 1986.

1987—Expansion

In 1987 Millie's received its first large national order. It was unexpected, and had been prompted by a small order to a local store in the Zeller's chain which had put Millie's on the supplier's list. A few months later, the president of Zeller's sent a letter to all suppliers soliciting funds for a charity. Shore replied with product samples and a letter stating if he had a contract he would be able to afford a donation. This resulted in an order for 500,000 bags and many of the stores sold out in two weeks. Internationally, Millie's received an order from a Taiwanese food importer whose representatives visited the plant and then ordered a container of chips (40,000 bags) six months later.

The sale of the building rented by Millie's provided an opportunity for expansion. Based on Shore's forecasted sales of $10 to $15 million in the next two years, Millie's moved into a $1.3 million, 17,000 sq. ft. plant across the harbour in Dartmouth's Burnside Industrial Park. The move was financed by a $250,000 loan from the Small Business Development Corporation, and accomplished during a two month summer shutdown caused by a potato shortage.

Shore perceived the need to compete in the conventional potato chip market, so the company launched a thinner chip called "Archie's." It gained wide distribution and was pegged at a price lower than the national producers' products. By the end of the year, Shore had appeared on the CBC's business program

"Venture," was negotiating a national contract with Boots Drug Stores, and was looking at the European and Asian markets. The company's annual sales were $3 million and it employed 35 people.

1988—The Demise

In 1988, consumer loyalty for the locally produced chip remained strong even though the chips had become increasingly greasy. Millie's had been trying to maximize the use of the frying oil to reduce costs, but had no way of testing the oil's quality.

By mid-year sales had slowed. The situation worsened when Millie's became caught in the cross fire of a price war between the national producers. Stated Shore, "If they want to shoot cannons at a mosquito they can, but they will make a mess of the wall." In addition, the federal government introduced a sales tax on snack foods which increased the price of chips to the consumer.

Distribution in the Maritimes became spotty when some of the wholesalers dropped the product due to falling sales. Shore continued to look for expansion in the Ontario market and approached John Miles to act as the Ontario broker. After a number of meetings, a tentative agreement was reached between the two parties. By year end, Shore was not returning Miles's phone calls, and by January 1989 no one was answering at Millie's until one day Miles's call was answered by a representative of Touche Ross, the receiver.

Questions

1. Why did Millie's fail?
2. What recommendations would you make to John Miles?

SOURCE: This case was prepared by Professor Scott B. Follows of Acadia University for the Atlantic Entrepreneurial Institute as a basis for classroom discussion, and is not meant to illustrate either effective or ineffective management.

WEISS MANUFACTURING COMPANY

E. Jerome McCarthy and Stanley J. Shapiro
Michigan State University and Simon Fraser University

Bill Carson is currently employed as a sales representative for a plastic goods manufacturer located in Montreal. He calls mostly on large industrial accounts such as refrigerator manufacturers who might need large quantities of custom-made products. He is on a straight salary of $20,000 from Weiss Manufacturing Company, an established thermoplastic moulder and manufacturer. Carl Weiss, the present owner, is nearing retirement age and has not developed anyone to run the business. He has agreed to sell the business to Robert Watson, a lawyer-entrepreneur, who has invited Bill Carson to invest and become the sales manager. Mr. Watson has agreed to give Carson his current salary plus expenses, plus a bonus of 1 percent of profits. However, Bill must invest to become part of the new company. He will obtain a 10 percent interest in the business for his $20,000 investment.

Weiss is well established in the industry, with a net worth of $150,000, sales of $1.5 million, and profits of $25,000 per year. As a percent of sales, cost of materials was 45 percent; direct labour, 13 percent; indirect factory labour, 15 percent; factory overhead, 13 percent; and sales overhead and general expenses, 13 percent. The company has not been making a large profit for several years but has been continually adding new machines or replacing those made obsolete by technological developments. The machinery is well maintained and modern, but most of it is similar to that owned by its many competitors. Most of the machines in the industry are standard. Special products are then made by using specially made dies with these machines.

Financially, the company seems to be in fairly good condition, at least as far as book value is concerned. The $20,000 investment would buy approximately $30,000 in assets.

Mr. Watson feels that with new management, the company has a real opportunity for profit. He expects to make some economies in the production process and hold custom moulding sales to the present $1 million level. The other major expectation is that he will be able to develop the proprietary line of products from a sales volume of about $500,000 to $2 million a year by adding several new "novelty items" normally sold in department stores. Bill Carson is expected to be a real asset here because of his sales experience.

Questions

1. What points should Bill Carson consider before making this decision? Discuss both the personal aspects and the potential successes of the firm.
2. Evaluate the financial implications of going ahead with the decision.

Directory of Supplementary Cases

Alan Berwick

Ray Klapstein
Dalhousie University

Alan Berwick had spent a total of sixteen years as a successful oil company service station lessee-operator[1] in Halifax. In the fall of 1988, he was approached by the owner of another service station who wanted to sell his operation to Berwick. Berwick rejected the offer, but the owner persisted. Berwick eventually agreed to consider the matter seriously, committing himself to a decision by early January, 1989. This was a genuine opportunity for Berwick to become the owner of his own operation for the first time; however, he had serious reservations. Since business was always slow during the week between Christmas and New Year's, Berwick took a few days off to focus his attention on the issue; he was resolved to reach a firm decision by the week's end.

The Man

Alan Berwick entered the service station business as a mechanic's apprentice in 1966. Four years later, when he was only 21, the oil company that owned the service station where he worked offered to lease a Halifax service station to him. His lack of training or experience in business management made him very hesitant to accept the offer, but the oil company persuaded him to become a lessee-operator. In six years he increased the service station's annual gasoline sales from 40,000 litres to 4 million litres. He was a good manager and the oil company was delighted with his performance. Nonetheless Berwick chose to leave the business. The service station demanded his full attention and left no time for his young family and no time for relaxation or vacations. In his words, "life had become all work and no play."

   Berwick then went to work as a delivery truck operator for a local bottling company. The job soon proved to be unchallenging, and he found himself in need of something more. He took a course in refrigeration and was promoted to a more demanding and rewarding job with the same employer, but found that this, too, was unfulfilling. After that, Berwick expanded his endeavours to include a chain of vending machines, dispensing his employer's products, but he still sought something more demanding and rewarding.

---

[1]Lessee-operators leased service station premises from an oil company and ran them on the same basis as an independent venture. They would buy the oil company's products and resell them to customers after adding a mark-up.

One day Berwick drove past a construction site on the edge of Halifax, where a sign announced it as the site for a new service station owned by Petro-Canada, the oil company with which he had previously been a lessee-operator. His first reaction had been that the site was a poor one, but it led him to reflect on the business and realize that he truly missed it. On the following morning he drove to the site, parked his car, and spent the day counting the number of vehicles that passed by. He was impressed by the volume of traffic. He repeated the exercise several times, always with the same result. He decided to discuss the new service station with his wife, Mary. He told her that he had not forgotten the long hours nor the headaches associated with operating a service station but, he told her, he felt his life wasn't going anywhere and he missed the business. Mary's evaluation of the situation was direct: Berwick was bored and frustrated, and there was not a real opportunity for advancement in his present work. She encouraged him to contact the oil company about the new service station, and assured him of her full support and assistance.

The Business

When Berwick had left the oil company and the service station business three years previously, he had left on good terms. Consequently, the oil company immediately offered the new service station to him, as its lessee-operator. Within the week he met with the company's representatives and signed a lease agreement.

The new service station opened in 1979. Gasoline sales in the first year were almost 3 million litres, with gross dollar sales of all products slightly exceeding $1 million. Gross sales had reached $2.9 million by 1988, but Berwick felt that future growth would be very limited: the service station's bays were working near capacity, and the size of the local market suggested there was little chance of significantly increasing gasoline sales. Management at the oil company continued to be pleased with Berwick's performance, and rated him as one of the company's ten best service station operators in Atlantic Canada. Mary Berwick became actively involved in the operation, acting as its bookkeeper. The Berwicks worked hard but enjoyed running the business as a family venture.

The Industry

The service station business in the Halifax metro area was very competitive. Gasoline prices were regulated by the Nova Scotia Board of Commissioners of Public Utilities (PUB).[2] The PUB used a complicated formula and included a wide range of factors in fixing price maxima. Although it set maxima only, the net effect of its intervention was that the major oil companies and their service stations did not compete on the basis of price: competition was based almost totally on service.

---

[2]Its mandate required balancing oil profitability considerations and the best interests of the consuming public.

The two most significant factors determining the level of success of a service station in metro Halifax were location and hours of operation. Hours of operation were regulated by local by-laws, and an oil company or a service station operator could do little to change a service station's permitted hours of operation. A good location could atone for a multitude of sins, but it was nearly impossible to turn a profit at a poor location. High traffic volume and easy access topped the list of requirements for a good location. Proximity to a residential neighbourhood from which to draw a customer base ranked second. The number of competitors, and their proximity, was also significant, as was the range of services and facilities offered by the service station itself. Finally, the presence of other service oriented operations (e.g., convenience stores) contributed to the volume of sales.

Given a good location, the remaining key to success was good management. A service orientation was the most important attribute of a good service station operator: he should be friendly and courteous, easy to talk to, and able to respond positively to customer needs and complaints. This served to emphasize the extreme importance of customer loyalty: repeat business was the life blood of any service station. A thorough knowledge of the business was equally important: the operator needed both to know what he was talking about and to establish customer confidence that he did. In addition, a good service station operator required the skills and attributes of any good business manager, including the ability to manage and motivate personnel, manage inventories and finances, and maintain an organized operation. The profile of an ideal operator, from an oil company perspective, also included an entrepreneurial drive to maximize the station's performance. Given the level of start-up costs, inventory financing, and cash flow requirements, a service station operator also required a net worth in the vicinity of $50,000.[3]

There were two types of relationships between an oil company and the operator of a service station bearing the company's name and selling its products. The more common was outright ownership of the service station by the oil company, with a lease contract between the company and the operator, who was called a lessee-operator. The lessee-operator had full operating control of the service station, and paid rent to the oil company. Typically, leases ran for a five year term with an option to renew, and included provision for the rental rate to be renegotiated at the end of the term.[4] The second type of relationship involved service stations which were owned by the operator, who was called an owner-operator. Supply contracts between owner-operators and oil companies also

---

[3]See Appendix 1 for details of the required investment and operating costs.

[4]Historically, there had been a tendency for oil companies to focus on sales and profit levels in establishing the amount of rent charged under a lease. In recent years, some had moved to a complex formula which reflected the appraised market value of the site, property tax expense, maintenance expense, and the nature of the facility (e.g., number of service bays). However, many lessee-operators remained suspicious about the change, concluding that good performance was still being rewarded by increased rent expense rather than increased profits.

typically ran for a five year term, but owner-operators had the advantage of a fixed mortgage and tax costs for land and buildings, not being subject to rent increases at the end of the term. Owner-operators also had the advantage of negotiating the provisions of a supply agreement from a much stronger bargaining position than lessee-operators: they had the benefit of an ever-present implied threat to contract with a different oil company.

The service station business in the Halifax area was a thriving one.[5] Sales remained strong through both good economic times and bad, and a service station with a good location and effective management was assured good sales, despite the high degree of competition.

The Company

Petro-Canada, a crown corporation, was a fully-integrated major oil company with a national chain of service stations. It had expanded into refining and marketing in eastern Canada with the acquisition of Petrofina Canada Inc. in 1981. Petrofina had been a well-established operation in the Maritime region, with a full network of service stations. After the takeover Petro-Canada maintained a policy of continually reviewing and monitoring the network; upgrading existing service stations; adding new ones in response to population trends and changing traffic patterns; and deleting stations in unattractive locations.

Petro-Canada was an aggressive petroleum products marketer. In addition to continually reviewing the service station network, it aggressively pursued sales growth through new product development, careful dealer selection, initial and ongoing dealer training and monitoring, and provision of a broad range of marketing supports for dealers. Marketing support included signage at service stations, mass-media advertising, and promotional programmes, all at little or no direct cost to the dealer.[6]

Petro-Canada provided a full range of TBA products[7] to its service station operators, in addition to gasolines and motor oils. While service stations were permitted to carry other TBA lines, the practice was discouraged and very few did.

Petro-Canada compared favourably with the other major oil companies on virtually all dimensions. Its marketing efforts were second to none, although they were matched by those of Imperial/Esso. It was an industry leader in new product development, notably because it had introduced a hydro-treating process for lubricants (used by the Big 3 North American auto manufacturers in the factory fill of new cars). It had also developed and introduced three grades of unleaded gasoline. The only competitors to improve their share of the Halifax area market in recent years had been Texaco and Ultramar, but neither had gained at

---

[5]See Appendix 2 for gasoline sales and numbers of service stations in the Halifax area, and Appendix 3 for average gross sales by category of product.

[6]Petro-Canada's promotional programmes are described in Appendix 5.

[7]TBA: Tires, Batteries, and Accessories, including fan belts, antifreeze, windshield washer fluid, etc.

Petro-Canada's expense. Imperial/Esso was the only competitor with its own full-range TBA line, while the others marketed a variety of TBA manufacturer's products.

The Proposal

The owner of a Petro-Canada service station in suburban Halifax had decided to sell his operation. Given the right buyer, he was prepared to take back a mortgage for 75% of the sale price at an interest rate of 12% per annum, amortized over 30 years.[8] The right buyer, in the seller's view, was Alan Berwick. He knew Berwick well and was familiar with his operation. He was convinced that Berwick's personality, drive and track record were precisely what was required to maximize the profitability of the service station and establish the return necessary to assure that mortgage payments would be covered. He would not offer to sell his service station to anyone else until Berwick made a decision.

To Alan Berwick, the proposal was one which required careful analysis. On the positive side, it presented an opportunity to become an owner-operator, continue in the business and with the product line with which he was thoroughly familiar, but without the constraints that were inherent in the lessee-operator role. He discussed the proposal with Petro-Canada and was told they would be pleased to act as his supplier if he made the acquisition, and encouraged him to consider operating both service stations. In addition, his research showed that no other established service station attractive to him was for sale in the Halifax area. The service station offered was worthy of serious consideration. Its location had all the attractive features of the station Berwick had been operating for nine years, but with two additional benefits: traffic volume past the location was 50% higher than at his present site and the service station was adjacent to a convenience store, thus attracting traffic directly to it. The Berwicks did not wish to invest their savings in the acquisition, but Berwick was assured by his banker that a second mortgage loan for 25% of the asking price would be available at 15% interest. On the negative side, the station was not properly equipped: the only necessary equipment already in the station was a single hoist in one of the bays, and a full inventory of tires and miscellaneous products for retail. The two service stations were virtually identical in other respects: they were the same size, each had two bays, and they served similar markets, suggesting that both would require the same level of supplies, equipment and personnel.[9]

---

[8]Selling price was $450,000; monthly mortgage payments would be $3,397; balance of purchase price could be financed at 15%/annum; property taxes were $8,000/annum. The service station was not legally incorporated and the seller had several other personal investments. He did not keep separate records for the station and was able to provide organized financial statements for the operation.

[9]Costs and expenses at Berwick's present location are presented in Appendix 1.

The competitive situations were also similar. Although gasoline sales at the two service stations in 1988 were approximately equal, sales for the remainder of the product line at the other station were only half the level Berwick had achieved. Berwick's analysis led him to the conclusion that the other location offered an opportunity to increase sales to 125% of those of his present operation for all items in the product line within two years. He based this conclusion on the greater traffic flow and proximity to a convenience store. Berwick became convinced that current sales were below potential levels because the current owner was unwilling to devote the necessary time and energy to ensure that customers were satisfied and that the operation was managed effectively. Gross margins for all items in the product line were the same for owner-operators and lessee-operators, so Berwick knew he could compute contribution levels that would help him determine fixed cost and interest coverage.

Alan Berwick determined that he had three options to consider:

1. Decline the offer;
2. Accept the offer and leave his current service station; and,
3. Accept the offer and continue as lessee-operator of his current service station, but hire a manager to be in charge of the new one.

The first option would limit the opportunity for future growth, but his current operation was profitable and had begun to allow time for other things. The second option would provide an opportunity for more growth, and independence from the oil company, but would bring with it the headaches and extra hours of work associated with a new venture for himself and Mary. The third option intrigued him most: it could provide the challenges and rewards of dramatic growth, but would demand an investment of money, time and energy by himself and Mary that would leave no opportunity for anything but work in at least the first year or two, and would include a need to identify, hire and train a reliable, competent and trustworthy manager.

Berwick presented the three options to Mary, and they discussed the implications of each for their personal lives. She indicated that she would be prepared to give her full support to whichever one he chose, but would leave the decision entirely to him. Given that, Berwick realized that he needed to fully analyze each of the three options. He sharpened his pencil and went to work.

Source: This case was prepared by Professor Ray Klapstein of Dalhousie University for the Atlantic Entrepreneurial Institute as a basis for classroom discussion, and is not meant to illustrate either effective or ineffective management. Some elements of this case have been disguised.

APPENDIX 1
ALAN BERWICK SERVICE STATION: COSTS IN 1988

Equipment[1]	Cost	Useful Life (Yrs.)	Capital Cost Allowance Rate (%)
Hoists	$ 16,000	20	20
Brake Lathe	6,000	10	20
Tire Changer	4,000	10	20
Wheel Balancer	4,000	10	20
Small Tools[2]	2,000	2	N/A
Scope/Analyzer	12,000	10	20
Computer Analyzer	2,000	10	20
Employee Uniforms	3,000	1	100

Inventory[3]	Cost		
Products Other Than Gasoline[4]	$ 10,000		

Annual Operating Expenses	Cost		
Rent	$ 40,000		
Insurance	3,500		
Electricity	7,200		
Service Vehicle	3,000		
Heat	5,000		
Salaries & Benefits[5]	260,000		
Equipment Maintenance & Repair	6,000		
Promotions/Advertising[6]	2,400		
Accounting Services	2,100		
Bank Charges	300		
Employee Uniforms: dry cleaning	3,000		
Licenses and Taxes[7]	2,500		
Discounts and Shortages	2,400		

[1]Equipment purchases could be financed at 15% per annum. Liquidation values were equivalent to book values.

[2]Mechanics supplied their own tools. The figure shown is for small tools, etc., supplied by the service station.

[3]Gasoline could be purchased on consignment. The financing charge was $0.0015/litre, due one week after sale.

[4]Required at start-up and maintained on a constant basis.

[5]Manager's salary and benefits are not included. The average salary, including benefits, for an employed manager was $35,000/annum. Figure includes equivalent of 3 full-time mechanics at $25,000/annum.

[6]Service station portion only. Most promotional campaigns and advertising were done by the oil companies, at little or no direct cost to the service station.

[7]Not including income tax.

SOURCE: Alan Berwick.

APPENDIX 2
GASOLINE SALES AND NUMBER OF SERVICE STATIONS IN THE HALIFAX AREA, BY OIL COMPANY, 1988

Oil Company	City of Halifax Gasoline Sales (000s of Litres)	Stations (#)	City of Dartmouth Gasoline Sales (000s of Litres)	Stations (#)	County of Halifax Gasoline Sales (000s of Litres)	Stations (#)
Irving	21,435	16	14,788	11	34,457	23
Imperial	23,141	9	17,878	8	39,277	19
Texaco	16,541	11	14,423	4	23,180	12
Ultramar	11,494	5	3,179	5	15,192	8
Petro-Canada	19,483	10	8,519	6	35,519	14
Shell	12,726	9	5,381	5	16,019	8
Olca					342	1

Note: The City of Halifax and Dartmouth are urban. The County of Halifax is both surburban and rural; approximately ⅓ of county gasoline sales and service stations were in the Halifax metro area.

SOURCE: Nova Scotia Board of Commissioners of Public Utilities.

APPENDIX 3
AVERAGE GROSS SALES PER 1,000 LITRES OF GASOLINE, FOR SERVICE STATIONS

Motor Oil	$ 8
Tires	14
Batteries	2
Parts & Accessories	45
Labour	50
Other	2

SOURCE: Analysis of industry data.

APPENDIX 4
ALAN BERWICK SERVICE STATION SALES REVENUE, 1988

Gasoline	$2,375,000
Motor Oil	35,000
Tires	50,000
Batteries	10,000
Parts & Accessories	225,000
Labour[1]	150,000
Other	8,000
	$2,853,000

[1]Customers billed at $30/hr.; mechanic's billable hours = 3 (40 hrs.) (49 weeks).

SOURCE: Alan Berwick.

APPENDIX 5
PETRO-CANADA PROMOTIONAL PROGRAMMES, 1987–1988

Commercial Credit Card—provided discounts to volume purchasers.

Women's Car Care Clinics—promoted through "pump toppers," kits were provided to dealers, and dealers provided an evening seminar at the service station, showing women customers the basics of how a car functions, tire changing, etc.

"Play Ball"—sponsorship of children/youth ball teams; the company provided brochures, etc., and dealers bought uniforms and put the service station's name on them.

Youth Soccer—parallel to "Play Ball."

Right Riders—the company provided program, materials, etc. to local Police Associations, which provided bicycle safety courses to children in the 5 to 12 years age bracket.

Local Promotions—Grand Openings, Anniversaries, Specials, Radio Remotes, Pump Toppers; cost shared equally by the company and the service station.

Regional Promotions—sales of promotional items (e.g., drinking glasses); no cost to service station.

National Promotions—same as regional, but on national scale.

Source: Consultations with Alan Berwick and company officials.

APPENDIX 6
FULL SERVICE WITH BAYS: STATISTICAL REPORT FOR HALIFAX

Gasoline Margin per Litre	$0.046
Gross Profit Percentages	
Gasoline	72.9%
Oil	35.0%
Tires	19.0%
Batteries	24.0%
Parts & Accessories	32.0%
Labour	96.0%
Other	30.0%
Total re: Sales Other Than Gasoline	59.0%
Sales Mix: Gasoline/Sales Other Than Gasoline	85%/15%
Total Expense as % of Total Gross Profit	85%
Wages as % of Total Gross Profit	41%
Average Annual Sales Other Than Gasoline/Bay	$102,420
Average Mechanic Productivity[1]	79.0%

Note: The figures given are industry averages.

[1] I.e., % of billable hours actually billed to customers.

SOURCE: *Service Station and Garage Management,* an industry periodical published by the Southam Business Information and Communications Group.

Video Delight

Dr. Mallika Das
Mount Saint Vincent University

Carla McDonald, Jennifer Smith, Peter Swain and Mark Swift were marketing students at a university in Halifax, Nova Scotia. As part of a marketing course, they were asked to conduct a research study for Video Delight, a Halifax video rental store. They were to examine consumer attitudes towards the store and its pricing policy. They were reviewing the details of the research study and other relevant information that they had collected and were to make recommendations on pricing and overall marketing strategy to the owner, Peter Thompson, by December 5th, 1988—in three weeks.

Mr. Thompson was concerned about the downturn in video rentals in his Halifax store. He attributed this primarily to the recent opening of Jumbo Video, a large chain, near his store. He was also interested in customer reaction to the new pricing policy that he had introduced in July, 1988.

The Company

Peter Thompson, a commerce graduate of Dalhousie University, had begun his video rental business with one small store located in a busy area of Halifax. Soon his store had expanded, and he now offered over 10,000 titles. According to Thompson, he had enough titles to compete with anyone. After five years in the business, Thompson had opened another branch in Bedford, 15 km from his Halifax outlet. Financially, the two outlets performed well. In fact, business had been so good that Thompson enlarged his Halifax outlet in early 1988. It was at this time that a new video outlet opened in the area. Mr. Thompson thought that the new competition was beginning to affect his volume of business.

The Industry

During the early to mid-eighties, when VCRs became very popular, many video outlets had sprung up in Halifax. In addition to the video rental outlets, many

This case was prepared by Dr. Mallika Das of Mount Saint Vincent University for the Atlantic Entrepreneurial Institute as a basis for classroom discussion. Some elements of this case have been disguised.

corner grocery stores and even some supermarkets had entered the field. Although these stores did not offer the same variety as video rental outlets, they offered consumers greater convenience.

By the latter part of the 1980's the proliferation of video rental outlets led to severe competition in the industry. Consumers had a lot of outlets from which to choose; consequently, attracting their attention was becoming more and more difficult. Many small operators had closed, and several corner grocery stores had gone out of the video rental business. For example, the number of video outlets on Video Delight's street had decreased from ten to five—one was the same size as Video Delight and the other three were smaller. Competition was still fierce, but as the industry matured fewer competitors were entering the market and the market stabilized.

At the same time another trend developed in the industry. National chain stores were formed. Several of them, like Jumbo and SuperVideo, were late entrants into the Atlantic region. However, by 1988 these stores had opened outlets in the Halifax-Dartmouth area, and they were beginning to expand. It was as part of this expansion that Jumbo had opened a store less than one block from Video Delight.

The larger chain stores had several advantages over smaller stores like Video Delight. They had more capital to work with, more buying power and usually could withstand intense competition for longer periods of time. With their modern, well-designed storefronts and interiors, large showrooms and greater advertising budgets, these stores posed a major problem to smaller video outlets such as Video Delight.

In Mr. Thompson's opinion, the smaller stores had some advantages too— their cost of operation was usually lower and many specialized in certain types of movies. For example, one of the stores near Video Delight specialized in art films and foreign language films. Video Delight carried a good selection of children's movies and Hollywood movie classics. The other two video outlets in the area were smaller and had no special "themes." Mr. Thompson thought that stores such as Video Delight had friendlier staff and offered more personalized service to their customers.

The Customer

According to Thompson, video rental customers could be classified into three groups. The first group consisted of ardent movie fans or those who rented at least one video a week. Some of these customers rented as many as 15 videos a month. The next group—the average viewers—rented anywhere from one to three movies a month. Those who rented less than one movie a month formed the last group. Mr. Thompson had a list of all his customers with details of their viewing patterns. For example, he could pick out the top 500 customers (in terms of the number of the videos rented).

Industry reports indicated that customers tended to rent videos from stores that were located in their neighbourhood or were, in some other way, conveniently located. For example, some chose stores that were on their way to work while others chose stores located next to a supermarket where they did their weekly grocery shopping. In the case of Video Delight, Thompson knew that nearly 80% of Video Delight's Halifax clients lived within three kilometres of his store. The Bedford store, which was located in the suburbs, drew customers from up to 12 km from the store.

Parking was another factor that affected business. However, Thompson thought that in the case of his Halifax outlet, closeness to downtown and busy retail centres made his customers less sensitive to parking problems. They recognized that if they wanted to shop at any of the stores in the neighbourhood, parking would be an issue and they might have to walk a little.

Many of Thompson's customers were young adults and families with young children. Quite often, parents and children came together and chose videos at the same time. The importance of children to the industry was reflected in the recent marketing strategies of some of the chain stores. Some of these stores offered free popcorn to children and showed in-store children's movies so that their parents could browse in peace.

Marketing Strategy

In the past, Video Delight had relied upon its extensive selection, a layout that made it easier for customers to find videos, a comfortable and homey setting, and good customer service to bring repeat clients. The store was located in an old building and had several small rooms. Each room contained a specific category of video movies and thus offered a more "private" setting to customers. While it did not carry as many multiple copies as the larger stores, it had a good variety of movies, including a better selection of old Hollywood classics than most other stores.

In July 1988, as part of his strategy to meet the new competition, Thompson changed his pricing policy. Previously he had been charging $1.99 per movie per day—the same as most of the stores in the neighbourhood. In July, Video Delight began charging $3.49 per movie for two days. Thompson thought that many customers found the single day rental inconvenient, and his method would give them the option of keeping the video for an extra day. If, however, the video was returned within 24 hours, the customer got a credit of $1 which could be applied against future rentals. The computerized system that Thompson had in place made it easy for him to keep track of the credits earned, and saved the customer the trouble of collecting coupons or making note of his/her return patterns.

The store's promotion strategy consisted mainly of pamphlets mailed to neighbouring households, a few ads in the *Mayflower* (the weekly TV guide distributed with the *Halifax Herald,* a local newspaper) and an occasional ad in the newspaper. As the store had been in the neighbourhood for a long time, Thompson thought that he need not advertise heavily anymore.

The Research Study

While he had some important information about his customers' needs, Thompson thought that he had to find out more about his customers, especially with the increased competition. Consequently, he contacted a local university to see if students in a marketing course would conduct a study for him. In particular, he was interested in learning about customer reactions to his main video outlet as well as their reactions to his new pricing policy.

The research study was conducted by the students as part of their course requirement. The students were asked to develop a questionnaire, collect and analyze data, and submit a report to Mr. Thompson. Carla, Jennifer, Peter and Mark developed a four page questionnaire and interviewed 200 people living near the Halifax Video Delight store. One hundred and forty of these people were drawn randomly from the telephone directory using a systematic sampling method. (The first three digits of the phone numbers were used to identify the area of interest.) These were primarily non-customers of Video Delight, although some (21) had rented videos from the store. The other 60 respondents were drawn, again using a systematic sampling approach, from the alphabetical list of the top 500 customers of Video Delight that Thompson had provided. The results of the study are found in Tables 1 to 6 and the questionnaire itself in Appendix 1. The interviews were conducted over the telephone during a two week period in October, 1988.

Conclusion

Carla, Jennifer, Peter and Mark were aware that they had to start writing their report for Mr. Thompson. Although they would have liked to have certain key financial and industry information before they made their recommendations, they knew that they had to manage with the information they had. They now also realized that there were weaknesses in their questionnaire; however, due to time constraints, they had no choice but to rely on the information they had already gathered.

Questions

1. How would you rate the research study? Did it achieve the objectives set forth by Mr. Thompson?
2. Evaluate the questionnaire and the research design.
3. Based on the data collected by this group, should Thompson re-evaluate his pricing strategy?
4. What recommendations (regarding other aspects of his marketing strategy) would you make to Thompson given the results of the study?
5. What other types of analyses would you like to perform using the data?

TABLE 1   Awareness of Video Outlets[1]

Store	Group 1 General Population	Group 2 Video Delight Customers
Jumbo Video	106	72
Video Delight	72	86
Store 3	40	21
Store 4	57	28
Store 5	39	18
Others	42	24

[1]Totals add up to more than 119 (140 less 21 Video Delight customers found in the general sample) and 81 (60 drawn from the customers list provided by Thompson plus 21 found in the general population) respectively as respondents mentioned more than one store.

SOURCE: Responses from Question 5 of survey (Appendix A).

TABLE 2   Most Favored Store

Store	Group 1 General Population	Group 2 Video Delight Customers
Jumbo Video	60	18
Video Delight	28	54
Others	31	9

SOURCE: Responses from Question 9 of survey (Appendix 1).

TABLE 3   Attributes Looked for in a Video Rental Outlet

Attribute	Overall Importance Rating[1]	Store Ratings Jumbo[2]	Store Ratings Video Delight[3]
Price	4.1	3.4	2.8
Selection	4.2	4.0	3.7
Location	3.8	3.7	3.7
Reservation System	1.7	3.2	2.9
Friendliness of Staff	2.5	2.8	3.6
Fast Service	3.5	2.7	3.8
Parking	2.7	2.9	2.8
Multiple Copies	3.2	3.9	3.2

[1] Results of Question 6, all 200 respondents.

[2] Results of Question 13 for customers of Jumbo Video alone.

[3] Results of Question 13 for customers of Video Delight alone.

SOURCE: Responses from Questions 6 and 13 of survey (Appendix 1).

TABLE 4 Main Reason for Choosing Video Outlet

	Jumbo Video Customers	*Video Delight Customers*
Price	40	18
Selection	56	45
Staff	17	24
Fast Service	9	16
Others	18	5

Respondents sometimes mentioned more than one reason.

SOURCE: Responses from Question 10 of survey (Appendix 1).

TABLE 5 Pricing Preferences

	General Sample[1]	*Video Delight Customers*[2]
Least Preferred Method		
Video Delight's Policy (A)	91	27
Pay when you take (B)	7	3
Pay when you return (C)	21	51
Most Preferred Method		
Video Delight's policy (A)	10	18
Pay when you take (B)	92	53
Pay when you return (C)	17	10

[1] Includes only non–Video Delight customers ($n = 119$).

[2] Video Delight sample includes respondents drawn from the general population who were customers of Video Delight ($n = 81$).

SOURCE: Responses from Question 7 of survey (Appendix 1).

TABLE 6 Age of Respondents

Age	*Video Delight Customers*	*Rest of Sample*
18 to 25	21	53
26 to 35	26	34
36 to 45	18	19
46 to 55	10	10
56 to 65	6	3

SOURCE: Responses from Question 15 of survey (Appendix 1).

APPENDIX 1
VIDEO DELIGHT SURVEY

Interviewer:	Date:
Time Start:	Phone #:
Time End:	Interview #:

Hello, my name is . . . and I am conducting a survey for a university marketing research course. I would like to ask you a few questions about video rental outlets or video stores. These questions will only take a few minutes.

Part I: Qualifiers

1. Are you over 18 years of age?   Yes   No

   (If "no" ask to speak to someone 18 years of age or over; if no one 18+ is in, terminate interview.)

2. Do you rent video movies?   Yes   No
   (If "no" terminate interview politely.)

3. If yes, how frequently do you rent video movies? (Read list.)
   a. 5 times or more per week
   b. 3 to 4 time a week
   c. 1 to 2 times a week
   d. Once every two weeks
   e. Once every month
   f. Less than once in a month

4. On average, how many movies do you usually rent per visit?   1   2   3   4+

   (If less than once in a month and only one movie per visit, terminate interview politely.)

Part II: Image and Related Issues

5. When you think of video rental stores, what stores, if any, come to mind? (Take down all names provided.)

a.	d.
b.	e.
c.	f.

6. On a scale of 1 to 5, "1" being not at all important, "5" being very important and "3" being neutral, I would like to find out how

Source: Company files.

important the following are to you when you choose a video rental store:

(Read list; if respondent needs assistance, please read the scale again.)

Price of rental	Fast service
Selection	Parking facility
Store location	Multiple copies
Reservation system	Other
Friendliness of staff	(Please specify)

7. Now, I am going to describe three different ways of pricing video movies. When I am finished, please tell me which one you prefer the most and which one you prefer the least.

   (If person is not sure of "least preferred," do not insist.)

   a. Each video costs $3.49 to rent; the rental is for 2 days; you get a credit of $1.00 toward future rentals if you return the video after one day.

   b. Each video costs $1.99 to rent per day; you pay when you take the video.

   c. Each video costs $1.99 to rent per day; you pay when you return the video.

   Most preferred _____   Least preferred _____

8. How many video stores do you rent videos from on a regular basis?   1   2   3   4+

9. Could you tell me the name of the store that you rent the most videos from, please?

   (If more than one, please take down all names; if Video Delight is mentioned, insert it in all the questions below; if not, use the name of one of the other companies mentioned above.)

10. The rest of the survey deals with the video store that you rent from most on a regular basis. Could you please tell me your reason for renting from _____ ?

   (Note down the top three answers; probe if necessary.)

   a.

   b.

   c.

11. How much does renting a video cost at _____ per movie; for _____ days?

12. How far is _____ from your house?   (kms/miles)

13. Using a 5 point scale with "1" being very bad, "5" being very good and "3" being neutral, how would you rate _____ on the following items?

   (Read list; if respondent needs assistance with the scale, please read it over again.)

Price of rental	Fast service
Selection	Parking facility
Store location	Multiple copies
Reservation system	Other
Friendliness of staff	(Please specify)

Part III: Demographic Information

For the purposes of analyzing the data we would like to get certain demographic details about yourself.

14. How many members are there in your household? Of these, how many are under the age of 18?

15. Which of the following age groups do you belong to?
    18–25   26–35   36–45   46–55   56–64   65+

16. Could you please tell me which one of the following groups your total household income would fall under?   under $15,000   under $30,000   under $45,000   under $60,000   over $60,000

Thank you very much for your time.

The Ship Shop

M.D. Beckman, Walter S. Good, and Caroline Dabrus
University of Manitoba

Richard Beck had just finished reading the latest issue of *Porthole* magazine[1] and was reflecting on the comments made in one of the articles and their relationship to a proposed business venture he was considering.

Sailing is becoming an increasingly popular pastime in Manitoba, he thought. Yet the industry has failed to recognize the potential that exists not only in sales but in after-sales service, in construction of mooring facilities, and in educational programs. With the industry's primary effort directed toward initial sales, there exists a gap between what the industry is providing and what the sailing public is demanding in Manitoba, causing many sailors to express concern over the absence of proper and adequate marine and service facilities. This was clearly laid out in the *Porthole* article. This gap suggests numerous opportunities for the development of various new business enterprises focusing on the after-sales concerns of the Manitoba sailor. However, the sailing industry in Manitoba is still in its infancy, and it may be too early to develop these opportunities. Further, the sailboat market is very competitive, and existing operations may limit the ability of a new business entity to become successful.

The following week Beck was to meet with two friends, Thomas Kregg and Gloria Roberts, to discuss a new venture proposal, The Ship Shop—a sailing retail and service outlet. In that meeting on August 25, Beck would indicate his decision as to whether or not he would support the venture. He recognized that his support was critical if the proposed venture was to become a reality, as he had not only the financial resources but also the managerial experience and sailing expertise that the other two individuals lacked. Further, should he support the venture, numerous decisions would have to be made immediately to prepare for the proposed November opening. Beck knew that entering the sailing market was a risky proposition, and he felt he needed more information on the market, on the competition, and on The Ship Shop before he could make his final decision.

The Sailing Industry and the Market

The Canadian sailing industry has been growing rapidly since the 1960s. From a few companies a decade earlier, the number of manufacturers had mushroomed to

---

[1]*Porthole* magazine is directed at the Manitoba sailing public, and publishes articles focusing on local events and concerns.

over 25 by 1978; their sales had increased similarly. Indeed, the largest manufacturer had increased sales by an average of 22 percent annually.

Increased expenditures and development had not occurred only with regard to initial boat sales. Other important aspects of the industry's growth were the expenditures made on harbourfront expansions and service and repair outlets. Facility development had generally increased in proportion with the increased number of boats and was considered by industry members as the key to its future success.

In contrast, Manitoba, with a system of lakes and waterways comparable to any in Canada, had not experienced a similar level of industry growth, particularly in terms of facility development. Sales of boats and equipment, though modest, had increased steadily throughout the decade, yet Manitoba had not developed adequate marine and service facilities to match. This lack of development had often been linked by industry members to a lack of confidence in the future of leisure sailing and to a lack of commitment on the part of a majority of boat retailers.

Manitoba's sales of sailboats had increased from 80 units in 1975 ($409,000 at retail) to 346 units in 1978 ($2,252,000 at retail), and were estimated to increase to at least 440 units in 1980 (approximately $2,864,000 at retail). Despite this steady increase in sales, many retailers were concerned that this growth would level off in the near future. In contrast, Thomas Kregg estimated that the market would realize even more dramatic growth. To support this argument, he referred Beck to three facts:

1. Membership in the Manitoba Sailing Association had increased on average 15 percent per year over the past four years, with current membership totalling over 1,000.
2. The Parks Branch of the Manitoba government estimated a more than 100 percent increase in sailboat ownership among cottage owners in Grand Beach.[2]
3. Several retailers had realized 25 to 30 percent sales increases annually.

Beck considered the main reason for the lack of development in both sales and facilities in Manitoba to be the overall lack of commitment on the part of retailers. This situation, he felt, was probably related to the extreme seasonality of sailboat sales. In general, retailers in Manitoba could be categorized into two groups. The first group included the large retailers of leisure products for whom sailboats represented a secondary or tertiary product in their product line. For these retailers, primary sales were derived from powerboats, motorboats, snowmobiles, and other leisure products, and therefore little emphasis was placed on sailboats. The second group consisted of individuals who were avid sailors and derived pleasure from operating a sailing business. In the majority of these cases, income from the

---

[2]Sailboat ownership increased from 0.4 percent of cottage owners in 1977 to 1.6 percent of cottage owners in 1978.

business was marginal and was a secondary source of income. They were generally employed on a full-time basis in another profession and therefore had limited time to spend on their sailing business.

Consumers' Buying Habits

Beck approached a part-time sailing dealer and accountant, Ivan Patterson, to see what he could learn about consumers' buying habits. Patterson observed that a recent article in *Porthole* summed up consumers as follows: "A major factor [in purchasing a boat], the price, which should provide an index of the materials and labour incorporated into the product, appears to be of lesser concern to the typical irrational sailor." Sailors tend to evaluate boats on their concept of how a boat should look, its colours and options, its sailing capabilities, and its racing class. Price is of secondary importance to the sailor, with the exception of potential sailors, who sometimes view price as a barrier. Patterson considered this secondary position of price to be important, particularly since prices seemed to be dictated by manufacturers. Manufacturers' list prices provided room for a 16 percent gross margin to the retailer on average.

In addition, Patterson pointed out that one of the major trends in the market was related to the popularity of different types of boats among customers. Whereas the dinghies and the traditional small-class boats[3] had been popular in the past, the current trend was toward the larger cruising yachts.[4] In particular, sales increased in this large-keelboat category as a result of sailors trading up every two to three years.[5] Even the novice sailor was making his initial acquisition a larger boat. These larger boats had more options and were suitable for a variety of water and weather conditions as well as racing. In general, however, Patterson felt that the attraction of these boats to consumers was in large part a function of their prestige. Given that the prices for boats in this category ranged from $8,000 to $51,000, cruisers could be considered status symbols. Patterson expected this trend to continue and believed even higher sales could be realized if there were more facilities for large cruising boats.

Growth in the cruising market, however, had not been at the expense of all the traditional sailing classes. Although there had been a downward trend in the market for dinghies, other small-boat classes, such as the Laser and, in particular, catamarans,[6] had demonstrated dramatic sales growth. In general, the smaller sailboats are capable of higher speeds and require more sailing expertise when

---

[3]Class sailboats are boats designated as belonging to an official class for racing and for which races are organized.

[4]Cruising yachts are sailboats that are usually 20 feet in length or more and have options such as cabins, engines, etc.

[5]This trade-up situation had created a large market for secondhand sailboats.

[6]The Laser is a brand sailboat, monohull, approximately 14 feet long. Catamarans are double-hulled boats, which possess greater speed capabilities than their monohull counterparts.

raced and therefore suit the serious racer. These boats often do not require mooring facilities. Prices in this category ranged from $1,000 to $6,000.

Competitors

A new retail and service outlet would face serious competition from several sources. Of particular concern would be Sampson's, Pier 7 and Lacwin Ltd., all of which were located in Winnipeg. Sampson's, in addition to selling sailboats, carried a line of motorboats, trailers, and campers and had an outlet catering to the winter downhill skiing industry. In terms of sailing craft, the firm sold the Hobie Cat catamaran on an exclusive basis. This catamaran was considered to be the most popular boat in its class, with an estimated 90 percent of the market. As a result of ever-increasing demand, however, Sampson's and Hobie Catamarans of Irvine, California, were considering the establishment of additional agents in Manitoba. Specifically they were looking for agents in Brandon and the Lake Winnipeg area in Manitoba or on Lake of the Woods in Ontario. The agent would sell Hobie Cats at a reduced margin, with a percentage of its sales being paid to Sampson's by the Hobie Catamaran Company.

Pier 7 was the exclusive local dealership for the Sol Cat (catamaran), the Laser, and the Taser, all of which were popular class boats for racing. Pier 7 combined its sailboat products with motorcycles, motorboats, skidoos, cross-country and downhill ski equipment, and a variety of related accessories. This wide product line had resulted in additional promotional expense for Pier 7 and necessitated the hiring of "specific product" staff. Despite Patterson's feeling that motorboats and sailboats did not mix, Pier 7 recorded a reasonable profit on sales of approximately 46 sailboat units of various types in 1978.

Lacwin Ltd. had the advantage of providing its customers with a wide variety of parts and accessories complementing their midsize and small-boat line. In addition, they offered custom rigging. Their product line, however, consisted of an inferior-quality line. In addition, as with other retail outlets, their marketing efforts had been negligible to date.

Patterson indicated that these retail outlets, as well as his own, were not doing as well as they might because they did not have lakeside facilities. Therefore, they were not able to offer mooring facilities, service and repair facilities, or any extensive educational programs to their customers.

There were, however, other outlets that did have a lakeside facility. The most notable competitor, Northern Marine, located at Northern Harbour on Lake of the Woods, had combined on-the-lake facilities with a retail office in Winnipeg. The firm specialized in large keelboats and had cornered a large share of the local cruise boat market. The firm had the exclusive dealership for C & C Yachts, the only Canadian manufacturer that offered a complete line of high-quality keelboats.[7] Northern Marine believed that much of its success was attributable to its lakeside facilities, which it operated on a concession basis.[8] Its extensive lakeside operation had been able to provide the financial resources needed to support the sale of larger and more expensive yachts. The firm was planning to expand its docking, storing, restaurant, and related facilities in anticipation of increased demand in the years to come.

A final competitor was Interlake Sail Ltd., which operated a lakeside facility on a concession basis on Lake Winnipeg. Its product line, however, was considered to be of inferior quality and of questionable popularity.

In general, Beck considered that he would describe the sailboat market as very competitive, resulting in gross margins for the industry as a whole rarely exceeding 15 percent. Promotional programs for sailing and sailing equipment, however, were negligible, and Beck believed this represented an opportunity for an aggressive firm.

The Ship Shop Proposal

In early August, Thomas Kregg and Gloria Roberts, both recent M.B.A. graduates and amateur sailors, had approached Beck with a proposal for a sailboat retail and service outlet, which they hoped he would invest in. The proposal was developed in recognition of an absence of adequate mooring and service facilities in Manitoba. The Ship Shop concept was designed to meet this perceived need in the industry. The proposal outlined the product and service offering as follows:

1. A retail outlet located in Winnipeg concentrating on sailboats and sailboat fittings and accessories.
2. A service outlet providing the sailor with mooring and docking space, as well as general service and repair facilities located on a lake.
3. An education centre intended to inform both the novice and the experienced sailor on sailing techniques, racing schedules, regattas, and other matters of interest. Both Kregg and Roberts felt there was a demand for educational programs, and therefore this program was included in the overall business plan. In particular, Roberts believed it could be used as an effective marketing tool.

The plan proposed that The Ship Shop's retail outlet carry sailboats, fittings, general marine equipment, educational aids (books, maps, etc.), and trailers.[9] With regard to sailboats, it was decided that the outlet should carry at least two lines of

---

[7]Due to current import duties and tariffs and the value of the Canadian dollar it was considered an advantage to have a Canadian supplier.

[8]The firm paid a concession fee for the right to use the facility's location.

[9]*Fittings* refers to trapeze harnesses, ropes, and other equipment necessary to make the sailboat operable. These fittings are parts that are often replaced.

boats. Kregg had suggested that the Hobie Cat catamarans and the O'Day line of cruising boats be considered. To sell Hobie Cats, however, The Ship Shop would have to arrange to become an agent at a fee that would reduce their gross margin on sales. This fee would be paid to Sampson's. Despite the disadvantage associated with paying an agency fee, Kregg judged that the product's increasing popularity would result in substantial sales volumes, thereby minimizing the effect of a reduced margin. In addition, he felt that there would be little difficulty in obtaining the Hobie Cat line.

The second proposed line, O'Day cruisers, was not carried by any other retailer in Manitoba despite the fact that the O'Day line represented the largest manufacturer of cruising boats in the world. These boats were considered to be of the highest quality. Further, the line had the advantage of being the most complete, offering models from day sailors to cruising yachts. This not only provided consumers with a wider selection base for the initial purchase but also gave them the opportunity to trade up in a line of boats they knew and understood. The manufacturer also guaranteed the product and offered an extensive one-year warranty policy. A disadvantage of the O'Day line, however, was that it was manufactured in the United States. Therefore, in addition to the purchase price of the boat, the shop would need to make allowances for tariff, duty, and exchange rates. Consequently, retail prices could be somewhat higher than competitive price levels.

The Ship Shop would also operate a used-boat section and would consider reselling boats brought in for trade-ups.

Fittings, educational aids, and trade-ins were of secondary importance, in terms of both the consumer's purchase decision and the retailer's product line, and were not considered the prime determinant of success or failure in a sailboat enterprise. They were, however, important sources of revenue for the retailer, providing profit margins in excess of sailboat sales. Further, fittings and trailers were thought of as part of the customer service function. Roberts felt that these products could play an important role in The Ship Shop's marketing program.

A focal point of The Ship Shop would be the mooring facilities for large cruisers that would offer the sailor the full use of repair facilities, supervision and security, and storage facilities in the winter. The buyer of a sailboat from The Ship Shop would be assured of year-round storage with security. This service, however, would not be restricted to Ship Shop customers; it would also be available to all requesting such a service on the lake. In addition, the lakeside facility would provide servicing and repair for cruisers and catamarans.[10] An on-location parts department would be necessary to handle the demand for repair parts.

The major problem in the development of this business plan was the selection of a site for a lakeside facility. Roberts believed that a site on Lake Winnipeg was preferable to one on Lake of the Woods, considering Northern Marine's current foothold in this area. There were three possible locations on Lake Winnipeg:

---

[10]Servicing would include haul-outs for cleaning, polishing, minor repairs, and the pumping out of holding tanks.

Grindstone Provincial Park, Gull Harbour, and Grand Beach. All three sites were to be developed by the parks branch of the provincial government. These sites would then be operated on a concession basis, private operators being selected by the government.[11] Grindstone and Gull Harbour were located approximately 130 miles north of Winnipeg, whereas Grand Beach was only 60 miles away. Both Gull Harbour and Grand Beach were developed park sites containing restaurants, resorts, and picnic sites. A number of facilities already existed in the Grand Beach area, whereas only modest docking facilities were available at Gull Harbour. There were no facilities at Grindstone.

The main risk involved in this concept was related to winning the concession rights to the government-constructed marina. If The Ship Shop was not selected as the operator, the firm would have to search for another location and would probably need to construct the appropriate facilities, thereby introducing unprojected construction and fixed-asset costs. Similarly, if the government postponed its marina development plans, the firm would also need to search for a new location.

Finally, the education program was seen as important insofar as sailing was still in its initial growth stage in Manitoba and therefore most Manitobans had a lot to learn about the sport. The Ship Shop would offer instructional sessions on the many aspects of sailing on a year-round basis. In winter, in-class instruction and seminars would be held in Winnipeg, and in summer the program would be expanded to include sailing instruction at the lakeside facility.

The Decision

Richard Beck had examined the financial projections prepared by Kregg (see Exhibits 1–8) and thought that if the projections were valid, the business venture represented a potentially sound investment. During the next few days, he would have to decide whether or not to participate in this venture. No matter what he decided, however, he would have to have some good reasons, particularly if he turned down his friend's offer.

EXHIBIT 1   Breakdown of Annual Wages

Richard Beck	$15,000
Sailing expert	18,000
Part-time salespeople	13,000
	46,000
Part-time secretary	6,000
Total	$52,000

Note: Part-time secretary's salary included under general administration.

---

[11]The government indicated that construction was proposed for the spring of 1980, to be completed in October. Concession fees varied but were estimated at $10,000 per year.

EXHIBIT 2   Management Team and Ownership

Richard Beck	President and General Manager
Thomas Kregg	Vice-President, Finance and Accounting
Gloria Roberts	Vice-President, Marketing

Mr. Beck will contribute $30,000 of the initial investment and will retain 50 percent ownership. Mr. Kregg and Ms. Roberts will contribute $15,000 each and will retain 25 percent ownership each.

EXHIBIT 3   Annual Location Costs, Retail Outlet

Rental charge ($/ft.)	$ 2.95
Taxes and utilities ($/ft.)	1.25
Total	$ 4.20
Total overhead (5,000 sq. ft.)	$21,000.00

EXHIBIT 4   Historical Sales Data

	1975			1976			1977			1978		
	L	*M*	*S*	*L*	*M*	*S*	*L*	*M*	*S*	*L*	*M*	*S*
Northern	10	—	2	15	—	5	28	—	8	33	—	12
Interlake	—	—	—	—	—	—	—	10	6	5	11	2
Sampson's	—	—	4	—	2	25	1	7	45	3	11	83
Pier 7	—	—	20	—	—	44	1	1	70	3	2	46
Lacwin	—	—	18	—	—	20	—	6	30	—	15	3
Redekopp	—	—	8	—	—	10	—	—	18	—	—	21
Others	5	3	10	7	8	15	9	9	25	12	12	30
Total ($000)	249	11	149	400	40	314	777	150	588	1,232	255	765

L = Large cruisers (21+ ft.)

M = Day sailors (18–21 ft.)

S = Dinghies and catamarans (less than 18 ft.)

EXHIBIT 5 **Sailboat Lines, 1978 Retail Base Prices**

Length	O'Day	C & C	Tanzer	Bayfield	Hinter Hoeller
20 ft.	$ 7,665				
22	8,728		$ 8,040		
23	11,524				
24		$12,125[1]			$ 9,700[1]
25	15,022		12,404	$16,350[2]	
26		22,995[1]	13,075		16,800[1]
27	20,586	26,450[1]			
29		34,450[1]		28,500[2]	
30	36,900[2]	32,700[1]			43,605[3]
32	44,022[2]			40,000[2]	
35					49,500[2]
37	51,790[2]				

[1] Price does not include sails or engine.

[2] Price includes sails and engine.

[3] Price includes engine.

All other prices include sails.

Note: O'Day prices were determined as follows:

(27' [cost price × exchange] × 17.5% duty × 9% fed. tax) × 16% profit = retail price

([13,197 × 1.05] × 17.5% × 9%) × 16% = $20,586 = retail price

SOURCE: *Boat Buyers Owner's Guide (1979).*

EXHIBIT 6 **Projected Cash Flow, Year 1: Nov. 1979–Nov. 1980 ($000)**

	N	D	J	F	M	A	M	J	J	A	S	O
Cash balance opening	60	5.2	134	81.9	28	13.1	2.8	42.8	54.5	56.9	55.7	48
Add:												
Cash receipts	1.1	3.1	10	11	37.4	44.3	60.1	58.3	18.6	12	5.5	3.5
Bank loan proceeds	—	150.0	—	—	—	—	—	—	—	—	—	—
Total receipts	1.1	153.1	10.0	11.0	37.4	44.3	60.1	58.3	18.6	12.0	5.5	3.5
Less disbursements:												
Labour	2.75	2.75	2.75	2.75	2.75	2.75	5.35	5.35	5.35	5.35	5.35	2.75
Utilities and taxes	.52	.52	.52	.52	.52	.52	.52	.52	.52	.52	.52	.52
Rent	1.23	1.23	1.23	1.23	1.23	1.23	1.23	1.23	1.23	1.23	1.23	1.23
General administration	1.00	1.00	1.00	1.00	1.00	1.00	1.00	1.00	1.00	1.00	1.00	1.00
Travel	—	1.00	—	—	1.00	1.00	1.00	1.00	1.00	1.00	—	—
Advertising	5.90	2.50	2.50	2.50	2.50	1.50	.40	.40	.40	.40	.40	.40
Concession fee	—	—	—	—	—	—	—	—	—	—	—	10.00
Operating	.16	.16	.16	.16	.16	.16	.16	.16	.16	.16	.16	.16
Interest	—	1.50	1.50	1.50	1.50	1.50	1.50	1.50	1.50	1.50	1.50	1.50
Cost of goods sold	41.34	13.90	52.20	54.20	41.66	44.90	10.00	36.50	6.00	3.00	3.00	12.00
Total disbursements	52.90	24.56	61.86	64.86	52.32	54.60	21.16	47.70	17.20	14.20	13.70	29.60
Cash increase (decrease)	(51.8)	128.5	(51.9)	(53.9)	(14.9)	(10.3)	38.9	10.6	1.4	(2.2)	(7.7)	(26.1)
Cash balance closing	5.2	133.8	81.9	28.0	13.1	2.8	42.8	54.5	56.9	55.7	48.0	21.9

EXHIBIT 7   Projected Pro Forma Income Statement ($000)

	1980	1981	1982	1983
Sales:				
Cruisers	132	288	339	508
Catamarans	32	87	186	331
Used boats	30	62	158	258
Fittings and options	49	112	172	252
Trailers	7	14	18	22
Education	2	4	5	6
Servicing	13	20	30	35
Total sales	265	587	908	1,412
Less average cost of goods sold (75%)	199	440	718	1,059
Gross margin	66	147	190	353
Less expenses:				
Wages and salaries	46	49	53	58
Utilities and taxes	6.25	6.6	7	7.4
Rent	15	16	16.5	17.5
General admin.	12	13	14	15
Travel	5	6	7	8
Advertising	19.8	15	15	16
Bad debts	2.6	3	3.5	3.8
Concession fee	10	15	18	20
Transportation	7	11	14	19
Operating	2	2.5	3	4
Interest	19.5	19.5	17.0	113.0
Total expenses	145.15	156.6	168.0	182.0
Net profit (loss)	$(79.15)	($ 9.6)	$ 22	$ 171

NOTES: Assume about 10% market share first year.

Neglects to add costs of running on-lake facility in terms of wages, equipment, etc.

Makes no estimate of cost of constructing facilities on lake.

EXHIBIT 8

**Catamaran Lines: 1978 Retail
Base Prices**

Length	Hobie Cat	Soltornado Cat
11 ft.	$1,445	
14	2,247	
15		—
16	3,043	
18	4,475	$3,700
20		$6,000

Class Boat Lines: 1978 Retail Base

Length	Bombadier	Laser
About 12 ft.	$1,200	
About 14 ft.		$1,500

Clovis Jewellers

D. Wesley Balderson
University of Lethbridge

Clovis Jewellers is a small jewellery store located in Brandon, Manitoba.[1] You have been called on by the owner to prepare an analysis of the business. The owners have supplied you with a detailed description of their operation and strategy. Critically evaluate each area described in the case.

Structure

Legal Structure.   Clovis Jewellers is an incorporated company under the name of Clovis Jewellers (1978) Limited. It is a privately held corporation. The only shareholders are Mr. and Mrs. Neudorf, each of whom owns 50 percent of the outstanding shares. As a corporation, Clovis Jewellers is authorized to issue an unlimited number of Class A, B, and C common shares. The only outstanding shares are 100 Class A shares. In the case of Clovis Jewellers, the shareholders are the owners, directors, and managers.

Financial Structure.   The capital structure of Clovis Jewellers is financed by a combination of debt and shareholder's equity. The debt constitutes roughly 75 percent of the capital and the shareholder's equity the other 25 percent. The shareholder's equity is made up of both class A share capital and retained earnings, of which the latter is by far the larger.

The debt financing is held with the Bank of Montreal and is in the form of a long-term loan. This loan is approximately $190,000. The first $150,000 is guaranteed through a provincial government small business assistance plan and therefore carries an interest rate of 9 percent; the remaining $40,000 carries a rate of prime plus 1½ percent. This long-term debt is covered by personal guarantees by Fred Meyer, a business associate of Mr. Neudorf, and from a mortgage on the Neudorfs' house.

The bank of Montreal has also authorized an operating line of credit to Clovis Jewellers with a ceiling of $20,000. This line of credit is used to assist Mr. Neudorf in managing the cash flow in the slower summer months.

Organizational Structure.   There are four levels of employees in Clovis Jewellers' organizational structure. (see Appendix 1). The first level is the manager and

---

[1]Although this case describes an actual business the names of the business and owners, as well as the location, have been changed.

is filled by Mr. Neudorf. The duties of this position include accounting and financial management, management of day-to-day store operations and gemologist/diamond expert. Mr. Neudorf works together with both the assistant manager and the sales staff.

The second level in the organization is the assistant manager and is filled by Mrs. Neudorf. She works as the assistant manager approximately 50 percent of the time and as a salesperson the remaining 50 percent. The duties of the assistant manager include purchasing of merchandise and control of inventory. The inventory control function is done on a very informal basis, usually by a simple visual check.

The third level in the organization includes the sales staff and the repair service administrator. The job of overseeing the repair service is held by one of the full-time salespersons and requires approximately 20 percent of her time. The number of salespersons varies with the time of year, ranging from six to seven at Christmastime to two or three during the summer months.

The fourth level in the organization is the goldsmith and repairperson. This position is filled by Mr. Neudorf and requires a great deal of his time. Mr. Neudorf works together with the repair service administrator when acting as goldsmith.

There are two positions outside of the four-level organization. One is an accountant, and the other is a lawyer. Mr. Neudorf hires these two professionals on a part-time basis as demand calls for them. Both the accountant and the lawyer interact only with Mr. Neudorf.

Personnel

Clovis Jewellers experiences very little employee turnover (one staff member every two or three years) and therefore does not engage in recruiting procedures on a regular basis. When a new staff member is needed, a small advertisement is placed in the classified section of Brandon's daily newspaper. Although an advertisement is always placed, most hiring results through word of mouth and other contacts with neighbouring businesspeople.

When selecting a new employee, Mr. and Mrs. Neudorf look for individuals with an outgoing, friendly personality. Usually the person is middle-aged and has sales experience. Application forms are screened based on these qualifications, and the applicant who best meets the qualifications is asked to come in for a personal interview. Unless there is more than one "ideal" applicant, the new employee is hired after only one interview.

The training supplied to new employees comes in two forms: product training and operations training. The product training requires the employee to learn a great deal about jewellery— a very complex area. The individual must gain knowledge about watches, diamonds, gemstones, and qualities of gold. This product training occurs as the person works in the showroom selling jewellery and takes approximately one month.

The operations training is less involved than the product training and is completed in the first week or two of employment. This training involves learning the daily routine carried out at Clovis Jewellers, as well as cash register and receipt-writing operations.

The method of employee remuneration is a straight hourly wage; no commissions are paid. Employees' hours are recorded in a payroll register, and employees are paid every two weeks based on the number of hours worked. Mr. Neudorf tried to introduce a commission pay plan in the past, but employee resistance forced him to shelve the plan.

Employee morale appears relatively high compared to other retail stores. Mr. Neudorf believes this is because he and his wife treat the sales staff with respect and as friends. The employees know the importance of selling to the company's well-being, and Mr. Neudorf continually reinforces this by verbally acknowledging an individual for his or her sales efforts. A further indication of high morale is the fact that Clovis Jewellers experiences an extremely low rate of absenteeism and lateness.

Marketing

Product. A majority of Clovis Jewellers' yearly sales consists of ring and precious stone jewellery; for this reason, its product mix heavily favours these two items. Ring sales are responsible for the single highest sales total; therefore, great emphasis is placed on the ring inventory when the product mix is evaluated. Clovis Jewellers is known for carrying good-quality merchandise; this is reflected in the purchasing habits and quality control employed at Clovis. However, Clovis has shifted to a lower-quality selection of rings and jewellery to compete with the competition. This shift appears to be temporary, as the better-quality lines remain.

Mr. Neudorf believes seasonal fluctuations in sales do not seriously affect the product mix. Relative sales of most items remain constant throughout the year.

Distribution. Clovis Jewellers is in the middle of a transition from using a traditional manufacturer-retailer distribution channel to a more direct channel. Jewellery and ring manufacturers are actually middlemen in the supply of diamonds and precious gems (the manufacturers buy the gemstones from large diamond and gemstone suppliers). This method of purchasing was more convenient for Mr. Neudorf but inevitably meant higher-priced merchandise. Mr. Neudorf has now made arrangements to buy diamonds directly from the source of supply and therefore has greatly reduced merchandise costs. This shift also gives Mr. Neudorf much greater control over diamond and gemstone quality.

Pricing. Mr. Neudorf uses several different methods in calculating the retail prices of the merchandise. Brand-name items such as watches are priced according to the manufacturer's suggested retail price, because Mr. Neudorf thinks customers will base their purchase decisions solely on price when shopping for brand names.

Merchandise whose quality the customer cannot differentiate easily, such as gold chains, are priced very competitively. Comparisons are often made with other jewellery stores to ensure that these items are priced competitively. Jewellery items such as earrings and pendants are priced according to a standard markup of keystone (50 percent), plus an additional 10 percent to make up for markdowns, which are often needed to sell the jewellery.

Mr. Neudorf finds rings the hardest items to price, as they carry no brand names or identifying trademarks. Each ring is priced individually, based on special features (or lack of them). A general markup formula is still used, but individual factors dictate the final selling price of the ring. For example, everyday solitaire engagement rings are priced below the standard markup, whereas individual modern engagement rings are priced above that markup.

Promotion. Clovis Jewellers uses a wide range of media in its advertising program, including a daily newspaper, a local television station, AM and FM radio stations, and flyers. Advertising is used to convey both a specific promotional method and corporate image advertising. Mr. Neudorf prepares much of his own advertising, especially radio and newspaper ads. He also gives the ads a personal touch by recording many of the radio ads himself and including his picture in several newspaper advertisements. Mr. Neudorf claims that Clovis Jewellers targets its selling toward middle-aged women, but this target is not evident in the advertising; rather, the advertising appears to be general, with no real objectives or target market in mind. The advertising budget is prepared by taking a percentage of projected sales. This target percentage is between 4 and 5 percent.

Mr. Neudorf uses many different forms of sales promotion throughout the year. These include diamond remount plans, jewellery repair sales, graduation promotions, Mother's Day promotions, and other general markdown sales. The number of sales promotions has increased over the past few years due to an increase in competition. The trend in promotions has switched from using them to enhance slow selling periods toward bettering higher selling periods. That is, they are now timed in conjunction with a month of already higher-than-average sales.

Personal selling is heavily used at Clovis Jewellers. Mr. Neudorf believes jewellery requires a substantial selling push and therefore uses in-store personal selling as a major marketing tool. Emphasis is on making every sale count, large or small. Monthly sales totals are updated every day and then compared to the projected sales for the month. This information is then passed on to the salespeople to keep them aware of the importance of selling.

Public relations can also be an effective marketing tool, especially in a close-knit community such as Brandon. Mr. Neudorf is involved with many community clubs and events, which give him a fair amount of low-cost public relations. Clovis Jewellers sponsors sporting events for persons with disabilities and is a member of both the Rotary Club of Brandon and the Brandon Chamber of Commerce (of which Mr. Neudorf has been president and is currently a director). Mr. Neudorf gives talks to local women's groups and at high school career days. He has also had much interaction with the Brandon City Council and has served on committees such as the Brandon Parking Commission.

Location and Layout

Location. Clovis Jewellers' trading area consists of the city of Brandon, surrounding towns and farmlands, and small communities that extend to the Ontario and Saskatchewan borders. The population of the area is slightly greater than 200,000, of which 55,000 live in the city of Brandon. The primary trading area (approximately 70 percent of the business) includes the entire city of Brandon and the surrounding towns of Virden, Souris, Minnedosa, and Neepawa.

The economy of Clovis Jewellers' trading area relies heavily on its two industries, farming and oil. Clovis Jewellers' sales experience large fluctuations due to the characteristics of each of these industries. The downturn in the oil industry has had a significant impact on the firm's profitability; sales have dropped significantly in the past three years.

Clovis Jewellers leases its site from a management firm located in Winnipeg. The basic rent is approximately $2,400 per month. On top of this expense, Clovis pays a yearly management, property tax, and insurance fee for the building. The building is a single-story structure located on Brandon's main downtown artery. The physical characteristics of the site follow the image Clovis is trying to portray; the storefront is pleasant and modern looking.

The buildings surrounding Clovis Jewellers host mostly banks and other independent retail stores. Several retail stores on the same city block appeal to Clovis's target market, including the Roset by Reid jewellery store located across the street. There is one vacant space on the street, located right next to Clovis Jewellers. The vacancy was caused by a fire over a year ago, and the building remains boarded up.

Clovis Jewellers is located on Ross Street, which is the center downtown street. Ross Street has angle parking on both sides and is busy every weekday from 9:00 A.M. until around 6:00 P.M. This heavy vehicle traffic is due to the large number of banks in the area that deal with a high volume of customers every day. Ross Street also experiences a high volume of pedestrian traffic during the day, as it is situated in the heart of Brandon's retail and office sector.

Layout. Clovis Jewellers' present location is 1,000 square feet. Eight hundred square feet are used as selling space and the remaining 200 for office and storage space. The showroom is divided among rings, gold chains, watches, gift items, diamond jewellery, and regular jewellery. Although space is allocated to each section according to proportion of total sales, the allocation is based on rough estimates of both percentage of sales and space used.

The layout of the store is designed to make efficient use of high-traffic areas. The engagement rings, which are classified as specialty goods, are located at the back of the store, a spot that would normally see low-traffic volume. The shopping goods such as watches and gold chains are located in high-traffic areas around the cash register and front entrance.

Merchandise is displayed in either a locked showcase or behind a showcase out of the customer's reach. This method of displaying is necessary due to the high value and small size of individual pieces of merchandise. Each display case is lighted by two spotlights dropped from the ceiling. Florescent lights light the general-purpose areas of the store; other lamps are suspended from the ceiling as part of the decor. The lighting appears adequate, as the store gives a "bright" first impression.

Purchasing and Inventory Control

Purchasing. Mrs. Neudorf is responsible for purchasing the majority of the required merchandise. The salespeople often assist her, especially when the purchasing is done in Clovis Jewellers' showroom. Purchasing is done through a combination of jewellery and gift show attendance and meetings with individual supplier representatives.

The trade shows Mr. and Mrs. Neudorf attend are held throughout Canada and the United States and include cities such as Hawaii, Vancouver, Brandon, Calgary, Winnipeg, and Toronto. Roughly 20 percent of total purchases are made at these trade shows. Mr. and Mrs. Neudorf attend them for the purpose of obtaining new products and ideas as well as the actual purchasing.

Eighty percent of purchasing is done in-store and with the help of the salespeople. Mrs. Neudorf prefers in-store purchasing because it gives her the undivided attention of the company representative and allows her to compare items with Clovis's existing merchandise. Each company representative visits Clovis Jewellers two or three times a year, usually in the spring and early fall.

Mr. Neudorf has arranged special payment terms with approximately 75 percent of his suppliers. The credit terms are usually 30/60 days, 30/60/90 days, 30/60/90/ 120 days, or even up to six months; most companies will give these terms free of any interest charges. Mr. Neudorf finds these terms necessary for cash flow management, as the majority of purchases are made during slow sales periods.

Mr. Neudorf maintains a tight level of quality control, inspecting each piece of jewellery before it is put on sale. Each item is checked for diamond or gemstone quality, quality of stone settings, and adequate stamping of gold quality. Items that do not meet the strict quality standards are returned to the supplier for exchange.

A purchasing budget is prepared by multiplying the target gross margin percentage by the budgeted sales figure. This total purchase figure is then spread out throughout the year according to monthly sales, with the majority of purchases made in the pre–Christmas season.

Inventory Control. No formal inventory control method is used at Clovis Jewellers. Mr. and Mrs. Neudorf rely on experience when it comes to controlling inventory levels. Visual inspections determine whether inventory levels are sufficient or need replenishing. No automatic reorder procedure is used; Mr. and Mrs. Neudorf believe automatic reordering would hurt rather than enhance sales because customers expect to find unique pieces of jewellery at Clovis.

Mr. Neudorf has insurance to cover fire, loss of merchandise stored in the safe, loss of customer goods stored in the safe, and business interruption (up to six months). Insurance to protect against theft of merchandise not stored in the safe is either not available or too expensive. All of the rings and diamond jewellery are placed in the safe after business hours; therefore, most of Clovis's inventory is insured in the event of a break-in. The business interruption insurance is related to inventory; a major loss or damage of inventory would not force Clovis Jewellers out of business, as the firm would continue to have a daily cash flow.

Accounting and Financial

Recording and Classifying. The daily and weekly recording and classifying done by the staff at Clovis Jewellers basically follows a one-write system, with the addition of certain journals and a daily cash summary. The one-write system, kept by Mr. Neudorf, is used to maintain all of the sundry (nonmerchandise) accounts as well as the company payroll. The nonmerchandise accounts are paid as they arise and therefore require almost daily attention; the payroll is calculated every two weeks.

A daily cash summary is prepared by Mr. Neudorf every weekday morning (Friday's and Saturday's are prepared on Monday). This cash summary includes a summary of the day's sales, both cash sales and charge sales; a summary of how the cash flow is distributed, including cash expenses and bank deposits; and a record of returned merchandise and cheques. The main purpose of this cash summary is to ensure that the cash transactions balance on a day-to-day basis.

Mr. Neudorf also keeps an accounts payable ledger, which he updates weekly. Proper managing of the accounts payable is important to Clovis Jewellers because it relies on trade credit to purchase all of its inventories. A journal of monthly purchases is kept to maintain control over the inventory and the merchandise purchases. Mrs. Neudorf is responsible for keeping this journal up to date; usually she adds all of the invoices to the journal at the end of the month, when a total can be calculated.

One final area in which recording is done on a day-to-day basis is the jewellery repair journal and record of ring sales. Clovis Jewellers has an extensive jewellery and watch repair department. The repair department is run by the sales staff and involves entering every repair job into a journal for easy reference. Because of the quick turnover of repair jobs (usually one to two days), they must be entered into the journal the same day they are received to prevent any bottlenecks in the system. Individual ring sales are also recorded in a book for quick reference as needed.

Budgeting. Five years ago, the budgeting process was almost nonexistent at Clovis Jewellers. Except for some very rough, off-the-top-of-the-head figures, no budgets were prepared. This has changed in the last few years, and although the budgetary process still needs improvement, it has taken a definite shape and form.

The process starts with a sales budget. This budget is prepared by looking at last year's sales and then updating them based on any special considerations for the upcoming year. The budget is prepared monthly and used to make regular comparisons to actual sales figures.

Once the sales budget is complete, a merchandise purchases budget is prepared based on the specific level of monthly sales. The purchases budget includes all shares of merchandise purchases, including the cost of repairs.

An expense budget is prepared by Mr. Neudorf. Again, previous years' expense totals are used. These expense totals are evaluated as being too high, too low, or correct over the past year and are then changed accordingly for the upcoming budgeted year. The budgeting of all the expense totals is very important, as it allows for better control of these expenses as they are incurred.

The final budget prepared is the cash flow project budget. This is done by combining the projected sales, merchandise payments, and expense budgets. This cash flow projection is very important for Clovis Jewellers, because the seasonal cash inflows it experiences often creates cash shortages; the cash flow analysis allows Mr. Neudorf to plan for these shortages.

Financial Statements.   Clovis Jewellers has a complete set of financial statements prepared once a year by a certified general accounting firm (see Appendix 2). The statements are prepared after January 31 of each year, which Mr. Neudorf has chosen as the year-end date due to the low volume of business and low inventory count that occur at this time. All financial statements are prepared showing the previous year's figures for purposes of easy comparison.

The balance sheet is prepared in the traditional format, with assets on the left side of the statement and liabilities and equity on the right. Current assets constitute roughly 75 percent of the total assets; inventory is the largest and most important part of the current assets. Clovis Jewellers has a long-term loan payable, which makes up the largest part of the total liabilities. This loan contract is held with the Bank of Montreal and carries personal guarantees from both Mr. Neudorf and his business associate, Fred Meyer.

An income statement is prepared based on sales and expense figures supplied by Mr. Neudorf. This statement does not include a detailed list of the operating expenses. For this purpose, a detailed statement of Operating Expenses is prepared. This statement lists each expense totalled for the year and in alphabetical order.

A statement of changes in financial position is also prepared at year end. This statement explains how funds were generated and used throughout the year. The purpose of this statement is to indicate any changes in the working capital of the business and explain how those changes occurred.

Planning

Long-Term Planning.   Management at Clovis Jewellers appears to be typical of most small businesses in that a serious lack of any long-term planning exists. The only long-term planning that has occurred is the signing of a five-year lease. Although this means of planning is extremely informal by even a liberal definition, it indicates that some consideration has been given to the long-range plans of Clovis Jewellers.

Short-Term Planning. Mr. Neudorf engages in a number of forms of short-term planning. Among them are budgeting for the upcoming year, planning promotions, and cash flow planning. Budgets are prepared early in the fiscal year and extend to the end of the year. The budgets include a sales budget, a purchases budget, and an expense budget. The budgetary process is still in the early stages of development, but an increased awareness on the part of Mr. Neudorf ensures that it will be an effective form of short-term planning in the future.

Promotions are planned on an informal basis; no concrete goals or objectives are stated. Most of the promotions are planned based on the success of the previous year's promotions. If a promotion proved successful one year, it is automatically considered for the next year. This method produces mixed results, as some promotions are successful one year and quite unsuccessful the next.

One area of short-range planning that requires attention is the planning of future cash flows. Mr. Neudorf prepares a complete cash flow analysis for the upcoming year based on projected sales, merchandise purchases, and expenses. This cash flow analysis does not always prove accurate due to extraordinary items that arise in the course of the year, but at least it gives Mr. Neudorf a plan for goals for which to aim.

APPENDIX 1
CLOVIS JEWELLERS: ORGANIZATIONAL STRUCTURE

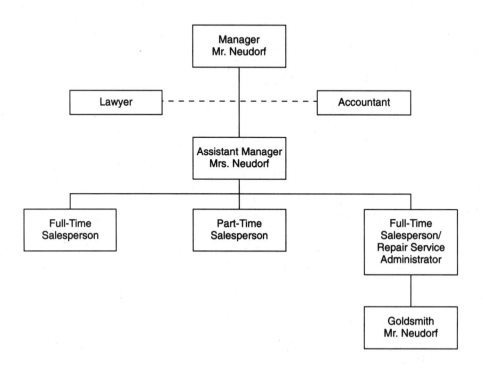

APPENDIX 2
CLOVIS JEWELLERS: FINANCIAL STATEMENTS

CLOVIS JEWELLERS (1978) LTD.
Balance Sheet
(Unaudited)
January 31, 1991

	1991	1990
Assets		
Current		
Cash	$ 24,886.15	$ 32,834.17
Accounts receivable (trade)	4,885.34	5,725.74
(shareholders)	18,186.40	18,462.84
Inventory	190,612.90	197,318.70
Prepaid expense	8,437.01	9,150.01
	247,007.80	263,490.46

Assets

Investments	1,045.00	—
Fixed	10,853.69	13,566.69
Other		
Goodwill less amortization	56,672.20	59,228.20
Incorporation costs	—	373.54
Due from Neudorf holdings	15,448.95	15,448.95
	$329,027.64	$352,107.84

Liabilities

Current:		
Accounts payable and accruals	$ 70,987.17	$ 92,214.96
Employee remittance payable	1,447.75	1,539.07
Corporation taxes payable	925.40	834.85
Current portion of long-term	11,316.00	8,000.00
	84,676.32	102,588.88
Long-Term	199,961.77	214,156.14
	214,683.09	316,745.02

Shareholders' Equity

Share Capital	$ 100.00	$ 100.00
Retained Earnings	44,289.55	35,262.82
	44,389.55	35,362.82
	$329,027.64	$352,107.84

CLOVIS JEWELLERS (1978) LTD.
Statement of Income
(Unaudited)
Year Ended January 31, 1991

	1991	1990
Sales	$420,559.99	$472,035.50
Cost of Sales	218,332.01	261,016.36
Gross Margin	202,227.98	211,019.14
Selling Expenses	192,626.33	210,073.57
Operating Income	9,601.65	945.57
Other Income:		
Interest earned	350.48	213.63
Gain from sale of assets	—	1,133.00
Income before Taxes	9,952.13	2,292.22
Income taxes	925.40	834.85
Net income	$ 9,026.73	$ 1,457.37

CLOVIS JEWELLERS (1978) LTD.
Statement of Operating Expenses
(Unaudited)
Year Ended January 31, 1991

	1991	1990
Operating Expense:		
Accounting	$ 761.20	$ 1,039.30
Advertising	11,024.93	33,265.13
Amortization	4,556.00	4,556.00
Auto expenses	1,794.77	3,146.33
Bank charges and interest	4,318.90	4,549.10
Canada pension plan	1,201.94	1,296.32
Donations	350.00	350.00
Depreciation	2,713.00	3,391.00
Equipment rental	4,200.00	2,700.00
Interest	28,016.38	30,747.77
Insurance	3,047.00	3,079.41
Legal expenses	448.54	80.09
Memberships and dues	510.00	587.74
Postage and stationery	1,382.82	2,388.12
Rent	28,965.29	28,175.00
Repairs and maintenance	432.41	464.59
Salaries	82,180.91	74,505.54
Security	711.39	681.25
Supplies	2,224.87	2,308.94
Taxes	2,603.75	3,144.88
Telephone	983.67	1,104.04
Travel and promotion	3,764.89	1,621.14
Unemployment insurance	2,492.46	2,539.19
Utilities	3,818.71	4,092.59
Workers' compensation	122.50	245.00
Total expenses	$192,626.33	$210,073.57

Movie Village

Stephen Tax under the Supervision of Walter S. Good
University of Manitoba

Dave Ringer, owner-manager of Movie Village, a video rental store, was contemplating the future of his business. The cool wet summer had been great for video rentals, and that had him worried. Everybody was talking about opening another store, and the market was getting saturated. The rental market was still experiencing some growth, but there were many challenges on the horizon. Dave was particularly concerned with his reliance on video rentals for almost all of his revenue. A variety of competitive forces, including new rental outlets in the vicinity of Movie Village, chain and franchise rental store expansions, actions by some of the movie studios, and the expected growth of pay television, were threatening his business and forcing Dave to consider some changes in his strategy.

The Video Rental Industry

The video/movie rental market developed through a marriage of the videocassette recorder (VCR) and the feature film industry. The VCR offered its owner two principal features: the ability to tape television programs for playback at a more convenient time and the ability to play rented or purchased movies or other prerecorded video products. A 1985 survey by the Bureau of Broadcast Measurement found that 57 percent of a typical user's VCR time was spent playing rented movies and 37 percent playing movies that had been recorded from television for playback at a different time.[1] The remaining 6 percent was used to tape television shows for later playback. The VCR, the survey declared, was essentially a movie machine.

The growth rate in VCR sales had been quite dramatic (see Exhibit 1). The VCR was expected to be in 30 percent of Canadian homes by the end of 1985. Industry observers believed that an eventual penetration of 80 percent of Canadian homes was not unreasonable to expect by 1995.[2]

There were two competing technologies in the VCR marketplace—VHS and Beta. The Beta system (designed by Sony) had approximately a 30 percent share, while the VHS system dominated with 70 percent. It was expected that both

---

[1] *Winnipeg Free Press,* October 16, 1985, p. 5.
[2] *Canadian Business* February 1984, p. 14.

EXHIBIT 1   Canadian VCR Sales By Year

Year	Units Sold
1980	45,000
1981	200,000
1982	430,000
1983	540,000
1984	950,000 (estimated)

SOURCE: Marketing, August 6, 1984, p. 8.

would continue to be available in the marketplace for many years. The two systems used different software (a VHS movie would not run on a Beta machine), which meant a movie rental retailer had to stock tapes in both formats to service the entire market.

Sony had recently introduced a new hardware system—8mm. This new product used much smaller tapes, which provided easier portability than either Beta or VHS hardware. The movie studios, however, were reluctant to develop prerecorded tapes until enough machines had been sold to suggest that the 8mm format would be successful. Consumers, on the other hand, were reluctant to purchase the 8mm hardware until there was an attractive selection of software on the market. This was essentially a chicken and egg problem. Many video retailers believed that broad acceptance of the 8mm format was still a few years away, but it would eventually have a significant impact on the market.[3]

The movie studios' goal was to maximize their profits from films by using all possible distribution methods, including movie theatres, pay TV, network TV, and cassette sales for resale or rental. The typical sequence of events was for a movie to first be shown in theatres, then be made available to video stores in cassette form for rental purposes. Sometime after the film's release for home rental, it might be shown on a pay television service such as First Choice/Superchannel or Home Box Office, and finally it might be shown on commercial network TV. In the home-rental market, the movie studios received all their revenue from the sale of cassettes to video distributors or video retailers. They did not receive a royalty or any share of the revenue received by the retailer from each rental.

Movies were rented to the public through a number of different types of outlets, such as specialty video rental stores (independent and chain operations), convenience stores, gas stations, food stores, drugstores, and some mass merchandisers.

Movie Village

Movie Village, located near the southwest corner of the fashionable Osborne Village shopping district in Winnipeg, opened for business in June 1984. Dave Ringer, a business communications graduate from the University of Manitoba in

---

[3]*Video Business*, August 19, 1985, pp. 1, 2.

1981, had spent a couple of years working, travelling, and analyzing a number of business opportunities before deciding to enter the video rental business. The growing market and the availability of what he thought was a viable location helped make up his mind.

Osborne Village was made up of a broad cross-section of people skewed somewhat toward the elderly, singles (not necessarily elderly), and childless couples covering all points of the income spectrum. "In his research Dave found his primary trading area, within a half-mile of the store, contained 12,000 to 14,000 people. Also a lot of people worked in the Village. Because of the abundance of video outlets in the city and the need for each customer to make two trips to his store (to rent and return the movie), most of Dave's business was from the immediate neighbourhood.

An important component of Dave's operation was his computerized information system. This system allowed Dave to keep tabs on his inventory, sales, and the frequency with which individual titles were rented. He could also take and record reservations and keep track of his membership file of 8,000 customers.[4]

Marketing Mix

Product. Dave rented movies and VCRs and sold blank tapes and a number of other accessories. His sales breakdown was as follows:

Movie rentals	92%
Blank tapes and accessories	5%
VCR rentals	3%

When Dave first opened for business, he also sold some hardware (VCRs and colour TVs), but found that the profit margins were small and the equipment took up a lot of space, tied up his working capital, and required too great a selling effort.

Dave stocked about 1,800 cassettes (total of VHS and Beta) representing approximately 1,100 different titles.[5] He purchased multiple copies of some of the new releases that were expected to be popular with the public. For example, he recently purchased 15 copies of *Ghostbusters.* By having multiple copies of these popular films available, Dave believed he was providing better service to his customers.

One particular problem Dave and other video retailers faced was the increasing number of new releases. When Movie Village first opened, about 150 new releases were offered by the studios each month. A year and a half later, the number had quadrupled to approximately 600. Dave felt it was important for him to change his product assortment continually and stock new releases. Studios and

---

[4] All renters had to be Movie Village members. This membership was free and helped Dave control his tape losses. The membership list was also used for direct-mail promotions.

[5] Dave kept a ratio of about 65 percent VHS versus 35 percent Beta.

distributors promoted their new products heavily, and customer demand for the newer films was very high for the first couple of months after they came out.

Dave obtained his movies from two local distributors. New releases cost him about $100 each, 60 percent of which he could get back if he returned the cassette within 40 days. The longer he kept the movie, the lower its return value. With a movie like *Ghostbusters,* Dave could buy 15 copies and return most of them within 40 days. Older movies could be purchased for between $40 and $80 each. Their resale value was quite low, less than $30. Dave usually rotated his older stock by trading in some of his inventory. He could take 100 movies in to his distributor and come out with 70 different ones. Dave spent about one-third of his previous month's revenue on new releases each month and also traded in some cassettes.

He used trade magazines and release lists provided by his distributors to make his purchase decisions. His computer provided him with data on the frequency with which each movie in the store was being rented. This information was useful in deciding which cassettes should be traded in.

Price.   The goal of Dave's pricing policy was to maximize his monthly revenue. This made sense, considering most of his costs were fixed in nature.

Dave charged $1.89 per movie rental on weekdays (Monday to Thursday) and $3.99 per movie on weekends (Friday to Sunday) and holidays. He also offered a number of price specials designed to increase his revenue up front and help build customer loyalty. His price deals included

1. A coupon providing 15 movie rentals for $25
2. A $30 fee for one movie per week through the calendar year (noncumulative)
3. A two-month summer special (July and August) whereby the customer paid $20 and could rent movies for 94¢ each during the two-month period
4. A special rental price of 94¢ for selected movies

Dave judged that these price promotions had increased his overall revenue.

Movie Village did not differentiate in price between new and old movies, despite the greater popularity of new releases, except in the case of his 94¢ specials. These tended to be older films that would otherwise have been in low demand. He was concerned that too many deals and specials might confuse his customers and sales staff.

Promotion.   Dave used a variety of promotional tools to stimulate repeat business by his current members and to attract non-members to his store. He regularly sent a direct mailing to all his members informing them of new releases and current specials. He also sent a coupon for a free movie rental to members on their birthdays and on the anniversaries of their membership.

Bulk mailings were periodically sent to all households within the store's trading area informing potential customers of price specials, store hours, new releases, and so on. Coupons for such specials as two rentals for the price of one were often included with this material to encourage the recipients to become members.

In addition, Dave had used contests to promote his store, most notably a "guess the weight" of a huge box of popcorn, to attract the attention of pedestrian traffic in the Village. The prizes were usually video equipment (VCRs and TVs).

A changeable outdoor sign hung over the entrance to the store. Dave found this sign useful for drawing attention to monthly promotions or price specials.

Promotion had become increasingly important to Movie Village because of the growing number of locations providing movie rentals. However, the limited geographic area served by Movie Village, as well as the considerable cost, precluded the use of any type of mass media advertising.

Sales and Expenses

Movie Village's sales revenue had grown slowly but steadily since its inception. Business would pick up considerably on long weekends, then settle back down, but to a slightly higher plateau. The store experienced a noticeable decline in business during the Folklorama multicultural festival during the second week in August. Dave had expected the whole summer to be slow, but the poor weather that year created what he considered to be an artificial boom.

A typical weekend day provided almost three times the revenue of a typical weekday ($850 compared to $300). The nine VCR rental machines owned by the store were rented primarily on weekends. For a typical month for Movie Village, see Exhibit 2.

Current Video Rental Competition

Dave had identified several important bases on which stores in the video rental business competed. These included convenience, service, selection, and price.

EXHIBIT 2 · Typical Monthly Revenue and Expenses for Movie Village

Revenues		Expenses	
Movie rentals	$16,000	Movie purchases	$ 5,000
Accessory sales	600	Employee wages	2,230
VCR rentals	400	Advertising	1,500
Total revenue	$17,000	Rent	750
		Administration	750
		Purchase of accessories	500
		Utilities	225
		Total expenses	$10,955

Convenience had several components from the viewpoint of the customer, including store hours, parking availability, and location on the street. Movie Village was open 10 A.M. to 10 P.M. on weekdays, and 10 A.M. to 11 P.M. on weekends. The store was located near the southwest corner of Osborne Street and River Avenue, a main intersection in the Village. This location had very limited available parking.

Customer service also had a number of elements. Some people just wanted to come in, get their movies, and get out. Movie Village had an efficient system, including a well-laid-out store and a fast, efficient check-out process. Other customers wanted help in finding and selecting a movie, and some even asked for a personal review.

Movie selection was important because many customers searched for a particular film. If the store did not carry it, or it was already rented, those customers were lost. Carrying multiple copies of popular films was essential if the store hoped to satisfy its customers.

While the rental price was important to many customers, Dave did not want to compete strictly on that basis. He felt it reduced his per-rental profit margin without a proportionate increase in volume.

Dave summarized the situation of his store in comparison to the four principal competitors in his trading area as follows:

1. California Connection was located right around the corner from Movie Village. It did not have as extensive a selection of movies, no Beta-format videocassettes were stocked, and it took longer to complete a transaction. Prices, however, were a bit lower.

2. Osborne Video was located on the opposite side of the street, the wrong side for customers on their way home from work or shopping downtown. Otherwise, it was quite similar to Movie Village.

3. The Shell gas station had a limited selection, and it took longer to rent a film. However, it was open 24 hours. Their staff was not particularly knowledgeable about the films they rented, but their prices—$1 on weekdays, $2 on weekends—were considerably lower than those at Movie Village.

4. Mac's Store was comparable to the Shell gas station.

Strategic Threats

There were a number of competitive challenges on the horizon that Dave believed seriously threatened the future viability of Movie Village if it continued on its present course. Those threats included:

1. Increasing traditional competition from other independent video rental stores in Movie Village's trading area

2. The growth of chain and franchised video operations throughout Winnipeg

3. The entry of new, nontraditional competitors (bookstores and record stores) into the video sales and rental market

4. Competition from other closely related entertainment vehicles (pay cable and satellite television)

5. Strategies being considered by the movie studios to increase their share of post-theatre movie revenues

Neighbourhood Competition. Dave had heard a rumour that a local Winnipeg chain specialty video store was planning to open an outlet in the vicinity of Movie Village. Historically, they had proven to be an aggressive marketer, using mass media advertising and loss-leader pricing (94¢ rental price specials) to build their business, although they did not carry multiple copies of many movies. Their entry into the local market could threaten Dave's volume of business and his ability to maintain his premium-pricing strategy.

Chain-Store Competition. According to the owner of the local Global Video stores, Winnipeg already had the highest number of video stores per capita in North America. Compounding this situation was the growth of national video chains and franchises.

Adventureland, a U.S.–based video franchise, was expected to have 1,000 outlets in the United States by the end of 1985 and 2,500 stores in the United States and Canada by the end of 1986. National Video, also an American company, already had over 1,000 franchised stores in the United States and Canada and had ambitious plans for further growth as well. Local chains such as Adi's and Star Time Video had been growing at a more modest rate. Each currently had six locations in Winnipeg.

Franchise operators offered their franchisees expertise in site selection, accounting and bookkeeping systems, merchandising, staffing, and the development of their product mix (most handled hardware in addition to rentals). They also used mass media advertising and could obtain quantity discounts on movie cassettes for their franchisees through central purchasing. By having multiple store locations in one city, the chains offered an added convenience to their customers, who could rent and return movies to a number of outlets.

The growth of the franchised stores added to what Dave perceived was rapidly becoming a saturated market. This concern was echoed by National Video president Ron Berger, who stated, "I can tell you right now the trend on the west coast (Los Angeles) is to video-store closings, and it's ferocious. All those undercapitalized mom-and-pops are collapsing due to oversaturation and their inability to develop the kind of systems and support programs they need to stay competitive. Most trends in this industry start in the west and slowly move across the country."[6]

The specialty video retailer had even more rivals with the entrance of nontraditional competitors such as book and record stores into the video market.

---

[6]*Video Business,* August 1985, p. 18.

Music/record stores were beginning to resemble home entertainment centres, and the fit, importance, and growth potential of video products in relation to their current product lines was apparent to many people in the business. According to one U.S. record store chain manager, "We are dealing with one group here. The record audience is also a video audience."[7] Record merchandisers were conceded to have larger promotion budgets and greater merchandising expertise than the small video store owner. Many of the large American record chains were beginning to offer video rentals and sales, especially of music videos.

Bookstores were also venturing into the video market, although primarily as resellers of video products rather than catering to the rental market. They tended to concentrate on the low-price segment, under $25 retail. Mainly three types of videos were being sold in these stores:

1. Older classic movies, drawn from the public domain
2. Children's material, from Disney cartoons to tie-ins with current toys
3. How-to tapes on things like exercising, cooking, and fixing your car

Video studios and distributors were very interested in the potential offered by bookstores as intermediaries for the sell-through market.[8] Bookstores, however, were not expected to have much of an impact on the rental market because of the high service requirements and the space and capital needed to stock an adequate level of inventory.

The Cable TV Challenge. On a broader basis, the movie rental business competed with a number of other forms of entertainment. In the post-theatre movie/video market, competition included network TV and cable television systems and satellite technologies for the reception of a wide range of specialty television services.

Basic cable TV services had a very high penetration rate in Winnipeg, about 85 percent of all households. However, the premium pay-TV service, Superchannel, had only a 3 percent penetration rate.[9] This premium channel cost a typical household $18 to connect plus a $16 monthly fee, and offered a variety of programming, including over 20 different movies per month. Marketing efforts to encourage increased acceptance of premium pay-TV services were expected to intensify.

Satellite dishes cost from $1,500 to over $5,000 and were designed to be used in rural locations where cable TV was not available. In recent years, however, they have begun to penetrate the urban residential market. They were selling in Canada at a rate of 70,000 units per year (1984) and increasing at an annual rate of 40%.[10]

---

[7]*Canadian Video Retailer* (May 1985), p.18.

[8]Sell-through referred to the sale of movie cassettes to individual end-users.

[9]Video Cable TV, Winnipeg. Basic cable included NBC, ABC, CBS, and PBS, as well as Canadian commercial networks and a variety of specialty services.

[10]*Marketing,* October 28, 1985, p. 20.

The satellite dish enabled a household to receive more than 30 American cable and local channels with no additional monthly charge. Some specialty channels were moving toward the scrambling of their satellite signal so that dish owners would not be able to receive their service unless they acquired a decoder and paid a monthly fee.

A longer-term threat posed by the cable industry was the possible implementation of pay-per-view (PPV) systems. These systems would allow basic cable subscribers to access premium channels, via addressable converters, for individual programs on a pay-per-view basis. The cost of plugging into such a system to view a movie might be in the neighbourhood of $4.

Movie Studio Actions. Another impending threat to the movie rental business came from the major movie studios (Paramount, 20th Century Fox, etc.). These studios controlled the availability of movies and were constantly looking for ways to increase their share of the post-theatre revenue a movie could generate.

The studios' strategy to date had been to manufacture cassette copies of their films and sell them to distributors who resold them at a high price to the video rental stores. The price of most new releases ($100 each to the retailer) was considered too high to attract much of a sell-through market. The studios, however, did not receive any royalty or other revenue when retailers rented the movie to their customers. Each prerecorded cassette cost the studios only about $8 to produce. While some "through selling" of the more popular movies had taken place even at this high price, some studios had recently begun to actively develop this market.

Some popular new releases were being sold directly to retailers for $29.95 U.S., with a suggested retail price of $39.95 U.S. Older movies were sold for somewhat less. However, the retailers the studios were using for this method of distribution were principally the mass merchandisers, bookstores, record stores, gift shops, and large video chains, not the independent video rental stores. The studios believed their movies could be more effectively merchandised by traditional gift-oriented and sales-oriented outlets than rental stores. In addition, since the studios planned to deal directly with the retailers, it would be easier for them to sell to a few large retail chains rather than thousands of small video stores. There were also some concerns that consumers might not purchase products from rental outlets because they feared that the cassettes may have been previously used for rental purposes.

Accentuating the problem for the specialty video stores was the apparent timing the studios were using in releasing their movies to each market segment. During the first two months of release, when a movie was most popular in the rental market, it would be sold to the retail rental stores for $100. After two months, it would be released for $29.95 U.S. to the sell-through outlets. Most video stores felt obliged to pay this higher price to have new releases available for their customers and keep up with the competition. Furthermore, it was unlikely that the resale value of new releases (60 percent within 40 days) could continue to be as high as it was presently given that the movies would be available for $29.95 U.S. shortly thereafter.

Strategic Options

Consideration of all of these issues convinced Dave that he needed to reduce his reliance on video rentals for such a large (92 percent) portion of his total revenue. He was considering a number of alternatives. Among them were

1. Developing a sell-through market in video cassettes
2. Expanding his geographic trading area
3. Increasing his accessory product sales
4. Diversifying his rental business to include compact discs (CDs) and similar items

The Sell-Through Market.   Dave was sceptical about his ability to sell a large number of movie cassettes at a projected price of $50 to $60.[11] However, he suspected that there might be a market for specialty videos such as children's films and cartoons, old classic movies, how-to cassettes, and sports and leisure instructional tapes such as Babe Winkleman's *Guide to Fishing* and similar programs. Dave thought these kinds of products had more value for multiple viewing and could be sold for gift and personal use if priced at $25 or less. Since most of these tapes were produced by independent studios and not the major motion picture companies, obtaining distribution rights would not be as difficult.

Jim Kartes, an American whose company was involved in specialty video production, believed that most people were reluctant to spend more than $20 U.S. on a video program.[12] His company produced such films as *Eight Minute Makeover* and *Colour Me Beautiful* in 30-minute formats that wholesaled to retailers for $6.99 U.S. These products apparently sold very well.

Dave calculated that with proper promotion, pricing, and merchandising he could sell 100 specialty cassettes a month. On average, he figured each cassette would cost him $15 and he could sell it for $25. He was also hoping that having these specialty videos for sale would increase the interest in his store from customers outside his current limited trading area.

Geographic Diversification.   Dave also considered opening another store, which by itself would not reduce his dependence on the rental business but would provide him with some geographic diversification.

A similar option was to acquire one or more video vending machines (VVMs). A VVM, costing approximately $35,000, could hold 500 cassettes for sale or rental purposes. The customer accessed the machine with a credit card. These VVMs

---

[11]The selling price is based on a typical retail price of $30 U.S., which at an exchange rate of $1.39 plus duty and a 10 percent federal tax brought the price to roughly $56.

[12]*Video Store*, July 1985, p. 90.

could be placed inside the current Movie Village location to make better use of the store's available space. This space, however, was presently at a premium because of the room needed to display new releases and promotional materials and the space taken up in storing the actual cassettes. The VVM would reduce the lineup at the counter during busy rental periods.

Another option would be to place the machine outside the store to provide customers with 24-hour service. The machines could also be placed around the city in other locations (indoor or outdoor) that Dave felt offered sufficient potential and where he was able to work out a satisfactory arrangement with the owner of the space.

Accessory Products.   Accessory products, including blank tapes, cassette cases, and VCR head cleaners, presently accounted for about 5 percent of Movie Village's revenue. Dave was interested in expanding the accessory portion of his business because of the high profit margin (around 40 percent) and the diversification opportunities it offered.

Success in the accessory market depended on carrying the right products at the right price points and promoting and merchandising them well. It was also important that the products' packaging and display materials, provided by the manufacturers, took up very little space, as product display areas were at a premium in Dave's store.

With the growth of the "home entertainment centre" concept, a number of accessory product manufacturers had developed specialized kits that performed one of two functions: They helped maintain the consumer's audio and video equipment, or they tied the consumer's audio and video equipment together into an integrated system. For example, the Discwasher company had developed a Video Starter Kit that showed the consumer how to tie all of the equipment together into a system that would allow him or her to realize all the possible benefits and utilize all the features of the VCR when used with cable TV. The company thought its product ideally should be sold as an add-on at the time of the hardware sale, but it was also a good item for video specialists, since new VCR owners tended to go to a video store when they had a question about hooking up the various components of their system.[13] That particular kit included a head cleaner, an A-B switch, a signal splitter, three coaxial RF cables, and an instruction manual. The suggested prices for the kit were $17.95 U.S. wholesale and $29.95 U.S. retail. There were also a number of other products, both related and unrelated to the video business, that accessory manufacturers were offering and Dave was considering carrying.

Compact Disc Rentals.   One final option Dave considered was building on his experience in the rental business to expand into other rental markets. Specifically, he was considering renting software for compact disc (CD) players.

The CD player, which read digital information on a doughnut-size disc via a laser beam, had a number of distinct advantages over records and audiotape cassettes. The quality of the sound was superior due to higher fidelity, and the CD

---

[13]*Video Business,* October 1985, p. 11.

was more durable and longer lasting because it was read by a laser beam. In contrast, sound was produced on a record by a diamond needle sliding over the vinyl surface. The CDs were also smaller and easier to store.

Dave believed that despite their current low level of market penetration—1 or 2 percent of Winnipeg homes—the CD player and software had greater potential for growth than the video market. Retail prices of CD players had dropped from about $1,500 a year ago to as low as $400. Software selection was expanding very rapidly, and prices were coming down as well. In addition, CD players were being heavily promoted by many retailers.

Despite these trends, however, CD software was still relatively expensive ($18 to $20 per disc retail) and limited in both the number of titles and the quantity of discs available in the stores. Dave believed that people would be reluctant to duplicate their record or cassette collections on CDs because of the cost. However, they might rent CDs to record onto audiotape cassettes (the quality of the sound would be superior to prerecorded cassettes or tapes copied from a record) or simply listen to on their CD players. In that way, they could use the compact discs to build up their collection of high-quality audiotapes or use the rental disc to help them decide whether they should purchase a disc of their own.

Dave was considering establishing a library of 500 to 600 CDs at an average wholesale cost of $14. He had a built-in customer base with his video business but realized he would have to attract additional customers from outside his primary trading area to make the CD rentals a viable proposition. He reasoned that a $1 daily rental fee would attract customers from outside his trading area and, perhaps, encourage them to rent the discs for a couple of days. This would reduce the inconvenience of having to rent a disc one day and return it the next. Dave was also excited about the complementary effect this additional customer traffic could have on his movie rental business.

Initially at least, Dave was considering only renting CDs because he did not have the space to properly display them for sale or the capital to invest in a large inventory. He had already discussed the possibility of starting joint promotional programs with some CD hardware retailers whereby Movie Village would give free memberships and assorted coupons for movie and CD rentals to purchasers of their players. A number of these retailers were enthusiastic about the promotion because one factor holding back their sales of CD players was the limited availability of the software.

Dave had heard of record stores that had previously tried to rent out CDs and failed. But Dave thought his store had an advantage over sales-oriented stores because it had the necessary system in place to effectively and efficiently handle software rentals.

Conclusion

Dave feared that a market shakeout was certain to occur in the near future, and he wanted to be a survivor. He had to select and implement a strategy to keep his business stable in the long term. Otherwise he would see his profits slowly dwindle away.

Endnotes

Chapter 1

1. Sabin Russell, "Now It's the World's Turn," *Venture*, September 1984, pp. 46–61.
2. "Canada's Entrepreneurial Revolution Advances," *Small Business*, June 1988, p. 24.
3. "The Entrepreneurial Numbers Game," *Inc.*, May 1986, pp. 31–36.
4. *Facts about Small Business and the U.S. Small Business Administration* (Washington, D.C.: Small Business Administration, 1979), pp. 2–6.
5. "The Entrepreneurial Numbers Game."
6. *Small Business in Canada* (Ottawa: Industry, Science and Technology Canada, 1991), p. 3.
7. *A Study of Job Creation in Canada, 1974–1982* (Statistical and Data Base Services, Department of Regional Industrial Expansion), 1985.
8. David Smith, "Why Small Business Is So Important" (budget brochure, Ministry of State for Small Business and Tourism, Government of Canada, 1984).
9. Lance H. K. Secretan, "How Should We Train the New Entrepreneurs?" *Journal of Small Business Canada*, Spring 1985, p. 21.
10. Michael Ryval, *Small Business Magazine,* June 1989, p. 86.
11. Thomas Peters and Robert H. Waterman, Jr., *In Search of Excellence* (New York: Harper & Row, 1982).
12. Ibid.
13. *Large Company ES-I Sample Survey* (Labour Division, Statistics Canada, May 1975).
14. R. Peterson, *Small Business—Building a Balanced Economy* (Erin, Ont.: Press Porcepie Ltd., 1977), p. 64.
15. *Small Business in Canada.*
16. Ibid.
17. Ibid.
18. Ibid.
19. Ibid.
20. Ibid.
21. "Taxation Statistics," in *Department of Regional Industrial Expansion Consultation Paper on Small Business* (Revenue Canada, February 1985).
22. Pat Thompson, "Characteristics of the Small Business Entrepreneur in Canada," *Journal of Small Business and Entrepreneurship* 4, no. 3 (Winter 1986–87), p. 5.

23. Ibid.

24. Ibid.

25. *Statistical Profile of Small Business in Canada, 1983* (Small Business Secretariat, quoted from report of Department of Regional Economic Expansion).

26. "Canada's Entrepreneurial Revolution Advances," *Small Business*, June 1988, p. 24.

27. Canadian Federation of Independent Business, projection made at the International Council of Independent Business Conference, Toronto, May 1984.

28. Robert Levering, Milton Moscowitz, and Michael Katz, *The 100 Best Companies to Work for in America, 1984* (Scarborough, N.Y.: New American Library, 1985).

29. Peters and Waterman, *In Search of Excellence.*

30. Ibid.

31. *Statistics on Foreign Ownership, Small versus Large* (Ottawa: Statistics Canada, Inter-Corporate Ownership, 1984), p. 252.

32. "Would You Want Your Son to Marry a Marketing Lady?" *Journal of Marketing*, January 1977, pp. 15–18.

33. Ivan I. Stefanovic, "Sidestepping Socialism in Yugoslavia," *Venture*, September 1984, p. 60.

34. Nelson A. Riis, Commons Debate, February 7, 1985, Ottawa, p. 2120.

35. Randall Litchfield, "Turn Change into Advantage," *Small Business Magazine,* June 1989, p. 19.

36. Joe Dangor, "Thriving on Change," *Small Business Magazine,* June 1989, p. 32.

37. Cathy Hilborn, "Recession Startups Not So Risky Business," *Profit Magazine,* July-August 1991, p. 8.

38. *The White Paper—Recent Cross Canada Consultations Inviting Submissions from Small Businesses* (Government of Canada, Ministry of State for Small Business).

39. John Bulloch,"Policy Guidelines to Help Make Your Venture Work," *The Financial Post Special Report*, November 24, 1984, p. 53.

Chapter 2

1. "Inc. and U.S.A. Today Survey of 500 Fastest Growing Private Companies," *Inc.*, June 1986, p. 48.

2. Ibid.

3. Pat Thompson, "Characteristics of the Small Business Entrepreneur in Canada," *Journal of Small Business and Entrepreneurship* 4, no. 3 (Winter 1986–87), p. 5.

4. Karl Vesper, "Freedom and Power: What Every Entrepreneur Craves," *Success*, May 1988, p. 48.

5. Thompson, "Characteristics of the Small Business Entrepreneur in Canada."

6. "Size Comparisons of Bankrupt Firms versus Non-Bankrupt Firms," *The Canadian Small Business Guide,* February 22, 1985, p. 5013.

7. *The Canadian Business Failure Record, 1984* (New York: Dun & Bradstreet, 1984), pp. 1–19.

8. David P. Boyd and David E. Gumpert, "Coping with Entrepreneurial Stress," *Harvard Business Review*, March-April 1983, pp. 44–64.

9. "Inc. Magazine and U.S.A. Today Survey."

10. Small Business Survey, Ron Rotenberg, Brock University, 1989.

11. Charles A. Garfield, *Peak Performers* (New York: William Morrow, 1985).

12. "A Nation of Entrepreneurs," *Report on Business Magazine,* October 1988, p. 62.

13. Thompson, "Characteristics of the Small Business Entrepreneur in Canada."

14. "A Nation of Entrepreneurs."

15. Carter Henderson, *Winners: The Successful Strategies Entrepreneurs Use to Build New Businesses* (New York: Holt, Rinehart and Winston, 1985), p. 178.

16. *The Canadian Business Failure Record, 1984.*

17. Ibid.

18. *Canadian Small Business Guide*, Part II, Vol. 43, February 22, 1985.

19. *Small Business and Special Surveys* (August 17, 1989, Statistics Canada).

20. Jeffrey A. Timmons, Leonard E. Smollen, and Alexander L. M. Dingee, *New Venture Creation: A Guide to Entrepreneurship* (Homewood, Ill.: Richard D. Irwin, 1985), p. 28.

Chapter 3

1. Raymond Kao, "Market Research and Small New-Venture Start-Up Strategy," *Journal of Small Business and Entrepreneurship*, Spring 1986, p. 36.

2. "Incubator Update," *Inc.*, January 1993, p. 49.

3. "Business Incubators Come of Age," *Entrepreneurial Manager's Newsletter*, May 1986, p. 5.

4. Examples are *Key Business Ratios* (Dun & Bradstreet); Statistics Canada; *Family Expenditures;* Census Tracts; Alberta Economic Development and Small Business.

Chapter 4

1. Donald Rumball, *The Entrepreneurial Edge* (Toronto: Key Porter Books, 1989), pp. 225–33.
2. Jerry White, "Canada's Free Trade Winners," *Small Business Magazine*, July-August 1990, p. 38.
3. *N.E.D.I. Notes* (Montreal: National Entrepreneurship Development Institute, January 1992), p. 5.

Chapter 5

1. Peter Thomas, "Negotiate to Win," *Profit Magazine,* October 1991, p. 34.

Chapter 6

1. *Franchise Annual* (St. Catharines, Ont.: Info Press, 1988).
2. Faye Rice, "How to Succeed at Cloning a Small Business," *Fortune*, October 28, 1985, p. 60.
3. *Small Business in Canada* (Industry, Science and Technology Canada, 1990), p. 41.
4. Cherise Clark, "The Future of Franchising," *Profit Magazine,* March 1992, p. 59.
5. *Franchise Annual.*
6. Gordon Brockhouse, "The Franchise Advantage," *Small Business Magazine*, July-August 1990, p. 48.
7. *Franchising in the Canadian Economy 1990–1992* (Toronto: Canadian Franchise Association and Price Waterhouse), p. 3.
8. Rice, "How to Succeed at Cloning."
9. U.S. Department of Commerce, *Franchising in the Economy, 1977–79* (Washington, D.C.: U.S. Government Printing Office, 1981), Table 3, p. 34.
10. Rice, "How to Succeed at Cloning."
11. Kenneth Barnes and Everett Banning, *Money Makers: The Secrets of Canada's Most Successful Entrepreneurs* (Toronto: McClelland & Stewart, 1985), p. 84.
12. Ibid., p. 72.
13. Ibid., p. 144.

Chapter 7

1. *The Canadian Business Failure Record, 1984* (Toronto: Dun & Bradstreet Business Education Division, 1983).

2. *Study of Business Startups in Canada* (Toronto: Decision Marketing Research Ltd., 1988).

3. "Venture Capital: More Money, Still Choosy," *The Magazine That's All about Small Business*, May 1984, p. 49.

4. "Risk Capital—Down but Not Out," *Profit Magazine*, December 1992, p. 60.

5. "Where Angels Dare," *Profit Magazine*, December 1992, p. 34.

6. Stanley Rich and David E. Gumpert, "Business Plans That Win $$$: Lessons from the MIT Enterprise Forum," *Venture*, June 1985, p. 72.

7. *Small Business Views the Banks* (Toronto: Canadian Federation of Independent Business, 1988).

8. Ibid.

9. "Venture Survey—Financing," *Venture*, October 1986, p. 24.

10. "Small Business Magazine's First Annual Survey of Canadian Entrepreneurs," *Small Business*, June 1987, pp. 49–50.

Chapter 8

1. Thomas J. Peters and Robert H. Waterman, Jr., *In Search of Excellence* (New York: Harper & Row, 1982), p. 156.

2. John Meyer, "Canada's Exports Reach Record High—Total Sales Top $90 Billion Mark," *Export Opportunity*, March 31, 1984, p. 1.

3. Report on Business, Globe and Mail, February 19, 1993, as reported by Statistics Canada for 1992.

4. *Federal/Provincial Action Report,* Canadian Federation of Independent Business, 1986.

5. Everet M. Rogers with F. Floyd Shoemaker, *Communication of Innovation* (New York: Free Press, 1971), p. 270.

Chapter 9

1. "Small Business Magazine's First Annual Survey of Canada's Entrepreneurs," *Small Business*, June 1987, pp. 49–53.

Chapter 11

1. Psychological Motivations Inc., "Dobbs Ferry, New York," *Venture*, May 1986, p. 26.

2. *Small Business in Canada, 1990* (Industry, Science and Technology Canada), p. 19.

3. Robert Levering, Milton Moscowitz, and Michael Katz, *The 100 Best Companies to Work for in America, 1984* (Scarborough, N.Y.: New American Library, 1985).

4. For a complete discussion, see Donald Rumball, *The Entrepreneurial Edge* (Toronto: Key Porter Books, 1989), pp. 159–79.

5. Frederick Herzberg, *Motivation to Work* (New York: John Wiley & Sons, 1959).

6. Abraham H. Maslow, *Motivation and Personality* (New York: Harper & Row, 1970).

7. "Small Business Magazine's First Annual Survey of Canada's Entrepreneurs," *Small Business*, June 1987, pp. 49–53.

8. Kenneth Blanchard and Robert Lorber, *Putting the One Minute Manager to Work* (New York: Berkley Books, 1984).

9. *Small Business in Canada, 1990,* p. 61.

Chapter 12

1. Brian Costello, *Your Money and How to Keep It* (Don Mills, Ont.: Stoddart Publishers, 1985), p. 14.

Chapter 13

1. "Canada's Fastest Growing Companies, 1992," *Profit Magazine*, June 1992, pp. 22–23.

2. Paul Weinberg, "Growing Pains," *The Magazine That's All about Small Business*, May 1984, p. 26.

3. Donald L. Sexton and Philip M. Van Auken, "Prevalence of Strategic Planning in Small Business," *Journal of Small Business Management*, July 1982, p. 20.

4. Richard M. Hodgetts, *Effective Small Business Management.* Reproduced by permission of Academic Press Inc., 1982, p. 197.

Chapter 14

1. P. C. Rosenblatt, L. deMik, R. M. Anderson, and P. A. Johnson, *The Family in Business* (San Francisco: Jossey-Bass, 1985), p. 5.

2. Jennifer Low, "Dad, When Are You Going to Let Go?", *Profit Magazine*, October 1991, p. 30.

3. S. I. Lansberg, "Managing Human Resources in Family Firms: The Problem of Institutional Overlap," *Organizational Dynamics*, Summer 1983, pp. 39–46.

4. Curtis Hartman, "Main Street Inc.," *Inc.*, June 1986, pp. 49–54.

5. B. Benson, "The Enigma of the Family-Owned Business," *Perspective* 10, no. 1 (1984), p. 26.

6. S. Birley, "Succession in the Family Firm: The Inheritor's View," *Journal of Small Business Management* 24, no. 3 (July 1986), p. 36.

7. Low, "Dad, When Are You Going to Let Go?", p. 28.

8. Marshall Paisner, "Myths about Succession," *Inc.*, October 1986, p. 146.

9. Rosenblatt, deMik, Anderson, and Johnson, *The Family in Business*, p. 274.

10. Birley, "Succession in the Family Firm."

11. Mark Stevens, "When to Take Your Company Public," *Entrepreneurial Manager's Newsletter* 7, no. 4 (1986), p. 4.

12. *Insolvency Bulletin,* Office of Superintendent of Bankruptcy Consumer and Corporate Affairs Canada, March 1992, Table 7-A.

13. William V. Curran, C.A., "Bankruptcy—What It Means," in *Running Your Own Business* (Ontario: Gage & Financial Post, 1982), pp. 104–107.

Index